17 대화를 듣고, 남자의 마지막 말에 대한 여자의 응답으로 가장 적절한 것을 고르시오.

Woman: _______________________________

① At 8 o'clock. But the hall is packed.

② In about thirty minutes. You can go in then.

③ It's in an hour. But you can go inside anytime.

④ It'll be tomorrow. I wish you a successful concert.

⑤ The concert starts at 7 p.m. You don't need to hurry.

[18~19] 대화를 듣고, 여자의 마지막 말에 대한 남자의 응답으로 가장 적절한 것을 고르시오.

18 **Man:** _______________________________

① Wow! Please give him my congratulations.

② Of course. Your dad will be so proud of you.

③ I'm sorry, but can you take another photo of me?

④ Yes. I think these eyeglass frames look good on you.

⑤ Great! Can you text me the exact location of the store?

19 **Man:** _______________________________

① Too bad. I already have a website.

② Really? This is exactly what I need.

③ Sure. I can introduce the coach to you.

④ That's amazing. Good luck with the marathon.

⑤ It is important that you finish without injuries.

20 다음 상황 설명을 듣고, Nora가 Justin에게 할 말로 가장 적절한 것을 고르시오.

Nora: Justin, _______________________________

① I'm afraid I can't help you anymore.

② your math skills have improved a lot.

③ cheer up! I'll help you during the break.

④ everyone loses confidence at some point.

⑤ I appreciate your help with the math problems.

Dictation Test 01

M3(17)_01_D

Dictation(받아쓰기)은 본문을 받아쓰면서 영어듣기의 집중력을 향상시키고 다양한 표현을 정리하기 위한 영어듣기 학습법입니다. 녹음을 다시 듣고, 빈칸에 알맞은 단어를 써 보세요.
※Dictation의 정답은 듣기 대본의 밑줄 친 부분을 확인하세요.

정답 p. 1

맞은 개수 / 총185개

그림정보파악(대화)

2025 영어듣기능력평가 1회 1번 변형

1. 대화를 듣고, 남자가 주문할 허리 벨트백을 고르시오.

①  ② 

③  ④ 

⑤ 

01

W: Welcome to Cycle Gear Shop.

M: Hi. Can I order 15 belt bags for my cycling club?

W: Sure. We have ready-made options, or you can _______________________.

M: I'd like to design the bags myself.

W: Okay. Do you want a single-bottle holder or a double-bottle holder?

M: A single-bottle holder, please.

W: Should the bags have __________ __________ for night riding?

M: Yes, definitely.

W: Would you like to add any initials or text?

M: Yes, please __________ the club's name "Road Wings" __________ __________ __________.

W: Perfect. I can have them ready by next Monday.

대화미언급

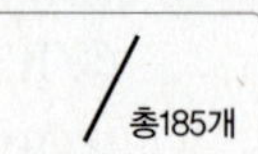

2025 영어듣기능력평가 1회 2번 변형

2. 대화를 듣고, City History Walking Tour 에 대해 언급되지 않은 것을 고르시오.
① 시작 날짜 ② 가이드 언어
③ 활동 내용 ④ 만남 장소
⑤ 참가 비용

02

(Telephone rings.)

M: Hello. This is City History Walking Tour.

W: Hi. Could you tell me about the tour? When does it run?

---

6 다음 그림의 상황에 가장 적절한 대화를 고르시오.

①   ②   ③   ④   ⑤

7 대화를 듣고, 여자가 남자에게 부탁한 일로 가장 적절한 것을 고르시오.

① 책 반납하기   ② 커피 사오기   ③ 여동생 데리고 오기
④ 도서관에서 책 빌려오기   ⑤ 여동생에게 우산 갖다 주기

8 다음을 듣고, 종이에 대해 언급되지 <u>않은</u> 것을 고르시오.

① 발명 지역   ② 사용 용도   ③ 제작 과정
④ 주요 원료   ⑤ 재활용 목적

9 다음을 듣고, 무엇에 관한 설명인지 고르시오.

① 청소기   ② 건조기   ③ 가습기   ④ 전기 난로   ⑤ 전기 포트

10 다음을 듣고, 두 사람의 대화가 <u>어색한</u> 것을 고르시오.

①   ②   ③   ④   ⑤

11번~20번 문제는 다음 페이지에 ➡

11 대화를 듣고, 대화 직후 남자가 할 일로 가장 적절한 것을 고르시오.

① 영수증 가지러 가기   ② 백화점에서 옷 사기   ③ 옷 수선 맡기기
④ 옷 환불 받기   ⑤ 코트에 단추 달기

12 다음 표를 보면서 대화를 듣고, 여자가 주문할 스포츠 물병을 고르시오.

	Model	Material	Size (liters)	Dishwasher Safe
①	A	Plastic	1.2	O
②	B	Plastic	2.0	O
③	C	Plastic	1.2	X
④	D	Stainless Steel	1.2	O
⑤	E	Stainless Steel	2.0	X

13 대화를 듣고, 두 사람이 미술 전시회에 가기로 한 날짜를 고르시오.

① 8월 5일   ② 8월 10일   ③ 8월 15일   ④ 8월 20일   ⑤ 8월 25일

14 대화를 듣고, 남자가 지난 주말에 한 일로 가장 적절한 것을 고르시오.

① 콘서트 가기   ② 공연 예약하기   ③ 달리기 훈련하기
④ 공원에서 야구하기   ⑤ 야구 경기 관람하기

15 다음을 듣고, 방송의 목적으로 가장 적절한 것을 고르시오.

① 자전거 동아리를 홍보하려고
② 자전거 관리 방법을 설명하려고
③ 새로운 도로교통법을 공지하려고
④ 교통사고 발생 시 행동수칙을 알리려고
⑤ 자전거를 안전하게 타는 법을 안내하려고

16 대화를 듣고, 남자가 지불할 금액을 고르시오.

① $3   ② $5   ③ $6   ④ $8   ⑤ $10

M: It runs every Saturday starting on May 10th. It
__________ __________ three hours, from 2:00
p.m. to 5:00 p.m.

W: In what language is the tour given?

M: It's __________ __________ both English and
Spanish.

W: What can I expect during the tour?

M: You'll visit __________ __________, museums,
and local markets.

W: Wonderful! How much is the fee?

M: It's 20 dollars __________ __________.

W: Perfect!

---

3. 대화를 듣고, 남자가 여자에게 전화한 목적으로 가장 적절한 것을 고르시오.
   ① 건강 관련 상담을 하려고
   ② 결제 금액 오류를 알리려고
   ③ 잘못 받은 약을 교환하려고
   ④ 약국 영업 시간을 물어보려고
   ⑤ 특정 약물의 재고 여부를 문의하려고

03 (Telephone rings.)

W: Good morning, City Pharmacy. How may I assist
you?

M: Hi, I'm calling about ________ ______________
I picked up yesterday.

W: Sure, what's the problem?

M: I received the __________ __________.

W: I'm terribly sorry about that. Can you tell me
which medication you were supposed to receive?

M: I was supposed to get more medicine for my
__________ __________ __________, but I got
medicine for allergies instead.

W: I __________ for the mix-up. We'll correct this
right away. Please bring back the wrong medicine,
and we'll give you the right one instead.

M: Thanks. I'll __________ __________ this
afternoon.

다음 페이지에 계속 ➡

4. 대화를 듣고, 여자가 탑승하려는 버스의 출발 시각을 고르시오.

① 2 p.m. ② 3 p.m.
③ 4 p.m. ④ 5 p.m.
⑤ 6 p.m.

04

M: Hello, how can I help you?

W: I'd like to buy one bus ticket to Jinju this afternoon.

M: Okay. What time do you want to leave?

W: The sooner, the better. When is the next bus?

M: The next bus is at 2 p.m., but it's ________ ________.

W: Then, what other times are available?

M: Buses also leave at 3 p.m. and 5 p.m.

W: I need to get there by 6 o'clock. So, I'll take the one ________ ________ 3 p.m. Here's my credit card.

M: Thanks. Here is your ticket. The __________ is number 4.

5. 대화를 듣고, 남자의 심정으로 가장 적절한 것을 고르시오.

① upset
② regretful
③ satisfied
④ shy
⑤ embarrassed

05

W: Welcome to Marley's Cleaners.

M: Hello. I'm ________ ________ ________ ________ my jacket.

W: Hello, Mr. Kim. Your jacket is ready.

M: It looks perfect. You really did ________ ________ ________ ________!

W: Of course. I'm familiar with that kind of stain. I also ________ ________ ________.

M: Wow! Thank you so much. They were ________. I forgot to mention it.

W: I'm glad you like the result.

M: I love it. The jacket looks almost new. You are the best cleaner in town.

W: You are too kind. Thanks.

6. 다음 그림의 상황에 가장 적절한 대화를 고르시오.

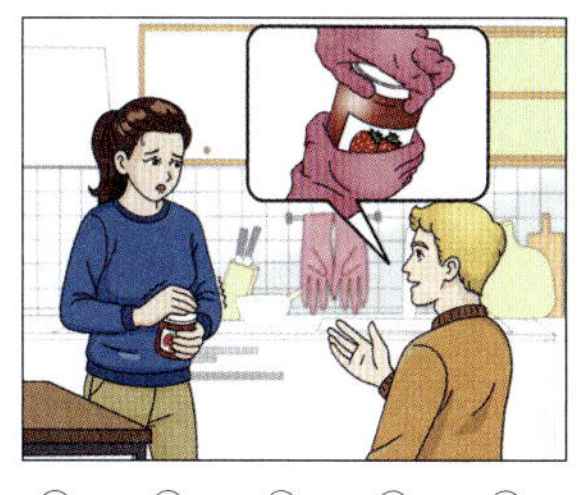

① ② ③ ④ ⑤

06

① W: Did you hear about the new ___________

___________?

M: Yes, I heard it's quite popular.

② W: Would you like some toast with strawberry jam?

M: Yes, please. That sounds delicious.

③ W: I love to travel to new places.

M: Me too! Exploring different cultures is

___________.

④ W: I can't open this jar. Can you help me?

M: Use rubber gloves. That should help you

___________ ___________ ___________

___________.

⑤ W: Hi, I'm looking for a pair of gloves.

M: How about these leather ones? They're one of

our bestsellers.

7. 대화를 듣고, 여자가 남자에게 부탁한 일로 가장 적절한 것을 고르시오.

① 책 반납하기
② 커피 사오기
③ 여동생 데리고 오기
④ 도서관에서 책 빌려오기
⑤ 여동생에게 우산 갖다 주기

07

M: Mom, I'm ___________ ___________ now!

W: Honey, are you going to the library?

M: Yes. I need to study for my finals.

W: Do you know ________ ________ ________ ________

right now?

M: She's working at the café next to the library.

W: Can you take an ________ umbrella with you and

________ ________ ________ your sister?

M: Sure. No problem.

8. 다음을 듣고, 종이에 대해 언급되지 <u>않은</u> 것을 고르시오.

① 발명 지역　② 사용 용도
③ 제작 과정　④ 주요 원료
⑤ 재활용 목적

08

W: Hello, students. Today, we'll talk about paper, one

of our most ___________ ___________. Paper was

first invented in ancient China around 2,000 years

ago. It quickly became an essential material for

___________ ___________. It is used in various

다음 페이지에 계속 ➡

ways, including for writing, printing, and packaging. The main materials used to make paper are wood pulp and water. Today, efforts are being made to ___________ ___________ to help save trees and reduce waste.

9. 다음을 듣고, 무엇에 관한 설명인지 고르시오.

① 청소기
② 건조기
③ 가습기
④ 전기 난로
⑤ 전기 포트

09 W: This is an electric home device which is very useful in winter. It ___________ has a water tank that needs to be ________ ________ ________. This device helps to increase the humidity in the air by ___________ ________ ________. This helps prevent dry skin, dry throats, and other problems caused by dry air. It is important to keep the water tank clean _______ ___________ ________ ___________ of bacteria.

10. 다음을 듣고, 두 사람의 대화가 <u>어색한</u> 것을 고르시오.

① ②
③ ④
⑤

10
① M: What do you want on your birthday?
 W: I just want a big cake.
② M: Please call us ________ ________ ________ ________.
 W: Yes, I will, Dad. Don't worry.
③ M: Can I borrow money from you?
 W: I'm sorry but I already ________ ________ ________ on my new camera.
④ M: I like this shirt but it's too small.
 W: Oh, we have that in other sizes, sir.
⑤ M: Do you ________ ________ ________ ________ when you go to school?
 W: Yes, I go to that school, too.

11. 대화를 듣고, 대화 직후 남자가 할 일로
    가장 적절한 것을 고르시오.
    ① 영수증 가지러 가기
    ② 백화점에서 옷 사기
    ③ 옷 수선 맡기기
    ④ 옷 환불 받기
    ⑤ 코트에 단추 달기

11
W: Welcome to Georgia's Clothing Store. May I help you?
M: Yes, I bought a coat two days ago, and these buttons __________ __________ __________ already.
W: Oh, I'm so sorry. What can we do for you?
M: Is it possible to __________ __________ __________?
W: Well, if you have the receipt, you can get the refund.
M: I see. Then, I think I'll go back to my house right now and __________ __________ __________.
W: Okay. We close at 8 p.m. So, please make sure you come back before 8.

2025 영어듣기능력평가 1회 12번 변형

12. 다음 표를 보면서 대화를 듣고, 여자가
    주문할 스포츠 물병을 고르시오.

	Model	Material	Size (liters)	Dishwasher Safe
①	A	Plastic	1.2	O
②	B	Plastic	2.0	O
③	C	Plastic	1.2	X
④	D	Stainless Steel	1.2	O
⑤	E	Stainless Steel	2.0	X

12
W: Timothy, I'm looking for a sports water bottle to take to the gym. Can you help me?
M: Sure! First, you need to __________ __________ __________. Which do you prefer, plastic or stainless steel?
W: I like plastic __________ __________ __________.
M: Okay. What about the size of the bottle?
W: It needs to __________ __________ my gym bag. So, it shouldn't be too large.
M: Then, you should choose one which is smaller than 1.5 liters.
W: Okay. If it's dishwasher safe, it's __________ __________ to clean, right?
M: Yes. You just need to put it in the dishwasher to __________ __________ __________.
W: Great. I'll order this one.

다음 페이지에 계속 ➡

13. 대화를 듣고, 두 사람이 미술 전시회에 가기로 한 날짜를 고르시오.

① 8월 5일
② 8월 10일
③ 8월 15일
④ 8월 20일
⑤ 8월 25일

13

M: Rachel, have you heard about the _____________ ________ __________ at the city gallery?

W: Yes, I saw the advertisement. Let's go check it out.

M: Sure. I saw that it will ________ ________ August 5th to 25th.

W: Why don't we go on August 10th? It's a Saturday, so we won't have to worry about school.

M: Sorry, it's my parents' wedding ____________ on the 10th. What about the 15th?

W: The 15th is a Thursday, right? I have dance club practice every Thursday. How about going on the 20th?

M: Great! That day ________ ________ ________.

14. 대화를 듣고, 남자가 지난 주말에 한 일로 가장 적절한 것을 고르시오.

① 콘서트 가기
② 공연 예약하기
③ 달리기 훈련하기
④ 공원에서 야구하기
⑤ 야구 경기 관람하기

14

W: Hi, Ethan. Did you enjoy the concert last weekend?

M: I couldn't go because all the tickets were ____________ ____________.

W: Oh, that's disappointing. Then what did you do last weekend?

M: I went to a baseball game with my dad.

W: Nice! Did the team you were ____________ ____________ win?

M: Yes, they did! They ____________ ____________ ____________ and scored four runs in the ninth inning.

W: Wow, that ____________ ____________ ____________ thrilling.

M: Yes, the whole crowd went wild!

W: Sounds amazing!

담화목적파악

15. 다음을 듣고, 방송의 목적으로 가장 적절한 것을 고르시오.

① 자전거 동아리를 홍보하려고
② 자전거 관리 방법을 설명하려고
③ 새로운 도로교통법을 공지하려고
④ 교통사고 발생 시 행동수칙을 알리려고
⑤ 자전거를 안전하게 타는 법을 안내하려고

15 W: Attention students. This is Mrs. Gibson, your vice principal. More and more students are riding their bikes to school. So, I'd like to give you some tips about how to ride a bike to school safely. First, wear a helmet to ___________ ___________ ___________. Also, get off your bike when you reach the schoolyard so that you don't ___________ ___________ other students. Third, use a bike lane when you ride your bike outside of the school area. Please follow these rules ___________ ___________ ___________.

고난도 수치계산(금액)

16. 대화를 듣고, 남자가 지불할 금액을 고르시오.

① $3 ② $5
③ $6 ④ $8
⑤ $10

16 W: Hello, how can I help you?

M: Hi. I'm looking to buy ________ __________.

W: Are you looking for something ________ __________?

M: Yes, I collect landmark magnets. How much are these Gyeongbokgung Palace magnets?

W: They're $3 each. ________ ________ ________ are the Seoul Tower magnets. They are $2 each.

M: Great! I'll take two Gyeongbokgung Palace magnets, and one Seoul Tower magnet.

W: Sure! Here you go. Do you want anything else?

M: No, ________ ________. Thanks.

다음 페이지에 계속 ➡

17. 대화를 듣고, 남자의 마지막 말에 대한 여자의 응답으로 가장 적절한 것을 고르시오.

Woman: ___________________

① At 8 o'clock. But the hall is packed.
② In about thirty minutes. You can go in then.
③ It's in an hour. But you can go inside anytime.
④ It'll be tomorrow. I wish you a successful concert.
⑤ The concert starts at 7 p.m. You don't need to hurry.

17

M: Hi. Can I go into the music hall, please?

W: I'm sorry, sir. The concert ___________ ___________. You cannot go in now.

M: I know I'm late, but I have my ticket here.

W: We cannot open the door ___________ ___________ ___________ of the concert.

M: Oh, no! My daughter is playing the violin in there.

W: Sorry. You have to ___________ ___________ ___________ ___________.

M: When is it?

W: In about thirty minutes. You can go in then.

2025 영어듣기능력평가 1회 18번 변형

18. 대화를 듣고, 여자의 마지막 말에 대한 남자의 응답으로 가장 적절한 것을 고르시오.

Man: ___________________

① Wow! Please give him my congratulations.
② Of course. Your dad will be so proud of you.
③ I'm sorry, but can you take another photo of me?
④ Yes. I think these eyeglass frames look good on you.
⑤ Great! Can you text me the exact location of the store?

18

W: What are you looking at on your phone, Minjae?

M: I'm trying to find a gift for my dad. He just ___________ ___________ at work.

W: That's awesome! Congratulations to him. How about a nice tie?

M: He already has so many of them. I'd like to get him something ___________ ___________.

W: That's so thoughtful of you. What about a framed photo of you and him with a message like "I'm proud of you."?

M: That's a wonderful idea! He'll love it.

W: There's a photo shop near our school that does ___________ ___________.

M: Great! Can you text me the exact location of the store?

19. 대화를 듣고, 여자의 마지막 말에 대한 남자의 응답으로 가장 적절한 것을 고르시오.

Man: _________________

① Too bad. I already have a website.
② Really? This is exactly what I need.
③ Sure. I can introduce the coach to you.
④ That's amazing. Good luck with the marathon.
⑤ It is important that you finish without injuries.

19
W: Hey, Fred. Is it true that you're running a half-marathon?
M: That's right, Brenda. Next month. My first time ever.
W: Great. How's your __________ ________?
M: I'm practicing, but it's not easy. ________ ________ ________ I have a coach.
W: Well, you don't need one. I know a website that can help.
M: A website? How did you ________ ________ about it?
W: I ran a half-marathon before. The website helped me a lot. Take a look.
M: Wow, ________ ________ ________. There are videos, too.
W: And, when you click here, they ________ ________ ________ ________ for you.
M: Really? This is exactly what I need.

2024 영어듣기능력평가 2회 20번 변형

20. 다음 상황 설명을 듣고, Nora가 Justin에게 할 말로 가장 적절한 것을 고르시오.

Nora: Justin, _________________

① I'm afraid I can't help you anymore.
② your math skills have improved a lot.
③ cheer up! I'll help you during the break.
④ everyone loses confidence at some point.
⑤ I appreciate your help with the math problems.

20
M: These days, Nora is having a __________ __________ __________ in math class. She often __________ __________ __________ the teacher's explanations. Justin, her classmate, kindly helps her understand how to complete the math problems during the breaks. After a few times, Nora starts to __________ __________ some confidence in math. So, she would like to thank Justin for his help. In this situation, what would Nora most likely say to Justin?

Nora: Justin, I appreciate your help with the math problems.

Words & Expressions Review 01

● 다음 단어를 암기하세요.

문제	번호	단어	뜻
1	1	belt bag	벨트백, 허리가방, 허리에 차는 가방
	2	reflective strip	반사띠
2	3	conduct	(특정한 활동을) 하다, 수행하다
	4	historic site	유적지
3	5	pharmacy	약국
	6	prescription	처방전
4	7	book	예약하다
	8	platform	승강장
5	9	take out	제거하다
	10	familiar with ~	~에 익숙한
6	11	explore	탐험하다
	12	fascinating	흥미로운, 매력적인
7	13	head out	출발하다, ~로 향하다
	14	extra	여분의
8	15	common	흔한
	16	necessity	필수품
	17	essential	필수적인, 극히 중요한
9	18	humidity	습도
	19	release	내뿜다, 방출하다
10	20	borrow	빌리다
	21	savings	모아둔 돈
11	22	come off	(~에서) 떨어지다
11	23	refund	환불
	24	receipt	영수증
12	25	material	재질
	26	fit in	~에 들어가다
13	27	convenient	편리한
	28	upcoming	곧 있을, 다가오는
14	29	sold out	매진된
	30	disappointing	실망스러운
	31	score	득점하다
15	32	vice principal	교감, 부교장
	33	get off	(탈것에서) 내리다
16	34	souvenir	기념품
	35	particular	특정한
17	36	in the middle of ~	~하는 도중에
	37	break	휴식 시간, 중단
18	38	promote	승진시키다, 진급시키다
	39	meaningful	의미 있는, 중요한
	40	thoughtful	사려 깊은, 친절한
19	41	injury	부상
	42	find out	~을 알게 되다, 알아내다
20	43	confidence	자신감
	44	appreciate	감사하다

● 왼쪽 단어장의 뜻이 보이지 않게 반으로 접고, 학습한 단어의 뜻을 아래 빈칸에 적어주세요.

1	particular		23	disappointing
2	appreciate		24	score
3	pharmacy		25	extra
4	reflective strip		26	in the middle of ~
5	explore		27	meaningful
6	sold out		28	necessity
7	fit in		29	fascinating
8	book		30	promote
9	platform		31	conduct
10	refund		32	prescription
11	convenient		33	thoughtful
12	confidence		34	take out
13	historic site		35	come off
14	find out		36	souvenir
15	injury		37	essential
16	borrow		38	belt bag
17	familiar with ~		39	get off
18	vice principal		40	head out
19	receipt		41	break
20	savings		42	common
21	release		43	humidity
22	upcoming		44	material

02회 중학영어듣기 모의고사

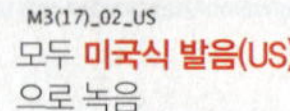

M3(17)_02_US
모두 **미국식 발음(US)**
으로 녹음

M3(17)_02_UK
20문제 중 5문제에 **영국식 발음**
(US+UK)을 포함하여 녹음

정답 및 해석 p. 7

1 대화를 듣고, 남자가 구입할 장난감 보관함을 고르시오.

①  ②  ③  ④  ⑤ 

2 대화를 듣고, Blue Pencil Contest에 관해 언급되지 <u>않은</u> 것을 고르시오.

① 주관사　　　② 주제　　　③ 마감기한　　　④ 심사 기준　　　⑤ 상금

3 대화를 듣고, 남자가 여자에게 전화한 목적으로 가장 적절한 것을 고르시오.

① 오븐을 판매하려고　　　② 수리 일정을 조정하려고
③ 구인 광고에 지원하려고　　　④ 예약 방법을 안내하려고
⑤ 고객센터 위치를 알려주려고

4 대화를 듣고, 여자가 고양이 건강 검진을 예약한 시각을 고르시오.

① 12 p.m.　　　② 1 p.m.　　　③ 2 p.m.　　　④ 3 p.m.　　　⑤ 4 p.m.

5 대화를 듣고, 여자의 심정으로 가장 적절한 것을 고르시오.

① excited　　　② nervous　　　③ glad　　　④ angry　　　⑤ bored

6 다음 그림의 상황에 가장 적절한 대화를 고르시오.

①   ②   ③   ④   ⑤

7 대화를 듣고, 여자가 남자에게 부탁한 일로 가장 적절한 것을 고르시오.

① 대신 일하기   ② 진로 상담해주기
③ 남동생과 놀아주기   ④ 아르바이트 구해주기
⑤ 연극 시사회에 같이 가기

8 다음을 듣고, Pet Nation에 관해 언급되지 <u>않은</u> 것을 고르시오.

① 제공 서비스   ② 보유 시설   ③ 지점   ④ 판매용품   ⑤ 예약 시스템

9 다음을 듣고, 어떤 장소에 관한 설명인지 고르시오.

① 약국   ② 병원   ③ 편의점   ④ 백화점   ⑤ 극장

10 다음을 듣고, 두 사람의 대화가 <u>어색한</u> 것을 고르시오.

①   ②   ③   ④   ⑤

11번~20번 문제는 다음 페이지에 ➡

11 대화를 듣고, 남자가 대화 직후에 할 일로 가장 적절한 것을 고르시오.

① 운송장 번호 찾기　　② 영수증 재발급받기　　③ 배송 일정 변경하기
④ 택배 물품 발송하기　　⑤ 문자 메시지 보내기

12 다음 표를 보면서 대화를 듣고, 여자가 주문할 블루투스 스피커를 고르시오.

	Model	Price	Weight	Battery Life
①	A	$100	950g	20 hours
②	B	$120	900g	20 hours
③	C	$130	750g	30 hours
④	D	$140	700g	40 hours
⑤	E	$160	600g	40 hours

13 대화를 듣고, 두 사람이 산에 갈 날짜를 고르시오.

① 10월 4일　　② 10월 5일　　③ 10월 11일
④ 10월 12일　　⑤ 10월 18일

14 대화를 듣고, 남자가 어제 한 일로 가장 적절한 것을 고르시오.

① 책 반납하기　　② 자전거 타기　　③ 조카 돌보기
④ 자료 조사하기　　⑤ 집 청소하기

15 다음을 듣고, 방송의 목적으로 가장 적절한 것을 고르시오.

① 체육 대회 일정을 공지하려고
② 농구 수행평가 일정을 알리려고
③ 점심시간 운동 활동을 장려하려고
④ 농구장 페인트 작업에 대해 안내하려고
⑤ 교내 체육시설 안전사고 예방을 강조하려고

16 대화를 듣고, 여자가 지불할 금액을 고르시오.

① $35　　② $40　　③ $55　　④ $70　　⑤ $105

17 대화를 듣고, 여자의 마지막 말에 대한 남자의 응답으로 가장 적절한 것을 고르시오.

Man: _______________________________

① You don't have to do that.　② I'm too tired to go there again.
③ OK. Let's visit them in two weeks.　④ I didn't know you didn't like children.
⑤ No. I don't want you to be in danger.

[18~19] 대화를 듣고, 남자의 마지막 말에 대한 여자의 응답으로 가장 적절한 것을 고르시오.

18 **Woman:** _______________________________

① I know, but I was so disappointed.
② Sure. I can help her with the party.
③ That's why I didn't have a fight with her.
④ That's right. So she didn't see the movie.
⑤ That's not true. She didn't have a choice.

19 **Woman:** _______________________________

① It's really sad that she is leaving.
② Then, let's prepare for the good-bye party.
③ I like the hat, too, but you should ask her first.
④ Don't worry. I don't want any expensive presents.
⑤ Why don't we split the cost? I'll pay for half.

20 다음 상황 설명을 듣고, Julian이 Leah에게 할 말로 가장 적절한 것을 고르시오.

Julian: Leah, _______________________________

① I think your new phone is amazing.
② can you introduce me to your friend?
③ I enjoy hanging out with you after school.
④ could you let me know which photo app it is?
⑤ can you teach me how to pose better for photographs?

Dictation Test 02

M3(17)_02_D

Dictation(받아쓰기)은 본문을 받아쓰면서 영어듣기의 집중력을 향상시키고 다양한 표현을 정리하기 위한 영어듣기 학습법입니다. 녹음을 다시 듣고, 빈칸에 알맞은 단어를 써 보세요.

※Dictation의 정답은 듣기 대본의 밑줄 친 부분을 확인하세요.　　　📖 정답 p. 7

맞은 개수 　 / 총176개

그림정보파악(대화)　　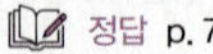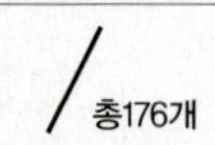

1. 대화를 듣고, 남자가 구입할 장난감 보관함을 고르시오.

01
W: Welcome. May I help you?

M: I'm looking for a toy storage box for my 4-year-old son.

W: I see. How about this type? It's a storage box with wheels ___________ ___________ ___________.

M: Oh, that seems very ___________. I like it.

W: Then, would you prefer one with a dinosaur character on the front or one without?

M: I'll go with the one with the dinosaur character. He loves dinosaurs.

W: Do you need handles on it? It'll be easier to carry around.

M: No, I don't think they're ___________.

W: Okay.

대화미언급

2. 대화를 듣고, Blue Pencil Contest에 관해 언급되지 않은 것을 고르시오.

① 주관사　　② 주제
③ 마감기한　④ 심사 기준
⑤ 상금

02
W: Frank, I was wondering if you are interested in participating in the Blue Pencil Contest.

M: Isn't that a writing contest ___________ ___________ Blue Pencil publishing company?

W: Yes, the ___________ ___________ this year is "Life."

M: Thanks for letting me know. When is ___________ ___________?

W: You need to ________ ________ ________ by
September 5th.

M: That's only two months away. I'd better start
writing today.

W: Good luck. The winner will receive $2,000
________ ________ ________.

M: Thank you. I'll do my best.

---

3. 대화를 듣고, 남자가 여자에게 전화한 목
적으로 가장 적절한 것을 고르시오.

① 오븐을 판매하려고
② 수리 일정을 조정하려고
③ 구인 광고에 지원하려고
④ 예약 방법을 안내하려고
⑤ 고객센터 위치를 알려주려고

03 (Telephone rings.)

W: Hello.

M: Hello, this is MG Customer Service. We received
your message about your oven ________ ________.

W: Oh, yes. I booked a ________ ________ on your
website for tomorrow.

M: Is it okay if we send the repair person this
afternoon? We have one slot open today.

W: One day early? That's great! Yes, I'm __________
this afternoon.

M: Good. Our repair person will call you for detailed
schedule.

W: All right. Thank you very much!

M: You're welcome.

4. 대화를 듣고, 여자가 고양이 건강 검진을
예약한 시각을 고르시오.

① 12 p.m.   ② 1 p.m.
③ 2 p.m.   ④ 3 p.m.
⑤ 4 p.m.

04 (Telephone rings.)

M: Good morning, Bright Veterinary Clinic. May I
help you?

W: Hi, I need to __________ __________ __________
for my cat's annual check-up.

M: Sure. When would you like to bring your cat
in? Just so you know, we have a __________
__________ from 12 p.m. to 1 p.m.

다음 페이지에 계속 ➡

W: Can I ___________ it for tomorrow?

M: Tomorrow afternoon works.

W: Great. How about 2 p.m.?

M: I'm sorry, but 2 p.m. is ___________ ___________.

  Would 3 p.m. work for you?

W: ____________, I have a meeting at 3 p.m. How

  about 4 p.m.?

M: 4 p.m. works. We'll see you and your cat then.

W: Perfect. Thank you so much.

5. 대화를 듣고, 여자의 심정으로 가장 적절
    한 것을 고르시오.

① excited   ② nervous
③ glad   ④ angry
⑤ bored

05 W: Have you had your wisdom teeth pulled out?

M: Yes. I had them ________ ________ a few years ago.

W: How was it?

M: To be honest with you, it was really painful.

W: Really? I'm going to ________ ________ tomorrow

  to have my wisdom teeth removed. I'm ________

  ________.

M: Oh, it's going to be okay.

W: I don't want to go. I'm ________ ________ the

  dentist.

6. 다음 그림의 상황에 가장 적절한 대화를
    고르시오.

① ② ③ ④ ⑤

06 ① M: Do you like my new wallpaper?

  W: Yes. You ________ ________ ________ ________.

② M: I really need to go to the restroom.

  W: Oh, no. The nearest one is 15 minutes away.

③ M: I always forget the password for my cellphone.

  W: How about ________ ________ ________

  somewhere?

④ M: Could you give me the password for the restroom?

W: Sure. It's ________ ________ ________ ________ right here.

⑤ M: Where can I find the toilet paper?

W: It's over there, in ________ 12.

7. 대화를 듣고, 여자가 남자에게 부탁한 일로 가장 적절한 것을 고르시오.
   ① 대신 일하기
   ② 진로 상담해주기
   ③ 남동생과 놀아주기
   ④ 아르바이트 구해주기
   ⑤ 연극 시사회에 같이 가기

07

W: Jason, do you have any plans this Friday?

M: Not yet.

W: Would you mind ________ ________ ________ me at my part-time job at the café on Friday night?

M: Oh, sure. Is everything alright?

W: Yes. My brother is ________ ________ a play that is ________ this Friday, and I have to go.

M: You are a wonderful sister to support your brother's career.

W: Thanks. I ________ ________ big time.

8. 다음을 듣고, Pet Nation에 관해 언급되지 않은 것을 고르시오.
   ① 제공 서비스
   ② 보유 시설
   ③ 지점
   ④ 판매용품
   ⑤ 예약 시스템

08

M: Welcome to Pet Nation! We are here for your ________ ________. Our services include pet grooming, dog training, and vet services. We also have a pet hotel and a grooming salon inside the center. There are 4 ________ around the city, so you can find us easily. We also sell ________ ________ ________ pet snacks and accessories. We are open 24 hours, so call us or visit us anytime.

다음 페이지에 계속 ➡

9. 다음을 듣고, 어떤 장소에 관한 설명인지 고르시오.

① 약국　　② 병원
③ 편의점　④ 백화점
⑤ 극장

09 W: This place sells many kinds of things. You can buy snacks, drinks, and even simple meals here. You can also buy ________ ________ such as toothbrushes and toilet paper, just to ________ ________ ________. In Korea, some medicines that don't require a prescription are sold here. This place usually ________ ________ ________ a small store and some are open 24 hours.

10. 다음을 듣고, 두 사람의 대화가 <u>어색한</u> 것을 고르시오.

① ② ③ ④ ⑤

10 ① W: Have you ________ ________ Chris Brown?
M: No. Who's that?
② W: ________ ________ ________?
M: I broke my sister's mirror.
③ W: Can you give me a hand?
M: I'd love to ________ ________ ________.
④ W: What are you going to do after school?
M: I'm going to play soccer.
⑤ W: ________ ________ will it take?
M: About 30 minutes.

2024 영어듣기능력평가 1회 11번 변형

11. 대화를 듣고, 남자가 대화 직후에 할 일로 가장 적절한 것을 고르시오.

① 운송장 번호 찾기
② 영수증 재발급받기
③ 배송 일정 변경하기
④ 택배 물품 발송하기
⑤ 문자 메시지 보내기

11 *(Telephone rings.)*
W: Hello, this is Quick Express Customer Service. How may I help you?
M: Hi, I want to check my ________ ________.

W: Sure. Could you give me your tracking number?

M: Oh, I'm not sure if I have it.

W: Are you the __________?

M: Yes, I am.

W: Then, the tracking number should be __________ __________ __________, or you would have received it as a text message.

M: Right. Let me check my phone. Just a second, I'll find it now.

W: Take your time.

---

12. 다음 표를 보면서 대화를 듣고, 여자가 주문할 블루투스 스피커를 고르시오.

	Model	Price	Weight	Battery Life
①	A	$100	950g	20 hours
②	B	$120	900g	20 hours
③	C	$130	750g	30 hours
④	D	$140	700g	40 hours
⑤	E	$160	600g	40 hours

12

M: Christine, what are you __________ __________ online?

W: I'm looking for a Bluetooth speaker. Can you help me choose one?

M: Sure. Are you searching for something __________?

W: Yeah, I can't spend more than 150 dollars.

M: Okay. You'll be __________ __________ __________ in your backpack, right?

W: Yeah, I don't want it to be heavier than my laptop which is 800 grams.

M: Okay. You have two options left, then.

W: This one looks good. It has __________ __________ __________ __________.

M: Yes, that seems like the better choice.

W: Thanks. I'll order this one then.

다음 페이지에 계속 ➡

13. 대화를 듣고, 두 사람이 산에 갈 날짜를 고르시오.

① 10월 4일 ② 10월 5일
③ 10월 11일 ④ 10월 12일
⑤ 10월 18일

13 M: Ellie, look at this picture! The leaves on the trees on Seorak Mountain have ________ ________ ________ red and yellow.

W: Wow! It's really beautiful!

M: Why don't we go to Seorak Mountain to see the ________ ________?

W: Sounds good. How about this Saturday, October 4th?

M: Oh, not this Saturday. I'm playing soccer on the 4th. How about the 11th?

W: Sorry, I have ________ ________ ________ that day. Perhaps we can go on Sunday. How about the 12th?

M: You know what? That's a great idea. Let's go on the 12th.

W: Great. See you then.

14. 대화를 듣고, 남자가 어제 한 일로 가장 적절한 것을 고르시오.

① 책 반납하기 ② 자전거 타기
③ 조카 돌보기 ④ 자료 조사하기
⑤ 집 청소하기

14 W: Sean, Kelvin and I are going to ride our bikes at the park. Do you want to join us?

M: I'd like to, but I need to do some research at the library.

W: ________ ________ ________ to do it yesterday?

M: I was. But I got a call from my sister on my way to the library.

W: What was it about?

M: She asked me to ________ ________ ________, Jason, because her babysitter called in ________.

W: I see. What did you do with your nephew yesterday?

M: We watched an animated film and I made him pancakes.

W: Sounds like you and Jason had a wonderful time together.

담화목적파악

15. 다음을 듣고, 방송의 목적으로 가장 적절한 것을 고르시오.
① 체육 대회 일정을 공지하려고
② 농구 수행평가 일정을 알리려고
③ 점심시간 운동 활동을 장려하려고
④ 농구장 페인트 작업에 대해 안내하려고
⑤ 교내 체육시설 안전사고 예방을 강조하려고

15

M: Hello, students. This is your P.E. teacher, Garry Wills. I want to let you know that you're not allowed to use the outdoor basketball court until tomorrow. I'm aware that many of you love to play basketball during lunchtime, but _________ _________ _______ __________ today, and it won't be dry until the next day. You can use the court _________ _________ _________ __________ as usual. It's almost lunchtime now. I hope you have a wonderful time. Thank you.

수치계산(금액)

16. 대화를 듣고, 여자가 지불할 금액을 고르시오.
① $35
② $40
③ $55
④ $70
⑤ $105

16

M: Welcome to Beauty Boutique. How can I assist you?

W: Hi, I'm ___________ __________ __________ some moisturizer.

M: Certainly. We have two options, regular and premium. The premium products have more powerful __________, so they work better.

W: That sounds great. How much are they?

M: A bottle of regular moisturizer is $20, while the premium one is $35.

W: I'll ___________ __________ the premium option.

M: Great choice. If you buy two premium products, you'll get one ___________ __________ for free.

다음 페이지에 계속 ➡

W: Oh, that's fantastic! I'll take __________

__________ __________ the premium moisturizer

then.

M: Excellent decision. Here you go.

W: Thanks. Let me pay with my card.

17. 대화를 듣고, 여자의 마지막 말에 대한 남자의 응답으로 가장 적절한 것을 고르시오.

Man: __________

① You don't have to do that.
② I'm too tired to go there again.
③ OK. Let's visit them in two weeks.
④ I didn't know you didn't like children.
⑤ No. I don't want you to be in danger.

17

W: I loved __________ __________ with those children. How about you?

M: Me, too. I thought an orphanage would be a __________ __________ __________ a depressing place, but the children were so nice and cute.

W: I'm a little tired, but I think it was nice to visit and do __________ __________ there.

M: I agree. I want to go there next weekend, too. What do you think?

W: I don't think I can. But I can go there the __________ __________ __________.

M: OK. Let's visit them in two weeks.

18. 대화를 듣고, 남자의 마지막 말에 대한 여자의 응답으로 가장 적절한 것을 고르시오.

Woman: __________

① I know, but I was so disappointed.
② Sure. I can help her with the party.
③ That's why I didn't have a fight with her.
④ That's right. So she didn't see the movie.
⑤ That's not true. She didn't have a choice.

18

M: What's the matter, Kelly? __________ __________ __________.

W: Dad, I had a fight with Jessica today.

M: I thought you were best friends with her. What went wrong?

W: We __________ __________ __________ __________ a movie together, but she went to see it with other people.

M: That's not nice, but maybe she __________ __________ __________.

W: She said she went to a birthday party and everyone went to see the movie together.

M: Oh, I see. She _______ _______ _______, then.

W: I know, but I was so disappointed.

고난도 **알맞은응답찾기**

19. 대화를 듣고, 남자의 마지막 말에 대한 여자의 응답으로 가장 적절한 것을 고르시오.

Woman: _______________

① It's really sad that she is leaving.
② Then, let's prepare for the good-bye party.
③ I like the hat, too, but you should ask her first.
④ Don't worry. I don't want any expensive presents.
⑤ Why don't we split the cost? I'll pay for half.

19

W: What are you doing, Sam?

M: I'm _______ _______ _______ for a good-bye present for Muriel.

W: Right. I have to buy one, too.

M: Do you have _______ _______ _______?

W: Not yet. What about you?

M: I want to get her a hat, but it's too expensive.

W: She's going to like it, hat or not.

M: Yeah, but this hat is _______ _______ _______ _______ _______.

W: Why don't we split the cost? I'll pay for half.

상황에적절한말찾기

2024 영어듣기능력평가 1회 20번 변형

20. 다음 상황 설명을 듣고, Julian이 Leah에게 할 말로 가장 적절한 것을 고르시오.

Julian: Leah, _______________

① I think your new phone is amazing.
② can you introduce me to your friend?
③ I enjoy hanging out with you after school.
④ could you let me know which photo app it is?
⑤ can you teach me how to pose better for photographs?

20

W: Julian has a close friend, Leah. They often _______ _______ and take a lot of pictures together. One day, Julian notices that Leah's photos are _______ _______ _______ than before. Leah explains that it's _______ _______ the new picture app on her phone. Julian thinks it's _______. So, he would like to ask her to tell him more about the app. In this situation, what would Julian most likely say to Leah?

Julian: Leah, could you let me know which photo app it is?

Words & Expressions Review 02

● 다음 단어를 암기하세요.

문제	번호	단어	뜻
1	1	storage	수납, 보관, 저장
	2	necessary	필요한
2	3	organize	조직하다, 개최하다
	4	publishing company	출판사
	5	theme	주제, 테마
3	6	slot	(명단/프로그램 등에 들어가는) 자리
	7	available	시간이 있는
	8	detailed	자세한, 상세한
4	9	unfortunately	안타깝게도, 불행하게도
5	10	wisdom tooth	사랑니
	11	pull out ~	~을 뽑다
6	12	make a choice	선택하다
	13	aisle	통로
7	14	fill in for A	A를 대신하여 일하다
	15	star in ~	~에서 주연을 맡다
	16	daily necessity	생활필수품
9	17	require	필요로 하다, 필요하다
	18	prescription	처방전
10	19	give A a hand	A를 도와주다
	20	status	(진행 과정상의) 상황
11	21	receipt	영수증
	22	receive	받다

문제	번호	단어	뜻
	23	search for	~을 찾다
12	24	affordable	적당한 가격의, 감당할 수 있는
	25	carry ~ around	~을 갖고 다니다
	26	option	선택(지)
13	27	turn	(~한 상태로) 변하다, 되다
	28	scenery	경치, 풍경
	29	gathering	(특정 목적을 위한) 모임
14	30	babysit	아이를 봐주다
	31	call in sick	전화로 아파서 못 간다고 하다
15	32	outdoor	실외의
	33	as usual	평상시처럼
16	34	moisturizer	수분 로션
	35	premium	고급의
	36	work	효과가 있다[나다]
	37	additional	추가적인, 추가의
17	38	orphanage	고아원
	39	depressing	우울한
	40	volunteer work	봉사 활동
18	41	wrong	잘못된
19	42	split	나누다
20	43	brilliant	훌륭한, 멋진
	44	hang out	시간을 보내다

M3(17)_W_02

● 왼쪽 단어장의 뜻이 보이지 않게 반으로 접고, 학습한 단어의 뜻을 아래 빈칸에 적어주세요.

1	additional	23	as usual
2	brilliant	24	affordable
3	work	25	slot
4	premium	26	fill in for A
5	call in sick	27	theme
6	search for	28	orphanage
7	prescription	29	require
8	status	30	hang out
9	moisturizer	31	outdoor
10	babysit	32	option
11	carry ~ around	33	publishing company
12	star in ~	34	detailed
13	wrong	35	give A a hand
14	turn	36	unfortunately
15	gathering	37	organize
16	storage	38	wisdom tooth
17	split	39	necessary
18	pull out ~	40	volunteer work
19	receive	41	receipt
20	scenery	42	daily necessity
21	depressing	43	aisle
22	available	44	make a choice

03회 중학영어듣기 모의고사

모두 **미국식 발음(US)**으로 녹음

20문제 중 5문제에 **영국식 발음 (US+UK)**을 포함하여 녹음

정답 및 해석 p. 13

1 대화를 듣고, 여자가 선택할 솜사탕을 고르시오.

①  ②  ③  ④  ⑤ 

2 대화를 듣고, 줄넘기 대회에 관해 언급되지 <u>않은</u> 것을 고르시오.

① 대회 요일 ② 장소 ③ 경기종목
④ 신청 방법 ⑤ 참가상품

3 대화를 듣고, 남자가 여자에게 전화한 목적으로 가장 적절한 것을 고르시오.

① 프린터를 사용하려고 ② 함께 파티에 가려고
③ 숙제를 같이 하려고 ④ 프린터를 사러 가려고
⑤ 함께 영문학 수업을 들으려고

4 대화를 듣고, 여자가 기차역에 마중 나갈 시각을 고르시오.

① 4 p.m. ② 5 p.m. ③ 6 p.m. ④ 7 p.m. ⑤ 8 p.m.

5 대화를 듣고, 여자의 심정으로 가장 적절한 것을 고르시오.

① bored ② proud ③ concerned
④ jealous ⑤ disappointed

6 다음 그림의 상황에 가장 적절한 대화를 고르시오.

①   ②   ③   ④   ⑤

7 대화를 듣고, 여자가 남자에게 부탁한 일로 가장 적절한 것을 고르시오.

① 빨래 꺼내기   ② 모터 교체하기   ③ 웹사이트 확인하기
④ 바이올린 수업 등록하기   ⑤ 세탁기의 전원 껐다 켜기

8 다음을 듣고, International Woodcraft Fair에 관해 언급되지 <u>않은</u> 것을 고르시오.

① 개최 장소   ② 개최 기간   ③ 참가 인원   ④ 입장 방법   ⑤ 후원사

9 다음을 듣고, 무엇에 관한 설명인지 고르시오.

① 김밥   ② 닭꼬치   ③ 떡볶이   ④ 순대   ⑤ 호떡

10 다음을 듣고, 두 사람의 대화가 <u>어색한</u> 것을 고르시오.

①   ②   ③   ④   ⑤

11번~20번 문제는 다음 페이지에 ➡

11 대화를 듣고, 남자가 대화 직후에 할 일로 가장 적절한 것을 고르시오.

① 훈련 계획 짜기　　　② 축구 팀 주장 선출하기　　　③ 방과 후 수업 신청하기
④ 축구 팀 가입 의사 묻기　　　⑤ 다음 경기 일정 확인하기

12 다음 표를 보면서 대화를 듣고, 남자가 주문할 텐트를 고르시오.

	Model	Capacity	Price	Number of Doors
①	A	2-person	$200	1
②	B	4-person	$250	1
③	C	4-person	$280	2
④	D	6-person	$330	3
⑤	E	6-person	$360	4

13 대화를 듣고, 남자가 코트를 찾아갈 날짜를 고르시오.

① 2월 2일　　　② 2월 4일　　　③ 2월 5일　　　④ 2월 6일　　　⑤ 2월 8일

14 대화를 듣고, 여자가 어제 한 일로 가장 적절한 것을 고르시오.

① 풍경 사진 찍기　　　② 시험공부하기　　　③ 자원봉사하기
④ 병문안 가기　　　⑤ 파티 준비하기

15 다음을 듣고, 방송의 목적으로 가장 적절한 것을 고르시오.

① 신규 입단 선수를 소개하려고　　　② 축구 시합 일정을 공지하려고
③ 입단 테스트 신청 절차를 안내하려고　　　④ 학생들의 체육대회 참가를 장려하려고
⑤ 준비 운동의 중요성에 대해 설명하려고

16 대화를 듣고, 여자가 지불할 금액을 고르시오.

① $7 ② $12 ③ $14 ④ $16 ⑤ $20

[17~19] 대화를 듣고, 여자의 마지막 말에 대한 남자의 응답으로 가장 적절한 것을 고르시오.

17 **Man:** _______________________________

① Today is a national holiday.
② Sure, let's look on the Internet.
③ His presentation was so boring.
④ It's important to know our history.
⑤ We're almost finished with our project.

18 **Man:** _______________________________

① No, I can't pick up the flowers today.
② My wife loves tulips. I'll get them instead.
③ Yes. I'd like to add a card with a message.
④ Please make sure to deliver them on time.
⑤ Could you prepare the arrangement in a flower pot?

19 **Man:** _______________________________

① I don't need acting lessons.
② Just relax and be yourself.
③ I'm afraid she might say no.
④ You never know until you try.
⑤ I don't have any questions.

20 다음 상황 설명을 듣고, Chad가 Bonnie에게 할 말로 가장 적절한 것을 고르시오.

Chad: Bonnie, _______________________________

① you'd better get your eyes checked out.
② you are using your smartphone too much.
③ how about taking a shower with cold water?
④ you can easily read articles on your cellphone.
⑤ washing your eyes with warm water may help you.

Dictation Test 03

M3(17)_03_D

Dictation(받아쓰기)은 본문을 받아쓰면서 영어듣기의 집중력을 향상시키고 다양한 표현을 정리하기 위한 영어듣기 학습법입니다. **녹음을 다시 듣고, 빈칸에 알맞은 단어를 써 보세요.**
※Dictation의 정답은 듣기 대본의 밑줄 친 부분을 확인하세요.

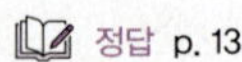 정답 p. 13

맞은 개수 / 총189개

그림정보파악(대화)

1. 대화를 듣고, 여자가 선택할 솜사탕을 고르시오.

①  ② 

③  ④ 

⑤

01

M: Hello. May I help you?

W: Hi. I'd like a cotton candy, please. It's for my daughter.

M: Sure. We have bear-shaped ones and rabbit-shaped ones. You can _________ _________ _________ _________ the samples here.

W: I'll go for a rabbit-shaped cotton candy. I think she'd like a rabbit better than a bear.

M: Okay. And if you _________ _________ _________, you'll _________ that some have small eyes, and some have big eyes. Which do you prefer?

W: Oh, the ones with big eyes look really pretty! Also, is it possible to _________ _________ _________ on one ear?

M: Of course! I'll make one for you right away.

대화미언급

2. 대화를 듣고, 줄넘기 대회에 관해 언급되지 <u>않은</u> 것을 고르시오.
① 대회 요일
② 장소
③ 경기종목
④ 신청 방법
⑤ 참가상품

02

M: Charlotte, are you entering the Annual Jump Rope Contest?

W: I'm not sure yet. The contest is next Saturday, right?

M: Yes. _________ _________ _________ at Star Stadium. I'm entering the contest.

W: Oh, really? What kind of jumps will you do?

M: The alternate foot jump and the double unders jump.

W: Right. Are there any other categories?

M: Sure. There are many other categories you can ________ ________. You should ________ ________.

W: Okay. Maybe I'll have a go.

M: Great. It'll be fun. Everyone will get a __________ bag as a participation prize, too.

W: That's nice. Do you want to practice together?

M: Yeah. Let's do that.

전화목적파악

3. 대화를 듣고, 남자가 여자에게 전화한 목적으로 가장 적절한 것을 고르시오.

① 프린터를 사용하려고
② 함께 파티에 가려고
③ 숙제를 같이 하려고
④ 프린터를 사러 가려고
⑤ 함께 영문학 수업을 들으려고

03 (Telephone rings.)

M: Hi, Annie. This is Tom.

W: Hi, Tom. What's up?

M: Annie, would you ________ ________ ________ ________?

W: Sure. What is it?

M: I need to ________ ________ my assignment for the English literature class. But I'm afraid my printer isn't working ________ ________. Can I use your printer?

W: Sure. But I'm going to my friend's birthday party tonight, so ________ ________ here before seven, okay?

M: OK. Thank you very much.

수치파악(시각)

4. 대화를 듣고, 여자가 기차역에 마중 나갈 시각을 고르시오.

① 4 p.m.　　② 5 p.m.
③ 6 p.m.　　④ 7 p.m.
⑤ 8 p.m.

04 (Cellphone rings.)

M: Hello.

W: Cameron, it's me. Are you on the train now?

M: Yes, the train left on time, at 4 p.m.

W: That's nice. I'll be ________ ________ ________ at 6 p.m. to pick you up.

다음 페이지에 계속 ➡

M: Come at 7. The train is delayed, and I need to

______ ______ ______ something at the

station.

W: Oh, did the train stop in the middle of the route

again?

M: Yes, there was a ______ ______-______.

W: Okay. I'll be there at 7 then.

M: Thanks. See you soon.

5. 대화를 듣고, 여자의 심정으로 가장 적절한 것을 고르시오.

① bored
② proud
③ concerned
④ jealous
⑤ disappointed

05 M: Mom, I'm home.

W: Andy, how was your speech contest?

M: Good. I ______ ______ ______ ______

______ and I quite enjoyed the contest.

W: I'm glad to hear that.

M: And guess what? I ______ ______ ______!

W: Wow, good for you! I knew you could do it.

M: Thank you, Mom. I still can't believe that I won.

W: Oh, you ______ ______. You practiced really

hard. I'm so happy for you.

6. 다음 그림의 상황에 가장 적절한 대화를 고르시오.

① ② ③ ④ ⑤

06 ① W: What time do you finish work here?

M: I finish at 6 p.m.

② W: Can I have a cheese cake, please?

M: Sorry. They are all ______ ______ today.

③ W: Where is the elevator?

M: It's ______ ______ ______.

④ W: Could you put my coffee _______ _______

_______, please?

M: Sure, no problem.

⑤ W: I have a high fever and runny nose.

M: You need to see a doctor.

---

7. 대화를 듣고, 여자가 남자에게 부탁한 일로 가장 적절한 것을 고르시오.

① 빨래 꺼내기
② 모터 교체하기
③ 웹사이트 확인하기
④ 바이올린 수업 등록하기
⑤ 세탁기의 전원 껐다 켜기

07

W: Dad, the washing machine isn't __________

__________.

M: What's wrong with it?

W: It's making a strange noise.

M: Have you tried __________ __________

__________ and on again?

W: Yes, I have, but it didn't help. I think there might be a problem with the motor.

M: Have you checked out the customer service center's website? They provide __________ ______________ in case we have a problem.

W: No, I haven't. I have to go now because I have a violin lesson. Could you check it out for me?

M: Sure. No problem.

---

8. 다음을 듣고, International Woodcraft Fair에 관해 언급되지 <u>않은</u> 것을 고르시오.

① 개최 장소
② 개최 기간
③ 참가 인원
④ 입장 방법
⑤ 후원사

08

W: Hello, everyone. Welcome to the International Woodcraft Fair at Riverside Complex. This event _______ _______ _______ two weeks until next Sunday. This year, over 200 woodcraft artists from 30 different countries _______ ______________.
It's a great chance to see world-class art. You can also buy beautiful wooden works _______ _______ _______. We give our thanks to our _______, Bailey Company. Enjoy!

다음 페이지에 계속 ➡

9. 다음을 듣고, 무엇에 관한 설명인지 고르시오.

① 김밥 ② 닭꼬치
③ 떡볶이 ④ 순대
⑤ 호떡

09 M: This is a delicious Korean street food that many people enjoy worldwide. It's _____________ _____________ its spicy and flavorful taste, and you can have it as a snack or a meal. In Korea, it's a favorite for street food lovers. The great thing is, it's very _____________ _____________ _____________. Just put some chewy rice cakes, fish cakes, and spicy sauce in a pan. Cook it until everything is soft and _____________ _____________ _____________, and you're done.

10. 다음을 듣고, 두 사람의 대화가 <u>어색한</u> 것을 고르시오.

①　　　②
③　　　④
⑤

10 ① M: _____________ _____________ _____________ _____________?

W: I've been pretty good.

② M: What is your _____________ _____________?

W: I like science the most.

③ M: You know what? Jacob failed the exam.

W: You are kidding! I can't believe it.

④ M: _____________ _____________ _____________ _____________ about your English teacher?

W: I think so, too.

⑤ M: _____________ _____________ do you go to the library?

W: I'd say about three times a month.

할일파악(대화직후)

11. 대화를 듣고, 남자가 대화 직후에 할 일로 가장 적절한 것을 고르시오.

① 훈련 계획 짜기
② 축구 팀 주장 선출하기
③ 방과 후 수업 신청하기
④ 축구 팀 가입 의사 묻기
⑤ 다음 경기 일정 확인하기

11
W: Eric, are you still on the school soccer team ____________ ____________?

M: Yes, but we lost two members who graduated last year.

W: Oh, then you must need more players for the next tournament.

M: Exactly. We need ____________ ____________ one more member to join the team soon.

W: How about asking Brian? I mean the new boy in our class. I heard that he ____________ ____________ ____________ a player at his previous school.

M: Really? I had no idea!

W: I think he'd be interested. You ____________ ____________ ____________.

M: That's a good suggestion, Trisha. I'll talk to him right now.

고난도 **도표정보파악**

12. 다음 표를 보면서 대화를 듣고, 남자가 주문할 텐트를 고르시오.

	Model	Capacity	Price	Number of Doors
①	A	2-person	$200	1
②	B	4-person	$250	1
③	C	4-person	$280	2
④	D	6-person	$330	3
⑤	E	6-person	$360	4

12
M: Chloe, I know you're an ________ camper. Can you help me buy a tent?

W: Sure, that sounds fun. How many people will be sleeping in the tent?

M: There will be three of us.

W: Then, you should ________ ________ ________ ________ ________ four or more people.

M: Okay, how much should I spend?

W: I wouldn't recommend spending more than $300.

M: Understood. Do you have ________ ________ ________?

W: You should also buy a tent which has ________ ________ two doors.

M: Thanks for your help. I'll buy this one then.

다음 페이지에 계속 ➡

13. 대화를 듣고, 남자가 코트를 찾아갈 날짜를 고르시오.

① 2월 2일　　② 2월 4일
③ 2월 5일　　④ 2월 6일
⑤ 2월 8일

13
W: You look great in that coat.
M: I like it, too. I'll take it. However, the sleeves are a bit long.
W: We can ＿＿＿＿＿＿ ＿＿＿＿＿＿ for ten dollars.
M: That sounds good. How long will it take?
W: Today is February 2, so you can ＿＿＿＿＿＿ ＿＿＿＿＿＿ ＿＿＿＿＿＿ ＿＿＿＿＿＿ next Monday, February 6.
M: Hmm… I have an event on Sunday. Can I get it earlier?
W: Let's see. (*pause*) Okay. We can ＿＿＿＿＿＿ ＿＿＿＿＿＿ ＿＿＿＿＿＿ by Saturday, February 4 after 5 p.m.
M: That sounds OK. What about tomorrow, February 3?
W: Sorry, that's too soon. Saturday is the ＿＿＿＿＿＿ ＿＿＿＿＿＿ ＿＿＿＿＿＿.
M: Okay, Saturday it is. Thank you.

14. 대화를 듣고, 여자가 어제 한 일로 가장 적절한 것을 고르시오.

① 풍경 사진 찍기
② 시험공부하기
③ 자원봉사하기
④ 병문안 가기
⑤ 파티 준비하기

14
M: Alicia, are you all right?
W: What do you mean?
M: Ron told me he saw you at the hospital yesterday. Were you sick?
W: No, I'm perfectly fine. I was ＿＿＿＿＿＿ ＿＿＿＿＿＿ ＿＿＿＿＿＿ in the hospital yesterday. He had surgery two days ago.
M: Oh, is he okay? Why did he need surgery?
W: He fell down and broke his arm. He's ＿＿＿＿＿＿ ＿＿＿＿＿＿ now.
M: That's a relief. When will he get out of the hospital?
W: Tomorrow. My sister and I are going to ＿＿＿＿＿＿ him a welcome home party.
M: Great!

15. 다음을 듣고, 방송의 목적으로 가장 적절한 것을 고르시오.

① 신규 입단 선수를 소개하려고
② 축구 시합 일정을 공지하려고
③ 입단 테스트 신청 절차를 안내하려고
④ 학생들의 체육대회 참가를 장려하려고
⑤ 준비 운동의 중요성에 대해 설명하려고

15
M: Hello, students. I'm the school football coach. If you've always wanted to join the football team, now is your chance. We're holding tryouts this Saturday. In order to __________ __________ __________ __________, you must register first. You can find the registration forms outside my office. After __________ __________ __________ __________, please hand it in to me by this Thursday. When your registration is complete, I'll __________ __________ about the time and place for the tryouts.

16. 대화를 듣고, 여자가 지불할 금액을 고르시오.

① $7   ② $12
③ $14   ④ $16
⑤ $20

16
M: Welcome to Super Smoothies.
W: Hi! I'd like a green smoothie and a protein shake, please.
M: Of course! The green smoothie is 5 dollars, and the protein shake is 7 dollars.
W: Great! I'll __________ __________ __________ __________. Oh, and do you have any energy bars?
M: Yes, they are 4 dollars each. But when you __________ __________ __________ a protein shake order, you can get it for 2 dollars.
W: That's a good deal! I'll take one energy bar __________ __________.
M: Excellent! How would you like to pay?
W: Here's my credit card.

다음 페이지에 계속 ➡

17. 대화를 듣고, 여자의 마지막 말에 대한 남자의 응답으로 가장 적절한 것을 고르시오.

Man: _________________

① Today is a national holiday.
② Sure, let's look on the Internet.
③ His presentation was so boring.
④ It's important to know our history.
⑤ We're almost finished with our project.

17

W: Thomas, I need help with my history presentation.

M: How can I help you?

W: I'm almost finished, but I need something in the introduction that will ________ ________ ________ ________.

M: Okay. Can you ________ ________ in your presentation?

W: Yeah, I think so. Do you think that would be helpful?

M: Yes. It's good to start with a short video to catch the interest of the audience.

W: That's a good idea. Can you ________ ________ ________ ________?

M: Sure, let's look on the Internet.

18. 대화를 듣고, 여자의 마지막 말에 대한 남자의 응답으로 가장 적절한 것을 고르시오.

Man: _________________

① No, I can't pick up the flowers today.
② My wife loves tulips. I'll get them instead.
③ Yes. I'd like to add a card with a message.
④ Please make sure to deliver them on time.
⑤ Could you prepare the arrangement in a flower pot?

18

(Cellphone rings.)

M: Hello?

W: Hi, this is Nadine's Flower Shop. Did you ________ ________ ________ for a dozen red roses?

M: Yes, that's correct. Is there an issue?

W: I'm afraid so. We've unexpectedly ________ ________ ________ red roses.

M: Oh, that's disappointing. My wife was really ________ ________ ________ them.

W: We sincerely apologize. You have the option to choose another flower arrangement or ________ ________ ________.

M: Hmm... What other flower options do you have available?

W: We have lilies, daisies, and tulips. Would any of those interest you?

M: My wife loves tulips. I'll get them instead.

19. 대화를 듣고, 여자의 마지막 말에 대한 남자의 응답으로 가장 적절한 것을 고르시오.

Man: _________________

① I don't need acting lessons.
② Just relax and be yourself.
③ I'm afraid she might say no.
④ You never know until you try.
⑤ I don't have any questions.

19

W: Hi, Jack!

M: Hey, Emily! I saw you at the coffee shop yesterday.

W: Really? Why didn't you come over and say hi?

M: I wanted to, but you were with Sarah, so I ____________ ________ ________.

W: Why? What's wrong?

M: She found out that I like her and now I don't know ________ ________ ________ around her.

W: If you really like her, why don't you ________ ________ ________ on a date?

M: I'm afraid she might say no.

20. 다음 상황 설명을 듣고, Chad가 Bonnie에게 할 말로 가장 적절한 것을 고르시오.

Chad: Bonnie, _________________

① you'd better get your eyes checked out.
② you are using your smartphone too much.
③ how about taking a shower with cold water?
④ you can easily read articles on your cellphone.
⑤ washing your eyes with warm water may help you.

20

W: Chad is reading an article about eye health. It says ____________ ____________ a digital screen for too long isn't good for your eyes. It also mentions that when your eyes feel dry, ____________ ____________ ____________ to them can help. While reading the article, he remembers that his friend Bonnie uses her cellphone a lot and often ____________ about dry eyes. Chad would like to tell Bonnie to ____________ ____________ ____________ with warm water whenever she has symptoms. In this situation, what would Chad most likely say to Bonnie?

Chad: Bonnie, washing your eyes with warm water may help you.

Words & Expressions Review 03

● 다음 단어를 암기하세요.

문제	번호	단어	뜻
2	☐ 1	category	부문, 범주
	☐ 2	reusable	재사용할 수 있는
3	☐ 3	assignment	숙제
	☐ 4	literature	문학
4	☐ 5	pick A up	A를 (차에) 태우러 가다
	☐ 6	mix-up	혼동, 혼란
5	☐ 7	try to + 동사원형	~하려고 노력하다
	☐ 8	do one's best	최선을 다하다
	☐ 9	quite	꽤, 상당히
	☐ 10	deserve	~을 받을 자격이 있다, ~을 받을 만하다
6	☐ 11	sold out	다 팔린, 매진된
	☐ 12	put	넣다, 놓다, 두다
7	☐ 13	properly	제대로, 적절히
	☐ 14	specific	구체적인
8	☐ 15	woodcraft	목각
	☐ 16	fair	박람회
	☐ 17	run	(공연 등이) 진행되다
	☐ 18	participate	참여하다
	☐ 19	world-class	세계 수준의
	☐ 20	sponsor	후원 업체, 후원자
9	☐ 21	delicious	맛있는
	☐ 22	flavorful	풍미 있는, 맛 좋은

문제	번호	단어	뜻
9	☐ 23	chewy	쫄깃한
	☐ 24	covered	버무려진, 뒤덮인
11	☐ 25	graduate	졸업하다
	☐ 26	previous	이전의, 전의
12	☐ 27	expert	전문가
	☐ 28	fit	(공간적으로) 들어가다, 크기가 맞다
	☐ 29	suggestion	제안, 의견
	☐ 30	at least	최소한, 적어도
13	☐ 31	shorten	줄이다
14	☐ 32	have surgery	수술받다
	☐ 33	relief	안심
	☐ 34	tryout	테스트, 적성 시험
15	☐ 35	complete	완료된, 완성된
	☐ 36	inform	알리다, 통지하다
16	☐ 37	protein	단백질
	☐ 38	add A to B	A를 B에 더하다
17	☐ 39	grab attention	관심을 끌다
	☐ 40	include	포함시키다
18	☐ 41	issue	(걱정거리가 되는) 문제
19	☐ 42	ask A out	A에게 데이트를 신청하다
20	☐ 43	apply	(물건을) 대다, (약 등을) 바르다
	☐ 44	symptom	증상

●왼쪽 단어장의 뜻이 보이지 않게 반으로 접고, 학습한 단어의 뜻을 아래 빈칸에 적어주세요.

1	reusable		23	pick A up	
2	shorten		24	complete	
3	put		25	try to + 동사원형	
4	fair		26	previous	
5	graduate		27	apply	
6	specific		28	literature	
7	tryout		29	woodcraft	
8	covered		30	category	
9	symptom		31	deserve	
10	properly		32	ask A out	
11	sponsor		33	assignment	
12	relief		34	issue	
13	include		35	inform	
14	sold out		36	run	
15	world-class		37	delicious	
16	do one's best		38	flavorful	
17	mix-up		39	chewy	
18	participate		40	quite	
19	suggestion		41	at least	
20	have surgery		42	expert	
21	add A to B		43	protein	
22	grab attention		44	fit	

04회 중학영어듣기 모의고사

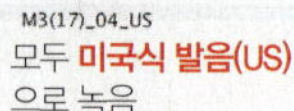

M3(17)_04_US
모두 **미국식 발음(US)** 으로 녹음

M3(17)_04_UK
20문제 중 5문제에 **영국식 발음 (US+UK)**을 포함하여 녹음

정답 및 해석 p. 19

1
대화를 듣고, 여자가 구입할 티셔츠로 가장 적절한 것을 고르시오.

① 　② 　③ 　④ 　⑤ 

2
대화를 듣고, Korea Apple Festival에 관해 언급되지 <u>않은</u> 것을 고르시오.

① 개최 시기　　② 행사 장소　　③ 프로그램
④ 참가비　　⑤ 기념품

3
대화를 듣고, 남자가 여자에게 전화한 목적으로 가장 적절한 것을 고르시오.

① 인터넷 서비스를 신청하려고　　② 할인 혜택에 대해 문의하려고
③ 인터넷 서비스를 중단하려고　　④ 케이블 TV 방송을 신청하려고
⑤ 더 빠른 인터넷 서비스를 신청하려고

4
대화를 듣고, 남자가 반려견을 목욕시킬 시각을 고르시오.

① 6 p.m.　　② 7 p.m.　　③ 8 p.m.　　④ 9 p.m.　　⑤ 10 p.m.

5
대화를 듣고, 남자의 심정으로 가장 적절한 것을 고르시오.

① scared　　② relaxed　　③ excited　　④ proud　　⑤ jealous

6 다음 그림의 상황에 가장 적절한 대화를 고르시오.

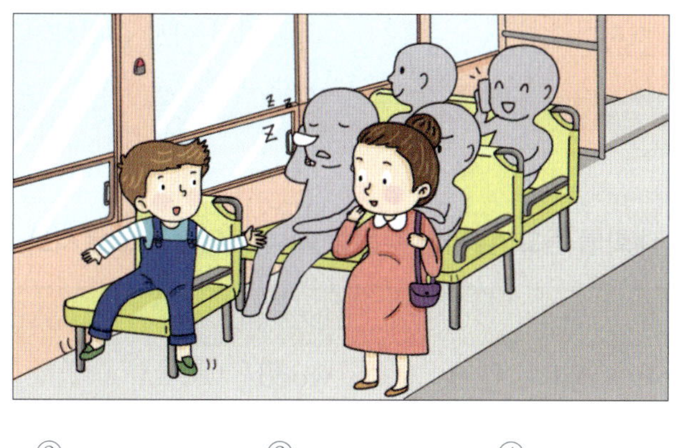

① ② ③ ④ ⑤

7 대화를 듣고, 남자가 여자에게 부탁한 일로 가장 적절한 것을 고르시오.

① 병원 방문하기 ② 이메일 보내기
③ 회의실 예약하기 ④ 발표자료 준비하기
⑤ 보험회사에 연락하기

8 다음을 듣고, MT Short Film Competition에 관해 언급되지 <u>않은</u> 것을 고르시오.

① 작품 길이 ② 출품 방법 ③ 접수 기간 ④ 결과 발표일 ⑤ 우승 상품

9 다음을 듣고, 어떤 직업에 관한 설명인지 고르시오.

① 라디오 진행자 ② 방송 연출자 ③ 지휘자
④ 공연 기획자 ⑤ 무대 디자이너

10 다음을 듣고, 두 사람의 대화가 <u>어색한</u> 것을 고르시오.

① ② ③ ④ ⑤

11번~20번 문제는 다음 페이지에 ➡

11 대화를 듣고, 여자가 할 일로 가장 적절한 것을 고르시오.

① 빨래하기　　　　　　　　　　② 세탁소에 옷 맡기기
③ 연습실에 셔츠 가져다주기　　④ 저녁 식사 준비하기
⑤ 과일 사기

12 다음 표를 보면서 대화를 듣고, 남자가 주문할 미니 테이블을 고르시오.

	Model	Price	Material	Foldable Table
①	A	$80	wood	×
②	B	$85	wood	○
③	C	$90	metal	×
④	D	$110	wood	○
⑤	E	$120	metal	×

13 대화를 듣고, 남자의 식당 예약 날짜를 고르시오.

① 6월 2일　　② 6월 3일　　③ 6월 4일　　④ 6월 5일　　⑤ 6월 6일

14 대화를 듣고, 남자가 아침에 한 일로 가장 적절한 것을 고르시오.

① 케이크 만들기　　② 결혼기념일 선물 사기　　③ 식탁 꾸미기
④ 꽃 사기　　　　　⑤ 여자 도와주기

15 다음을 듣고, 방송의 목적으로 가장 적절한 것을 고르시오.

① 연간회원권의 특전을 홍보하려고　　② 놀이기구 이용 안전수칙을 설명하려고
③ 미아의 인상착의를 공지하려고　　　④ 놀이공원의 즐길 거리를 안내하려고
⑤ 우천으로 행사가 취소되었음을 알리려고

16 대화를 듣고, 남자가 지불할 금액을 고르시오.

① $12　　② $18　　③ $24　　④ $30　　⑤ $36

17 대화를 듣고, 남자의 마지막 말에 이어질 여자의 응답으로 가장 적절한 것을 고르시오.

Woman: _______________________________________

① You should exercise regularly. ② I can teach you how to do that.

③ I really enjoyed watching the video. ④ Doing simple yoga postures is easy.

⑤ Then do exercises you can do outdoors.

[18~19] 대화를 듣고, 여자의 마지막 말에 대한 남자의 응답으로 가장 적절한 것을 고르시오.

18 **Man:** _______________________________________

① Good. Be careful not to catch a cold.

② Please use a tissue to wipe your nose.

③ Sorry. I don't remember telling you that.

④ Okay. I'll sneeze into my elbow this time.

⑤ I'll make sure to wear a mask like you said.

19 **Man:** _______________________________________

① Yes, Monet's paintings are truly amazing.

② The fire was put out soon, and no one was hurt.

③ You are lucky. Our museum has many great paintings.

④ We do not know yet. It depends on the level of damage.

⑤ No paintings suffered damage, but we closed the room for safety.

20 다음 상황 설명을 듣고, George가 기사에게 할 말로 가장 적절한 것을 고르시오.

George: _______________________________________

① The driver drives the bus so smoothly.

② Could you tell me when the bus arrives?

③ Do you have my cellphone by any chance?

④ I think someone left this cellphone on the bus.

⑤ There's a passenger who fell asleep back there.

Dictation Test 04

M3(17)_04_D

Dictation(받아쓰기)은 본문을 받아쓰면서 영어듣기의 집중력을 향상시키고 다양한 표현을 정리하기 위한 영어듣기 학습법입니다. **녹음을 다시 듣고, 빈칸에 알맞은 단어를 써 보세요.**
※Dictation의 정답은 듣기 대본의 밑줄 친 부분을 확인하세요.

정답 p. 19

맞은 개수 / 총171개

고난도 그림정보파악(대화)

1. 대화를 듣고, 여자가 구입할 티셔츠로 가장 적절한 것을 고르시오.

①  ② 

③  ④ 

⑤ 

01

M: Welcome to Happy Kids. How can I help you?

W: I'm looking for a T-shirt for my nephew. He's 4 years old.

M: Okay. Would you like a long-sleeved one or a short-sleeved one?

W: I think a ________-________ ________ would be better because the weather is getting warmer.

M: True. How about this one with a dinosaur? It's very popular.

W: Um… No, I'm sure ________ ________ ________ a car.

M: Okay. You can choose between two types. One has a round neck and the other has a V-neck.

W: I'll take the one with ________ ________ ________. It looks nicer.

M: Sure. That's a good choice.

대화미언급

2. 대화를 듣고, Korea Apple Festival에 관해 언급되지 <u>않은</u> 것을 고르시오.

① 개최 시기
② 행사 장소
③ 프로그램
④ 참가비
⑤ 기념품

02

W: Ryan, I saw an online advertisement about the Korea Apple Festival.

M: I saw that, too. It's ________ ________ ________ held in late September, right?

W: You're right. It's going to be held at Central Park this year.

M: Good. Will there be any interesting festival programs?

W: Yes, I'm hoping to ___________ ________ their apple pie baking program.

M: Great. I also heard that there will be ________ ___________.

W: Yes, they will be giving out free tumblers, but only for the first 100 visitors.

M: Okay. Let's go early on the first day then.

3. 대화를 듣고, 남자가 여자에게 전화한 목적으로 가장 적절한 것을 고르시오.

① 인터넷 서비스를 신청하려고
② 할인 혜택에 대해 문의하려고
③ 인터넷 서비스를 중단하려고
④ 케이블 TV 방송을 신청하려고
⑤ 더 빠른 인터넷 서비스를 신청하려고

03 (Telephone rings.)

M: Hello? Is this "Fast Connect?"

W: Yes, how may I help you?

M: I would like to ___________ my Internet service.

W: OK. Is there a problem with your service?

M: No, not at all. I'm ________ ________ another city.

W: I understand. Is there anything else I can help you with?

M: Oh, is there a penalty for ___________ ________ ________?

W: No, you've used the service for more than 3 years. So, there won't be any penalties.

4. 대화를 듣고, 남자가 반려견을 목욕시킬 시각을 고르시오.

① 6 p.m.   ② 7 p.m.
③ 8 p.m.   ④ 9 p.m.
⑤ 10 p.m.

04 M: Mom, you're late for the dinner with your friends.

W: The dinner is at 7 p.m., honey. It's only 6. Aren't you going out, too?

M: Yes. I'm going to play basketball with Karl. I'm leaving now.

W: Okay. Oh, can you ________ ________ ________ ________ ________ when you get back?

M: Sure. But, she's going to have to wait. I ________ ________ ________ until 8 p.m.

다음 페이지에 계속 ➡

W: That's all right. Just don't forget to ________ her.

M: I'll bathe her at 9 p.m. after I take a shower.

W: All right. Have a good evening.

5. 대화를 듣고, 남자의 심정으로 가장 적절한 것을 고르시오.

① scared
② relaxed
③ excited
④ proud
⑤ jealous

05 W: Hey, Adam. Why the ________ ________?

M: Candice, listen. You know I have a crush on this girl.

W: The new girl in our school? Sure.

M: I kind of ________ ________ ________ the other day, and she said no.

W: I remember. Something happened?

M: Yeah, she is ________ ________ ________ Brian now!

W: Oh, dear. Brian from our class?

M: Yes! She said yes to him. I can't believe this. Don't I look better than Brian?

W: Um, I'm not going to answer that question.

M: I hate him. I ________ him, and I hate him.

6. 다음 그림의 상황에 가장 적절한 대화를 고르시오.

① ② ③ ④ ⑤

06 ① M: You should be quiet when you're on ________ ____________.

W: Okay. I'll keep that in mind.

② M: Would you close your legs a little bit?

W: Oh, sorry. I was ____________.

③ M: How many stops are ________ until Daehan Hospital?

W: There's only one more stop to go.

④ M: You can sit here, ma'am. I'm ________ ________ at the next stop.

W: Thanks for giving me your seat.

⑤ M: Are you tired? You ________ ________ ________.

W: Yes, I didn't sleep very well last night.

7. 대화를 듣고, 남자가 여자에게 부탁한 일로 가장 적절한 것을 고르시오.

① 병원 방문하기
② 이메일 보내기
③ 회의실 예약하기
④ 발표자료 준비하기
⑤ 보험회사에 연락하기

07 *(Cellphone rings.)*

W: Hello, Mark.

M: Hi, Karen. I'm afraid I have to ________ ________ ________ ________ today.

W: Is everything okay?

M: Well, I need to take my son to the hospital. He has a ________ ________.

W: I'm sorry to hear that. Then, I guess you won't be able to attend the meeting this afternoon.

M: No, so I __________ the meeting until tomorrow. I've just sent an e-mail to let people know.

W: I see. Is there anything else you need?

M: Yes. Could you ________ the meeting room for 2 p.m. tomorrow?

W: Sure, no problem.

8. 다음을 듣고, MT Short Film Competition 에 관해 언급되지 <u>않은</u> 것을 고르시오.

① 작품 길이
② 출품 방법
③ 접수 기간
④ 결과 발표일
⑤ 우승 상품

08 W: Hello, everyone. I'm proud to announce that the MT Short Film Competition is just ________ ________ ________. We accept short films no longer than 10 minutes of any genre. To enter the competition, you must ________ ________ ________ as an MP4 file along with your application form. The submission period is from October 1st to November 30th. The winners will be announced on our website on December 15th. For more details, ________ ________ ________ email us at shortfilm@mothertongue.com. Thanks!

다음 페이지에 계속 ➡

9. 다음을 듣고, 어떤 직업에 관한 설명인지 고르시오.
① 라디오 진행자　② 방송 연출자
③ 지휘자　　　　④ 공연 기획자
⑤ 무대 디자이너

09 W: People who have this job lead a group of instrumentalists or singers to make music __________ __________ __________ __________. They use their gestures to set the tempo, volume, rhythm and so on in a performance. They also __________ the music and __________ __________ to the musicians. To have this job, you need to have broad knowledge about music and be skilled at many aspects of giving music performances.

10. 다음을 듣고, 두 사람의 대화가 <u>어색한</u> 것을 고르시오.
①　　　　②
③　　　　④
⑤

10 ① M: I saw that movie last night with some friends.
W: Do you __________ it?
② M: Do you think it will rain today?
W: I honestly can't tell if it will.
③ M: Can you remember where you left your bag?
W: __________ __________ __________ bags and shoes is horrible.
④ M: I'm going to see Jeremy this afternoon.
W: Really? Tell him I said "Hi."
⑤ M: When is Mr. Godfrey __________ __________ __________ Bangkok?
W: He said he won't return until Monday evening.

11. 대화를 듣고, 여자가 할 일로 가장 적절한 것을 고르시오.
① 빨래하기
② 세탁소에 옷 맡기기
③ 연습실에 셔츠 가져다주기
④ 저녁 식사 준비하기
⑤ 과일 사기

11 (*Cellphone rings.*)
M: Hello, Mom.
W: Hi, Nathan. Are you on your way?
M: Not yet. I'm still practicing for the dance contest.

W: I see. Can you buy some peaches on your way home?

M: Sure. ________ ________ ________ dinner tonight?

W: No, your dad is cooking. It's going to be delicious!

M: Wow! I'm looking forward to it. By the way, is my favorite shirt ________? I want to wear it to tomorrow's practice.

W: It's not, but I'll wash it right away. It'll be ________ ________ __________.

M: Thanks, Mom. See you at home!

12. 다음 표를 보면서 대화를 듣고, 남자가 주문할 미니 테이블을 고르시오.

	Model	Price	Material	Foldable Table
①	A	$80	wood	×
②	B	$85	wood	○
③	C	$90	metal	×
④	D	$110	wood	○
⑤	E	$120	metal	×

12

M: Hey, I'm thinking about buying a mini table. Can you give me some advice?

W: Sure! What do you want to use it for?

M: I need it for my small apartment, mainly as a compact workspace for my laptop.

W: OK. What's your budget for it?

M: I'm hoping to __________ __________ __________ $100.

W: All right. How about the material? Wood or metal?

M: I __________ __________ __________ __________ because it looks nicer.

W: That's a good choice. Lastly, do you want a foldable table?

M: Of course. I have __________ __________, so a foldable one won't __________ __________ __________ __________.

W: Great. Then you should order this one.

다음 페이지에 계속 ➡

13. 대화를 듣고, 남자의 식당 예약 날짜를 고르시오.

① 6월 2일 ② 6월 3일
③ 6월 4일 ④ 6월 5일
⑤ 6월 6일

13 (Telephone rings.)

W: Thank you for calling Panda Chinese Restaurant. How may I help you?

M: I'd like to ________ ________ ________ for this Sunday evening, June 5.

W: I'm sorry, sir. We are ________ ________ on Sunday. However, we have just a few tables left on Friday evening.

M: You mean June 3?

W: Yes. I can give you a table ________ ________ ________.

M: Sounds great. Please book a table under the name of Jason for 4 people at 6 p.m.

W: Thank you. Your reservation ________ ________ for Friday at 6.

14. 대화를 듣고, 남자가 아침에 한 일로 가장 적절한 것을 고르시오.

① 케이크 만들기
② 결혼기념일 선물 사기
③ 식탁 꾸미기
④ 꽃 사기
⑤ 여자 도와주기

14 W: Mmm, smells good. What are you making, Tom?

M: I'm baking a cake. Today is my parents' ________ ________, so I am throwing them a party.

W: Aww, that's so sweet. Do you need any help? I'm free right now.

M: Thank you so much! Can you ________ ________ ________ with those flowers?

W: No problem. Wow, the flowers are beautiful!

M: My mom loves flowers, so I bought them this morning.

W: Your mom will be ________ ________ ________ ________.

15. 다음을 듣고, 방송의 목적으로 가장 적절한 것을 고르시오.
   ① 연간회원권의 특전을 홍보하려고
   ② 놀이기구 이용 안전수칙을 설명하려고
   ③ 미아의 인상착의를 공지하려고
   ④ 놀이공원의 즐길 거리를 안내하려고
   ⑤ 우천으로 행사가 취소되었음을 알리려고

15
W: Good afternoon, visitors! Thank you for visiting Wonderland amusement park. Here are a few shows that will make ________ __________ ________ ________. First, a live music show by the award-winning musical group Mariachi begins at noon. Second, a Christmas Fantasy Parade will ________ ________ along Main Street at 4 p.m. Lastly, a __________ ________ show starts at 7 p.m. at the central castle. We hope you enjoy your time at Wonderland. Thank you.

16. 대화를 듣고, 남자가 지불할 금액을 고르시오.
   ① $12   ② $18
   ③ $24   ④ $30
   ⑤ $36

16
W: Welcome to the National History Museum.

M: How much is ________ ________ ________ an adult?

W: It's 12 dollars.

M: ________ ________ a kid? My son is five years old. Is he free?

W: I'm sorry. Only ________ ________ three years old are free. It's six dollars for your son.

M: I see. Then I need two adult tickets and one child ticket for my son.

W: Okay. ________ ________ ________, please.

다음 페이지에 계속 ➡

17. 대화를 듣고, 남자의 마지막 말에 이어질 여자의 응답으로 가장 적절한 것을 고르시오.

Woman: ___________________

① You should exercise regularly.
② I can teach you how to do that.
③ I really enjoyed watching the video.
④ Doing simple yoga postures is easy.
⑤ Then do exercises you can do outdoors.

17

M: Hi, Lisa. How are you __________ __________ with the yoga __________ I taught you last week?

W: Hi, Matthew. I'm doing them every day! Thanks to you, I found the perfect exercises for me.

M: I'm glad you're __________ __________ __________ __________.

W: You know what? It would be great if you'd make a video of the yoga postures and upload it online.

M: Why do you think so?

W: Because you teach so well! A lot of people are looking for simple exercises they can do at home.

M: That sounds interesting, but I don't know how to __________ videos.

W: I can teach you how to do that.

18. 대화를 듣고, 여자의 마지막 말에 대한 남자의 응답으로 가장 적절한 것을 고르시오.

Man: ___________________

① Good. Be careful not to catch a cold.
② Please use a tissue to wipe your nose.
③ Sorry. I don't remember telling you that.
④ Okay. I'll sneeze into my elbow this time.
⑤ I'll make sure to wear a mask like you said.

18

M: (*Sneezing sound*)

W: Ethan, please cover your mouth properly when you sneeze.

M: I did, Mom. I covered my mouth with my hands.

W: I know, but you might be __________ __________ to others that way.

M: Oh, I didn't know that.

W: The __________ __________ for sneezing is to sneeze into the inside of your elbow.

M: Wait, Mom. I feel another __________ __________ __________.

W: Remember what I just told you!

M: Okay. I'll sneeze into my elbow this time.

---

19. 대화를 듣고, 여자의 마지막 말에 대한 남자의 응답으로 가장 적절한 것을 고르시오.

Man: ___________________

① Yes, Monet's paintings are truly amazing.
② The fire was put out soon, and no one was hurt.
③ You are lucky. Our museum has many great paintings.
④ We do not know yet. It depends on the level of damage.
⑤ No paintings suffered damage, but we closed the room for safety.

19

M: Welcome to City Museum. How may I help you?

W: I just saw the ________ ________ . Is it true that the Monet Room is closed?

M: Yes, ma'am. I'm ________ ________ .

W: No! Why? I came all the way from Chicago to see Monet's paintings!

M: We are really sorry. There was ________ ________ ________ in that room yesterday.

W: Well, when will it reopen? I'm ________ ________ in the city for a few days.

M: We do not know yet. It depends on the level of damage.

20. 다음 상황 설명을 듣고, George가 기사에게 할 말로 가장 적절한 것을 고르시오.

George: ___________________

① The driver drives the bus so smoothly.
② Could you tell me when the bus arrives?
③ Do you have my cellphone by any chance?
④ I think someone left this cellphone on the bus.
⑤ There's a passenger who fell asleep back there.

20

M: George is on the express bus on his way to see his grandparents. He falls asleep, and when he wakes up, the bus is arriving at his destination. As he prepares to get off, he ________ ________ ________ next to his seat. He thinks that someone ________ ________ ________ ________ . So, he decides to take it to the driver and tell him ________ ________ ________ . In this situation, what would George most likely say to the driver?

George: I think someone left this cellphone on the bus.

Words & Expressions Review 04

● 다음 단어를 암기하세요.

문제	번호	단어	뜻
1	☐ 1	long-sleeved	긴팔의, 긴 소매의
	☐ 2	short-sleeved	반팔의, 짧은 소매의
2	☐ 3	annual	연례의
3	☐ 4	discontinue	중단하다
4	☐ 5	give A a bath	A를 목욕시키다
	☐ 6	bathe	목욕시키다, 씻기다
5	☐ 7	have a crush on A	A에게 반하다
	☐ 8	go out with ~	~와 사귀다, 교제하다
	☐ 9	keep in mind	명심하다
6	☐ 10	careless	부주의한
	☐ 11	give one's seat	자리를 양보하다
7	☐ 12	take the day off	하루 쉬다, 하루 휴가를 내다
	☐ 13	attend	참석하다
	☐ 14	postpone	연기하다, 미루다
	☐ 15	reserve	예약하다
	☐ 16	competition	(경연) 대회, 시합, 경쟁(자)
	☐ 17	around the corner	코앞에 와 있는, 아주 가까운
	☐ 18	no longer than ~	~보다 길지 않은
8	☐ 19	submit	제출하다
	☐ 20	along with	~과 함께
	☐ 21	submission	제출
	☐ 22	feel free to + 동사	마음 편히 ~하다
9	☐ 23	unified	통합된, 통일된
	☐ 24	interpret	해석하다, 설명하다
10	☐ 25	taste	취향, 맛
	☐ 26	horrible	끔찍한
11	☐ 27	look forward to ~	~을 기대하다
12	☐ 28	compact	(공간이) 작은
	☐ 29	fully booked	모두 예약된
13	☐ 30	reservation	예약
	☐ 31	confirm	확정하다, 확인하다
14	☐ 32	anniversary	기념일
	☐ 33	amusement park	놀이공원
15	☐ 34	take place	벌어지다, 일어나다
	☐ 35	spectacular	장관인, 장관을 이루는
16	☐ 36	free	무료의
17	☐ 37	get on with ~	~을 해나가다
	☐ 38	posture	자세, 태도
18	☐ 39	sneeze	재채기하다
	☐ 40	germ	세균, 병균
19	☐ 41	reopen	다시 문을 열다
	☐ 42	It depends on ~	~에 달려 있다
20	☐ 43	fall asleep	잠들다
	☐ 44	get off	내리다

M3(17)_W_04

●왼쪽 단어장의 뜻이 보이지 않게 반으로 접고, 학습한 단어의 뜻을 아래 빈칸에 적어주세요.

1	spectacular	23	no longer than ~
2	submit	24	annual
3	postpone	25	reservation
4	long-sleeved	26	fall asleep
5	It depends on ~	27	germ
6	sneeze	28	keep in mind
7	give A a bath	29	taste
8	take place	30	feel free to + 동사
9	have a crush on A	31	bathe
10	unified	32	reopen
11	discontinue	33	amusement park
12	reserve	34	confirm
13	around the corner	35	short-sleeved
14	free	36	interpret
15	careless	37	get off
16	take the day off	38	fully booked
17	anniversary	39	compact
18	along with	40	go out with ~
19	look forward to ~	41	attend
20	posture	42	competition
21	get on with ~	43	submission
22	give one's seat	44	horrible

04 회 단어

05회 중학영어듣기 모의고사

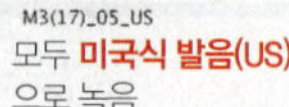

M3(17)_05_US
모두 **미국식 발음(US)** 으로 녹음

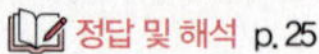

M3(17)_05_UK
20문제 중 5문제에 **영국식 발음 (US+UK)**을 포함하여 녹음

정답 및 해석 p.25

---

1 대화를 듣고, 남자가 구입할 필러를 고르시오.

① 　② 　③ 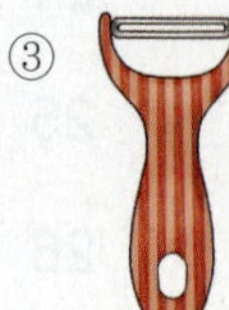　④ 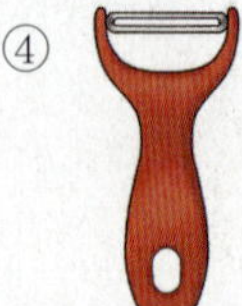　⑤ 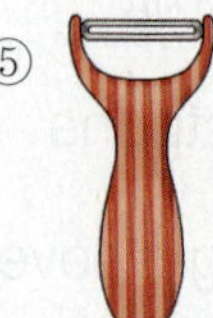

---

2 대화를 듣고, 필라테스 강습에 관해 언급되지 <u>않은</u> 것을 고르시오.

① 지도강사　　② 수업 난이도　　③ 강습시간
④ 수업료　　⑤ 준비물

---

3 대화를 듣고, 남자가 여자에게 전화한 목적으로 가장 적절한 것을 고르시오.

① 자동차 수리를 예약하려고　　② 항공권 예약을 변경하려고
③ 도로 교통 상황을 알리려고　　④ 렌트카 서비스를 이용하려고
⑤ 차를 태워줄 것을 부탁하려고

---

4 대화를 듣고, 남자가 집에서 나설 시각을 고르시오.

① 4 p.m.　　② 5 p.m.　　③ 6 p.m.　　④ 7 p.m.　　⑤ 8 p.m.

---

5 대화를 듣고, 남자의 심정으로 가장 적절한 것을 고르시오.

① peaceful　　② angry　　③ calm
④ excited　　⑤ scared

---

6 다음 그림의 상황에 가장 적절한 대화를 고르시오.

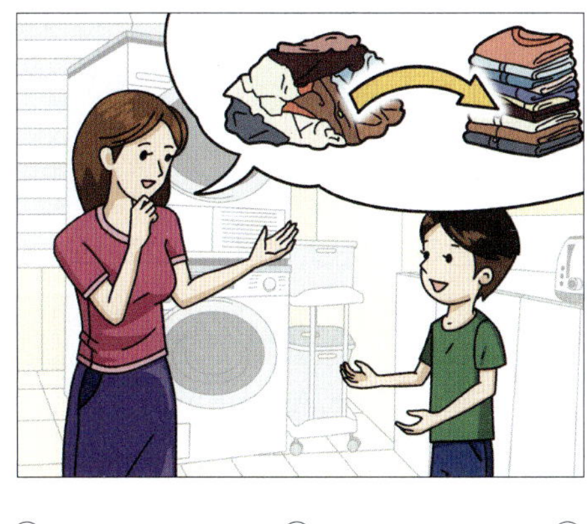

①　　　　②　　　　③　　　　④　　　　⑤

7 대화를 듣고, 여자가 남자에게 부탁한 일로 가장 적절한 것을 고르시오.

① 반창고 사오기　　　② 신발 구매하기　　　③ 신발 교환하기
④ 자동차 태워주기　　　⑤ 병원 데려다 주기

8 다음을 듣고, 학교 밴드 오디션에 관해 언급되지 <u>않은</u> 것을 고르시오.

① 접수 기한　　　② 개최 장소　　　③ 심사위원
④ 준비사항　　　⑤ 합격자 발표일

9 다음을 듣고, 어떤 장소에 관한 설명인지 고르시오.

① 약국　　　② 법원　　　③ 병원　　　④ 헬스장　　　⑤ 수영장

10 다음을 듣고, 두 사람의 대화가 <u>어색한</u> 것을 고르시오.

①　　　　②　　　　③　　　　④　　　　⑤

11번~20번 문제는 다음 페이지에 ➡

11 대화를 듣고, 남자가 할 일로 가장 적절한 것을 고르시오.

① 케이크 찾아오기　　　② 초대장 만들기　　　③ 다이어리 사기
④ 집에 들르기　　　　　⑤ 책 읽기

12 다음 표를 보면서 대화를 듣고, 두 사람이 주문할 냄비를 고르시오.

	Model	Size (inch)	Material	Detachable Handle
①	A	7	Aluminum	X
②	B	8	Aluminum	O
③	C	9	Aluminum	X
④	D	10	Stainless steel	O
⑤	E	11	Stainless steel	X

13 대화를 듣고, 여자가 네일 스튜디오를 예약한 날짜를 고르시오.

① 10월 10일　　　　② 10월 11일　　　　③ 10월 15일
④ 10월 16일　　　　⑤ 10월 17일

14 대화를 듣고, 여자가 지난 주말에 한 일을 고르시오.

① 할머니 댁 방문하기　　② 콘서트 가기　　　③ 과제하기
④ 사과 농장 가기　　　　⑤ 콘서트 예매하기

15 다음을 듣고, 방송의 목적으로 가장 적절한 것을 고르시오.

① 환경 보호 후원금을 요청하려고
② 환경 오염의 심각성을 설명하려고
③ 해양 생물 보호 캠페인을 소개하려고
④ 쓰레기 청소 자원봉사자를 모집하려고
⑤ 플라스틱 쓰레기를 줄이는 방법을 알려주려고

16 대화를 듣고, 여자가 지불할 금액을 고르시오.

① $16　　　② $20　　　③ $24　　　④ $30　　　⑤ $36

17 대화를 듣고, 남자의 마지막 말에 이어질 여자의 응답으로 가장 적절한 것을 고르시오.

Woman: ___________________________________

① I'm really happy to hear that.
② When did you take the exam?
③ I guess we can't discount that.
④ Of course, I don't want you to go.
⑤ Take it easy. You'll get it next time.

[18~19] 대화를 듣고, 여자의 마지막 말에 대한 남자의 응답으로 가장 적절한 것을 고르시오.

18 **Man:** ___________________________________

① How often do you exercise?
② All right! I can't wait to start.
③ I used to swim there every week.
④ Health is the most important thing.
⑤ Our school has many after-school programs.

19 **Man:** ___________________________________

① His movie is good.
② Shall I ask him for you?
③ You can meet him anytime.
④ He's not very kind to his fans.
⑤ I don't need to know his name.

20 다음 상황 설명을 듣고, Jude가 Monica에게 할 말로 가장 적절한 것을 고르시오.

Jude: ___________________________________

① How was your shopping today?   ② Do you like going shopping?
③ Why don't you buy this jacket?   ④ Which color looks best on me?
⑤ You look great in blue.

Dictation Test 05

M3(17)_05_D

Dictation(받아쓰기)은 본문을 받아쓰면서 영어듣기의 집중력을 향상시키고 다양한 표현을 정리하기 위한 영어듣기 학습법입니다. **녹음을 다시 듣고, 빈칸에 알맞은 단어를 써 보세요.**

※Dictation의 정답은 듣기 대본의 밑줄 친 부분을 확인하세요.　　📖 정답 p. 25

맞은 개수 　／ 총181개

2024 영어듣기능력평가 2회 1번 변형

그림정보파악(대화)

1. 대화를 듣고, 남자가 구입할 필러를 고르시오.

① ② ③ ④ ⑤

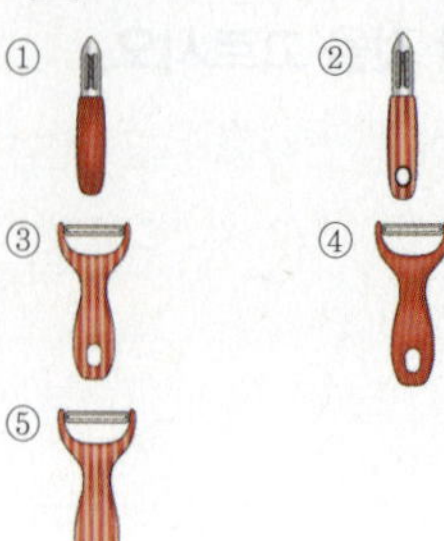

01

W: May I help you?

M: Hi, I'm ___________ ___________ a vegetable peeler.

W: Sure. What type of blade do you want—vertical or Y-shaped?

M: I'll take the Y-shaped one.

W: Would you like a striped handle or a plain one?

M: I'll take the striped one.

W: Do you want a hole at the end of the handle so you can ___________ ___________?

M: No, I don't need that ___________.

W: Okay.

대화미언급

2. 대화를 듣고, 필라테스 강습에 관해 언급되지 <u>않은</u> 것을 고르시오.

① 지도강사
② 수업 난이도
③ 강습시간
④ 수업료
⑤ 준비물

02

(*Telephone rings.*)

M: Hello. Everyday Pilates Center. How may I help you?

W: Hi. I'd like to ___________ ___________ ___________ a one-on-one Pilates lesson.

M: Okay. Do you have a teacher ___________ ___________?

W: Yes. I read about Sarah Kim on your website.

M: Oh, Sarah is a popular teacher. She has a ___________ ___________ at 4 p.m. on Saturdays.

W: That's perfect. I'd like a one-hour lesson every week. How much is it?

M: It's 40 dollars an hour.

W: Right. Is there anything I ________ ________

________?

M: You just need to bring your own Pilates clothes. We have everything else you need here.

W: Okay. Thanks.

🇺🇸🇬🇧

3. 대화를 듣고, 남자가 여자에게 전화한 목적으로 가장 적절한 것을 고르시오.

① 자동차 수리를 예약하려고
② 항공권 예약을 변경하려고
③ 도로 교통 상황을 알리려고
④ 렌트카 서비스를 이용하려고
⑤ 차를 태워줄 것을 부탁하려고

03 *(Cellphone rings.)*

M: Hi, Rachel. It's Joseph.

W: Hi. What's going on?

M: I have a bit of a dilemma. I'm supposed to pick up my parents from the airport tomorrow, but my car __________ __________.

W: Oh, no. What do you need?

M: I was wondering if you could __________ __________ __________ __________ to the airport tomorrow morning.

W: Of course, I'd be happy to help. What time do you need to be there?

M: Their flight lands at 10 a.m., so if we leave by 9:00, that should give us __________ __________ __________.

W: Sounds good. I'll be there at 9:00 sharp.

M: I __________ __________ __________, Rachel. Thanks a lot.

4. 대화를 듣고, 남자가 집에서 나설 시각을 고르시오.

① 4 p.m.   ② 5 p.m.
③ 6 p.m.   ④ 7 p.m.
⑤ 8 p.m.

04 W: Bradley, when does the football game start?

M: At 7 p.m., Mom. But, I have to get to the stadium by 6 p.m.

W: Why? Are you going to stop by the souvenir store?

M: Yes, we can ________ ________ ________ with our tickets.

다음 페이지에 계속 ➡

W: Good. It takes about an hour to get to the stadium. So, make sure to leave early.

M: I'll leave home at 5 p.m. Paul and I will take the subway.

W: Good idea. You can ________ ________ ________ -________ ________, then.

M: Yes! I'm so excited!

5. 대화를 듣고, 남자의 심정으로 가장 적절한 것을 고르시오.

① peaceful
② angry
③ calm
④ excited
⑤ scared

05 W: Hey, Jim! Did you hear about the new movie, *Jinx*?

M: Of course! I've wanted to see that movie since ________ ________ ________ ________!

W: Really? Then, are you going to the premiere?

M: No… Unfortunately, I couldn't ________ ________ ________.

W: Oh, really? Guess what I have?

M: You're ________ ________ ________! Do you have a ticket?

W: Yes! In fact, I have two tickets, so you can come with me!

M: Oh my gosh! This is ________ ________ ________ ________ true!

6. 다음 그림의 상황에 가장 적절한 대화를 고르시오.

① ② ③ ④ ⑤

06 ① M: How much is this ________ ________?

W: It's 800 dollars.

② M: I'd like to buy some jeans.

W: The jeans are right over there in aisle 6.

③ M: Can you pick up my jacket from the dry cleaner's?

W: Sure. I'll ________ ________ ________ after work.

④ M: Do you want me to help you with anything?

W: Yes. Get the clean laundry out of the dryer and

__________ __________.

⑤ M: I've spilled some soda on my shirt.

W: We should __________ __________ __________

__________ immediately.

7. 대화를 듣고, 여자가 남자에게 부탁한 일로 가장 적절한 것을 고르시오.
   ① 반창고 사오기
   ② 신발 구매하기
   ③ 신발 교환하기
   ④ 자동차 태워주기
   ⑤ 병원 데려다 주기

07 M: Hey, Katie. Are you ready to go?

W: Hi, Mike. Before we go, can I sit here for a few

more minutes?

M: What's the matter?

W: Actually, my feet are ________ ________. I ________

________ ________.

M: Oh, how did that happen?

W: It's because of these new shoes that I bought. They

don't ________ ________.

M: Is there anything that I can do to help?

W: Could you buy me some bandages? I want to put

some bandages on my heels.

M: Sure. Wait here for a minute.

8. 다음을 듣고, 학교 밴드 오디션에 관해 언급되지 않은 것을 고르시오.
   ① 접수 기한 ② 개최 장소
   ③ 심사위원 ④ 준비사항
   ⑤ 합격자 발표일

08 M: Hello, I'm Eric Kim, leader of the school band,

Rock Stars. We're looking for new members

now. If you're good at music, ________ ________

________ the audition by next Friday. The

audition will be held on October 10 in the main

hall. ________ ________ ________ ________ two

music teachers and us. The new members will be

________ on October 11. For more information,

check the notice on the school website.

다음 페이지에 계속 ➡

9. 다음을 듣고, 어떤 장소에 관한 설명인지 고르시오.

① 약국　　　② 법원
③ 병원　　　④ 헬스장
⑤ 수영장

09 W: This is an important place that is _________ _________ people's health. Many adults regularly receive _________ _________ here. This place provides people with physical _________ and also mental therapy. Some people might stay at this place for multiple days to receive _________. Mostly, people go to this place when they feel sick or when they get injured.

10. 다음을 듣고, 두 사람의 대화가 <u>어색한</u> 것을 고르시오.

①　　②
③　　④
⑤

10 ① W: Excuse me. Where is the post office?

M: _________ _________ and turn right at the corner.

② W: Hello. May I speak to John?

M: _________. Who's this, please?

③ W: Who's that in the picture?

M: That's Mahatma Gandhi. Don't you _________ him?

④ W: Have you ever heard about Mother Teresa?

M: My mother doesn't _________ _________ _________.

⑤ W: Fall is a very beautiful season.

M: Yes, it is. That's why it's my _________ season.

11. 대화를 듣고, 남자가 할 일로 가장 적절한 것을 고르시오.
    ① 케이크 찾아오기
    ② 초대장 만들기
    ③ 다이어리 사기
    ④ 집에 들르기
    ⑤ 책 읽기

11

W: Richard, are you ________ ________ Valerie's birthday party?

M: Yes! You're coming, too, right?

W: Yes. Can you do me a favor? Can you ________ ________ a cake at Molly's Bakery?

M: Sure. Is that your present for her?

W: Yes. I already ________ ________ ________. It's just that I don't have time to go pick it up.

M: Don't worry. I'll do it now. The bakery is not ________ ________ my house.

W: Thanks. What's your present?

M: I bought her a diary. I got her a book last year, but it seems that she likes writing better than reading!

12. 다음 표를 보면서 대화를 듣고, 두 사람이 주문할 냄비를 고르시오.

	Model	Size (inch)	Material	Detachable Handle
①	A	7	Aluminum	X
②	B	8	Aluminum	O
③	C	9	Aluminum	X
④	D	10	Stainless steel	O
⑤	E	11	Stainless steel	X

12

W: Phil, what are you looking at online?

M: We need a new saucepan. Can you help me choose one?

W: Sure. I think an 8-inch to 10-inch saucepan would ________ ________ us.

M: You're right. 7-inch saucepans are too small, and 11-inch ones are too big. Now, let's choose the material.

W: I prefer aluminum saucepans. They are ________ ________ ________ stainless steel saucepans.

M: I agree. Look! There is a saucepan with a ________ ________.

W: Do you think we should buy that one?

M: Definitely! It will save ________ ________ when we keep it in the cupboard.

W: That's an excellent point! Let's order it.

다음 페이지에 계속 ➡

13. 대화를 듣고, 여자가 네일 스튜디오를 예약한 날짜를 고르시오.

① 10월 10일 ② 10월 11일
③ 10월 15일 ④ 10월 16일
⑤ 10월 17일

13 *(Telephone rings.)*

M: Hello, Glamour Nail Studio. How can I assist you?

W: Hi, I'd like to schedule a manicure ___________.
Do you have any availability on October 10th?

M: I'm sorry, but we're ___________ ___________ on
that day. How about October 11th?

W: Unfortunately, I have a busy schedule ___________
___________.

M: I understand. So, October 12th to the 15th won't
___________ ___________ you. How about October
16th?

W: Hmm. Can I book for Sunday, October 17th
instead?

M: Certainly. Would 3 p.m. work for you?

W: Yes, that's perfect. Can you please book it
___________ ___________ ___________, Jasmine?

M: Absolutely. We'll see you then.

14. 대화를 듣고, 여자가 지난 주말에 한 일을 고르시오.

① 할머니 댁 방문하기
② 콘서트 가기
③ 과제하기
④ 사과 농장 가기
⑤ 콘서트 예매하기

14 W: Hello! Did you have a ________ ________?

M: Yes. I went to my grandmother's farm and helped
her pick apples. How was your weekend?

W: Well, it ________ ________.

M: Why? What happened?

W: My boyfriend and I ________ ________ ________
go to a concert, but we didn't go.

M: Why?

W: I had a huge fight with him. So I just stayed home
and ________ ________ ________.

M: Oh, has he called you yet?

W: No, not yet.

15. 다음을 듣고, 방송의 목적으로 가장 적절한 것을 고르시오.

① 환경 보호 후원금을 요청하려고
② 환경 오염의 심각성을 설명하려고
③ 해양 생물 보호 캠페인을 소개하려고
④ 쓰레기 청소 자원봉사자를 모집하려고
⑤ 플라스틱 쓰레기를 줄이는 방법을 알려주려고

15 M: Hello. This is *Save Our Blue Planet*. Thousands of sea animals are harmed by plastic waste. Here are some ways to __________ __________ __________. First, take your own bags and containers to the grocery store. Second, say "no" to straws and get a ____________ ____________ __________ instead of a paper cup. Third, buy as few packaged products as possible. Your small actions can __________ __________ __________ ____________ and save animals in the ocean. Thank you.

16. 대화를 듣고, 여자가 지불할 금액을 고르시오.

① $16   ② $20
③ $24   ④ $30
⑤ $36

16 M: Welcome to Fresh Mart. How can I help you?

W: Hi. I'm looking to buy some coffee beans.

M: Sure. We have two options __________, regular and premium. The premium beans are __________ __________.

W: Sounds good. How much are they?

M: A bag of regular beans is $8, and the premium beans are $12 per bag.

W: I'll get the premium ones.

M: Great choice. We also have a __________ __________. If you buy two bags of coffee beans, you get a third bag for __________ price.

W: That's fantastic! I'll take three bags of premium beans __________ __________.

M: Wonderful. Here you go.

W: Thanks. Here's my credit card.

다음 페이지에 계속 ➡

17. 대화를 듣고, 남자의 마지막 말에 이어질 여자의 응답으로 가장 적절한 것을 고르시오.

Woman: _________________

① I'm really happy to hear that.
② When did you take the exam?
③ I guess we can't discount that.
④ Of course, I don't want you to go.
⑤ Take it easy. You'll get it next time.

17

W: Hey, Nick. Why the _________ _________?

M: I didn't get my driver's license yet. I've been trying _________ _________ _________, but I just keep failing.

W: What's the problem?

M: The written test is easy, but I always _________ _________ on the driving course.

W: Oh, you mean the one that looks like the letter, "S"?

M: Yes. I will _________ _________ that course.

W: Take it easy. You'll get it next time.

18. 대화를 듣고, 여자의 마지막 말에 대한 남자의 응답으로 가장 적절한 것을 고르시오.

Man: _________________

① How often do you exercise?
② All right! I can't wait to start.
③ I used to swim there every week.
④ Health is the most important thing.
⑤ Our school has many after-school programs.

18

W: Mike, look at this news article! It says most students _________ _________ at all and it's causing a lot of health problems.

M: I _________ _________. I should work out as well, but I can't seem to find anything interesting to do.

W: Why don't you take a swimming class after school?

M: Swimming? That's a great idea!

W: I've been in a class since last year, and it _________ _________ _________ _________.

M: I didn't know you were in a swimming class. I'd love to join you.

W: You're going to love it! The class is on Wednesday and Friday.

M: All right! I can't wait to start.

19. 대화를 듣고, 여자의 마지막 말에 대한 남자의 응답으로 가장 적절한 것을 고르시오.

Man: ________________

① His movie is good.
② Shall I ask him for you?
③ You can meet him anytime.
④ He's not very kind to his fans.
⑤ I don't need to know his name.

19
M: There are so many people over there. What's going on in the park?

W: I don't know. Is there a ________ ________?

M: There is! Look! I can see the actor. I forget his name.

W: Let me see. Oh! That's Ian Holland! I like him so much.

M: He is ________ ________ ________.

W: He is handsome all the time.

M: Why don't you go and ________ ________ ________ ________?

W: I can't! How can I speak to him? I can't even look at him.

M: Shall I ask him for you?

---

20. 다음 상황 설명을 듣고, Jude가 Monica에게 할 말로 가장 적절한 것을 고르시오.

Jude: ________________

① How was your shopping today?
② Do you like going shopping?
③ Why don't you buy this jacket?
④ Which color looks best on me?
⑤ You look great in blue.

20
W: Jude and her friend Monica go shopping together. Jude ________ ________ ________ a nice jacket. After an hour shopping, she finds a jacket she likes. However, she can't ________ ________ the color. She likes both the black and the blue, but she has to ________ ________. So she ________ ________ ________ Monica's opinion on the jacket. In this situation, what would Jude say to Monica?

Jude: Which color looks best on me?

Words & Expressions Review 05

● 다음 단어를 암기하세요.

문제	번호	단어	뜻
1	1	blade	칼날
	2	hang	걸다, 매달다
2	3	free slot	빈자리, 공석
4	4	get to ~	~에 도착하다
	5	stop by ~	~에 들르다
	6	make sure	반드시 (~하도록) 하다
	7	rush-hour	(출퇴근) 혼잡 시간대
5	8	premiere	(영화, 연극의) 시사회
	9	pull one's leg	놀리다, 농담을 던지다
6	10	aisle	(상점이나 극장 같은 곳의) 통로
	11	fold	(옷 등을) 개다
	12	stain	얼룩, 오염
7	13	sore	아픈, 따가운
	14	barely	거의 ~ 아니게
	15	bandage	반창고, 붕대
8	16	judge	심사하다, 판단하다
	17	announce	발표하다, 알리다
9	18	receive	받다, 받아들이다
	19	physical examination	신체검사
	20	therapy	치료, 요법
	21	treatment	치료, 처치
	22	get injured	다치다, 부상을 입다

문제	번호	단어	뜻
10	23	recognize	알아보다
11	24	far from	~과 거리가 먼
	25	work	효과가 있다, 잘 맞다
12	26	detachable	분리할 수 있는
	27	storage	저장, 보관
13	28	schedule	일정을 잡다
	29	work for	~에게 문제없다, 괜찮다
14	30	be supposed to + 동사	~하기로 되어 있다
	31	have a fight with A	A와 싸우다
15	32	pollution	오염
	33	reusable	재사용할 수 있는
	34	freshly	갓[막] …한
16	35	roast	(콩 등을) 볶다
	36	promotion	판촉 (행사)
	37	in total	총합으로
17	38	long face	우울한 얼굴
	39	driver's license	운전면허
18	40	work out	운동하다
	41	stay fit	건강을 유지하다
19	42	shooting	촬영, 발사
	43	in person	직접, 몸소
20	44	decide	결정하다

●왼쪽 단어장의 뜻이 보이지 않게 반으로 접고, 학습한 단어의 뜻을 아래 빈칸에 적어주세요.

1	stop by ~		23	long face
2	promotion		24	have a fight with A
3	pull one's leg		25	decide
4	bandage		26	shooting
5	treatment		27	sore
6	detachable		28	premiere
7	work out		29	free slot
8	recognize		30	get injured
9	rush-hour		31	reusable
10	driver's license		32	in person
11	be supposed to + 동사		33	get to ~
12	aisle		34	barely
13	judge		35	schedule
14	in total		36	stain
15	make sure		37	work for
16	far from		38	fold
17	physical examination		39	stay fit
18	roast		40	freshly
19	announce		41	pollution
20	storage		42	receive
21	hang		43	work
22	blade		44	therapy

05
회
단어

06회 중학영어듣기 모의고사

M3(17)_06_US
모두 **미국식 발음(US)**
으로 녹음

M3(17)_06_UK
20문제 중 5문제에 **영국식 발음**
(US+UK)을 포함하여 녹음

정답 및 해석 p. 31

1 대화를 듣고, 남자가 구입할 화분을 고르시오.

①  ②  ③  ④  ⑤ 

2 대화를 듣고, 콘서트에 관해 언급되지 <u>않은</u> 것을 고르시오.

① 가수 이름 ② 시작 시각 ③ 종료 시각 ④ 티켓 가격 ⑤ 공연 장소

3 대화를 듣고, 여자가 남자에게 전화한 목적으로 가장 적절한 것을 고르시오.

① 미용실 위치를 문의하려고 ② 예약 시간을 변경하려고
③ 가격을 문의하려고 ④ 스타일을 논의하려고
⑤ 예약 날짜를 확인하려고

4 대화를 듣고, 여자가 등록할 테니스 수업 시각을 고르시오.

① 1 p.m. ② 2 p.m. ③ 4 p.m. ④ 5 p.m. ⑤ 7 p.m.

5 대화를 듣고, 남자의 심정으로 가장 적절한 것을 고르시오.

① relaxed ② envious ③ apologetic
④ satisfied ⑤ happy

6 다음 그림의 상황에 가장 적절한 대화를 고르시오.

①   ②   ③   ④   ⑤

7 대화를 듣고, 여자가 남자에게 부탁한 일로 가장 적절한 것을 고르시오.

① 의자 갖다주기   ② 테이프 자르기   ③ 그림 그려주기
④ 청소 같이 하기   ⑤ 동아리 홍보하기

8 다음을 듣고, Bake Sale에 관해 언급되지 <u>않은</u> 것을 고르시오.

① 개최 날짜   ② 행사 목적   ③ 행사 장소
④ 행사 시간   ⑤ 판매품

9 다음을 듣고, 무엇에 대한 설명인지 고르시오.

① 축구   ② 농구   ③ 하키   ④ 핸드볼   ⑤ 미식축구

10 다음을 듣고, 두 사람의 대화가 어색한 것을 고르시오.

①   ②   ③   ④   ⑤

11번~20번 문제는 다음 페이지에 ➡

11 대화를 듣고, 여자가 대화 직후에 할 일로 가장 적절한 것을 고르시오.

① 커피 원두 가져오기 ② 일회용 컵 구매하기 ③ 주차요금 결제하기
④ 음료 주문하기 ⑤ 가방 구입하기

12 다음 표를 보면서 대화를 듣고, 두 사람이 선택할 프로그램을 고르시오.

	Program	Time	Activity	Milk/Cheese Tasting
①	A	9:00 ~ 11:00 a.m.	Milk Cow Feeding	X
②	B	9:00 ~ 11:30 a.m.	Cheese Making	O
③	C	2:00 ~ 4:30 p.m.	Milk Cow Feeding	O
④	D	2:00 ~ 4:00 p.m.	Milk Cow Feeding	X
⑤	E	2:00 ~ 4:00 p.m.	Cheese Making	X

13 대화를 듣고, 두 사람이 롤러코스터를 타러 가기로 한 날짜를 고르시오.

① 6월 5일 ② 6월 15일 ③ 6월 19일 ④ 6월 25일 ⑤ 6월 29일

14 대화를 듣고, 여자가 주말에 한 일로 가장 적절한 것을 고르시오.

① 재즈 콘서트 관람하기 ② 헤드폰 구매하기 ③ 콘서트 예매하기
④ 악기 연습하기 ⑤ 병문안 가기

15 다음을 듣고, 방송의 목적으로 가장 적절한 것을 고르시오.

① 등산 시 주의사항을 공지하려고
② 수해복구 자원봉사를 독려하려고
③ 일기예보의 중요성을 설명하려고
④ 집중호우 시 행동요령을 안내하려고
⑤ 물놀이 사고 예방법을 알려주려고

16 대화를 듣고, 여자가 지불해야 할 금액으로 가장 적절한 것을 고르시오.

① $15   ② $20   ③ $30   ④ $35   ⑤ $40

17 대화를 듣고, 여자의 마지막 말에 대한 남자의 응답으로 가장 적절한 것을 고르시오.

Man: _______________________________________

① No. I wasn't paid to do the work.   ② Right. Their future depends on us.

③ Yes. I think I want to be a dog trainer.   ④ Great! You should follow your dreams.

⑤ Sure. You can come with me next time.

[18~19] 대화를 듣고, 남자의 마지막 말에 대한 여자의 응답으로 가장 적절한 것을 고르시오.

18 **Woman:** _______________________________________

① I play tennis three times a week.

② Of course, you can borrow mine.

③ Okay. I hope we can get a good deal.

④ I'm sorry that I can't help you with that.

⑤ I heard you won the game. Congratulations!

19 **Woman:** _______________________________________

① My friends are always hungry.   ② I'll have a vegetarian sandwich.

③ She can prepare the ingredients.   ④ Just a little bit of mustard, please.

⑤ I'd like to have some potato chips.

20 다음 상황 설명을 듣고, David가 Allison에게 할 말로 가장 적절한 것을 고르시오.

David: _______________________________________

① Tell me. How can you write so well?

② It's okay. I have already read the book.

③ Don't worry. I'm going to return the book.

④ Thank you. I was looking for it everywhere.

⑤ You already have one. Why don't you sell it?

Dictation Test 06

M3(17)_06_D

Dictation(받아쓰기)은 본문을 받아쓰면서 영어듣기의 집중력을 향상시키고 다양한 표현을 정리하기 위한 영어듣기 학습법입니다. 녹음을 다시 듣고, 빈칸에 알맞은 단어를 써 보세요.
※Dictation의 정답은 듣기 대본의 밑줄 친 부분을 확인하세요.　정답 p. 31

맞은 개수 　／　총187개

그림정보파악(대화)

1. 대화를 듣고, 남자가 구입할 화분을 고르시오.

① 　② 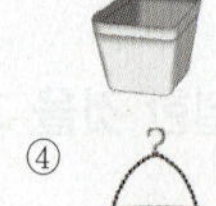

③ 　④

⑤

01

W: Welcome to Fun Flowers. How can I help you?

M: Hi, I'd like to buy a flower pot.

W: Sure. We have round pots and square pots.

M: I think the round pots look prettier.

W: Okay. What do you think of the _________ one? It's a popular model.

M: Hmm… I like the ________ model more.

W: Sure. The pot _________ ________ two styles. One has a hanger and the other does not.

M: I like the one with the ________. I was thinking of hanging the flower pot on the wall.

W: Good choice! I'm sure you'll make good use of it.

대화미언급

2. 대화를 듣고, 콘서트에 관해 언급되지 <u>않</u>은 것을 고르시오.
① 가수 이름
② 시작 시각
③ 종료 시각
④ 티켓 가격
⑤ 공연 장소

02

W: Jonathan, _________ _________ ___________ ________ going to a concert with me this Friday?

M: This Friday? Who's the singer?

W: It's Brian Jackson. Actually, I got two tickets from my aunt.

M: Really? He's my favorite!

W: Great! The concert starts at 7 p.m. and will be finished around 10 p.m.

M: That sounds great. _________ _________ _________

_________?

W: The concert is at Robin's Hall on 16th Street.

_________ _________ _________ _________ at 6:30 in

front of the hall?

M: Okay. Thank you, Susan.

3. 대화를 듣고, 여자가 남자에게 전화한 목적으로 가장 적절한 것을 고르시오.

① 미용실 위치를 문의하려고
② 예약 시간을 변경하려고
③ 가격을 문의하려고
④ 스타일을 논의하려고
⑤ 예약 날짜를 확인하려고

03 *(Telephone rings.)*

M: Hello, this is Natural Beauty Salon.

W: Hello, my name is Tiffany Lee. I _________ _________

_____________ at 6 p.m. today.

M: Yes, Tiffany. How can I help you?

W: I'm getting a perm today, and I was wondering

about the price.

M: Well, it depends on the _________ _________

_________ _________.

W: Oh, I see.

M: If you come 10 minutes early, we can _________

_________.

W: Thanks. Then, I'll be there at 5:50.

4. 대화를 듣고, 여자가 등록할 테니스 수업 시각을 고르시오.

① 1 p.m.　　② 2 p.m.
③ 4 p.m.　　④ 5 p.m.
⑤ 7 p.m.

04 M: Mary, did you register for tennis lessons yet?

W: Not yet, Dad. I haven't decided _________ _________

_________ the 4 p.m. class or the 7 p.m. class.

M: Don't you think it'll be a little tight to take the 4

p.m. class?

W: Yeah, I might not _________ _________ _________ the

class in time after school.

다음 페이지에 계속 ➡

M: So, you shouldn't take the 4 p.m. class.

W: You're right. The 7 p.m. class is ________ ________ ________ because I can eat dinner at 5 p.m. and then go to the class.

M: That's a good plan.

W: I'll go register now.

5. 대화를 듣고, 남자의 심정으로 가장 적절한 것을 고르시오.

① relaxed
② envious
③ apologetic
④ satisfied
⑤ happy

05

M: Kimberly, can I talk to you for a second?

W: Sure. What's up?

M: Remember the book I borrowed from you last week?

W: *War and Peace?* Do you like it? It's a bit long, isn't it?

M: Um, yes, it's fine. I'm really sorry, but I ________ ________ ________ to you.

W: Why?

M: My little cousin came over and drew pictures ________ ________ ________ when I was in another room.

W: Oh... it's my favorite novel.

M: I know. I'm so sorry. I'll buy you ________ ________ ________. I've already ordered one.

W: That's kind. Thank you, Dale.

6. 다음 그림의 상황에 가장 적절한 대화를 고르시오.

①   ②
③   ④
⑤

06

① M: Are you paying in ________ ________ ________ ________ ________?

W: In cash. Here you are.

② M: Is this your first time visiting Korea?

W: Actually, this is my fifth visit to Korea.

③ M: Excuse me. Do you have this shirt ________ ________ ________ ________?

W: Sure, let me get it for you.

④ M: How much money would you like to exchange?

W: I'd like to change ________ ________ ________

________ ________.

⑤ M: What is the purpose of your visit?

W: I'm here for business.

7. 대화를 듣고, 여자가 남자에게 부탁한 일로 가장 적절한 것을 고르시오.
   ① 의자 갖다주기
   ② 테이프 자르기
   ③ 그림 그려주기
   ④ 청소 같이 하기
   ⑤ 동아리 홍보하기

07

M: Hey, Katelynn! What are you doing?

W: Well, I'm trying to ________ ________ ________ on the bulletin board.

M: Do you need my help?

W: Hmm… I can ________ it.

M: I think the board is too high to reach.

W: I'll ________ ________ ________ ________.

M: Okay, that will do!

W: Oh, wait… Could you cut the tape while I'm holding the poster?

M: Sure, why not?

W: Thank you!

8. 다음을 듣고, Bake Sale에 관해 언급되지 않은 것을 고르시오.
   ① 개최 날짜   ② 행사 목적
   ③ 행사 장소   ④ 행사 시간
   ⑤ 판매품

08

W: Hello, students. I'd like to ________ you all about the Bake Sale we will be having on June 9. We are holding this event to ________ ________ for our local animal rescue. It will be held in our cafeteria. There will be a variety of ________ ________ such as brownies, cookies, cakes, and more. So, come to the bake sale and enjoy some delicious desserts. Please bring your family and friends ________ ________. Thank you.

다음 페이지에 계속 ➡

9. 다음을 듣고, 무엇에 대한 설명인지 고르시오.

① 축구
② 농구
③ 하키
④ 핸드볼
⑤ 미식축구

09 W: This is the world's most popular team sport. The game is ________ ________ a rectangular grass field and there is a goal at each end of the field. Two teams move the ball ________ ________ ________ kick it into the goal. The only player on each team who can touch the ball ________ ________ ________ stands in front of the goal. The other players must use their feet, knees, head and chest to ________ the ball. If a player touches the ball with his hands, it is considered a foul and a free kick is given to ________ ________ ________.

10. 다음을 듣고, 두 사람의 대화가 <u>어색한</u> 것을 고르시오.

① ②
③ ④
⑤

10 ① M: ________ ________ ________ ________ ________, ma'am?

W: I will have a chicken salad.

② M: What's wrong? You ________ ________.

W: I think I lost my wallet.

③ M: Who's calling, please?

W: This is Emily speaking.

④ M: When shall we meet?

W: ________ ________ ________ the concert hall.

⑤ M: May I help you?

W: Yes, please. I am looking for men's shirts.

11. 대화를 듣고, 여자가 대화 직후에 할 일로 가장 적절한 것을 고르시오.

① 커피 원두 가져오기
② 일회용 컵 구매하기
③ 주차요금 결제하기
④ 음료 주문하기
⑤ 가방 구입하기

11
M: Hello, welcome to Nature Coffee.

W: Hi. Can I have ___________ ___________ ___________ white coffee, please?

M: Sure. Do you need anything else?

W: Um, actually, I have ___________ ___________ ___________ coffee beans. Can you grind them for me?

M: Of course.

W: How much is it to ___________ ___________ ___________?

M: Oh, there's no charge if you buy a cup of coffee.

W: That's great! Let me get the bag of beans right away. It's in my car.

M: ___________ ___________ ___________.

12. 다음 표를 보면서 대화를 듣고, 두 사람이 선택할 프로그램을 고르시오.

	Program	Time	Activity	Milk/Cheese Tasting
①	A	9:00 ~ 11:00 a.m.	Milk Cow Feeding	X
②	B	9:00 ~ 11:30 a.m.	Cheese Making	O
③	C	2:00 ~ 4:30 p.m.	Milk Cow Feeding	O
④	D	2:00 ~ 4:00 p.m.	Milk Cow Feeding	X
⑤	E	2:00 ~ 4:00 p.m.	Cheese Making	X

12
M: Hey, look at this schedule on the website. There are farm experience programs.

W: Oh, I like farms. Why don't we ___________ ___________ ___________ one over the weekend?

M: Sounds good. Which do you prefer, a morning or afternoon program?

W: An afternoon program. I want to ___________ ___________ ___________ ___________.

M: Right. How about experiencing a milk cow feeding?

W: Sounds good. Do you want to do the tasting, too?

M: Sure. Then, let's sign up for this program.

W: Okay. ___________ ___________ ___________.

다음 페이지에 계속 ➡

13. 대화를 듣고, 두 사람이 롤러코스터를 타러 가기로 한 날짜를 고르시오.

① 6월 5일
② 6월 15일
③ 6월 19일
④ 6월 25일
⑤ 6월 29일

13

W: Hi, Tom. What are you looking at on your laptop?

M: I'm ________ ________ the Awesome Amusement Park website. They're opening a new rollercoaster soon.

W: Oh, really? I love rollercoasters! When is it opening?

M: It's opening on June 5th.

W: Great! We should ___________ _________ ________ ________ together.

M: Yeah, we should. How about going on June 15th? I think it'll be ________ __________ then.

W: Hmm... I have a student council meeting on the 15th. How about June 19th?

M: No problem! I'm ________ ________ ________.

14. 대화를 듣고, 여자가 주말에 한 일로 가장 적절한 것을 고르시오.

① 재즈 콘서트 관람하기
② 헤드폰 구매하기
③ 콘서트 예매하기
④ 악기 연습하기
⑤ 병문안 가기

14

M: Ella, how was your weekend? Didn't you say that you were going to a jazz concert?

W: Yeah, but the show ________ __________ at the last minute.

M: Really? What happened?

W: The musician got food poisoning, so he couldn't ________.

M: I'm sorry to hear that. Did you do anything else?

W: Yes, I bought these new headphones. Here, ___________ ________ ________ ________.

M: Wow, the sound is amazing! I really like them.

W: Thanks. I really like them as well.

15. 다음을 듣고, 방송의 목적으로 가장 적절한 것을 고르시오.

① 등산 시 주의사항을 공지하려고
② 수해복구 자원봉사를 독려하려고
③ 일기예보의 중요성을 설명하려고
④ 집중호우 시 행동요령을 안내하려고
⑤ 물놀이 사고 예방법을 알려주려고

15 W: Hello. This is *Today's Safety Tip*. When _________ _________ _________ is expected, don't go near streams, rivers or beaches. Try to _________ _________ if you can, and close all the windows. Then, keep track of weather updates on TV, radio, or the Internet. On the road, avoid going near ___________ _________ as things may fall from above. Heavy rain can be very dangerous. _________ _________, everyone.

---

16. 대화를 듣고, 여자가 지불해야 할 금액으로 가장 적절한 것을 고르시오.

① $15　　② $20
③ $30　　④ $35
⑤ $40

16 M: Hello, may I help you?

W: Hi, I'm looking for a Mother's Day present.

M: Do you have anything _________ _________?

W: Well... My mom likes tea. How much are these _________ _________?

M: The big one is 20 dollars, and the small one is 15 dollars.

W: Then, I'd like to buy one of each.

M: Okay, your _________ will be 35 dollars.

W: Can I use this coupon?

M: Sure. You can get a five-dollar ___________ from the total price.

W: Okay. I'll pay by credit card.

다음 페이지에 계속 ➡

17. 대화를 듣고, 여자의 마지막 말에 대한 남자의 응답으로 가장 적절한 것을 고르시오.

Man: _______________

① No. I wasn't paid to do the work.
② Right. Their future depends on us.
③ Yes. I think I want to be a dog trainer.
④ Great! You should follow your dreams.
⑤ Sure. You can come with me next time.

17
W: Hi, Tom. How was your summer vacation?

M: Hi, Angela. I spent some time working at an ________ ________.

W: Wow! How did you decide to do that during your vacation?

M: I'm thinking of becoming a dog trainer so I wanted to have some real experience with dogs.

W: That's a very good idea. So, how was it?

M: It was very tough but extremely __________. I still miss some of the dogs I cared for there.

W: So, I guess you became more ________ ________ what you want to do in the future?

M: Yes. I think I want to be a dog trainer.

18. 대화를 듣고, 남자의 마지막 말에 대한 여자의 응답으로 가장 적절한 것을 고르시오.

Woman: _______________

① I play tennis three times a week.
② Of course, you can borrow mine.
③ Okay. I hope we can get a good deal.
④ I'm sorry that I can't help you with that.
⑤ I heard you won the game. Congratulations!

18
M: Sharon, did you know that the badminton club is ________ ________ new members?

W: Yes, I saw the poster on the board.

M: Me, too. Would you like to ________ ________ ________ with me?

W: Sure. Sounds fun.

M: The poster says we need to bring our own racket. Do you have one?

W: No, I ________ ________ ________ badminton before.

M: I don't have one, either.

W: Oh, I just remembered that the sporting goods store on Sierra Street is having a ________ ________.

M: The one that has just opened? That's great. Let's go and ________ ________ ________.

W: Okay. I hope we can get a good deal.

19. 대화를 듣고, 남자의 마지막 말에 대한 여자의 응답으로 가장 적절한 것을 고르시오.

Woman: _________________
① My friends are always hungry.
② I'll have a vegetarian sandwich.
③ She can prepare the ingredients.
④ Just a little bit of mustard, please.
⑤ I'd like to have some potato chips.

19
M: Welcome to Sandy's Sandwiches. How may I help you?
W: _________ _________ __________ a vegetarian sandwich for me?
M: How about the mushroom sandwich? It is one of our most popular menu items.
W: Do you have any other __________ ________?
M: Yes, we have an avocado sandwich that is also quite popular.
W: Sounds good. I'll have that one.
M: Okay. _________ _________ _________ ________ would you like?
W: Just a little bit of mustard, please.

20. 다음 상황 설명을 듣고, David가 Allison에게 할 말로 가장 적절한 것을 고르시오.

David: _________________
① Tell me. How can you write so well?
② It's okay. I have already read the book.
③ Don't worry. I'm going to return the book.
④ Thank you. I was looking for it everywhere.
⑤ You already have one. Why don't you sell it?

20
M: David is having a birthday party at home. Allison, one of his friends, ________ _________ ________ ________ as a present. There is even a beautiful handwritten message inside. However, when Allison finds the same book already on his shelf, ________ ________ ________. David hasn't read the book yet, and he bought it just a few days ago. So, he wants to tell her that he can just ________ ________ ________ he bought. In this situation, what would David most likely say to Allison?
David: Don't worry. I'm going to return the book.

Words & Expressions Review 06

● 다음 단어를 암기하세요.

문제	번호	단어	뜻
1	☐ 1	striped	줄무늬가 있는
	☐ 2	plain	무늬가 없는, 밋밋한
	☐ 3	hanger	(옷 따위를 거는) 고리, 걸이
	☐ 4	make good use of	~을 잘 활용하다
2	☐ 5	actually	사실은, 실제로는
	☐ 6	around	~쯤, 약
3	☐ 7	beauty salon	미용실
	☐ 8	length	길이
	☐ 9	discuss	상의하다
4	☐ 10	tight	(여유가 없이) 빠듯한, 빡빡한
	☐ 11	in time	제시간에, 시간 맞춰
5	☐ 12	for a second	잠시
	☐ 13	all over	곳곳에
	☐ 14	copy	(책 · 신문 등의) 한 부
6	☐ 15	credit card	신용카드
	☐ 16	exchange	환전하다, 교환하다
	☐ 17	purpose	목적
	☐ 18	business	일, 업무
7	☐ 19	handle	처리하다, 다루다
	☐ 20	remind	다시 한번 알려주다, 상기시키다
8	☐ 21	raise funds	기금을 모으다, 자금을 조달하다
	☐ 22	a variety of	여러 가지의
9	☐ 23	field	경기장, 들판
	☐ 24	in order to + 동사	~하기 위해
	☐ 25	consider	간주하다, 고려하다
	☐ 26	opposing team	상대팀
11	☐ 27	grind	(곡식 등을 잘게) 갈다, 빻다
	☐ 28	no charge	무료의, 무료인
13	☐ 29	crowded	붐비는, 복잡한
	☐ 30	get cancel(l)ed	취소되다
14	☐ 31	perform	공연하다, 연주하다
	☐ 32	give ~ a try	~을 한번 해보다
	☐ 33	localized	국지적인
15	☐ 34	keep track of ~	~을 놓치지 않도록 하다
	☐ 35	avoid	피하다
	☐ 36	construction site	공사장, 건설 현장
16	☐ 37	get a discount	할인을 받다
17	☐ 38	animal shelter	동물 보호소
	☐ 39	rewarding	보람 있는
18	☐ 40	look for ~	~을 찾다
	☐ 41	goods	용품, 상품, 제품
19	☐ 42	vegetarian	채식주의자의, 채식의
20	☐ 43	handwritten	손으로 쓴
	☐ 44	shelf	책꽂이

● 왼쪽 단어장의 뜻이 보이지 않게 반으로 접고, 학습한 단어의 뜻을 아래 빈칸에 적어주세요.

1	striped	23	all over
2	opposing team	24	crowded
3	avoid	25	get cancel(l)ed
4	handwritten	26	construction site
5	grind	27	raise funds
6	remind	28	field
7	beauty salon	29	rewarding
8	keep track of ~	30	tight
9	around	31	discuss
10	for a second	32	localized
11	no charge	33	exchange
12	perform	34	goods
13	copy	35	make good use of
14	animal shelter	36	get a discount
15	consider	37	credit card
16	shelf	38	in time
17	business	39	in order to + 동사
18	hanger	40	length
19	a variety of	41	give ~ a try
20	vegetarian	42	plain
21	actually	43	handle
22	purpose	44	look for ~

07회 중학영어듣기 모의고사

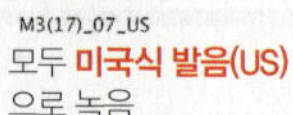

M3(17)_07_US
모두 **미국식 발음(US)** 으로 녹음

M3(17)_07_UK
20문제 중 5문제에 **영국식 발음 (US+UK)**을 포함하여 녹음

정답 및 해석 p. 37

1
대화를 듣고, 여자가 구입할 종이 접시를 고르시오.

① 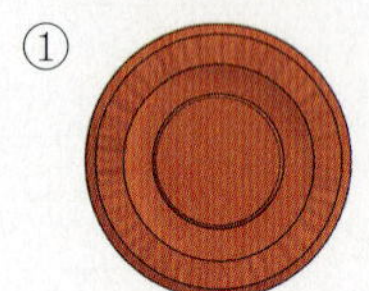 ② 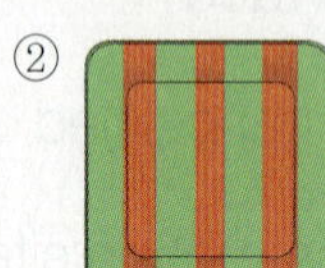 ③ 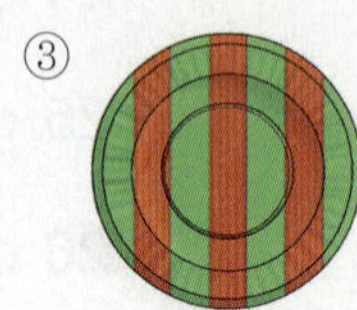 ④  ⑤ 

2
대화를 듣고, Heavenly Voice Contest에 관해 언급되지 않은 것을 고르시오.

① 결승 진출자   ② 우승 상금   ③ 심사 위원   ④ 방영 시각   ⑤ 방영 요일

3
대화를 듣고, 여자가 남자에게 전화한 목적으로 가장 적절한 것을 고르시오.

① 분실물을 찾기 위해서 ② 환불을 요청하기 위해서
③ 배송지 주소를 변경하기 위해서 ④ 상품의 재고를 확인하기 위해서
⑤ 세일 행사 기간을 물어보기 위해서

4
대화를 듣고, 두 사람이 만나기로 한 시각을 고르시오.

① 1 p.m.   ② 2 p.m.   ③ 3 p.m.   ④ 4 p.m.   ⑤ 5 p.m.

5
대화를 듣고, 남자의 심정으로 가장 적절한 것을 고르시오.

① excited   ② pleased   ③ regretful   ④ bored   ⑤ jealous

6 다음 그림의 상황에 가장 적절한 대화를 고르시오.

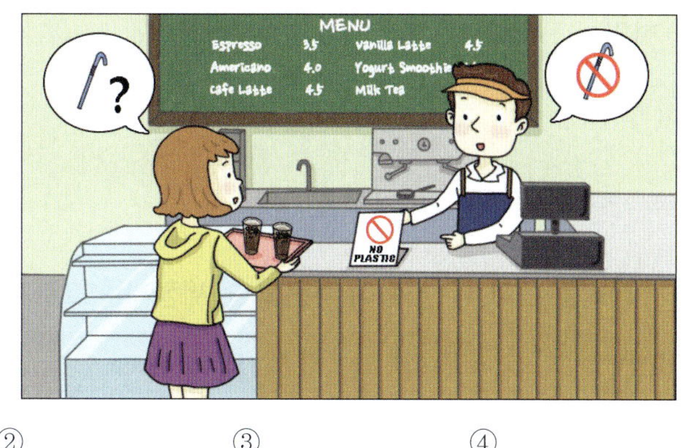

①   ②   ③   ④   ⑤

7 대화를 듣고, 남자가 여자에게 부탁한 일로 가장 적절한 것을 고르시오.

① 휴가용 짐 싸기　　　② 표 예매하기　　　③ 회의에 참석하기
④ 버스 시간 변경하기　　　⑤ 샌드위치 사오기

8 다음을 듣고, Ben Hicks에 대해 언급되지 <u>않은</u> 것을 고르시오.

① 출생 연도　　　② 성장 환경　　　③ 취미 생활
④ 대학 전공　　　⑤ 수상 경력

9 다음을 듣고, 무엇에 관한 설명인지 고르시오.

① 냉장고　　　② 노트북　　　③ 데스크탑　　　④ 세탁기　　　⑤ 스마트폰

10 다음을 듣고, 두 사람의 대화가 <u>어색한</u> 것을 고르시오.

①   ②   ③   ④   ⑤

11번~20번 문제는 다음 페이지에 ➡

11 대화를 듣고, 남자가 대화 직후에 할 일로 가장 적절한 것을 고르시오.

① 친구와 축구 하기　　　② 친구에게 전화하기　　　③ 저녁 준비 도와주기
④ 공항에 가기　　　　　⑤ 공원에 산책 가기

12 다음 표를 보면서 대화를 듣고, 두 사람이 주문할 손 세정제를 고르시오.

	Product	Price	Fragrance	Type
①	A	$8	vanilla	liquid
②	B	$10	lavender	foam
③	C	$12	lavender	liquid
④	D	$14	vanilla	foam
⑤	E	$16	lavender	liquid

13 대화를 듣고, 두 사람이 음악 축제에 갈 날짜를 고르시오.

① 7월 20일　　　② 7월 21일　　　③ 7월 22일　　　④ 7월 23일　　　⑤ 7월 24일

14 대화를 듣고, 여자가 추석에 한 일을 고르시오.

① 연날리기　　　　② 무용 관람　　　　③ 게임
④ 엄마 고향 방문　　⑤ 송편 빚기

15 다음을 듣고, 방송의 목적으로 가장 적절한 것을 고르시오.

① 학교 식당을 소개하려고
② 교내 체육 대회를 안내하려고
③ 실내 환기의 중요성을 설명하려고
④ 과학 발명품 경진대회 참여를 장려하려고
⑤ 실외 활동 시 신발 갈아 신기를 권고하려고

16 대화를 듣고, 여자가 지불할 금액을 고르시오.

① $4　　　② $5　　　③ $12　　　④ $15　　　⑤ $20

17 대화를 듣고, 여자의 마지막 말에 대한 남자의 응답으로 가장 적절한 것을 고르시오.

Man: _______________________________

① Well, haste makes waste.
② No pain, no gain.
③ Yeah, when it rains, it pours.
④ I learned that unity is strength.
⑤ Ah, well, you have to look before you leap.

[18~19] 대화를 듣고, 남자의 마지막 말에 대한 여자의 응답으로 가장 적절한 것을 고르시오.

18 **Woman:** _______________________________

① OK. Please put a lot of ice in the water.
② Good idea. I will download it right away.
③ I don't think it will help boost my energy.
④ Maybe not. I shouldn't use my phone too often.
⑤ Thanks for the advice. I will call and make a reservation.

19 **Woman:** _______________________________

① Sure. The salmon contains healthy fat.
② Thanks. I appreciate you taking care of it.
③ Right. The food is for dinner, so no hurry.
④ Wait. I think they have the wrong delivery address.
⑤ No. Cook the chicken first and forget about the salad.

20 다음 상황 설명을 듣고, Peter가 Jenna에게 할 말로 가장 적절한 것을 고르시오.

Peter: _______________________________

① I should go and buy some water.
② You'd better not sit still for too long.
③ Do you want to take a walk with me?
④ Can you wake me up after five minutes?
⑤ You're not allowed to eat and drink here.

Dictation Test 07

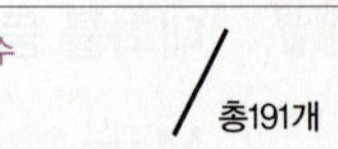

M3(17)_07_D

Dictation(받아쓰기)은 본문을 받아쓰면서 영어듣기의 집중력을 향상시키고 다양한 표현을 정리하기 위한 영어듣기 학습법입니다. 녹음을 다시 듣고, 빈칸에 알맞은 단어를 써 보세요.
※Dictation의 정답은 듣기 대본의 밑줄 친 부분을 확인하세요.

정답 p. 37

맞은 개수 / 총191개

고난도 | 그림정보파악(대화)

1. 대화를 듣고, 여자가 구입할 종이 접시를 고르시오.

① 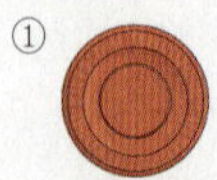　②  

③ 　④  

⑤ 

01

M: Hello. What can I do for you?

W: Hi, I'm __________ ________ __________ ______ and I'd like to buy some paper plates.

M: Okay. Here are the samples of what we ________ ________ ________. There are square ones and round ones.

W: Oh, I like the round plates. I'll choose from among those ones.

M: Sure. They come in two styles, ________ ________ ________.

W: I like the striped ones more.

M: These ones have the words 'Merry Christmas' ________ ________ ________. Would you like to buy them?

W: Yes. That's just what I was looking for. I'll take them.

M: Okay.

대화미언급

2. 대화를 듣고, Heavenly Voice Contest 에 관해 언급되지 **않은** 것을 고르시오.

① 결승 진출자　② 우승 상금
③ 심사 위원　④ 방영 시각
⑤ 방영 요일

02

M: Do you watch the Heavenly Voice Contest program?

W: Yes. I'm really ________ about the ________.

M: Who do you think will win between Daniel and Ella?

W: I'm ________ ________ Ella, so I hope she wins.

M: Me, too. She'll get a million dollars in prize money if she wins.

W: Right. I hope the judges will be generous with her this time.

M: Yes. They've been a little ________ ________ her.

W: Let's see what happens this week. The program is on Saturday, right?

M: Yes. It's going to be so fun!

3. 대화를 듣고, 여자가 남자에게 전화한 목적으로 가장 적절한 것을 고르시오.
   ① 분실물을 찾기 위해서
   ② 환불을 요청하기 위해서
   ③ 배송지 주소를 변경하기 위해서
   ④ 상품의 재고를 확인하기 위해서
   ⑤ 세일 행사 기간을 물어보기 위해서

03 (Telephone rings.)

M: Hello. This is City Outfitter.

W: Hello. I was at your shop this morning and I think I ________ ________ ________ there.

M: Your purse? We do not have any purses in our ________ ________ ________.

W: Oh, no! Could you check the fitting room? I think I left it there.

M: One moment, please. (Pause) Is it a purple purse with a dog keychain on it?

W: Yes! That's mine!

M: We will ________ ________ ________ ________ for you.

W: Thank you so much! I will be there soon!

4. 대화를 듣고, 두 사람이 만나기로 한 시각을 고르시오.
   ① 1 p.m.   ② 2 p.m.
   ③ 3 p.m.   ④ 4 p.m.
   ⑤ 5 p.m.

04 [Cellphone rings.]

W: Good morning, Dad.

M: Hi, Jane. I ________ ________ ________ see you. When is your arrival time?

W: It was supposed to be 1 p.m., but the flight ________ ________ ________ due to a mechanical problem.

M: I'm sorry to hear that. Let me know what time to ________ ________ ________.

다음 페이지에 계속 ➡

W: The flight attendant says the arrival time may be 3 p.m.

M: Okay. I'll wait for you in front of the __________ ________ gate.

W: I need to find my luggage, so it will take me _______ _______ _______.

M: OK. Then, let's meet at 4 p.m.

W: Sure, Dad. I'll text you the flight number so you can find the gate number.

5. 대화를 듣고, 남자의 심정으로 가장 적절한 것을 고르시오.

① excited   ② pleased
③ regretful   ④ bored
⑤ jealous

05 W: David, why do you look so down?

M: I _______ _______ my little brother this morning. He cried a lot.

W: What happened?

M: He broke my old toy and I _______ _______ _______ him.

W: Hmm, that can happen.

M: He's only five years old, and I was _______ _______ _______ _______.

W: Did you try to talk to him after that?

M: I tried, but he's still so down. I _______ _______ _______ at him like that.

6. 다음 그림의 상황에 가장 적절한 대화를 고르시오.

①   ②   ③   ④   ⑤

06 ① W: May I _______ _______ _______?

M: Yes, I'd like a vanilla latte, please.

② W: Hi, I'm here to interview for the part-time job.

M: Oh, I'll be with you in a moment.

③ W: Excuse me, where can I find a straw?

M: _____________ plastics _________ ___________

from cafés.

④ W: I think you got my order wrong.

M: I'm very sorry. I'll make your drinks again right

away.

⑤ W: I'm sorry, but can I have these ________

_________ ________?

M: Sure! No problem.

7. 대화를 듣고, 남자가 여자에게 부탁한 일로 가장 적절한 것을 고르시오.

① 휴가용 짐 싸기
② 표 예매하기
③ 회의에 참석하기
④ 버스 시간 변경하기
⑤ 샌드위치 사오기

07 W: Pete, are you ready to ________ ________ ________

___________ tomorrow?

M: I'm all set, but I have one problem.

W: The bus? Don't worry. I already bought the

tickets.

M: No. It's the meeting I have tomorrow. It ends at

five.

W: The bus leaves at six, so we ________ ________

________.

M: OK, then. But can you buy me a sandwich? I won't

have time to buy anything before we ________

________ ________ ________.

W: No problem.

다음 페이지에 계속 ➡

8. 다음을 듣고, Ben Hicks에 대해 언급되
   지 <u>않은</u> 것을 <u>고르시오</u>.
   ① 출생 연도   ② 성장 환경
   ③ 취미 생활   ④ 대학 전공
   ⑤ 수상 경력

08 W: Hello, class. Today we'll learn about Ben Hicks, the famous space scientist. He was born in Seattle in 1969. He _________ _________ in a poor family. But he found hope and joy in math and science. He _________ _________ _________ _________ school and up to scholarships. He studied space science in college and started working at NASA. When he was 27, he became the youngest winner of the National Science Award. Since then, he has made many discoveries that _________ _________ _________ space travel.

9. 다음을 듣고, 무엇에 관한 설명인지 고르
   시오.
   ① 냉장고
   ② 노트북
   ③ 데스크탑
   ④ 세탁기
   ⑤ 스마트폰

09 M: It is one of the most popular types of _________ _________. The screen is located on the inside of the upper lid and the keyboard is on the inside of the lower lid. Sometimes the screens are _________. It folds shut for transportation and it is _________ _________ mobile use. It can be used for many different purposes from gaming to writing a report. Its name originated from the fact that it can be placed on _________ _________ _________ when being used.

10. 다음을 듣고, 두 사람의 대화가 <u>어색한</u>
    것을 <u>고르시오</u>.
    ①   ②
    ③   ④
    ⑤

10 ① M: Do you know what this means?
   W: Yes, I've _________ _________ once.
② M: Do you know who he is?
   W: I have no idea.
③ M: Can you _________ _________ how to drive a car?
   W: I'm sorry, but I have no time.

④ M: Why do you think he's rude?

W: He talks ________ ________ in the classroom.

⑤ M: Are you okay?

W: Sure. Don't worry.

11. 대화를 듣고, 남자가 대화 직후에 할 일로 가장 적절한 것을 고르시오.

① 친구와 축구 하기
② 친구에게 전화하기
③ 저녁 준비 도와주기
④ 공항에 가기
⑤ 공원에 산책 가기

11

M: Mom, I'm going to the park, now.

W: You mean now? We're supposed to pick up your dad ________ ________ ________ at 4 o'clock, remember?

M: Is it today? I thought it was tomorrow.

W: Your dad is coming today. Sweetie, I told you yesterday at dinner.

M: At dinner? Oh, you're right. But, ________ __________ ________ play soccer with Brian at 3 o'clock today.

W: I think you'd better cancel that. ________ ________ ________ play soccer on the weekend?

M: Okay. I'll call him ________ ________ and tell him I can't play today.

12. 다음 표를 보면서 대화를 듣고, 두 사람이 주문할 손 세정제를 고르시오.

	Product	Price	Fragrance	Type
①	A	$8	vanilla	liquid
②	B	$10	lavender	foam
③	C	$12	lavender	liquid
④	D	$14	vanilla	foam
⑤	E	$16	lavender	liquid

12

M: Honey, are you going to buy something online?

W: Yes, I'm looking for some hand soap. We're ________ ________ ________ ________.

M: OK, let's check together. I don't think we should spend more than $15.

W: I agree. I don't want to spend too much on hand soap.

M: Right. How about the __________?

W: __________ ________ vanilla. We've used vanilla for a long time.

M: Okay. Then, we have two options left.

W: How about getting foam soap? I ________ ________ ________ ________.

M: Me, too. Let's order it.

다음 페이지에 계속 ➡

13. 대화를 듣고, 두 사람이 음악 축제에 갈 날짜를 고르시오.

① 7월 20일 ② 7월 21일
③ 7월 22일 ④ 7월 23일
⑤ 7월 24일

13

W: Hi, Max! What are you up to?

M: Hey, Christine! I'm just __________ __________ some event listings online. There's a music festival in the park next weekend.

W: Oh, that sounds like fun! When is it?

M: It's __________ __________ from July 20th to July 24th.

W: Nice! We should definitely go together. How about July 21st?

M: July 21st sounds good, but I have a family gathering that day. How about July 22nd?

W: July 22nd __________ __________ __________. Let's mark it on our calendars!

M: Okay. See you then.

14. 대화를 듣고, 여자가 추석에 한 일을 고르시오.

① 연날리기 ② 무용 관람
③ 게임 ④ 엄마 고향 방문
⑤ 송편 빚기

14

M: Where were you last week?

W: My whole family celebrated Chuseok in Daegu, which is my father's hometown. There were a lot of __________ __________ for Chuseok.

M: Sounds like you had fun. Did you join any events?

W: No, we didn't. We __________ __________ __________ __________ watch a dance, but it was cancelled because of the bad weather.

M: Oh, that's too bad.

W: It was okay. I __________ __________ __________ my cousins instead.

15. 다음을 듣고, 방송의 목적으로 가장 적절한 것을 고르시오.

① 학교 식당을 소개하려고
② 교내 체육 대회를 안내하려고
③ 실내 환기의 중요성을 설명하려고
④ 과학 발명품 경진대회 참여를 장려하려고
⑤ 실외 활동 시 신발 갈아 신기를 권고하려고

15 W: Good afternoon, students. The weather is getting warmer every day, and a lot of you are __________ __________ __________. Getting fresh air is good for you and for your studies. However, it seems that many of you are enjoying your time outside while wearing your indoor shoes. This isn't __________, since your shoes bring all the dust and dirt from outside into your classrooms. Next time when you head outdoors, please __________ __________ __________. You can protect everybody's health by doing so. Thank you.

16. 대화를 듣고, 여자가 지불할 금액을 고르시오.

① $4 ② $5
③ $12 ④ $15
⑤ $20

16 M: Welcome to Happy Mart.

W: Hi, I'm looking to buy some strawberries.

M: We have __________ __________ __________: organic strawberries and locally grown strawberries. The organic ones are slightly larger __________ __________.

W: How much are they?

M: A pound of organic strawberries is $5, while the locally grown ones are $4 per pound.

W: I'll take the organic strawberries.

M: Great choice! We also have a __________ __________. If you buy three pounds of strawberries, you get one more pound __________ __________.

W: Wonderful! I'll take three pounds of organic strawberries, then.

M: Here they are.

W: Thank you! I'll pay with cash.

다음 페이지에 계속 ➡

17. 대화를 듣고, 여자의 마지막 말에 대한 남자의 응답으로 가장 적절한 것을 고르시오.

Man: ___________

① Well, haste makes waste.
② No pain, no gain.
③ Yeah, when it rains, it pours.
④ I learned that unity is strength.
⑤ Ah, well, you have to look before you leap.

17
W: Hey, how was your trip over the weekend?
M: It was terrible. We ________ ________ ________ ________ on the way.
W: Oh, dear. So, what happened?
M: It was the ________ ________ ________ ________ when we arrived.
W: You got to the hotel, anyway.
M: Yeah, but they ________ ________ our booking, and we had no room.
W: What?
M: So, we ________ ________ ________, and the next morning it rained.
W: I'm so sorry to hear that.
M: Yeah, when it rains, it pours.

---

18. 대화를 듣고, 남자의 마지막 말에 대한 여자의 응답으로 가장 적절한 것을 고르시오.

Woman: ___________

① OK. Please put a lot of ice in the water.
② Good idea. I will download it right away.
③ I don't think it will help boost my energy.
④ Maybe not. I shouldn't use my phone too often.
⑤ Thanks for the advice. I will call and make a reservation.

18
W: Zack, what's that sound? I think it's coming from your phone.
M: Oh, it's my new app. It ________ ________ to drink water every two hours.
W: I heard that drinking plenty of water has a lot of health benefits.
M: That's right. It increases your energy and ________ ________ ________.
W: I tried to do that before, but it wasn't easy.
M: It wasn't easy for me, either. That's why I've ________ this app.
W: It sounds really useful.
M: It also sends you messages like "You ________ ________ ________ by now."
W: That's really interesting.
M: You should try it out.
W: Good idea. I will download it right away.

19. 대화를 듣고, 남자의 마지막 말에 대한 여자의 응답으로 가장 적절한 것을 고르시오.

Woman: _______________

① Sure. The salmon contains healthy fat.
② Thanks. I appreciate you taking care of it.
③ Right. The food is for dinner, so no hurry.
④ Wait. I think they have the wrong delivery address.
⑤ No. Cook the chicken first and forget about the salad.

19 (*Cellphone rings.*)

W: Charlie? What's up?

M: Hey, Abigail. I'm at the shop. You wanted a chicken salad for lunch, right?

W: Yes. Is there a problem?

M: They ___________ ___________ ___________ chicken. Can I get you any other salad?

W: Sure. What do they have?

M: They have tuna, salmon, and egg.

W: Hmm, I'm ___________ ___________ salmon. Other than that, I'm fine with anything.

M: All right. I've ___________ ___________ mine along with a tuna salad for you. I'll be there as soon as I can.

W: Thanks. I appreciate you taking care of it.

20. 다음 상황 설명을 듣고, Peter가 Jenna에게 할 말로 가장 적절한 것을 고르시오.

Peter: _______________

① I should go and buy some water.
② You'd better not sit still for too long.
③ Do you want to take a walk with me?
④ Can you wake me up after five minutes?
⑤ You're not allowed to eat and drink here.

20 W: Peter and Jenna are studying at the study café. After a few hours, Peter starts to feel sleepy. He tries drinking cold water and doing some stretches to shake off his sleepiness, but he _______ _______ _______. Peter can't concentrate on his studies. He thinks it _______ _______ _______ _______ he took a nap for a few minutes. So, he wants to ask Jenna to _______ _______ _______ after five minutes. In this situation, what would Peter most likely say to Jenna?

Peter: Can you wake me up after five minutes?

Words & Expressions Review 07

● 다음 단어를 암기하세요.

문제	번호	단어	뜻
1	☐ 1	plain	무늬가 없는, 무지의
2	☐ 2	cheer for	~를 응원하다
	☐ 3	judge	심사위원, 심판
4	☐ 4	mechanical	기계적인
	☐ 5	flight attendant	승무원
5	☐ 6	pleased	기쁜
	☐ 7	regretful	후회하는
6	☐ 8	take an order	주문을 받다
	☐ 9	disposable	일회용의
7	☐ 10	be all set	준비가 다 되다
	☐ 11	get on ~	~에 타다
8	☐ 12	scholarship	장학금
	☐ 13	discovery	발견
9	☐ 14	transportation	이동, 운반
	☐ 15	be suitable for ~	~에 적합하다
	☐ 16	mobile	이동식의, 이동하는
	☐ 17	lap	무릎
10	☐ 18	rude	무례한
11	☐ 19	be supposed to + 동사	~하기로 되어 있다
	☐ 20	be out of ~	~을 다 써서 없다, ~이 떨어지다
12	☐ 21	fragrance	향, 향기
	☐ 22	anything but	~이 결코 아닌

문제	번호	단어	뜻
13	☐ 23	take place	(준비되거나 계획된 일이) 개최되다, 열리다
	☐ 24	definitely	꼭, 분명히, 절대로
	☐ 25	family gathering	가족 모임
	☐ 26	mark	표시하다, 기록하다
14	☐ 27	hometown	고향
15	☐ 28	outdoors	야외에서
	☐ 29	indoor	실내의, 실내용의
	☐ 30	hygienic	위생적인, 청결한
	☐ 31	variety	종류
16	☐ 32	organic	유기농의
	☐ 33	locally grown	현지에서 기른
	☐ 34	flat tire	바람 빠진 타이어
17	☐ 35	mix up ~	~을 혼동하다
	☐ 36	booking	예약
	☐ 37	remind	상기시키다, 생각나게 하다
18	☐ 38	plenty of	많은
	☐ 39	regulate	조절하다, 조정하다
	☐ 40	install	설치하다
19	☐ 41	allergic	알레르기가 있는
	☐ 42	contain	~이 들어[함유되어] 있다
20	☐ 43	concentrate	집중하다
	☐ 44	take a nap	낮잠 자다

● 왼쪽 단어장의 뜻이 보이지 않게 반으로 접고, 학습한 단어의 뜻을 아래 빈칸에 적어주세요.

1	outdoors		23	scholarship
2	definitely		24	remind
3	flat tire		25	family gathering
4	rude		26	be suitable for ~
5	hometown		27	install
6	contain		28	indoor
7	take an order		29	be all set
8	regretful		30	organic
9	locally grown		31	disposable
10	take place		32	regulate
11	discovery		33	mix up ~
12	take a nap		34	booking
13	get on ~		35	fragrance
14	plain		36	mobile
15	hygienic		37	anything but
16	mark		38	judge
17	be out of ~		39	be supposed to + 동사
18	flight attendant		40	transportation
19	allergic		41	lap
20	cheer for		42	mechanical
21	pleased		43	plenty of
22	variety		44	concentrate

08회 중학영어듣기 모의고사

M3(17)_08_US
모두 **미국식 발음(US)** 으로 녹음

M3(17)_08_UK
20문제 중 5문제에 **영국식 발음 (US+UK)**을 포함하여 녹음

정답 및 해석 p. 43

1 대화를 듣고, 여자가 구입할 액자를 고르시오.

① 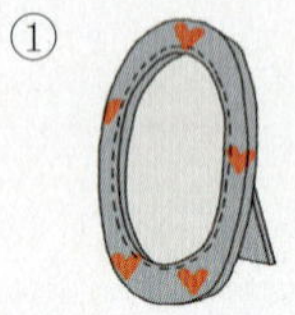　② 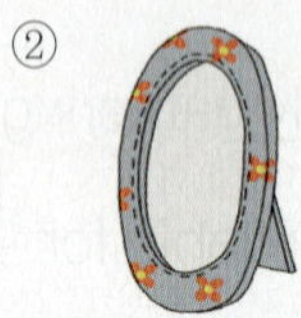　③ 　④ 　⑤ 

2 대화를 듣고, 헬스 PT에 관해 언급되지 <u>않은</u> 것을 고르시오.

① 운동 목적　　　② 목표 체중　　　③ 목표 달성 기간
④ PT 시간　　　⑤ 식단 관리 여부

3 대화를 듣고, 여자가 남자에게 전화한 목적으로 가장 적절한 것을 고르시오.

① 잠옷을 구매하려고
② 할인 쿠폰을 사용하려고
③ 매장의 위치를 물어보려고
④ 잠옷의 사이즈를 변경하려고
⑤ 배송 누락에 대해 문의하려고

4 대화를 듣고, 두 사람이 만나기로 한 시각을 고르시오.

① 2 p.m.　　② 3 p.m.　　③ 4 p.m.　　④ 5 p.m.　　⑤ 6 p.m.

5 대화를 듣고, 남자의 심정으로 가장 적절한 것을 고르시오.

① bored　　　② relaxed　　　③ jealous
④ satisfied　　⑤ frustrated

6 다음 그림의 상황에 가장 적절한 대화를 고르시오.

①   ②   ③   ④   ⑤

7 대화를 듣고, 남자가 여자에게 부탁한 일로 가장 적절한 것을 고르시오.

① 케이크 만들기   ② 선물 고르기   ③ 풍선 가져오기
④ 파티 장소 장식하기   ⑤ 생일카드 구입하기

8 다음을 듣고, Golden Science Fair에 관해 언급되지 <u>않은</u> 것을 고르시오.

① 주최 기관   ② 개최 장소   ③ 참가자 수   ④ 참가 비용   ⑤ 후원 기관

9 다음을 듣고, 어떤 동물에 관한 설명인지 고르시오.

① 악어   ② 거북이   ③ 개구리   ④ 캥거루   ⑤ 카멜레온

10 다음을 듣고, 두 사람의 대화가 <u>어색한</u> 것을 고르시오.

①   ②   ③   ④   ⑤

11번~20번 문제는 다음 페이지에 ➡

11 대화를 듣고, 남자가 대화 직후에 할 일로 가장 적절한 것을 고르시오.

① 방 청소하기 ② 입장권 예매 취소하기 ③ 학생증 가져오기
④ 증강현실 체험하기 ⑤ 게임 대회 참가하기

12 다음 표를 보면서 대화를 듣고, 여자가 구입할 가방을 고르시오.

	Bag	Color	Size	Chest Strap
①	A	Black	Large	O
②	B	Black	Small	X
③	C	Black	Large	X
④	D	Red	Large	O
⑤	E	Red	Small	X

13 대화를 듣고, 집들이 날짜를 고르시오.

① 11월 26일 ② 11월 27일 ③ 12월 4일
④ 12월 5일 ⑤ 12월 6일

14 대화를 듣고, 남자가 어제 한 일로 가장 적절한 것을 고르시오.

① 파티 참석하기 ② 할머니 댁 방문하기 ③ 가족 사진 찍기
④ 케이크 만들기 ⑤ 사진 앨범 주문하기

15 다음을 듣고, 방송의 목적으로 가장 적절한 것을 고르시오.

① 온라인 쇼핑몰을 홍보하려고 ② 재래 시장 이용을 장려하려고
③ 세일 상품에 대해 안내하려고 ④ 매장의 영업 마감을 공지하려고
⑤ 물건이 품절됐음을 알려주려고

16 대화를 듣고, 남자가 지불할 금액을 고르시오.

① $3 ② $5 ③ $7 ④ $10 ⑤ $12

17 대화를 듣고, 남자의 마지막 말에 대한 여자의 응답으로 가장 적절한 것을 고르시오.

Woman: _______________________________________

① Great! Please text it to me now.

② Yes. I ordered a pair online yesterday.

③ Can you tell me where the bowling alley is?

④ Is the club meeting on Tuesday or Thursday?

⑤ Those shoes are more expensive than I thought.

[18~19] 대화를 듣고, 여자의 마지막 말에 대한 남자의 응답으로 가장 적절한 것을 고르시오.

18 **Man:** _______________________________________

① You can relieve sneezing by treating your allergies.

② Place it in indirect sunlight and water it monthly.

③ It is a perfect choice for a housewarming gift.

④ Gardening helps reduce stress.

⑤ It'll be delivered tomorrow.

19 **Man:** _______________________________________

① Please take this medicine three times a day.

② I'll call the school and explain the situation.

③ I got caught in the rain on the way home.

④ Being late for school is not a good habit.

⑤ You can invite all your friends.

20 다음 상황 설명을 듣고, Emily가 Liam에게 할 말로 가장 적절한 것을 고르시오.

Emily: _______________________________________

① Can you hand me some tissues?

② Why don't you order one more dish?

③ Please stop talking with your mouth full.

④ I need to use the bathroom for a second.

⑤ Could you be quiet while watching the movie?

Dictation Test 08

M3(17)_08_D

Dictation(받아쓰기)은 본문을 받아쓰면서 영어듣기의 집중력을 향상시키고 다양한 표현을 정리하기 위한 영어듣기 학습법입니다. **녹음을 다시 듣고, 빈칸에 알맞은 단어를 써 보세요.**
※Dictation의 정답은 듣기 대본의 밑줄 친 부분을 확인하세요. 정답 p. 43

맞은 개수 / 총182개

---

1. 대화를 듣고, 여자가 구입할 액자를 고르시오.

① 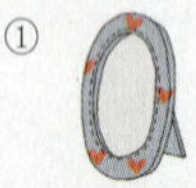 ② 

③  ④ 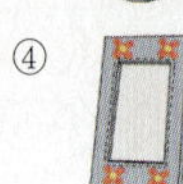

⑤

01

M: What can I do for you?

W: I can't decide on which one to buy. Every frame is so pretty and unique.

M: This oval shaped frame ________ ________ ____________ is very popular in our store.

W: It's pretty, but I have an oval frame ________ ________. I want to try a rectangular frame this time.

M: Then how about this one with the stars?

W: ________ ________ is too retro. I like this rectangular frame ________ ________.

M: That's a good one, too. It ________ ________ with classic furniture.

W: I think so, too. I'll take it.

---

2. 대화를 듣고, 헬스 PT에 관해 언급되지 <u>않은</u> 것을 고르시오.

① 운동 목적
② 목표 체중
③ 목표 달성 기간
④ PT 시간
⑤ 식단 관리 여부

02

W: Hi, I'd like to sign up for a personal training program.

M: Welcome. Let me help you with that. What's the purpose of your exercise?

W: I want to lose some weight and ________ ________ ________.

M: Okay. Do you have a specific weight goal in mind?

W: Well, I want to _______ _______ _______ 55 kg.

M: And how quickly do you want to achieve your goal?

W: I hope I can get there within three to four months.

M: Alright. Now let's talk about diet. Are you ___________ _______ _______?

W: No, I'd like some help with that.

M: Okay, then. Let's check your _______ _______ and go over some more details.

3. 대화를 듣고, 여자가 남자에게 전화한 목적으로 가장 적절한 것을 고르시오.

① 잠옷을 구매하려고
② 할인 쿠폰을 사용하려고
③ 매장의 위치를 물어보려고
④ 잠옷의 사이즈를 변경하려고
⑤ 배송 누락에 대해 문의하려고

03 *[Telephone rings.]*

M: Hello, this is Comfy Wear Company.

W: Hello, I ordered some pajamas online. Your website says _______ _______ ___________, but I never got them.

M: Really? Do you have your order number?

W: Yes, I have it here. It's PJ469.

M: *[Typing sound]* Oh, the package _______ _______ _______ _______. We're very sorry. Would you like a refund or _________?

W: Please send them again.

M: Okay. We'll send your pajamas as soon as possible. We'll also send you a 30 percent discount coupon for a future order. We apologize again _______ _______ ___________.

W: That's okay. Thanks for the coupon.

다음 페이지에 계속 ➡

4. 대화를 듣고, 두 사람이 만나기로 한 시각을 고르시오.

① 2 p.m.　　② 3 p.m.
③ 4 p.m.　　④ 5 p.m.
⑤ 6 p.m.

04

M: Mina, did you hear that professor Kim's __________ __________ will be held on Saturday afternoon?

W: Yes, I did. I'll definitely be there. I think that he is the best professor on campus.

M: I think so, too. How about we go together?

W: Sounds great! Do you know when the ceremony starts?

M: It starts at 5 p.m. When shall we meet?

W: It'll be held in the campus auditorium. So, how about at the __________ __________ at 3 p.m.?

M: I think that's too early. What about 4 p.m.?

W: That's better. See you then.

5. 대화를 듣고, 남자의 심정으로 가장 적절한 것을 고르시오.

① bored
② relaxed
③ jealous
④ satisfied
⑤ frustrated

05

W: Josh, are you okay? You __________ __________.

M: What should I do? I can't enter the contest now.

W: The video contest? Why? What's wrong?

M: When I finished editing the video, my computer __________.

W: Oh, no. Did you save the file?

M: I'm sure I did.

W: Then you'll be fine. __________ __________ for the contest is tomorrow.

M: Yeah, but the service center can't fix my computer until tomorrow.

W: Are you sure? Is there any way you can __________ the file?

M: No. I don't know what to do. __________ __________ __________ __________ __________ are useless now.

6. 다음 그림의 상황에 가장 적절한 대화를 고르시오.

① ② ③ ④ ⑤

06 ① W: How much is this ___________ ___________ ___________?

M: It's 3 dollars.

② W: Can you help me find my phone?

M: Sure. I think I see it ___________ ___________ ___________.

③ W: May I see your ticket, please?

M: Sure, here it is.

④ W: I'm sorry I'm late.

M: It's okay. I ___________ a little late, too.

⑤ W: It looks like it's going to rain.

M: Really? I didn't bring my umbrella.

7. 대화를 듣고, 남자가 여자에게 부탁한 일로 가장 적절한 것을 고르시오.

① 케이크 만들기
② 선물 고르기
③ 풍선 가져오기
④ 파티 장소 장식하기
⑤ 생일카드 구입하기

07 *(Cellphone rings.)*

W: Hi, Hojin. Are we ready for Juri's birthday party?

M: Nearly. I've bought the cake, and you're ________ ________ ________, right?

W: Yes. How about the balloons?

M: ________ ________ ________. We've decorated the room nicely.

W: Great. Is there anything else I can do?

M: Actually, that's why I called you. Can you ________ ________ ___________ __________ on your way here?

W: Sure. I'll get a really cute one!

다음 페이지에 계속 ➡

8. 다음을 듣고, Golden Science Fair에 관해 언급되지 <u>않은</u> 것을 고르시오.

① 주최 기관　② 개최 장소
③ 참가자 수　④ 참가 비용
⑤ 후원 기관

08 W: The Golden Science Fair is for middle school students ______ ______ ______. It was initiated to help develop our future scientists. It's hosted by the Golden Science Center, and is held every May. This year, the fair ______ ______ ______ the Capital Convention Center. Around 600 students from 423 schools participated. They ______ ______ awards totaling $5,000. Special thanks go to Triangle Corporation for their ______ and volunteer efforts.

9. 다음을 듣고, 어떤 동물에 관한 설명인지 고르시오.

① 악어
② 거북이
③ 개구리
④ 캥거루
⑤ 카멜레온

09 W: This animal is a reptile that can be found in warm countries such as Australia and Africa. It has thick skin and a powerful jaw ______ ______ ______ ______. It has a long tail that helps it swim and move on land. It is a great swimmer and can ______ ______ ______ for a long time underwater. It is a good hunter and eats fish, birds, and mammals. Some people wear shoes and bags ______ ______ ______ ______.

10. 다음을 듣고, 두 사람의 대화가 <u>어색한</u> 것을 고르시오.

①　②
③　④
⑤

10 ① M: I really want to ______ ______ ______ of this scenery.
W: Oh, do you want me to be in it?
② M: How about going to the beach?
W: I'm not ______ ______ ______ ______ that.
③ M: Do you know where James is?
W: He went to the restroom.

④ M: Do you have ________ ___________?

W: No, I don't like rock and roll music very much.

⑤ M: I didn't know that he had a daughter.

W: Me, ________.

11. 대화를 듣고, 남자가 대화 직후에 할 일로 가장 적절한 것을 고르시오.

① 방 청소하기
② 입장권 예매 취소하기
③ 학생증 가져오기
④ 증강현실 체험하기
⑤ 게임 대회 참가하기

11

W: Jake, I hear that a new AR experience park just opened in the area.

M: What's AR?

W: Augmented Reality. You can experience a whole new artificial world ___________ __________ it were real.

M: Does it include gaming experience, too?

W: Of course. Do you want to __________ __________ __________?

M: Sure. I'm free today. Let's go now.

W: Okay. By the way, we can get a __________ __________. Do you have your student ID?

M: I think I left it in my room. I'll __________ __________ __________ right now.

W: Okay. I'll meet you downstairs.

2025 영어듣기능력평가 1회 12번 변형

12. 다음 표를 보면서 대화를 듣고, 여자가 구입할 가방을 고르시오.

	Bag	Color	Size	Chest Strap
①	A	Black	Large	O
②	B	Black	Small	X
③	C	Black	Large	X
④	D	Red	Large	O
⑤	E	Red	Small	X

12

W: Patrick, I want to get a new bag for school. What do you think about this one?

M: You mean the red one? I think black would __________ __________ more of your outfits.

W: You're right. Black is __________ __________ __________. What about the size? Small or large?

M: I'd go with the large one. You carry a lot of books.

다음 페이지에 계속 ➡

W: That _________ _________. Do you think I
should get one with a chest strap?

M: Yes, absolutely. My bag has a chest strap and
it's really comfortable. It _________ the straps
_________ _________.

W: That sounds perfect. I'll choose that one.

13. 대화를 듣고, 집들이 날짜를 고르시오.
① 11월 26일
② 11월 27일
③ 12월 4일
④ 12월 5일
⑤ 12월 6일

13

M: I'm going to have a housewarming party soon.
When would be good for you?

W: _________ _________ this Friday, November 27.

M: I have a dinner meeting with a client on that day.
How about next Friday? I mean December 4.

W: Sorry, but I have other plans with my friends
_________ _________. I'm free on the next weekend,
though.

M: Then, is Saturday evening okay for you?
December 5?

W: Yes. _________ _________ anytime after 6 on that
day.

M: Good. Then I'll see you next Saturday.

14. 대화를 듣고, 남자가 어제 한 일로 가장
적절한 것을 고르시오.
① 파티 참석하기
② 할머니 댁 방문하기
③ 가족 사진 찍기
④ 케이크 만들기
⑤ 사진 앨범 주문하기

14

W: Bill, what are you going to do next Saturday?

M: I'm going to go to my grandmother's birthday
party.

W: Oh, what present are you going to give to her?

M: I made her _________ _________ _________ of our
family members.

W: What a meaningful gift! How did you make it?

M: I ordered it by ________ ________ ____________

yesterday. It was ________ ________ ________.

W: That sounds interesting. I can use it to make one

for my mom's birthday.

M: Sure. I'll show you the application.

15. 다음을 듣고, 방송의 목적으로 가장 적절한 것을 고르시오.

① 온라인 쇼핑몰을 홍보하려고
② 재래 시장 이용을 장려하려고
③ 세일 상품에 대해 안내하려고
④ 매장의 영업 마감을 공지하려고
⑤ 물건이 품절됐음을 알려주려고

15

M: Good evening, guests. Thank you for visiting

our shopping center today. The current time is

9:45 p.m. We wanted to let you know that the

shopping center ________ ________ ________

in 15 minutes. At this time, we ask that you bring

________ __________ ________ to the cash

registers. If you need any assistance, our staff

members will be ________ ________ ________

________. Thank you for shopping with us. We

hope you visit us again soon.

16. 대화를 듣고, 남자가 지불할 금액을 고르시오.

① $3   ② $5
③ $7   ④ $10
⑤ $12

16

W: Welcome! What would you like to order?

M: Hi, I ________ ________ ________ ________ a

double cheeseburger combo.

W: That will be $7. Would you like to add any sides to

your combo?

M: Let's see... How much is the salad?

W: It's $3 ________ ________ ________ ________ and $5

for the large salad.

M: Okay. I'll have the small salad then.

W: Sure! Will ________ ________ ________?

M: Yeah, that's it. Thank you.

다음 페이지에 계속 ➡

17. 대화를 듣고, 남자의 마지막 말에 대한 여자의 응답으로 가장 적절한 것을 고르시오.

Woman: ___________________
① Great! Please text it to me now.
② Yes. I ordered a pair online yesterday.
③ Can you tell me where the bowling alley is?
④ Is the club meeting on Tuesday or Thursday?
⑤ Those shoes are more expensive than I thought.

17

M: Lily, you are coming to our bowling club next week, aren't you?

W: Of course. I'm so excited. But I haven't bought shoes yet.

M: You can always ________ them from the ________ ________.

W: I want my own shoes, though. Do you know any stores that sell them?

M: Oh, I know a place where you can buy them at a ____________ ________.

W: Really? Where is it?

M: Wait! I have the store name and number in my phone. *[Pause]* Found it!

W: Great! Please text it to me now.

18. 대화를 듣고, 여자의 마지막 말에 대한 남자의 응답으로 가장 적절한 것을 고르시오.

Man: ___________________
① You can relieve sneezing by treating your allergies.
② Place it in indirect sunlight and water it monthly.
③ It is a perfect choice for a housewarming gift.
④ Gardening helps reduce stress.
⑤ It'll be delivered tomorrow.

18

M: Hello, how can I help you?

W: Hi, I'd like to buy a plant for my home. Could you recommend something easy to grow?

M: How about this sansevieria? It's a popular plant for people who are ________ ________ ________.

W: Why is it popular?

M: It cleans the air and relieves allergies, not to mention how easy it is to take care of.

W: Perfect! I'll take it. Can I ________ ________ ________?

M: Certainly. Please write your address on this form.

W: Here you are. Are there any ________ ________ ________ ________ this plant?

M: Place it in indirect sunlight and water it monthly.

19. 대화를 듣고, 여자의 마지막 말에 대한 남자의 응답으로 가장 적절한 것을 고르시오.

Man: _________________

① Please take this medicine three times a day.
② I'll call the school and explain the situation.
③ I got caught in the rain on the way home.
④ Being late for school is not a good habit.
⑤ You can invite all your friends.

19

M: Are you okay, Ashley? You are coughing a lot and look sick.

W: I feel terrible, Dad. I think I'm ________ ________ ________ the flu.

M: You shouldn't have run home in the rain yesterday.

W: It wasn't raining hard, so I didn't think it would be a problem. Sorry.

M: You ________ ________ ________ and see the doctor now.

W: Now, Dad? What about school?

M: Your health is more important, Ashley.

W: I know, but my teachers and friends will worry about me.

M: I'll call the school and explain the situation.

20. 다음 상황 설명을 듣고, Emily가 Liam에게 할 말로 가장 적절한 것을 고르시오.

Emily: _________________

① Can you hand me some tissues?
② Why don't you order one more dish?
③ Please stop talking with your mouth full.
④ I need to use the bathroom for a second.
⑤ Could you be quiet while watching the movie?

20

W: Emily and Liam are having lunch together at a restaurant. While they are eating, Liam talks to Emily while there is food in his mouth. She is ________ ________ ________ __________ because some of the food comes ________ ________ ________ ________. So, she wants to ask him to ________ ________ while he is eating. In this situation, what would Emily most likely say to Liam?

Emily: Please stop talking with your mouth full.

Words & Expressions Review 08

● 다음 단어를 암기하세요.

문제	번호	단어	뜻
1	☐ 1	frame	액자, 틀
2	☐ 2	get in shape	몸매를 가꾸다, 몸을 단련하다
	☐ 3	order number	주문 번호
3	☐ 4	reship	재배송하다
	☐ 5	inconvenience	불편, 애로
	☐ 6	professor	교수
4	☐ 7	be held	열리다
	☐ 8	on campus	교내에서, 대학에서
5	☐ 9	pale	(안색이) 창백한, 핼쑥한
	☐ 10	retrieve	복구하다, 되찾다
6	☐ 11	arrive	도착하다
	☐ 12	be going to	~할 것이다
7	☐ 13	decorate	꾸미다, 장식하다
	☐ 14	initiate	시작하다, 개시하다
8	☐ 15	develop	성장시키다, 개발하다
	☐ 16	sponsorship	후원
	☐ 17	reptile	파충류
9	☐ 18	jaw	턱
	☐ 19	made from ~	~으로 만든
	☐ 20	scenery	풍경, 경치
10	☐ 21	mood	기분, 분위기
	☐ 22	bandage	붕대

문제	번호	단어	뜻
	☐ 23	augmented reality	증강 현실
11	☐ 24	artificial	인공[인조]의
	☐ 25	as if	마치 …인 것처럼
13	☐ 26	housewarming party	집들이
	☐ 27	present	선물
14	☐ 28	meaningful	의미 있는
	☐ 29	application	애플리케이션
	☐ 30	cash register	계산대
15	☐ 31	assistance	도움
	☐ 32	order	주문하다, 명령하다
16	☐ 33	double	두 배의
	☐ 34	add	추가하다, 더하다
	☐ 35	borrow	빌리다, 대여하다
17	☐ 36	bowling alley	볼링장
	☐ 37	discounted price	할인된 가격
	☐ 38	relieve	완화시키다
18	☐ 39	allergy	알레르기
	☐ 40	not to mention ~	~은 말할 것도 없이
19	☐ 41	come down with	(병에) 걸리다
	☐ 42	habit	습관, 버릇
20	☐ 43	annoyed	짜증이 난
	☐ 44	behavior	행동

M3(17)_W_08

●왼쪽 단어장의 뜻이 보이지 않게 반으로 접고, 학습한 단어의 뜻을 아래 빈칸에 적어주세요.

1	meaningful	23	bandage
2	inconvenience	24	initiate
3	not to mention ~	25	relieve
4	order number	26	annoyed
5	borrow	27	mood
6	as if	28	arrive
7	get in shape	29	decorate
8	professor	30	scenery
9	reship	31	pale
10	augmented reality	32	be going to
11	application	33	on campus
12	artificial	34	bowling alley
13	be held	35	come down with
14	develop	36	add
15	housewarming party	37	assistance
16	double	38	discounted price
17	retrieve	39	habit
18	behavior	40	order
19	cash register	41	present
20	made from ~	42	reptile
21	allergy	43	frame
22	sponsorship	44	jaw

09회 중학영어듣기 모의고사

M3(17)_09_US
모두 **미국식 발음(US)**
으로 녹음

M3(17)_09_UK
20문제 중 5문제에 **영국식 발음
(US+UK)**을 포함하여 녹음

정답 및 해석 p. 49

1 대화를 듣고, 여자가 선택할 손거울을 고르시오.

①  ②  ③  ④  ⑤ 

2 대화를 듣고, Technology Fair에 관해 언급되지 <u>않은</u> 것을 고르시오.

① 행사 주제 ② 행사 장소 ③ 입장료
④ 프로그램 ⑤ 종료일

3 대화를 듣고, 남자가 여자에게 전화한 목적으로 가장 적절한 것을 고르시오.

① 도서 반납 기한을 연장하려고 ② 회원 가입 정보를 변경하려고
③ 도서관 카드를 재발급 받으려고 ④ 도서관 운영 시간을 확인하려고
⑤ 전자책 대출 방법을 문의하려고

4 대화를 듣고, 남자가 탑승하려는 기차의 출발 시각을 고르시오.

① 12 p.m. ② 1 p.m. ③ 2 p.m. ④ 3 p.m. ⑤ 4 p.m.

5 대화를 듣고, 남자의 심정으로 가장 적절한 것을 고르시오.

① calm ② anxious ③ relieved ④ regretful ⑤ satisfied

6 다음 그림의 상황에 가장 적절한 대화를 고르시오.

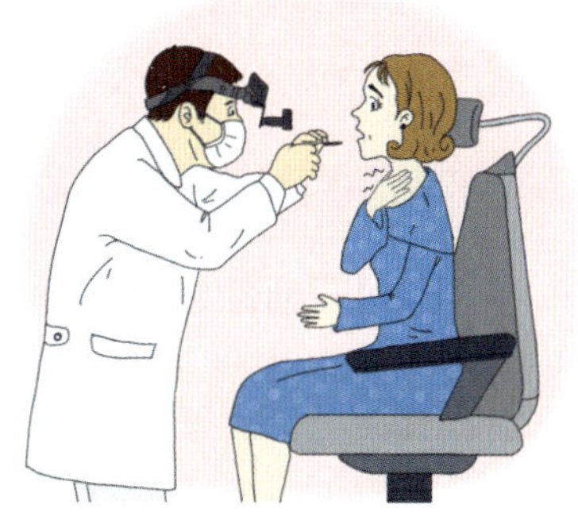

①   ②   ③   ④   ⑤

7 대화를 듣고, 여자가 남자에게 부탁한 일로 가장 적절한 것을 고르시오.

① 저녁 만들기   ② 수업 등록하기   ③ 요리 재료 사기
④ 컴퓨터 고쳐주기   ⑤ 요리 강좌 홍보하기

8 다음을 듣고, Food Festival에 대해 언급되지 <u>않은</u> 것을 고르시오.

① 장소   ② 날짜   ③ 주제   ④ 특별 상품   ⑤ 입장료

9 다음을 듣고, 무엇에 관한 설명인지 고르시오.

① 바다   ② 호수   ③ 동굴   ④ 늪지대   ⑤ 우물

10 다음을 듣고, 두 사람의 대화가 <u>어색한</u> 것을 고르시오.

①   ②   ③   ④   ⑤

11번~20번 문제는 다음 페이지에 ➡

11 대화를 듣고, 여자가 할 일로 가장 적절한 것을 고르시오.

① 샤워하기　　　　② 머핀 만들기　　　　③ 쓰레기 버리기
④ 이웃집 방문하기　　⑤ 기계 고치기

12 다음 표를 보면서 대화를 듣고, 두 사람이 구매할 텔레비전을 고르시오.

	Model	Size (inches)	Screen Type	Connectivity
①	A	55	Curved	Wireless
②	B	55	Flat	HDMI Cable
③	C	65	Flat	Wireless
④	D	65	Flat	HDMI Cable
⑤	E	65	Curved	Wireless

13 대화를 듣고, 여자가 취재를 가기로 한 날짜를 고르시오.

① 8월 10일　　　　② 8월 11일　　　　③ 8월 12일
④ 8월 13일　　　　⑤ 8월 14일

14 대화를 듣고, 여자가 주말에 한 일로 가장 적절한 것을 고르시오.

① 만화책 읽기　　　② 예방 접종 맞기　　　③ 영화 보기
④ 온라인 쇼핑하기　　⑤ 할머니 뵈러 가기

15 다음을 듣고, 방송의 목적으로 가장 적절한 것을 고르시오.

① 도서관 회원증 발급 절차를 설명하려고
② 공사 일정 지연을 공지하려고
③ 교무실 출입 예절을 지도하려고
④ 중고 책 기부 방법을 알리려고
⑤ 희망 도서 신청 방법을 안내하려고

16 대화를 듣고, 남자가 받게 될 거스름돈으로 적절한 것을 고르시오.

① $30　　　② $40　　　③ $50　　　④ $60　　　⑤ $70

17 대화를 듣고, 여자의 마지막 말에 대한 남자의 응답으로 가장 적절한 것을 고르시오.

Man: _______________________________________

① Thanks. I just do what I can.
② You're such a cute little boy.
③ No, I don't see her every day.
④ No, I didn't eat all the candies.
⑤ Besides, my cousins are really sweet.

[18~19] 대화를 듣고, 남자의 마지막 말에 대한 여자의 응답으로 가장 적절한 것을 고르시오.

18 **Woman:** _______________________________________

① Well, we're not in a hurry after all.
② Don't worry. The theater is open until late.
③ Still, drivers don't need to be kind all the time.
④ That's what I'm saying. He should not drive so fast.
⑤ He should pull over if he wants to use his cellphone.

19 **Woman:** _______________________________________

① That sounds good. I'll take the deal.
② Okay. I just wanted to buy a new bed.
③ Thank you, but a double bed is just fine.
④ No problem. I hope you enjoy your stay.
⑤ I'm sorry, but you booked the wrong hotel.

20 다음 상황 설명을 듣고, Mary가 Peter에게 할 말로 가장 적절한 것을 고르시오.

Mary: _______________________________________
① I'm encountering problems with my laptop.
② Would it be okay if I borrowed your charger?
③ Would you mind if I have another cup of coffee?
④ Where can I find a coffee shop that's laptop-friendly?
⑤ When are you thinking of wrapping up and going home?

Dictation Test 09

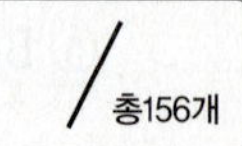

M3(17)_09_D

Dictation(받아쓰기)은 본문을 받아쓰면서 영어듣기의 집중력을 향상시키고 다양한 표현을 정리하기 위한 영어듣기 학습법입니다. **녹음을 다시 듣고, 빈칸에 알맞은 단어를 써 보세요.**

※Dictation의 정답은 듣기 대본의 밑줄 친 부분을 확인하세요.

정답 p. 49

맞은 개수 / 총 156개

그림정보파악(대화)

1. 대화를 듣고, 여자가 선택할 손거울을 고르시오.

①  ② 

③  ④ 

⑤ 

01

M: Hello, how can I help you?

W: I'm ___________ ___________ a hand mirror for my friend.

M: We have square-shaped and round-shaped mirrors. Which one would your friend like?

W: I think she would like a round-shaped one. Oh, there are designs ___________ ___________ ___________.

M: Yes. These flower designs are popular.

W: I want a mirror with the flower design.

M: Good choice. We can also put your friend's name on it. It will only take a few minutes.

W: Wonderful! Put 'Alice' ___________ ___________ ___________, please.

M: Okay. I'll be right back.

대화미언급

2. 대화를 듣고, Technology Fair에 관해 언급되지 않은 것을 고르시오.

① 행사 주제
② 행사 장소
③ 입장료
④ 프로그램
⑤ 종료일

02

W: Steve, did you know that the Technology Fair is going on right now?

M: Yes. The theme of the fair this year is 'AI and ___________ robots.'

W: I'm really interested in domestic robots these days.

M: I'm sure you can get a lot of information there.

W: Do you know where the fair is ___________ ___________?

M: It's being held at Lincoln Center downtown.

W: Tickets are only 7 dollars each for students. Do you want to go with me?

M: Definitely.

W: How about going next weekend?

M: We have to go this weekend. The fair ends on August 25th.

W: I see. Let's go this weekend then.

3. 대화를 듣고, 남자가 여자에게 전화한 목적으로 가장 적절한 것을 고르시오.

① 도서 반납 기한을 연장하려고
② 회원 가입 정보를 변경하려고
③ 도서관 카드를 재발급 받으려고
④ 도서관 운영 시간을 확인하려고
⑤ 전자책 대출 방법을 문의하려고

03 *(Telephone rings.)*

W: Good afternoon. City Library. How may I help you?

M: Hi. I'm ___________ ___________ visit the library today, but I think I've lost my library card.

W: I'm sorry to hear that. May I have your full name, please?

M: Brian Johnson.

W: *(Typing sound)* ___________ ___________ ___________ that for you... Yes, I found your record in our system.

M: Can I get a new card?

W: Of course! But you'll need to visit the library with your ID. There's also a ___________ ___________ of $2.

M: I understand. Thank you for your help.

4. 대화를 듣고, 남자가 탑승하려는 기차의 출발 시각을 고르시오.

① 12 p.m.　② 1 p.m.
③ 2 p.m.　④ 3 p.m.
⑤ 4 p.m.

04 W: Hello, how may I help you?

M: I'd like to buy four tickets for the express train to Busan this afternoon.

W: Okay. Would you like first class or economy class?

M: Economy class, please.

W: Sure. You can buy tickets for trains ___________ ___________ 12 p.m., 2 p.m. or 4 p.m.

M: What about the 1 p.m. train?

다음 페이지에 계속 ➡

W: I'm afraid tickets are _________ _________ for that one.

M: I see. The 12 p.m. train _________ _________ _________ any time for lunch. So, _________ _________ the one leaving at 2 p.m.

W: Okay. Would you like four adult tickets?

M: That's right.

5. 대화를 듣고, 남자의 심정으로 가장 적절한 것을 고르시오.

① calm   ② anxious
③ relieved   ④ regretful
⑤ satisfied

05

W: Hi, Jiho. You don't look so well. Is there something wrong?

M: Hello, Mrs. Hills. I'm feeling _________ about the school play tomorrow.

W: What's the matter?

M: During rehearsal last week, I _________ _________ _________ several times. It was awful.

W: Don't be silly. You've practiced so much more since then. You'll be great tomorrow.

M: But what if I make the same mistakes again?

W: I don't think you will. But even if you forget some lines, just _________ _________ _________ and the audience won't notice.

M: I'm not sure if I'll be able to do that.

6. 다음 그림의 상황에 가장 적절한 대화를 고르시오.

① ② ③ ④ ⑤

06

① W: That's a really ugly painting.

M: Yeah, it does not suit this restaurant.

② W: You _________ _________ _________ _________.

M: Oh, I didn't know. I'm so sorry.

③ W: Why is it so noisy in here?

M: The TV is on. I'll turn the volume down.

④ W: My throat really hurts. I can't even drink water.

M: Okay, let me take a look. Say "Ah."

⑤ W: What _________ _________ _________ the problem?

M: The oven is broken. It's okay, I'll fix it.

7. 대화를 듣고, 여자가 남자에게 부탁한 일로 가장 적절한 것을 고르시오.

① 저녁 만들기
② 수업 등록하기
③ 요리 재료 사기
④ 컴퓨터 고쳐주기
⑤ 요리 강좌 홍보하기

07

W: Hey, did you hear about the cooking class happening next Saturday?

M: No, I missed that. ___________ ___________ will they be covering?

W: They're offering a variety, from Italian pasta dishes to Indian curries.

M: That sounds exciting! Should we ___________ ___________ ___________ it?

W: Definitely. The announcement mentioned that registration is now open online. Plus, there's a ___________ for early birds.

M: Oh, I'm usually good at online registration.

W: Perfect! In that case, could you ___________ ___________ ___________ ___________?

M: Of course, I'll take care of it right now.

8. 다음을 듣고, Food Festival에 대해 언급되지 **않은** 것을 고르시오.

① 장소   ② 날짜
③ 주제   ④ 특별 상품
⑤ 입장료

08

W: Ladies and gentlemen, I am ___________ ___________ ___________ this year's Food Festival. Thanks to the incredible support of our sponsors, it will be held at City Park. On September 15th, ___________ ___________ ___________ enjoy a feast like never before! The theme of the festival will be "Flavors of the World." Some lucky attendees will receive gourmet food baskets ___________ ___________ ___________. Don't miss out on this opportunity to sample delicious dishes from various cultures!

다음 페이지에 계속 ➡

9. 다음을 듣고, 무엇에 관한 설명인지 고르시오.

① 바다　　　　② 호수
③ 동굴　　　　④ 늪지대
⑤ 우물

09 W: This is a natural ＿＿＿＿＿＿ ＿＿＿＿＿. It is created when slowly-moving water dissolves rocks. It is ＿＿＿＿ ＿＿＿＿ ＿＿＿＿ hold a person. Its size can be small like a single room, but it also can be a long tunnel-like passage. Animals like bats, fish, snakes and spiders are found in the dark parts of this. Also, ＿＿＿＿ ＿＿＿＿ often drew pictures on the walls of this.

10. 다음을 듣고, 두 사람의 대화가 <u>어색한</u> 것을 고르시오.

①　　　　②
③　　　　④
⑤

10 ① M: I bought a box of chocolates for you on my trip.

W: Thank you. They're really delicious.

② M: How often do you ＿＿＿＿ ＿＿＿＿?

W: I work out every day.

③ M: Which do you prefer, meat or fish?

W: I ＿＿＿＿ ＿＿＿＿ ＿＿＿＿ ＿＿＿＿.

④ M: Who should I talk to about changing a reservation?

W: I can help you with that.

⑤ M: Can I ＿＿＿＿ ＿＿＿＿ ＿＿＿＿ ＿＿＿＿?

W: Okay. Let's meet at 7.

11. 대화를 듣고, 여자가 할 일로 가장 적절한 것을 고르시오.
　① 샤워하기
　② 머핀 만들기
　③ 쓰레기 버리기
　④ 이웃집 방문하기
　⑤ 기계 고치기

11
W: Honey, what are you doing?

M: I'm _______ _______ _______. Our back yard is like a jungle.

W: Last night, you said our lawn mower was broken. Have you fixed it already?

M: No, I borrowed a lawn mower from Jerry next door.

W: That's very sweet of him. Do you need a hand?

M: It's okay. I'm done here. I'm about to _______ the machine to Jerry.

W: Wait. I'll _______ _______ _______. Take them with you. He loves them.

M: Okay. I'll go and take a shower, then.

12. 다음 표를 보면서 대화를 듣고, 두 사람이 구매할 텔레비전을 고르시오.

	Model	Size (inches)	Screen Type	Connectivity
①	A	55	Curved	Wireless
②	B	55	Flat	HDMI Cable
③	C	65	Flat	Wireless
④	D	65	Flat	HDMI Cable
⑤	E	65	Curved	Wireless

12
M: Honey, which television should we buy?

W: We should definitely get a large one. There's that saying, "_______ _______, _______ _______!"

M: I agree. Let's buy a 65-inch model.

W: Okay. Should we buy one with a curved screen?

M: No. I don't like curved screens. I believe that TV screens _______ _______ _______.

W: Then, we have two options left.

M: Let's choose the one that has the wireless connection.

W: Okay. Then we can connect the smartphone to the TV without cables. Let's buy that one.

다음 페이지에 계속 ➡

13. 대화를 듣고, 여자가 취재를 가기로 한 날짜를 고르시오.

① 8월 10일　　② 8월 11일
③ 8월 12일　　④ 8월 13일
⑤ 8월 14일

13 *(Telephone rings.)*

M: Hello, this is Denny's Pizzeria.

W: Hello, this is Sarah Simpson and I'm a journalist at K magazine.

M: Oh, hello. How can I help you?

W: I've heard your restaurant ＿＿＿＿ ＿＿＿＿ ＿＿＿＿ and I'd like to write an article about it.

M: Thank you. That would be wonderful.

W: So, can I visit the restaurant on August 11 around 3?

M: Um... We'll be closed from August 10 to 12 for vacation. Can you ＿＿＿＿ ＿＿＿＿ on August 13 instead?

W: I'm only available after 5 p.m. on that day. Will that be okay?

M: No problem. I'll see you on August 13 at 5 p.m.

W: Okay, see you then.

14. 대화를 듣고, 여자가 주말에 한 일로 가장 적절한 것을 고르시오.

① 만화책 읽기
② 예방 접종 맞기
③ 영화 보기
④ 온라인 쇼핑하기
⑤ 할머니 뵈러 가기

14 M: Olivia, how was your weekend? You said that you were going to visit your grandmother.

W: Yes, but she told me ＿＿＿＿ ＿＿＿＿ ＿＿＿＿.

M: Why would she say that? What happened?

W: She ＿＿＿＿ ＿＿＿＿ ＿＿＿＿, so she didn't want to infect me.

M: I see… I hope she ＿＿＿＿ ＿＿＿＿ soon. How did you spend your weekend then?

W: I just stayed at home and read some comic books.

M: Oh, what did you read?

W: I read *The Fabulous Five*. You should read it, too!

15. 다음을 듣고, 방송의 목적으로 가장 적절한 것을 고르시오.

① 도서관 회원증 발급 절차를 설명하려고
② 공사 일정 지연을 공지하려고
③ 교무실 출입 예절을 지도하려고
④ 중고 책 기부 방법을 알리려고
⑤ 희망 도서 신청 방법을 안내하려고

15 W: Good afternoon, students. We're happy to announce that we have finished ______________ our school library. Our library now has more space to ______________ more books. If there are books that you want the library to purchase, please let us know. You can _______ _______ _______ on our school website. Please fill out and submit the book purchase request form that can be found on the online library menu. Your requests will be reviewed by our librarian and then considered for purchase. Thank you.

16. 대화를 듣고, 남자가 받게 될 거스름돈으로 적절한 것을 고르시오.

① $30 　　② $40
③ $50 　　④ $60
⑤ $70

16 W: May I help you?

M: I'm looking for a T-shirt.

W: Then, please come _______ _______. This is the men's section.

M: Hmm, I like this grey one. How much is this?

W: It's 60 dollars, sir.

M: That's a _______ _______. I thought this store was having a sale.

W: I'm really sorry, but the sale is only on women's clothing.

M: I see. I guess I'll _______ _______ _______. Here's a 100 dollars.

W: Thank you. Here's your change.

다음 페이지에 계속 ➡

17. 대화를 듣고, 여자의 마지막 말에 대한 남자의 응답으로 가장 적절한 것을 고르시오.

Man: _________________

① Thanks. I just do what I can.
② You're such a cute little boy.
③ No, I don't see her every day.
④ No, I didn't eat all the candies.
⑤ Besides, my cousins are really sweet.

17

W: Hey, Michael. What are you going to do tomorrow?

M: I'm not sure yet. Why?

W: I just thought that maybe we could go to the __________ ________ tomorrow.

M: Oh, sorry, but I can't. I just remembered that I'm visiting my aunt tomorrow ________ ________.

W: As usual? You mean, you visit her every weekend? Why?

M: She lives alone since all her children have ________ ________. I don't want her to be lonely.

W: Oh. That's so ________ ________ ________.

M: Thanks. I just do what I can.

18. 대화를 듣고, 남자의 마지막 말에 대한 여자의 응답으로 가장 적절한 것을 고르시오.

Woman: _________________

① Well, we're not in a hurry after all.
② Don't worry. The theater is open until late.
③ Still, drivers don't need to be kind all the time.
④ That's what I'm saying. He should not drive so fast.
⑤ He should pull over if he wants to use his cellphone.

18

W: This bus is slow.

M: It's the traffic. Don't worry. We ________ ________ ________.

W: How many more stops before we get to the theater?

M: Hmm... three. Oh, look at that man in the car!

W: In ________ ________ ________? What's he doing?

M: He's driving and talking on his cellphone at the same time.

W: Isn't that dangerous, ________ ________ ________ is slow?

M: Of course it is. I hope he stops doing that.

W: He should pull over if he wants to use his cellphone.

19. 대화를 듣고, 남자의 마지막 말에 대한 여자의 응답으로 가장 적절한 것을 고르시오.

Woman: ________________

① That sounds good. I'll take the deal.
② Okay. I just wanted to buy a new bed.
③ Thank you, but a double bed is just fine.
④ No problem. I hope you enjoy your stay.
⑤ I'm sorry, but you booked the wrong hotel.

19

M: Welcome to Sunnyside Hotel. Did you ________ ________ ________?

W: Yes, a twin-bed room under the name of Lee.

M: Let me see… I'm sorry, but we're ________ ________ twin-bed rooms. Is a double-bed room okay?

W: No. There are two of us, and I ________ twin beds.

M: Right. It's our fault. So, if you stay in a double-bed room just for tonight, we'll ________ ________ ________ ________ you.

W: How?

M: We'll move you to a twin-bed room tomorrow, and give you free breakfast for your ________ ________.

W: That sounds good. I'll take the deal.

20. 다음 상황 설명을 듣고, Mary가 Peter에게 할 말로 가장 적절한 것을 고르시오.

Mary: ________________

① I'm encountering problems with my laptop.
② Would it be okay if I borrowed your charger?
③ Would you mind if I have another cup of coffee?
④ Where can I find a coffee shop that's laptop-friendly?
⑤ When are you thinking of wrapping up and going home?

20

W: Mary is studying for a midterm exam with her friend, Peter. They are in a coffee shop. She's using her laptop to ________ ________ ________ ________ for the exam, but the battery is low. Peter uses the same model as Mary's, and his laptop seems ________ ________. So, Mary decides to ask Peter if she can ________ ________ ________. In this situation, what would Mary most likely say to Peter?

Mary: Would it be okay if I borrowed your charger?

Words & Expressions Review 09

● 다음 단어를 암기하세요.

문제	번호	단어	뜻
1	1	a few	조금의
2	2	domestic	가정용의, 집안의
3	3	record	정보, 기록
4	4	express train	급행 열차
	5	economy class	일반석, 이코노미 클래스
5	6	uneasy	불안한, 우려되는
	7	awful	끔찍한
	8	make up	지어내다, 만들어내다
6	9	suit	어울리다
7	10	cuisine	요리
	11	registration	등록
8	12	feast	축제
	13	attendee	참석자
	14	miss out	(좋은 기회를) 놓치다
	15	sample	맛보다, 시식하다
9	16	underground	지하의
	17	dissolve	녹이다, 용해하다
	18	passage	통로, 복도
	19	bat	박쥐, 방망이
	20	ancient	고대의
10	21	reservation	예약
11	22	mow the lawn	잔디를 깎다
11	23	need a hand	도움이 필요하다
12	24	saying	옛말, 속담
	25	journalist	기자
13	26	make it	가다, 참석하다
	27	available	시간이 있는
14	28	catch the flu	독감에 걸리다
	29	infect	병을 옮기다, 감염시키다
	30	announce	알리다
	31	renovate	수리하다, 개조하다
15	32	accommodate	수용하다, 공간을 제공하다
	33	purchase	구매하다
	34	make a request	요청하다
16	35	change	거스름돈, 변화
17	36	abroad	해외로, 해외에(서)
	37	traffic	교통(량)
18	38	lane	차선, 도로
	39	at the same time	동시에
	40	pull over	차를 세우다
19	41	make it up to	~에게 보상하다
	42	look up	찾아보다
20	43	material	자료
	44	charge	충전하다

●왼쪽 단어장의 뜻이 보이지 않게 반으로 접고, 학습한 단어의 뜻을 아래 빈칸에 적어주세요.

1 look up		23 catch the flu	
2 accommodate		24 ancient	
3 make it up to		25 suit	
4 a few		26 make a request	
5 purchase		27 available	
6 saying		28 journalist	
7 mow the lawn		29 cuisine	
8 sample		30 traffic	
9 miss out		31 change	
10 registration		32 charge	
11 economy class		33 dissolve	
12 attendee		34 awful	
13 domestic		35 abroad	
14 express train		36 bat	
15 material		37 underground	
16 announce		38 make up	
17 feast		39 need a hand	
18 uneasy		40 at the same time	
19 passage		41 renovate	
20 lane		42 pull over	
21 infect		43 reservation	
22 make it		44 record	

10회 중학영어듣기 모의고사

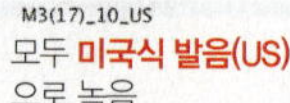

모두 **미국식 발음(US)** 으로 녹음

20문제 중 5문제에 **영국식 발음 (US+UK)**을 포함하여 녹음

📖 정답 및 해석 p. 55

1 대화를 듣고, 남자가 주문할 깃발을 고르시오.

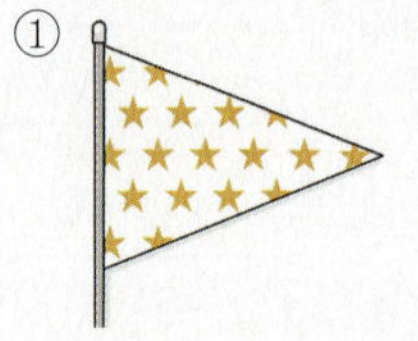

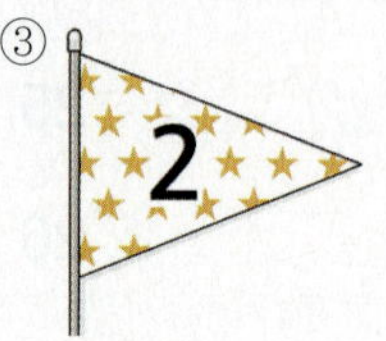

2 대화를 듣고, Oracle Bath Salt에 관해 언급되지 <u>않은</u> 것을 고르시오.

① 효과　　② 성분　　③ 무게　　④ 향기　　⑤ 가격

3 대화를 듣고, 남자가 여자에게 전화한 목적으로 가장 적절한 것을 고르시오.

① 환불을 요청하려고
② 주소 변경을 알리려고
③ 주문 수량을 변경하려고
④ 제품 입고 날짜를 확인하려고
⑤ 상품 미도착에 대해 문의하려고

4 대화를 듣고, 두 사람이 만나기로 한 시각을 고르시오.

① 3 p.m.　　② 4 p.m.　　③ 5 p.m.　　④ 7 p.m.　　⑤ 8 p.m.

5 대화를 듣고, 남자의 심정으로 가장 적절한 것을 고르시오.

① sad　　② proud　　③ annoyed
④ shocked　　⑤ sorry

6 다음 그림의 상황에 가장 적절한 대화를 고르시오.

① ② ③ ④ ⑤

7 대화를 듣고, 여자가 남자에게 부탁한 일로 가장 적절한 것을 고르시오.

① 학교에 연락하기
② 아들의 조퇴 허락하기
③ 아이의 성적 상담하기
④ 치과 예약 변경하기
⑤ 생물 수업 참관하기

8 다음을 듣고, Autumn Program에 관해 언급되지 <u>않은</u> 것을 고르시오.

① 지연 사유
② 진행 기간
③ 인원 제한
④ 제공 강좌
⑤ 대상 연령

9 다음을 듣고, 무엇에 관한 설명인지 고르시오.

① 농구
② 축구
③ 배구
④ 야구
⑤ 핸드볼

10 다음을 듣고, 두 사람의 대화가 <u>어색한</u> 것을 고르시오.

① ② ③ ④ ⑤

11번~20번 문제는 다음 페이지에 ➡

11 대화를 듣고, 여자가 대화 직후에 할 일로 가장 적절한 것을 고르시오.

① 도서관에 들르기
② 컵 가지러 가기
③ 사물함 신청하기
④ 주변 카페 찾아보기
⑤ 쿠폰 다운로드하기

12 다음 표를 보면서 대화를 듣고, 두 사람이 구매할 매트리스를 고르시오.

	Model	Size	Firmness	Trial Period
①	A	Queen	Hard	100 days
②	B	Queen	Soft	60 days
③	C	King	Hard	60 days
④	D	King	Soft	100 days
⑤	E	King	Hard	100 days

13 대화를 듣고, 두 사람이 영화를 관람할 날짜를 고르시오.

① 10월 7일
② 10월 8일
③ 10월 9일
④ 10월 10일
⑤ 10월 11일

14 대화를 듣고, 여자가 지난 토요일에 한 일로 가장 적절한 것을 고르시오.

① 가족여행하기
② 영화 감상하기
③ 전시회 관람하기
④ 미술대회 참가하기
⑤ 동생 숙제 도와주기

15 다음을 듣고, 방송의 목적으로 가장 적절한 것을 고르시오.

① 분리수거 방법을 설명하려고
② 도로 공사 일정을 공지하려고
③ 새로운 공원 개장을 홍보하려고
④ 봄철 산불 예방 수칙을 고지하려고
⑤ 국립 공원 이용 규칙을 안내하려고

16 대화를 듣고, 남자가 지불할 금액을 고르시오.

① $15
② $25
③ $30
④ $45
⑤ $50

17 대화를 듣고, 남자의 마지막 말에 대한 여자의 응답으로 가장 적절한 것을 고르시오.

Woman: _______________________________________

① Thanks. You've been a lot of help.

② No problem. I can give you a hand.

③ Sorry. Volunteer work is not my thing.

④ Okay. Wash your hands before serving meals.

⑤ Of course. We always welcome a helping hand.

[18~19] 대화를 듣고, 여자의 마지막 말에 대한 남자의 응답으로 가장 적절한 것을 고르시오.

18 **Man:** _______________________________________

① It is our pleasure to serve our customers.

② Yes, toy trains are very popular these days.

③ Don't worry. Your son is going to like the present.

④ I'll go and see if we have any stock left in storage.

⑤ Will you come with me, please? I can arrange the party.

19 **Man:** _______________________________________

① I reserved a table for 4 people. ② A wooden table would be perfect.

③ I'm afraid it's not on sale right now. ④ I'd like to spend as little as possible.

⑤ It was delivered to the wrong address.

20 다음 상황 설명을 듣고, Sally가 Joe에게 할 말로 가장 적절한 것을 고르시오.

Sally: Joe, _______________________________________

① have you seen any trash cans around here?

② we should come here again next week.

③ can I put my book in your empty bag?

④ you shouldn't leave the bottle behind.

⑤ would you like to drink some water?

Dictation Test 10

M3(17)_10_D

Dictation(받아쓰기)은 본문을 받아쓰면서 영어듣기의 집중력을 향상시키고 다양한 표현을 정리하기 위한 영어듣기 학습법입니다. **녹음을 다시 듣고, 빈칸에 알맞은 단어를 써 보세요.**
※Dictation의 정답은 듣기 대본의 밑줄 친 부분을 확인하세요. 📖 정답 p. 55

맞은 개수 ____ / 총160개

2025 영어듣기능력평가 1회 1번 변형

그림정보파악(대화)

1. 대화를 듣고, 남자가 주문할 깃발을 고르시오.

01
W: Welcome to The Flag Company.

M: Hello. Can I order 25 spirit flags for my students?

W: Certainly! We have ___________-___________ options, or you can design your own.

M: I'd prefer to design the flags myself.

W: Excellent! What shape would you like, square or triangular?

M: Triangular, please.

W: Should they have ___________ like stars or hearts on them?

M: Stars would be nice.

W: Do you want to add any text or a ___________?

M: Yes, please print the class number, 2, in the middle of each flag.

W: Perfect. We'll have your order completed by next Friday.

대화미언급

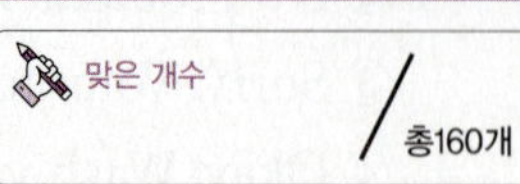

2. 대화를 듣고, Oracle Bath Salt에 관해 언급되지 않은 것을 고르시오.
   ① 효과　　② 성분
   ③ 무게　　④ 향기
   ⑤ 가격

02
M: Hey, Sue. What do you think of Oracle Bath Salt? I think I'll get some for Grace.

W: That's a good idea. Its ___________ ___________ are really helping me.

M: Really? Grace said she wanted something just like that.

W: It's ___________ ___________ minerals and natural oils, so she'll like it.

M: Do you recommend ___________ ___________?

W: Lavender and rosemary are popular, although I prefer peppermint.

M: I see. Do you know how much it is?

W: Yeah. It's 12 dollars a bottle, but it's _________ _________ _________.

M: Okay. Thanks.

전화목적파악

3. 대화를 듣고, 남자가 여자에게 전화한 목적으로 가장 적절한 것을 고르시오.

① 환불을 요청하려고
② 주소 변경을 알리려고
③ 주문 수량을 변경하려고
④ 제품 입고 날짜를 확인하려고
⑤ 상품 미도착에 대해 문의하려고

03 *(Telephone rings.)*

W: Yellow Shopping Mall. How may I help you?

M: Hello. My name is Chris Walker. __________ __________ about the order I made for a shirt.

W: *(Typing sound)* Yes, Mr. Walker. I see that you ordered a shirt on June 2nd.

M: That's right. I got a text message saying the __________ __________ __________, but I never received the package.

W: Really? It's possible there was a mistake with the delivery. We'll send you another shirt.

M: How long will it take?

W: Two days. Or, would you like a __________?

M: No, I can wait. Could you send it right away?

W: Of course. We're very sorry. And thank you for __________ __________.

수치파악(시각)

4. 대화를 듣고, 두 사람이 만나기로 한 시각을 고르시오.

① 3 p.m.　　② 4 p.m.
③ 5 p.m.　　④ 7 p.m.
⑤ 8 p.m.

04 W: Hey, David. Are you going to _________ _________ _________ at the gym today?

M: Yeah, I think I will go work out around 3 p.m. Why?

W: I was going to ask if you wanted to go work out together.

M: Sure! I'll go with you. What time were you planning to go?

다음 페이지에 계속 ➡

W: I was thinking around 5 p.m. Would that work for you?

W: I was thinking around 5 p.m. Would that work for you?

M: _________ _________ _________. I am going to have dinner with my friends at that time.

W: How about after dinner? Maybe at 8 p.m.?

M: I think I can _________ _________ then.

W: Okay! I'll see you at the gym.

---

5. 대화를 듣고, 남자의 심정으로 가장 적절한 것을 고르시오.
   ① sad
   ② proud
   ③ annoyed
   ④ shocked
   ⑤ sorry

05

W: Look! The girl in the yellow swimsuit swims very fast.

M: Yeah, she is _________ _________ _________.

W: Yes, I can see that.

M: She also won the _________ _________ last month.

W: Oh, you know her well!

M: Of course I do. She is my youngest _________.

W: That's why you _________ _________!

---

6. 다음 그림의 상황에 가장 적절한 대화를 고르시오.

① ② ③ ④ ⑤

06

① W: What are you doing now?

   M: I'm _________ _________ my daughter.

② W: Honey, did we buy soy sauce?

   M: Hold on. Let me _________ the cart.

③ W: That'll be 87 dollars _________ _________.

   M: What? I think there must be a _________.

④ W: Do you have a coin? We need one for the cart.

   M: Yeah. I have one right here.

⑤ W: I can't find my phone. Can you call it?

   M: Okay. I'm calling now.

7. 대화를 듣고, 여자가 남자에게 부탁한 일
   로 가장 적절한 것을 고르시오.
   ① 학교에 연락하기
   ② 아들의 조퇴 허락하기
   ③ 아이의 성적 상담하기
   ④ 치과 예약 변경하기
   ⑤ 생물 수업 참관하기

07 *(Cellphone rings.)*

M: Hello?

W: Hello, Mr. Bowman, this is Mike's mother.

M: Oh, hi, Mrs. Myers.

W: I'm sorry, but can I ________ ________ ________

________ from school an hour early today?

M: May I ask what this is about?

W: It's my fault. I ________ ____________ ________

classes end late today when I made Mike's

________ ____________.

M: It's OK. His last class is biology. I'll let the teacher

know. By the way, I'm very happy with Mike's

grades. He's doing well.

W: Thank you very much.

8. 다음을 듣고, Autumn Program에 관해
   언급되지 않은 것을 고르시오.
   ① 지연 사유   ② 진행 기간
   ③ 인원 제한   ④ 제공 강좌
   ⑤ 대상 연령

08 W: Hello, listeners! Cornville Community Center's

Autumn Program begins next week. This

long-awaited program ________ ________

________ because of the recent typhoons. Still, it

will run ________ ________ ________ as usual, and

end in late November. The program will offer

many classes such as farming, gardening, and

even creative writing. The program is for those

who are 12 years ________ ________ ________

________. Please visit the website to learn more.

다음 페이지에 계속 ➡

9. 다음을 듣고, 무엇에 관한 설명인지 고르시오.

① 농구　　② 축구
③ 배구　　④ 야구
⑤ 핸드볼

09 M: This is a sport that uses a ball. This sport is usually played on a wooden court. You can score points by putting the ball through the opponent's hoop. The hoop is _______ and it is 10 feet above the ground. You need to use your hands to control the ball, however, you are _______ _______ _______ touch the ball with your feet.

10. 다음을 듣고, 두 사람의 대화가 <u>어색한</u> 것을 고르시오.

①　　②
③　　④
⑤

10 ① M: The weather is _______ _______.

W: Yeah. It is almost winter.

② M: You must not eat this food.

W: What's wrong with it?

③ M: What should I do _______ _______ _______?

W: How about changing your eating habits?

④ M: What are you going to do this summer vacation?

W: It _______ _______. I went to Jejudo with my family.

⑤ M: Will you watch the new James Bond movie with me today?

W: I am sorry. I _______ _______ _______.

11. 대화를 듣고, 여자가 대화 직후에 할 일로 가장 적절한 것을 고르시오.

① 도서관에 들르기
② 컵 가지러 가기
③ 사물함 신청하기
④ 주변 카페 찾아보기
⑤ 쿠폰 다운로드하기

11 M: Torrie, we've been in the library for two hours now. I can't focus anymore.

W: Yeah, _______, _______. Let's go outside and get some coffee.

M: Okay. Oh, wait. I need to bring this cup with me.

W: Why?

M: Well, if we bring our own cup to the cafe, they

_____________ _____________ _____________ _____________

on coffee.

W: Really? That's brilliant. It's to help protect the

environment, right?

M: Yes. If you have a _____________ _____________ with

you…

W: I have one in my locker. I'll go get it right away.

M: Sure. _____________ _____________ _____________.

---

12. 다음 표를 보면서 대화를 듣고, 두 사람
이 구매할 매트리스를 고르시오.

	Model	Size	Firmness	Trial Period
①	A	Queen	Hard	100 days
②	B	Queen	Soft	60 days
③	C	King	Hard	60 days
④	D	King	Soft	100 days
⑤	E	King	Hard	100 days

12 M: Honey, which mattress should we buy?

W: Let's buy a large mattress. Our old mattress felt a

bit small.

M: I agree. Let's get a king size mattress then.

W: Okay. Should we choose a _________ mattress?

M: Yes. I ___________ get a better sleep when using a

hard mattress.

W: Then, we have two options to choose from.

M: Let's choose the one that offers the longer

_________ _________.

W: Yes. Then, we'll have more time to test out the

mattress before deciding if we want to _________

_________.

다음 페이지에 계속 ➡

13. 대화를 듣고, 두 사람이 영화를 관람할 날짜를 고르시오.

① 10월 7일
② 10월 8일
③ 10월 9일
④ 10월 10일
⑤ 10월 11일

13

M: Would you like to ________ ________ ________ ________ tomorrow?

W: I'd love to, but I'm busy all day tomorrow. How about this Saturday?

M: You mean October 11? It's my ____________ ________.

W: Then how about Wednesday, October 8?

M: We can't see a movie on Wednesday. We have a ________ ________ on Thursday.

W: You're right. Then let's see a movie on Thursday after the test. So it's ________ ________ ________ October 9.

M: That's a good idea. I'll buy tickets on Thursday ________ 7.

14. 대화를 듣고, 여자가 지난 토요일에 한 일로 가장 적절한 것을 고르시오.

① 가족여행하기
② 영화 감상하기
③ 전시회 관람하기
④ 미술대회 참가하기
⑤ 동생 숙제 도와주기

14

M: Caroline, did you hear the news about Mia?

W: Yes. She ________ ________ ________ at the city art contest.

M: There's a special exhibition going on for the winners.

W: That's right. It's at the city art center.

M: I want to go and see her painting. Do you want to come with me?

W: Thanks for asking, but I ________ ________ ________ ____________ with my sister last Saturday.

M: Really? How did you like it?

W: It was very interesting. I'm sure you'll enjoy it.

M: OK. I'll ________ ________ I go.

15. 다음을 듣고, 방송의 목적으로 가장 적절한 것을 고르시오.

① 분리수거 방법을 설명하려고
② 도로 공사 일정을 공지하려고
③ 새로운 공원 개장을 홍보하려고
④ 봄철 산불 예방 수칙을 고지하려고
⑤ 국립 공원 이용 규칙을 안내하려고

15 W: Attention, visitors to Elm National Park. During your visit, please follow these rules. First, _________ _________ the trail so you don't get lost. Second, fires are __________. Third, take any trash back home with you so we can keep _________ _________ _________. I hope you have fun. Safe trekking!

16. 대화를 듣고, 남자가 지불할 금액을 고르시오.

① $15   ② $25
③ $30   ④ $45
⑤ $50

16 W: Welcome to Meow Pet Store.

M: Hi there. I need to purchase some cat food.

W: We have two options available: regular brand and premium brand. The premium brand __________ __________ __________.

M: How much does each brand cost?

W: The regular brand is $15 per bag, and the premium brand is $25 per bag.

M: I'll __________ __________ the regular brand. Any discounts available?

W: Yes, if you buy two bags, you can get $5 __________ __________ __________ __________.

M: In that case, I'll take two bags of the regular brand.

W: Great! Anything else you need?

M: No, that will be all.

다음 페이지에 계속 ➡

17. 대화를 듣고, 남자의 마지막 말에 대한 여자의 응답으로 가장 적절한 것을 고르시오.

Woman: _______________

① Thanks. You've been a lot of help.
② No problem. I can give you a hand.
③ Sorry. Volunteer work is not my thing.
④ Okay. Wash your hands before serving meals.
⑤ Of course. We always welcome a helping hand.

17

M: Are you doing _______ _______ this weekend, Katie?

W: I'm going to do volunteer work at a nursing home.

M: That's nice. What do you do there?

W: Nothing special. I help to _______ _______ and clean the rooms.

M: Isn't it hard?

W: _______ _______ others is not always easy, but it's _______ _______. It feels great to see the happy faces of those I have helped.

M: Oh, I see now. Can I come with you next time?

W: Of course. We always welcome a helping hand.

---

18. 대화를 듣고, 여자의 마지막 말에 대한 남자의 응답으로 가장 적절한 것을 고르시오.

Man: _______________

① It is our pleasure to serve our customers.
② Yes, toy trains are very popular these days.
③ Don't worry. Your son is going to like the present.
④ I'll go and see if we have any stock left in storage.
⑤ Will you come with me, please? I can arrange the party.

18

W: Excuse me. Can you help me please?

M: What can I do for you, ma'am?

W: I saw a toy here yesterday that was _______ _______ _______ my son, but I can't find it now.

M: What does it look like?

W: It's a train with animals _______ _______ _______ _______.

M: It seems that all of the trains we had on display are _______ _______.

W: Oh, no. I really want that toy for my son's birthday.

M: I'll go and see if we have any stock left in storage.

19

19. 대화를 듣고, 여자의 마지막 말에 대한 남자의 응답으로 가장 적절한 것을 고르시오.

Man: _______________

① I reserved a table for 4 people.
② A wooden table would be perfect.
③ I'm afraid it's not on sale right now.
④ I'd like to spend as little as possible.
⑤ It was delivered to the wrong address.

W: Hello. Welcome to Sweet Home Furniture Store. What can I do for you?

M: Hi, I'm _______ _______ a dining table.

W: Okay. We have many sizes of dining tables. For example, the smallest one seats 2 people, and the biggest one will seat 10 to 12 people.

M: I need one that _______ _______ 4 chairs.

W: Alright. What shape would you prefer, a _______ one or an _______ one?

M: I would prefer a rectangular one.

W: Okay. Do you have a _______ _______________ _______?

M: I'd like to spend as little as possible.

20

20. 다음 상황 설명을 듣고, Sally가 Joe에게 할 말로 가장 적절한 것을 고르시오.

Sally: Joe, _______________

① have you seen any trash cans around here?
② we should come here again next week.
③ can I put my book in your empty bag?
④ you shouldn't leave the bottle behind.
⑤ would you like to drink some water?

W: Sally is at the park. She is having a good time with her friends. It is _______ _______ and they are about to leave. One of her friends, Joe, is about to leave his empty water bottle on the bench. After noticing what he is about to do, she thinks it's wrong. So, she decides to tell Joe that he should _______ _______ his trash. In this situation, what would Sally most likely say to Joe?

Sally: Joe, you shouldn't leave the bottle behind.

Words & Expressions Review 10

● 다음 단어를 암기하세요.

문제	번호	단어	뜻
1	1	flag	깃발
	2	spirit	기운, 열성
	3	slogan	구호
2	4	packed with	~으로 가득한
	5	scent	향, 향기
3	6	package	택배, 소포
	7	refund	환불
	8	patience	인내, 참을성
4	9	go work out	운동하러 가다
	10	around	~쯤, 약
	11	make it	제시간에 도착하다
5	12	excellent	뛰어난, 훌륭한
6	13	soy sauce	간장
	14	check	확인하다, 알아보다
7	15	fault	잘못, 단점
	16	make an appointment	예약하다, 만날 약속을 하다
	17	biology	생물학
8	18	long-awaited	오래 기다려온
	19	typhoon	태풍
	20	run	운영하다, 달리다
	21	offer	제공하다
9	22	wooden	나무로 된, 목재의

문제	번호	단어	뜻
9	23	feet	피트(길이의 단위로 약 30cm)
10	24	lose weight	체중을 줄이다
11	25	focus	집중하다
12	26	definitely	확실히, 분명히
	27	trial period	체험 기간
13	28	all day	하루 종일
15	29	prohibit	금지하다
	30	trekking	트레킹, 등산
16	31	nutrient	영양소, 영양분
	32	serve	(음식을) 제공하다, 차려주다
17	33	care for	~를 돌보다, 보살피다
	34	worth	~할 가치가 있는
18	35	stock	재고(품)
	36	look for	~을 찾다
	37	seat	좌석이 있다
19	38	rectangular	직사각형의
	39	oval	타원형의
	40	price range	가격대
	41	get	~해지다
20	42	pick up	~을 치우다
	43	trash can	쓰레기통
	44	leave ~ behind	~을 두고 가다

●왼쪽 단어장의 뜻이 보이지 않게 반으로 접고, 학습한 단어의 뜻을 아래 빈칸에 적어주세요.

1	get		23	prohibit
2	scent		24	feet
3	run		25	all day
4	worth		26	leave ~ behind
5	spirit		27	flag
6	seat		28	check
7	price range		29	wooden
8	fault		30	excellent
9	soy sauce		31	stock
10	make an appointment		32	packed with
11	pick up		33	focus
12	care for		34	slogan
13	look for		35	typhoon
14	oval		36	package
15	trekking		37	around
16	offer		38	nutrient
17	biology		39	definitely
18	refund		40	long-awaited
19	go work out		41	trash can
20	rectangular		42	lose weight
21	serve		43	patience
22	trial period		44	make it

정답 및 해석 p. 61

1

대화를 듣고, 여자가 만들고 있는 냄비 받침을 고르시오.

①  ②  ③  ④  ⑤ 

2

대화를 듣고, Sunshine Bazaar에 관해 언급되지 <u>않은</u> 것을 고르시오.

① 행사 목적 ② 기부 대상 ③ 행사 일시
④ 행사 장소 ⑤ 판매 물품

3

대화를 듣고, 남자가 여자에게 전화한 목적으로 가장 적절한 것을 고르시오.

① 권투 장갑을 구매하려고 ② 수업 신청을 취소하려고
③ 새로운 수업을 추천하려고 ④ 수업 준비물을 알아보려고
⑤ 수업을 온라인으로 전환하려고

4

대화를 듣고, 두 사람이 만나기로 한 시각을 고르시오.

① 11 a.m. ② 12 p.m. ③ 1 p.m. ④ 2 p.m. ⑤ 3 p.m.

5

대화를 듣고, 남자의 심정으로 가장 적절한 것을 고르시오.

① upset ② bored ③ regretful
④ satisfied ⑤ embarrassed

6 대화를 듣고, 그림 상황에 가장 적절한 것을 고르시오.

① ② ③ ④ ⑤

7 대화를 듣고, 여자가 남자에게 부탁한 일로 가장 적절한 것을 고르시오.

① 빵 배달하기 ② 블로그에 홍보 리뷰 쓰기
③ 손님 응대하기 ④ 개점 이벤트용 쿠폰 만들기
⑤ 고객에게 연락하기

8 다음을 듣고, Sunnyside Children's Bookstore에 관해 언급되지 <u>않은</u> 것을 고르시오.

① 위치 ② 영업 시간 ③ 서적 종류 ④ 주차 안내 ⑤ 할인 혜택

9 다음을 듣고, 무엇에 관한 설명인지 고르시오.

① 세탁기 ② 냉장고 ③ 진공청소기
④ 에어컨 ⑤ 공기청정기

10 다음을 듣고, 두 사람의 대화가 <u>어색한</u> 것을 고르시오.

① ② ③ ④ ⑤

11번~20번 문제는 다음 페이지에 ➡

11 대화를 듣고, 남자가 할 일로 가장 적절한 것을 고르시오.

① 교무실에 들르기　　　② 역사 리포트 쓰기　　　③ 컴퓨터실에 들르기
④ 프린터기 수리하기　　⑤ 답장 이메일 보내기

12 다음 표를 보면서 대화를 듣고, 여자가 구입할 모자를 고르시오.

	Model	Color	Brim	Chin Strap
①	A	Beige	Wide	×
②	B	Beige	Short	○
③	C	Blue	Wide	○
④	D	Blue	Short	×
⑤	E	Beige	Wide	○

13 대화를 듣고, 남자가 Wellington's Chocolate Factory에 방문할 날짜를 고르시오.

① 5월 4일　　　② 5월 11일　　　③ 5월 18일　　　④ 5월 25일　　　⑤ 5월 31일

14 대화를 듣고, 남자가 여름방학에 한 일로 가장 적절한 것을 고르시오.

① 낚시하기　　　② 요리 배우기　　　③ 수영 강습 받기
④ 식당에서 일하기　　⑤ 삼촌 댁 방문하기

15 다음을 듣고, 방송의 목적으로 가장 적절한 것을 고르시오.

① 교내 체육 활동을 장려하려고　　　② 물품 대여 서비스를 소개하려고
③ 분실물 찾는 방법을 안내하려고　　④ 중고물품 판매 행사를 홍보하려고
⑤ 학교 시설 이용 예절을 지도하려고

16 대화를 듣고, 남자가 지불할 금액을 고르시오.

① $36　　　② $45　　　③ $50　　　④ $54　　　⑤ $60

17 대화를 듣고, 여자의 마지막 말에 대한 남자의 응답으로 가장 적절한 것을 고르시오.

Man: ___________________________________

① No. This bag is not hand-made.

② Well, I don't like buying used things.

③ That's right. Your items will be popular.

④ Yes. But be aware that they close if it rains.

⑤ I'm sorry. I can't go to the park this weekend.

[18~19] 대화를 듣고, 남자의 마지막 말에 대한 여자의 응답으로 가장 적절한 것을 고르시오.

18 **Woman:** ___________________________________

① No way. The stairs are too slippery.

② Not at all. You can go grocery shopping.

③ Good idea. Let's start exercising tomorrow.

④ Could you? I'll make you a nice, big dinner.

⑤ That's right. The elevator is working fine now.

19 **Woman:** ___________________________________

① With coding, you can make a robot move.

② We are currently not accepting new members.

③ Maybe next time. I'm kind of busy at the moment.

④ I'd like to congratulate you on winning the competition.

⑤ Sure! I'll give you his phone number so you can call him.

20 다음을 듣고, Dean이 친구에게 할 말로 가장 알맞은 것을 고르시오.

Dean: ___________________________________

① Will you join me?　　　② Why don't we go some other time?

③ Can you be there on time?　　　④ Make sure to bring your umbrella.

⑤ I have another appointment tomorrow.

Dictation Test 11

M3(17)_11_D

Dictation(받아쓰기)은 본문을 받아쓰면서 영어듣기의 집중력을 향상시키고 다양한 표현을 정리하기 위한 영어듣기 학습법입니다. **녹음을 다시 듣고, 빈칸에 알맞은 단어를 써 보세요.**

※Dictation의 정답은 듣기 대본의 밑줄 친 부분을 확인하세요.

정답 p. 61

맞은 개수 / 총180개

고난도 | 그림정보파악(대화)

1. 대화를 듣고, 여자가 만들고 있는 냄비 받침을 고르시오.

① 
② 
③ 
④ 
⑤ 

01

M: Stacy, what are you making with that clay?

W: I'm making a pot mat for my kitchen.

M: You made a ___________ ___________.

W: Thanks. I first tried to make a star, but it didn't work out so well. So, I changed the shape.

M: I see. Is that ___________ ___________ ___________ ___________?

W: Yes! I wanted to put my cat, Luna's face on it.

M: That's lovely. Why don't you ___________ ___________ ___________ to it?

W: Good idea. I'll write her name right away.

대화미언급

2. 대화를 듣고, Sunshine Bazaar에 관해 언급되지 **않은** 것을 고르시오.

① 행사 목적   ② 기부 대상
③ 행사 일시   ④ 행사 장소
⑤ 판매 물품

02

W: Randy, you should come to the Sunshine Bazaar with me.

M: What's the Sunshine Bazaar?

W: It's a sales event designed to ___________ ___________ for a local charity.

M: Sounds interesting. Tell me more.

W: The profits will go to a ___________ ___________ ___________.

M: Great. When is it?

W: It'll be held this weekend from 10 a.m. to 6 p.m.

M: Do you know what kinds of items we can buy?

W: Yes. From pencils to clothes, all kinds of items will be sold. I even heard there will be _______________ ____________ such as headsets and tablets.

M: Cool. I've been thinking of buying a headset. I'll definitely be there.

3. 대화를 듣고, 남자가 여자에게 전화한 목적으로 가장 적절한 것을 고르시오.
① 권투 장갑을 구매하려고
② 수업 신청을 취소하려고
③ 새로운 수업을 추천하려고
④ 수업 준비물을 알아보려고
⑤ 수업을 온라인으로 전환하려고

03 *(Telephone rings.)*

W: Hello, this is Midtown Boxing Academy.

M: Hi, I'm in the boxing class that's starting this Friday. I'd like to check if I _________ _________ _________ anything to the class.

W: Which level are you in?

M: Basic level.

W: Then, there's nothing you need to bring to the class. We _________ ___________ that you will need.

M: Really? Not even gloves? I was going to bring my brother's old ones.

W: We have gloves for beginners here, but you can bring your own if you prefer. Just remember to wear ____________ _______________.

M: I will. Thank you.

4. 대화를 듣고, 두 사람이 만나기로 한 시각을 고르시오.
① 11 a.m.   ② 12 p.m.
③ 1 p.m.   ④ 2 p.m.
⑤ 3 p.m.

04 M: Hey, Bridget. What time do you want to _________ _________ our history project together?

W: Umm… Do you have time after school today? Because I am free after 4 p.m.

M: I have to go to the volunteer center after school, so I can't meet today. Are you _________ _________ _________ ___________?

다음 페이지에 계속 ➡

W: Yeah! I have tennis practice from 11 a.m. to 1 p.m. on Saturday, but ______ ______ ______ I am free.

M: Okay! Then, do you want to meet at 2 p.m. on Saturday?

W: Let's meet at 3 p.m., ______ ______ ______ ______. Sometimes tennis practice ends later than usual.

M: Sounds good! I will see you then.

5. 대화를 듣고, 남자의 심정으로 가장 적절한 것을 고르시오.

① upset
② bored
③ regretful
④ satisfied
⑤ embarrassed

05

W: Hello. Welcome to Lily's Cake House.

M: Hi. I'm here to pick up a cake ______ ______ a few days ago.

W: Okay. May I have your name?

M: Tom Bradley. It's a ______ ______ cake.

W: Oh, I remember. Please wait a minute. [Pause] Here's your cake.

M: Wow! It's beautiful. It's amazing how you ______ ______ ______ on the cake.

W: That's our specialty. I'm glad you like it.

M: It's perfect. I'm sure my wife will be very ______ ______ ______.

W: Great! Have a nice day.

6. 대화를 듣고, 그림 상황에 가장 적절한 것을 고르시오.

① ② ③ ④ ⑤

06

① W: It's so hot outside.

M: Yes, it is. Maybe we shouldn't ride a bike today.

② W: I ______ ______ ______ from the department store.

M: Did you buy me a bike?

③ W: Please don't ______ ______ ______ ______.

M: I won't. You don't have to worry.

④ W: Did you see that car?

M: I did. The driver is very careless.

⑤ W: Does this come _______ _______ _________ ________?

M: Yes. It also comes with a front basket of your choice.

7. 대화를 듣고, 여자가 남자에게 부탁한 일로 가장 적절한 것을 고르시오.

   ① 빵 배달하기
   ② 블로그에 홍보 리뷰 쓰기
   ③ 손님 응대하기
   ④ 개점 이벤트용 쿠폰 만들기
   ⑤ 고객에게 연락하기

07
W: Thank you for coming, Shawn. So, what do you think?

M: It's very nice! You must have worked hard to open this bakery.

W: It wasn't easy _______ _______ ________. But then I started to get a few regular customers.

M: I'm so proud of you. I'm sure you'll get more regulars sooner or later.

W: Thank you. _________ _______ _______, could you help me to get more customers?

M: Sure! What can I do for you?

W: Can you _________ _________ ________ of my bakery on your blog?

M: Sure thing. No problem.

8. 다음을 듣고, Sunnyside Children's Bookstore에 관해 언급되지 <u>않은</u> 것을 고르시오.

   ① 위치   ② 영업 시간
   ③ 서적 종류   ④ 주차 안내
   ⑤ 할인 혜택

08
W: Good afternoon! Are you looking for quality books for your kids? Then, come to Sunnyside Children's Bookstore, _________ _________ downtown Chicago. We are open Monday through Saturday from 10 a.m. to 9 p.m. We are closed on Sunday. We have thousands of picture books, non-fiction books, middle-grade novels, and even _________ _______ for adults. If you apply for a membership on our website, you can _______ _______ _______ ________.

For more information, visit our website, www.thescbookstore.com. Thank you.

다음 페이지에 계속 ➡

9. 다음을 듣고, 무엇에 관한 설명인지 고르시오.

① 세탁기   ② 냉장고
③ 진공청소기   ④ 에어컨
⑤ 공기청정기

09 W: This is an electronic home device. You can use this __________ __________ __________. It usually looks like a rectangle or a tube. You can change the suction power based on what you're cleaning. People use it to __________ __________ dust, dirt, and messes from carpets and floors. It's easy to use and helps you __________ __________ __________. That's why almost everyone has one at home or uses one __________ __________ __________.

10. 다음을 듣고, 두 사람의 대화가 <u>어색한</u> 것을 고르시오.

①   ②
③   ④
⑤

10 ① M: You know John, don't you?

W: Of course, I do. He is __________ __________ my best friends.

② M: Do you have __________ __________ this afternoon?

W: Not really. Why?

③ M: __________ __________ stop here?

W: No, I don't.

④ M: Will you join the science club?

W: No, I'd rather join the drama club.

⑤ M: Where do you usually __________ __________?

W: At school.

11. 대화를 듣고, 남자가 할 일로 가장 적절한 것을 고르시오.

① 교무실에 들르기
② 역사 리포트 쓰기
③ 컴퓨터실에 들르기
④ 프린터기 수리하기
⑤ 답장 이메일 보내기

11

W: Ted, did you finish your history report?

M: Yes, I just need to print it.

W: You do know that the printer at the computer lab is broken, right?

M: What? This is ________ ________ ________ I've heard about this.

W: It's been broken for about a week.

M: ________ ________ ________ to Ms. Smith's office to see if I can ________ ________ ________ by e-mail.

W: Hurry, class starts in 15 minutes.

2025 영어듣기능력평가 1회 12번 변형

도표정보파악

12. 다음 표를 보면서 대화를 듣고, 여자가 구입할 모자를 고르시오.

	Model	Color	Brim	Chin Strap
①	A	Beige	Wide	×
②	B	Beige	Short	○
③	C	Blue	Wide	○
④	D	Blue	Short	×
⑤	E	Beige	Wide	○

12

W: Jonathan, I'm picking out a hat for the summer. How do you like this blue one?

M: I think beige would __________ __________ __________ better.

W: You're right. Beige is __________ __________. Should I get a wide brim or a short brim?

M: Go for a wide brim. It'll __________ you __________ the sun.

W: That's a good idea. Do you think I need one with a chin strap?

M: __________. It'll stay on even when it's windy.

W: Great. I'll get that one.

다음 페이지에 계속 ➡

13. 대화를 듣고, 남자가 Wellington's Chocolate Factory에 방문할 날짜를 고르시오.

① 5월 4일
② 5월 11일
③ 5월 18일
④ 5월 25일
⑤ 5월 31일

13 *(Telephone rings.)*

W: Wellington's Chocolate Factory. How may I help you?

M: Hello. This is Harry Winters from Leigh Middle School. I'd like to ________ ________ ________ for my students.

W: Hello, Mr. Winters. There's a tour every Tuesday in May, __________ on May 4th.

M: Can I book a tour for May 11th?

W: Of course. But if ________ ________ ________ ________ on May 18th, that would be better.

M: Why? What's special about that day?

W: On that day, you'll ________ ________ ________ ________ ________ our new line of chocolate products.

M: Wonderful. We'll visit on May 18th, then.

W: Good choice.

14. 대화를 듣고, 남자가 여름방학에 한 일로 가장 적절한 것을 고르시오.

① 낚시하기
② 요리 배우기
③ 수영 강습 받기
④ 식당에서 일하기
⑤ 삼촌 댁 방문하기

14 W: Daniel, how was your summer vacation? You said you were going to learn ________ ________ ________, right?

M: Oh, my uncle was going to teach me but he couldn't do it.

W: Why not?

M: He's a cook and his restaurant got very busy.

W: I see. Then did you do something else?

M: Yes. I wanted to try something new, so I ________ ________ with my dad.

W: Sounds fun! How was it?

M: It was great. I had so much fun.

15. 다음을 듣고, 방송의 목적으로 가장 적절한 것을 고르시오.

① 교내 체육 활동을 장려하려고
② 물품 대여 서비스를 소개하려고
③ 분실물 찾는 방법을 안내하려고
④ 중고물품 판매 행사를 홍보하려고
⑤ 학교 시설 이용 예절을 지도하려고

15 W: Good morning, students. To make school life easier for our students, we're opening a _________ _________ called 'School Market.' You can borrow pens, slippers, umbrellas, soccer balls and many more items from the market. There's _________ _________, but you need to return the items on time and take good care of them. To borrow items, please go to the student meeting room. The market will be _________ _________ during lunchtime. I hope many of you will _________ from it. Thank you.

16. 대화를 듣고, 남자가 지불할 금액을 고르시오.

① $36 ② $45
③ $50 ④ $54
⑤ $60

16 W: Welcome to Blossom Flower Shop. How can I assist you?

M: Hi, I'm _________ _________ some flowers for a special occasion.

W: Absolutely! We have two choices: a bouquet of _________ _________ or a bouquet of just one type of flower like roses or lilies.

M: How much are they?

W: The mixed bouquet is $30, while the single flower arrangements _________ _________ $20 to $25.

M: I'll go for the mixed bouquet. Can I _________ _________ _________ if I buy two bouquets?

W: Certainly! If you purchase two bouquets, we offer a 10% discount.

M: Perfect! I'll take two of the mixed bouquets.

W: Excellent choice! Let me help you pay at the counter.

다음 페이지에 계속 ➡

17. 대화를 듣고, 여자의 마지막 말에 대한 남자의 응답으로 가장 적절한 것을 고르시오.

Man: _______________

① No. This bag is not hand-made.
② Well, I don't like buying used things.
③ That's right. Your items will be popular.
④ Yes. But be aware that they close if it rains.
⑤ I'm sorry. I can't go to the park this weekend.

17
W: That's a nice canvas bag you have there, Stewart.
M: Thanks, Tiffany. I really like it. _______________, it is one-hundred percent hand-made.
W: Really? Where did you get it?
M: I bought it _______ _______ _______ _______ in Riverside Park.
W: I thought they only sold food.
M: No, they sell _______ _______ _______ _______. Their hand-made items are especially good.
W: Why didn't I know that? I should go there. They're open _______ _______, right?
M: Yes. But be aware that they close if it rains.

18. 대화를 듣고, 남자의 마지막 말에 대한 여자의 응답으로 가장 적절한 것을 고르시오.

Woman: _______________

① No way. The stairs are too slippery.
② Not at all. You can go grocery shopping.
③ Good idea. Let's start exercising tomorrow.
④ Could you? I'll make you a nice, big dinner.
⑤ That's right. The elevator is working fine now.

18
(Door keypad lock opening sound)
W: Honey, I'm home.
M: Hey, why are you panting?
W: The elevator is _______ _______ _______, so I had to walk up the stairs.
M: Oh, honey, it's only _______ _______ of stairs. You really need to exercise more.
W: Thanks for pointing that out. But, we have a bigger issue _______ _______.
M: What's that?
W: Our groceries will _______ _______ soon. So, someone has to go down and come back up again.
M: Okay. That someone must be me, I guess?
W: Could you? I'll make you a nice, big dinner.

19. 대화를 듣고, 남자의 마지막 말에 대한 여자의 응답으로 가장 적절한 것을 고르시오.

Woman: _________________

① With coding, you can make a robot move.
② We are currently not accepting new members.
③ Maybe next time. I'm kind of busy at the moment.
④ I'd like to congratulate you on winning the competition.
⑤ Sure! I'll give you his phone number so you can call him.

19

M: Hi, Gemma! What club are you in at school?

W: I'm in the robotics club. We make and control robots.

M: Cool! I'm thinking about joining, too.

W: That'd be great! We can work on robot projects as a team and ___________ ___________ together.

M: Yeah, it sounds fun. But I don't know much about robots.

W: Don't worry! Our club is ___________ ___________ everyone. We'll teach you all about robotics.

M: Thanks, that's ___________. I'll think about joining.

W: If you need help, I can ___________ you to our club leader. He knows a lot about robots.

M: Thanks! That'd be helpful.

W: <u>Sure! I'll give you his phone number so you can call him.</u>

20. 다음을 듣고, Dean이 친구에게 할 말로 가장 알맞은 것을 고르시오.

Dean: _________________

① Will you join me?
② Why don't we go some other time?
③ Can you be there on time?
④ Make sure to bring your umbrella.
⑤ I have another appointment tomorrow.

20

M: Dean ___________ ___________ ___________ to the water park tomorrow with his friend Ted. Before he goes, he checks the weather report for tomorrow. Unfortunately, it says it's going to rain ___________ ___________ ___________. He's very disappointed, but he calls his friend to ___________ ___________ ___________. In this situation, what would Dean most likely say to his friend?

Dean: <u>Why don't we go some other time?</u>

Words & Expressions Review 11

● 다음 단어를 암기하세요.

문제	번호	단어	뜻
1	1	clay	점토
	2	pot mat	냄비 받침
	3	work out	(일이) 잘 풀리다
	4	shape	모양
2	5	bazzar	바자회
	6	charity	자선[구호] 단체
	7	foundation	재단
	8	secondhand	중고의
3	9	bring	가져오다
	10	provide	제공하다
	11	comfortable	편안한, 편한
5	12	anniversary	기념일
6	13	get back	돌아오다
	14	let go of ~	~을 놓다
	15	careless	부주의한
	16	adjustable	조절 가능한
7	17	regular customer	단골손님
	18	speaking of which	말이 나와서 말인데
	19	downtown	시내의, 도심의
8	20	selected	선별된, 엄선된
	21	apply for ~	~을 신청하다
9	22	device	기기, 장치, 기구
9	23	suction	흡입, 빨아들이기
10	24	join	가입하다, 합류하다
11	25	submit	제출하다
	26	match	(색깔·무늬 등이 서로) 어울리다, 맞다
12	27	outfit	옷차림, 복장
	28	neutral	중립적인, 중간색의
	29	brim	(모자의) 챙
13	30	book	예약하다
	31	make it	참석하다, 가다
	32	charge	요금
15	33	on time	제때에, 시간을 어기지 않고
	34	meeting room	회의실
	35	benefit from	~로부터 혜택을 입다
16	36	bouquet	꽃다발, 부케
	37	amazingly	놀랍게도
17	38	all kinds of	온갖 종류의
	39	aware	알고 있는, 의식하고 있는
18	40	pant	(숨을) 헐떡이다
	41	out of order	고장 난
19	42	reassuring	안심시키는
	43	currently	현재, 지금
20	44	unfortunately	안타깝게도

M3(17)_W_11

●왼쪽 단어장의 뜻이 보이지 않게 반으로 접고, 학습한 단어의 뜻을 아래 빈칸에 적어주세요.

1	device		23	pot mat
2	anniversary		24	charity
3	on time		25	provide
4	benefit from		26	currently
5	downtown		27	out of order
6	match		28	regular customer
7	comfortable		29	submit
8	suction		30	book
9	let go of ~		31	reassuring
10	bouquet		32	join
11	selected		33	brim
12	adjustable		34	apply for ~
13	charge		35	amazingly
14	make it		36	outfit
15	neutral		37	get back
16	shape		38	pant
17	secondhand		39	meeting room
18	all kinds of		40	foundation
19	bring		41	clay
20	aware		42	bazzar
21	work out		43	speaking of which
22	unfortunately		44	careless

11회 단어

12회 중학영어듣기 모의고사

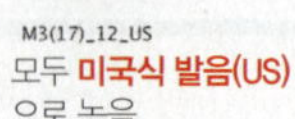

모두 **미국식 발음(US)**
으로 녹음

M3(17)_12_US

20문제 중 5문제에 **영국식 발음
(US+UK)**을 포함하여 녹음

M3(17)_12_UK

정답 및 해석 p. 67

1 대화를 듣고, 남자가 구입할 수영 모자를 고르시오.

①  ②  ③  ④  ⑤ 

2 대화를 듣고, Super Soccer Class에 관해 언급되지 <u>않은</u> 것을 고르시오.

① 기간　　　② 시간　　　③ 장소　　　④ 참가비　　　⑤ 신청 방법

3 대화를 듣고, 남자가 여자에게 전화한 목적으로 가장 적절한 것을 고르시오.

① 식당 예약을 하려고
② 식당 메뉴에 대해 문의하려고
③ 식당의 운영시간을 문의하려고
④ 식당에 주차가 가능한지 문의하려고
⑤ 식당에 반려견 동반이 가능한지 문의하려고

4 대화를 듣고, 두 사람이 만날 시각을 고르시오.

① 4:00 p.m.　　② 4:30 p.m.　　③ 5:00 p.m.　　④ 5:30 p.m.　　⑤ 6:00 p.m.

5 대화를 듣고, 여자의 심정으로 가장 적절한 것을 고르시오.

① angry　　　② sad　　　③ happy　　　④ thankful　　　⑤ excited

6 다음 그림의 상황에 가장 적절한 대화를 고르시오.

① ② ③ ④ ⑤

---

7 대화를 듣고, 여자가 남자에게 부탁한 일로 가장 적절한 것을 고르시오.

① 정비소에서 자동차 찾아오기
② 식당 예약 시간 변경하기
③ 부모님께 문자 보내기
④ 기차표 예매하기
⑤ 렌트카 빌리기

---

8 다음을 듣고, Warm Glow에 관해 언급되지 <u>않은</u> 것을 고르시오.

① 개업 시기   ② 업종   ③ 제품 특징   ④ 구매 방법   ⑤ 회원 특전

---

9 다음을 듣고, 무엇에 관한 설명인지 고르시오.

① 매
② 독수리
③ 올빼미
④ 까마귀
⑤ 비둘기

---

10 다음을 듣고, 두 사람의 대화가 <u>어색한</u> 것을 고르시오.

① ② ③ ④ ⑤

11번~20번 문제는 다음 페이지에 ➡

11 대화를 듣고, 남자가 대화 직후에 할 일로 가장 적절한 것을 고르시오.

① 샴푸 하기   ② 머리 말리기   ③ 미용실 가기
④ 스타일북 보기   ⑤ 머리 파마 하기

12 다음 표를 보면서 대화를 듣고, 남자가 선택할 비타민 제품을 고르시오.

	Product	Vitamin	Type	Quantity
①	A	Vitamin A	Jellies	30
②	B	Vitamin A	Jellies	60
③	C	Vitamin A	Pills	30
④	D	Vitamin C	Pills	60
⑤	E	Vitamin C	Pills	30

13 대화를 듣고, 두 사람이 도자기 수업을 받을 날짜를 고르시오.

① 7월 25일   ② 7월 26일   ③ 7월 27일   ④ 7월 28일   ⑤ 7월 29일

14 대화를 듣고, 남자가 지난 주말에 한 일로 가장 적절한 것을 고르시오.

① 가족 여행 가기   ② 영어 과제 하기
③ 봉사활동 하기   ④ 영화 보러 가기
⑤ 올림픽 경기 관람하기

15 다음을 듣고, 방송의 목적으로 가장 적절한 것을 고르시오.

① 영화 관람 예절을 안내하려고   ② 비상시 대피 방법을 알리려고
③ 개봉 예정 영화를 홍보하려고   ④ 영화관 방역 일정을 공지하려고
⑤ 관람객 인원 제한을 설명하려고

16 대화를 듣고, 남자가 지불해야 할 금액으로 가장 적절한 것을 고르시오.

① $16   ② $18   ③ $20   ④ $34   ⑤ $36

17 대화를 듣고, 남자의 마지막 말에 대한 여자의 응답으로 가장 적절한 것을 고르시오.

Woman: ______________________________________

① Yes, purple is my favorite color.

② You saved my life! I'll be there soon.

③ Thank you so much. I'll buy the purse.

④ There were too many people at the mall.

⑤ Good, because it's hard to find what I like.

[18~19] 대화를 듣고, 여자의 마지막 말에 대한 남자의 응답으로 가장 적절한 것을 고르시오.

18 **Man:** ______________________________________

① I am busy after school.　　② Sorry, I don't remember.

③ Let's go hiking tomorrow.　　④ I bought shoes last week.

⑤ Sure, we can go together.

19 **Man:** ______________________________________

① Great! I can't wait to meet her.

② OK. Let's look it up in the dictionary.

③ My family lived in China for 5 years.

④ I usually watch movies on weekends.

⑤ How do you pronounce this in Chinese?

20 다음 상황 설명을 듣고, Naomi가 Phil에게 할 말로 가장 적절한 것을 고르시오.

Naomi: Phil, ______________________________________

① could you take a photo of us?

② I think we need to change rows.

③ can you see me through the camera?

④ when did you clean up the classroom?

⑤ you should dress up for the group photo.

Dictation Test 12

M3(17)_12_D

Dictation(받아쓰기)은 본문을 받아쓰면서 영어듣기의 집중력을 향상시키고 다양한 표현을 정리하기 위한 영어듣기 학습법입니다. **녹음을 다시 듣고, 빈칸에 알맞은 단어를 써 보세요.**

※Dictation의 정답은 듣기 대본의 밑줄 친 부분을 확인하세요.

📖 정답 p. 67

맞은 개수 / 총181개

그림정보파악(대화)

🇺🇸🇬🇧

1. 대화를 듣고, 남자가 구입할 수영 모자를 고르시오.

① 
②  
③ 
④ 
⑤  

01

W: Hi, Jake. What are you ________ ________?

M: Hi, Letty. I'm looking at swimming caps. I need a new one. Can you ________ ________ ________ ________?

W: Sure. Let's see. How would you like a dolphin on the cap?

M: Sure, I like dolphins. They are ________ ________.

W: Okay. There are caps with one dolphin and caps with two dolphins.

M: The caps with two dolphins look nice.

W: Good. How about ________ ________ ________ ________ 'SPLASH?'

M: It's nice. I'll get that one. Thanks for your help.

대화미언급

2. 대화를 듣고, Super Soccer Class에 관해 언급되지 <u>않은</u> 것을 고르시오.

① 기간　② 시간
③ 장소　④ 참가비
⑤ 신청 방법

02

W: Jamie, have you heard about Super Soccer Class?

M: Yeah, I love soccer so I'm interested in the class. How about you?

W: Me, too. I think it's a good chance to learn how to play soccer.

M: The class _________ from August 3 to 14, right?

W: Yes, it is from 8 to 9:30 every weekday morning.

M: _________ _________, the class is free!

W: Sounds great. How can we sign up for the class?

M: We need to fill out the form on the website.

W: Let's _________ _________ right away.

3. 대화를 듣고, 남자가 여자에게 전화한 목적으로 가장 적절한 것을 고르시오.

① 식당 예약을 하려고
② 식당 메뉴에 대해 문의하려고
③ 식당의 운영시간을 문의하려고
④ 식당에 주차가 가능한지 문의하려고
⑤ 식당에 반려견 동반이 가능한지 문의하려고

03 *(Telephone rings.)*

W: Hello. This is Forest Restaurant. How can I help you?

M: Hi. I have some questions about your menu.

W: Okay. What would you like to know?

M: My daughter is vegan. Do you have any _________ _________?

W: Yes, we have some dishes with tofu.

M: Oh, okay. Also, I _________ _________ _________ peanuts, so is there anything on the menu without peanuts in it?

W: Yes, we do have a peanut-free menu as well.

M: _________ _________ _________. Okay, thank you so much.

W: No problem. Just ask your waiter about the items on the menu and he can explain them _________ _________ _________.

다음 페이지에 계속 ➡

4. 대화를 듣고, 두 사람이 만날 시각을 고
   르시오.
   ① 4:00 p.m.   ② 4:30 p.m.
   ③ 5:00 p.m.   ④ 5:30 p.m.
   ⑤ 6:00 p.m.

04
M: I'm thinking about learning how to play the guitar.

W: That's great. I can give you some tips if you'd like.

M: Really? I didn't know you played the guitar. It would be really helpful if you could.

W: Why don't we ________ ________ ________ ________ after school?

M: That sounds good. How about we meet at 5:00 p.m.?

W: I can't. I have to go to the dentist at 4:30 p.m. I'll ________ ________ ________ 5:30 p.m.

M: Oh, okay. Does 6:00 p.m. work for you?

W: Sure, see you then. We can have dinner while we talk.

M: All right. Dinner is on me.

5. 대화를 듣고, 여자의 심정으로 가장 적절
   한 것을 고르시오.
   ① angry   ② sad
   ③ happy   ④ thankful
   ⑤ excited

05
M: Sally, you look so ________. What's up?

W: I went to piano class today.

M: And?

W: There was a little boy, and he kept __________ ________.

M: Oh, no. What did you do?

W: I told the teacher to stop him, but she ________ ________ for not being patient with him.

M: That's so ________. You must have been very mad.

6. 다음 그림의 상황에 가장 적절한 대화를 고르시오.

① ②
③ ④
⑤

06 ① W: Do we have milk? I want to have some cereal.

M: ＿＿＿＿ ＿＿＿＿ ＿＿＿＿ check the fridge?

② W: Would you like plastic or paper bags?

M: Plastic bags, please. Thank you.

③ W: This product is ＿＿＿＿ ＿＿＿＿, ＿＿＿＿

＿＿＿＿ ＿＿＿＿.

M: Oh, really? I'll go grab another one.

④ W: The pears are ＿＿＿＿ ＿＿＿＿ online.

M: Let's order some right now.

⑤ W: There's ＿＿＿＿ ＿＿＿＿ on the top shelf.

M: Let's put these books there then.

2024 영어듣기능력평가 2회 7번 변형

7. 대화를 듣고, 여자가 남자에게 부탁한 일로 가장 적절한 것을 고르시오.

① 정비소에서 자동차 찾아오기
② 식당 예약 시간 변경하기
③ 부모님께 문자 보내기
④ 기차표 예매하기
⑤ 렌트카 빌리기

07 W: Honey, when did you say we're going to get our car back from the ＿＿＿＿＿ ＿＿＿＿＿?

M: It won't be ready until next week. Why are you asking about it?

W: Didn't I tell you that my parents are ＿＿＿＿＿ ＿＿＿＿＿ ＿＿＿＿＿ this weekend?

M: Oh, right! Are they taking the train?

W: Yes, they are. So, we definitely need a car to ＿＿＿＿＿ ＿＿＿＿＿ ＿＿＿＿＿ at the station and drive them around.

M: We should rent a car for the weekend then.

W: Could you ＿＿＿＿＿ ＿＿＿＿＿ ＿＿＿＿＿ it, please?

M: Okay, I will.

다음 페이지에 계속 ➡

8. 다음을 듣고, Warm Glow에 관해 언급되
지 <u>않은</u> 것을 고르시오.
① 개업 시기　② 업종
③ 제품 특징　④ 구매 방법
⑤ 회원 특전

08 W: Are you looking for a new experience, or a way to relax? __________ you want, you can find it at Warm Glow. We produce ________ ________ ________ ________ 100% handmade candles. Our candles are different because they are long-lasting and ________ ________. Visit our website now. You can ________ ________ ________ online, or over the phone. Also, our members always receive discounts.

9. 다음을 듣고, 무엇에 관한 설명인지 고르
시오.
① 매　　　　② 독수리
③ 올빼미　　④ 까마귀
⑤ 비둘기

09 W: This is a bird. It has excellent eyesight and hearing. It has very powerful claws to help it ________ ________ ________ ________. It can rotate its neck 270 degrees. It is very ________ ________ ________ and its night vision allows it to catch prey at night. Its feathers allow it to fly silently. It ________ ________ ________ its hooting sound.

10. 다음을 듣고, 두 사람의 대화가 <u>어색한</u>
것을 고르시오.
①　　　　　②
③　　　　　④
⑤

10 ① W: Would you please help me ________ ________ ________?
M: Sure. I'd be glad to.
② W: Can you tell me the way to the post office?
M: Sorry, I'm new here, too.
③ W: ________ ________ ________ ________ New York?
M: You're really good.
④ W: I decided to learn Japanese.
M: That's a ________ ________.
⑤ W: What are you reading?
M: A story about a ________ painter.

11. 대화를 듣고, 남자가 대화 직후에 할 일로 가장 적절한 것을 고르시오.

① 샴푸 하기
② 머리 말리기
③ 미용실 가기
④ 스타일북 보기
⑤ 머리 파마 하기

11

W: Hi, how are you today? What can I do for you?

M: I'd like to change my hairstyle.

W: Do you have ________ ________ ________ ________?

M: I was thinking of getting a perm, but I'm not sure if that's the right choice.

W: Here, ________ ________ ________ ________ our stylebook. It has photos of different hairstyles.

M: Wow, thanks. There are lots of photos here!

W: ________ ________ ________. You can choose what style you prefer and show it to me.

M: Okay, I will. Give me a minute, please.

12. 다음 표를 보면서 대화를 듣고, 남자가 선택할 비타민 제품을 고르시오.

	Product	Vitamin	Type	Quantity
①	A	Vitamin A	Jellies	30
②	B	Vitamin A	Jellies	60
③	C	Vitamin A	Pills	30
④	D	Vitamin C	Pills	60
⑤	E	Vitamin C	Pills	30

12

M: Hello, I'm looking for some vitamins for my son.

W: Do you have anything __________ in mind?

M: He says his eyes ________ ________ easily these days. Do you have anything for that?

W: Vitamin A is really good for your eyes. Vitamin A comes in two types: jellies and pills.

M: My son would love the jellies. Then, he won't have ________ ________ ________ ________.

W: Great! Do you want the smaller quantity, just in case he doesn't like them?

M: Okay. I will take that one.

다음 페이지에 계속 ➡

13. 대화를 듣고, 두 사람이 도자기 수업을 받을 날짜를 고르시오.

① 7월 25일 ② 7월 26일
③ 7월 27일 ④ 7월 28일
⑤ 7월 29일

13

M: Have you thought about when we should take ___________ ___________ ___________?

W: Not yet. What about you, Fred?

M: I'm still deciding. Why don't we plan it together for next month?

W: Sounds like a good idea. How about Saturday, July 27th?

M: Well... Saturdays are usually busy for me. What about July 28th?

W: Hmm... I have a friend's birthday party on the 28th. Does July 26th work for you?

M: July 26th ___________ ___________. I don't have any other plans then.

W: Okay, ___________ ___________ ___________ July 26th for our pottery class.

14. 대화를 듣고, 남자가 지난 주말에 한 일로 가장 적절한 것을 고르시오.

① 가족 여행 가기
② 영어 과제 하기
③ 봉사활동 하기
④ 영화 보러 가기
⑤ 올림픽 경기 관람하기

14

W: Hey, Dave. How was your weekend?

M: Oh, hey, Cindy! It was very meaningful.

W: Why? What did you do?

M: I ___________ ___________ ___________ this event called the Hand-in-Hand Mini Olympics.

W: What's that?

M: It's an event for kids with ___________. I ___________ ___________ ___________ them complete the games as a team.

W: That's so nice of you. It must have been worth it.

M: It really was. I'm going to participate next year as well.

15. 다음을 듣고, 방송의 목적으로 가장 적절한 것을 고르시오.

① 영화 관람 예절을 안내하려고
② 비상시 대피 방법을 알리려고
③ 개봉 예정 영화를 홍보하려고
④ 영화관 방역 일정을 공지하려고
⑤ 관람객 인원 제한을 설명하려고

15 W: Hello and welcome to ABC Cinema. Before you enjoy your movie, let me ________ ________ a few rules to keep in mind. First, ________ ________ the seat in front of you. Second, please ________ ________ your cellphone. The light from your phone can be very _________ for other people. Lastly, put all trash in the trash can when you exit the theater. Please keep these rules in mind to ________ for everyone's comfort. Have a good time.

16. 대화를 듣고, 남자가 지불해야 할 금액으로 가장 적절한 것을 고르시오.

① $16   ② $18
③ $20   ④ $34
⑤ $36

16 M: Excuse me, I'd like to buy two adult bus tickets to New York.

W: They are 10 dollars each.

M: Can I buy ________ ________ here, too?

W: Yes, it'll cost 8 dollars more for each person.

M: Okay, I'll buy two return tickets. How much is it ________ ________?

W: It's 36 dollars.

M: I have a two-dollar ________ ________ here. Can I use it?

W: Let me see. (*pause*) Yes, you can.

M: All right. Here's my credit card.

다음 페이지에 계속 ➡

17. 대화를 듣고, 남자의 마지막 말에 대한 여자의 응답으로 가장 적절한 것을 고르시오.

Woman: _______________

① Yes, purple is my favorite color.
② You saved my life! I'll be there soon.
③ Thank you so much. I'll buy the purse.
④ There were too many people at the mall.
⑤ Good, because it's hard to find what I like.

17 *(Telephone rings.)*

M: Hello, Happy Mall _________-_________-_________.

W: Hello. I'm calling about my purse. I think I left it _________ _________ _________ on the first floor.

M: Okay. What does your purse look like?

W: It's purple with a gold button.

M: I have one _________ _________ _________ _________ _________. What's in it?

W: Some cash, a student ID, and a family photo.

M: Please tell me your name.

W: Tina Evans.

M: Okay, I have _________ _________ _________ _________.

W: You saved my life! I'll be there soon.

18. 대화를 듣고, 여자의 마지막 말에 대한 남자의 응답으로 가장 적절한 것을 고르시오.

Man: _______________

① I am busy after school.
② Sorry, I don't remember.
③ Let's go hiking tomorrow.
④ I bought shoes last week.
⑤ Sure, we can go together.

18 M: Hey, Alice. Are you doing anything after school?

W: No, I _________ _________ _________ _________. What about you?

M: I'm thinking of going shopping at the mall.

W: What are you _________ _________?

M: I want to look at some hiking shoes.

W: I didn't know you liked to _________ _________.

M: Yeah, I went for the first time last week, and it was really fun.

W: Well, I could use some new shoes as well. Can I _________ _________ you?

M: Sure, we can go together.

19. 대화를 듣고, 여자의 마지막 말에 대한 남자의 응답으로 가장 적절한 것을 고르시오.

Man: ________________

① Great! I can't wait to meet her.
② OK. Let's look it up in the dictionary.
③ My family lived in China for 5 years.
④ I usually watch movies on weekends.
⑤ How do you pronounce this in Chinese?

19

W: Hi, Patrick. What's wrong? You look worried.

M: Hi, Amy. I was just thinking about ________ ________ ________ my Chinese pronunciation.

W: Oh, I see.

M: How come your pronunciation is so good?

W: Didn't I tell you that my sister is ________ ________ Chinese in college?

M: Wow! Cool!

W: She is helping me on weekends. Why don't you join us this weekend?

M: That would be awesome! I hope she'll be okay with it.

W: I'm sure she ________ ________ ________ ________ a friend. I will call you this Saturday.

M: Great! I can't wait to meet her.

20. 다음 상황 설명을 듣고, Naomi가 Phil에게 할 말로 가장 적절한 것을 고르시오.

Naomi: Phil, ________________

① could you take a photo of us?
② I think we need to change rows.
③ can you see me through the camera?
④ when did you clean up the classroom?
⑤ you should dress up for the group photo.

20

W: Naomi is a middle school student. Today is class photo day. When the photographer ________ ________ ________ ________, Phil, one of her classmates, is standing in the row in front of her. Phil happens to be a tall boy, and Naomi ________ ________ he will block her in the photo. So, she would like to ask Phil to change places with her. In this situation, what would Naomi most likely say to Phil?

Naomi: Phil, I think we need to change rows.

Words & Expressions Review 12

● 다음 단어를 암기하세요.

문제	번호	단어	뜻
2	1	run	운영하다, 제공하다
3	2	be allergic to ~	~에 알레르기가 있다
	3	in detail	자세하게
4	4	tip	(실용적인, 작은) 조언
	5	bother	괴롭히다, 귀찮게 하다
	6	scold	혼내다
5	7	patient	참을성 있는, 환자
	8	unfair	불공평한
	9	mad	몹시 화가 난, 미친
6	10	fridge	냉장고
	11	grab	가져오다
7	12	repair shop	정비소, 수리점
	13	rent	빌리다
	14	produce	생산하다
	15	a wide range of	다양한, 광범위한
	16	handmade	수제의
8	17	long-lasting	오래 지속되는
	18	highly scented	향이 풍부한
	19	place an order	주문하다
	20	claw	(동물·새의) 발톱
9	21	prey	(사냥 동물의) 먹이, 사냥감
	22	rotate	회전하다

문제	번호	단어	뜻
9	23	silently	조용히
11	24	think of -ing	~하려고 생각하다
	25	give ~ a minute	~에게 잠시 시간을 주다
12	26	have ~ in mind	~을 생각하다
	27	quantity	양, 수량
13	28	pottery	도자기
	29	work for + 사람	(일정이나 계획이) ~에게 맞다, 괜찮다
	30	meaningful	의미 있는, 중요한
14	31	disability	(신체적, 정신적) 장애
	32	worth	~할 가치가 있는
	33	go over	살펴보다, 검토하다
	34	avoid	피하다, 회피하다
15	35	distracting	방해가 되는
	36	ensure	보장하다, 확보하다
	37	comfort	편안함, 안락
16	38	cost	비용이 들다
17	39	lost-and-found	분실물 센터
	40	pronounce	발음하다
19	41	How come ~?	어째서, 왜 ~?
	42	major in	~을 전공하다
20	43	set up	준비하다
	44	row	줄, 열

●왼쪽 단어장의 뜻이 보이지 않게 반으로 접고, 학습한 단어의 뜻을 아래 빈칸에 적어주세요.

1	work for + 사람	23	patient
2	claw	24	avoid
3	place an order	25	have ~ in mind
4	go over	26	handmade
5	scold	27	prey
6	ensure	28	pottery
7	rotate	29	silently
8	be allergic to ~	30	run
9	a wide range of	31	produce
10	mad	32	rent
11	How come ~?	33	disability
12	major in	34	fridge
13	give ~ a minute	35	worth
14	highly scented	36	repair shop
15	cost	37	long-lasting
16	meaningful	38	quantity
17	pronounce	39	think of -ing
18	comfort	40	in detail
19	tip	41	set up
20	lost-and-found	42	grab
21	unfair	43	row
22	bother	44	distracting

13회 중학영어듣기 모의고사

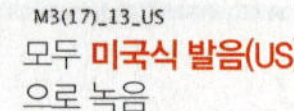

M3(17)_13_US
모두 **미국식 발음(US)**
으로 녹음

M3(17)_13_UK
20문제 중 5문제에 **영국식 발음**
(US+UK)을 포함하여 녹음

정답 및 해석 p. 73

1 대화를 듣고, 남자가 선택할 고무동력기를 고르시오.

① ② ③ ④ ⑤

2 대화를 듣고, Eco Adventure Day에 관해 언급되지 <u>않은</u> 것을 고르시오.

① 진행 장소 ② 시작 시각 ③ 신청 방법
④ 활동 내용 ⑤ 유의 사항

3 대화를 듣고, 남자가 여자에게 전화한 목적으로 가장 적절한 것을 고르시오.

① 신청 도서 입고를 알리려고 ② 독서 모임 가입을 권유하려고
③ 도서관 자원봉사를 신청하려고 ④ 연체 도서의 반납을 촉구하려고
⑤ 도서관 카드 재발급을 요청하려고

4 대화를 듣고, 에어컨 수리 기사가 방문할 시각을 고르시오.

① 2 p.m. ② 3 p.m. ③ 4 p.m. ④ 5 p.m. ⑤ 6 p.m.

5 대화를 듣고, 남자의 심정으로 가장 적절한 것을 고르시오.

① worried ② bored ③ relieved ④ curious ⑤ proud

6 다음 그림의 상황에 가장 적절한 대화를 고르시오.

①   ②   ③   ④   ⑤

7 대화를 듣고, 여자가 남자에게 부탁한 일로 가장 적절한 것을 고르시오.

① 책 반납일 연장하기   ② 문자 메시지 보내기
③ 독서실 자리 예약하기   ④ 스터디 그룹에 받아주기
⑤ 예약 도서 대신 수령하기

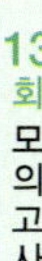

8 다음을 듣고, 학급 체험학습에 관해 언급되지 <u>않은</u> 것을 고르시오.

① 장소   ② 프로그램   ③ 복장
④ 준비물   ⑤ 종료 시간

9 다음을 듣고, 무엇에 관한 설명인지 고르시오.

① 커피   ② 김밥   ③ 컵라면   ④ 도시락   ⑤ 아이스크림

10 다음을 듣고, 두 사람의 대화가 <u>어색한</u> 것을 고르시오.

①   ②   ③   ④   ⑤

11번~20번 문제는 다음 페이지에 ➡

11 대화를 듣고, 여자가 대화 직후에 할 일로 가장 적절한 것을 고르시오.

① 연습실 가기　　　　　② 지원서 제출하기　　　　　③ 텀블링 연습하기
④ 댄스 안무 짜기　　　　⑤ 치어리더 보러 가기

12 다음 표를 보면서 대화를 듣고, 두 사람이 선택할 수업을 고르시오.

	Class	Language	No. of Classes(per week)	Time
①	A	Italian	3	9:00 ~ 11:00 a.m.
②	B	Italian	2	2:00 ~ 4:00 p.m.
③	C	French	3	2:00 ~ 4:00 p.m.
④	D	French	3	9:00 ~ 11:00 a.m.
⑤	E	French	2	2:00 ~ 4:00 p.m.

13 대화를 듣고, 남자의 치과 예약 날짜를 고르시오.

① 4월 10일　　　② 4월 11일　　　③ 4월 12일　　　④ 4월 13일　　　⑤ 4월 14일

14 대화를 듣고, 여자가 어제 한 일로 가장 적절한 것을 고르시오.

① 영상 편집하기　　　　② 학교 촬영하기　　　　③ 카메라 수리하기
④ 아이디어 회의하기　　⑤ 공모전 참가 신청하기

15 다음을 듣고, 방송의 목적으로 가장 적절한 것을 고르시오.

① 해수욕장 축제를 홍보하려고　　　　② 해수욕장 안전수칙을 안내하려고
③ 해수욕장 이용시간 변경을 공지하려고　④ 수상 스포츠 동아리 가입을 독려하려고
⑤ 수상 스포츠 강습 프로그램을 소개하려고

16 대화를 듣고, 여자가 지불해야 할 금액으로 가장 적절한 것을 고르시오.

① $70　　　② $75　　　③ $80　　　④ $85　　　⑤ $90

17 대화를 듣고, 여자의 마지막 말에 대한 남자의 응답으로 가장 적절한 것을 고르시오.

Man: ____

① Congratulations! I'm glad you passed.

② Don't worry. I'm sure you will do great!

③ Thanks for the tip. I should definitely try it out.

④ Awesome! That will certainly improve my writing.

⑤ I agree. Let's talk to our teacher about the deadline.

[18~19] 대화를 듣고, 남자의 마지막 말에 대한 여자의 응답으로 가장 적절한 것을 고르시오.

18 **Woman:** ____

① Sure. Feel free to look around.

② No problem. We have smaller sizes.

③ I'm afraid we don't have a bigger size.

④ I'm sorry, but I can't give you a refund.

⑤ Yes. This is the same shirt in a different size.

19 **Woman:** ____

① I'm so excited about our trip.

② Thanks, I'll go check the drawers.

③ Did you pack your cell phone charger?

④ We have to leave the house in two hours.

⑤ You can't board the plane without your passport.

20 다음 상황 설명을 듣고, Steve가 Katie에게 할 말로 가장 적절한 것을 고르시오.

Steve: Katie, ____

① I'll make up for my rude behavior.

② the test was harder than I expected.

③ don't be disappointed by the test results.

④ I didn't know that math was your favorite subject.

⑤ can you give me a hand with the test next week?

Dictation Test 13

M3(17)_13_D

Dictation(받아쓰기)은 본문을 받아쓰면서 영어듣기의 집중력을 향상시키고 다양한 표현을 정리하기 위한 영어듣기 학습법입니다. 녹음을 다시 듣고, 빈칸에 알맞은 단어를 써 보세요.

※Dictation의 정답은 듣기 대본의 밑줄 친 부분을 확인하세요.

📖 정답 p. 73

맞은 개수 / 총168개

그림정보파악(대화)

1. 대화를 듣고, 남자가 선택할 고무동력기를 고르시오.

①  ② 

③  ④ 

⑤ 

01
W: Hi, Roger. What are you doing here?

M: Hey, Brittany. I need to buy a __________ __________ model airplane kit for Science Day at school. Can you help me choose one?

W: Sure. How many sets of wings do you want for your model airplane?

M: I'd like 2 sets of wings.

W: Then let's look at the design. Would you like star __________ on the wings?

M: Yes. I think stars will make it __________ __________.

W: Okay. Then how about this one with four stars?

M: Cool! I'll get that one. Thanks for helping me.

대화미언급

2024 영어듣기능력평가 2회 2번 변형

2. 대화를 듣고, Eco Adventure Day에 관해 언급되지 <u>않은</u> 것을 고르시오.

① 진행 장소 ② 시작 시각
③ 신청 방법 ④ 활동 내용
⑤ 유의 사항

02
M: Are you excited about Eco Adventure Day?

W: Absolutely! It'll __________ __________ at Blue Forest Park on June 3.

M: What time does the program begin?

W: It starts at 8:30 a.m.

M: What are we going to do there?

W: We'll plant trees and __________ __________ the hiking trail.

M: Sounds meaningful!

W: By the way, they said we should __________

__________ __________ because the paths might

be muddy.

M: Good to know.

3. 대화를 듣고, 남자가 여자에게 전화한 목적으로 가장 적절한 것을 고르시오.

① 신청 도서 입고를 알리려고
② 독서 모임 가입을 권유하려고
③ 도서관 자원봉사를 신청하려고
④ 연체 도서의 반납을 촉구하려고
⑤ 도서관 카드 재발급을 요청하려고

03 *(Cellphone rings.)*

W: Hello?

M: Hi, this is Chris calling from Sunshine Library. Am I speaking with Emily Parker?

W: Yes, speaking.

M: The book ________ __________, *The Secret Plan*, has arrived and is ready for pickup.

W: Oh, that's great news! Can I pick it up tomorrow?

M: Sure! We're open from 9 a.m. to 6 p.m., so you can ________ ________ _______ during those hours.

W: Perfect! Is there anything I need to bring with me?

M: No. You _______ ________ ________ ________ your library card.

W: Thank you, Chris. I appreciate the call.

4. 대화를 듣고, 에어컨 수리 기사가 방문할 시각을 고르시오.

① 2 p.m.   ② 3 p.m.
③ 4 p.m.   ④ 5 p.m.
⑤ 6 p.m.

04 *(Telephone rings.)*

W: VR Electronics Service Center. How may I help you?

M: Hi. My air conditioner ________ ________. Could you send a repairperson?

W: Sure. ________ ________ we can send someone is Thursday. Is that okay?

M: Yes. But I won't be home in the morning.

다음 페이지에 계속 ➡

W: I see. Then, is 2 p.m. okay for you?

M: I'm afraid not. Could you ________ ________

6 p.m. ________?

W: I'm sorry, but they get off at 6.

M: I see. Then how about 5 p.m.?

W: Okay. I'll ________ ________ ________ at 5.

M: Thank you.

5. 대화를 듣고, 남자의 심정으로 가장 적절한 것을 고르시오.

① worried
② bored
③ relieved
④ curious
⑤ proud

05

W: So, how did it go with the doctor?

M: What do you mean?

W: You said you were taking your cat to ________

________.

M: Oh, right! He's fine. Thank goodness.

W: Nothing is ________ ________ ________, then? You were so worried.

M: Well, he is ________-________, and he is being lazy. That's why he isn't moving very much.

W: He just needs to go on a diet.

M: Exactly. It's ________ ________ ________ ________ my chest. I really thought he was sick.

W: Well, I'm glad he's fine.

6. 다음 그림의 상황에 가장 적절한 대화를 고르시오.

① ②
③ ④
⑤

06 ① W: Look at that tiger ________ ________ ________. It looks so scary.

M: Yes, it is. Let's take a picture of it.

② W: Hello, sir. Can I help you?

M: Yes. I'm looking for a teddy bear for my daughter.

③ W: Do you want me to ________ ________ ________?

M: Yes, first as a bear, then as a tiger.

④ W: Did you watch the documentary on bears last
      night?

   M: Yes, I did. It was so __________.

⑤ W: Can I _______ this baby tiger?

   M: No, you are _______ _______ _______ do it.

부탁(요청)한일파악

7. 대화를 듣고, 여자가 남자에게 부탁한 일로 가장 적절한 것을 고르시오.

① 책 반납일 연장하기
② 문자 메시지 보내기
③ 독서실 자리 예약하기
④ 스터디 그룹에 받아주기
⑤ 예약 도서 대신 수령하기

07 *(Cellphone rings.)*

M: Hi, Karen.

W: Hi, Joel. Are you still at the library?

M: Yeah, I just finished up with my study group. I'm __________ __________ __________. Why?

W: I got a message that the __________ __________ __________ is now available, but I can't go pick it up today.

M: Oh, really? Do you want me to get it for you?

W: Could you, please? I'll send my library card to your phone.

M: Sure. Just one book?

W: Yes. I __________ __________ __________ __________.

M: Hey, no problem. I'll bring it to you later.

고난도　담화미언급

8. 다음을 듣고, 학급 체험학습에 관해 언급되지 <u>않은</u> 것을 고르시오.

① 장소　　② 프로그램
③ 복장　　④ 준비물
⑤ 종료 시간

08 W: Hello, students. Let me tell you about tomorrow's _______ _______ _______ to Daehan Youth Sports Center. You need to be there by 9 a.m. You can take bus number 23 or 38 to get there. You're going to have a chance to experience exciting sports such as _______ _______ _______.
Please wear casual clothes or athletic wear for the programs. And, don't forget to bring your lunch. Thank you.

다음 페이지에 계속 ➡

9. 다음을 듣고, 무엇에 관한 설명인지 고르시오.

① 커피　　② 김밥
③ 컵라면　　④ 도시락
⑤ 아이스크림

09 M: This is a food. Many people eat this as a meal. It's very __________ and easy to eat. So, many people reach for it when they are busy. There are various recipes for this, __________ __________ the ingredients. To make this, spread rice on a dried sheet of seaweed. Then, put eggs, carrots, ham and all the other ingredients on top, and roll it up. Finally, __________ __________ __________ bite-sized pieces so you can eat it.

10. 다음을 듣고, 두 사람의 대화가 <u>어색한</u> 것을 고르시오.

①　　　②
③　　　④
⑤

10
① M: Do they allow dogs in this apartment building?

W: There's a __________ pet shop where I get all my supplies.

② M: My elbows are swollen and they really hurt.

W: Soak them in warm water. That'll ease the pain.

③ M: Do you need money for your school trip?

W: No, it's okay. Everything __________ __________ __________ for us.

④ M: How did you get to be that __________ __________ __________?

W: I've been practicing every day since I was nine years old.

⑤ M: What's the __________ of this restaurant?

W: I think they serve a fusion of Asian and European foods.

11. 대화를 듣고, 여자가 대화 직후에 할 일
로 가장 적절한 것을 고르시오.

① 연습실 가기
② 지원서 제출하기
③ 텀블링 연습하기
④ 댄스 안무 짜기
⑤ 치어리더 보러 가기

11

W: Hey, Chris. Did you hear about the cheerleading team _________ at our school?

M: No, I didn't.

W: Well, there is going to be one, and I'm going to try out.

M: Good for you! How are you going to _____________ _________ _________?

W: I need to practice my tumbling skills, and make up some dance ___________.

M: Wow, that's a lot of work. Are you going to the practice room right now?

W: Actually, I'm going to the principal's office. I have to _________ _________ _____________ first.

12. 다음 표를 보면서 대화를 듣고, 두 사람
이 선택할 수업을 고르시오.

	Class	Language	No. of Classes (per week)	Time
①	A	Italian	3	9:00 ~ 11:00 a.m.
②	B	Italian	2	2:00 ~ 4:00 p.m.
③	C	French	3	2:00 ~ 4:00 p.m.
④	D	French	3	9:00 ~ 11:00 a.m.
⑤	E	French	2	2:00 ~ 4:00 p.m.

12

M: Hey, why don't we learn a foreign language this winter?

W: Good idea. Actually, I want to learn French. I'd like to go to France someday.

M: Me, too. Will three classes a week _________ _________ _________?

W: Not at all. It's better to learn fast, and winter break is _________ _________ _________.

M: Right. How about taking classes in the morning?

W: That _________ _________ _________.

M: Okay. Let's go and sign up now.

다음 페이지에 계속 ➡

13. 대화를 듣고, 남자의 치과 예약 날짜를 고르시오.

① 4월 10일
② 4월 11일
③ 4월 12일
④ 4월 13일
⑤ 4월 14일

13

W: Mr. Park, when ___________ ___________ ___________ for your next dental appointment?

M: Do you have anything available on April 12?

W: I'm afraid we don't. Dr. Lee is fully booked ___________ ___________.

M: Then how about April 13?

W: I'm sorry, ___________ ___________ that day. Are you available on April 14?

M: Yes, I am. How about 11 o'clock?

W: ___________ ___________ ___________ the schedule. *(pause)* Oh, we have 11 o'clock open. I'll schedule you at 11 next week.

14. 대화를 듣고, 여자가 어제 한 일로 가장 적절한 것을 고르시오.

① 영상 편집하기
② 학교 촬영하기
③ 카메라 수리하기
④ 아이디어 회의하기
⑤ 공모전 참가 신청하기

14

W: Hey, Brandon. What's up?

M: Hey, Cathy. Have you heard about the school ___________ ___________ ___________?

W: Yeah, I saw the notice a few days ago.

M: I thought you would be interested. So, are you applying?

W: Of course! In fact, I ___________ ___________ the ___________ yesterday.

M: Really? Who is on your team?

W: Nick and Becky.

M: Wow! You guys are the dream team. I hope your team ___________ ___________ ___________.

15. 다음을 듣고, 방송의 목적으로 가장 적절한 것을 고르시오.

① 해수욕장 축제를 홍보하려고
② 해수욕장 안전수칙을 안내하려고
③ 해수욕장 이용시간 변경을 공지하려고
④ 수상 스포츠 동아리 가입을 독려하려고
⑤ 수상 스포츠 강습 프로그램을 소개하려고

15 W: Welcome to Sunset Beach. Before you start swimming in the ocean, let me remind you of a few things. First, please don't ___________ ___________ the water except during the hours when swimming is _________. At other times, the ocean may be dangerous to swim in or the ___________ may not be there to help you. Second, make sure you always wear your life jacket when ______________ _________ water activities. Have a good time and _________ _________, everyone!

16. 대화를 듣고, 여자가 지불해야 할 금액으로 가장 적절한 것을 고르시오.

① $70
② $75
③ $80
④ $85
⑤ $90

16 M: Good morning. How can I help you?

W: I'd like to buy tickets for the music concert tomorrow.

M: Great. Tickets are 70 dollars for VIP seats and 40 dollars for standard seats.

W: Two ___________ _________, please.

M: Thank you. The _________ _________ _________ 80 dollars.

W: Oh, is this a catalog for the concert program?

M: Yes, it is. The price of the _________ is 5 dollars.

W: I'll take one catalog. Here's a 100-dollar bill.

다음 페이지에 계속 ➡

17. 대화를 듣고, 여자의 마지막 말에 대한 남자의 응답으로 가장 적절한 것을 고르시오.

Man: _______________

① Congratulations! I'm glad you passed.
② Don't worry. I'm sure you will do great!
③ Thanks for the tip. I should definitely try it out.
④ Awesome! That will certainly improve my writing.
⑤ I agree. Let's talk to our teacher about the deadline.

17

W: Hi, Alex! Have you finished your essay for writing class?

M: No, not yet. We still have time. Isn't it due next Friday?

W: I don't think so. It's due this Friday.

M: Let me check. *[Pause]* Oh, you're right! I often _______ _______ _______ _______.

W: Why don't you use a time management app?

M: A time management app? Please tell me more about it.

W: It _______ _______ _______ the deadlines for all your important tasks.

M: That sounds really helpful!

W: I've been using it for quite a while now and I _______ _______ _______ _______.

M: Thanks for the tip. I should definitely try it out.

18. 대화를 듣고, 남자의 마지막 말에 대한 여자의 응답으로 가장 적절한 것을 고르시오.

Woman: _______________

① Sure. Feel free to look around.
② No problem. We have smaller sizes.
③ I'm afraid we don't have a bigger size.
④ I'm sorry, but I can't give you a refund.
⑤ Yes. This is the same shirt in a different size.

18

W: Good morning, how may I help you?

M: Hi. I bought this shirt yesterday, and I'd like to _______ _______ for another.

W: Sure. May I ask why you would like to exchange it?

M: It's a little tight for me. I think I've _______ _______ recently.

W: I see. Then I'll get you a bigger one right away.

M: Actually, I want to _______ _______ _______ around and find a different shirt. Is that OK?

W: Sure. Feel free to look around.

19. 대화를 듣고, 남자의 마지막 말에 대한 여자의 응답으로 가장 적절한 것을 고르시오.

Woman: _______________

① I'm so excited about our trip.
② Thanks, I'll go check the drawers.
③ Did you pack your cell phone charger?
④ We have to leave the house in two hours.
⑤ You can't board the plane without your passport.

19

M: Honey, are you _______ _______ _______ our trip?

W: No, I still have to pack a few more things. Have you finished packing your stuff?

M: Yeah, I'm finished. Do you need any help?

W: Well… Can you find my passport for me? I _______ _______ _______ find it.

M: Did you lose your passport? That's bad news.

W: I don't think I actually lost it. It should be _______ _______ _______.

M: Did you check the drawers in the living room? I think I saw it there.

W: Thanks, I'll go check the drawers.

상황에적절한말찾기

20. 다음 상황 설명을 듣고, Steve가 Katie에게 할 말로 가장 적절한 것을 고르시오.

Steve: Katie, _______________

① I'll make up for my rude behavior.
② the test was harder than I expected.
③ don't be disappointed by the test results.
④ I didn't know that math was your favorite subject.
⑤ can you give me a hand with the test next week?

20

M: Steve is a middle school student. He _______ _______ _______ the math test next week. He didn't do very well last time, and he wants to _______ _______ _______ it this time. He knows that one of his classmates, Katie, is really good at math. She always gets an A. So, he would like to ask Katie if she can help him _______ _______ the test. In this situation, what would Steve most likely say to Katie?

Steve: Katie, can you give me a hand with the test next week?

Words & Expressions Review 13

● 다음 단어를 암기하세요.

문제	번호	단어	뜻	문제	번호	단어	뜻
1	1	decoration	장식, 무늬	10	23	supplies	물품
	2	awesome	아주 멋진, 굉장한		24	swollen	부푼, 부어오른
2	3	by the way	그런데		25	ease	(고통 등을) 덜어 주다
	4	waterproof	방수의	11	26	specialty	전문, 특제품
	5	muddy	진흙투성이의, 진흙의		27	tryout	테스트, 적성 시험
3	6	drop by	잠깐 들르다, 불시에 찾아가다		28	prepare	준비하다
4	7	get off	퇴근하다	12	29	break	휴가, 휴식
	8	set ~ up	(약속 · 회의 등을) 잡다, 마련하다	13	30	appointment	예약, 약속
5	9	vet	수의사		31	off	(근무, 일을) 쉬는
	10	go on a diet	다이어트를 하다		32	promotional	홍보의
6	11	cage	(짐승의) 우리, 새장	14	33	contest	공모전, 대회
	12	touching	감동적인		34	turn in	～을 제출하다
7	13	reserve	예약하다		35	application	신청서, 지원서
	14	available	이용 가능한	15	36	allowed	허용된, 허가 받은
8	15	indoor	실내의		37	participate in	～에 참가하다
	16	rock climbing	암벽 등반	16	38	standard	일반적인, 보통의
9	17	convenient	간편한, 편리한	17	39	confused	헷갈려 하는, 혼란스러워하는
	18	reach for	～을 찾다, 손을 뻗다	18	40	exchange	교환하다
	19	seaweed	해조, 해초		41	gain weight	살찌다, 체중이 늘다
	20	ingredient	재료, 구성 요소	19	42	drawer	서랍
	21	slice	자르다		43	board	(배, 기차, 버스, 비행기 등에) 타다
	22	bite-sized	한입 크기의	20	44	make up for	～을 만회하다

● 왼쪽 단어장의 뜻이 보이지 않게 반으로 접고, 학습한 단어의 뜻을 아래 빈칸에 적어주세요.

1	indoor	23	bite-sized
2	muddy	24	set ~ up
3	slice	25	ingredient
4	touching	26	application
5	allowed	27	standard
6	promotional	28	rock climbing
7	seaweed	29	by the way
8	contest	30	convenient
9	available	31	reach for
10	make up for	32	go on a diet
11	reserve	33	appointment
12	cage	34	gain weight
13	awesome	35	exchange
14	get off	36	swollen
15	break	37	supplies
16	drawer	38	turn in
17	waterproof	39	confused
18	off	40	vet
19	board	41	decoration
20	prepare	42	drop by
21	specialty	43	participate in
22	ease	44	tryout

13
회
단
어

정답 및 해석 p. 79

1 대화를 듣고, 여자가 구입할 부츠로 가장 적절한 것을 고르시오.

①  ②  ③   ④   ⑤ 

2 대화를 듣고, Cosypod earphones에 관해 언급되지 <u>않은</u> 것을 고르시오.

① 가격 　　　　　② 배터리 지속시간 　　　　　③ 방수기능
④ 제조사 　　　　　⑤ 색상

3 대화를 듣고, 남자가 여자에게 전화한 목적으로 가장 적절한 것을 고르시오.

① 시험 범위를 물어보려고 　　　　② 숙제가 무엇인지 물어보려고
③ Karen의 안부를 물어보려고 　　　④ 숙제를 도와달라고 부탁하려고
⑤ 선생님께 말을 전해달라고 하려고

4 대화를 듣고, 남자가 등록할 수영 수업 시각을 고르시오.

① 6 a.m. 　　　② 7 a.m. 　　　③ 6 p.m. 　　　④ 7 p.m. 　　　⑤ 8 p.m.

5 대화를 듣고, 남자의 심정으로 가장 적절한 것을 고르시오.

① bored 　　　　　② happy 　　　　　③ upset
④ jealous 　　　　　⑤ surprised

6 다음 그림의 상황에 가장 적절한 대화를 고르시오.

①   ②   ③   ④   ⑤

7 대화를 듣고, 여자가 남자에게 부탁한 일로 가장 적절한 것을 고르시오.

① 택시 부르기   ② 남동생과 놀아주기   ③ 안내 책자 가져오기
④ 병원에 데려다주기   ⑤ 헬스클럽 다니기

8 다음을 듣고, Venice Water Park에 관해 언급되지 <u>않은</u> 것을 고르시오.

① 개업 날짜   ② 위치   ③ 시설
④ 할인   ⑤ 운영 시간

9 다음을 듣고, 무엇에 관한 설명인지 고르시오.

① 계단   ② 휠체어   ③ 무빙워크
④ 엘리베이터   ⑤ 에스컬레이터

10 다음을 듣고, 두 사람의 대화가 <u>어색한</u> 것을 고르시오.

①   ②   ③   ④   ⑤

11번~20번 문제는 다음 페이지에 ➡

11 대화를 듣고, 여자가 할 일로 가장 적절한 것을 고르시오.

① 사다리 내리기 ② 정리용 박스 구입하기 ③ 중고책 구입하기
④ 진공청소기 가져오기 ⑤ 층계 청소하기

12 다음 축제 배치도를 보면서 대화를 듣고, 두 사람이 샌드위치 부스를 열 구역을 고르시오.

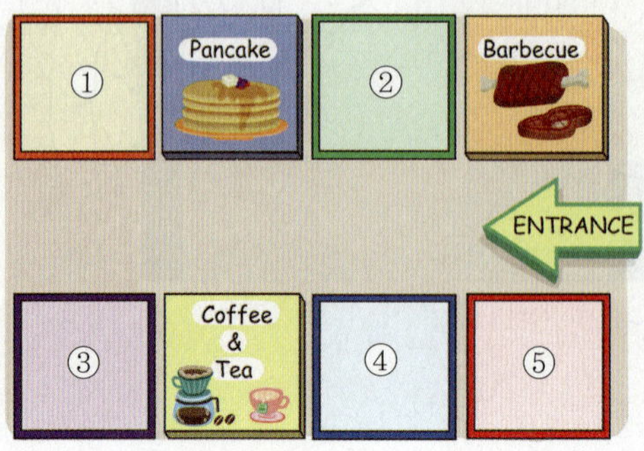

13 대화를 듣고, 두 사람이 국립 박물관에 가기로 한 날짜를 고르시오.

① 5월 17일 ② 5월 18일 ③ 5월 20일
④ 5월 24일 ⑤ 5월 27일

14 대화를 듣고, 남자가 어제 한 일로 가장 적절한 것을 고르시오.

① 책 빌리기 ② 여행 계획하기 ③ 분실물 신고하기
④ 과학 숙제하기 ⑤ 도서 주문하기

15 다음을 듣고, 방송의 목적으로 가장 적절한 것을 고르시오.

① 변경된 교칙을 알리려고
② 운동회 준비 사항을 안내하려고
③ 식목일 행사 참여를 권유하려고
④ 학교 급식실 공사 일정을 안내하려고
⑤ 학교 현장 학습 관련 지침을 공지하려고

16 대화를 듣고 남자가 지불할 금액을 고르시오.

① $13 ② $18 ③ $23 ④ $28 ⑤ $33

17 대화를 듣고, 여자의 마지막 말에 대한 남자의 응답으로 가장 적절한 것을 고르시오.

Man: _______________________________

① I see. I hope you get well soon.

② That's why you couldn't visit her.

③ Yes. Being with family is the best thing.

④ It's good that she wasn't in a car accident.

⑤ I'm sorry your grandmother got hurt badly.

[18~19] 대화를 듣고, 남자의 마지막 말에 대한 여자의 응답으로 가장 적절한 것을 고르시오.

18 **Woman:** _______________________________

① I don't think so. I have a family trip.

② OK. I wish I could go to the trip with you.

③ Yes. You might be able to take Kevin's place.

④ Sure. But you already handed in the application form.

⑤ You're right. She doesn't know anything about the trip.

19 **Woman:** _______________________________

① Too bad. Better luck next time.

② No problem. I can do that for you.

③ That's great! I hope he will allow us to take it.

④ You're right! Taking the stairs will be much faster.

⑤ Never mind. I've already registered for another class.

20 다음 상황 설명을 듣고, Nick이 Claire에게 할 말로 가장 적절한 것을 고르시오.

Nick: Claire, _______________________________

① could you change seats with me?

② when will the bus arrive at school?

③ is it okay to open the window for a while?

④ would you mind closing the window, please?

⑤ I'm worried that we might be late for school.

Dictation Test 14

M3(17)_14_D

Dictation(받아쓰기)은 본문을 받아쓰면서 영어듣기의 집중력을 향상시키고 다양한 표현을 정리하기 위한 영어듣기 학습법입니다. 녹음을 다시 듣고, 빈칸에 알맞은 단어를 써 보세요.
※Dictation의 정답은 듣기 대본의 밑줄 친 부분을 확인하세요. 📖 정답 p. 79

맞은 개수 / 총192개

그림정보파악(대화) 🇺🇸🇬🇧

1. 대화를 듣고, 여자가 구입할 부츠로 가장 적절한 것을 고르시오.

① ②

③ ④

⑤

01
M: How may I help you?

W: I'm looking for some winter boots for myself.

M: Okay. These tall boots are popular this year. They look very trendy.

W: Well, I ________ ________ ________. Do you have any?

M: Sure. How about these ones with zippers on the side?

W: Oh, they look very nice! I think the zippers will be ________, too.

M: We also have the same design with heels.

W: Um... I like the flat ones better, ________ ________ ________. I'll take those ones.

M: Sure. That's a good choice.

대화미언급 🇺🇸🇬🇧

2. 대화를 듣고, Cosypod earphones에 관해 언급되지 않은 것을 고르시오.

① 가격
② 배터리 지속시간
③ 방수기능
④ 제조사
⑤ 색상

02
W: Hey, Nathan. You use the wireless earphones, 'Cosypod,' don't you?

M: Yes, I use them all the time. Why?

W: I'm tired of ________ ________ ________ ________. So, I'm thinking of getting new wireless ones.

M: Good idea. They're really comfortable, and mine only cost $50.

W: That's cheaper than I thought. How long do they stay charged?

M: They ________ ________ 5 hours once charged.

W: That will be long enough. Do they have any additional functions?

M: Well, they provide ________ __________ and they are waterproof.

W: I see. What colors do they come in?

M: ________ ________ ________ white, black and gold.

W: Okay, thanks.

3. 대화를 듣고, 남자가 여자에게 전화한 목적으로 가장 적절한 것을 고르시오.

① 시험 범위를 물어보려고
② 숙제가 무엇인지 물어보려고
③ Karen의 안부를 물어보려고
④ 숙제를 도와달라고 부탁하려고
⑤ 선생님께 말을 전해달라고 하려고

03 (Telephone rings.)

M: Hi, Karen. It's me, Alex.

W: Oh, hi. Are you okay? Ms. Gage told us that you couldn't ________ ________ school because you were sick.

M: I feel ________ ________ now. Thank you for asking.

W: You're welcome. Why did you ________ ________?

M: I wanted to ________ ________ what today's homework is.

W: It is reading our history textbook from page 11 to 15.

M: Thanks. See you tomorrow!

4. 대화를 듣고, 남자가 등록할 수영 수업 시각을 고르시오.

① 6 a.m.　　② 7 a.m.
③ 6 p.m.　　④ 7 p.m.
⑤ 8 p.m.

04 (Telephone rings.)

W: Hello, Daymoon Community Center.

M: Hi, I'd like to ________ ________ the basic swimming lesson program on Monday and Wednesday.

W: Okay. What time do you want to register for?

M: I want the morning class. ________ ________ ________ or 7 a.m. is fine.

W: Sorry, but the morning classes are both full.

다음 페이지에 계속 ➡

M: Oh, I see. Then which class is _________?

W: There are still a few spots available for evening lessons.

M: Then, I'd like to _________ _________ _________ the 7 p.m. class.

W: Sure. Can I have your name, please?

M: It's Kevin Lee.

W: All right. Please bring your ID card on the first day.

5. 대화를 듣고, 남자의 심정으로 가장 적절한 것을 고르시오.
   ① bored
   ② happy
   ③ upset
   ④ jealous
   ⑤ surprised

05

W: Ron, what's wrong?

M: You know my parents _________ a dog last week, right?

W: Yes, I remember. You were so excited.

M: He is very sick. I don't think his _________ _________ took care of him _________.

W: Oh, no! But, will he be okay?

M: I'm not sure. I just wish there were more I _________ _________ _________ _________.

W: I'm so sorry, Ron.

M: I don't know what I'd do without him.

6. 다음 그림의 상황에 가장 적절한 대화를 고르시오.

   ①   ②
   ③   ④
   ⑤

06

① W: Hello, how may I help you?

   M: I'm here to _________ _________ _________ new contact lenses.

② W: Excuse me. You dropped your wallet.

   M: Oh, my. Thank you for letting me know.

③ W: Can you cover your right eye and read this letter?

   M: Um… I can't _________ _________ _________.

④ W: Oh, no. I forgot to bring my glasses.

M: Don't worry. I'll show you my notes later.

⑤ W: Can you __________ __________ __________

the cafeteria?

M: Sure. It's this way.

7. 대화를 듣고, 여자가 남자에게 부탁한 일로 가장 적절한 것을 고르시오.

① 택시 부르기
② 남동생과 놀아주기
③ 안내 책자 가져오기
④ 병원에 데려다주기
⑤ 헬스클럽 다니기

07 W: John, are you going to ________ ________?

M: Yes, I am. Why?

W: I'm thinking of joining.

M: That's great. ________ ________ ________.

W: Not today. I have to take my brother to the

hospital.

M: Right. Can I ________ ________ ________ ________ on

my way?

W: It's OK. We're taking a taxi. But can you bring me

a __________ from the gym?

M: Sure, no problem.

8. 다음을 듣고, Venice Water Park에 관해 언급되지 않은 것을 고르시오.

① 개업 날짜   ② 위치
③ 시설   ④ 할인
⑤ 운영 시간

08 W: Do you want to have some excitement this

summer? Then, come to the Venice Water Park.

Our new park will open for the summer on

May 30. It's conveniently located in Venice,

and is ________ __________ from the city. You

can enjoy a variety of __________ at the park

including swimming pools, water slides, water

playgrounds, and more. ________ ________

________ ________, we will offer 40% off tickets

until June 30. Please visit our website to find out

more!

다음 페이지에 계속 ➡

9. 다음을 듣고, 무엇에 관한 설명인지 고르시오.

① 계단
② 휠체어
③ 무빙워크
④ 엘리베이터
⑤ 에스컬레이터

09 W: This is a ________ ________ ____________. You use it to go up and down between floors. It is usually square in shape. You can press the number button on the wall inside to ________ ________ ________ you want to go to. People use this instead of taking the stairs in a building. It's very ________ and saves time. That's why most tall buildings these days have one of these inside.

10. 다음을 듣고, 두 사람의 대화가 <u>어색한</u> 것을 고르시오.

①　　　②
③　　　④
⑤

10 ① W: How long do I have to wait to get my order?

M: It will arrive in two days.

② W: Why don't we ________ ________ ________ for 30 minutes?

M: That sounds great.

③ W: I can't start my computer.

M: Have you checked that it's plugged in?

④ W: Isn't it cold in here?

M: I'll get you something to ________ ________.

⑤ W: Where is the fitting room?

M: I'll clean my room ________ ________ ________.

11. 대화를 듣고, 여자가 할 일로 가장 적절
한 것을 고르시오.
① 사다리 내리기
② 정리용 박스 구입하기
③ 중고책 구입하기
④ 진공청소기 가져오기
⑤ 충계 청소하기

11
W: Honey, aren't we supposed to ________ ________
________ ________ today?
M: You're right. ________ ________ ________ some
boxes up to put things in.
W: Then let's do it now. Oh, what do you want to do
with the books?
M: The books in the attic? We don't read them
anymore, so let's sell them.
W: Good idea. Are the boxes upstairs?
M: Yes, I'll move them to the attic.
W: Then, I'll bring the vacuum cleaner. ________
________ ________ lots of dust.

12. 다음 축제 배치도를 보면서 대화를 듣고,
두 사람이 샌드위치 부스를 열 구역을 고
르시오.

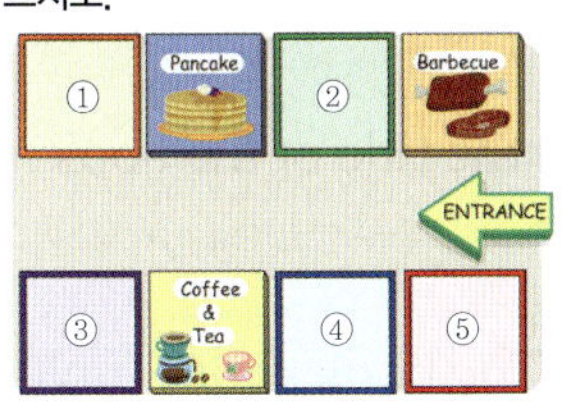

12
W: The school food festival is next week. Where shall
we set up our sandwich booth?
M: I think we should ________ ________ ________ next
to the barbecue booth.
W: I agree. There could be too much smoke.
M: How about the place ________ ________ ________
________ of the pancake booth?
W: Well, let's try to avoid the sections at the far
end. We'll sell more if we're ________ ________
________ ________.
M: Right. Then we have two choices left.
W: Why don't we go directly next to the coffee
and tea booth? Those drinks ________ ________
________ our sandwiches.
M: Sounds perfect!

다음 페이지에 계속 ➡

13. 대화를 듣고, 두 사람이 국립 박물관에 가기로 한 날짜를 고르시오.

① 5월 17일
② 5월 18일
③ 5월 20일
④ 5월 24일
⑤ 5월 27일

13

W: Hey, Liam. How about going to the National Museum on our trip?

M: But we are traveling to a ________ ________. The National Museum is in Seoul.

W: They ________ ________ ________. It's right in the city we are visiting.

M: Oh, good. Then, let's go there on May 17th.

W: That's the first day of our trip. We won't have time.

M: How about ________ ________ ________? On the 18th.

W: We booked a visit to a petting zoo on the 18th. How about May 24th?

M: That's ________ ________ ________ of the trip. Sounds great.

14. 대화를 듣고, 남자가 어제 한 일로 가장 적절한 것을 고르시오.

① 책 빌리기
② 여행 계획하기
③ 분실물 신고하기
④ 과학 숙제하기
⑤ 도서 주문하기

14

W: Thomas, I can't remember the title of the book ________ ________.

M: Which one do you mean? The book about travel to Peru?

W: No. It was science fiction. Something about space travel.

M: Oh, it's *Mike 8*. That's the title.

W: Right. Can I ________ ________ ________ ________?

M: You can. But you'll have to wait for a couple of days.

W: Why? Did someone else borrow it?

M: No, I lost it. So I ________ ________ ________ online yesterday.

W: I see. You really like the book!

15. 다음을 듣고, 방송의 목적으로 가장 적절한 것을 고르시오.

① 변경된 교칙을 알리려고
② 운동회 준비 사항을 안내하려고
③ 식목일 행사 참여를 권유하려고
④ 학교 급식실 공사 일정을 안내하려고
⑤ 학교 현장 학습 관련 지침을 공지하려고

15 W: Attention, students! This is Mrs. Clarkson, your school principal. We have a field trip _________ next Wednesday to Seoul Botanic Park and I'd like to provide you with _________ _________ _________. First, we'll meet in the school courtyard at 8:30 a.m. Second, wear comfortable clothing and footwear since we'll be _________ _________ a lot. Finally, bring a packed lunch and a water bottle as we will be _________ _________ _________ _________ _________. Let's all stay safe and have fun!

16. 대화를 듣고 남자가 지불할 금액을 고르시오.

① $13　　② $18
③ $23　　④ $28
⑤ $33

16 W: Hello, sir. How can I help you?

M: How much is it for the chocolate cake and the muffins?

W: The chocolate cake is $6 a piece and muffins are $5 each.

M: I'd like three pieces of chocolate cake and two peanut butter muffins, please.

W: Okay. If you _________ _________ _________ and get a membership, you can get $5 _________ _________ _________.

M: Oh, I'll do it then. *[Pause]* I've done it.

W: Can I see your phone, please? Okay, now you can _________ _________ _________.

M: Thanks. I'll pay by credit card.

다음 페이지에 계속 ➡

17. 대화를 듣고, 여자의 마지막 말에 대한 남자의 응답으로 가장 적절한 것을 고르시오.

Man: ___________________

① I see. I hope you get well soon.
② That's why you couldn't visit her.
③ Yes. Being with family is the best thing.
④ It's good that she wasn't in a car accident.
⑤ I'm sorry your grandmother got hurt badly.

17

M: Hi, Laura. Why didn't you come to school yesterday?

W: My grandmother was in a ________ __________, so my family went to see her.

M: I'm ________ _______ _______ that. I hope she didn't get hurt too badly.

W: Luckily, she didn't ________ _______ at all. She was just a little shocked by the accident.

M: I understand. So, you went to comfort her.

W: That's right. I think she _______ ______ _______ after seeing us.

M: Yes. Being with family is the best thing.

18. 대화를 듣고, 남자의 마지막 말에 대한 여자의 응답으로 가장 적절한 것을 고르시오.

Woman: ___________________

① I don't think so. I have a family trip.
② OK. I wish I could go to the trip with you.
③ Yes. You might be able to take Kevin's place.
④ Sure. But you already handed in the application form.
⑤ You're right. She doesn't know anything about the trip.

18

W: Josh, are you going on the ________ _______ next month?

M: No, ________ _______ _______. How about you?

W: I'm going. It'll be really exciting, and I'm looking forward to it. Why aren't you going?

M: I really want to, but I forgot to ________ _______ the application form. I'm very disappointed.

W: Well, I heard that Kevin handed in the form but can't go because he has ________ _______ _______.

M: Really? Then I should go and talk to Mrs. Park about it.

W: Yes. You might be able to take Kevin's place.

19. 대화를 듣고, 남자의 마지막 말에 대한 여자의 응답으로 가장 적절한 것을 고르시오.

Woman: _______________

① Too bad. Better luck next time.
② No problem. I can do that for you.
③ That's great! I hope he will allow us to take it.
④ You're right! Taking the stairs will be much faster.
⑤ Never mind. I've already registered for another class.

19

M: Hi, Sally! Have you signed up for the computer coding class?

W: Unfortunately, it was ________ ________ ________ when I tried.

M: I couldn't register, either. I guess a lot of students wanted to take that class.

W: What are you going to do now?

M: I'm ________ ________ ________ ________ online.

W: There's an online coding class?

M: Yes, but if we want to take it online, we are ________ ________ ________ ________ Mr. Smith first.

W: I see. Then let's go together to talk to him now. Do you know where his office is?

M: It's ________ ________ ________ ________ in this building.

W: That's great! I hope he will allow us to take it.

20. 다음 상황 설명을 듣고, Nick이 Claire에게 할 말로 가장 적절한 것을 고르시오.

Nick: Claire, _______________

① could you change seats with me?
② when will the bus arrive at school?
③ is it okay to open the window for a while?
④ would you mind closing the window, please?
⑤ I'm worried that we might be late for school.

20

M: Nick is a middle school student. Today, he is ________ ________ ________ ________ from school by bus as usual. Claire, his classmate is sitting in the seat in front of him. The window by her seat is ________ ________. The wind is blowing pretty hard and after a few minutes, Nick starts to feel cold. So, he would like to ask Claire if she could ________ ________ ________ beside her. In this situation, what would Nick most likely say to Claire?

Nick: Claire, would you mind closing the window, please?

Words & Expressions Review 14

● 다음 단어를 암기하세요.

문제	번호	단어	뜻
1	1	trendy	최신 유행의
	2	convenient	편리한
2	3	deal with	~을 다루다, 처리하다
	4	waterproof	방수의
3	5	textbook	교과서
4	6	register for	~에 등록하다
	7	available	이용할 수 있는, 구할 수 있는
5	8	adopt	입양하다
	9	previous	이전의
	10	owner	주인, 소유자
	11	properly	제대로, 적절히
6	12	letter	글자, 문자
	13	note	(기억을 돕기 위한) 메모
7	14	gym	체육관
	15	give A a ride	A를 태워주다
	16	brochure	(안내용) 책자
8	17	be located in ~	~에 위치하다
	18	a variety of	다양한, 각종
10	19	plug in	플러그를 꽂다, 전원을 연결하다
	20	clear out	청소하다
11	21	attic	다락
	22	upstairs	위층에, 2층에

문제	번호	단어	뜻
11	23	vacuum cleaner	진공청소기
12	24	set up	설치하다
13	25	rural area	지방, 시골 지역
	26	the day after	그 다음날, 익일
	27	recommend	추천하다
14	28	a couple of days	이틀 정도
	29	copy	(책, 신문 등의) 한 부
15	30	botanic park	식물원
	31	guideline	지침, 가이드라인
	32	courtyard	안뜰, 안마당
	33	packed lunch	도시락
16	34	install	설치하다
17	35	shocked	충격을 받은
	36	comfort	위로하다, 위로, 편안
18	37	hand in ~	~을 제출하다
	38	application form	신청서
19	39	sign up for	~에 등록하다, 신청하다
	40	consult	상의하다, 상담하다
20	41	on one's way home	집으로 돌아가는 길에
	42	as usual	평소대로, 늘 그렇듯이
	43	wide open	활짝 열린, 크게 벌어진
	44	pretty	꽤, 어느 정도

● 왼쪽 단어장의 뜻이 보이지 않게 반으로 접고, 학습한 단어의 뜻을 아래 빈칸에 적어주세요.

1	deal with	23	convenient
2	adopt	24	copy
3	recommend	25	letter
4	plug in	26	waterproof
5	a couple of days	27	install
6	attic	28	previous
7	set up	29	botanic park
8	a variety of	30	as usual
9	gym	31	register for
10	available	32	comfort
11	brochure	33	properly
12	hand in ~	34	packed lunch
13	note	35	upstairs
14	application form	36	vacuum cleaner
15	clear out	37	the day after
16	rural area	38	guideline
17	be located in ~	39	consult
18	courtyard	40	pretty
19	trendy	41	give A a ride
20	sign up for	42	shocked
21	on one's way home	43	textbook
22	wide open	44	owner

정답 및 해석 p. 85

1 대화를 듣고, 여자가 구입할 스노글로브를 고르시오.

①  ②  ③  ④  ⑤ 

2 대화를 듣고, 스케이트 강습에 관해 언급되지 <u>않은</u> 것을 고르시오.

① 강습 시간 ② 강습 장소 ③ 수업료
④ 지도 강사 ⑤ 준비물

3 대화를 듣고, 여자가 남자에게 전화한 목적으로 가장 적절한 것을 고르시오.

① 녹음실 위치를 확인하려고 ② 녹음기 주문을 취소하려고
③ 녹음 일정을 변경하려고 ④ 교재 편집을 맡기려고
⑤ 대본 집필을 부탁하려고

4 대화를 듣고, 남자가 예약한 애견 미용실 시각을 고르시오.

① 9 a.m. ② 10 a.m. ③ 12 p.m. ④ 3 p.m. ⑤ 5 p.m.

5 대화를 듣고, 남자의 심정으로 가장 적절한 것을 고르시오.

① scared ② shy ③ regretful
④ excited ⑤ disappointed

6 다음 그림의 상황에 가장 적절한 대화를 고르시오.

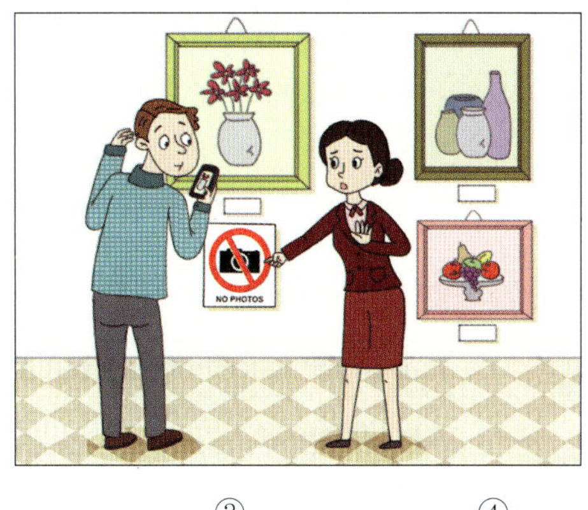

① ② ③ ④ ⑤

7 대화를 듣고, 남자가 여자에게 부탁한 일로 가장 적절한 것을 고르시오.

① 약 사다 주기　　② 병원 같이 가기　　③ 과일 사다 주기
④ 건강 검진 받기　　⑤ 시장에 데려다주기

8 다음을 듣고, 분실물에 대해 언급되지 <u>않은</u> 것을 고르시오.

① 발견 장소　　② 발견 시간　　③ 색깔
④ 크기　　⑤ 보관 장소

9 다음을 듣고, 무엇에 관한 설명인지 고르시오.

① 보일러　　② 냉장고　　③ 선풍기
④ 에어컨　　⑤ 가습기

10 다음을 듣고, 두 사람의 대화가 <u>어색한</u> 것을 고르시오.

① ② ③ ④ ⑤

11번~20번 문제는 다음 페이지에 ➡

11 대화를 듣고, 여자가 대화 직후에 할 일로 가장 적절한 것을 고르시오.

① 연습 일정 조정하기 ② 대회 규칙 확인하기 ③ 대회 파트너 제안하기
④ 코치에게 조언 구하기 ⑤ 배드민턴 라켓 구입하기

12 다음 표를 보면서 대화를 듣고, 남자가 구입할 탁상용 선풍기를 고르시오.

	Table Fans	Fan Size	Working Time	Color
①	A	17 cm	9 hours	Blue
②	B	17 cm	9 hours	White
③	C	17 cm	7 hours	Blue
④	D	13 cm	9 hours	White
⑤	E	13 cm	7 hours	Blue

13 대화를 듣고, 두 사람이 봉사 활동을 하기로 한 날짜를 고르시오.

① 8월 1일 ② 8월 7일 ③ 8월 14일
④ 8월 21일 ⑤ 8월 28일

14 대화를 듣고, 남자가 어제 한 일로 가장 적절한 것을 고르시오.

① 농구 경기 관람하기 ② 방과 후 수업 듣기 ③ 농구 연습하기
④ 병원 가기 ⑤ 학원 가기

15 다음을 듣고, 방송의 목적으로 가장 적절한 것을 고르시오.

① 교무실에서의 예절을 알리려고 ② 학교 웹사이트 이용을 권장하려고
③ 학교 행사 날짜의 변경을 알리려고 ④ 운동장에서의 안전 규칙을 설명하려고
⑤ 일시적인 정문 사용 불가를 알리려고

16 대화를 듣고, 남자가 지불할 금액을 고르시오.

① $80 ② $99 ③ $102 ④ $107 ⑤ $110

17 대화를 듣고, 남자의 마지막 말에 대한 여자의 응답으로 가장 적절한 것을 고르시오.

Woman: _______________________________________

① I'd like to pay by credit card, please.

② Yes, a laptop bag would be convenient to have.

③ Buy a laptop and get a wireless mouse for free!

④ Then, I'll take this laptop. Thanks for helping me.

⑤ No, touch-screens consume more power than regular displays.

[18~19] 대화를 듣고, 여자의 마지막 말에 대한 남자의 응답으로 가장 적절한 것을 고르시오.

18 **Man:** _______________________________________

① What's for dinner? I'm hungry.

② I used to be a marathon runner.

③ I feel tired today. Let's start tomorrow.

④ An apple a day keeps the doctor away.

⑤ I've never seen you at the gym.

19 **Man:** _______________________________________

① That's a great idea. Let's go watch the play.

② I don't think you relate to the character.

③ I'm going to arrive late at school.

④ Just believe in yourself. Go for it!

⑤ I'm afraid I might not do well.

20 다음 상황 설명을 듣고, Kevin이 Erin에게 할 말로 가장 적절한 것을 고르시오.

Kevin: Erin, _______________________________________

① would you like a hamster for your birthday?

② you're really good at taking care of animals.

③ caring for a pet takes a lot of time and effort.

④ there are many useful video clips on the Internet.

⑤ watching videos is not the best way to learn new things.

Dictation Test 15

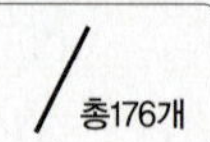

M3(17)_15_D

Dictation(받아쓰기)은 본문을 받아쓰면서 영어듣기의 집중력을 향상시키고 다양한 표현을 정리하기 위한 영어듣기 학습법입니다. 녹음을 다시 듣고, 빈칸에 알맞은 단어를 써 보세요.
※Dictation의 정답은 듣기 대본의 밑줄 친 부분을 확인하세요.

📖 정답 p. 85

맞은 개수 / 총176개

---

1. 대화를 듣고, 여자가 구입할 스노글로브를 고르시오.

①  ② 

③  ④ 

⑤ 

01

M: What are you looking for, Daisy?

W: Hey, Jim. I want to buy a snow globe _________ _________ _________ of Paris. I collect snow globes.

M: I didn't know that. Then, how about this snow globe with a French girl holding the flag? It looks cute.

W: Well, I _________ _________ a globe with the Eiffel Tower.

M: What about this one? It has a _________ beside the tower.

W: Cool. And I like the word 'PARIS' _________ _________ the snow globe. I'll buy this one.

---

2. 대화를 듣고, 스케이트 강습에 관해 언급되지 <u>않은</u> 것을 고르시오.

① 강습 시간
② 강습 장소
③ 수업료
④ 지도 강사
⑤ 준비물

02

M: Felicity, I'm going to take skating lessons. Are you interested?

W: Yeah, I am. When are the lessons?

M: They're every Saturday, from 10 a.m. to 12 p.m.

W: Cool. They're at the Central Ice Rink, right?

M: That's right. _________ _________ _________ _________?

W: No, I've never skated. How much do we have to pay?

M: It's 10 dollars _________ ________. We can learn all

the basic skills during 4 sessions.

W: Okay. Is there anything we need to bring?

M: No. We can ________ ________ ________ ________

there.

W: Great. Let's sign up!

3. 대화를 듣고, 여자가 남자에게 전화한 목적으로 가장 적절한 것을 고르시오.

① 녹음실 위치를 확인하려고
② 녹음기 주문을 취소하려고
③ 녹음 일정을 변경하려고
④ 교재 편집을 맡기려고
⑤ 대본 집필을 부탁하려고

03 *(Telephone rings.)*

W: Hello, is this Andrew Bint's phone?

M: Yes, who's this, please?

W: Hi, this is Michelle from your ________

__________ __________. Is it a good time to talk?

M: Sure, what can I do for you?

W: ________ ________ ________ ________ your

recording schedule. Can we record on Friday from

1:30 to 3:30 instead of Wednesday? The scripts are

not ready yet. Sorry.

M: That's all right. ________ ________ ________

my schedule first. *(pause)* I think I can. So the

recording is on Friday.

W: Right. Thanks a lot. Have a nice day!

다음 페이지에 계속 ➡

4. 대화를 듣고, 남자가 예약한 애견 미용실
   시각을 고르시오.

   ① 9 a.m.　　② 10 a.m.
   ③ 12 p.m.　　④ 3 p.m.
   ⑤ 5 p.m.

04 *[Telephone rings.]*

W: This is Selena's pet salon. How can I help you?

M: Hi, I'd like to get my dog _________. Can I _________

_________ _________ at 9 a.m. tomorrow?

W: Sorry, but we open at 10 a.m. And we are _________

_________ tomorrow morning.

M: Then, is there a time available in the afternoon?

W: We have _________ at 3 p.m. and 5 p.m.

M: I can come in at 5. I'll visit then.

W: All right. Can I have your dog's name, please?

M: Her name is Coco.

W: I've got Coco on the list. We'll see you tomorrow.

5. 대화를 듣고, 남자의 심정으로 가장 적절
   한 것을 고르시오.

   ① scared　　② shy
   ③ regretful　　④ excited
   ⑤ disappointed

05 W: Bill, you look different today.

M: I'm _________ _________ _________ person, Martha. I

got onto the school basketball team finally!

W: Really? That's great! You really wanted to join the

team.

M: I practiced hard last summer. And the coach

_________ _________ this time.

W: I'm so happy for you. So, can I see you on court at

the next match?

M: I hope so. I _________ _________ for the first practice!

W: Good luck to you!

6. 다음 그림의 상황에 가장 적절한 대화를 고르시오.

① ② ③ ④ ⑤

06 ① W: _________ _________ go to an art gallery today?

M: Maybe next time. I'm too tired today.

② W: I'm afraid you're not allowed to take photos here.

M: Oh, I didn't see the sign. Sorry.

③ W: What are you going to draw for the art contest?

M: I'm going to draw some flowers _________

_________ _________.

④ W: Excuse me. Could you take a picture for us?

M: Sure. Let me _________ _________ _________.

⑤ W: You shouldn't use your cell phone during the concert.

M: Don't worry. I've already _________ _________

_________.

7. 대화를 듣고, 남자가 여자에게 부탁한 일로 가장 적절한 것을 고르시오.

① 약 사다 주기
② 병원 같이 가기
③ 과일 사다 주기
④ 건강 검진 받기
⑤ 시장에 데려다주기

07 M: Hey, where are you _________ _________?

W: I'm going to the market for some fruit.

M: Can you _________ _________ _________, too?

W: No problem.

M: Thanks. I had my checkup at the hospital last week, and the doctor said that I need to eat healthy.

W: That's what _________ _________ _________ you every day.

M: I know. I'm really going to try to _________ my lifestyle this time.

다음 페이지에 계속 ➡

8. 다음을 듣고, 분실물에 대해 언급되지 <u>않</u>은 것을 고르시오.

① 발견 장소
② 발견 시간
③ 색깔
④ 크기
⑤ 보관 장소

08 M: May I ________ ________ ________, please? We've found a cellphone. It was found on a chair in the ________ ________ ________ ________ lunch time. It is a black smartphone with cute puppy stickers ________ ________ ________. If you are looking for a phone like this, you will be able to find your phone at the ________ ________ on the second floor.

9. 다음을 듣고, 무엇에 관한 설명인지 고르시오.

① 보일러
② 냉장고
③ 선풍기
④ 에어컨
⑤ 가습기

09 M: This is an electric home device. You usually use this during the summer. It comes in many different shapes. It sometimes can be ________ ________ ________ ________ or ceiling. People commonly use this when they need to cool the room. Sometimes, it is used to ________ ________ ________ ________. However, if you use this device too much, you could get sick. Moreover, your electricity bill could ________ ________ ________ ________ ________ if you use it too much.

10. 다음을 듣고, 두 사람의 대화가 <u>어색한</u> 것을 고르시오.

①   ②
③   ④
⑤

10

① M: What did you do on Sunday?

   W: I played video games all day.

② M: How long does it take to get to school?

   W: It takes about 15 minutes _________ _________.

③ M: Do you _________ _________ _________ in the

     morning?

   W: No, I usually don't have time to do that.

④ M: Why didn't you come to basketball practice

     today?

   W: One of my hobbies is playing basketball.

⑤ M: Where did you buy that scarf?

   W: I didn't buy it. I _________ _________ _________

     _________.

2024 영어듣기능력평가 2회 11번 변형

11. 대화를 듣고, 여자가 대화 직후에 할 일로 가장 적절한 것을 고르시오.

① 연습 일정 조정하기
② 대회 규칙 확인하기
③ 대회 파트너 제안하기
④ 코치에게 조언 구하기
⑤ 배드민턴 라켓 구입하기

11

M: Maria, are you planning to __________

     __________ the school badminton tournament?

W: I wanted to, but all the singles matches are already

   full.

M: Oh, that's too bad. What about the mixed

   doubles?

W: __________ __________ __________ try that, but I

   don't have a partner.

M: How about asking Allen? He's really good at

   badminton.

W: That's a great idea! Do you think he would want

     to be my partner?

M: I'm sure he would. You should ask him before

     __________ __________ does.

W: You're right. I'll go ask him right now.

다음 페이지에 계속 ➡

12. 다음 표를 보면서 대화를 듣고, 남자가 구입할 탁상용 선풍기를 고르시오.

	Table Fans	Fan Size	Working Time	Color
①	A	17 cm	9 hours	Blue
②	B	17 cm	9 hours	White
③	C	17 cm	7 hours	Blue
④	D	13 cm	9 hours	White
⑤	E	13 cm	7 hours	Blue

12
W: Hi, how may I help you?
M: Hello, I'm looking for a ________ ________ for my desk.
W: All right. We have two sizes, 17 cm and 13 cm.
M: I think the bigger one would be better.
W: Okay. The fans are ________, and they can ________ ________ 9 hours or 7 hours.
M: I'm in the office for at least 8 hours, so, I'd prefer the one that runs ________ ________.
W: Sure. There are two colors, blue and white.
M: I'll take the blue one.
W: Okay. Please wait a second.

13. 대화를 듣고, 두 사람이 봉사 활동을 하기로 한 날짜를 고르시오.
① 8월 1일
② 8월 7일
③ 8월 14일
④ 8월 21일
⑤ 8월 28일

13
M: Brenda, have you decided where ________ ________?
W: I'm thinking of helping out at a local farm. What about you, Nick?
M: I'm thinking of doing the same. You know, August 7th is blueberry ________ ________.
W: Oh, I can't volunteer that day. Why don't you join me the week after that? We can still pick other fruit.
M: I have a cooking class on August 14th. What about August 21st?
W: August 21st ________ ________ ________!
M: Then, let's go on that day.

14. 대화를 듣고, 남자가 어제 한 일로 가장 적절한 것을 고르시오.
① 농구 경기 관람하기
② 방과 후 수업 듣기
③ 농구 연습하기
④ 병원 가기
⑤ 학원 가기

14
W: Hey, Glen. I didn't see you at the ________ yesterday.
M: Hi, Diane. Yeah, I couldn't go.
W: Why not?
M: Two days ago, I played basketball after school with some friends, and I ________ ________ ________.

W: Oh, no! Are you okay?

M: I'm okay, but I went to the hospital yesterday __________ __________ __________.

W: What did the doctor say?

M: The doctor said that it's not a serious injury.

W: __________ __________ __________.

15. 다음을 듣고, 방송의 목적으로 가장 적절한 것을 고르시오.

① 교무실에서의 예절을 알리려고
② 학교 웹사이트 이용을 권장하려고
③ 학교 행사 날짜의 변경을 알리려고
④ 운동장에서의 안전 규칙을 설명하려고
⑤ 일시적인 정문 사용 불가를 알리려고

15

W: Hello, students. Attention, please. As you already know, we __________ __________ __________ our main gate. Starting Monday, you won't be able to use the main gate for two weeks. We're sorry for the inconvenience, but it's __________ for your safety. You can use the back gate from July 6th to 20th. Detailed information is __________ on our school website. If you have any questions, please contact your teacher or come to the teachers' office.

2025 영어듣기능력평가 1회 16번 변형

16. 대화를 듣고, 남자가 지불할 금액을 고르시오.

① $80 ② $99
③ $102 ④ $107
⑤ $110

16

W: Welcome to Speedy Car Rental!

M: Hi, how much does it cost to rent a car for one day?

W: It's 80 dollars.

M: I also need __________.

W: Insurance is 30 dollars, but we __________ a 10% __________ on the car rental if you are renting the car for just one day.

M: Oh, that's nice. You mean I can get a discount on the total price?

W: The 10% discount __________ __________ the car rental only. The insurance isn't included in the discount.

M: All right, that's __________. I'll use my card to pay.

다음 페이지에 계속 ➡

17. 대화를 듣고, 남자의 마지막 말에 대한 여자의 응답으로 가장 적절한 것을 고르시오.

Woman: ___________________

① I'd like to pay by credit card, please.
② Yes, a laptop bag would be convenient to have.
③ Buy a laptop and get a wireless mouse for free!
④ Then, I'll take this laptop. Thanks for helping me.
⑤ No, touch-screens consume more power than regular displays.

17
M: Welcome to Bright Electronics. How can I help you?

W: Hi, ___________ ___________ ___________ purchasing a new laptop.

M: Sure. Are you looking for a standard size or something ___________ ___________ like a notebook?

W: I need a standard size laptop.

M: All right. Do you prefer a touchscreen or a regular display?

W: I think a regular display will ___________ ___________ ___________ better.

M: Great. Would you also like to add any accessories like a mouse or a laptop bag?

W: Yes, a laptop bag would be convenient to have.

---

18. 대화를 듣고, 여자의 마지막 말에 대한 남자의 응답으로 가장 적절한 것을 고르시오.

Man: ___________________

① What's for dinner? I'm hungry.
② I used to be a marathon runner.
③ I feel tired today. Let's start tomorrow.
④ An apple a day keeps the doctor away.
⑤ I've never seen you at the gym.

18
W: Honey, how was your checkup this morning?

M: The doctor said everything's fine, but he did mention that I ___________ ___________ ___________ ___________.

W: He's definitely right about that. You haven't exercised in ages.

M: Okay, I'll start exercising, but I don't know where to start.

W: You can always ___________ ___________ ___________ ___________.

M: I think you're right. Why don't you start jogging ___________ ___________ ___________ ?

W: Hmm… Okay. Then let's start tonight, shall we?

M: I feel tired today. Let's start tomorrow.

19. 대화를 듣고, 여자의 마지막 말에 대한 남자의 응답으로 가장 적절한 것을 고르시오.

Man: _______________

① That's a great idea. Let's go watch the play.
② I don't think you relate to the character.
③ I'm going to arrive late at school.
④ Just believe in yourself. Go for it!
⑤ I'm afraid I might not do well.

19
W: I'm so nervous. I wonder if I should just back out of the play.
M: What's the matter? You've been waiting to be in this play for so long.
W: I know, but I'm afraid I might _______ _______.
M: We both know how much you wanted to get the part in the school play. Don't let this opportunity _______ _______ _______. You're a great performer!
W: You really think so?
M: Of course!
W: Hmm… You're right. I should _______ _______ _______. Thanks a lot, Phil.
M: Just believe in yourself. Go for it!

20. 다음 상황 설명을 듣고, Kevin이 Erin에게 할 말로 가장 적절한 것을 고르시오.

Kevin: Erin, _______________

① would you like a hamster for your birthday?
② you're really good at taking care of animals.
③ caring for a pet takes a lot of time and effort.
④ there are many useful video clips on the Internet.
⑤ watching videos is not the best way to learn new things.

20
M: Erin gets a hamster from her parents on her birthday. She always wanted a pet, so she is _______. But she doesn't know _______ _______ _______ _______ of a hamster. Erin asks her classmate, Kevin, who also has a pet hamster, where to start. When Kevin first got his pet, he _______ _______ _______ _______ _______ from video clips on the Internet. So, Kevin would like to suggest to Erin that she watch video clips online. In this situation, what would Kevin most likely say to Erin?
Kevin: Erin, there are many useful video clips on the Internet.

Words & Expressions Review 15

● 다음 단어를 암기하세요.

문제	번호	단어	뜻
1	1	souvenir	기념품
	2	flag	깃발
2	3	session	수업[강의] 시간
	4	gear	(특정 활동에 필요한) 장비
3	5	agency	회사, 기관
	6	record	녹음하다
	7	script	대본
4	8	groom	손질하다, 다듬다
	9	available	이용할 수 있는
	10	opening	빈자리, 공석
5	11	regretful	후회하는
6	12	take a picture	사진을 찍다
	13	turn ~ off	(전기, 가스, 수도 등을) 끄다
	14	be off to ~	~로 가다
7	15	checkup	건강 검진, 대조, 검사
	16	lifestyle	생활 방식
	17	school cafeteria	학교 식당
8	18	principal	교장, 주요한
	19	office	사무실
	20	hang	걸리다, 걸다, 매달리다
9	21	bring ~ down	~을 낮추다, 줄이다
	22	humidity	습도

문제	번호	단어	뜻
9	23	end up	(결국) ~이 되다
	24	on foot	걸어서
10	25	make (the) bed	침대[잠자리]를 정리하다
	26	by oneself	직접, 도움을 받지 않고
11	27	participate in	~에 참가하다
12	28	portable	휴대용의
	29	run	작동하다
13	30	local	지역의, 현지의
	31	work for	~에게 문제없다, 좋다
	32	sprain	삐다, 접지르다
14	33	injury	부상, 상처
	34	that's a relief	다행이다, 안심이다
15	35	renovate	수리하다, 개조하다
	36	detailed	자세한
16	37	insurance	보험, 보험료
17	38	consume	소비하다
	39	mention	말하다, 언급하다
18	40	in ages	오랫동안
	41	used to + 동사	예전에는 ~이었다[했다]
19	42	mess up	망치다, 엉망으로 만들다
20	43	effort	노력, 수고
	44	thrilled	매우 기뻐하는, 흥분된

●왼쪽 단어장의 뜻이 보이지 않게 반으로 접고, 학습한 단어의 뜻을 아래 빈칸에 적어주세요.

1	gear	23	agency
2	that's a relief	24	humidity
3	principal	25	make (the) bed
4	portable	26	local
5	used to + 동사	27	effort
6	end up	28	take a picture
7	flag	29	injury
8	be off to ~	30	hang
9	lifestyle	31	work for
10	insurance	32	office
11	on foot	33	record
12	script	34	session
13	school cafeteria	35	in ages
14	regretful	36	mess up
15	available	37	detailed
16	mention	38	groom
17	sprain	39	checkup
18	participate in	40	renovate
19	by oneself	41	run
20	turn ~ off	42	thrilled
21	consume	43	souvenir
22	opening	44	bring ~ down

정답 및 해석 p. 90

1 대화를 듣고, 남자가 구입할 쓰레기통을 고르시오.

①  ② 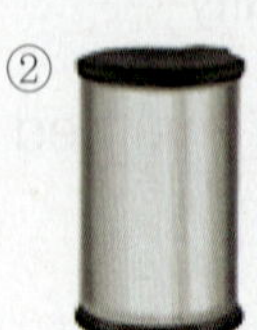 ③  ④  ⑤ 

2 대화를 듣고, Green Art Workshop에 대해 언급되지 <u>않은</u> 것을 고르시오.

① 시작 날짜 ② 워크숍 운영시간 ③ 준비물
④ 활동 내용 ⑤ 참가 비용

3 대화를 듣고, 남자가 여자에게 전화한 목적으로 가장 적절한 것을 고르시오.

① 신규 헬스장을 홍보하려고 ② 헬스장 회원권을 양도하려고
③ 헬스장 샤워실 폐쇄를 안내하려고 ④ 피트니스 수업 일정을 확인하려고
⑤ 헬스장 회원권 연장을 문의하려고

4 대화를 듣고, 남자가 선택한 병원 진료 시각을 고르시오.

① 2 p.m. ② 3 p.m. ③ 4 p.m. ④ 5 p.m. ⑤ 6 p.m.

5 대화를 듣고, 여자의 심정으로 가장 적절한 것을 고르시오.

① scared ② relaxed ③ happy
④ sad ⑤ jealous

6 다음 그림의 상황에 가장 적절한 대화를 고르시오.

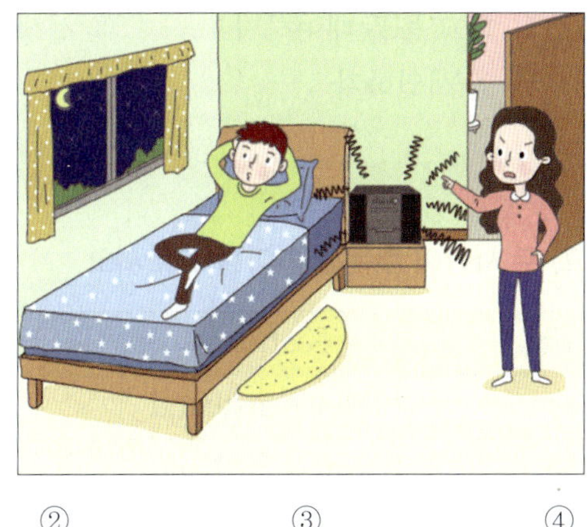

①   ②   ③   ④   ⑤

7 대화를 듣고, 남자가 여자에게 부탁한 일로 가장 적절한 것을 고르시오.

① 책 구매하기   ② 강의실 예약하기
③ 팀 과제 제출하기   ④ 발표 자료 인쇄하기
⑤ 발표 연습에 대해 피드백 주기

8 다음을 듣고, 음악회에 관해 언급되지 <u>않은</u> 것을 고르시오.

① 목적   ② 날짜   ③ 티켓 가격   ④ 연주곡   ⑤ 공연 참가자

9 다음을 듣고, 무엇에 관한 설명인지 고르시오.

① 창문   ② 거울   ③ 유리컵   ④ 접시   ⑤ 카메라

10 다음을 듣고, 두 사람의 대화가 <u>어색한</u> 것을 고르시오.

①   ②   ③   ④   ⑤

11번~20번 문제는 다음 페이지에 ➡

11 대화를 듣고, 여자가 대화 직후에 할 일로 가장 적절한 것을 고르시오.

① 박람회 주제 정하기　　② 학교 물품 대여하기　　③ 선생님께 문의하기
④ 포스터 만들기　　⑤ 앱 시연하기

12 다음 표를 보면서 대화를 듣고, 두 사람이 주문할 치마를 고르시오.

	Model	Material	Feature	Pocket
①	A	Linen	Elastic waistband	×
②	B	Linen	Elastic waistband	○
③	C	Linen	Zipper	×
④	D	Cotton	Elastic waistband	○
⑤	E	Cotton	Zipper	×

13 대화를 듣고, 두 사람이 야시장에 갈 날짜를 고르시오.

① 5월 7일　　② 5월 14일　　③ 5월 21일
④ 6월 14일　　⑤ 6월 21일

14 대화를 듣고, 여자가 어제 한 일로 가장 적절한 것을 고르시오.

① 문학수업 듣기　　② 과제 제출하기　　③ 도서 대출하기
④ 독서 동아리 가입하기　　⑤ 도서 목록 작성하기

15 다음을 듣고, 방송의 목적으로 가장 적절한 것을 고르시오.

① 학교 행사 참여 방법을 안내하려고　　② 휴대전화 사용 제한을 공지하려고
③ 새 스마트폰 제품을 홍보하려고　　④ 교내 안전 수칙을 설명하려고
⑤ 습득된 분실물을 알리려고

16 대화를 듣고, 남자가 블라우스를 사기 위해 지불해야 할 총 금액이 얼마인지 고르시오.

① $20　　② $31　　③ $40　　④ $41　　⑤ $50

17 대화를 듣고, 남자의 마지막 말에 대한 여자의 응답으로 가장 적절한 것을 고르시오.

Woman: ______________________________

① He lives in Brazil now.　② He is the fastest player.

③ He liked to pass the ball.　④ He scored over 1,200 goals.

⑤ He was the best on his team.

[18~19] 대화를 듣고, 여자의 마지막 말에 대한 남자의 응답으로 가장 적절한 것을 고르시오.

18 **Man:** ______________________________

① OK. Let's work together on the report.

② That's great! I would really appreciate it.

③ Too bad. You must miss your sister a lot.

④ In that case, you'd better report to the teacher.

⑤ Sure. He gave me positive feedback on my report.

19 **Man:** ______________________________

① I hope so. But I don't have enough storage space.

② I don't want to become addicted to online games.

③ I used to live in Spain, so I'm good at speaking Spanish.

④ All right, I'll give it a shot. Thanks for telling me about it.

⑤ Learning a foreign language helps improve your memory.

20 다음 상황 설명을 듣고, Helen이 친구에게 할 말로 가장 적절한 것을 고르시오.

Helen: ______________________________

① Why is photography prohibited in this room?

② How long do you want to stay at the gallery?

③ Which painting do you want to take a picture of?

④ Do you want to see the paintings in another room?

⑤ Please look at that sign. We can't take pictures here.

Dictation Test 16

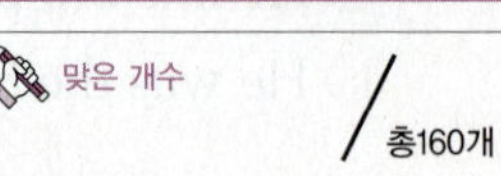
M3(17)_16_D

Dictation(받아쓰기)은 본문을 받아쓰면서 영어듣기의 집중력을 향상시키고 다양한 표현을 정리하기 위한 영어듣기 학습법입니다. **녹음을 다시 듣고, 빈칸에 알맞은 단어를 써 보세요.**
※Dictation의 정답은 듣기 대본의 밑줄 친 부분을 확인하세요.

📖 정답 p. 90

맞은 개수 / 총160개

그림정보파악(대화)

1. 대화를 듣고, 남자가 구입할 쓰레기통을 고르시오.

① ② ③ ④ ⑤

01
W: Welcome to the Home Market. How can I help you?

M: I'm looking for a trash can for my house.

W: I see. Would you ________ a big one or a smaller one?

M: I'll be putting the trash can in my bedroom, so I think a ________ ________ would be nice.

W: All right. Would you prefer a rectangular one or a round one?

M: The round one looks more stylish. The design will match my room.

W: Okay. It ________ ________ two styles. One has a pedal and the other doesn't.

M: I'll take the one with a pedal. It is more ________ to use.

W: Good choice.

2025 영어듣기능력평가 1회 **2번 변형**

대화미언급

2. 대화를 듣고, Green Art Workshop에 대해 언급되지 **않은** 것을 고르시오.

① 시작 날짜
② 워크숍 운영시간
③ 준비물
④ 활동 내용
⑤ 참가 비용

02
(Telephone rings.)

M: Hello. This is Green Art Workshop.

W: Hi. I'm ________ ________ the art workshop. When does it begin?

M: It begins on August 5th.

W: How long does it last?

M: It __________ _________ two days, from 10:00 a.m. to 3:00 p.m.

W: That's great. What kind of activities are included?

M: Participants can try pottery, watercolor painting, and collage making.

W: Sounds fun! How much is the fee for the two-day workshop?

M: It's 50 dollars per person.

W: Wonderful! I'll __________ __________ _________ it.

3. 대화를 듣고, 남자가 여자에게 전화한 목적으로 가장 적절한 것을 고르시오.
   ① 신규 헬스장을 홍보하려고
   ② 헬스장 회원권을 양도하려고
   ③ 헬스장 샤워실 폐쇄를 안내하려고
   ④ 피트니스 수업 일정을 확인하려고
   ⑤ 헬스장 회원권 연장을 문의하려고

03 *(Cellphone rings.)*

W: Hello?

M: Hi, is this Sarah? This is John from FlexFit Gym.

W: Hi, John. Yes, this is Sarah.

M: Due to a pipe ________ issue, our showers will be ________ ______ __________ starting tomorrow.

W: Oh, no! How long will the showers be closed?

M: Approximately one week.

W: I guess I'll have to go home to shower during the repairs. Thanks for the ________ _______, though.

M: I'm so sorry. As compensation for the inconvenience, we'll _______ your membership by one week.

W: Thank you, John. I appreciate it.

4. 대화를 듣고, 남자가 선택한 병원 진료 시각을 고르시오.
   ① 2 p.m.
   ② 3 p.m.
   ③ 4 p.m.
   ④ 5 p.m.
   ⑤ 6 p.m.

04 *(Telephone rings.)*

W: Dr. Howard's office. May I help you?

M: Yes. This is Brad Lee. I'm not going to be able to make it _______ ________ __________ today.

다음 페이지에 계속 ➡

W: No problem, Mr. Lee. Would you like to

___________?

M: Yes. Can I come in next Tuesday at 5 p.m.?

W: I'm sorry, but 5 p.m. is already ________. Does

3 p.m. work for you?

M: No, I could get there by 4 p.m., though.

W: 4 p.m. works for us, too. I'll reschedule your

appointment to 4 p.m. next Tuesday, then.

M: Great. Thanks a lot.

5. 대화를 듣고, 여자의 심정으로 가장 적절한 것을 고르시오.

① scared
② relaxed
③ happy
④ sad
⑤ jealous

05 M: What's wrong, Nina? Why are you just standing

in front of your locker?

W: Jay, the lock on my locker is ________.

M: What? What happened?

W: I don't know. I just came from class and ________

________ ________ ________.

M: Somebody picked the lock?!

W: I think so. Now I'm afraid to open it.

M: But you need to check ________ ________ ________

________.

W: I'm more afraid that somebody put something in

there.

M: Like what?

W: How should I know? It could be anything.

6. 다음 그림의 상황에 가장 적절한 대화를 고르시오.

① ② ③ ④ ⑤

06 ① W: You should go to bed.

M: I know, but let me just finish this drawing first.

② W: Do you want to go for a walk?

M: Not now. I prefer taking a walk at night.

③ W: Your music is too loud. ________ ________

________ ________ ________?

M: Sure. I'll do it right away.

④ W: Where can I buy headphones?

M: You should go to the music section over there.

⑤ W: You shouldn't ________ ________ ________

________ at night.

M: I'm sorry. I won't do it again.

---

7. 대화를 듣고, 남자가 여자에게 부탁한 일로 가장 적절한 것을 고르시오.

① 책 구매하기
② 강의실 예약하기
③ 팀 과제 제출하기
④ 발표 자료 인쇄하기
⑤ 발표 연습에 대해 피드백 주기

07 W: Nathan, what's up? You look ________ ________

________.

M: Hi, Amy. I have a presentation this afternoon and I

can't stop thinking about it.

W: Don't worry. You'll do fine.

M: I'm really nervous. I don't think I practiced enough.

W: If your presentation is in the afternoon, why don't

you practice now?

M: Maybe I should. Can you ________ ________

________?

W: Sure! What do you want me to do?

M: Could you listen to my practice presentation and

________ ________ ________ ________?

W: Sure, no problem.

8. 다음을 듣고, 음악회에 관해 언급되지 <u>않</u>은 것을 고르시오.

① 목적　　② 날짜
③ 티켓 가격　　④ 연주곡
⑤ 공연 참가자

08 W: Hello, students. This is Anna, the president of

the student council. I'm happy to invite you to a

concert to ________ ________ to help our friend

다음 페이지에 계속 ➡

Helen, who is bravely fighting cancer. The concert will __________ __________ on July 11th from 6 to 8 p.m. in the school auditorium. You can now __________ __________ for $20 from the student council. During the concert, our school orchestra and a school band will play beautiful music. Thank you.

9. 다음을 듣고, 무엇에 관한 설명인지 고르시오.

① 창문 ② 거울
③ 유리컵 ④ 접시
⑤ 카메라

09 M: This is a familiar object seen everywhere. It allows you to view your __________ ____________. It is made of glass, so it is breakable. When you look at yourself in this, the image you see __________ __________. In other words, you see everything on the ___________ __________ from how another person sees you. It is also __________ __________ every car. You can see on the right, left and in the back with this while driving. What is it?

10. 다음을 듣고, 두 사람의 대화가 <u>어색한</u> 것을 고르시오.

① ②
③ ④
⑤

10 ① M: What are you studying now?
  W: I'm studying science for an exam next week.
② M: __________ __________ __________ __________ I turn off the air conditioner?
  W: Not at all. I was feeling a bit cold myself.
③ M: Which bus goes to the airport?
  W: It will __________ __________ __________ to get there.
④ M: It was the best musical I've ever seen.
  W: I __________ __________ __________ you.
⑤ M: May I borrow your book?
  W: Sure. I'll give it to you when I'm done.

11. 대화를 듣고, 여자가 대화 직후에 할 일로 가장 적절한 것을 고르시오.

① 박람회 주제 정하기
② 학교 물품 대여하기
③ 선생님께 문의하기
④ 포스터 만들기
⑤ 앱 시연하기

11
W: Anton, what should we do for the science fair?
M: I'm not sure. I don't want to make an app like last time.
W: Yeah, me, neither. What about making something ____________ ____________, like fireworks?
M: That sounds interesting! It'll definitely ____________ ____________.
W: And I'm sure we can borrow materials from the school, too.
M: Great. But, wait. Are we allowed to ____________ ____________? The fair is indoors.
W: Why not? As long as we follow safety protocols it should be okay.
M: I think we should ____________ ____________ ____________ first, to be certain.
W: Okay. I'll do it right now.

12. 다음 표를 보면서 대화를 듣고, 두 사람이 주문할 치마를 고르시오.

	Model	Material	Feature	Pocket
①	A	Linen	Elastic waistband	×
②	B	Linen	Elastic waistband	○
③	C	Linen	Zipper	×
④	D	Cotton	Elastic waistband	○
⑤	E	Cotton	Zipper	×

12
M: Honey, have you decided which summer skirt to buy for our daughter, Sally?
W: It's harder than I thought. I could use your opinion.
M: No problem. It is for summer, so a linen skirt would be ____________ ____________.
W: I agree. Linen absorbs moisture and dries quickly, which ____________ ____________ ____________ for the summer.
M: Okay. Should we get a skirt with an elastic waistband or one with a zipper?
W: Sally would feel ____________ ____________ with an elastic waistband.
M: You're right. Now, we have two options left. Do you want one with pockets or no pockets?
W: In my opinion, the skirt with pockets doesn't ____________ ____________ ____________.
M: You have a point. Let's order this one, then.

다음 페이지에 계속 ➡

13. 대화를 듣고, 두 사람이 야시장에 갈 날짜를 고르시오.

① 5월 7일
② 5월 14일
③ 5월 21일
④ 6월 14일
⑤ 6월 21일

13

M: Look, Heather! The Han River night market is finally back.

W: Really? Why don't we go there together?

M: Yeah, sure! Let's see. It will be _________ every Sunday for one month only starting on May 7th.

W: How about going on the first day, May 7th? The night market will _________ _________ _________ with all the crowds.

M: True, but I can't go that night. I _________ _________ _________ my family on the 7th. How about the 14th?

W: I can't go on the 14th. I'm going to a musical that night.

M: Then, is the 21st okay with you?

W: Yeah, the 21st _________ _________. Let's go then.

14. 대화를 듣고, 여자가 어제 한 일로 가장 적절한 것을 고르시오.

① 문학수업 듣기
② 과제 제출하기
③ 도서 대출하기
④ 독서 동아리 가입하기
⑤ 도서 목록 작성하기

14

M: Katelyn, have you finished the literature homework?

W: Not yet. How about you?

M: I _________ _________ _________. It's too hard. How can I pick the right book?

W: Well, the list our teacher gave us is very long. So, I went to the library yesterday.

M: And?

W: I asked the librarian to _________ _________ the least popular books. And I came home with one of them.

M: How did it help you?

W: _________ _________ _________ _________, it saved me time _________ a book.

M: Okay. Not a bad idea. I think I'll do the same.

15. 다음을 듣고, 방송의 목적으로 가장 적절한 것을 고르시오.

① 학교 행사 참여 방법을 안내하려고
② 휴대전화 사용 제한을 공지하려고
③ 새 스마트폰 제품을 홍보하려고
④ 교내 안전 수칙을 설명하려고
⑤ 습득된 분실물을 알리려고

15
W: Good afternoon, students. This is your teacher Mrs. Hill speaking. A valuable item was ________ ________ ________ our school's Lost and Found. It's a smartphone of the Milky Way brand. It's white with gold star stickers on the back. It was found in the women's restroom on the second floor. It's locked, so the owner will need to ________ ________ to prove that it belongs to her. If the phone ________ ________ ________, come to my office as soon as you can. Thank you.

고난도 수치계산(금액)

16. 대화를 듣고, 남자가 블라우스를 사기 위해 지불해야 할 총 금액이 얼마인지 고르시오.

① $20　　② $31
③ $40　　④ $41
⑤ $50

16
W: What can I do for you, sir?

M: I'm looking for a ________ ________ my sister.

W: Okay. How about this blouse? It's the most ________ item.

M: It looks nice. How much is it?

W: The ________ ________ is 50 dollars, but we're giving a 20% discount this week.

M: Oh, that's great. I'll ________ ________.

W: Do you want it gift-wrapped? It will cost one more dollar.

M: Yes, please.

다음 페이지에 계속 ➡

17. 대화를 듣고, 남자의 마지막 말에 대한 여자의 응답으로 가장 적절한 것을 고르시오.

Woman: _________________

① He lives in Brazil now.
② He is the fastest player.
③ He liked to pass the ball.
④ He scored over 1,200 goals.
⑤ He was the best on his team.

17

W: Hi, Carl. Did you see the sports documentary on TV last night?

M: No. What was it about?

W: It was about the famous Brazilian soccer player, Pele.

M: I've never heard of him. Can you tell me something about him?

W: He was an amazing ________ ________.

M: Was he the best?

W: Well, he ________ ________ ________ ________ for most goals.

M: Really? What is the record?

W: He scored over 1,200 goals.

18. 대화를 듣고, 여자의 마지막 말에 대한 남자의 응답으로 가장 적절한 것을 고르시오.

Man: _________________

① OK. Let's work together on the report.
② That's great! I would really appreciate it.
③ Too bad. You must miss your sister a lot.
④ In that case, you'd better report to the teacher.
⑤ Sure. He gave me positive feedback on my report.

18

W: Hi, Adrian! How is your history report going?

M: Hi, Joyce! I've just finished my first draft. I've ________ a lot of ________ ________ it.

W: I'm sure you have.

M: But I think I need someone to give me some feedback.

W: Oh, why don't you ask your brother? Isn't he a college student?

M: He is, but he's ________ ________-________ ________ these days. I hardly see him.

W: Then, I will ask my sister. She loves history.

M: Are you sure? I would be ________ ________ ________ ________.

W: No problem. I'm sure she will be happy to help you.

M: That's great! I would really appreciate it.

알맞은응답찾기

19. 대화를 듣고, 여자의 마지막 말에 대한 남자의 응답으로 가장 적절한 것을 고르시오.

Man: ___________________

① I hope so. But I don't have enough storage space.
② I don't want to become addicted to online games.
③ I used to live in Spain, so I'm good at speaking Spanish.
④ All right, I'll give it a shot. Thanks for telling me about it.
⑤ Learning a foreign language helps improve your memory.

19 M: You seem to be busy with your phone these days. What are you doing?

W: I've been learning Spanish with a new language app.

M: Oh, really? Is it ___________ ___________ the app you used before?

W: Definitely. It has fun games and short lessons that ___________ ___________ ___________.

M: That sounds interesting. Is it free to use?

W: Yes, the basic version is free, and you can pay for ___________ ___________ if you want. You should try it.

M: That's a great idea. Does it work for other languages, too?

W: Yes, they have over 20 languages to choose from.

M: All right, I'll give it a shot. Thanks for telling me about it.

상황에적절한말찾기

20. 다음 상황 설명을 듣고, Helen이 친구에게 할 말로 가장 적절한 것을 고르시오.

Helen: ___________________

① Why is photography prohibited in this room?
② How long do you want to stay at the gallery?
③ Which painting do you want to take a picture of?
④ Do you want to see the paintings in another room?
⑤ Please look at that sign. We can't take pictures here.

20 W: Helen is visiting an art gallery with her friend. Taking pictures is allowed in most parts of the gallery, so they take a lot of pictures. However, when they enter one room, there is a sign saying that they ___________ ___________ ___________ in that particular room. Not noticing this sign, her friend starts to take pictures as in other rooms. So, Helen wants to ask her friend to ___________ ___________ ___________. In this situation, what would Helen most likely say to her friend?

Helen: Please look at that sign. We can't take pictures here.

Words & Expressions Review 16

● 다음 단어를 암기하세요.

문제	번호	단어	뜻	문제	번호	단어	뜻
1	1	stylish	세련된, 멋진	10	23	air conditioner	에어컨
	2	match	어울리다	11	24	visually	시각적으로
	3	come in ~	(상품 등이) ~으로 나오다		25	attractive	매력적인, 멋진
2	4	watercolor painting	수채화		26	attention	주의, 주목
	5	collage	콜라주, 모음	12	27	absorb	흡수하다
3	6	leakage	누수		28	elastic	고무로 된
	7	maintenance	보수, 정비	13	29	alive	활기찬, 생기 있는
	8	heads up	알림, 경고	14	30	point out	알려주다, 가리키다
	9	compensation	보상		31	at the very least	최소한, 적어도
4	10	reschedule	일정을 변경하다		32	Lost and Found	분실물 센터
5	11	lock	자물쇠	15	33	unlock	잠금 해제하다
	12	missing	없어진, 실종된		34	belong to	~ 것이다, 소유이다
6	13	take a walk	산책하다	16	35	give a discount	할인해 주다
	14	turn ~ down	~을 줄이다		36	gift-wrapped	선물용으로 포장된
7	15	anxious	불안한, 걱정하는	17	37	hear of + 명사	~에 대해 듣다
	16	feedback	피드백, 반응, 의견		38	hold	(기록, 타이틀 등을) 보유하다
8	17	raise funds	기금을 모으다		39	draft	초고, 초안
	18	auditorium	강당	18	40	hardly	거의 ~할 수 없다
	19	reflection	(거울에 비친) 모습, 반사		41	grateful	고마워하는, 감사하는
9	20	reversed	반대의, 뒤집힌	19	42	motivate	동기를 부여하다
	21	opposite	반대의, ~ 맞은편의		43	particular	특정한
10	22	turn off	(전기, 가스, 수도 등을) 끄다	20	44	notice	알아채다

● 왼쪽 단어장의 뜻이 보이지 않게 반으로 접고, 학습한 단어의 뜻을 아래 빈칸에 적어주세요.

1	maintenance		23	reschedule
2	give a discount		24	belong to
3	draft		25	attractive
4	collage		26	missing
5	compensation		27	auditorium
6	at the very least		28	heads up
7	grateful		29	hardly
8	particular		30	visually
9	motivate		31	raise funds
10	hold		32	elastic
11	alive		33	turn off
12	come in ~		34	anxious
13	turn ~ down		35	reversed
14	notice		36	hear of + 명사
15	feedback		37	attention
16	gift-wrapped		38	opposite
17	watercolor painting		39	air conditioner
18	stylish		40	Lost and Found
19	absorb		41	lock
20	match		42	point out
21	take a walk		43	unlock
22	leakage		44	reflection

16
회
단
어

17 회 중학영어듣기 모의고사

M3(17)_17_US
모두 **미국식 발음(US)**
으로 녹음

M3(17)_17_UK
20문제 중 5문제에 **영국식 발음**
(US+UK)을 포함하여 녹음

정답 및 해석 p. 97

1 대화를 듣고, 남자가 출력할 스티커를 고르시오.

①  ②  ③  ④  ⑤ 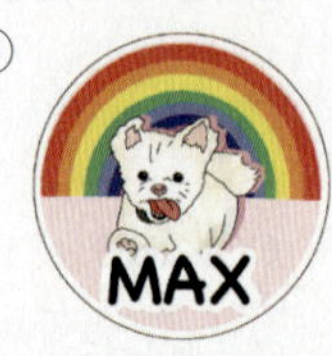

2 대화를 듣고, Junior Cooking Challenge에 관해 언급되지 <u>않은</u> 것을 고르시오.

① 진행 장소　　　　② 시작 시각　　　　③ 활동 내용
④ 유의 사항　　　　⑤ 신청 방법

3 대화를 듣고, 여자가 남자에게 전화한 목적으로 가장 적절한 것을 고르시오.

① 자원봉사 소감을 공유하려고　　　② 봉사 활동 일정을 안내하려고
③ 유기견 입양에 대해 상의하려고　　④ 봉사 동아리 가입 방법을 문의하려고
⑤ 동물 보호소 자원봉사 참여를 권하려고

4 대화를 듣고, 남자가 등록할 수영 수업 시각을 고르시오.

① 6 a.m.　　② 7 a.m.　　③ 4 p.m.　　④ 5 p.m.　　⑤ 7 p.m.

5 대화를 듣고, 여자의 심정으로 가장 적절한 것을 고르시오.

① upset　　　　② regretful　　　　③ delighted
④ bored　　　　⑤ embarrassed

6 다음 그림의 상황에 가장 적절한 대화를 고르시오.

①   ②   ③   ④   ⑤

7 대화를 듣고, 여자가 남자에게 부탁한 일로 가장 적절한 것을 고르시오.

① 토마토 구매하기   ② 스파게티 요리하기
③ 샐러드 소스 만들기   ④ 배달 음식 주문하기
⑤ 지하철역까지 태워주기

8 다음을 듣고, Student Computer Lab에 관해 언급되지 <u>않은</u> 것을 고르시오.

① 구비 장비   ② 위치   ③ 이용 가능 시간
④ 이용 시 주의 사항   ⑤ 인터넷 속도 개선

9 다음을 듣고, 무엇에 대한 설명인지 고르시오.

① 창던지기   ② 배구   ③ 양궁   ④ 허들   ⑤ 사격

10 다음을 듣고, 두 사람의 대화가 <u>어색한</u> 것을 고르시오.

①   ②   ③   ④   ⑤

11번~20번 문제는 다음 페이지에 ➡

11 대화를 듣고, 여자가 할 일로 가장 적절한 것을 고르시오.

① 돈 넣을 상자 가져오기 ② 시럽 구입하기 ③ 교실에서 의자 가져오기
④ 가격표 만들기 ⑤ 아이스크림 기계 빌리기

12 다음 표를 보면서 대화를 듣고, 두 사람이 주문할 태블릿 PC를 고르시오.

	Model	Screen Size(inches)	Color	Storage(GB)
①	A	11	White	128
②	B	11	Grey	128
③	C	11	White	256
④	D	13	Grey	128
⑤	E	13	Grey	256

13 대화를 듣고, 두 사람이 팝업스토어를 가기로 한 날짜를 고르시오.

① 9월 10일 ② 9월 15일 ③ 9월 16일
④ 9월 17일 ⑤ 9월 20일

14 대화를 듣고, 여자가 지난 주말에 한 일로 가장 적절한 것을 고르시오.

① 산책하기 ② 캠프파이어 하기 ③ 나무 심기
④ 블루베리 따기 ⑤ 농작물 구매하기

15 다음을 듣고, 방송의 목적으로 가장 적절한 것을 고르시오.

① 스포츠센터 이용규칙을 안내하려고 ② 새로운 운동복 브랜드를 홍보하려고
③ 스포츠센터 직원 채용을 공지하려고 ④ 규칙적인 운동의 중요성을 강조하려고
⑤ 키 성장에 효과적인 운동을 소개하려고

16 대화를 듣고, 여자가 지불할 금액을 고르시오.

① $20 ② $25 ③ $30 ④ $35 ⑤ $40

17 대화를 듣고, 여자의 마지막 말에 대한 남자의 응답으로 가장 적절한 것을 고르시오.

Man: ______________________________________

① I'll pick it up this Friday. ② I need six candles, please.
③ No, I didn't get any messages. ④ My daughter loves strawberries.
⑤ Yes, please write "Happy Birthday, Amy" on it.

[18~19] 대화를 듣고, 남자의 마지막 말에 대한 여자의 응답으로 가장 적절한 것을 고르시오.

18 **Woman:** ______________________________________

① Awesome. We have your size in stock.
② Good. I'll make sure the sneakers are in.
③ That's wonderful. I'll buy a pair right now.
④ Oh, I didn't know that. Thanks for the tip.
⑤ Of course. You can use the coupons today.

19 **Woman:** ______________________________________

① Great. He said he could come.
② Of course. I owe you a big one.
③ Really? I'm glad he answered your call.
④ Sure. I can give a lecture at your event.
⑤ Sorry. We'll have to wait until October.

20 다음 상황 설명을 듣고, Elliot이 Sarah에게 할 말로 가장 적절한 것을 고르시오.

Elliot: ______________________________________
① Why don't you stay at my house?
② Let's call or text each other often.
③ I'm moving to a faraway province.
④ It's exciting to spend time with you.
⑤ Do you have any plans for the summer?

Dictation Test 17

M3(17)_17_D

Dictation(받아쓰기)은 본문을 받아쓰면서 영어듣기의 집중력을 향상시키고 다양한 표현을 정리하기 위한 영어듣기 학습법입니다. **녹음을 다시 듣고, 빈칸에 알맞은 단어를 써 보세요.**
※Dictation의 정답은 듣기 대본의 밑줄 친 부분을 확인하세요.

정답 p. 97

맞은 개수 / 총186개

그림정보파악(대화)

1. 대화를 듣고, 남자가 출력할 스티커를 고르시오.

① 
② 
③ 
④ 
⑤ 

01
W: Hi, Carl. What are you doing on your ___________?

M: I'm ___________ a sticker using a photo of my dog. Can you help me out?

W: Sure. Let's choose the sticker shape first. Do you want a circle-shaped sticker?

M: Yes, that sounds good.

W: It seems that you can add other pictures like flowers and rainbows to the sticker ___________ ___________.

M: Okay. I'll add a picture of a rainbow then.

W: Good. Your dog's name is 'Max,' isn't it? Why don't you put his name on the sticker as well?

M: That's a great idea. I think we're done! I'll ___________ ___________ ___________.

대화미언급

2024 영어듣기능력평가 2회 2번 변형

2. 대화를 듣고, Junior Cooking Challenge에 관해 언급되지 <u>않은</u> 것을 고르시오.

① 진행 장소　　② 시작 시각
③ 활동 내용　　④ 유의 사항
⑤ 신청 방법

02
M: Mia, are you participating in this year's Junior Cooking Challenge?

W: Yes! It'll be held at the Downtown ___________ ___________ this Saturday.

M: Do you know when it starts?

W: The challenge begins at 2 p.m.

M: What are we going to make?

W: We'll ___________ ___________ and decorate cookies.

M: Yum! That sounds delicious.

W: Oh, and remember to ___________ ___________ your hair for safety and sanitation.

M: Good tip.

3. 대화를 듣고, 여자가 남자에게 전화한 목적으로 가장 적절한 것을 고르시오.
   ① 자원봉사 소감을 공유하려고
   ② 봉사 활동 일정을 안내하려고
   ③ 유기견 입양에 대해 상의하려고
   ④ 봉사 동아리 가입 방법을 문의하려고
   ⑤ 동물 보호소 자원봉사 참여를 권하려고

03 (*Cellphone rings.*)

M: Hi, Emily.

W: Hi, David. I have a question for you. Are you still interested in volunteer work?

M: Of course. I love ________ ________ ________ the community. Why do you ask?

W: Our local animal shelter is organizing an adoption event, and we need volunteers to ________ ________ ________ ____________.

M: Oh, that's wonderful.

W: Would you like to join us? I know that you love animals.

M: Well, let me think about it. When do you need to know by?

W: We ________ ________ ____________ the volunteer schedule by this Friday.

M: OK. I'll let you know by tomorrow.

4. 대화를 듣고, 남자가 등록할 수영 수업 시각을 고르시오.
   ① 6 a.m.　　② 7 a.m.
   ③ 4 p.m.　　④ 5 p.m.
   ⑤ 7 p.m.

04 W: Harry, have you decided which swimming class to take?

M: Mom, I'm thinking about taking the afternoon class at 5 p.m.

W: Don't you think you will be too tired after school?

M: School finishes around 4 p.m., so I can ________ ________ ________ ________ ________.

W: But you often ________ ________ ________ your classmates after school to work on school projects.

다음 페이지에 계속 ➡

M: Hm… You're right, Mom.

W: Why don't you take a morning lesson? They have classes at 6 a.m. and 7 a.m.

M: That's a better idea. 6 a.m. is too early for me. I will ________ ________ ________ the 7 a.m. class.

W: Sounds good.

5. 대화를 듣고, 여자의 심정으로 가장 적절한 것을 고르시오.

① upset
② regretful
③ delighted
④ bored
⑤ embarrassed

05

M: Ms. Wallace, thank you for coming by our shop.

W: Thank you for calling me. So, where is it?

M: Here. It just ________ ________ ________ ________. Is this the clock you were looking for?

W: Oh, my! Yes!

M: It wasn't easy to find a clock this old ________ ________ ________.

W: I can imagine. This antique clock looks the same as the one in my grandparents' photo.

M: Will you take it?

W: Of course! I ________ ________ ________ ________ it to my granny.

M: I'm so glad you like it.

W: Thank you for finding this. It ________ ________ ________ to me.

6. 다음 그림의 상황에 가장 적절한 대화를 고르시오.

①　　②
③　　④
⑤

06

① M: Can I help you with anything?

　 W: Sure. Please ________ ________ ________ for me, will you?

② M: Can you do the dishes while I clean the living room?

　 W: I can't. I'm ________ ________ ________ the baby.

③ M: We need to buy some beef for dinner.

　 W: Okay. Let's go to the meat section over there.

④ M: There's something in my soup.

　W: Oh, no. I'll call the waiter and complain.

⑤ M: What are you doing in the kitchen?

　W: I'm trying to _______ _______ _______. It's not working.

부탁(요청)한일파악

7.　대화를 듣고, 여자가 남자에게 부탁한 일로 가장 적절한 것을 고르시오.

① 토마토 구매하기
② 스파게티 요리하기
③ 샐러드 소스 만들기
④ 배달 음식 주문하기
⑤ 지하철역까지 태워주기

07 (*Telephone rings.*)

M: Hello.

W: Honey, it's me. Are you on your way home?

M: Yeah, I'm on the subway. I think I'll be home in 30 minutes.

W: Good. I'm making spaghetti for dinner.

M: That sounds delicious. I can't wait _______ _______ _______.

W: I was trying to make a salad as well, but I'm out of _____________.

M: Oh, what are you missing? I can buy whatever you need.

W: Then, can you buy some tomatoes on your way home?

M: No problem. _______ _______ _______ _______.

고난도 **담화미언급**

8.　다음을 듣고, Student Computer Lab에 관해 언급되지 <u>않은</u> 것을 고르시오.

① 구비 장비
② 위치
③ 이용 가능 시간
④ 이용 시 주의 사항
⑤ 인터넷 속도 개선

08 W: Good morning, students! Our school now has a Student Computer Lab. There are personal computers, printers, and scanners _____________ _______ _______ _______. The lab is on the second floor, inside the library. It is _______ _______ _______ _______. When using the lab, please do not store files or user names. Also, you cannot _______ _______ _______ _______ inside the lab. To access the wireless network, please ask our librarian, Mr. Banks.

다음 페이지에 계속 ➡

---

9. 다음을 듣고, 무엇에 대한 설명인지 고르시오.

① 창던지기   ② 배구
③ 양궁   ④ 허들
⑤ 사격

09 W: This sport first ________ ________ ________ a skill used in hunting and in battle. Now it is one of the most popular Olympic sports. A player aims to shoot an arrow ________ ________ ________ with the use of a bow. To win, a player needs to ________ ________ as close to the center of a target as possible. Determination and ____________ are very important for the players of this sport.

10. 다음을 듣고, 두 사람의 대화가 <u>어색한</u> 것을 고르시오.

①   ②
③   ④
⑤

10 ① M: Hello. Can I ________ ________ Minji?

W: Speaking. Who's calling, please?

② M: What did the ________ ________ say?

W: It's going to be sunny and warm.

③ M: Where shall we meet?

W: ____________ at three o'clock.

④ M: May I see your ticket and passport, please?

W: Yes. Here you are.

⑤ M: What are you ________ ________?

W: Beethoven's 3rd symphony.

11. 대화를 듣고, 여자가 할 일로 가장 적절한 것을 고르시오.

① 돈 넣을 상자 가져오기
② 시럽 구입하기
③ 교실에서 의자 가져오기
④ 가격표 만들기
⑤ 아이스크림 기계 빌리기

11 M: Hey, Becky. Is our ________ ________ ________ for the school food festival?

W: Almost. The ice cream machine is fantastic!

M: _______ _______. Do we have a box for the

money?

W: Dan will bring us one.

M: Great. Oh, we don't have any chairs _______

_______ _______.

W: Can you bring some from our classroom? I'll

make a sign for the ice cream prices.

M: Sure. But Jenny's already made the sign. Why don't

you get _______ _______ for the ice cream?

W: OK. I'll go and buy some.

M: Thanks.

12. 다음 표를 보면서 대화를 듣고, 두 사람
이 주문할 태블릿 PC를 고르시오.

	Model	Screen Size (inches)	Color	Storage (GB)
①	A	11	White	128
②	B	11	Grey	128
③	C	11	White	256
④	D	13	Grey	128
⑤	E	13	Grey	256

12

M: Honey, what are you doing?

W: I'm looking for a tablet PC for our daughter. Can

we _______ _______ one together?

M: Sure. Do you have anything in mind?

W: Not yet. Do you think we should buy one with a

bigger screen?

M: I guess 11 inches will be big enough for her.

W: Okay. The 11-inch models _______ _______

two colors. She said she likes white _______

_______ grey.

M: Then we should choose the white one. How about

the storage?

W: She will mainly use it for taking lectures online.

She won't need a lot of storage space for that.

M: I agree. Let's get her the one _______

_______ _______.

W: Great. Let's order this one.

다음 페이지에 계속 ➡

13. 대화를 듣고, 두 사람이 팝업스토어를 가기로 한 날짜를 고르시오.

① 9월 10일
② 9월 15일
③ 9월 16일
④ 9월 17일
⑤ 9월 20일

13

M: Hey, Nicole. What are you doing?

W: Oh, hey, Paul. I was looking at this pop-up store's Instagram account.

M: What kind of pop-up store is it?

W: It's a clothing brand __________ _________ street fashion.

M: I like street fashion. Can I go with you?

W: Sure. The pop-up store _________ ________ _________ _______ September 10th to 20th.

M: I would like to go on the weekend. Does ________ the 16th or 17th _______ ________ _______?

W: I have something on the 17th. But I think the 16th would work for me.

M: Perfect!

14. 대화를 듣고, 여자가 지난 주말에 한 일로 가장 적절한 것을 고르시오.

① 산책하기
② 캠프파이어 하기
③ 나무 심기
④ 블루베리 따기
⑤ 농작물 구매하기

14

M: Leona, how was your weekend? Did you go to the farm ________ _________ ________?

W: Yes. The farm is my aunt and uncle's. It was so nice!

M: Sounds like you had a good time.

W: I ________ ________ ________ a lot. I'm just sorry that it rained. We couldn't have a campfire.

M: Oh, too bad. What did you do to help them?

W: I did some work in the fields. I planted new blueberry bushes, too.

M: That's nice. ________ ________ ________ ________ a farm.

W: Come with me next time.

15. 다음을 듣고, 방송의 목적으로 가장 적절한 것을 고르시오.

① 스포츠센터 이용규칙을 안내하려고
② 새로운 운동복 브랜드를 홍보하려고
③ 스포츠센터 직원 채용을 공지하려고
④ 규칙적인 운동의 중요성을 강조하려고
⑤ 키 성장에 효과적인 운동을 소개하려고

15 W: Welcome to Sports Village, _________ _________ _________ sports center in town! Before you start your exciting adventure, let me tell you about our rules. First, you should be 120 cm or over to use our facilities. Second, if you wear __________ shoes like slippers or high heels, you will not be able to __________ _________ some sports activities for safety reasons. Third, no outside food or drink is _________. Have a great time.

16. 대화를 듣고, 여자가 지불할 금액을 고르시오.

① $20　　② $25
③ $30　　④ $35
⑤ $40

16 M: Welcome to Happy Camping. How may I help you?

W: I'd like to _________ _________ __________ for this weekend.

M: It's 25 dollars for four people. The cost of electricity is included.

W: I'll take it. Can I rent a tent?

M: It's 15 dollars. You can also get a grill for 10 dollars.

W: I'll _________ _________ the tent. Can I use this discount coupon?

M: Sure. You can _________ _________ _________ _________ with the coupon.

W: Okay, here's my credit card.

다음 페이지에 계속 ➡

17. 대화를 듣고, 여자의 마지막 말에 대한 남자의 응답으로 가장 적절한 것을 고르시오.

Man: ________________

① I'll pick it up this Friday.
② I need six candles, please.
③ No, I didn't get any messages.
④ My daughter loves strawberries.
⑤ Yes, please write "Happy Birthday, Amy" on it.

17

W: Hello, how can I help you?

M: Hi, ________ ________ ________ ________ a birthday cake for my daughter.

W: Fantastic! How old is she?

M: She'll be 6 this Friday.

W: Excellent! We have vanilla, chocolate, and strawberry cakes. ________ ________ ________ ________ ________?

M: I'll go with a vanilla cake. And can I have strawberry filling in it?

W: Of, course. Would you like to ________ ________ ________ on the cake?

M: Yes, please write "Happy Birthday, Amy" on it.

18. 대화를 듣고, 남자의 마지막 말에 대한 여자의 응답으로 가장 적절한 것을 고르시오.

Woman: ________________

① Awesome. We have your size in stock.
② Good. I'll make sure the sneakers are in.
③ That's wonderful. I'll buy a pair right now.
④ Oh, I didn't know that. Thanks for the tip.
⑤ Of course. You can use the coupons today.

18

M: Hi. What can I do for you?

W: Hi, I'm looking for the new Max series sneakers. I heard that you sell them.

M: Yes, we do. What size do you need? ________ ________ ________ size 240 at the moment.

W: Oh, no. I wear size 240. When will you ________ ________ ________?

M: Probably by tomorrow morning.

W: Alright. I'll come back then.

M: Before you come back, I'd ________ that you download our app. You can get discount coupons on it.

W: Oh, I didn't know that. Thanks for the tip.

19. 대화를 듣고, 남자의 마지막 말에 대한 여자의 응답으로 가장 적절한 것을 고르시오.

Woman: _______________

① Great. He said he could come.
② Of course. I owe you a big one.
③ Really? I'm glad he answered your call.
④ Sure. I can give a lecture at your event.
⑤ Sorry. We'll have to wait until October.

19
W: Mr. Austin, you know I'm __________ __________ __________ the School Career Day, right?

M: Sure, Ms. Webster. What's the matter?

W: I want to __________ a fashion designer as one of the lecturers, and I hear that you have one as a close friend.

M: Oh, yes. A shoe designer. Do you want me to __________ __________?

W: Could you, please?

M: No problem. When is the event?

W: It's October 10th. Am I asking too early?

M: Not at all. He's a __________ busy man, so I think it's safe to ask early on. Just give me a day __________ __________.

W: Of course. I owe you a big one.

20. 다음 상황 설명을 듣고, Elliot이 Sarah에게 할 말로 가장 적절한 것을 고르시오.

Elliot: _______________
① Why don't you stay at my house?
② Let's call or text each other often.
③ I'm moving to a faraway province.
④ It's exciting to spend time with you.
⑤ Do you have any plans for the summer?

20
M: Elliot and Sarah are close friends. Elliot finds out that Sarah will spend her whole summer vacation in a __________ __________ with her family. He is a little disappointed that he cannot __________ __________ __________ with her for the next few months. So, he wants to ask her to __________ __________ __________ __________ as often as possible. In this situation, what would Elliot most likely say to Sarah?

Elliot: Let's call or text each other often.

Words & Expressions Review 17

● 다음 단어를 암기하세요.

문제	번호	단어	뜻
1	1	create	만들어 내다
2	2	culinary	요리의
	3	sanitation	위생
3	4	organize	준비하다, 조직하다
	5	finalize	마무리 짓다
4	6	rest	쉬다
	7	meet up with	~와 만나다
	8	work on	~에 대한 작업을 하다
5	9	come by	잠깐 들르다
	10	abroad	해외에서
	11	antique	골동품인
6	12	stir	젓다, 섞다
	13	section	구역, 구획
7	14	on one's way home	집에 오는 길에
	15	be out of ~	~이 떨어지다, 품절되다
8	16	access	접속하다, 접근하다
	17	wireless	무선의
	18	librarian	사서
9	19	arrow	화살
	20	bow	활
	21	determination	결단력, 결정
	22	concentration	집중력, 집중
10	23	passport	여권
	24	symphony	교향곡
11	25	sign	표지판
12	26	come in	(상품 등이) 나오다
	27	mainly	주로
13	28	account	(정보 서비스) 계정
	29	known for	~으로 유명한
14	30	field	밭, 들판
	31	bush	관목, 덤불
15	32	indoor	실내의, 실내용의
16	33	campsite	캠핑 자리
	34	electricity	전기
17	35	filling	(파이 등 음식의) 소[속]
	36	pick ~ up	~을 찾다[찾아오다]
18	37	have A in stock	A의 재고가 있다
	38	invite	초청하다, 초대하다
19	39	or so	~정도, 쯤
	40	give a lecture	강연하다
	41	faraway	먼
20	42	province	지방
	43	disappointed	실망한
	44	contact	연락하다

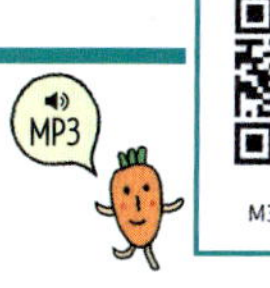

M3(17)_W_17

● 왼쪽 단어장의 뜻이 보이지 않게 반으로 접고, 학습한 단어의 뜻을 아래 빈칸에 적어주세요.

1	finalize	23	contact
2	work on	24	bow
3	sign	25	passport
4	known for	26	account
5	bush	27	come by
6	come in	28	province
7	abroad	29	organize
8	have A in stock	30	stir
9	sanitation	31	filling
10	pick ~ up	32	give a lecture
11	symphony	33	concentration
12	campsite	34	create
13	indoor	35	arrow
14	section	36	be out of ~
15	access	37	culinary
16	meet up with	38	invite
17	librarian	39	wireless
18	field	40	disappointed
19	rest	41	mainly
20	or so	42	on one's way home
21	antique	43	electricity
22	faraway	44	determination

17
회
단
어

18회 중학영어듣기 모의고사

M3(17)_18_US
모두 **미국식 발음(US)** 으로 녹음

M3(17)_18_UK
20문제 중 5문제에 **영국식 발음 (US+UK)**을 포함하여 녹음

정답 및 해석 p. 103

1 대화를 듣고, 여자가 구입할 자전거를 고르시오.

①  ②  ③  ④  ⑤ 

2 대화를 듣고, Summer Sports Camp에 관해 언급되지 <u>않은</u> 것을 고르시오.

① 시작 날짜　　② 기간　　③ 프로그램 내용
④ 비용　　⑤ 신청 방법

3 대화를 듣고, 여자가 남자에게 전화한 목적으로 가장 적절한 것을 고르시오.

① 친구의 전화번호를 물으려고　　② 노래를 추천하려고
③ 책을 주문하려고　　④ 함께 도서관에 가려고
⑤ 함께 콘서트에 가려고

4 대화를 듣고, 두 사람이 만나기로 한 시각을 고르시오.

① 11 a.m.　　② 12 p.m.　　③ 1 p.m.　　④ 2 p.m.　　⑤ 3 p.m.

5 대화를 듣고, 남자의 심정으로 가장 적절한 것을 고르시오.

① upset　　② sorry　　③ happy
④ bored　　⑤ embarrassed

6 다음 그림의 상황에 가장 적절한 대화를 고르시오.

①   ②   ③   ④   ⑤

7 대화를 듣고, 여자가 남자에게 부탁한 일로 가장 적절한 것을 고르시오.

① 공연 예매하기   ② 관람 후기 올리기   ③ 지역 센터 방문하기
④ 연극 동아리 소개하기   ⑤ 예고편 동영상 시청하기

8 다음을 듣고, Special Interview of Jefferson에 대해 언급되지 <u>않은</u> 것을 고르시오.

① 방송 요일   ② 방송 시간   ③ 초대 손님
④ 방송 내용   ⑤ 경품 추첨

9 다음을 듣고, 무엇에 관한 설명인지 고르시오.

① 메모지   ② 펜   ③ 스티커
④ 스테이플러   ⑤ 자

10 다음을 듣고, 두 사람의 대화가 <u>어색한</u> 것을 고르시오.

①   ②   ③   ④   ⑤

11번~20번 문제는 다음 페이지에 ➡

11 대화를 듣고, 남자가 대화 후에 할 일로 적절한 것을 고르시오.

① 친구 만나기   ② 침대 정리하기   ③ 빨래하기
④ 설거지하기   ⑤ 바닥 걸레질하기

12 다음 표를 보면서 대화를 듣고, 두 사람이 주문할 의류 건조기를 고르시오.

	Model	Price	Smart Functions	Color
①	A	$720	×	white
②	B	$760	○	white
③	C	$810	○	black
④	D	$860	×	black
⑤	E	$950	○	white

13 대화를 듣고, 여자가 미용실에 갈 날짜를 고르시오.

① 3월 9일   ② 3월 11일   ③ 3월 15일
④ 3월 16일   ⑤ 3월 18일

14 대화를 듣고, 남자가 어제 한 일로 가장 적절한 것을 고르시오.

① 트럼펫 구매하기   ② 악기 수리 맡기기   ③ 바이올린 연습하기
④ 캠프 참가 신청하기   ⑤ 포스터 만들기

15 다음을 듣고, 방송의 목적으로 가장 적절한 것을 고르시오.

① 교환 학생 프로그램을 홍보하려고   ② 홈스테이 제공 가정을 모집하려고
③ 새로 오신 선생님을 소개하려고   ④ 미국의 한 지역을 소개하려고
⑤ 가을 학기 시작을 공지하려고

16 대화를 듣고, 남자가 지불해야 할 금액으로 가장 적절한 것을 고르시오.

① $6   ② $7   ③ $8   ④ $9   ⑤ $10

17 대화를 듣고, 남자의 마지막 말에 대한 여자의 응답으로 가장 적절한 것을 고르시오.

Woman: ____________________________________

① I'm afraid I can't wait that long.

② We're sorry, but we're out of sushi.

③ I think I'll get sushi from another place.

④ Thanks for waiting. Your order will arrive soon.

⑤ Sorry for the mix-up. We'll get you the right one.

[18~19] 대화를 듣고, 여자의 마지막 말에 대한 남자의 응답으로 가장 적절한 것을 고르시오.

18 **Man:** ____________________________________

① Giving presentations is hard for me.

② How often should I water the plants?

③ I will give you some candles I've made.

④ Don't worry. You will do better next time.

⑤ Sounds great! I'll wait for you at the main gate.

19 **Man:** ____________________________________

① I'm going to fail history class.

② You are very kind, but no thanks.

③ Did you send me another e-mail before?

④ That's great. I'll e-mail you the file right now.

⑤ Thank goodness! Can you send it to me, please?

20 다음 상황 설명을 듣고, Tiffany가 Mr. Wilson에게 할 말로 가장 적절한 것을 고르시오.

Tiffany: Mr. Wilson, ____________________________________

① I'm sorry, but I have injured my leg.

② I believe we can do better at the match.

③ I'm afraid I can't participate in the tournament.

④ I think it's time for me to start practicing again.

⑤ I heard the tournament will take place in our town.

Dictation Test 18

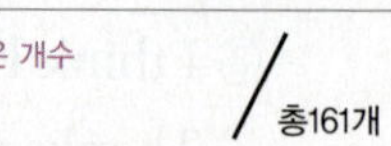

M3(17)_18_D

Dictation(받아쓰기)은 본문을 받아쓰면서 영어듣기의 집중력을 향상시키고 다양한 표현을 정리하기 위한 영어듣기 학습법입니다. **녹음을 다시 듣고, 빈칸에 알맞은 단어를 써 보세요.**
※Dictation의 정답은 듣기 대본의 밑줄 친 부분을 확인하세요.

📖 정답 p. 103

맞은 개수 / 총161개

---

1. 대화를 듣고, 여자가 구입할 자전거를 고르시오.

①  ② 

③  ④ 

⑤ 

01
W: I'm looking for a bicycle for my son. Can you __________ __________?

M: Can he ride a two-wheel bicycle?

W: No, he needs a four-wheel bicycle.

M: Okay, ma'am. This four-wheel bicycle with __________ __________ __________ is nice.

W: I see. Do you have any other models?

M: Yes. Please come this way. This four-wheel bicycle has an adjustable back, so a child __________ __________ __________ the bike seat. It has a front basket, too.

W: Oh, I like it. I'll take it.

---

2. 대화를 듣고, Summer Sports Camp에 관해 언급되지 <u>않은</u> 것을 고르시오.
① 시작 날짜
② 기간
③ 프로그램 내용
④ 비용
⑤ 신청 방법

02
W: Paul, are you interested in Summer Sports Camp?

M: Oh, I love summer sports. When is it?

W: It __________ __________ July 20th.

M: How long is the camp?

W: It's a week, from Monday to Sunday.

M: I think I can join. So, you mean we'll be doing summer sports like scuba-diving and waterskiing?

W: Exactly. And the program also includes __________ __________.

M: Sounds good! I'll ask my mom if I can _______ _______ _______.

W: Tell Mr. Anderson if you want to _______ _______ the camp. He'll give you more details about it.

3. 대화를 듣고, 여자가 남자에게 전화한 목적으로 가장 적절한 것을 고르시오.
① 친구의 전화번호를 물으려고
② 노래를 추천하려고
③ 책을 주문하려고
④ 함께 도서관에 가려고
⑤ 함께 콘서트에 가려고

03 (*Telephone rings.*)

W: Hello, can I _______ _______ Michael?

M: This is he. Who's calling, please?

W: Hi, it's me, Anne. Do you have _______ _______ today?

M: Not really. I just need to pick up some books from the library. Why?

W: Would you like to go to a hip hop concert tonight? I got _______ _______.

M: I'm sorry, but I don't like hip hop music very much.

W: Oh, I didn't know that. Hmm, whom should I go with, then?

M: Ask Kenny. I heard that he's _______ _______ hip hop.

W: Really? Great! Thanks, Michael.

4. 대화를 듣고, 두 사람이 만나기로 한 시각을 고르시오.
① 11 a.m.   ② 12 p.m.
③ 1 p.m.   ④ 2 p.m.
⑤ 3 p.m.

04 M: Hey, Diane. You like the actor Kim Dong Hun, right?

W: Yes, I love him. Why?

M: I have two tickets for the premiere of his latest movie. _______ _______ _______ _______ go with me?

W: I'd love to! When is it?

M: It's at 2 p.m. this Saturday. _______ _______ _______ an hour to get there from my place, so we should meet up at 1 p.m.

다음 페이지에 계속 ➡

W: Hmm… How about we meet a little earlier and
________ ________ ________ before we go?

M: That sounds great! Let's meet at 12 p.m. at my
place.

W: Okay, I'll see you then.

5. 대화를 듣고, 남자의 심정으로 가장 적절
한 것을 고르시오.

① upset   ② sorry
③ happy   ④ bored
⑤ embarrassed

05 M: Mom, can I ________ ________ ________ Mike on
Friday evening?

W: Sure. Just don't be out too late.

M: But this is special. Guess what, Mom? I'm going to
the football match!

W: Really? You said the tickets were ________
________.

M: Mike got the tickets as a birthday present, and he's
taking me!

W: That's amazing. You really wanted to go to the
match.

M: I know. I'm so excited that he asked me.

W: That's great news. Is ________ ________ ________
________?

M: Yeah, Mike's dad is taking us.

W: Good.

6. 다음 그림의 상황에 가장 적절한 대화를
고르시오.

①   ②
③   ④
⑤

06 ① W: What seems to be the problem?

M: I'll have to open it up and check what's wrong.

② W: Where can I ________ ________ ________
________?

M: You'll need to take it to the computer repair
shop.

③ W: Where did you buy that scarf?

M: I didn't buy it. My girlfriend made it for me.

④ W: Don't forget to ________ ________ ________

________ when you leave the room.

M: Okay. I won't forget.

⑤ W: I'd like to order a cheeseburger and a Diet Coke.

M: Okay, that will be 10 dollars.

---

7. 대화를 듣고, 여자가 남자에게 부탁한 일로 가장 적절한 것을 고르시오.
① 공연 예매하기
② 관람 후기 올리기
③ 지역 센터 방문하기
④ 연극 동아리 소개하기
⑤ 예고편 동영상 시청하기

07

W: Hey, Adam. Did you hear about the new play at the community theater?

M: No, what is it about?

W: It's a comedy about student life. I saw a short __________ __________ online, and it looked really funny.

M: Sounds interesting. Are tickets __________ __________ already?

W: Yes. And there's a 15 percent discount for members of the community learning center.

M: Really? I'm a member!

W: Great! Could you __________ __________ for both of us, then?

M: Sure thing. I'll do it __________ __________.

---

8. 다음을 듣고, Special Interview of Jefferson에 대해 언급되지 <u>않은</u> 것을 고르시오.

① 방송 요일
② 방송 시간
③ 초대 손님
④ 방송 내용
⑤ 경품 추첨

08

W: Good afternoon, Jefferson Middle School students. This is Colin from the school broadcasting club. Starting next week, we will ________ ________ ________ of Special Jefferson Interviews every Friday. It'll be from 12 p.m. to 12:30 p.m. The guests will be our ________ ________ ________. They will talk about topics such as grades, activities, friends, and more. You can ________ ________ ________ school-wide broadcasting, or on the school app. Thank you.

다음 페이지에 계속 ➡

9. 다음을 듣고, 무엇에 관한 설명인지 고르시오.

① 메모지
② 펜
③ 스티커
④ 스테이플러
⑤ 자

09 M: This is a type of stationery. You can use this to ______ ______. It is usually square in shape. You can write or draw anything on this. People usually use this when they need to leave a message or ______ ______ ______ ______ something. Some of these are sticky on the back. It's usually packaged in bundles so you can ______ ______ a page from the whole pack.

10. 다음을 듣고, 두 사람의 대화가 <u>어색한</u> 것을 고르시오.

①　　　　②
③　　　　④
⑤

10
① M: Do you have tickets for the show at 2:30?
W: I'm sorry, sir. We're all ______ ______.
② M: May I check your baggage?
W: Sure, here you are.
③ M: ______ ______ is it to send a letter to China?
W: It will arrive tomorrow.
④ M: Could you show me the way to Seoul City Hall?
W: Sure. It's not ______ ______ here.
⑤ M: I'm looking for something for my father's birthday.
W: How about this watch?

11. 대화를 듣고, 남자가 대화 후에 할 일로 적절한 것을 고르시오.

① 친구 만나기
② 침대 정리하기
③ 빨래하기
④ 설거지하기
⑤ 바닥 걸레질하기

11
M: Mom, do you need any help cleaning the house?
W: Are you sure? Aren't you going out with your friends?
M: Nah, I just want to stay home today.

W: Wow, that's a first. Did you ________ ________

________?

M: Yes. I also put the dirty clothes in the laundry.

W: I'm impressed. Help me ________ ________

________ then. Oh wait, you might drop the

plates.

M: Hahaha... You're right. How about I just ________

________ ________?

W: That's a great idea.

12. 다음 표를 보면서 대화를 듣고, 두 사람
이 주문할 의류 건조기를 고르시오.

	Model	Price	Smart Functions	Color
①	A	$720	×	white
②	B	$760	○	white
③	C	$810	○	black
④	D	$860	×	black
⑤	E	$950	○	white

12

W: Honey, I think we need a clothes dryer.

M: I agree. It will be ____________ in any type of

weather. Let's find one online.

W: How much can we ________?

M: I don't think we can afford to spend more than

$900.

W: You're right. Look, some of the dryers have smart

functions.

M: With the smart functions, we can check ________

________ ____________ on our app.

W: Then we should get one with those functions.

M: Now, we have two options left.

W: A black one would go well with our ________

________.

M: I agree! Let's order this one.

다음 페이지에 계속 ➡

13. 대화를 듣고, 여자가 미용실에 갈 날짜를 고르시오.

① 3월 9일 ② 3월 11일
③ 3월 15일 ④ 3월 16일
⑤ 3월 18일

13 *(Telephone rings.)*

W: Hello?

M: Hello. This is Jason from J's Hair Salon. You ________ ________ __________ on March 15 at 9 o'clock, right?

W: Yes, I did.

M: I'm really sorry, but I'll be ________ ________ ________ on business that day. So I'm calling to reschedule you for another day and time.

W: I see. Do you have ________ __________ on March 16 or March 18?

M: How about March 18 at 11?

W: That sounds good. I'll see you ________ ________ then.

14. 대화를 듣고, 남자가 어제 한 일로 가장 적절한 것을 고르시오.

① 트럼펫 구매하기
② 악기 수리 맡기기
③ 바이올린 연습하기
④ 캠프 참가 신청하기
⑤ 포스터 만들기

14 W: Hey, Nate. What's up?

M: Hi, Brenda. Have you heard about the classical music camp?

W: Yeah. I saw a poster on the school website. Are you going?

M: Yes. I need to __________ my trumpet skills.

W: Me, too. I haven't practiced the violin ________ ________ ________. How about practicing together?

M: Sure, but not today. My trumpet is at the __________ ________ ________.

W: Why? What happened?

M: It's broken so I took it there yesterday.

W: I see. I hope it's ________ soon.

15. 다음을 듣고, 방송의 목적으로 가장 적절
한 것을 고르시오.
① 교환 학생 프로그램을 홍보하려고
② 홈스테이 제공 가정을 모집하려고
③ 새로 오신 선생님을 소개하려고
④ 미국의 한 지역을 소개하려고
⑤ 가을 학기 시작을 공지하려고

15 W: Hello, students. This is your vice principal. I have a special _____________ today. As you know, we have a __________ __________ ___________ with Franklin Middle School in Arizona. This September, we will have three exchange students, so we are looking for families to ________ the students. They will be staying from September until the end of November. This will be a great __________ for you to learn about a new culture. If you are interested, please contact Mr. Harbour.

16. 대화를 듣고, 남자가 지불해야 할 금액으
로 가장 적절한 것을 고르시오.
① $6　　② $7
③ $8　　④ $9
⑤ $10

16 W: May I take your order?

M: One cheeseburger and one Coke, please.

W: Okay. Your total comes to 8 dollars.

M: Oh, wait. Do you have any combo meals?

W: Yes. For a dollar more, you can add French fries to your order.

M: Great. ________ ________ that combo meal.

W: Thank you. For here or ________ ________?

M: To go, please. I can get a two-dollar discount on the to-go order, right?

W: Oh, I'm sorry, that discount event ________ last month.

M: All right. Here's my credit card.

다음 페이지에 계속 ➡

17. 대화를 듣고, 남자의 마지막 말에 대한 여자의 응답으로 가장 적절한 것을 고르시오.

Woman: _______________

① I'm afraid I can't wait that long.
② We're sorry, but we're out of sushi.
③ I think I'll get sushi from another place.
④ Thanks for waiting. Your order will arrive soon.
⑤ Sorry for the mix-up. We'll get you the right one.

17 (Cellphone rings.)

M: Hello?
W: Hi, this is Sushi King. Did you __________ __________ __________ for two sushi combos for delivery?
M: Yes, I did. Is there a problem?
W: We're swamped with orders, and our delivery drivers __________ __________ at the moment.
M: Oh, no! Does that mean my order won't be delivered?
W: We're __________ __________ __________ to manage the situation, but it might take an extra 45 minutes for your order to arrive.
M: I see. We're really __________ sushi, so we'll wait for it.
W: Thanks for waiting. Your order will arrive soon.

18. 대화를 듣고, 여자의 마지막 말에 대한 남자의 응답으로 가장 적절한 것을 고르시오.

Man: _______________

① Giving presentations is hard for me.
② How often should I water the plants?
③ I will give you some candles I've made.
④ Don't worry. You will do better next time.
⑤ Sounds great! I'll wait for you at the main gate.

18 M: Jessica, how is your school presentation going?
W: I've finished writing it, but I need some practice presenting it.
M: What's your topic?
W: I'm going to talk about how to make scented candles and how they __________ __________ __________.
M: That sounds interesting! My topic is the benefits of having indoor plants.
W: Philip! Why don't we __________ __________ and review each other's work?
M: That's a very good idea. Then we can __________ __________ to our presentations.
W: Since the presentations are tomorrow, let's meet after school today.
M: Sounds great! I'll wait for you at the main gate.

19. 대화를 듣고, 여자의 마지막 말에 대한 남자의 응답으로 가장 적절한 것을 고르시오.

Man: ________________

① I'm going to fail history class.
② You are very kind, but no thanks.
③ Did you send me another e-mail before?
④ That's great. I'll e-mail you the file right now.
⑤ Thank goodness! Can you send it to me, please?

19
W: Mr. Yoon, ________ ________ ________ that computer for hours now.

M: I'm looking for a file, but I can't find it.

W: Is the file for a class?

M: Yes, it's for the third grade. ________ ________ ________ I lost it.

W: What is it about?

M: It's about Korean history.

W: Isn't that the one you e-mailed to all of the history teachers last week? I got it.

M: Did I? Oh, yes! ________ ________ ________ ________ ?

W: Of course I did.

M: Thank goodness! Can you send it to me, please?

20. 다음 상황 설명을 듣고, Tiffany가 Mr. Wilson에게 할 말로 가장 적절한 것을 고르시오.

Tiffany: Mr. Wilson, ________

① I'm sorry, but I have injured my leg.
② I believe we can do better at the match.
③ I'm afraid I can't participate in the tournament.
④ I think it's time for me to start practicing again.
⑤ I heard the tournament will take place in our town.

20
M: Tiffany is on the field hockey team. During a practice a month ago, she injured her ankle. She has missed practice since then and has ________ ________ ________. Now, a tournament is coming up and she feels she cannot just rest any longer. So, she decides to tell her coach, Mr. Wilson that she would like to ________ ________ ________ ________. In this situation, what would Tiffany most likely say to Mr. Wilson?

Tiffany: Mr. Wilson, I think it's time for me to start practicing again.

Words & Expressions Review 18

● 다음 단어를 암기하세요.

문제	번호	단어	뜻
1	1	recommend	추천하다
	2	adjustable	조정 가능한
2	3	apply for	~을 신청하다
	4	details	세부 사항, 정보
3	5	free ticket	공짜 표
	6	be into ~	~에 빠져 있다
4	7	premiere	시사회
	8	Would you like to + 동사?	너는 ~하고 싶니?
	9	take	(시간이) 걸리다
5	10	come along	함께 가다
6	11	open ~ up	~을 열다, 따다, 펴다
	12	laptop	노트북, 휴대용 컴퓨터
	13	repair shop	수리점
	14	turn off	(전기·가스·수도 등을) 끄다
7	15	preview	예고편
	16	on sale	판매 중인
	17	discount	할인
8	18	broadcasting	방송
	19	air	방송하다
	20	fellow	학우의, 동등한 위치의
	21	via	(특정한 사람·시스템 등을) 통하여
9	22	stationery	문구류

문제	번호	단어	뜻
	23	convey	전달하다
9	24	package	포장하다
10	25	tear off	떼어내다, 찢어내다
	26	baggage	짐, 수하물
11	27	make one's bed	침대를 정리하다
	28	laundry	세탁물
	29	impressed	감동을 받은
	30	mop the floor	(대걸레로) 바닥을 닦다
12	31	decor	실내 장식
13	32	be out of town	도시를 떠나 있다
	33	reschedule	일정을 변경하다
14	34	classical	클래식의, 고전의
	35	upgrade	개선하다
	36	for a while	한동안
	37	instrument	악기
	38	broken	고장 난
	39	fix	수리하다
15	40	vice principal	교감 선생님
	41	host	(손님을) 묵게 하다
17	42	overwhelm	(너무 많은 일로) 어쩔 줄 모르게 만들다
19	43	save	저장하다, 구하다
20	44	patiently	끈기 있게, 참을성 있게

●왼쪽 단어장의 뜻이 보이지 않게 반으로 접고, 학습한 단어의 뜻을 아래 빈칸에 적어주세요.

1	make one's bed	23	host
2	save	24	recommend
3	overwhelm	25	patiently
4	details	26	be out of town
5	adjustable	27	upgrade
6	free ticket	28	preview
7	on sale	29	convey
8	impressed	30	classical
9	air	31	broken
10	via	32	premiere
11	reschedule	33	fix
12	discount	34	Would you like to + 동사?
13	laptop	35	come along
14	for a while	36	be into ~
15	instrument	37	laundry
16	package	38	stationery
17	apply for	39	vice principal
18	turn off	40	mop the floor
19	decor	41	take
20	fellow	42	baggage
21	tear off	43	broadcasting
22	open ~ up	44	repair shop

19회 중학영어듣기 모의고사

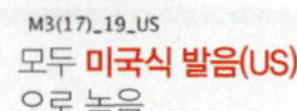

M3(17)_19_US

모두 **미국식 발음(US)**으로 녹음

M3(17)_19_UK

20문제 중 5문제에 **영국식 발음 (US+UK)**을 포함하여 녹음

정답 및 해석 p. 109

1 대화를 듣고, 여자가 만든 열쇠 고리를 고르시오.

①  ②  ③  ④  ⑤ 

2 대화를 듣고, English Speech Contest에 관해 언급되지 <u>않은</u> 것을 고르시오.

① 대회 요일　　　② 장소　　　③ 주제
④ 발표 시간　　　⑤ 우승 상품

3 대화를 듣고, 여자가 남자에게 전화한 목적으로 가장 적절한 것을 고르시오.

① 환불을 받으려고　　　② 옷을 수선하려고　　　③ 옷을 추가 주문하려고
④ 옷을 교환하려고　　　⑤ 가게 위치를 물으려고

4 대화를 듣고, 두 사람이 만나기로 한 시각을 고르시오.

① 10 a.m.　　② 12 p.m.　　③ 1 p.m.　　④ 3 p.m.　　⑤ 5 p.m.

5 대화를 듣고, 여자의 심정으로 가장 적절한 것을 고르시오.

① satisfied　　② regretful　　③ lonely　　④ happy　　⑤ bored

6 다음 그림의 상황에 가장 적절한 대화를 고르시오.

① ② ③ ④ ⑤

7 대화를 듣고, 남자가 여자에게 부탁한 일로 가장 적절한 것을 고르시오.

① 아이 데려오기 ② 차에 기름 넣기 ③ 시장에 다녀오기
④ 퇴근 시간 앞당기기 ⑤ 자동차 정비소에 가기

8 다음을 듣고, 자원봉사 프로그램에 관해 언급되지 <u>않은</u> 것을 고르시오.

① 활동 목적 ② 활동 지역 ③ 활동 기간 ④ 참가 연령 ⑤ 참가 비용

9 다음을 듣고, 무엇에 관한 설명인지 고르시오.

① 상어 ② 돌고래 ③ 참치
④ 문어 ⑤ 바다거북

10 다음을 듣고, 두 사람의 대화가 <u>어색한</u> 것을 고르시오.

① ② ③ ④ ⑤

11번~20번 문제는 다음 페이지에 ➡

11 대화를 듣고, 여자가 대화 직후에 할 일로 가장 적절한 것을 고르시오.

① 요리하기 　　　　② 집 꾸미기 　　　　③ 저녁 메뉴 정하기
④ 할머니께 전화하기 　　⑤ 생일 선물 구입하기

12 다음 표를 보면서 대화를 듣고, 두 사람이 주문할 스탠드를 고르시오.

	Model	Price	Arm	Brightness Adjustment
①	A	$39	Fixed	○
②	B	$35	Adjustable	×
③	C	$25	Adjustable	○
④	D	$20	Adjustable	×
⑤	E	$15	Fixed	×

13 대화를 듣고, 두 사람이 예약할 날짜를 고르시오.

① 10월 9일 　　　　② 10월 10일 　　　　③ 10월 16일
④ 10월 17일 　　　⑤ 10월 18일

14 대화를 듣고, 여자가 어제 한 일로 가장 적절한 것을 고르시오.

① 파이 굽기 　　　　② 요리 가르치기 　　　　③ 아르바이트 하기
④ 수프 만들기 　　　⑤ 가족 모임 참석하기

15 다음을 듣고, 방송의 목적으로 가장 적절한 것을 고르시오.

① 졸업생들을 축하하려고 　　　　② 학교 도서관을 소개하려고
③ 도서 대출 방법을 설명하려고 　　④ 미납 도서 반납을 촉구하려고
⑤ 졸업식 장소 변경을 공지하려고

16 대화를 듣고 여자가 지불할 금액을 고르시오.

① $40 　　　② $50 　　　③ $60 　　　④ $70 　　　⑤ $80

17 대화를 듣고, 남자의 마지막 말에 대한 여자의 응답으로 가장 적절한 것을 고르시오.

Woman: _______________________________

① I would like to go to a K-pop concert.

② Let's keep our fingers crossed for him.

③ I'm disappointed that the audition is canceled.

④ I want to become a world-famous singer.

⑤ Please do not make any loud noises.

[18~19] 대화를 듣고, 여자의 마지막 말에 대한 남자의 응답으로 가장 적절한 것을 고르시오.

18 **Man:** _______________________________

① I think it was delivered yesterday.

② Your computer has been repaired.

③ We received the order on Sunday.

④ It will certainly arrive by tomorrow.

⑤ I'm not sure why it wasn't delivered.

19 **Man:** _______________________________

① It's a bit sore, but I'll manage.

② You should learn how to cook, too.

③ No, I don't need to go to the hospital.

④ Sure! I'll teach you how to chop vegetables.

⑤ Don't forget safety comes first in the kitchen.

20 다음을 듣고, Cynthia가 엄마에게 할 말로 가장 적절한 것을 고르시오.

Cynthia: _______________________________

① Should I see a doctor?   ② I'll be home soon.

③ Can you drop me off at school?   ④ Are you ready to go?

⑤ Can you pick me up at school now?

Dictation Test 19

M3(17)_19_D

Dictation(받아쓰기)은 본문을 받아쓰면서 영어듣기의 집중력을 향상시키고 다양한 표현을 정리하기 위한 영어듣기 학습법입니다. **녹음을 다시 듣고, 빈칸에 알맞은 단어를 써 보세요.**
※Dictation의 정답은 듣기 대본의 밑줄 친 부분을 확인하세요.

정답 p. 109

맞은 개수 / 총189개

그림정보파악(대화)

1. 대화를 듣고, 여자가 만든 열쇠 고리를 고르시오.

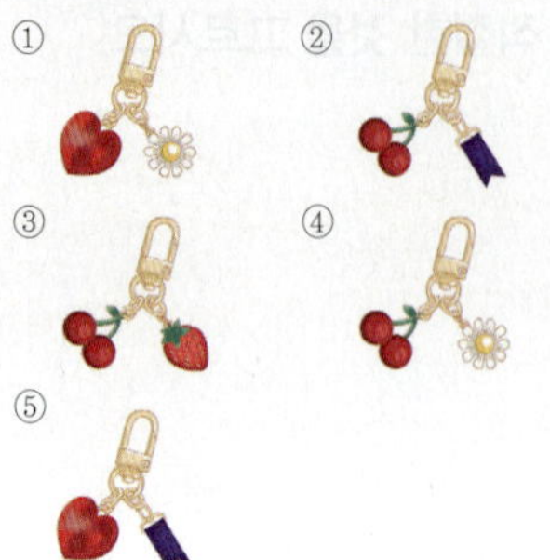

01

M: Joan, what is that __________ __________ __________ __________?

W: It's a key chain. I make key chains as a hobby. They're really easy to make.

M: Wow! It looks great. I like the cherries on it.

W: Well, I thought __________ __________ would give it a refreshing energy. Besides, it is my favorite fruit.

M: I see. And there's __________ __________ __________ on it.

W: Yes. I wanted to add a strap, but I was __________ __________ __________ them. So, I put a flower on it instead.

M: That's awesome.

대화미언급

2. 대화를 듣고, English Speech Contest 에 관해 언급되지 <u>않은</u> 것을 고르시오.

① 대회 요일
② 장소
③ 주제
④ 발표 시간
⑤ 우승 상품

02

M: Sarah, have you heard about the __________ English speech contest at our school?

W: Yeah, the contest is next Wednesday, isn't it?

M: Yes, it's going to be held in the school auditorium.

W: Can the students __________ __________ about anything they want?

M: No, they must speak about a topic __________ __________ education.

W: Interesting. Are you participating in the contest?

M: Yes, I'm planning to talk about the importance of
   reading books.
W: That's a great topic. Will there be any prizes for
   the winners?
M: Yes, the top three contestants ________ ________
   __________ certificates and scholarships.
W: Oh, I might consider participating, too.
M: Good luck if you decide to join!

3. 대화를 듣고, 여자가 남자에게 전화한 목
   적으로 가장 적절한 것을 고르시오.

   ① 환불을 받으려고
   ② 옷을 수선하려고
   ③ 옷을 추가 주문하려고
   ④ 옷을 교환하려고
   ⑤ 가게 위치를 물으려고

03 *(Telephone rings.)*

M: Hello. Denny and George's. How may I help you?
W: Hi. I bought ________ ________ ________ pants at
   your store, and I found that a part of it was torn.
M: I'm sorry, ma'am. Would you like to get an
   __________ or a refund?
W: I want to get a __________.
M: Okay, ma'am. Do you have the receipt?
W: Yes, I have it.
M: Well, come by the store __________ and we'll give
   you a refund.
W: OK. Thanks.

4. 대화를 듣고, 두 사람이 만나기로 한 시
   각을 고르시오.

   ① 10 a.m.   ② 12 p.m.
   ③ 1 p.m.   ④ 3 p.m.
   ⑤ 5 p.m.

04 [Cellphone rings.]

M: Hey, Phoebe.
W: Hi, Carl. You promised to teach me ________
   ________ __________. Can we start tomorrow?
M: Tomorrow sounds good. When do you want to
   meet?
W: I was thinking 10 a.m. ________ ________ ________
   then?
M: I'm afraid not. I have to finish my homework by
   noon. What about 1 p.m.?

다음 페이지에 계속 ➡

W: I'm ________ ________ ________ Sylvia at that

time. Is 3 p.m. okay?

M: Yeah. See you then at Gate Park. Don't ________

________ ________ your skateboard!

W: Sure thing. Bye.

5. 대화를 듣고, 여자의 심정으로 가장 적절
한 것을 고르시오.

① satisfied
② regretful
③ lonely
④ happy
⑤ bored

05 M: I got an "A" on my English test.

W: Really? That's great. Please don't ask me ________

________ ________.

M: Is it that bad?

W: Well, I got a "C" on my test. I think my mom will

be ________ ____________.

M: ________ ________! You'll do better next time.

W: Well, to be honest with you, I didn't study

________ ________ for the test. I played mobile

games every night.

M: You know what? There is a saying, "As you sow,

so you reap."

W: I know that, too. Whew… I ________ ________

studied harder. What should I do now?

6. 다음 그림의 상황에 가장 적절한 대화를
고르시오.

① ②
③ ④
⑤

06 ① W: Our car is parked on what floor?

M: It's on the 2nd ___________ ________. I'll press

the button.

② W: Do you ________ ________ the window?

M: Of course not.

③ W: What time and where should we meet?

M: How about six?

④ W: Do you need ________ ________ the market?

M: Oh, can you get some ice cream?

⑤ W: This escalator is slow.

M: Yes. I ________ ________ ________ faster.

7. 대화를 듣고, 남자가 여자에게 부탁한 일로 가장 적절한 것을 고르시오.

① 아이 데려오기
② 차에 기름 넣기
③ 시장에 다녀오기
④ 퇴근 시간 앞당기기
⑤ 자동차 정비소에 가기

07 M: Honey, will you be ________ ________ ________ after work tonight?

W: No. I have to pick up some groceries.

M: Do you have ________ ________ ________ ________ after that?

W: Not really, why?

M: Can you ________ ________ ________ to the auto repair shop as well?

W: Why's that?

M: It's time to change the oil.

W: Okay. I'll ________ ________ ________ it.

8. 다음을 듣고, 자원봉사 프로그램에 관해 언급되지 <u>않은</u> 것을 고르시오.

① 활동 목적　② 활동 지역
③ 활동 기간　④ 참가 연령
⑤ 참가 비용

08 M: Hello, listeners. The Hands Foundation is looking for enthusiastic teenagers. The Foundation's summer volunteer program is now recruiting students to ________ ________ at farms during the busiest time of the year. The activities will ________ ________ in mid-southern areas. The program starts on June 1st, and ends on the 14th. It's open to all students __________ the ages of 13 and 17. Please ________ ________ May 20th.

다음 페이지에 계속 ➡

담화화제추론

9. 다음을 듣고, 무엇에 관한 설명인지 고르시오.

① 상어　　　② 돌고래
③ 참치　　　④ 문어
⑤ 바다거북

09 M: This animal lives in the ocean but is not a fish. It uses _________ _________ _________ and must come to the surface for air. It is very intelligent and often _________ _________ _________. It _________ _________ _________ its friendly image. It swims gracefully in the water. People enjoy watching it jump and spin out of the water. It is widely loved, _________, and _________.

어색한대화찾기

10. 다음을 듣고, 두 사람의 대화가 <u>어색한</u> 것을 고르시오.

①　　　　②
③　　　　④
⑤

10 ① W: Can I borrow this book for a few days?

M: Of course.

② W: I'm ________ ________ ________ seeing her again.

M: You don't have to look for it.

③ W: Do you sell blue jeans?

M: Sure. What's your size?

④ W: I have a ________ _________ tomorrow.

M: I hope everything goes well.

⑤ W: How would you like your steak?

M: ________-________, please.

할일파악(대화직후)

11. 대화를 듣고, 여자가 대화 직후에 할 일로 가장 적절한 것을 고르시오.

① 요리하기
② 집 꾸미기
③ 저녁 메뉴 정하기
④ 할머니께 전화하기
⑤ 생일 선물 구입하기

11 W: Dad, Mom's birthday is __________ __________. We should get something special for her.

M: Okay. What do you have in mind?

W: Let's _________ her a surprise birthday party at home. We should also surprise Mom by inviting Grandma.

M: I like that idea! We'll need to ___________ the house and prepare some food then.

W: I'll ___________ ___________ ___________ the decorations. Can you help me with the menu? What should we make?

M: Hmm… I'll think about the menu.

W: Okay. While you're thinking, I'm going to ___________ ___________.

M: Good idea.

12. 다음 표를 보면서 대화를 듣고, 두 사람이 주문할 스탠드를 고르시오.

	Model	Price	Arm	Brightness Adjustment
①	A	$39	Fixed	○
②	B	$35	Adjustable	×
③	C	$25	Adjustable	○
④	D	$20	Adjustable	×
⑤	E	$15	Fixed	×

12

M: Honey, are you still ___________ for desk lamps online?

W: Yes. I'm trying to choose the right one for our son's desk. Can you help me?

M: Sure. Let's see. I think spending more than $30 is too much.

W: I agree. Let's look for ones that are ___________ ___________ $30. Should we choose one with an adjustable arm or a fixed arm?

M: An adjustable arm would be better because then the light ___________ ___________ ___________.

W: Okay. Then, two options are left, a lamp with ___________ ___________ or one without.

W: Let's get one with brightness adjustment. That way, he can adjust it ___________ ___________ his needs.

W: Good idea. Let's order this one.

다음 페이지에 계속 ➡

13. 대화를 듣고, 두 사람이 예약할 날짜를 고르시오.

① 10월 9일
② 10월 10일
③ 10월 16일
④ 10월 17일
⑤ 10월 18일

13

W: Dad, the International Air Show is finally starting next month.

M: You've been ________ ________ ________ it for so long! Let's buy tickets right away.

W: Great! It starts on October 9th and ends on the 18th.

M: Should we go on ________ ________?

W: Sorry, Dad. I have to go to Eric's birthday party that day.

M: Then what about the 17th?

W: Look, Dad. We should go on the 16th ________ ________ the 17th. On that day, visitors can get in the planes that are ________ ________.

M: Awesome! Let's book the tickets for that day.

14. 대화를 듣고, 여자가 어제 한 일로 가장 적절한 것을 고르시오.

① 파이 굽기
② 요리 가르치기
③ 아르바이트 하기
④ 수프 만들기
⑤ 가족 모임 참석하기

14

M: Hi, Abby. How was your cooking class today?

W: Hi, Peter. I learned how to make chicken soup. I'll make it for our next family dinner.

M: Sounds yummy. It makes me feel hungry.

W: ________ ________ ________ lunch yet?

M: No. I was too busy doing my part-time job.

W: ________ ________ ________ ________ some soup left. I do have some pie left, though instead. I baked it yesterday. Would you like it?

M: Of course! Thanks. You're a ________ ________.

W: You're welcome.

15. 다음을 듣고, 방송의 목적으로 가장 적절한 것을 고르시오.

① 졸업생들을 축하하려고
② 학교 도서관을 소개하려고
③ 도서 대출 방법을 설명하려고
④ 미납 도서 반납을 촉구하려고
⑤ 졸업식 장소 변경을 공지하려고

15 W: Good afternoon, students. This is an announcement from your student council. First of all, congratulations on your graduation! We also wanted to ________ ________ __________ to remind you once again to return all books to the library. The librarian delivered the list of students with ____________ library items a week ago, but some __________ still have not returned their books. All books borrowed from the library ________ ________ __________ before your graduation ceremony. We would appreciate the return of these items as soon as possible. Thank you.

16. 대화를 듣고 여자가 지불할 금액을 고르시오.

① $40　　② $50
③ $60　　④ $70
⑤ $80

16 M: Hi, can I help you?

W: I'm ________ ________ toys for my twin daughters. They are 4.

M: How about these ________ _______?

W: How much are they?

M: The small ones are $30 each, and the big ones are $40 each.

W: That's ________ expensive.

M: We have a ________ __________ this week. You can get a $10 discount if you spend more than $50.

W: Oh, great. I'll take two large ones, please. Here is my credit card.

다음 페이지에 계속 ➡

17. 대화를 듣고, 남자의 마지막 말에 대한 여자의 응답으로 가장 적절한 것을 고르시오.

Woman: ___________________

① I would like to go to a K-pop concert.
② Let's keep our fingers crossed for him.
③ I'm disappointed that the audition is canceled.
④ I want to become a world-famous singer.
⑤ Please do not make any loud noises.

17

M: Kelly, did you hear about John's K-pop audition?

W: I heard that he passed the first round.

M: Wow! _________ _________ _________ _________ _________.

W: Yes, but he still needs to pass the second round of the audition.

M: Well, he is __________ at singing, so I'm sure he'll pass the next round.

W: I heard that _________ _________ _________ more time for this round, so he has to dance as well.

M: I see. I hope he doesn't make any mistakes.

W: Let's keep our fingers crossed for him.

18. 대화를 듣고, 여자의 마지막 말에 대한 남자의 응답으로 가장 적절한 것을 고르시오.

Man: ___________________

① I think it was delivered yesterday.
② Your computer has been repaired.
③ We received the order on Sunday.
④ It will certainly arrive by tomorrow.
⑤ I'm not sure why it wasn't delivered.

18

(*Telephone rings.*)

M: Hello, Charley's Electronics Store.

W: Hi, I ordered a _________ __________ through the Internet but it hasn't _________ __________ _________.

M: OK. May I have your name, please?

W: It's Elena Park. I _________ _________ _________ three days ago, on Sunday evening.

M: I see. Well, I think the delivery has been delayed because the order _________ _________ on the weekend. I'm very sorry.

W: That's OK. Can you check when it will be delivered?

M: It will certainly arrive by tomorrow.

19

19. 대화를 듣고, 여자의 마지막 말에 대한 남자의 응답으로 가장 적절한 것을 고르시오.

Man: _________________

① It's a bit sore, but I'll manage.
② You should learn how to cook, too.
③ No, I don't need to go to the hospital.
④ Sure! I'll teach you how to chop vegetables.
⑤ Don't forget safety comes first in the kitchen.

W: Owen, what happened to your hand? It looks like it's _________ _________!

M: Oh, it's nothing serious. I accidentally cut it while cooking yesterday.

W: That sounds painful. How did it happen?

M: I _________ _________ _________ and I accidentally _________ my finger with the knife.

W: Ouch, that must have hurt. Did you get it checked by a doctor?

M: Yeah, the doctor said it's _________ _________ _________ _________ and would heal quickly.

W: That's good to hear. Is it _________ _________ a lot?

M: It's a bit sore, but I'll manage.

20

20. 다음을 듣고, Cynthia가 엄마에게 할 말로 가장 적절한 것을 고르시오.

Cynthia: _________________

① Should I see a doctor?
② I'll be home soon.
③ Can you drop me off at school?
④ Are you ready to go?
⑤ Can you pick me up at school now?

W: Cynthia is _________ _________ now. However, she doesn't feel well. She has a _________ _________ and a headache. Her teacher tells her to go home and _________ _________ _________. So Cynthia decides to call her mom to say that she's sick. She wants her mom to _________ _________ _________ and take her home. In this situation, what would Cynthia say to her mom?

Cynthia: Can you pick me up at school now?

Words & Expressions Review 19

● 다음 단어를 암기하세요.

문제	번호	단어	뜻
1	1	dangle	매달리다, 달랑거리다
	2	besides	게다가, ~외에
	3	run out of	~이 다 떨어지다
2	4	award	수여하다
	5	certificate	증명서, 증서
	6	scholarship	장학금
3	7	a pair of	한 벌의, 한 쌍의
	8	tear	찢다
	9	get an exchange	교환하다
	10	come by	잠깐 들르다
5	11	Cheer up!	기운 내!
	12	to be honest	솔직히 말하자면
	13	saying	속담, 격언
	14	sow	뿌리다, 심다
	15	reap	거두다, 수확하다
6	16	basement	지하층
	17	escalator	에스컬레이터
7	18	groceries	식료품류
	19	as well	~도, ~뿐만 아니라
	20	take care of ~	~을 처리하다
8	21	enthusiastic	열정적인, 열렬한
	22	recruit	모집하다

문제	번호	단어	뜻
8	23	register	등록하다
9	24	breathe	숨 쉬다
	25	intelligent	똑똑한, 지능이 높은
10	26	well-done	(고기가) 잘 익혀진
11	27	come up	다가오다
	28	throw a party	파티를 열다
12	29	arm	거치대
	30	direct	(어떤 방향으로) 돌리다
13	31	display	전시, 진열
14	32	life saver	생명의 은인
15	33	outstanding	아직 처리되지 않은
	34	appreciate	고마워하다
16	35	stuffed animal	봉제 동물 인형
	36	promotion	홍보 활동
	37	proud of ~	~을 자랑스러워하는
17	38	marvelous	훌륭한, 놀라운
	39	allot	할당하다
18	40	place an order	주문을 하다
	41	delay	지연시키다, 미루다
19	42	chop	다지다, 썰다
	43	nick	(칼로) 베다
20	44	fever	열, 발열

● 왼쪽 단어장의 뜻이 보이지 않게 반으로 접고, 학습한 단어의 뜻을 아래 빈칸에 적어주세요.

1	promotion	23	escalator
2	register	24	groceries
3	enthusiastic	25	place an order
4	a pair of	26	recruit
5	certificate	27	throw a party
6	marvelous	28	well-done
7	run out of	29	come by
8	appreciate	30	take care of ~
9	as well	31	direct
10	arm	32	stuffed animal
11	outstanding	33	basement
12	proud of	34	delay
13	fever	35	get an exchange
14	besides	36	life saver
15	saying	37	nick
16	display	38	allot
17	intelligent	39	breathe
18	to be honest	40	award
19	reap	41	tear
20	sow	42	Cheer up!
21	chop	43	come up
22	scholarship	44	dangle

19회 단어

20회 중학영어듣기 모의고사

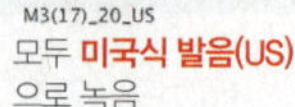

모두 **미국식 발음(US)** 으로 녹음

20문제 중 5문제에 **영국식 발음 (US+UK)**을 포함하여 녹음

정답 및 해석 p. 114

1 대화를 듣고, 여자가 구입할 책가방을 고르시오.

①  ②  ③  ④  ⑤ 

2 대화를 듣고, ABC Scooter Rental에 관해 언급되지 <u>않은</u> 것을 고르시오.

① 대여료 ② 스쿠터 종류 ③ 운영 시간
④ 가게 위치 ⑤ 대여 준비물

3 대화를 듣고, 여자가 남자에게 전화한 목적으로 가장 적절한 것을 고르시오.

① 배송지 주소를 바꾸려고 ② 재고가 있는지 확인하려고
③ 잘못 배송된 옷을 교환하려고 ④ 온라인 주문 방법을 문의하려고
⑤ 주문 수량을 수정하려고

4 대화를 듣고, 두 사람이 영화를 보기로 한 시각을 고르시오.

① 9 a.m. ② 11 a.m. ③ 2 p.m. ④ 4 p.m. ⑤ 6 p.m.

5 대화를 듣고, 여자의 심정으로 가장 적절한 것을 고르시오.

① sorry ② excited ③ jealous
④ annoyed ⑤ thankful

6 다음 그림의 상황에 가장 적절한 대화를 고르시오.

① ② ③ ④ ⑤

7 대화를 듣고, 여자가 남자에게 부탁한 일로 가장 적절한 것을 고르시오.

① 사진 보여주기 ② 참고서적 찾기
③ 여행 계획표 공유하기 ④ 여행 후기 알려주기
⑤ 여행 블로그 찾기

8 다음을 듣고, River Opera House에 관해 언급되지 <u>않은</u> 것을 고르시오.

① 개관 연도 ② 내부 시설 ③ 회원 특전
④ 대관 비용 ⑤ 교육 프로그램

9 다음을 듣고, 무엇에 관한 설명인지 고르시오.

① 전기차 ② 배 ③ 비행기 ④ 자전거 ⑤ 기차

10 대화를 듣고, 두 사람의 대화가 <u>어색한</u> 것을 고르시오.

① ② ③ ④ ⑤

11번~20번 문제는 다음 페이지에 ➡

11 대화를 듣고, 남자가 대화 후에 할 일로 적절한 것을 고르시오.

① 친구 만나기　　　② 책 사기　　　③ 점심 먹기
④ 영화 보기　　　⑤ 집으로 가기

12 다음 표를 보면서 대화를 듣고, 남자가 구입할 티셔츠를 고르시오.

	Model	Neck Line	Color	Cooling Cotton
①	A	U-neck	White	○
②	B	U-neck	Black	×
③	C	V-neck	Black	○
④	D	V-neck	White	×
⑤	E	V-neck	White	○

13 대화를 듣고, 두 사람이 베이비 페어에 가기로 한 날짜를 고르시오.

① 8월 9일　　　② 8월 10일　　　③ 8월 11일
④ 8월 12일　　　⑤ 8월 13일

14 대화를 듣고, 여자가 어제 한 일로 가장 적절한 것을 고르시오.

① 쇼핑하기　　　② 요리 강좌 듣기　　　③ 쿠키 굽기
④ 책 읽기　　　⑤ 친구 만나기

15 다음을 듣고, 방송의 목적으로 가장 적절한 것을 고르시오.

① 올바른 마스크 착용 방법을 알리려고
② 교실 내 공기 청정기의 사용법을 안내하려고
③ 미세 먼지가 심할 때 행동 요령을 공지하려고
④ 호흡기 질환에 도움이 되는 음식을 소개하려고
⑤ 미세 먼지가 건강에 미치는 영향을 설명하려고

16 대화를 듣고, 여자가 지불할 금액을 고르시오.

① $3　　　　② $5　　　　③ $8　　　　④ $10　　　　⑤ $11

17 대화를 듣고, 남자의 마지막 말에 대한 여자의 응답으로 가장 적절한 것을 고르시오.

Woman: ______________________________________

① I've tried, but she wouldn't listen to me.

② OK. I will have a heart-to-heart talk with her.

③ No problem. I will help you find a new house.

④ Exactly. I'd better find a new place right away.

⑤ Thank you for the advice on how to keep it clean.

[18~19]　대화를 듣고, 여자의 마지막 말에 대한 남자의 응답으로 가장 적절한 것을 고르시오.

18 **Man:** ______________________________________

① Okay. I hope he says yes.　　② My report is due next Friday.

③ History is my favorite subject.　　④ I can't believe I got a C on the test.

⑤ We'd better start the project right away.

19 **Man:** ______________________________________

① Oh. This food is so delicious.　　② You forgot to give me my change.

③ No. I just want something to drink.　　④ Sure. I'll follow you there.

⑤ Just go straight and turn left.

20 다음 상황 설명을 듣고, Ms. Lee가 Bruce에게 할 말로 가장 적절한 것을 고르시오.

Ms. Lee: Bruce, ______________________________________

① you have to practice your kicks more.

② you have all that is needed inside you.

③ Taekwondo is a wonderful sport, isn't it?

④ the tournament will be over before you know.

⑤ I didn't know you had entered the tournament.

Dictation Test 20

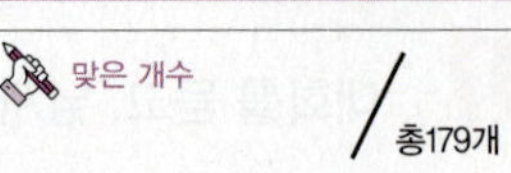

M3(17)_20_D

Dictation(받아쓰기)은 본문을 받아쓰면서 영어듣기의 집중력을 향상시키고 다양한 표현을 정리하기 위한 영어듣기 학습법입니다. **녹음을 다시 듣고, 빈칸에 알맞은 단어를 써 보세요.**
※Dictation의 정답은 듣기 대본의 밑줄 친 부분을 확인하세요.

정답 p. 114

맞은 개수 / 총179개

그림정보파악(대화)

1. 대화를 듣고, 여자가 구입할 책가방을 고르시오.

① ② ③ ④ ⑤

01

M: Hello. Welcome to Everything Backpack! How can I help you?

W: Hi. I am ________ ________ a backpack for my daughter.

M: Okay. Here are the backpack __________. Would you like a backpack with wheels or ________ ________?

W: I think the ones with wheels will be better, because her backpack can be very heavy sometimes.

M: I see… So, would your daughter like a backpack with a cat or a rabbit?

W: Oh, __________ a rabbit! She loves rabbits!

M: Okay, sounds good! Would you like a backpack with or without side pockets?

W: I will take the one ________ ________ ________. Thank you.

대화미언급

2. 대화를 듣고, ABC Scooter Rental에 관해 언급되지 <u>않은</u> 것을 고르시오.

① 대여료
② 스쿠터 종류
③ 운영 시간
④ 가게 위치
⑤ 대여 준비물

02

(Telephone rings.)

M: Hello, ABC Scooter Rental. How can I assist you today?

W: Hi, I'm interested in renting a scooter for the weekend. How much is the ________ ________?

M: Our rental fees start at $30 per day.

W: That sounds __________. What are your ________ ________?

M: We are open from 9 a.m. to 6 p.m.

W: Great, and where is your shop _________?

M: We are located on Main Street, right next to the park.

W: Excellent. Do I need to bring anything when renting a scooter?

M: Yes, you need to bring your driver's license.

W: I see. Thank you, I'll _________ _________ this weekend.

M: You're welcome. We look forward to seeing you.

3. 대화를 듣고, 여자가 남자에게 전화한 목적으로 가장 적절한 것을 고르시오.

① 배송지 주소를 바꾸려고
② 재고가 있는지 확인하려고
③ 잘못 배송된 옷을 교환하려고
④ 온라인 주문 방법을 문의하려고
⑤ 주문 수량을 수정하려고

03 (Telephone rings.)

M: Hello, this is Every Kind of Clothes You Can Think of.

W: Hi, I'm calling about the _________ _________ for my online order.

M: Okay. How can I help you?

W: I just _________ _________ _________ from your online store, but I __________ used my old address as my shipping address.

M: So, you need to _________ your shipping address?

W: Yes. Would that be possible?

M: Of course. Can I get your order number and the new shipping address?

W: My order number is 158347 and the new shipping address is 303 Madison St., New York City.

M: Okay. I've _________ the address for your order.

4. 대화를 듣고, 두 사람이 영화를 보기로 한 시각을 고르시오.

① 9 a.m.　　② 11 a.m.
③ 2 p.m.　　④ 4 p.m.
⑤ 6 p.m.

04 W: Hey, Mike! The movie, *Adventure Galaxy* _________ _________ __________ this Saturday.

M: I know! Let's watch it together in 3D.

W: Of course. Let me _________ _________ _________ on my phone.

다음 페이지에 계속 ➡

M: Are there any shows in the morning?

W: Hmm… There's one at 9 a.m. and another at 11 a.m., but they're not in 3D.

M: Is there anything before 6 p.m.?

W: There's one at 2 p.m., and it's in 3D. The tickets for 4 p.m. are ________ ________.

M: All right. 2 p.m. ________ for me.

W: Me, too. Let's buy the tickets now.

5. 대화를 듣고, 여자의 심정으로 가장 적절한 것을 고르시오.

① sorry　② excited
③ jealous　④ annoyed
⑤ thankful

05

M: Hello, Angela. Is there something wrong?

W: Hi, Matthew. It's my sister again.

M: What happened?

W: Did I tell you before that she ________ ________ my clothes and shoes?

M: Yes, you did. What did she take this time?

W: My new trainers. I was really ________ ________ ________ wearing them today.

M: Oh, no. I guess she didn't even ask you if she could wear them.

W: She never does. I think it is so rude.

M: I agree. You should talk to her about this.

W: I will. I've ________ ________.

6. 다음 그림의 상황에 가장 적절한 대화를 고르시오.

①　②　③　④　⑤

06

① M: Can I help you?

W: Yes, I'm ________ ________ a laptop.

② M: What are you doing now?

W: I'm studying for the test.

③ M: Why ________ ________ ________?

W: I got a poor grade in English.

④ M: I've lost some weight.

W: Good for you. You look ________ ________.

⑤ M: You look so happy. Why is that?

W: Guess what? I got _______ _______ _______ on

the English test.

7. 대화를 듣고, 여자가 남자에게 부탁한 일
로 가장 적절한 것을 고르시오.

① 사진 보여주기
② 참고서적 찾기
③ 여행 계획표 공유하기
④ 여행 후기 알려주기
⑤ 여행 블로그 찾기

07 W: Hey, Patrick. How was your trip to Europe?

M: Hey, Gina. It was fantastic. I want to go again

soon.

W: What was the best thing about your trip?

M: I would say it was the beautiful scenery.

W: I guess that's _______ _______ _______ _______.

I'm planning a trip to Europe myself.

M: Oh, you are?

W: Yeah. So, can you share your __________

and _______ with me? I want to have some

information for when I plan my own trip.

M: Sure. I have __________ __________ _____ _______

_______. I'll send it to you when I get home.

W: Thanks.

8. 다음을 듣고, River Opera House에 관해
언급되지 않은 것을 고르시오.

① 개관 연도   ② 내부 시설
③ 회원 특전   ④ 대관 비용
⑤ 교육 프로그램

08 M: Welcome to River Opera House. We opened in

1999 as a hub for local artists. Besides two concert

halls, we house three __________ _______, as well

as training facilities. You can enjoy all of these

amenities at a __________ _______ when you

become a member of the River Opera House. The

_______ membership fee is $200. We also run

_______ educational programs for the general

public. _______ _______ __________, please visit

our website.

다음 페이지에 계속 ➡

9. 다음을 듣고, 무엇에 관한 설명인지 고르시오.

① 전기차 ② 배
③ 비행기 ④ 자전거
⑤ 기차

09 M: This is a method of transportation. It allows you to travel long distances. It can ______________ hundreds of people. It can go across not only continents but also oceans. Its design is ________ ________ ________. People usually take this to go to foreign countries. There are staff who ________ ________ ________ ________ on it while cruising.

10. 대화를 듣고, 두 사람의 대화가 <u>어색한</u> 것을 고르시오.

①　　　　②
③　　　　④
⑤

10 ① M: What course do you want to ________ ________ ________?

W: Maybe music or fine arts.

② M: Are you ready? We're leaving in five minutes.

W: Wait, I'll just get my jacket.

③ M: Where did you spend spring break?

W: We ________ ________ ________ visit our grandfather in Italy.

④ M: Are you going to the cafeteria for lunch?

W: No, I brought ________ ________ ________.

⑤ M: Oh no, I left my homework at home!

W: Let's go back and get it.

11. 대화를 듣고, 남자가 대화 후에 할 일로 적절한 것을 고르시오.

① 친구 만나기 ② 책 사기
③ 점심 먹기 ④ 영화 보기
⑤ 집으로 가기

11 M: Hey, Pippa! What are you doing here?

W: I'm going to ________ ________ ________ my friend. What about you?

M: I just bought some books.

W: I see. Do you want to join us? We're going to have lunch at Steakland.

M: Mmm. I don't think I can.

W: Come on. We might ________ ________ ________ ________, too.

M: Nah, maybe next time. I have to be home early. ________ ________ ________ ________ today.

W: Oh, okay. Tell her Happy Birthday for me then. See you around.

12. 다음 표를 보면서 대화를 듣고, 남자가 구입할 티셔츠를 고르시오.

	Model	Neck Line	Color	Cooling Cotton
①	A	U-neck	White	○
②	B	U-neck	Black	×
③	C	V-neck	Black	○
④	D	V-neck	White	×
⑤	E	V-neck	White	○

12

W: Honey, don't you need some T-shirts? They are ________ ________.

M: Great! I need some for this summer. What kind of T-shirts do they have?

W: They have T-shirts with ________ ________ of neck lines, U-neck and V-neck.

M: I prefer V-necks. I ________ ________ ________ V-necks.

W: What color do you want, white or black?

M: I want white T-shirts.

W: Then, you have two options left. Do you need T-shirts ________ ________ cooling cotton?

M: Sure. They are helpful in the summer.

W: I agree. Then, pick that one.

다음 페이지에 계속 ➡

13. 대화를 듣고, 두 사람이 베이비 페어에 가기로 한 날짜를 고르시오.

① 8월 9일
② 8월 10일
③ 8월 11일
④ 8월 12일
⑤ 8월 13일

13

M: Honey, did you hear that there's going to be a baby fair in town this summer?

W: Oh, really? We should go ________ ________ ________. When is it taking place?

M: It's ________ ________ ________ August 9th to 13th.

W: How about going on August 10th? Do you have any plans for that day?

M: Yes, I have a dinner appointment with a client on the 10th. What about the 11th?

W: We have a family gathering ________ ________ the 11th. Are you free on August 12th?

M: Yes, it's a Saturday. We can spend the ________ ________ ________ the fair together.

14. 대화를 듣고, 여자가 어제 한 일로 가장 적절한 것을 고르시오.

① 쇼핑하기
② 요리 강좌 듣기
③ 쿠키 굽기
④ 책 읽기
⑤ 친구 만나기

14

W: Jake, I have something for you.

M: Wow, chocolate cookies? ________ ________ ________! Thank you.

W: I remember you saying that you love chocolate cookies.

M: That's really nice of you. Where did you buy these?

W: Actually, I made them ________ yesterday.

M: What? You must be ________ at baking.

W: Well, it's not that difficult if you have a good ________.

M: Oh, really? How long did it ________ to make these?

W: About an hour.

15. 다음을 듣고, 방송의 목적으로 가장 적절한 것을 고르시오.

① 올바른 마스크 착용 방법을 알리려고
② 교실 내 공기 청정기의 사용법을 안내하려고
③ 미세 먼지가 심할 때 행동 요령을 공지하려고
④ 호흡기 질환에 도움이 되는 음식을 소개하려고
⑤ 미세 먼지가 건강에 미치는 영향을 설명하려고

15 M: Hello, students. This is Mr. Anderson, your principal. The fine dust problem is ________ ________ these days. Today, I'd like to tell you what to do when the fine dust ________ ________ ________. First of all, close all the windows and turn on the ________ ________ in the classroom. Second, drink plenty of water as ________ as possible. Finally, make sure to wear a mask when you go out. Keep these tips in mind to ________ ________ ________. Thank you.

16. 대화를 듣고, 여자가 지불할 금액을 고르시오.

① $3 ② $5
③ $8 ④ $10
⑤ $11

16 M: Hello. How can I help you?

W: Hi. I'd like to pay for my PC bang ________.

M: Sure. Can you tell me your seat number?

W: I used PC number 11.

M: *[Typing sounds]* Okay, you ________ ________ ________ ________ the PC for five hours, so it's five dollars. Did you order food?

W: Yes, I ordered two cup noodles.

M: Okay, that's three dollars for the cup noodles and five dollars for your PC session.

W: All right. Here you go.

다음 페이지에 계속 ➡

17. 대화를 듣고, 남자의 마지막 말에 대한 여자의 응답으로 가장 적절한 것을 고르시오.

Woman: ___________________

① I've tried, but she wouldn't listen to me.
② OK. I will have a heart-to-heart talk with her.
③ No problem. I will help you find a new house.
④ Exactly. I'd better find a new place right away.
⑤ Thank you for the advice on how to keep it clean.

17

W: Hi, Peter! Are you busy at the moment?

M: Not really. Do you need some help?

W: Yes. Can you help me look for ________ ________ ________ ________?

M: Oh, are you thinking of moving out?

W: Yes. I'm having some problems with my roommate.

M: That's too bad. Can I ask what the problem is?

W: She doesn't ________ ________. The living room and the kitchen are always ________.

M: Have you talked to her about it?

W: No, I haven't. Do you think I should?

M: Of course. I'm sure you can ________ ________ ________ through communication.

W: OK. I will have a heart-to-heart talk with her.

18. 대화를 듣고, 여자의 마지막 말에 대한 남자의 응답으로 가장 적절한 것을 고르시오.

Man: ___________________

① Okay. I hope he says yes.
② My report is due next Friday.
③ History is my favorite subject.
④ I can't believe I got a C on the test.
⑤ We'd better start the project right away.

18

W: Hi, Andy. Who is ________ ________ ________ for the history project?

M: Actually, I was thinking about you. We worked together last year and we did an excellent job.

W: I was thinking the same! I have so many good ideas for this project.

M: I knew ________ ________, but we still need one more person. Do you know anyone?

W: How about Paul? I heard him say he ________ ________ ________ ________ history.

M: That's great! Do you know his phone number?

W: Yes. I'll call him right now.

M: Okay. I hope he says yes.

19. 대화를 듣고, 여자의 마지막 말에 대한 남자의 응답으로 가장 적절한 것을 고르시오.

Man: _________________

① Oh. This food is so delicious.
② You forgot to give me my change.
③ No. I just want something to drink.
④ Sure. I'll follow you there.
⑤ Just go straight and turn left.

19

W: Hey, Mike. Can you please do me a favor?

M: Yeah, sure. What is it?

W: Can you ________ ________ ________ ________ my bags? I'll just leave them here beside you.

M: Why? ________ ________ ________ ________?

W: I'm just going to the bathroom.

M: Okay. Hmmm. Can you get me a soda ________? There's a food stall near the bathroom.

W: Sure. Is there ________ ________ you want?

M: No. I just want something to drink.

20. 다음 상황 설명을 듣고, Ms. Lee가 Bruce에게 할 말로 가장 적절한 것을 고르시오.

Ms. Lee: Bruce, _________________

① you have to practice your kicks more.
② you have all that is needed inside you.
③ Taekwondo is a wonderful sport, isn't it?
④ the tournament will be over before you know.
⑤ I didn't know you had entered the tournament.

20

W: Ms. Lee is a Taekwondo coach. She is coaching one of her students, Bruce for the local Taekwondo tournament. 15-year-old Bruce ________ ________ ________ for three months. On the day of the tournament, Ms. Lee sees that Bruce is very nervous and his kick isn't ________ ________ ________ ________. So, Ms. Lee would like to tell him that he has the power to win. In this situation, what would Ms. Lee most likely say to Bruce?

Ms. Lee: Bruce, you have all that is needed inside you.

Words & Expressions Review 20

● 다음 단어를 암기하세요.

문제	번호	단어	뜻
1	1	selection	전시품
	2	side pocket	옆 주머니
2	3	rental fee	대여료, 사용료
	4	reasonable	(가격이) 합리적인, 적정한
3	5	make a purchase	구매하다, 구입하다
	6	accidentally	실수로, 잘못하여
	7	switch	변경하다, 바꾸다
4	8	sold out	표가 매진된
5	9	happen	일어나다, 발생하다
	10	trainer	운동화
	11	have had enough	더 이상 못 참다, 지긋지긋하다
6	12	long face	우울한 얼굴
	13	lose weight	살이 빠지다, 체중이 줄다
7	14	scenery	풍경, 경치
	15	itinerary	여행 일정(표)
8	16	hub	중심지
	17	amenity	편의 시설
	18	inspire	영감을 주다
9	19	attend to	~를 응대하다, 돌보다
	20	cruise	순항하다
10	21	spend	(시간을) 보내다, 쓰다
	22	spring break	봄 방학

문제	번호	단어	뜻
11	23	meet up with A	A를 만나다
	24	See you around.	또 봐.. 잘 있어.
12	25	thin	(사람·몸 등이) 마른, 가는
	26	made of	~으로 만든
13	27	check ~ out	(흥미로운 것을) 살펴보다
	28	scheduled	예정된, 계획된
14	29	talented	재능이 있는
	30	fine dust	미세먼지
15	31	air purifier	공기청정기
	32	keep ~ in mind	명심하다, 유념하다
16	33	session	시간, 기간
	34	log in	접속하다, 로그인하다
	35	move out	이사를 나가다
17	36	resolve	(문제 등을) 해결하다
	37	heart-to-heart	솔직한, 마음을 터놓고 하는
18	38	project	과제, 연구 프로젝트
	39	be due	(제출 기한이) ~까지이다
	40	keep an eye on ~	~을 계속 지켜보다
19	41	afterwards	나중에, 그 뒤에
	42	stall	매점, 노점
20	43	tournament	토너먼트
	44	usual	평소의

M3(17)_W_20

● 왼쪽 단어장의 뜻이 보이지 않게 반으로 접고, 학습한 단어의 뜻을 아래 빈칸에 적어주세요.

1	amenity	23	hub
2	keep an eye on ~	24	itinerary
3	side pocket	25	log in
4	made of	26	cruise
5	meet up with A	27	talented
6	accidentally	28	check ~ out
7	attend to	29	long face
8	scheduled	30	rental fee
9	trainer	31	inspire
10	have had enough	32	See you around.
11	spring break	33	fine dust
12	lose weight	34	switch
13	sold out	35	resolve
14	tournament	36	selection
15	be due	37	heart-to-heart
16	usual	38	move out
17	project	39	stall
18	reasonable	40	afterwards
19	happen	41	air purifier
20	scenery	42	spend
21	keep ~ in mind	43	thin
22	session	44	make a purchase

21회 중학영어듣기 모의고사

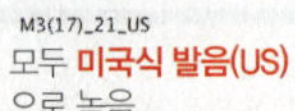

M3(17)_21_US
모두 **미국식 발음(US)** 으로 녹음

M3(17)_21_UK
20문제 중 5문제에 **영국식 발음 (US+UK)**을 포함하여 녹음

정답 및 해석 p. 121

1 대화를 듣고, 여자가 구입할 쇼핑 카트를 고르시오.

①  ②  ③  ④  ⑤ 

2 대화를 듣고, Max Energy Drink에 관해 언급되지 <u>않은</u> 것을 고르시오.

① 효과　　② 맛　　③ 용량　　④ 가격　　⑤ 부작용

3 대화를 듣고, 여자가 남자에게 전화한 목적으로 가장 적절한 것을 고르시오.

① 콘서트에 초대하려고
② 이사 계획을 알리려고
③ 노래 수업을 의뢰하려고
④ 합창단 입단을 제안하려고
⑤ 콘서트 티켓 구매를 요청하려고

4 대화를 듣고, 두 사람이 만나기로 한 시각을 고르시오.

① 5 p.m.　　② 6 p.m.　　③ 7 p.m.　　④ 8 p.m.　　⑤ 10 p.m.

5 대화를 듣고, 남자의 심정으로 가장 적절한 것을 고르시오.

① angry　　② excited　　③ sorry　　④ shy　　⑤ satisfied

6 다음 그림의 상황에 가장 적절한 대화를 고르시오.

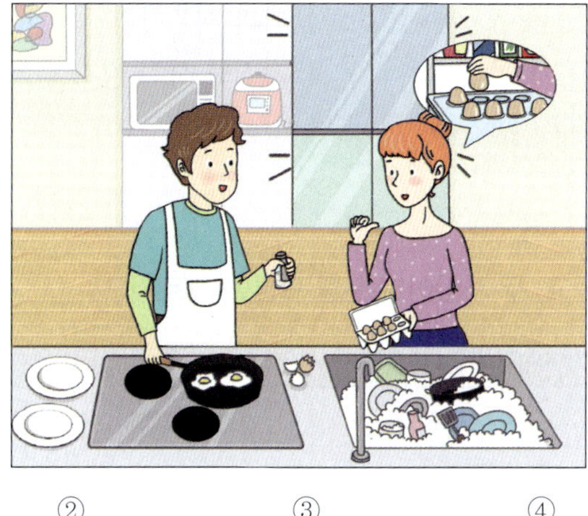

①   ②   ③   ④   ⑤

7 대화를 듣고, 여자가 남자에게 부탁한 일로 가장 적절한 것을 고르시오.

① 아파트 주소 확인해 주기   ② 상자 옮겨 주기
③ 층간 소음 문제 해결해 주기   ④ 난방기 작동법 알려 주기
⑤ 휴대폰 번호 알려 주기

8 다음을 듣고, Cornell Fitness Club에 관해 언급되지 <u>않은</u> 것을 고르시오.

① 개업 날짜   ② 구비 시설   ③ 위치
④ 제공 프로그램   ⑤ 회원권 가격

9 다음을 듣고, 무엇에 대한 설명인지 고르시오.

① 빈대떡   ② 떡국   ③ 송편   ④ 한과   ⑤ 가래떡

10 다음을 듣고, 두 사람의 대화가 <u>어색한</u> 것을 고르시오.

①   ②   ③   ④   ⑤

11번~20번 문제는 다음 페이지에 ➡

11 대화를 듣고, 남자가 대화 직후에 할 일로 가장 적절한 것을 고르시오.

① 앱 다운받기
② 커피 제조하기
③ 회원 가입하기
④ 수집품 사진 찍기
⑤ 도장에 새길 문구 정하기

12 다음 표를 보면서 대화를 듣고, 두 사람이 주문할 드론을 고르시오.

	Model	Range of Control	Flying Time	Price
①	A	50 m	5 minutes	$30
②	B	70 m	5 minutes	$50
③	C	100 m	10 minutes	$90
④	D	150 m	20 minutes	$100
⑤	E	200 m	40 minutes	$150

13 대화를 듣고, 남자와 여자가 병문안을 가기로 한 날짜를 고르시오.

① 8월 20일　　② 8월 21일　　③ 8월 22일　　④ 8월 23일　　⑤ 8월 24일

14 대화를 듣고, 여자가 어제 한 일로 가장 적절한 것을 고르시오.

① 경기 관람하기
② 탁구 연습하기
③ 탁구화 구매하기
④ 동아리 가입하기
⑤ 동영상 촬영하기

15 다음을 듣고, 방송의 목적으로 가장 적절한 것을 고르시오.

① 교통약자석을 비워두도록 당부하려고
② 에어컨 사용을 자제하도록 촉구하려고
③ 지하철 이용 시 안전 수칙을 설명하려고
④ 열차 고장에 따른 정차에 대해 공지하려고
⑤ 열차 내 약냉방 칸 운영에 대해 안내하려고

16 대화를 듣고, 여자가 지불할 금액을 고르시오.

① $9　　② $15　　③ $18　　④ $20　　⑤ $23

17 대화를 듣고, 여자의 마지막 말에 이어질 남자의 응답으로 가장 적절한 것을 고르시오.

Man: ___________________________________

① Sure thing. Let me just get it for you.

② Thanks for lending me the tape measure.

③ Why are you going to redesign your room?

④ All right. We'll buy the drawers tomorrow.

⑤ Yes, that seems like enough space for your drawers.

[18~19] 대화를 듣고, 남자의 마지막 말에 대한 여자의 응답으로 가장 적절한 것을 고르시오.

18 **Woman:** ___________________________________

① No problem. I can pay with cash.

② Yes. It would be useful to have them.

③ No, I don't have any pockets on my clothes.

④ I'd like a refund for the bag with the metal strap.

⑤ I'm sorry, but we don't have any clothes that match.

19 **Woman:** ___________________________________

① Yes, I think law is an important subject.

② They know because they are good people.

③ Well, they obviously chose to ignore the law.

④ You should write more articles about factories.

⑤ It's just a piece of news. Don't read too much into it.

20 다음을 듣고, 수지가 점원에게 할 말로 가장 적절한 것을 고르시오.

Suji: ___________________________________

① I'd like to pay in cash.　　② Do you have a stain remover?

③ I bought this at a bargain.　　④ Can you lower the price a little bit?

⑤ When does the sale start?

Dictation Test 21

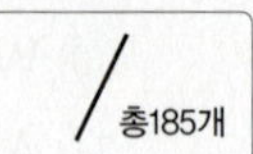

M3(17)_21_D

Dictation(받아쓰기)은 본문을 받아쓰면서 영어듣기의 집중력을 향상시키고 다양한 표현을 정리하기 위한 영어듣기 학습법입니다. **녹음을 다시 듣고, 빈칸에 알맞은 단어를 써 보세요.**
※Dictation의 정답은 듣기 대본의 밑줄 친 부분을 확인하세요.

📖 정답 p. 121

맞은 개수 / 총185개

고난도 그림정보파악(대화)

1. 대화를 듣고, 여자가 구입할 쇼핑 카트를 고르시오.

①  ② 

③  ④ 

⑤ 

01
M: Hello, do you need some help?

W: Hello, I'm looking for a grocery cart for my grandmother.

M: How about this one with bears on it?

W: It's cute, but I think it's too young for my grandma. I like that ________ - ________ ________.

M: Okay. It comes in two types, one with a zipper and one with a buckle.

W: Hmm… I prefer the one that ________ ________ ________ ________.

M: All right. What about the wheels? I recommend the three-wheel design. It can climb stairs.

W: Sure, I'll take your suggestion. Please give me the one with the ________ - ________ ________.

M: Excellent choice.

대화미언급

2. 대화를 듣고, Max Energy Drink에 관해 언급되지 **않은** 것을 고르시오.

① 효과　　② 맛
③ 용량　　④ 가격
⑤ 부작용

02
M: Chloe, does the new Max Energy Drink help ________ ________ ________?

W: Yes, I drank a can of it a few hours ago and I still don't feel sleepy.

M: What does it taste like?

W: Similar to orange juice, but it has a ________ ________ ________.

M: I should drink one as well. How much is it?

W: One can is five dollars, but don't drink more than one can per day.

M: Oh, are there ________ ________?

W: Yes, if you drink too much of it, it might make you dizzy.

M: OK. I'll ________ ________ ________ that.

3. 대화를 듣고, 여자가 남자에게 전화한 목적으로 가장 적절한 것을 고르시오.

① 콘서트에 초대하려고
② 이사 계획을 알리려고
③ 노래 수업을 의뢰하려고
④ 합창단 입단을 제안하려고
⑤ 콘서트 티켓 구매를 요청하려고

03 *(Cellphone rings.)*

M: Hi, Olivia.

W: Hi, Daniel. Can I ask you something?

M: Of course. What is it?

W: I think you said once that you ________ ________ ________ in a choir as a tenor. Is that right?

M: Yes. It was about two years ago. Why do you ask?

W: Well, someone in my choir has moved to a different city and now we're ________ ________ a tenor.

M: Oh, I see.

W: How about ________ the choir? We sing at concerts and have lots of fun.

M: Sounds interesting. Do I have to decide right now?

W: No, you can ________ ________ ________ ________ to think about it.

M: Okay. Then I'll let you know by Monday.

4. 대화를 듣고, 두 사람이 만나기로 한 시각을 고르시오.

① 5 p.m. ② 6 p.m.
③ 7 p.m. ④ 8 p.m.
⑤ 10 p.m.

04 *(Cellphone rings.)*

W: Hi, Ben! What's up?

M: Hey, Emily! I just found out about an outdoor concert happening tonight. Are you ________ ________ going?

다음 페이지에 계속 ➡

W: Oh, that sounds fun! When does it start and end?

M: It starts at 6 p.m. and goes until 10 p.m.

W: Hmm, I have a dance class at 8 p.m. Can we
___________ ___________?

M: Sure, we can catch the opening acts. How about
meeting up at 6 p.m.?

W: Let's meet earlier than that. I want to grab a front
row seat ___________ ___________.

M: Okay, sounds good. Let's meet near the main
stage ___________ 5 p.m.

W: All right, see you there!

5. 대화를 듣고, 남자의 심정으로 가장 적절
한 것을 고르시오.
① angry
② excited
③ sorry
④ shy
⑤ satisfied

05 W: Hello, I booked a table under the name of Darla.

M: Miss Darla? I ___________ ___________ ___________ ___________
you. I'm afraid we cannot serve you this evening.

W: Really? What's wrong?

M: There was a small fire in the kitchen. We have to
close the restaurant ___________ ___________ ___________.

W: Oh, dear. Is anyone hurt?

M: Thankfully, no. But this will ___________ ___________
___________ for the evening.

W: Don't worry about it. We can eat somewhere else.

M: All the same, I ___________ ___________. Hopefully
we'll see you again soon.

6. 다음 그림의 상황에 가장 적절한 대화를
고르시오.

① ② ③ ④ ⑤

06 ① W: I ___________ ___________ an egg sandwich for
lunch.

M: I'm afraid we don't have any eggs.

② W: What are you doing right now?

M: I'm ordering some dishes online.

③ W: Shall I ___________ ___________ ___________
___________ in the fridge?

M: Yes, please. I won't need any more of them.

④ W: Where is the refrigerator section?

M: It's over there. Please follow me.

⑤ W: Can you make some fried eggs for me?

M: Sorry, but __________ __________ __________ the dishes.

---

7. 대화를 듣고, 여자가 남자에게 부탁한 일로 가장 적절한 것을 고르시오.

① 아파트 주소 확인해 주기
② 상자 옮겨 주기
③ 층간 소음 문제 해결해 주기
④ 난방기 작동법 알려 주기
⑤ 휴대폰 번호 알려 주기

07

M: Hello, are you _______ _______ this apartment?

W: Yes. I'm Katelin. It's nice to meet you.

M: Hi, I'm Rick. I live in 203. That's _______ _______ _______ _______! Let me help you.

W: That's very kind, but my friends are helping, so it's OK.

M: Well, welcome anyway. If you need anything, just let me know.

W: Actually, I don't know how to _______ _______ _______-_______ _______. Can you come inside and show me how?

M: No problem.

---

8. 다음을 듣고, Cornell Fitness Club에 관해 언급되지 <u>않은</u> 것을 고르시오.

① 개업 날짜   ② 구비 시설
③ 위치   ④ 제공 프로그램
⑤ 회원권 가격

08

M: Cornell Fitness Club is looking for new members! We _______ _______ on July 3. We have top-quality exercise equipment, lockers, shower rooms, and a lounge. The club is _________ _______ in the city center. We have both group and personal exercise programs for all ages. You can enjoy all of these services _______ _______ _______ _______. Visit us today, and find out more.

다음 페이지에 계속 ➡

9. 다음을 듣고, 무엇에 대한 설명인지 고르시오.

① 빈대떡　　② 떡국
③ 송편　　　④ 한과
⑤ 가래떡

09 W: This is _________ _________ during one of the Korean holidays. It is a rice cake and it is _________ like a half-moon. It is usually _________ _________ sesame seeds, chestnut paste, or beans. When you cook this, you _________ it over a layer of pine needles. There is a belief that if you make this pretty, you will have pretty children and a good-looking partner _________ _________ _________.

10. 다음을 듣고, 두 사람의 대화가 <u>어색한</u> 것을 고르시오.

①　　　②
③　　　④
⑤

10 ① M: Why don't we _________ _________ tomorrow?

W: That sounds like a great idea.

② M: Who runs faster?

W: I'm _________ a business.

③ M: What's the matter? You _________ _________.

W: My mom is very sick.

④ M: What's your _________ subject?

W: I like English best.

⑤ M: How much does it cost?

W: It costs 20 dollars.

11. 대화를 듣고, 남자가 대화 직후에 할 일로 가장 적절한 것을 고르시오.

① 앱 다운받기
② 커피 제조하기
③ 회원 가입하기
④ 수집품 사진 찍기
⑤ 도장에 새길 문구 정하기

11

W: Hi, what can I get you?

M: Hi, one cappuccino, please.

W: All right. It's 3 dollars. Do you have a stamp card?

M: No. What is it?

W: We give you one stamp for each coffee that you buy. When you __________ eight stamps, you get one coffee __________ __________.

M: That's good. How can I get the stamp card?

W: First, you need to __________ __________ __________ on your cellphone.

M: Okay. I'll do it now.

12. 다음 표를 보면서 대화를 듣고, 두 사람이 주문할 드론을 고르시오.

	Model	Range of Control	Flying Time	Price
①	A	50 m	5 minutes	$30
②	B	70 m	5 minutes	$50
③	C	100 m	10 minutes	$90
④	D	150 m	20 minutes	$100
⑤	E	200 m	40 minutes	$150

12

M: Bella, I'm planning to buy a drone for our son as a birthday gift.

W: Do you __________ __________ __________ __________?

M: I'm thinking of buying one on this list. Can you help me choose one?

W: Sure. What about __________ __________ __________?

M: I think we need over 75 m of range of control.

W: Right. And our son doesn't need more than 30 minutes of flying time.

M: Okay. Then we have __________ __________ __________.

W: Let's get the cheaper one.

M: Okay. I'll order this one.

다음 페이지에 계속 ➡

13. 대화를 듣고, 남자와 여자가 병문안을 가기로 한 날짜를 고르시오.

① 8월 20일
② 8월 21일
③ 8월 22일
④ 8월 23일
⑤ 8월 24일

13
M: Hey, Julie! I'm going to visit Matt in the hospital. Do you want to join me?

W: Of course I do. Why don't we go ________ ________ ________ tomorrow? I mean on August 21.

M: Sorry, I can't go that day, but I can ________ ________ on Friday, August 23.

W: Friday is the busiest day for me. Well, can you go ________ ________ Thursday, August 22 or Saturday, August 24?

M: Thursday is fine with me.

W: That's good. I'm ________ ________ Thursday, too.

2024 영어듣기능력평가 1회 14번 변형

14. 대화를 듣고, 여자가 어제 한 일로 가장 적절한 것을 고르시오.

① 경기 관람하기
② 탁구 연습하기
③ 탁구화 구매하기
④ 동아리 가입하기
⑤ 동영상 촬영하기

14
M: Amy, I heard you're __________ __________ __________ our table tennis club.

W: Yeah. I __________ my application form last week. You've been in the club for a while, right?

M: Yes, for a year now. It's fun but you need to practice __________ __________ __________ __________.

W: I know. I've been watching tutorial videos to learn the basic techniques.

M: That's a good start.

W: Also, yesterday, I bought new table tennis shoes at the sports store.

M: Good for you! If you need __________ __________, just let me know.

W: Thanks. I'm excited to start playing with everyone!

15. 다음을 듣고, 방송의 목적으로 가장 적절한 것을 고르시오.

① 교통약자석을 비워두도록 당부하려고
② 에어컨 사용을 자제하도록 촉구하려고
③ 지하철 이용 시 안전 수칙을 설명하려고
④ 열차 고장에 따른 정차에 대해 공지하려고
⑤ 열차 내 약냉방 칸 운영에 대해 안내하려고

15 M: Hello, passengers. Our train is fully air-conditioned, but due to individual preferences ___________ ____________, we have compartments with milder air-conditioning. ___________ ________ the compartment you are in, you might feel cold. If you ________ ________ ________ the cold, please move to a compartment with milder air-conditioning. We appreciate your cooperation and understanding in creating a comfortable environment for ___________ ________ ________.

16. 대화를 듣고, 여자가 지불할 금액을 고르시오.

① $9   ② $15
③ $18   ④ $20
⑤ $23

16 M: Hello. Welcome to Healthy Bites Cafe.

W: Hi. I'd like an avocado salad and a grilled chicken wrap, please.

M: ___________. The avocado salad is 9 dollars, and the grilled chicken wrap is 6 dollars. Do you need ____________ ________?

W: How much is a banana smoothie?

M: It's 5 dollars. But if you order it with your salad and wrap, it's only 3 dollars.

W: That's ________ ________ ________. I'll ________ a banana smoothie to my order as well.

M: Great choice. How would you like to pay?

W: I'll ________ ________ my credit card.

다음 페이지에 계속 ➡

17. 대화를 듣고, 여자의 마지막 말에 이어질 남자의 응답으로 가장 적절한 것을 고르시오.

Man: ________________

① Sure thing. Let me just get it for you.
② Thanks for lending me the tape measure.
③ Why are you going to redesign your room?
④ All right. We'll buy the drawers tomorrow.
⑤ Yes, that seems like enough space for your drawers.

17 M: What's that?

W: I'm just ________ ________ some room design ideas.

M: Oh, are you going to redo your bedroom?

W: I'm planning on it. I need ________ ________ for my clothes.

M: Sounds like a big project.

W: It is. By the way, do you have a ________ ________ that I can borrow? I need to see how much space I have for new drawers.

M: Sure thing. Let me just get it for you.

18. 대화를 듣고, 남자의 마지막 말에 대한 여자의 응답으로 가장 적절한 것을 고르시오.

Woman: ________________

① No problem. I can pay with cash.
② Yes. It would be useful to have them.
③ No, I don't have any pockets on my clothes.
④ I'd like a refund for the bag with the metal strap.
⑤ I'm sorry, but we don't have any clothes that match.

18 M: Hello. May I help you?

W: Yes, I'd like to buy a bag.

M: Sure. We have ________ ________ ________ of bags this season. What size are you looking for?

W: I'd like a small one with a long strap.

M: Okay. Would you like a ________ strap or a ________ strap?

W: Oh, a leather strap would be better for me. Metal straps ________ ________ ________ ________ on my clothes.

M: Sure. Do you also need ________ ________ ________ inside the bag?

W: Yes. It would be useful to have them.

19. 대화를 듣고, 남자의 마지막 말에 대한 여자의 응답으로 가장 적절한 것을 고르시오.

Woman: ___________________

① Yes, I think law is an important subject.
② They know because they are good people.
③ Well, they obviously chose to ignore the law.
④ You should write more articles about factories.
⑤ It's just a piece of news. Don't read too much into it.

19

W: This is awful.

M: What's the matter, Miranda?

W: It's this news article that I'm reading.

M: What is it about?

W: It's about a factory that's ___________ ___________ into the river.

M: Dumping chemicals? That's terrible! There are people who ________ ________ ________ ________.

W: Tell me about it. The article says the factory has been doing it for years.

M: How can they do it? Don't they know it's ________ ________ ________?

W: Well, they obviously chose to ignore the law.

20. 다음을 듣고, 수지가 점원에게 할 말로 가장 적절한 것을 고르시오.

Suji: ___________________

① I'd like to pay in cash.
② Do you have a stain remover?
③ I bought this at a bargain.
④ Can you lower the price a little bit?
⑤ When does the sale start?

20

W: Suji is in a clothing shop. She ________ ________ ________ the T-shirt she really likes. When she is about to pay for it, she finds a small stain on it. She asks the ________ to give her another one, but the clerk says it is ________ ________ ________ in stock. She really wants to buy that T-shirt, even if there's a ________ on it. So she wants to ask the clerk if she can ________ ________ ________. In this situation, what would Suji say to the clerk?

Suji: Can you lower the price a little bit?

Words & Expressions Review 21

● 다음 단어를 암기하세요.

문제	번호	단어	뜻
1	1	grocery	식료품점
	2	recommend	추천하다
2	3	bitter	맛이 쓴
	4	side effect	부작용
3	5	choir	합창단, 성가대
	6	be short of	~이 부족하다
4	7	catch	~을 보대[듣다], ~에 참석하다
	8	in advance	미리, 사전에
5	9	reason	이유, 까닭
	10	ruin	망치다, 파괴하다
	11	all the same	그래도, 그럼에도 불구하고
6	12	put ~ back	~을 다시 제자리에 갖다 놓다
	13	fridge	냉장고
	14	section	부분, 부문, 구획
7	15	move into ~	~로 이사[이동]하다
	16	actually	사실은, 실제로
	17	exercise equipment	운동 장비
8	18	conveniently	편리하게
	19	be located in ~	~에 위치하다
9	20	be filled with ~	~으로 가득 차다
	21	steam	찌다, 증기
10	22	run	달리다, 운영하다

문제	번호	단어	뜻
11	23	stamp	도장
	24	for free	무료로
12	25	have ~ in mind	~을 생각하다, 염두에 두다
13	26	the day after tomorrow	내일모레
	27	make time	(~하는 데) 시간을 내다
	28	apply	신청하다, 지원하다
14	29	submit	제출하다
	30	tutorial	설명, 지도, 학습
15	31	individual	개인의, 개별의
	32	sensitive	민감한, 예민한
16	33	grilled	구운
	34	redo	다시 하다
17	35	storage	수납공간, 창고
	36	tape measure	줄자
18	37	strap	끈, 줄
	38	match	어울리다
	39	dump	버리다
19	40	obviously	분명히
	41	ignore	무시하다
	42	be about to + 동사	막 ~하려고 하다
20	43	stain	얼룩
	44	at a bargain	싼값으로

M3(17)_W_21

● 왼쪽 단어장의 뜻이 보이지 않게 반으로 접고, 학습한 단어의 뜻을 아래 빈칸에 적어주세요.

1	ruin	23	storage
2	actually	24	grilled
3	bitter	25	fridge
4	in advance	26	grocery
5	tutorial	27	reason
6	tape measure	28	conveniently
7	for free	29	the day after tomorrow
8	put ~ back	30	strap
9	catch	31	section
10	apply	32	all the same
11	redo	33	have ~ in mind
12	be short of	34	ignore
13	obviously	35	be located in ~
14	exercise equipment	36	make time
15	be about to + 동사	37	sensitive
16	run	38	stain
17	dump	39	recommend
18	submit	40	match
19	side effect	41	choir
20	be filled with ~	42	move into ~
21	at a bargain	43	stamp
22	individual	44	steam

22회 중학영어듣기 모의고사

M3(17)_22_US
모두 **미국식 발음(US)** 으로 녹음

M3(17)_22_UK
20문제 중 5문제에 **영국식 발음 (US+UK)**을 포함하여 녹음

정답 및 해석 p. 126

1

대화를 듣고, 여자가 선택할 의자를 고르시오.

①  ②  ③  ④  ⑤ 

2

대화를 듣고, World Camping Fair에 관해 언급되지 <u>않은</u> 것을 고르시오.

① 개최 시기　　② 행사 장소　　③ 프로그램
④ 참가비　　⑤ 기념품

3

대화를 듣고, 남자가 여자에게 전화한 목적으로 가장 적절한 것을 고르시오.

① 주문을 취소하려고　　② 배송지를 변경하려고
③ 주문 수량을 확인하려고　　④ 새로운 제품을 홍보하려고
⑤ 택배 배달 지연을 알리려고

4

대화를 듣고, 여자가 참여할 댄스 수업 시각을 고르시오.

① 7 a.m.　　② 8 a.m.　　③ 5 p.m.　　④ 6 p.m.　　⑤ 7 p.m.

5

대화를 듣고, 남자의 심정으로 가장 적절한 것을 고르시오.

① shy　　② worried　　③ bored　　④ nervous　　⑤ pleased

6 다음 그림의 상황에 가장 적절한 대화를 고르시오.

① ② ③ ④ ⑤

7 대화를 듣고, 남자가 여자에게 부탁한 일로 가장 적절한 것을 고르시오.

① 차에 태워주기 ② 자동차 수리하기 ③ 출근 시간 미루기
④ 컴퓨터 업데이트 하기 ⑤ 노트북을 수리점에 맡기기

8 다음을 듣고, Future of Environment에 대해 언급되지 <u>않은</u> 것을 고르시오.

① 주제 ② 길이 ③ 작성 방법
④ 발표 순서 ⑤ 채점 기준

9 다음을 듣고, 무엇에 관한 설명인지 고르시오.

① 세탁기 ② 다리미 ③ 믹서기 ④ 냉장고 ⑤ 전자레인지

10 다음을 듣고, 두 사람의 대화가 <u>어색한</u> 것을 고르시오.

① ② ③ ④ ⑤

11번~20번 문제는 다음 페이지에 ➡

11 대화를 듣고, 남자가 대화 직후에 할 일로 가장 적절한 것을 고르시오.

① 당근 썰기　　　　② 치즈 사오기　　　　③ 스테이크 굽기
④ 수프 만들기　　　⑤ 감자 다듬기

12 다음 표를 보면서 대화를 듣고, 여자가 주문할 스마트워치를 고르시오.

	Model	Face	Battery Life	Strap
①	A	Round	48 hours	Leather
②	B	Round	36 hours	Leather
③	C	Round	60 hours	Metal
④	D	Square	48 hours	Leather
⑤	E	Square	36 hours	Metal

13 대화를 듣고, 두 사람이 컵라면 박물관에 가기로 한 날짜를 고르시오.

① 10월 14일　　　　② 10월 16일　　　　③ 10월 20일
④ 10월 22일　　　　⑤ 10월 25일

14 대화를 듣고, 남자가 어제 한 일로 가장 적절한 것을 고르시오.

① 피아노 연습하기　　② 사촌과 통화하기　　③ 기차표 예매하기
④ 방학 숙제하기　　　⑤ 섬에 놀러가기

15 다음을 듣고, 방송의 목적으로 가장 적절한 것을 고르시오.

① 엘리베이터 공사의 일정을 안내하려고
② 관리 사무소의 새로운 위치를 알리려고
③ 이사할 때의 지침을 준수하도록 요청하려고
④ 대형 쓰레기의 올바른 폐기 방법을 설명하려고
⑤ 건물 사용 시 불편 신고 접수 방법을 공지하려고

16 대화를 듣고, 여자가 지불할 금액을 고르시오.

① $10　　　② $12　　　③ $15　　　④ $17　　　⑤ $27

17 대화를 듣고, 여자의 마지막 말에 대한 남자의 응답으로 가장 적절한 것을 고르시오.

Man: ______________________________

① Sorry but my watch is broken.
② The waiter gave us the wrong food.
③ I hope I'm not already late.
④ We'll be there at around 6:30.
⑤ I'm not sure what time I had lunch.

[18~19] 대화를 듣고, 남자의 마지막 말에 대한 여자의 응답으로 가장 적절한 것을 고르시오.

18 **Woman:** ______________________________

① You'd better go and see a doctor.
② I will donate some books and clothes.
③ Don't worry. We will get there on time.
④ Please eat all the vegetables on your plate.
⑤ Thank you so much for telling me about this.

19 **Woman:** ______________________________

① That sounds great. Let's plan a visit.
② Sorry, I've already watched the show.
③ No problem. I'll tell you how to get there.
④ I agree. Robots will help us with many things.
⑤ Sure. I'd love to join the science club with you.

20 다음을 듣고, 희수가 택시기사에게 할 말로 가장 적절한 것을 고르시오.

Huisu: ______________________________

① Can you drive slowly?
② How long will it take to go there?
③ Can you drop me off here?
④ Where is the nearest bus stop?
⑤ Can you take another route?

Dictation Test 22

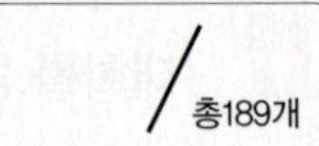

Dictation(받아쓰기)은 본문을 받아쓰면서 영어듣기의 집중력을 향상시키고 다양한 표현을 정리하기 위한 영어듣기 학습법입니다. **녹음을 다시 듣고, 빈칸에 알맞은 단어를 써 보세요.**
※Dictation의 정답은 듣기 대본의 밑줄 친 부분을 확인하세요.

정답 p. 126

맞은 개수 / 총189개

그림정보파악(대화)

1. 대화를 듣고, 여자가 선택할 의자를 고르시오.

① ②

③ ④

⑤

01

M: Hello, how can I assist you today?

W: Hi, I'm ___________ ___________ a nice chair for my computer desk.

M: We have chairs ___________ ___________ and chairs without wheels. Which type do you prefer?

W: I need a chair that has wheels. It will help me move more freely within my room.

M: All right. Do you need a chair that ___________ ___________ to support your arms and hands?

W: Yes, I need armrests, but I don't want a headrest. I've found that a headrest lowers my ___________.

M: I understand. Then, I think this chair would be perfect for you.

W: Yes, that looks perfect. I'll take it.

대화미언급

2. 대화를 듣고, World Camping Fair에 관해 언급되지 않은 것을 고르시오.

① 개최 시기
② 행사 장소
③ 프로그램
④ 참가비
⑤ 기념품

02

W: Honey, look at this poster about the World Camping Fair.

M: Oh, it's in the first week of next month. We should go.

W: Yes. It'll ___________ ___________ ___________ the Grand Convention Center. That's only 10 minutes away by car.

M: Great. Will there be any programs for kids?

W: Yes, it says here that there's a tumbler printing
program.

M: Cool. Our kids will love that.

W: Yeah. And we'd better ________ ________ ________
________ ________. They are 9 dollars each.

M: Okay. Let's buy them today!

3. 대화를 듣고, 남자가 여자에게 전화한 목적으로 가장 적절한 것을 고르시오.
   ① 주문을 취소하려고
   ② 배송지를 변경하려고
   ③ 주문 수량을 확인하려고
   ④ 새로운 제품을 홍보하려고
   ⑤ 택배 배달 지연을 알리려고

03 *(Cellphone rings.)*

W: Hello?

M: Hello, this is Fast Delivery Service. Is this Natalia
Shin?

W: Yes, this is she.

M: I am calling to let you know that your delivery
will ________ ________.

W: Oh no… Could I ask why? And how long is it
going to be delayed?

M: Because of the heavy rain, our storage area
________. So, it will be at least a week before we
________ ________ any products.

W: I see… I guess I have no choice ________ ________
wait. Thank you for calling me to let me know.

M: Thank you. I'm very sorry for the ____________.

4. 대화를 듣고, 여자가 참여할 댄스 수업 시각을 고르시오.
   ① 7 a.m.   ② 8 a.m.
   ③ 5 p.m.   ④ 6 p.m.
   ⑤ 7 p.m.

04 *(Telephone rings.)*

M: Hello, Herington Dance Studio. How may I help
you?

W: Hi, this is Julia Dunkin, and I'd like to ________
________ ________ ________ tomorrow.

M: Okay. What time is your class?

W: 7 a.m. but I'd like to change it to ____________
________ ________ ________.

다음 페이지에 계속 ➡

M: Sure. What time?

W: Can I join the 5 p.m. class?

M: I'm afraid that class is already ________.

W: Oh, that's too bad. How about the 6 p.m. class?

M: You are in luck. We have ________ ________ ________. I will sign you up for that class.

W: That's great! Thank you so much.

5. 대화를 듣고, 남자의 심정으로 가장 적절한 것을 고르시오.

① shy
② worried
③ bored
④ nervous
⑤ pleased

05

W: Hey, why didn't you come to our club meeting yesterday?

M: My brother was sick. I had to take him to the hospital.

W: I'm ________ ________ ________ ________. What did the doctor say?

M: The doctor said it's a ________ ________.

W: That's too bad. Is he okay now?

M: His fever's down, but he still has a ________ ________. I feel sorry for him.

W: Oh, I hope he ________ ________ ________.

M: Thanks.

6. 다음 그림의 상황에 가장 적절한 대화를 고르시오.

① ②
③ ④
⑤

06

① M: I am ________. I need food right now!

W: Okay, calm down! Let's go get some food.

② M: Excuse me, where can I find the restroom?

W: Oh, the restroom is right next to the entrance.

③ M: Would you like a ________ ________ ________ ________ for your items?

W: I will have a paper bag, please. Thank you.

④ M: Where can I find light bulbs?

W: You can find them in aisle number 7.

⑤ M: Can I have a cup of black coffee with ________

________ ________ ________?

W: Sure, no problem. Here you go.

7. 대화를 듣고, 남자가 여자에게 부탁한 일
   로 가장 적절한 것을 고르시오.
   ① 차에 태워주기
   ② 자동차 수리하기
   ③ 출근 시간 미루기
   ④ 컴퓨터 업데이트 하기
   ⑤ 노트북을 수리점에 맡기기

07 W: Honey, ________ ________?

M: My laptop's not working.

W: What happened?

M: It ________ while I was updating this software, and
   I don't have time to ________ ________ ________.

W: You have to go to work, don't you?

M: Yes. Could you take my laptop to the computer
   ________ ________ while I'm at work?

W: Of course, I'm happy to ________.

8. 다음을 듣고, Future of Environment에
   대해 언급되지 <u>않은</u> 것을 고르시오.
   ① 주제   ② 길이
   ③ 작성 방법   ④ 발표 순서
   ⑤ 채점 기준

08 W: Attention, class. I have a new __________ for you
   called Future of the Environment. You will write
   an essay about what our ________ __________
   will be like in the future. The essay should be
   ________ ________ ________ 1,000 words. Pick
   out a book on the topic, write a review of it and
   submit your review before the end of the term.
   Grades will ________ ________ ________ clarity of
   presentation, flow of ideas, and correct sentence
   structure. I will post __________ ________ on the
   school website.

다음 페이지에 계속 ➡

9. 다음을 듣고, 무엇에 관한 설명인지 고르시오.

① 세탁기　　② 다리미
③ 믹서기　　④ 냉장고
⑤ 전자레인지

09 M: This is a common electronic device that can be found in the house. Usually, this can be found in the kitchen. People use this to store food and drinks. It ________ ________ many different designs and sizes, but usually, it is rectangular. People can use this to ________ ________ ________ and even freeze things. Its cold temperature lowers bacteria reproduction and reduces the ________ ________ ________.

10. 다음을 듣고, 두 사람의 대화가 어색한 것을 고르시오.

①　　②
③　　④
⑤

10 ① M: It looks like it's going to rain.

W: Oh, no! I didn't bring my umbrella.

② M: What time do you normally go to bed?

W: Somewhere __________ 11 p.m. and midnight.

③ M: I think these shoes are __________ __________ for me.

W: Let's try on some bigger shoes then.

④ M: What did you think of the movie?

W: It wasn't a good movie, but I've seen worse.

⑤ M: How long can you __________ __________ __________ underwater?

W: I can hold onto your things for you.

11. 대화를 듣고, 남자가 대화 직후에 할 일로 가장 적절한 것을 고르시오.

① 당근 썰기
② 치즈 사오기
③ 스테이크 굽기
④ 수프 만들기
⑤ 감자 다듬기

11

M: Mom, what's all this?

W: Hi, honey. I'm preparing a special dinner. Your father __________ __________!

M: That's great! Is there anything I can help you with?

W: Can you __________ some carrots for me?

M: I'm on it. Are they for the salad?

W: Yes. The potatoes and steaks are ready, but I can't find any cheese for the salad.

M: Oh, I __________ __________ __________ __________. I'll go and buy some at the store.

W: Thanks, honey. I'll have the __________ __________ when you get back.

12. 다음 표를 보면서 대화를 듣고, 여자가 주문할 스마트워치를 고르시오.

	Model	Face	Battery Life	Strap
①	A	Round	48 hours	Leather
②	B	Round	36 hours	Leather
③	C	Round	60 hours	Metal
④	D	Square	48 hours	Leather
⑤	E	Square	36 hours	Metal

12

M: Natalie, what are you looking at on your phone?

W: I'm trying to buy a smartwatch. You have one; can you help me choose one?

M: Sure. Let's choose the face of the watch first. Which do you __________, round or square?

W: I'd like a round one better.

M: OK. Then, what about the battery life?

W: I don't want to __________ __________ __________ it too often.

M: Then, why don't you choose one that lasts at least 48 hours?

W: Great. Leather straps __________ __________ __________ casual outfits, right?

M: Yes. Leather straps are a __________ __________ for casual outfits than metal straps.

W: All right. I'll order this one.

다음 페이지에 계속 ➡

13. 대화를 듣고, 두 사람이 컵라면 박물관에 가기로 한 날짜를 고르시오.

① 10월 14일 ② 10월 16일
③ 10월 20일 ④ 10월 22일
⑤ 10월 25일

13

M: Hi, Mandy. Have you heard that a Cup Noodles Museum is opening in Seoul?

W: Yes. It was really popular in Japan, and I'm so glad that it's coming to Seoul.

M: Do you know when it will open?

W: On October 14th. Would you like to ___________ ___________?

M: Sounds great! Are you free on October 16th?

W: I'm afraid not. I have to do some ___________ ___________ that day. How about October 22nd?

M: I'm going camping with my dad on the 22nd. Are you available on the 25th?

W: October 25th ___________ ___________ ___________. I will see you then.

14. 대화를 듣고, 남자가 어제 한 일로 가장 적절한 것을 고르시오.

① 피아노 연습하기
② 사촌과 통화하기
③ 기차표 예매하기
④ 방학 숙제하기
⑤ 섬에 놀러가기

14

W: Richard, do you have any plans for the summer?

M: I'm thinking of ___________ ___________ ___________. How about you?

W: I'm taking piano lessons. My cousin says playing the piano is ___________ ___________ ___________.

M: I think your cousin is right.

W: Where are you planning to go, ___________ ___________ ___________?

M: To the southern part of the country.

W: Will you visit the islands, too?

M: Of course. I just booked my train ticket yesterday.

W: Cool. I'm sure you'll have a wonderful vacation.

15. 다음을 듣고, 방송의 목적으로 가장 적절한 것을 고르시오.
① 엘리베이터 공사의 일정을 안내하려고
② 관리 사무소의 새로운 위치를 알리려고
③ 이사할 때의 지침을 준수하도록 요청하려고
④ 대형 쓰레기의 올바른 폐기 방법을 설명하려고
⑤ 건물 사용 시 불편 신고 접수 방법을 공지하려고

15 W: Good afternoon, residents! This is Alice Walker from the management office. We have been __________ __________ __________ from residents about disturbances caused by people who are __________ __________. So, I'd like to ask you to follow these guidelines when you move out. First, contact the management office to __________ __________ __________ two weeks before moving out. Second, do not park your moving truck in front of the building entrance. Finally, __________ __________ __________ __________ in the proper area for pickup. Thank you for your cooperation.

16. 대화를 듣고, 여자가 지불할 금액을 고르시오.
① $10 　　② $12
③ $15 　　④ $17
⑤ $27

16 M: Hello! Welcome to Paws Pet Supplies.

W: Hi. I'm looking to __________ __________ __________ for my dog.

M: Sure. We have two types. __________ is a basic leash, __________ __________ __________ is a retractable leash.

W: How much does each cost?

M: The basic leash is 10 dollars, and the retractable leash is 15 dollars.

W: I'll buy the retractable leash.

M: Sure! When you __________ a leash, you can also get a chew toy for 2 dollars.

W: That's perfect. I'll buy one chew toy, too.

M: Okay. How would you like to pay?

W: I'll __________ __________ __________.

다음 페이지에 계속 ➡

17. 대화를 듣고, 여자의 마지막 말에 대한 남자의 응답으로 가장 적절한 것을 고르시오.

Man: _______________

① Sorry but my watch is broken.
② The waiter gave us the wrong food.
③ I hope I'm not already late.
④ We'll be there at around 6:30.
⑤ I'm not sure what time I had lunch.

17

W: Napoli Restaurant. How may I help you?

M: Hi there! _______ _______ _______ _______ a table for dinner tonight, please.

W: Sure. _______ _______ _______, sir?

M: Seven.

W: Okay. We have _______ _______ _______ for you. May I get your name?

M: I'm John Powell. Powell is spelled P-O-W-E-L-L.

W: Okay. Got it, sir. Oh, I forgot to ask, what time will you be _______?

M: We'll be there at around 6:30.

18. 대화를 듣고, 남자의 마지막 말에 대한 여자의 응답으로 가장 적절한 것을 고르시오.

Woman: _______________

① You'd better go and see a doctor.
② I will donate some books and clothes.
③ Don't worry. We will get there on time.
④ Please eat all the vegetables on your plate.
⑤ Thank you so much for telling me about this.

18

W: Hi, Daniel, where are you going?

M: I'm on my way to the blood donation center. I donate blood _______ _______ _______ _______.

W: Blood donation?

M: I think it's a great way to help other people. Plus there are _______ _______ _______ for the donor as well.

W: Really?

M: At the blood donation center they will check your pulse, blood pressure, body temperature, and more. They will tell you if _______ _______ _______.

W: I _________ ________ ________ that. Can I join you?

M: Sure. They always need more people.

W: Thank you so much for telling me about this.

19. 대화를 듣고, 남자의 마지막 말에 대한 여자의 응답으로 가장 적절한 것을 고르시오.

Woman: _____________________

① That sounds great. Let's plan a visit.
② Sorry, I've already watched the show.
③ No problem. I'll tell you how to get there.
④ I agree. Robots will help us with many things.
⑤ Sure. I'd love to join the science club with you.

19 M: Joyce, did you know that there's an AI robot show at the City Tech Center?

W: Yes. Actually, I was thinking of ___________ ___________ ___________.

M: I've already seen it twice, but I'd love to go again.

W: Oh, I didn't know you ___________ ___________ robots and AI.

M: I'm fascinated by how much the technology has ___________. Do you enjoy things like that too?

W: Absolutely. I find it amazing how ___________ ___________ ___________ robots are becoming.

M: Me, too. Would you like to see the show together?

W: That sounds great. Let's plan a visit.

20. 다음을 듣고, 희수가 택시기사에게 할 말로 가장 적절한 것을 고르시오.

Huisu: _____________________

① Can you drive slowly?
② How long will it take to go there?
③ Can you drop me off here?
④ Where is the nearest bus stop?
⑤ Can you take another route?

20 M: Huisu _________ _________ _________ meet his girlfriend for lunch at 12 o'clock. However, he gets up late in the morning. He gets ready ________ ________ ________ and takes a taxi. Unfortunately, he soon gets stuck in a ________ ________. It's already 11:45. Now he wants to ________ ________ the taxi to transfer to the subway. In this situation, what would Huisu say to the taxi driver?

Huisu: Can you drop me off here?

Words & Expressions Review 22

● 다음 단어를 암기하세요.

문제	번호	단어	뜻
1	1	assist	돕다, 도와주다
	2	productivity	생산성
2	3	fair	박람회
	4	in advance	사전에, 미리
3	5	delay	지연하다, 연기하다
	6	flood	침수되다, 물에 잠기다
	7	ship out	~을 발송하다, 보내다
4	8	be in luck	운이 좋다, 재수가 좋다
	9	spot	자리, 장소
5	10	severe	(태풍·병 등이) 심한, 중한
	11	feel sorry for	~를 불쌍하게 여기다
	12	get well	(병이) 낫다, 회복하다
6	13	starve	몹시 배고프다, 굶주리다
	14	aisle	통로
7	15	freeze	멈추다, 얼다
	16	be at work	일하고 있다
8	17	be based on ~	~에 기초하다
	18	clarity	명확성, 명료성
9	19	store	보관하다, 저장하다
	20	rate	속도
	21	spoilage	(음식의) 부패
10	22	hold one's breath	숨을 참다

문제	번호	단어	뜻
10	23	underwater	물 속에서
	24	hold onto	~을 맡아두다, 간수하다
11	25	promote	승진[진급]시키다
	26	I'm on it.	알겠어요., 제가 할게요.
	27	last	지속되다
12	28	leather	가죽
	29	metal	금속
13	30	do volunteer work	자원봉사 일을 하다
	31	resident	주민, 거주자
15	32	complaint	항의, 불편
	33	disturbance	소란, 소동, 방해
	34	cooperation	협조, 협력, 협동
	35	reserve	예약하다
17	36	available	이용할 수 있는
	37	spell	철자를 말하다
18	38	on a regular basis	정기적으로
	39	donor	헌혈자, 기증자
19	40	fascinate	매료시키다
	41	advance	(지식·기술 등이) 진보하다
	42	lifelike	실제 같은, 진짜 같은
20	43	in a hurry	서둘러
	44	traffic jam	교통체증

● 왼쪽 단어장의 뜻이 보이지 않게 반으로 접고, 학습한 단어의 뜻을 아래 빈칸에 적어주세요.

1	traffic jam	23	aisle
2	hold onto	24	resident
3	ship out	25	be in luck
4	starve	26	productivity
5	do volunteer work	27	reserve
6	in a hurry	28	assist
7	metal	29	cooperation
8	get well	30	be based on ~
9	disturbance	31	flood
10	clarity	32	I'm on it.
11	fair	33	leather
12	spot	34	spell
13	spoilage	35	feel sorry for
14	last	36	on a regular basis
15	complaint	37	store
16	be at work	38	advance
17	promote	39	rate
18	underwater	40	freeze
19	hold one's breath	41	lifelike
20	available	42	fascinate
21	severe	43	donor
22	in advance	44	delay

23회 중학영어듣기 모의고사

M3(17)_23_US
모두 **미국식 발음(US)** 으로 녹음

M3(17)_23_UK
20문제 중 5문제에 **영국식 발음 (US+UK)**을 포함하여 녹음

정답 및 해석 p. 133

1 대화를 듣고, 두 사람이 구입할 풍선을 고르시오.

①  ②  ③  ④  ⑤ 

2 대화를 듣고, Youth Festival에 관해 언급되지 <u>않은</u> 것을 고르시오.

① 행사 장소 ② 참가자 나이 ③ 참가 기념품
④ 행사 기간 ⑤ 참가 비용

3 대화를 듣고, 여자가 남자에게 전화한 목적으로 가장 적절한 것을 고르시오.

① 식당의 위치를 문의하기 위해서 ② 구인공고에 대해 문의하기 위해서
③ 저녁 예약을 하기 위해서 ④ 식당의 영업 시간을 확인하기 위해서
⑤ 분실물을 찾기 위해서

4 대화를 듣고, 인터넷 수리기사가 방문하기로 한 시각을 고르시오.

① 9 a.m. ② 11 a.m. ③ 1 p.m. ④ 3 p.m. ⑤ 5 p.m.

5 대화를 듣고, 여자의 심정으로 가장 적절한 것을 고르시오.

① proud ② bored ③ jealous
④ relieved ⑤ frustrated

6 다음 그림의 상황에 가장 적절한 대화를 고르시오.

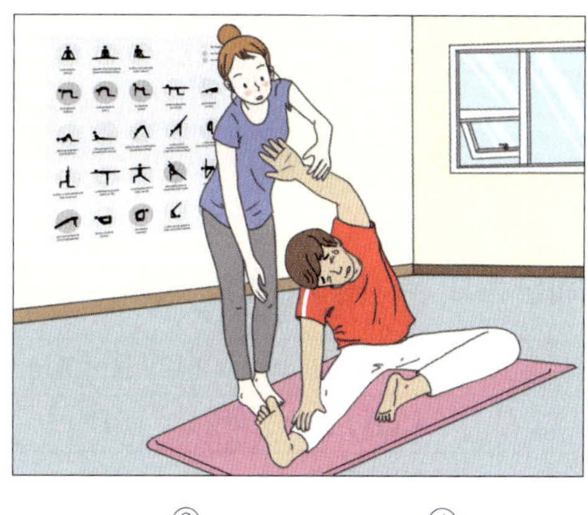

①   ②   ③   ④   ⑤

7 대화를 듣고, 여자가 남자에게 부탁한 일로 가장 적절한 것을 고르시오.

① 난방 켜기   ② 영어 숙제 돕기   ③ 감기약 사다 주기
④ 도서관에서 책 빌리기   ⑤ 도서관에 책 반납하기

8 다음을 듣고, National Express에 관해 언급되지 <u>않은</u> 것을 고르시오.

① 보유 차량 수   ② 수리 센터   ③ 운행 노선
④ 예매 방법   ⑤ 고객 센터 전화번호

9 다음을 듣고, 무엇에 관한 설명인지 고르시오.

① 식혜   ② 김밥   ③ 비빔밥   ④ 떡볶이   ⑤ 불고기

10 다음을 듣고, 두 사람의 대화가 <u>어색한</u> 것을 고르시오.

①   ②   ③   ④   ⑤

11번~20번 문제는 다음 페이지에 ➡

11 대화를 듣고, 남자가 대화 직후에 할 일로 가장 적절한 것을 고르시오.

① 신분증 찾기 ② 수영하기 ③ 가방 보관하기
④ 객실에 짐 풀기 ⑤ 지갑 구매하기

12 다음 표를 보면서 대화를 듣고, 두 사람이 구입할 영화 표를 고르시오.

	Movie	Time	3D / Regular	Dubbed / Subtitled
①	A	4:00 PM	3D	Dubbed
②	B	4:00 PM	3D	Subtitled
③	C	4:00 PM	Regular	Subtitled
④	D	4:45 PM	3D	Dubbed
⑤	E	4:45 PM	Regular	Subtitled

13 대화를 듣고, 두 사람이 예약할 날짜를 고르시오.

① 7월 27일 ② 7월 28일 ③ 7월 29일
④ 7월 30일 ⑤ 7월 31일

14 대화를 듣고, 남자가 어제 한 일로 가장 적절한 것을 고르시오.

① 자전거 타기 ② 차고 청소하기 ③ 동영상 시청하기
④ 자전거 수리하기 ⑤ 봉사활동 참여하기

15 다음을 듣고, 방송의 목적으로 가장 적절한 것을 고르시오.

① 식단 관리의 중요성을 설명하려고 ② 학교 요리 동아리를 홍보하려고
③ 제품의 영양 성분을 안내하려고 ④ 음식물 쓰레기 줄이기를 촉구하려고
⑤ 새로운 영양사를 소개하려고

16 대화를 듣고, 남자가 지불할 금액을 고르시오.

① $7 ② $8 ③ $9 ④ $10 ⑤ $11

17 대화를 듣고, 남자의 마지막 말에 대한 여자의 응답으로 가장 적절한 것을 고르시오.

Woman : ___________________________________

① Sure! My e-mail is jenny@gmail.com.
② Don't worry. I can walk home by myself.
③ Okay, we can watch the movie on Wednesday.
④ I couldn't finish because my computer was broken.
⑤ No, thank you. I already ate lunch with my friends.

18 대화를 듣고, 여자의 마지막 말에 대한 남자의 응답으로 가장 적절한 것을 고르시오.

Man : ___________________________________

① I've never been a huge fan of opera.
② That sounds good. I'll check it out later.
③ Right. I think you should really quit the club.
④ No problem! Let me know if you need any more help.
⑤ Sorry. I'm not interested in playing a musical instrument.

19 대화를 듣고, 남자의 마지막 말에 대한 여자의 응답으로 가장 적절한 것을 고르시오.

Woman : ___________________________________

① No, I stayed at home yesterday.
② Yes, I'll text you his number right now.
③ I'm sorry. I can't go with you tomorrow.
④ Okay, I'm moving out of town next week.
⑤ Great! I hope you get to know each other.

20 다음 상황 설명을 듣고, Peter가 웨이터에게 할 말로 가장 적절한 것을 고르시오.

Peter : ___________________________________
① At what time does this café open and close?
② Can I have another blueberry muffin, please?
③ Excuse me, I think I received the wrong drink.
④ Is there a quiet place where I can study for my exam?
⑤ Excuse me, do you know where I can find the bathroom?

Dictation Test 23

M3(17)_23_D

Dictation(받아쓰기)은 본문을 받아쓰면서 영어듣기의 집중력을 향상시키고 다양한 표현을 정리하기 위한 영어듣기 학습법입니다. **녹음을 다시 듣고, 빈칸에 알맞은 단어를 써 보세요.**
※Dictation의 정답은 듣기 대본의 밑줄 친 부분을 확인하세요.

 정답 p. 133

맞은 개수 / 총187개

고난도 그림정보파악(대화)

1. 대화를 듣고, 두 사람이 구입할 풍선을 고르시오.

①  ② 

③  ④ 

⑤ 

01

W: Chris, we have to buy some balloons for Judy's welcome home party. Which kind do you like?

M: How about these ________-________ ones?

W: Hmm… I think the round ones look better. How about these ones ________ ________ ________ on them?

M: Well, I think they are too simple. Hey, look at these.

W: Which ones ________ ________ ________? The ones with stars, or the ones with flowers?

M: The ones with stars look nice to me.

W: Oh, I think so, too. Let's buy them right now.

대화미언급

2. 대화를 듣고, Youth Festival에 관해 언급되지 <u>않은</u> 것을 고르시오.

① 행사 장소
② 참가자 나이
③ 참가 기념품
④ 행사 기간
⑤ 참가 비용

02

W: Justin! I heard that the Youth Festival is ________ ________ at Han River Park.

M: What is a Youth Festival?

W: It's a festival for youth ____________ ________ ________ of 15 and 24! There are many things to eat and events to ____________ ________.

M: Okay. That's it?

W: No! There will be famous artists coming to perform and they are ____________ ________, too.

M: So, when is this festival?

W: It starts today and ends next Friday. Do you want to go with me?

M: Sure, __________ __________?

W: But, there is an entrance fee of $10. Are you okay with that?

M: No problem!

3. 대화를 듣고, 여자가 남자에게 전화한 목적으로 가장 적절한 것을 고르시오.
   ① 식당의 위치를 문의하기 위해서
   ② 구인공고에 대해 문의하기 위해서
   ③ 저녁 예약을 하기 위해서
   ④ 식당의 영업 시간을 확인하기 위해서
   ⑤ 분실물을 찾기 위해서

03 *(Telephone rings.)*

M: Hello, this is The Grill Restaurant. How can I help you?

W: Hi, I would like to __________ __________ __________ for four people at 8 p.m. tomorrow.

M: Sure, I'll check. *(pause)* I'm afraid all the tables are __________ __________ 8 p.m.

W: Well… Is there another time that is available?

M: How about 7?

W: That sounds good! I'll make a reservation under the name Brown.

M: Okay, may I __________ __________ __________ __________, please?

W: 310-555-9024.

4. 대화를 듣고, 인터넷 수리기사가 방문하기로 한 시각을 고르시오.
   ① 9 a.m.   ② 11 a.m.
   ③ 1 p.m.   ④ 3 p.m.
   ⑤ 5 p.m.

04 *(Cellphone rings.)*

M: OZ Wireless, how can I help you?

W: Hi, I'm calling because I've __________ __________ __________ __________.

M: We're very sorry for the inconvenience. Have you tried rebooting your computer?

W: Yes, even the router, but nothing has changed.

다음 페이지에 계속 ➡

M: I see. We'll send someone to your house. Are you
___________ on Saturday at 9 a.m.?

W: No, I have a yoga lesson in the morning. How
about at 1 p.m.?

M: Sorry, that time's ___________ _________. What
about at 3 p.m.?

W: That's fine by me.

M: All right. Someone will visit you then.

W: Okay, thanks.

5. 대화를 듣고, 여자의 심정으로 가장 적절
한 것을 고르시오.

① proud
② bored
③ jealous
④ relieved
⑤ frustrated

05

M: Evelyn, is there something wrong?

W: Yes, Lucas. I was ___________ _________ my
résumé for a job application, but it's ___________
_____________.

M: What do you mean?

W: Well, I edited it for the last time, but then deleted
everything in the file ________ _________.

M: Did you save the file with everything deleted?

W: That's right. And the ___________ to submit it is in
10 minutes.

M: Oh, no. What can you do?

W: It's ___________. I can't rewrite my résumé in
10 minutes.

M: Is there no solution to this?

W: No. I can't believe I ________ _________ ___________
in this way.

6. 다음 그림의 상황에 가장 적절한 대화를
고르시오.

① ② ③
④ ⑤

06

① W: Stephen, where are you going?

M: I'm going to the library to ________ some books.

② W: How long have you been in sales?

M: I've worked in sales for 6 years.

③ W: Hello. How may I help you?

M: I'd like to return this shirt. It's too small for me.

④ W: You have to _______ _______ _______ further

than that.

M: I'm trying my best, but it's difficult.

⑤ W: Do you know the way to the gym?

M: Yes, go straight down this road and _______

_______ at the corner.

7. 대화를 듣고, 여자가 남자에게 부탁한 일로 가장 적절한 것을 고르시오.

① 난방 켜기
② 영어 숙제 돕기
③ 감기약 사다 주기
④ 도서관에서 책 빌리기
⑤ 도서관에 책 반납하기

07 M: _______ _______ _______ _______, Sojin?

W: I'm working on my English homework.

M: Is it going well?

W: Yes, but I have to read some more books.

M: I see. I'm _______ _______ _______ _______ the

library. Do you need anything?

W: It's OK. I have all the books I need. Can you just

_______ _______ _______ _______ as you go

out?

M: Sure. It's really cold in here.

8. 다음을 듣고, National Express에 관해 언급되지 않은 것을 고르시오.

① 보유 차량 수　② 수리 센터
③ 운행 노선　④ 예매 방법
⑤ 고객 센터 전화번호

08 M: Thank you for using National Express. We own

200 _______-_______ buses. Putting safety

first, we run 11 repair centers for these vehicles.

We recently added two extra lines, and now we

operate 30 express bus lines _______ _______

_______ _______. You can buy tickets through

our website, or by calling our 24-hour _______

_______ center. We value our customers'

satisfaction above all.

다음 페이지에 계속 ➡

9. 다음을 듣고, 무엇에 관한 설명인지 고르시오.

① 식혜　　② 김밥
③ 비빔밥　　④ 떡볶이
⑤ 불고기

09 W: This is a traditional Korean dish. It is a bowl of rice ________ ________ various vegetables, eggs, and beef. Before eating it, you need to ________ ________ ________ ________ together. It's basically served with red pepper paste, but other sauces like soy sauce may replace it. A spoon of sesame oil is also a common addition. The city of Jeonju ________ ________ ________ ________ the most popular version of this.

10. 다음을 듣고, 두 사람의 대화가 <u>어색한</u> 것을 고르시오.

①　　②
③　　④
⑤

10 ① W: Is it OK if I sit here?

M: I'm sorry but this ________ ________ ________.

② W: Thank you so much for your kindness.

M: Don't mention it.

③ W: Would you do me a ________?

M: Sure. What is it?

④ W: What is your favorite subject?

M: I love ________ ________.

⑤ W: How was the exam?

M: It wasn't difficult.

11. 대화를 듣고, 남자가 대화 직후에 할 일로 가장 적절한 것을 고르시오.

① 신분증 찾기
② 수영하기
③ 가방 보관하기
④ 객실에 짐 풀기
⑤ 지갑 구매하기

11

W: Welcome to Sunny Beach Resort. How can I assist you?

M: Hi, I'd like to rent a beach chair and umbrella.

W: Sure. Would you prefer a full-day rental or a half-day?

M: Just a half-day, please.

W: All right. We ___________ ___________ ___________ for seniors.

M: Oh, that's wonderful to know.

W: Could you please show me your ID to ___________ ___________ ___________?

M: Of course. Give me a second to find it in my purse.

W: ___________ ___________ ___________.

12. 다음 표를 보면서 대화를 듣고, 두 사람이 구입할 영화 표를 고르시오.

	Movie	Time	3D / Regular	Dubbed / Subtitled
①	A	4:00 PM	3D	Dubbed
②	B	4:00 PM	3D	Subtitled
③	C	4:00 PM	Regular	Subtitled
④	D	4:45 PM	3D	Dubbed
⑤	E	4:45 PM	Regular	Subtitled

12

M: Hey, Grace. It's 3 o'clock now and we need to ___________ our movie tickets.

W: Oh, right. We were going to watch that new animated movie.

M: Yes. So, the next one starts at 4:00 p.m. and then there's another one at 4:45 p.m.

W: 4:00 p.m. ___________ ___________ ___________. I don't want to wait until 4:45 p.m.

M: Okay. Then, do you want 3D or just a regular movie?

W: They have 3D? 3D sounds really good to me!

M: Do you prefer a ___________ ___________ ___________ movie?

W: Subtitles, of course! I want to hear the real actors' voices.

M: Me, too. I'll ___________ ___________ ___________ now.

다음 페이지에 계속 ➡

13. 대화를 듣고, 두 사람이 예약할 날짜를 고르시오.

① 7월 27일
② 7월 28일
③ 7월 29일
④ 7월 30일
⑤ 7월 31일

13

M: Lizzy! I heard Joanna Swift is going to have a concert in Seoul this summer. Do you want to go together?

W: Yes, I would love to! I love her songs. When are __________ __________?

M: Let's see. The concert dates are July 27th through 31st.

W: Are there __________ __________ __________ on July 29th or 30th?

M: Unfortunately, tickets for the weekend are sold out. How about Friday, July 28th?

W: Well, that's not the best date for me, but I have __________ __________ for July 27th. So, Friday it is!

M: Okay. Sounds good. I will __________ __________ __________ for that day.

한일파악

2024 영어듣기능력평가 2회 **14번 변형**

14. 대화를 듣고, 남자가 어제 한 일로 가장 적절한 것을 고르시오.

① 자전거 타기
② 차고 청소하기
③ 동영상 시청하기
④ 자전거 수리하기
⑤ 봉사활동 참여하기

14

W: David, did you participate in the school volunteer day yesterday?

M: No, I didn't.

W: Really? I thought you had __________ __________ __________ it!

M: I was in my garage all day yesterday.

W: Oh, were you cleaning it out?

M: No. I was __________ __________ __________ __________ that had been broken for months.

W: Isn't it hard to do that yourself?

M: I watched a bicycle repair video online last weekend. It didn't look too difficult, so I tried it __________ __________ __________.

W: That's awesome! Why don't we go for a bike ride sometime?

M: Great idea.

15. 다음을 듣고, 방송의 목적으로 가장 적절한 것을 고르시오.

① 식단 관리의 중요성을 설명하려고
② 학교 요리 동아리를 홍보하려고
③ 제품의 영양 성분을 안내하려고
④ 음식물 쓰레기 줄이기를 촉구하려고
⑤ 새로운 영양사를 소개하려고

15 M: Good morning, students! Welcome to our weekly school broadcast, "Food for Thought." Today, we'd like to talk about ________ ________. Did you know that a large amount of food is wasted every day? This has become a serious problem for our environment. However, we students can make a difference. Let's start by ________ ________ ________ ________ ________ and finishing our meals in the school cafeteria. Let's ________ ________ before wasting food.

16. 대화를 듣고, 남자가 지불할 금액을 고르시오.

① $7　　② $8
③ $9　　④ $10
⑤ $11

16 W: Hello, what can I get for you?

M: Hi, I'd like to order one medium popcorn and one large Coke.

W: Sure, that will be $8. Do you ________ ________ ________?

M: Hmm… I'm sorry, but I'd like to ________ ________ ________. One large popcorn and one large Coke, please.

W: No problem. That will be $10. By the way, if you show us your movie ticket, you can ________ ________ ________ ________ ________.

M: Oh, really? That's great! Here's my movie ticket.

W: Thanks! So, one large popcorn and one large Coke, right?

M: That's right.

다음 페이지에 계속 ➡

17. 대화를 듣고, 남자의 마지막 말에 대한 여자의 응답으로 가장 적절한 것을 고르시오.

Woman: _______________

① Sure! My e-mail is jenny@gmail.com.
② Don't worry. I can walk home by myself.
③ Okay, we can watch the movie on Wednesday.
④ I couldn't finish because my computer was broken.
⑤ No, thank you. I already ate lunch with my friends.

17

M: Hey, Jenny. How was your mid-term exam?

W: Awful! I think I failed my math test.

M: Don't worry. I'm sure you did fine. (*pause*) By the way, if you need any help, I know this online tutoring website that I _______ _______ _______.

W: Online tutoring?

M: Yeah, the tutoring teachers make difficult subjects easy to understand. I _______ _______ _______ through this tutoring site.

W: Hmm... Maybe I should get some help.

M: If you are interested, I can _______ _______ _______ _______.

W: Sure! My e-mail is jenny@gmail.com.

18. 대화를 듣고, 여자의 마지막 말에 대한 남자의 응답으로 가장 적절한 것을 고르시오.

Man: _______________

① I've never been a huge fan of opera.
② That sounds good. I'll check it out later.
③ Right. I think you should really quit the club.
④ No problem! Let me know if you need any more help.
⑤ Sorry. I'm not interested in playing a musical instrument.

18

W: Dan, did you pick which club you want to join?

M: No, I'm _______ _______ _______ _______. There are too many clubs at our school.

W: What are your _______? I'm sure there must be a club for you.

M: I like singing and listening to music.

W: Oh, there's an opera club where they sing classical music.

M: Uh... I'm _______ _______ _______ pop songs.

W: Then how about joining the band? I saw a poster that says the band is recruiting a new singer.

M: That sounds good. I'll check it out later.

19. 대화를 듣고, 남자의 마지막 말에 대한 여자의 응답으로 가장 적절한 것을 고르시오.

Woman: ___________________

① No, I stayed at home yesterday.
② Yes, I'll text you his number right now.
③ I'm sorry. I can't go with you tomorrow.
④ Okay, I'm moving out of town next week.
⑤ Great! I hope you get to know each other.

19

W: Hi, Mark! You'll never guess _________ _________ _________ _________ yesterday!

M: I have no idea. Who did you meet?

W: I met Mr. Watterson, our elementary school home room teacher! You remember him, right?

M: Of course, how could I forget? I haven't seen him in ages. How is he?

W: He's retired now, and he just _________ _________ our neighborhood a couple of days ago.

M: Really? I should _________ _________ _________ _________ him. Did you get his cell number?

W: Yes, I'll text you his number right now.

20. 다음 상황 설명을 듣고, Peter가 웨이터에게 할 말로 가장 적절한 것을 고르시오.

Peter: ___________________

① At what time does this café open and close?
② Can I have another blueberry muffin, please?
③ Excuse me, I think I received the wrong drink.
④ Is there a quiet place where I can study for my exam?
⑤ Excuse me, do you know where I can find the bathroom?

20

W: Peter went to the café to read some books. He ordered a blueberry muffin and an iced latte. However, when _________ _________ _________ _________, he noticed that the drink wasn't an iced latte, but a chocolate drink instead. He realized that the waiter _________ _________ _________ the orders and given him the wrong drink. So, Peter wants to ask if he could _________ _________ _________ _________. In this situation, what would Peter most likely say to the waiter?

Peter: Excuse me, I think I received the wrong drink.

Words & Expressions Review 23

● 다음 단어를 암기하세요.

문제	번호	단어	뜻
1	1	round	둥근, 원형의
2	2	youth	청년, 젊은이
	3	perform	공연하다, 연주하다
	4	screen	(영화를) 상영하다
	5	entrance fee	입장료
3	6	book	(식당, 호텔 등을) 예약하다
4	7	reboot	재부팅하다
5	8	finish off ~	~을 마무리하다
	9	résumé	이력서
	10	hopeless	가망 없는, 절망적인
	11	ruin	망치다
6	12	extend	뻗다, 늘이다
	13	try one's best	최선을 다하다
7	14	work on ~	~에 노력을 들이다
	15	go well	(일이) 잘 되어가다
8	16	value	소중히 여기다, 가치
	17	satisfaction	만족
	18	above all	무엇보다도
9	19	traditional	전통적인
	20	ingredient	재료
10	21	kindness	친절
	22	favor	부탁, 호의

문제	번호	단어	뜻
11	23	verify	확인하다, 입증하다
12	24	subtitled	자막 처리가 된
	25	dubbed	더빙된
13	26	scheduled	예정된
14	27	clean out	깨끗이 치우다
	28	fix	고치다
15	29	waste	쓰레기, 낭비, 낭비하다
	30	serious	심각한, 진지한
	31	make a difference	변화를 가져오다, 차별을 두다
	32	think twice	신중히 생각하다, 재고하다, 숙고하다
16	33	What can I get for you?	(상점에서) 무엇을 주문하시겠어요?
	34	anything else	그 밖의 다른 것
	35	get a discount	할인을 받다
17	36	understand	이해하다
	37	improve	향상시키다, 개선하다
18	38	pick	고르다, 선택하다
	39	recruit	모집하다, 채용하다
	40	retired	퇴직한, 은퇴한
19	41	move	이사하다, 이주하다
	42	get to know	알게 되다
20	43	instead	대신에
	44	realize	깨닫다, 알아차리다

● 왼쪽 단어장의 뜻이 보이지 않게 반으로 접고, 학습한 단어의 뜻을 아래 빈칸에 적어주세요.

1	book	23	improve
2	What can I get for you?	24	realize
3	favor	25	kindness
4	screen	26	satisfaction
5	finish off ~	27	move
6	understand	28	scheduled
7	value	29	anything else
8	extend	30	perform
9	pick	31	subtitled
10	ingredient	32	entrance fee
11	hopeless	33	waste
12	reboot	34	recruit
13	clean out	35	résumé
14	retired	36	go well
15	serious	37	fix
16	verify	38	think twice
17	work on ~	39	instead
18	get to know	40	make a difference
19	traditional	41	dubbed
20	above all	42	get a discount
21	ruin	43	youth
22	round	44	try one's best

1

대화를 듣고, 남자가 구입할 자석을 고르시오.

①  ②  ③ 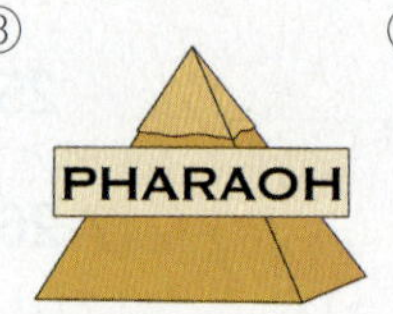 ④  ⑤ 

2

대화를 듣고, 건물에 관해 언급되지 **않은** 것을 고르시오.

① 이름　　　　　② 높이　　　　　③ 층 수
④ 완공 시기　　　⑤ 건설 기간

3

대화를 듣고, 여자가 남자에게 전화한 목적으로 가장 적절한 것을 고르시오.

① 배달 주문을 취소하려고　　　② 배달 주소지를 변경하려고
③ 음식을 추가로 주문하려고　　　④ 식사 예약 시간을 조정하려고
⑤ 초인종을 누르지 말도록 요청하려고

4

대화를 듣고, 남자가 미용실을 예약한 시각을 고르시오.

① 7 a.m.　　　② 8 a.m.　　　③ 9 a.m.　　　④ 10 a.m.　　　⑤ 11 a.m.

5

대화를 듣고, 여자의 심정으로 가장 적절한 것을 고르시오.

① nervous　　　② sorry　　　③ amazed
④ bored　　　⑤ envious

6 다음 그림의 상황에 가장 적절한 대화를 고르시오.

①   ②   ③   ④   ⑤

7 대화를 듣고, 남자가 여자에게 부탁한 일로 가장 적절한 것을 고르시오.

① 과제물 제출하기   ② 농구공 반납하기
③ 과학 책 빌려주기   ④ 컴퓨터로 문서 작성하기
⑤ 고장 난 컴퓨터 살펴보기

8 다음을 듣고, Han Sports Center에 관해 언급되지 <u>않은</u> 것을 고르시오.

① 체육관   ② 요가실   ③ 실내 수영장
④ 매점   ⑤ 샤워실

9 다음을 듣고, 무엇에 관한 설명인지 고르시오.

① 기린   ② 독수리   ③ 타조   ④ 사자   ⑤ 북극곰

10 다음을 듣고, 두 사람의 대화가 <u>어색한</u> 것을 고르시오.

①   ②   ③   ④   ⑤

11번~20번 문제는 다음 페이지에 ➡

11 대화를 듣고, 여자가 대화 직후에 할 일로 가장 적절한 것을 고르시오.

① 교복 다리기　　　② 운동화 빨기　　　③ 미용실에 가기
④ 사진관 방문하기　　⑤ 친구 만나러 가기

12 다음 표를 보면서 대화를 듣고, 남자가 주문할 로봇 청소기를 고르시오.

	Model	Price	Noise Level	Controller Type
①	A	$600	75dB	Remote Controller
②	B	$700	68dB	Remote Controller
③	C	$800	68dB	Mobile App
④	D	$1,000	65dB	Mobile App
⑤	E	$1,100	65dB	Mobile App

13 대화를 듣고, 여자가 소파를 받기로 한 날짜를 고르시오.

① 1월 19일　　　② 1월 20일　　　③ 1월 21일
④ 1월 22일　　　⑤ 1월 23일

14 대화를 듣고, 남자가 어제 한 일로 가장 적절한 것을 고르시오.

① 가족과 외식하기　　② 봉사활동 하기　　③ 영화 관람하기
④ 공원으로 소풍 가기　　⑤ 양로원 방문하기

15 다음을 듣고, 방송의 목적으로 가장 적절한 것을 고르시오.

① 학교 입학 절차를 설명하려고
② 보건실 이용에 대해 안내하려고
③ 교사와 가깝게 지낼 것을 당부하려고
④ 정부의 새로운 보건 정책에 대해 소개하려고
⑤ 신입생의 건강 상태에 대해 학교에 알리도록 유도하려고

16 대화를 듣고, 여자가 지불해야 할 이번 달 통신비로 가장 적절한 것을 고르시오.

① $30　　　② $40　　　③ $50　　　④ $80　　　⑤ $100

17 대화를 듣고, 여자의 마지막 말에 대한 남자의 응답으로 가장 적절한 것을 고르시오.

Man: _______________________________________

① It is impossible for me to get such a vocal training.
② I'll take the free lessons for tenors over the weekend.
③ Yes, I'd like to recommend my friend for the mixed choir.
④ Unfortunately, I don't have time during the weekend.
⑤ Perhaps you'd like to join me at the choir.

18 대화를 듣고, 남자의 마지막 말에 대한 여자의 응답으로 가장 적절한 것을 고르시오.

Woman: _______________________________________

① It's so kind of you to help her.
② I don't think I can make it to the party.
③ Okay. I will call and make a reservation.
④ That's a great idea! She'd love the cake.
⑤ Wonderful! I could use a fresh pair of eyes.

19 대화를 듣고, 여자의 마지막 말에 대한 남자의 응답으로 가장 적절한 것을 고르시오.

Man: _______________________________________

① Andy will have difficulty moving to a new place.
② I think I should call a repair person to fix the elevator.
③ You need to be honest and get all the help you can get.
④ Why don't we make some calls and gather a few more friends?
⑤ I'm thinking of getting him an indoor plant as a housewarming gift.

20 다음 상황 설명을 듣고, Hazel이 Patrick에게 할 말로 가장 적절한 것을 고르시오.

Hazel: Patrick, _______________________________________

① how about organizing a workshop by yourself?
② I think you will be an excellent AI educator one day.
③ you can get a certificate after completing the course.
④ why don't you sign up for the AI workshop with me?
⑤ field experience is an advantage when searching for a job.

Dictation Test 24

M3(17)_24_D

Dictation(받아쓰기)은 본문을 받아쓰면서 영어듣기의 집중력을 향상시키고 다양한 표현을 정리하기 위한 영어듣기 학습법입니다. **녹음을 다시 듣고, 빈칸에 알맞은 단어를 써 보세요.**
※Dictation의 정답은 듣기 대본의 밑줄 친 부분을 확인하세요.

정답 p. 139

맞은 개수 / 총190개

그림정보파악(대화)

1. 대화를 듣고, 남자가 구입할 자석을 고르시오.

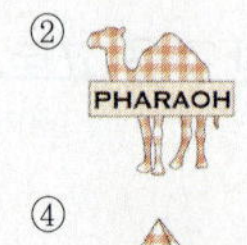
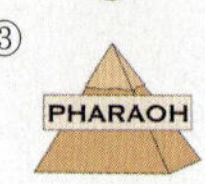
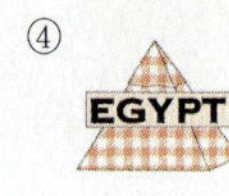

01
W: Welcome to the Desert Gift Shop. Did you enjoy your trip?

M: I did. Thank you. The desert was great. I want to buy a magnet ____________ ____________ it by.

W: Sure. We have camel-shaped and triangle-shaped magnets. Both designs are popular.

M: I'll choose the triangle-shaped one. It ____________ ____________ of the pyramids.

W: Good choice. They come in two styles, plain and checkered.

M: Oh, the checkered style looks nice.

W: All right. Then, how about this one ____________ ____________ ____________ "Pharaoh" on it? It ____________ the ancient rulers.

M: Great! I'll take it.

대화미언급

2. 대화를 듣고, 건물에 관해 언급되지 **않은** 것을 고르시오.
① 이름　　② 높이
③ 층 수　　④ 완공 시기
⑤ 건설 기간

02
W: Honey, I am glad that we joined this city tour. Isn't it fun?

M: It's really entertaining. What's that building over there? It's really tall!

W: I'll ____________ ____________ ____________ on my smartphone. *(pause)* That must be "The Razor Tower."

M: "The Razor Tower?" That's an interesting name. ____________ ____________ ____________ ____________?

W: It's 500 meters in height.

M: Wow! How many floors are there?

W: It says on their website that there are 100 floors.

M: Incredible! I wonder how long it took to build that thing.

W: Their website says that it took eight years to complete the building.

M: That's a lot of hard work.

---

3. 대화를 듣고, 여자가 남자에게 전화한 목적으로 가장 적절한 것을 고르시오.

① 배달 주문을 취소하려고
② 배달 주소지를 변경하려고
③ 음식을 추가로 주문하려고
④ 식사 예약 시간을 조정하려고
⑤ 초인종을 누르지 말도록 요청하려고

03 *(Telephone rings.)*

M: Hello. This is Happy Chicken. How can I help you?

W: Hi. I ordered a fried chicken and a chicken salad ___________ ___________ about 30 minutes ago.

M: Yes, your order is ___________ ___________ ___________.

W: Great. Could I ask you a favor?

M: Sure, what is it?

W: There's a baby sleeping at home. Please tell the delivery person ___________ ___________ ___________ the doorbell.

M: Of course. I'll tell him to text you ___________ ___________ ___________.

W: Thank you so much. That would really help.

---

4. 대화를 듣고, 남자가 미용실을 예약한 시각을 고르시오.

① 7 a.m.
② 8 a.m.
③ 9 a.m.
④ 10 a.m.
⑤ 11 a.m.

04 *(Telephone rings.)*

W: Good evening, Happy Hair Salon. How may I help you?

M: Hello, I'd like to _______ _______ _______ ___________ for this Sunday.

W: Let me check, please. *(pause)* The only time we have on Sunday is in the morning.

M: That's fine. What time do you open?

다음 페이지에 계속 ➡

W: We open at 11 a.m. on weekdays and 9 a.m. on weekends. Would you like to come at 9 a.m.?

M: No, that's ________ ________ ________. Can I make an appointment for 10 a.m.?

W: Okay. May I ________ ________ ________, please?

M: It's Owen Wilson.

W: Thank you, Mr. Wilson. We'll see you on Sunday.

5. 대화를 듣고, 여자의 심정으로 가장 적절한 것을 고르시오.

① nervous
② sorry
③ amazed
④ bored
⑤ envious

05
W: Mr. Bates, you wanted to see me?

M: Yes, Hannah. What do you think of ________ ________ ________ for our school leaflet?

W: Me? But, there are better looking students than me.

M: It's ________ ________ ________ ________. I think you'd be a great representative of our school.

W: Wow, that's a nice surprise! I feel ________.

M: I'll take that ________ ________ ________.

W: Yes, sir. I can't believe you picked me.

M: I wasn't the only one.

6. 다음 그림의 상황에 가장 적절한 대화를 고르시오.

① ② ③
④ ⑤

06
① M: Your dog is so cute. What's his name?
   W: Thanks! His name is "Cookies."
② M: May I pet your dog?
   W: I'm sorry, but he doesn't like ________ ________ ________ strangers.

③ M: Do you know where Central Park is?

W: Sure! You just need to walk __________ ______ for 5 minutes.

④ M: Excuse me, ma'am. ______ ______ ______ __________ in this park.

W: I'm sorry. I'll leave right away.

⑤ M: Why don't we ______ ______ ______ ______ tomorrow?

W: Okay! Let's meet at the park.

7. 대화를 듣고, 남자가 여자에게 부탁한 일로 가장 적절한 것을 고르시오.

① 과제물 제출하기
② 농구공 반납하기
③ 과학 책 빌려주기
④ 컴퓨터로 문서 작성하기
⑤ 고장 난 컴퓨터 살펴보기

07

W: Hi, Ben. What happened to your arm?

M: Hi, Nancy. I broke it yesterday during a basketball game.

W: Oh, no! It must hurt a lot.

M: It's okay, but it's ________ __________. I really need to finish my science assignment, but I can't do very much with this arm.

W: We have to ________ ______ __________ by tomorrow, don't we? Well, I'm free this afternoon if you need any help.

M: Oh, then can you ________ ______ ______ ______ my report? I can't do any typing on my computer.

W: Sure! Let's go to your house and do it right now.

M: Great. Thanks!

8. 다음을 듣고, Han Sports Center에 관해 언급되지 않은 것을 고르시오.

① 체육관　　　② 요가실
③ 실내 수영장　　④ 매점
⑤ 샤워실

08

W: Hello, students. Welcome to Han Sports Center. I'm Nicole Newman, the manager of the center. Let me tell you about ________ __________. Right inside the hallway, you can find ________ ________ ________ you can exercise. On the second floor, there's a hall where you can learn yoga. We also

다음 페이지에 계속 ➡

have an indoor swimming pool. Please _______ _______ _______ _______ the proper clothing for each facility. Showers and lockers are __________ _______ the ground floor. Thank you for listening.

9. 다음을 듣고, 무엇에 관한 설명인지 고르시오.

① 기린　　　② 독수리
③ 타조　　　④ 사자
⑤ 북극곰

09 W: This is a wild animal, but you can also see it in a zoo. This animal is usually found in Africa. It's the tallest animal _______ _______ _______.
It _______ _______ _______ its beautiful long neck. It has big eyes and two little horns. It also _______ _______ _______ _______ on its body.
It likes to eat leaves and fruit. It's a peaceful animal on the savannah.

10. 다음을 듣고, 두 사람의 대화가 <u>어색한</u> 것을 고르시오.

①　　　②
③　　　④
⑤

10 ① W: I have a __________ _______ _______ at the meeting tomorrow.
M: Good luck. I'm sure you'll do well.
② W: Why don't we play basketball after lunch?
M: Sounds good. I'll meet you at the gym.
③ W: Excuse me. This is not what I ordered.
M: I'm sorry. _______ _______ _______ _______ a mistake.
④ W: Could you show me how to use this machine?
M: Of course. Just press the red button on the top.
⑤ W: How long _______ _______ _______ _______ in Seoul?
M: It is a great place to live.

11. 대화를 듣고, 여자가 대화 직후에 할 일로 가장 적절한 것을 고르시오.

① 교복 다리기
② 운동화 빨기
③ 미용실에 가기
④ 사진관 방문하기
⑤ 친구 만나러 가기

11

W: Colin, don't you need to ___________ ___________ ___________?

M: I'm getting it tomorrow, Mom.

W: Isn't your graduation ___________ ___________ tomorrow?

M: It's the day after tomorrow.

W: Oh, right. Then, I'll iron your school uniform tomorrow.

M: Thanks, Mom. I'm going to ___________ ___________ ___________ my friends now.

W: ___________ ___________ your black sneakers. I'll wash your white ones right now.

M: Oh, are they for the photo shoot?

W: Yes. I think they'll ___________ ___________ with your uniform.

M: Okay. See you, Mom!

12. 다음 표를 보면서 대화를 듣고, 남자가 주문할 로봇 청소기를 고르시오.

	Model	Price	Noise Level	Controller Type
①	A	$600	75dB	Remote Controller
②	B	$700	68dB	Remote Controller
③	C	$800	68dB	Mobile App
④	D	$1,000	65dB	Mobile App
⑤	E	$1,100	65dB	Mobile App

12

M: Maya, I'm trying to buy a robot vacuum cleaner. Can you help me out?

W: Sure. Have you ___________ ___________ your options?

M: Yes. I'm considering buying one of these.

W: What's your ___________?

M: I can spend up to 900 dollars.

W: Alright. The noise level should be low so it ___________ ___________ your pets.

M: Great point. I think a noise level lower than 70dB will do. What controller type should I choose?

W: Get one that ___________ ___________ ___________ ___________ a mobile app. It'll be more useful than a remote controller.

M: Okay. I'll order this one.

다음 페이지에 계속 ➡

13. 대화를 듣고, 여자가 소파를 받기로 한 날짜를 고르시오.

① 1월 19일
② 1월 20일
③ 1월 21일
④ 1월 22일
⑤ 1월 23일

13 (*Cellphone rings.*)

W: Hello?

M: Hello, this is Ashley Furniture. Is this Ms. Bennett?

W: Yes, hi. This is about the sofa, right?

M: Yes, it is. I'm sorry, but I'm afraid we won't be able to ___________ ___________ ___________ on January 20.

W: Is there a problem?

M: There was a system error. Can we deliver it on the 21st instead?

W: I'm ___________ ___________ ___________ on that day. How about January 22?

M: Well, if you are available in the morning, we ___________ ___________ ___________ on the 19th.

W: That sounds good! Can you come by 10 a.m.?

M: Sure! We'll see you on January 19, then.

W: Thank you.

14. 대화를 듣고, 남자가 어제 한 일로 가장 적절한 것을 고르시오.

① 가족과 외식하기
② 봉사활동 하기
③ 영화 관람하기
④ 공원으로 소풍 가기
⑤ 양로원 방문하기

14 W: Hi, Jeff. How was your ___________ ___________ ___________ yesterday?

M: Oh, it didn't happen.

W: You didn't go to the movies?

M: No, the theater was being renovated, so we just ___________ ___________ ___________.

W: I'm sorry to hear that. You were really looking forward to this movie.

M: It's okay. We had a good time anyway.

W: Oh, did you and your club members do something fun?

M: Yeah, we went to Riverside Park, and enjoyed a ___________ ___________.

W: That's nice!

15. 다음을 듣고, 방송의 목적으로 가장 적절한 것을 고르시오.

① 학교 입학 절차를 설명하려고
② 보건실 이용에 대해 안내하려고
③ 교사와 가깝게 지낼 것을 당부하려고
④ 정부의 새로운 보건 정책에 대해 소개하려고
⑤ 신입생의 건강 상태에 대해 학교에 알리도록 유도하려고

15 W: Hello, new students. Your health and wellbeing are very important to us, so we ask you _________ _________ _________ _________ if you have any allergies or medical conditions. Here is how to do it: go to your teacher, or any teacher, and tell them about your health __________. Emails are also welcome. If you don't want to do it yourself, ask one of your parents to do it for you. Any information you share with us will _________ _________ _____________. So, don't be shy. Let us help you! Thank you.

16. 대화를 듣고, 여자가 지불해야 할 이번 달 통신비로 가장 적절한 것을 고르시오.

① $30
② $40
③ $50
④ $80
⑤ $100

16 *(Telephone rings.)*

M: Best Mobile, how may I help you?

W: Hi, I'm using the $30 __________ _________, but I'm always _________ _________ _________.

M: Okay, then you could get the unlimited data plan priced at $100.

W: That's too expensive.

M: Then, how about the $50 plan that includes 12GB of data?

W: Great! I'll _________ my plan to $50. So, how much _________ _________ _________ for this month?

M: Today is September 15, so you'll have to pay half of the monthly bill for both the old and new plans.

W: Okay, then it would be $15 plus $25.

M: That's correct.

다음 페이지에 계속 ➡

17. 대화를 듣고, 여자의 마지막 말에 대한 남자의 응답으로 가장 적절한 것을 고르시오.

Man: _______________

① It is impossible for me to get such a vocal training.
② I'll take the free lessons for tenors over the weekend.
③ Yes, I'd like to recommend my friend for the mixed choir.
④ Unfortunately, I don't have time during the weekend.
⑤ Perhaps you'd like to join me at the choir.

17

M: Hello, is this where I can __________ ______ for the community choir?

W: Yes, you've come to the right place. Which one are you here to join?

M: You mean there is more than one?

W: Of course! We have a mixed choir as well as single-gender choirs.

M: They all sound inviting, but I don't have a specific preference. Are there any __________ __________ __________?

W: We happen to have open spots in all three choirs, actually. But you'll have to audition for the mixed-gender choir. It is short on tenors.

M: ______ ______ __________ ______ I am a tenor! I have a couple of years of experience in my church choir as well.

W: __________ __________. Would you like to sign up for an audition over the weekend?

M: Unfortunately, I don't have time during the weekend.

18. 대화를 듣고, 남자의 마지막 말에 대한 여자의 응답으로 가장 적절한 것을 고르시오.

Woman: _______________

① It's so kind of you to help her.
② I don't think I can make it to the party.
③ Okay. I will call and make a reservation.
④ That's a great idea! She'd love the cake.
⑤ Wonderful! I could use a fresh pair of eyes.

18

M: Ruth, what's wrong? You look __________.

W: Hi, Jim. I'm sure you know about Linda's birthday party this weekend.

M: Of course. All our classmates are invited.

W: Yes… The problem is that I haven't decided ______ ______ give her.

M: Don't worry. You know Linda. She will like whatever you give her.

W: We're best friends and we have known ______ ______ since we were babies. It's __________ ______ to choose presents for her.

M: I see. Actually, I haven't bought her anything yet,
________. Let's go to the mall together this Friday.

W: Wonderful! I could use a fresh pair of eyes.

19. 대화를 듣고, 여자의 마지막 말에 대한 남자의 응답으로 가장 적절한 것을 고르시오.

Man: ________________

① Andy will have difficulty moving to a new place.
② I think I should call a repair person to fix the elevator.
③ You need to be honest and get all the help you can get.
④ Why don't we make some calls and gather a few more friends?
⑤ I'm thinking of getting him an indoor plant as a housewarming gift.

19

W: About our friend Andy's move, you're coming __________ __________ __________, right?

M: That's right. Are you coming, too?

W: Yes. But, I just heard bad news. Andy says there's no elevator in the building.

M: Uh-oh. What floor is he __________ __________?

W: Third.

M: That's not that bad. I think we'll need __________ __________ __________, though.

W: Yes, especially with the furniture and __________. Any suggestions?

M: Why don't we make some calls and gather a few more friends?

2025 영어듣기능력평가 1회 20번 변형

20. 다음 상황 설명을 듣고, Hazel이 Patrick에게 할 말로 가장 적절한 것을 고르시오.

Hazel: Patrick, ________________

① how about organizing a workshop by yourself?
② I think you will be an excellent AI educator one day.
③ you can get a certificate after completing the course.
④ why don't you sign up for the AI workshop with me?
⑤ field experience is an advantage when searching for a job.

20

M: Hazel is going to register for the practical AI workshop that'll be held at the local youth education center. She wants to get as much information as possible about __________ -__________ artificial intelligence. She is excited to learn about how best to use AI and how it'll change jobs in the future. She __________ __________ that her friend, Patrick is also interested in this field. So, she would like to suggest that Patrick __________ __________ the workshop as well. In this situation, what would Hazel most likely say to Patrick?

Hazel: Patrick, why don't you sign up for the AI workshop with me?

Words & Expressions Review 24

● 다음 단어를 암기하세요.

문제	번호	단어	뜻
1	1	remind A of B	A에게 B를 생각나게 하다
	2	ruler	통치자, 지배자
	3	entertaining	재미있는, 즐거움을 주는
2	4	look ~ up	(정보를) 찾아보다, 검색하다
	5	height	높이
3	6	order	주문하다, 주문
4	7	make an appointment	예약하다, 만날 약속을 하다
	8	leaflet	홍보 책자, 전단
5	9	representative	대표, 대리인
	10	honored	영광스러운, 명예로운
	11	inconvenient	불편한, 곤란한
7	12	assignment	과제, 임무
	13	type	타자를 치다
8	14	facility	시설
	15	proper	적절한, 적당한
	16	horn	뿔
9	17	unique	독특한, 특이한
	18	peaceful	온화한, 평온한, 조용한
10	19	mistake	착오, 실수, 잘못
	20	press	누르다
11	21	graduation	졸업
	22	the day after tomorrow	(내일) 모레

문제	번호	단어	뜻
11	23	iron	다림질하다
12	24	narrow down	좁히다, 줄이다
	25	budget	예산, 비용
	26	deliver	배달하다
13	27	error	오류, 실수
	28	available	시간이 있는
	29	gathering	모임
14	30	renovate	수리하다, 개조하다
	31	put ~ off	(시간, 날짜를) 연기하다, 미루다
15	32	allergy	알레르기
	33	medical condition	질병
	34	monthly	매월의
16	35	short of ~	~이 부족한
	36	include	포함시키다
	37	sign up for A	A를 신청하다
17	38	choir	합창단
	39	specific	특정한, 구체적인
	40	preference	선호
18	41	concerned	걱정하는, 염려하는
19	42	appliance	가전제품
	43	practical	실용적인
20	44	cutting-edge	최첨단의

●왼쪽 단어장의 뜻이 보이지 않게 반으로 접고, 학습한 단어의 뜻을 아래 빈칸에 적어주세요.

1	leaflet	23	horn
2	put ~ off	24	available
3	unique	25	honored
4	choir	26	include
5	graduation	27	renovate
6	gathering	28	peaceful
7	allergy	29	make an appointment
8	short of ~	30	cutting-edge
9	inconvenient	31	appliance
10	medical condition	32	practical
11	type	33	iron
12	specific	34	concerned
13	monthly	35	order
14	error	36	ruler
15	sign up for A	37	press
16	height	38	mistake
17	budget	39	assignment
18	entertaining	40	the day after tomorrow
19	proper	41	preference
20	narrow down	42	remind A of B
21	deliver	43	representative
22	facility	44	look ~ up

2026 17차 개정판

마더텅 100% 실전대비 MP3 중학 영어듣기 24회 모의고사 3학년

발행 17차 개정판 3쇄(2026년 1월 31일)

Chief Editorial Director 서은숙   **Editorial Directors** 이혜빈, 최민정, 최은조, 박상우, 신준기, 김현수, 이윤정, 강수민, 김다영

English Editors Christopher Swafford, Jordan Sanders   **책임 원고 검수** 서은숙, 신재진   **감수** 강산(EBSi 수능영어 강사)

Writers 신재진, 유예슬, 이용진, 김경미, 박선주, 장정문, 남현정, 박상우, 박새미, 신주희, 박헌준, 배기현, 최동렬, 홍유진, 김선혜, 이장원, 김두리, 김유한, 김창범, 노영선, 민희성, 박근혜, 박재민, 손은진, 이찬희, 이상미, 조아라, 허혜경, 손필헌, 호현, 박희나, 정수지, 신은경, 김지야, 권주연, 하은옥, 김현수, 김현정, 탁나희, 안명은, 박주현, 조승희, 이지오, Steve McLeod, Arvin Adams, Janine Davis, Iris James, Lorelei Rivers, Tristan Hughes, Liz Stewart

단어 및 해석 집필 정하은, 김현수, 박상우, 선대훈, 황희진, 송현석, 권은정, 김택, 이정현

원어민 감수 Kathy O'Handley

Audio 녹음 김지야, 이영재, 백찬솔, 손정은, 이승아, 이승민, 정하은   **Audio 편집** 와이알미디어, Netiline, 이형구

Audio 감수 신소미, 신순화, 김다영, 이미경, 차선화, 유지원, 최은조, 이은영, 선대훈, 변선영, 신의진, 박새미, 신재진, 한기범, 장지현, 허은혜, 황혜진, 손정은, 이혜경, 김수정, 김주현, 조재윤, 이상미, 백경빈, 장시은, 정다혜, 문은아, 이슬기, 이한주, 신진실, 유윤정, 이윤정

Voice Actors 임승미, April Lynn, Laura-Leigh, Margaret Chung, Tony Ruse, Peter Bint, Monique Dami Lee, Janet Lee, Shane Hahm, Josh Smith, Anna Sue, 이지나, Alexander Jensen, Josh Schwartzy

교정 신소미, 박상우, 이혜빈, 최민정, 정은주, 신재진, 이은영, 윤숙경, 김효진, 김하나, 김단, 장정문, 임홍일, 이영재, 임하람, 장지현, 김현, 하은옥, 김주현, 선대훈, 이승민, 신영은, 최소영, 오정훈, 성은혜, 홍성경, 남현정, 양희송, 정새로나, 이한주, 신진실, 장신혜, 이옥현, 변선영, 유윤정, 정현희, 신순화, 임현해, 김다영, 신준기, 이윤정, 조수성

표지디자인 김연실   **내지디자인** 김연실, 양은선, 양정혜   **인디자인편집** 고연화, 최송실, 양은선, 정은영, 박경아

Illustrators 정제욱, 이혜승, 박현주, 이은경, 이지은, 박우선, 양은선

제작 이주영   **발행인** 문숙영   **발행처** ㈜ 마더텅 (Mother Tongue Co., Ltd.)

주소 서울시 금천구 가마산로 96 708호   **팩스** 02-3142-9126   **홈페이지** www.toptutor.co.kr

등록번호 제1-2423호 (1999년 1월 8일)

마더텅 교재를 풀면서 궁금한 점이 생기셨나요?

교재 관련 내용 문의나 오류신고 사항이 있으면 아래 문의처로 보내 주세요!

문의하신 내용에 대해 성심성의껏 답변해 드리겠습니다.

또한 교재의 **내용 오류** 또는 **오·탈자, 그 외 수정이 필요한 사항**에 대해 가장 먼저 신고해 주신 분께는 감사의 마음을 담아 네이버페이 포인트 1천 원 을 보내 드립니다!

＊기한: 2026년 12월 31일 ＊오류신고 이벤트는 당사 사정에 따라 조기 종료될 수 있습니다. ＊홈페이지에 게시된 정오표 기준으로 최초 신고된 오류에 한하여 상품권을 보내 드립니다.

● **카카오톡** mothertongue @ **이메일** mothert1004@toptutor.co.kr 🏠 **홈페이지** www.toptutor.co.kr ▫ **교재Q&A게시판**

🎧 **고객센터 전화** 1661-1064(07:00~22:00) ✉ **문자** 010-6640-1064(문자수신전용)

 **모바일로 교재 MP3 재생 방법** 마더텅의 교재 MP3는 모바일 스트리밍/다운로드를 지원합니다.

1 아래의 QR 코드 접속

2 스타플레이어 어플 설치

▶▶ SKIP (특정 부분을 건너 뛰어 뒤로 가거나 앞으로 다시 가서 듣고 싶은 경우)

1

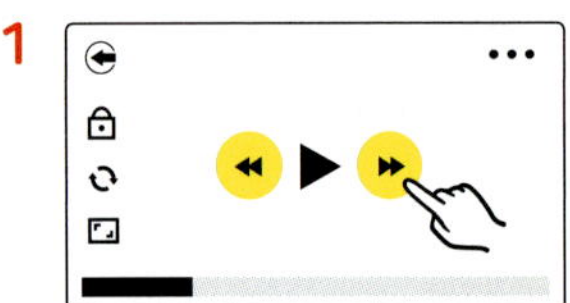

재생 버튼 양쪽의 화살표를 누르면 앞으로 가거나 뒤로 갈 수 있습니다.

2

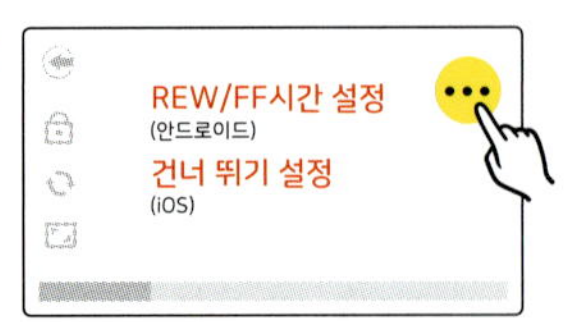

우측 상단의 점 세 개 버튼을 누르면 REW/FF시간 설정 (안드로이드) 건너 뛰기 설정 (iOS) 가능

구간반복 (특정 구간을 반복 재생하고 싶은 경우)

1. 좌측 또는 우측 하단 구간반복 아이콘 누르면 빨간 선 활성화

2. 선의 양쪽 끝점을 이동하여 원하는 반복재생 구간 설정 가능

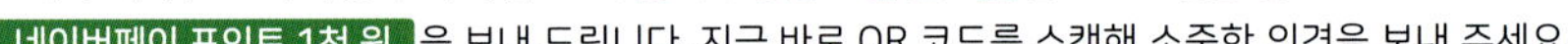

마더텅 학습 교재 이벤트에 참여해 주세요. 참여해 주신 분께 선물을 드립니다.

이벤트 1 1분 간단 교재 사용 후기 이벤트

마더텅은 고객님의 소중한 의견을 반영하여 보다 좋은 책을 만들고자 합니다.
교재 구매 후, <교재 사용 후기 이벤트>에 참여해 주신 모든 분께는 감사의 마음을 담아
네이버페이 포인트 1천 원을 보내 드립니다. 지금 바로 QR 코드를 스캔해 소중한 의견을 보내 주세요!

이벤트 2 중학영어듣기 인증샷 이벤트

SNS에 <중학영어듣기> 인증샷을 올려 주시면 참여해 주신 모든 분께 감사의 마음을 담아
네이버페이 포인트 2천 원을 보내 드립니다. 지금 바로 QR 코드를 스캔해 작성한 게시물의 URL을 입력해 주세요!

필수 태그 #마더텅 #중학영어듣기

이벤트 3 마더텅 우편 이벤트

본 교재의 24회 고난도 모의고사 페이지를 오려서 마더텅으로 보내 주세요!
추첨을 통해 소정의 상품을 보내 드립니다.

참여 방법 24회 고난도 모의고사(p.368~371) 풀이 및 채점 완료
→ 해당 페이지를 모두 오려서 마더텅에 발송(우편, 택배 등) → QR 코드를 스캔하고 발송 인증

주소 (08501) 서울특별시 금천구 가마산로 96, 대륭테크노타운 8차 708호, 마더텅 이벤트 담당자 앞 / 010-6640-1064

※ 이벤트 기간: 2026년 12월 31일까지 (*해당 이벤트는 당사 사정에 따라 조기 종료될 수 있습니다.) ※ 자세한 사항은 해당 QR 코드를 스캔하거나 홈페이지 이벤트 공지 글을 참고해 주세요. ※ 당사 사정에 따라 이벤트의 내용이나 상품이 변경될 수 있으며 변경 시 홈페이지에 공지합니다. ※ 만 14세 미만은 부모님께서 신청해 주셔야 합니다. ※ 상품은 이벤트 참여일로부터 4~5일(영업일 기준) 내에 발송됩니다. (단, 이벤트 3은 예외) ※ 동일 교재로 세 가지 이벤트 모두 참여 가능합니다. (단, 같은 이벤트 중복 참여는 불가합니다.)

2026 17차 개정판

마더텅 100% 실전대비 MP3 중학영어듣기 24회 모의고사 3학년

정답과 해석

MOTHERTONGUE
마더텅출판사
since 1999.4.1.

학습계획표 **24**회 완성

- ✔ 100% 실전대비 MP3 중학영어듣기 24회 모의고사를 100% 활용할 수 있도록 도와주는 학습계획표입니다. 계획표를 활용하여 학습 일정을 계획하고 자신의 성적을 체크해 보세요. 스스로 학습 현황을 체크하면서 공부하는 습관은 문제집을 끝까지 푸는 데 도움을 줍니다.
- ✔ 계획은 도중에 틀어질 수 있습니다. 하지만 계획을 세우고 지키는 과정은 그 자체로 효율적인 학습에 큰 도움이 됩니다. 학습 중 계획이 변경될 경우에 대비해 마더텅 홈페이지에서 학습계획표 PDF 파일을 제공하고 있습니다.

회	학습날짜	문항수	학습결과		딕테이션 맞은 갯수
1회		20	맞음	개	
2회		20	맞음	개	
3회		20	맞음	개	
4회		20	맞음	개	
5회		20	맞음	개	
6회		20	맞음	개	
7회		20	맞음	개	
8회		20	맞음	개	
9회		20	맞음	개	
10회		20	맞음	개	
11회		20	맞음	개	
12회		20	맞음	개	
13회		20	맞음	개	
14회		20	맞음	개	
15회		20	맞음	개	
16회		20	맞음	개	
17회		20	맞음	개	
18회		20	맞음	개	
19회		20	맞음	개	
20회		20	맞음	개	
21회		20	맞음	개	
22회		20	맞음	개	
23회		20	맞음	개	
24회		20	맞음	개	

Listening Test
영어듣기 모의고사 01회

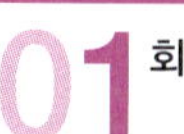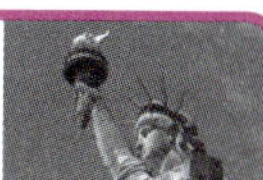

|정|답|

01 ③	02 ④	03 ③	04 ②	05 ③
06 ④	07 ⑤	08 ③	09 ③	10 ⑤
11 ①	12 ①	13 ④	14 ⑤	15 ⑤
16 ④	17 ②	18 ⑤	19 ②	20 ⑤

01 그림정보파악(대화)   ▶ 정답 ③

듣·기·대·본

W: Welcome to Cycle Gear Shop.

M: Hi. Can I order 15 belt bags for my cycling club?

W: Sure. We have ready-made options, or you can design your own.

M: I'd like to design the bags myself.

W: Okay. Do you want a single-bottle holder or a double-bottle holder?

M: A single-bottle holder, please.

W: Should the bags have reflective strips for night riding?

M: Yes, definitely.

W: Would you like to add any initials or text?

M: Yes, please print the club's name "Road Wings" on the front.

W: Perfect. I can have them ready by next Monday.

우·리·말·해·석

여: Cycle Gear Shop(자전거 용품점)에 오신 것을 환영합니다.

남: 안녕하세요. 제 사이클링 동호회를 위해 벨트백 15개를 주문할 수 있을까요?

여: 물론이죠. 저희는 기성 제품이 있고, 아니면 직접 디자인할 수도 있어요.

남: 제가 직접 그 벨트백들을 디자인하고 싶어요.

여: 알겠습니다. 한 개의 물병 홀더를 원하시나요, 아니면 두 개의 물병 홀더를 원하시나요?

남: 한 개의 물병 홀더로 해 주세요.

여: 그 벨트백들에 야간 주행용 반사띠가 있어야 할까요?

남: 네, 반드시요.

여: 이니셜이나 글을 추가하시겠어요?

남: 네, 앞면에 동호회명 "Road Wings"를 인쇄해 주세요.

여: 좋습니다. 다음 주 월요일까지 준비해 드릴 수 있습니다.

단·어·및·표·현

belt bag 벨트백, 허리가방, 허리에 차는 가방

ready-made 기성품의

reflective strip 반사띠

02 대화미언급   ▶ 정답 ④

듣·기·대·본

(*Telephone rings.*)

M: Hello. This is City History Walking Tour.

W: Hi. Could you tell me about the tour? When does it run?

M: It runs every Saturday starting on May 10th. It lasts about three hours, from 2:00 p.m. to 5:00 p.m.

W: In what language is the tour given?

M: It's conducted in both English and Spanish.

W: What can I expect during the tour?

M: You'll visit historic sites, museums, and local markets.

W: Wonderful! How much is the fee?

M: It's 20 dollars per person.

W: Perfect!

우·리·말·해·석

(전화벨이 울린다.)

남: 안녕하세요. 여기는 시 역사 도보 투어입니다.

여: 안녕하세요. 투어에 대해 알려 주실 수 있나요? 언제 운영되나요?

남: 5월 10일부터 시작해서 매주 토요일에 운영됩니다. 약 세 시간 동안 진행되며, 오후 2시부터 5시까지입니다.

여: 투어는 어떤 언어로 제공되나요?

남: 영어와 스페인어 둘 다로 진행됩니다.

여: 투어 동안 어떤 것을 기대할 수 있나요?

남: 유적지들, 박물관들, 그리고 지역 시장들을 방문하게 됩니다.

여: 좋네요! 참가 비용은 얼마인가요?

남: 한 사람당 20달러입니다.

여: 완벽하네요!

단·어·및·표·현

run [rʌn] [동] (서비스 등을) 운영하다, (행사 등이) 진행되다

conduct [kəndʌ́kt] [동] (특정한 활동을) 하다, 수행하다

historic site 유적지

fee [fiː] [명] 비용, 요금

per [pəːr] [전] ~당

03 전화목적파악   ▶ 정답 ③

듣·기·대·본

(*Telephone rings.*)

W: Good morning, City Pharmacy. How may I assist you?

M: Hi, I'm calling about the prescription I picked up yesterday.

W: Sure, what's the problem?

M: I received the wrong medication.

W: I'm terribly sorry about that. Can you tell me which medication you were supposed to receive?

M: I was supposed to get more medicine for my high blood pressure, but I got medicine for allergies instead.

W: I apologize for the mix-up. We'll correct this right away. Please bring back the wrong medicine, and we'll give you the right one instead.

M: Thanks. I'll come by this afternoon.

우·리·말·해·석

(전화벨이 울린다.)

여: 안녕하세요, City 약국입니다. 제가 어떻게 도와드릴까요?

남: 안녕하세요, 저는 어제 들고 왔던 처방전 때문에 전화하고 있습니다.

여: 네, 무슨 문제인가요?

남: 전 잘못된 약을 받았어요.

여: 그것에 대해 대단히 죄송합니다. 당신은 어떤 약을 받기로 했었는지 말씀해주실 수 있나요?

남: 저는 제 고혈압 약을 더 받기로 되어 있었지만, 대신 알레르기 약을 받았어요.

여: 뒤바뀜에 사과드립니다. 저희는 이것을 지금 바로 정정할게요. 잘못된 약을 가져와 주세요, 그러면 저희가 대신 당신께 맞는 약을 드리

겠습니다.
남: 감사해요. 전 오늘 오후에 잠깐 들를게요.

단·어·및·표·현
pharmacy [fά:rməsi] 똉 약국
prescription [priskrípʃən] 똉 처방전
medication [mèdəkéiʃən] 똉 약
terribly [térəbli] 뵝 대단히, 너무
be supposed to ~하기로 되어있다
high blood pressure 고혈압
correct [kərékt] 똑 정정하다, 바로잡다
come by 잠깐 들르다

04 수치파악(시각) ▶ 정답 ②

듣·기·대·본
M: Hello, how can I help you?
W: I'd like to buy one bus ticket to Jinju this afternoon.
M: Okay. What time do you want to leave?
W: The sooner, the better. When is the next bus?
M: The next bus is at 2 p.m., but it's fully booked.
W: Then, what other times are available?
M: Buses also leave at 3 p.m. and 5 p.m.
W: I need to get there by 6 o'clock. So, I'll take the one leaving at 3 p.m. Here's my credit card.
M: Thanks. Here is your ticket. The platform is number 4.

우·리·말·해·석
남: 안녕하세요, 어떻게 도와드릴까요?
여: 저는 오늘 오후에 진주로 가는 버스표를 한 장 사고 싶어요.
남: 네. 언제 출발하고 싶으신가요?
여: 빠를수록 좋아요. 다음 버스는 언제 있어요?
남: 다음 버스는 오후 2시에 있는데, 예약이 다 찼어요.
여: 그러면, 다른 시간은 언제 가능한가요?
남: 버스는 오후 3시와 오후 5시에도 출발해요.
여: 저는 6시 정각까지 그곳에 도착해야 해요. 그래서, 저는 오후 3시에 출발하는 버스로 할게요. 여기 제 신용카드요.
남: 감사합니다. 여기 당신의 표가 있어요. 승강장은 4번이에요.

단·어·및·표·현
leave [li:v] 똑 출발하다, 떠나다
book [buk] 똑 예약하다
platform [plǽtfɔ:rm] 똉 승강장

05 심정추론 ▶ 정답 ③

듣·기·대·본
W: Welcome to Marley's Cleaners.
M: Hello. I'm here to pick up my jacket.
W: Hello, Mr. Kim. Your jacket is ready.
M: It looks perfect. You really did take out the stain!
W: Of course. I'm familiar with that kind of stain. I also fixed the buttons.
M: Wow! Thank you so much. They were loose. I forgot to mention it.
W: I'm glad you like the result.
M: I love it. The jacket looks almost new. You are the best cleaner in town.
W: You are too kind. Thanks.

우·리·말·해·석
① 속상한 ② 후회하는 ③ 만족하는 ④ 수줍은 ⑤ 창피한

여: Marley의 세탁소에 오신 것을 환영합니다.
남: 안녕하세요. 저는 제 재킷을 찾으러 왔어요.
여: 안녕하세요, 김 선생님. 당신의 재킷은 준비 되었습니다.
남: 완벽해 보이네요. 당신은 얼룩을 정말 제거해 주셨네요!
여: 당연하죠. 저는 그런 종류의 얼룩에 익숙합니다. 저는 또한 단추들도 손봤습니다.
남: 왜! 정말 감사합니다. 그것들은 헐거워져 있었거든요. 그것을 말한다는 것을 잊어버렸습니다.
여: 결과에 만족하신다니 다행이네요.
남: 아주 맘에 들어요. 재킷이 거의 새 것처럼 보여요. 당신은 도시 최고의 세탁전문가예요.
여: 당신은 너무 다정하시네요. 감사합니다.

단·어·및·표·현
take out 제거하다
stain [stein] 똉 (지우기 힘든) 얼룩
familiar with ~에 익숙한
loose [lu:s] 똉 (떨어질 것처럼) 헐거워진
mention [ménʃən] 똑 말하다, 언급하다

06 그림상황에적절한대화찾기 ▶ 정답 ④

듣·기·대·본
① W: Did you hear about the new art exhibit?
   M: Yes, I heard it's quite popular.
② W: Would you like some toast with strawberry jam?
   M: Yes, please. That sounds delicious.
③ W: I love to travel to new places.
   M: Me too! Exploring different cultures is fascinating.
④ W: I can't open this jar. Can you help me?
   M: Use rubber gloves. That should help you get a better grip.
⑤ W: Hi, I'm looking for a pair of gloves.
   M: How about these leather ones? They're one of our bestsellers.

우·리·말·해·석
① 여: 너는 새 미술 전시회에 대해 들었니?
   남: 응, 나는 그것이 꽤 인기 있다고 들었어.
② 여: 딸기잼을 바른 토스트를 좀 먹을래?
   남: 응, 부탁해. 맛있겠다.
③ 여: 나는 새로운 곳으로 여행가는 걸 좋아해.
   남: 나도! 다른 문화를 탐험하는 건 흥미로워.
④ 여: 난 이 병을 못 열겠어. 너는 나를 도와줄 수 있니?
   남: 고무장갑들을 써봐. 그건 네가 더 잘 잡는 데 도움이 될 거야(그렇게 하면 손에 힘이 더 잘 들어갈 거야).
⑤ 여: 안녕하세요, 저는 장갑 한 켤레를 찾고 있어요.
   남: 이 가죽으로 된 것들은 어떠세요? 저희의 베스트셀러 중 하나예요.

단·어·및·표·현
exhibit [igzíbit] 똉 전시회, 전람회
explore [iksplɔ́:r] 똑 탐험하다
fascinating [fǽsənèitiŋ] 똉 흥미로운, 매력적인
rubber gloves 고무장갑
grip [grip] 똉 단단히 붙잡음
leather [léðər] 똉 가죽으로 된

07 부탁(요청)한일파악 ▶ 정답 ⑤

듣·기·대·본

M: Mom, I'm heading out now!
W: Honey, are you going to the library?
M: Yes. I need to study for my finals.
W: Do you know where your sister is right now?
M: She's working at the café next to the library.
W: Can you take an extra umbrella with you and give it to your sister?
M: Sure. No problem.

우·리·말·해·석

남: 엄마, 저 지금 출발해요!
여: 얘야, 도서관에 가는 거니?
남: 네. 기말 시험을 위해 공부해야 해요.
여: 지금 네 여동생이 어디 있는지 아니?
남: 도서관 옆 카페에서 일하고 있어요.
여: 여분의 우산을 가져가서 네 여동생에게 줄 수 있겠니?
남: 그럼요. 문제없어요.

단·어·및·표·현

head out 출발하다

08 담화미언급 ▶ 정답 ③

듣·기·대·본

W: Hello, students. Today, we'll talk about paper, one of our most common necessities. Paper was first invented in ancient China around 2,000 years ago. It quickly became an essential material for recording information. It is used in various ways, including for writing, printing, and packaging. The main materials used to make paper are wood pulp and water. Today, efforts are being made to recycle paper to help save trees and reduce waste.

우·리·말·해·석

여: 안녕하세요, 학생 여러분들. 오늘, 우리는 우리의 가장 흔한 필수품 중 하나인 종이에 대해 얘기해볼 거예요. 종이는 약 2,000년 전에 고대 중국에서 처음으로 발명됐어요. 그것은 빠르게 정보를 기록하는 필수적인 재료가 되었어요. 그것은 필기, 인쇄, 그리고 포장을 포함한 다양한 방식으로 사용됐어요. 종이를 만드는 데 사용되는 주 재료는 목재 펄프와 물이예요. 오늘날, 나무들을 보호하고 쓰레기 줄이는 것을 돕기 위해 종이를 재활용하는 노력이 이루어지고 있어요.

단·어·및·표·현

common [kámən] [형] 흔한
necessity [nəsésəti] [명] 필수품
ancient [éinʃənt] [형] 고대의
essential [əsénʃəl] [형] 필수적인, 극히 중요한
material [mətí(:)əriəl] [명] (물건의) 재료
recycle [ri:sáikl] [동] 재활용하다

09 담화화제추론 ▶ 정답 ③

듣·기·대·본

W: This is an electric home device which is very useful in winter. It commonly has a water tank that needs to be filled with water. This device helps to increase the humidity in the air by releasing water vapor. This helps prevent dry skin, dry throats, and other problems caused by dry air. It is important to keep the water tank clean to prevent the growth of bacteria.

우·리·말·해·석

여: 이것은 겨울에 매우 유용한 가전제품입니다. 이것은 보통 물로 채워야 하는 수조가 있습니다. 이 기기는 수증기를 내뿜는 것으로 대기 중의 습도를 높이는 데 도움이 됩니다. 이것은 건조한 피부, 건조한 목, 그리고 건조한 대기로 인해 발생되는 다른 문제들을 예방하는 데 도움이 됩니다. 박테리아의 증식을 방지하기 위해 수조를 깨끗하게 유지하는 것이 중요합니다.

단·어·및·표·현

commonly [kámənli] [부] 보통, 흔히
humidity [hju:mídəti] [명] 습도
release [rilí:s] [동] 내뿜다, 방출하다
water vapor 수증기
prevent [privént] [동] 예방하다, 방지하다

10 어색한대화찾기 ▶ 정답 ⑤

듣·기·대·본

① M: What do you want on your birthday?
W: I just want a big cake.
② M: Please call us when you get there.
W: Yes, I will, Dad. Don't worry.
③ M: Can I borrow money from you?
W: I'm sorry but I already used my savings on my new camera.
④ M: I like this shirt but it's too small.
W: Oh, we have that in other sizes, sir.
⑤ M: Do you always take the bus when you go to school?
W: Yes, I go to that school, too.

우·리·말·해·석

① 남: 너의 생일에 무엇을 원하니?
여: 그냥 큰 케이크를 원해.
② 남: 거기에 도착하면 우리에게 전화하렴.
여: 네, 그럴게요, 아빠. 걱정 마세요.
③ 남: 내가 너에게 돈을 좀 빌릴 수 있을까?
여: 미안하지만 내 새 카메라에 모아둔 돈을 이미 써버렸어.
④ 남: 저는 이 셔츠가 좋지만 이건 너무 작아요.
여: 오, 그건 다른 사이즈도 있어요, 손님.
⑤ 남: 너는 학교 갈 때 항상 버스를 타니?
여: 응, 나도 그 학교에 다녀.

단·어·및·표·현

savings [séiviŋz] [명] 모아둔 돈, 저축 금액

11 할일파악(대화직후) ▶ 정답 ①

듣·기·대·본

W: Welcome to Georgia's Clothing Store. May I help you?
M: Yes, I bought a coat two days ago, and these buttons have come off already.
W: Oh, I'm so sorry. What can we do for you?
M: Is it possible to get a refund?
W: Well, if you have the receipt, you can get the refund.
M: I see. Then, I think I'll go back to my house right now and get my receipt.
W: Okay. We close at 8 p.m. So, please make sure you

come back before 8.

우·리·말·해·석

여: Georgia의 옷 가게에 오신 것을 환영합니다. 도와드릴까요?

남: 네, 이틀 전에 코트를 샀는데, 이 단추들이 벌써 떨어졌습니다.

여: 오, 죄송합니다. 어떻게 해 드릴까요?

남: 환불을 받는 것이 가능한가요?

여: 음, 영수증을 갖고 계신다면 환불을 받을 수 있습니다.

남: 알겠습니다. 그러면, 당장 집으로 돌아가서 영수증을 가져와야겠네요.

여: 좋습니다. 저희는 오후 8시에 문을 닫습니다. 그러니 꼭 8시 전에 돌아오도록 해주세요.

단·어·및·표·현

clothing [klóuðiŋ] 몡 옷

get a refund 환불을 받다

12 도표정보파악 ▶ 정답 ①

듣·기·대·본

W: Timothy, I'm looking for a sports water bottle to take to the gym. Can you help me?

M: Sure! First, you need to choose the material. Which do you prefer, plastic or stainless steel?

W: I like plastic since it's lighter.

M: Okay. What about the size of the bottle?

W: It needs to fit in my gym bag. So, it shouldn't be too large.

M: Then, you should choose one which is smaller than 1.5 liters.

W: Okay. If it's dishwasher safe, it's more convenient to clean, right?

M: Yes. You just need to put it in the dishwasher to get it washed.

W: Great. I'll order this one.

우·리·말·해·석

	모델	재질	크기 (리터)	식기세척기 사용 가능
①	A	플라스틱	1.2	O
②	B	플라스틱	2.0	O
③	C	플라스틱	1.2	X
④	D	스테인리스 스틸	1.2	O
⑤	E	스테인리스 스틸	2.0	X

여: Timothy, 나는 헬스장에 가지고 갈 스포츠 물병을 찾고 있어. 도와줄 수 있어?

남: 물론이지! 먼저, 재질을 선택해야 해. 플라스틱이 좋아, 아니면 스테인리스 스틸이 좋아?

여: 더 가벼워서 플라스틱이 좋아.

남: 알겠어. 그럼 물병 크기는 어때?

여: 내 헬스장 가방에 들어가야 해. 그래서 너무 크면 안 돼.

남: 그럼 1.5리터보다 작은 걸 고르는 게 좋겠어.

여: 알겠어. 식기세척기 사용 가능이면 세척하기가 더 편해, 맞지?

남: 응. 세척하려면 그냥 식기세척기에 넣기만 하면 돼.

여: 좋아. 이걸로 주문할게.

단·어·및·표·현

material [mətí(:)əriəl] 몡 재질

fit in ~에 들어가다

dishwasher safe 식기세척기 사용 가능

convenient [kənví:njənt] 톙 편리한

13 수치파악(날짜) ▶ 정답 ④

듣·기·대·본

M: Rachel, have you heard about the upcoming art exhibition at the city gallery?

W: Yes, I saw the advertisement. Let's go check it out.

M: Sure. I saw that it will run from August 5th to 25th.

W: Why don't we go on August 10th? It's a Saturday, so we won't have to worry about school.

M: Sorry, it's my parents' wedding anniversary on the 10th. What about the 15th?

W: The 15th is a Thursday, right? I have dance club practice every Thursday. How about going on the 20th?

M: Great! That day works for me.

우·리·말·해·석

남: Rachel, 너는 시립 미술관에서 곧 있을 미술 전시회에 대해 들어봤니?

여: 응, 나는 광고를 봤어. 가서 확인해보자.

남: 그래. 나는 그것이 8월 5일에서 25일까지 진행될 거라고 봤어.

여: 우리 8월 10일에 가는 게 어때? 토요일이라서 우리는 학교에 대해 걱정할 필요가 없어.

남: 미안, 10일은 우리 부모님의 결혼기념일이야. 15일은 어때?

여: 15일은 목요일이지, 맞지? 나는 매주 목요일에 댄스 동아리 연습이 있어. 20일에 가는 게 어때?

남: 좋아! 그 날은 괜찮아.

단·어·및·표·현

upcoming [ʌ́pkʌ̀miŋ] 톙 곧 있을, 다가오는

advertisement [æ̀dvərtáizmənt] 몡 광고

run [rʌn] 통 (얼마의 기간 동안) 계속되다

work for (특정 일시 · 상황 등이) ~에게 문제없다, 좋다

14 한일파악 ▶ 정답 ⑤

듣·기·대·본

W: Hi, Ethan. Did you enjoy the concert last weekend?

M: I couldn't go because all the tickets were sold out.

W: Oh, that's disappointing. Then what did you do last weekend?

M: I went to a baseball game with my dad.

W: Nice! Did the team you were cheering for win?

M: Yes, they did! They came from behind and scored four runs in the ninth inning.

W: Wow, that must have been thrilling.

M: Yes, the whole crowd went wild!

W: Sounds amazing!

우·리·말·해·석

여: 안녕, Ethan. 지난 주말에 콘서트 재밌었어?

남: 표가 다 매진돼서 못 갔어.

여: 아, 그거 실망이었겠다. 그럼 지난 주말엔 뭐 했어?

남: 아빠랑 야구 경기에 갔어.

여: 좋았겠다! 네가 응원하는 팀이 이겼어?

남: 응, 이겼어! 9회에 역전해서 4점을 득점했어.

여: 와, 그거 정말 짜릿했겠다.

남: 응, 모든 관중이 열광했어!

여: 정말 멋지다!

단·어·및·표·현

sold out 매진된

disappointing [dìsəpɔ́intiŋ] 형 실망스러운
come from behind 역전하다
score [skɔ:r] 동 득점하다
run [rʌn] 형 (야구에서) 득점
inning [íniŋ] 형 (야구에서 9회 중의 한) 회
thrilling [θríliŋ] 형 짜릿한, 스릴 있는
go wild 열광하다

15 담화목적파악　　　　　▶ 정답 ⑤

듣·기·대·본

W: Attention students. This is Mrs. Gibson, your vice principal. More and more students are riding their bikes to school. So, I'd like to give you some tips about how to ride a bike to school safely. First, wear a helmet to protect your head. Also, get off your bike when you reach the schoolyard so that you don't bump into other students. Third, use a bike lane when you ride your bike outside of the school area. Please follow these rules to keep safe.

우·리·말·해·석

여: 학생 여러분들 주목하세요. 저는 여러분의 교감 선생님인 Mrs. Gibson 이에요. 점점 더 많은 학생들이 학교에 그들의 자전거를 타고 옵니다. 그래서, 저는 여러분에게 안전하게 학교에 자전거를 타고 오는 방법에 대해 몇 가지 조언을 주고 싶습니다. 우선, 여러분의 머리를 보호하기 위해 헬멧을 착용하세요. 또한, 다른 학생들과 부딪히지 않도록 학교 운동장에 도착하면 자전거에서 내리세요. 셋째, 학교 구역 밖에서 자전거를 탈 때는 자전거 도로를 이용하세요. 안전을 지키기 위해 이 규칙들을 준수해 주세요.

단·어·및·표·현

vice principal 교감, 부교장
protect [prətékt] 동 보호하다
get off (탈것에서) 내리다
bump into 부딪치다

16 수치계산(금액)　　　　　▶ 정답 ④

듣·기·대·본

W: Hello, how can I help you?
M: Hi. I'm looking to buy some souvenirs.
W: Are you looking for something in particular?
M: Yes, I collect landmark magnets. How much are these Gyeongbokgung Palace magnets?
W: They're $3 each. Next to those are the Seoul Tower magnets. They are $2 each.
M: Great! I'll take two Gyeongbokgung Palace magnets, and one Seoul Tower magnet.
W: Sure! Here you go. Do you want anything else?
M: No, that's it. Thanks.

우·리·말·해·석

여: 안녕하세요, 어떻게 도와드릴까요?
남: 안녕하세요. 저는 기념품을 좀 사려고 보고 있어요.
여: 특별히 찾고 있는 것이 있나요?
남: 네, 저는 랜드마크 자석을 모아요. 이 경복궁 자석들은 얼마예요?
여: 그것들은 각각 3달러입니다. 그것들 바로 옆에 있는 것은 서울 타워 자석입니다. 그것들은 각각 2달러입니다.

남: 훌륭해요! 저는 경복궁 자석 2개와 서울 타워 자석 1개를 살게요.
여: 그럼요! 여기 있습니다. 그 밖의 다른 것을 원하세요?
남: 아니요, 그게 다예요. 고마워요.

단·어·및·표·현

souvenir [sù:vəníər] 형 기념품
That's it. 그것이 다다.

17 알맞은응답찾기　　　　　▶ 정답 ②

듣·기·대·본

M: Hi. Can I go into the music hall, please?
W: I'm sorry, sir. The concert has started. You cannot go in now.
M: I know I'm late, but I have my ticket here.
W: We cannot open the door in the middle of the concert.
M: Oh, no! My daughter is playing the violin in there.
W: Sorry. You have to wait until the break.
M: When is it?
W: In about thirty minutes. You can go in then.

우·리·말·해·석

① 8시입니다. 하지만 홀이 만원입니다.
② 약 30분 후입니다. 그때 들어가실 수 있습니다.
③ 한 시간 후입니다. 하지만 언제든지 들어가실 수 있습니다.
④ 내일일 것입니다. 성공적인 콘서트가 되길 기원합니다.
⑤ 콘서트는 오후 7시에 시작합니다. 서두르실 필요가 없습니다.

남: 안녕하세요. 음악당 안으로 들어가도 될까요?
여: 죄송합니다, 선생님. 콘서트가 시작되었습니다. 지금 들어가실 수 없습니다.
남: 제가 늦은 것은 알지만, 여기 제 표가 있는데요.
여: 저희는 콘서트 도중에 문을 열 수 없습니다.
남: 아, 안 돼요! 저 안에서 제 딸이 바이올린을 연주하고 있어요.
여: 미안합니다. 휴식 시간까지 기다리셔야 합니다.
남: 그게 언제죠?
여: 약 30분 후입니다. 그때 들어가실 수 있습니다.

단·어·및·표·현

break [breik] 형 휴식 시간, 중단

18 알맞은응답찾기　　　　　▶ 정답 ⑤

듣·기·대·본

W: What are you looking at on your phone, Minjae?
M: I'm trying to find a gift for my dad. He just got promoted at work.
W: That's awesome! Congratulations to him. How about a nice tie?
M: He already has so many of them. I'd like to get him something more meaningful.
W: That's so thoughtful of you. What about a framed photo of you and him with a message like "I'm proud of you."?
M: That's a wonderful idea! He'll love it.
W: There's a photo shop near our school that does custom frames.
M: Great! Can you text me the exact location of the store?

우·리·말·해·석

① 우와! 그에게 꼭 내 축하를 전해줘.

② 물론이지. 네 아버지가 너를 정말 자랑스러워 하실 거야.
③ 미안한데, 너는 내 사진 하나 더 찍어줄 수 있어?
④ 응. 난 이 안경테가 너에게 잘 어울리는 것 같아.
⑤ 좋아! 그 가게의 정확한 위치를 내게 문자로 보내줄 수 있어?

여: 민재야, 너는 네 핸드폰에서 뭘 보고 있어?
남: 나는 내 아빠를 위한 선물을 찾으려고 하는 중이야. 그는 직장에서 막
　　승진하셨거든.
여: 멋지다! 그에게 축하드린다고 전해줘. 멋진 넥타이는 어때?
남: 그는 이미 그것들을 너무 많이 가지고 있어. 나는 그에게 더 의미 있는
　　걸 드리고 싶어.
여: 너는 참 사려 깊다. "나는 당신이 자랑스러워요" 같은 메시지가 새겨진
　　너와 그의 액자 사진은 어때?
남: 그거 좋은 생각이다! 아빠가 그것을 아주 좋아할 거야.
여: 우리 학교 근처에 맞춤 액자를 해주는 사진관이 있어.
남: **좋아! 그 가게의 정확한 위치를 내게 문자로 보내줄 수 있어?**

promote [prəmóut] 동 승진시키다, 진급시키다
meaningful [míːniŋfəl] 형 의미 있는, 중요한
thoughtful [θɔ́ːtfəl] 형 사려 깊은, 친절한
custom [kʌ́stəm] 형 맞춤의

19 알맞은응답찾기　　　　　　　　　▶ 정답 ②

듣·기·대·본

W: Hey, Fred. Is it true that you're running a half-marathon?
M: That's right, Brenda. Next month. My first time ever.
W: Great. How's your preparation going?
M: I'm practicing, but it's not easy. It's not like I have a
　　coach.
W: Well, you don't need one. I know a website that can
　　help.
M: A website? How did you find out about it?
W: I ran a half-marathon before. The website helped me a
　　lot. Take a look.
M: Wow, so many details. There are videos, too.
W: And, when you click here, they make a practice plan for
　　you.
M: Really? This is exactly what I need.

우·리·말·해·석

① 유감이야. 난 이미 웹사이트를 알고 있어.
② 정말? 이건 정확히 내가 필요한 거야.
③ 그래. 내가 너에게 코치를 소개해 줄게.
④ 대단해. 마라톤 잘하길 바라.
⑤ 네가 부상 없이 끝내는 게 중요해.

여: 얘, Fred. 네가 하프 마라톤을 한다는 것이 사실이니?
남: 맞아, Brenda. 다음 달이야. 내 인생에서 처음 해보는 거야.
여: 대단하다. 준비는 어떻게 되어가고 있어?
남: 난 연습 중이지만 쉽지 않아. 내게 코치가 있는 건 아니니까.
여: 글쎄, 넌 코치가 필요 없어. 난 도움을 줄 수 있는 웹사이트를 알고 있어.
남: 웹사이트? 너는 그것에 대해 어떻게 알게 되었어?
여: 나는 전에 하프 마라톤을 했어. 그 웹사이트가 날 많이 도와줬어. 한
　　번 봐봐.
남: 와, 정말 많은 정보가 있네. 영상도 있어.
여: 그리고 네가 여기를 클릭하면 그들은 널 위한 연습 계획도 만들어줘.
남: **정말? 이건 정확히 내가 필요한 거야.**

run a marathon 마라톤을 하다, 마라톤에서 뛰다
preparation [prèpəréiʃən] 명 준비
find out ~을 알게 되다, 알아내다
details [ditéilz] 명 정보(사항)
injury [índʒəri] 명 부상

20 상황에적절한말찾기　　　　　　　　▶ 정답 ⑤

듣·기·대·본

M: These days, Nora is having a hard time keeping up in
　　math class. She often fails to understand the teacher's
　　explanations. Justin, her classmate, kindly helps her
　　understand how to complete the math problems during
　　the breaks. After a few times, Nora starts to gain back
　　some confidence in math. So, she would like to thank
　　Justin for his help. In this situation, what would Nora
　　most likely say to Justin?
Nora: Justin, I appreciate your help with the math
　　　problems.

우·리·말·해·석

① 유감이지만 너를 더 이상 도와줄 수 없을 것 같아.
② 너의 수학 실력이 많이 늘었어.
③ 기운 내! 쉬는 시간에 내가 도와줄게.
④ 누구나 어느 순간에 자신감을 잃기도 해.
⑤ 수학 문제를 도와줘서 고마워.

남: 요즘 Nora는 수학 수업을 따라가는 데 어려움을 겪고 있다. 그녀는 선
　　생님의 설명을 이해하는 데 자주 실패한다. 같은 반 친구인 Justin이 그
　　녀가 수학 문제 푸는 법을 이해하도록 쉬는 시간 동안 친절하게 도와준
　　다. 몇 번 (그렇게 도와준) 후, Nora는 수학에 대한 자신감을 조금씩 되
　　찾기 시작한다. 그래서 그녀는 Justin에게 도와줘서 고맙다고 하고 싶어
　　한다. 이 상황에서, Nora는 Justin에게 뭐라고 말하겠는가?
Nora: Justin, **수학 문제를 도와줘서 고마워.**

have a hard time -ing ~하는 데 어려움을 겪다
keep up (뒤떨어지지 않도록) 따라가다
gain back (잃었던 것을) 되찾다
confidence [kánfidəns] 명 자신감
appreciate [əpríːʃièit] 동 감사하다

Words & Expressions Review

1. 특정한	2. 감사하다	3. 약국
4. 반사띠	5. 탐험하다	6. 매진된
7. ~에 들어가다	8. 예약하다	9. 승강장
10. 환불	11. 편리한	12. 자신감
13. 유적지	14. ~을 알게 되다, 알아내다	15. 부상
16. 빌리다	17. ~에 익숙한	18. 교감, 부교장
19. 영수증	20. 모아둔 돈	21. 내뿜다, 방출하다
22. 곧 있을, 다가오는	23. 실망스러운	24. 득점하다
25. 여분의	26. ~하는 도중에	27. 의미 있는, 중요한
28. 필수품	29. 흥미로운, 매력적인	30. 승진시키다, 진급시키다
31. (특정한 활동을) 하다, 수행하다	32. 처방전	33. 사려 깊은, 친절한

34. 제거하다	35. (~에서) 떨어지다	36. 기념품
37. 필수적인, 극히 중요한	38. 벨트백, 허리가방, 허리에 차는 가방	39. (탈것에서) 내리다
40. 출발하다, ~로 향하다	41. 휴식 시간, 중단	42. 흔한
43. 습도	44. 재질	

Listening Test

영어듣기 모의고사 02회

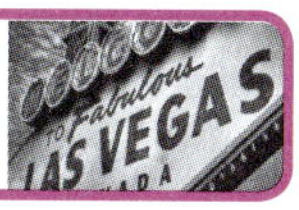

|정|답|

01 ④	02 ④	03 ②	04 ⑤	05 ②
06 ④	07 ①	08 ⑤	09 ③	10 ③
11 ①	12 ④	13 ④	14 ③	15 ④
16 ④	17 ③	18 ①	19 ⑤	20 ④

01 그림정보파악(대화) ▶ 정답 ④

듣·기·대·본

W: Welcome. May I help you?
M: I'm looking for a toy storage box for my 4-year-old son.
W: I see. How about this type? It's a storage box with wheels on the bottom.
M: Oh, that seems very practical. I like it.
W: Then, would you prefer one with a dinosaur character on the front or one without?
M: I'll go with the one with the dinosaur character. He loves dinosaurs.
W: Do you need handles on it? It'll be easier to carry around.
M: No, I don't think they're necessary.
W: Okay.

우·리·말·해·석

여: 어서 오세요. 제가 도와드릴까요?
남: 저는 네 살 난 아들을 위한 장난감 수납 상자를 찾고 있어요.
여: 알겠습니다. 이런 종류는 어떠세요? 이것은 아래에 바퀴가 달린 수납 상자예요.
남: 오, 그거 정말 실용적인 것 같네요. 마음에 들어요.
여: 그렇다면 앞면에 공룡 캐릭터가 있는 걸로 하시겠어요, 아니면 없는 걸로 하시겠어요?
남: 공룡 캐릭터가 있는 걸로 할게요. 그는 공룡을 정말 좋아해요.
여: 그것에 손잡이가 달린 게 필요하신가요? 들고 다니기 더 쉬울 거예요.
남: 아니요, 그건 필요하지 않을 것 같아요.
여: 알겠습니다.

단·어·및·표·현

storage [stɔ́:ridʒ] [명] 수납, 보관, 저장
practical [prǽktikəl] [형] 실용적인
necessary [nèsəséri] [형] 필요한

02 대화미언급 ▶ 정답 ④

듣·기·대·본

W: Frank, I was wondering if you are interested in participating in the Blue Pencil Contest.
M: Isn't that a writing contest organized by Blue Pencil publishing company?
W: Yes, the writing theme this year is "Life."
M: Thanks for letting me know. When is the deadline?
W: You need to submit your entry by September 5th.
M: That's only two months away. I'd better start writing today.
W: Good luck. The winner will receive $2,000 as a prize.
M: Thank you. I'll do my best.

우·리·말·해·석

여: Frank, 나는 네가 Blue Pencil 대회에 참가하는 것에 관심이 있는지 궁금해하고 있었어.
남: 그것은 Blue Pencil 출판사가 주최하는 글쓰기 대회 아니야?
여: 응, 올해의 글쓰기 주제는 "삶"이야.
남: 나에게 알려줘서 고마워. 기한이 언제야?
여: 너는 9월 5일까지 네 응모작을 제출해야 해.
남: 그것은 겨우 두 달밖에 안 남았잖아. 나는 오늘 글쓰기를 시작해야겠네.
여: 행운을 빌어. 우승자는 상으로 2,000달러를 받을 거야.
남: 고마워. 나는 최선을 다할 거야.

단·어·및·표·현

organize [ɔ́:rgənàiz] [동] 조직하다, 개최하다
submit [səbmít] [동] 제출하다
entry [éntri] [명] 응모작

03 전화목적파악 ▶ 정답 ②

듣·기·대·본

(*Telephone rings.*)
W: Hello.
M: Hello, this is MG Customer Service. We received your message about your oven being broken.
W: Oh, yes. I booked a repair service on your website for tomorrow.
M: Is it okay if we send the repair person this afternoon? We have one slot open today.
W: One day early? That's great! Yes, I'm available this afternoon.
M: Good. Our repair person will call you for detailed schedule.
W: All right. Thank you very much!
M: You're welcome.

우·리·말·해·석

(전화벨이 울린다.)
여: 여보세요.
남: 안녕하세요, 여기는 MG 소비자 서비스센터입니다. 저희는 댁의 오븐이 고장 났다는 메시지를 받았습니다.
여: 오, 맞아요. 저는 당신들의 웹사이트에서 내일로 수리 서비스를 예약해 뒀어요.
남: 혹시 저희가 오늘 오후에 수리 기사를 보내드려도 괜찮으실까요? 저희가 오늘 한 자리가 비어서요.
여: 하루 일찍요? 그건 너무 좋죠! 네, 전 오늘 오후에 시간이 돼요.

남: 잘 됐네요. 자세한 일정은 저희 수리 기사가 전화를 드릴 겁니다.
여: 알겠어요. 정말 감사합니다!
남: 천만에요.

slot [slɑt] 몡 (명단/프로그램 등에 들어가는) 자리, (가느다란) 구멍
available [əvéiləbl] 몧 (사람들을 만날) 시간이 있는, 이용할 수 있는
detailed [díːteild] 몧 자세한, 상세한

04　수치파악(시각)　　▶ 정답 ⑤

듣·기·대·본

(*Telephone rings.*)

M: Good morning, Bright Veterinary Clinic. May I help you?
W: Hi, I need to <u>schedule an appointment</u> for my cat's annual check-up.
M: Sure. When would you like to bring your cat in? Just so you know, we have a <u>lunch break</u> from 12 p.m. to 1 p.m.
W: Can I <u>schedule</u> it for tomorrow?
M: Tomorrow afternoon works.
W: Great. How about 2 p.m.?
M: I'm sorry, but 2 p.m. is <u>already booked</u>. Would 3 p.m. work for you?
W: <u>Unfortunately</u>, I have a meeting at 3 p.m. How about 4 p.m.?
M: 4 p.m. works. We'll see you and your cat then.
W: Perfect. Thank you so much.

우·리·말·해·석

(전화벨이 울린다.)

남: 안녕하세요, Bright 동물 병원입니다. (무엇을) 도와드릴까요?
여: 안녕하세요, 저는 제 고양이의 연간 정기검진 예약을 잡아야 해요.
남: 네. 당신은 언제 당신의 고양이를 데려오시고 싶으세요? 참고로 말씀드리자면 저희는 오후 12시부터 오후 1시까지 점심 시간이 있습니다.
여: 제가 내일로 일정을 잡을 수 있을까요?
남: 내일 오후 괜찮습니다.
여: 좋아요. 오후 2시 괜찮나요?
남: 죄송하지만, 오후 2시는 이미 예약이 되었습니다. 오후 3시는 당신께 괜찮으신가요?
여: 안타깝게도, 저는 오후 3시에 회의가 있어요. 오후 4시는 어떤가요?
남: 오후 4시 괜찮습니다. 저희는 그때 당신과 당신 고양이를 뵙겠습니다.
여: 완벽하네요. 매우 감사합니다.

veterinary clinic 동물병원
schedule [skédʒuːl] 통 일정을 잡다
appointment [əpɔ́intmənt] 몡 예약, 약속
check-up 정기검진
lunch break 점심 시간
unfortunately [ʌnfɔ́ːrtʃənətli] 凰 안타깝게도, 불행하게도

05　심정추론　　▶ 정답 ②

듣·기·대·본

W: Have you had your wisdom teeth pulled out?
M: Yes. I had them <u>pulled out</u> a few years ago.
W: How was it?
M: To be honest with you, it was really painful.
W: Really? I'm going to <u>the dentist</u> tomorrow to have my wisdom teeth removed. <u>I'm really scared.</u>

M: Oh, it's going to be okay.
W: I don't want to go. <u>I'm afraid of</u> the dentist.

우·리·말·해·석

① 신이 난　② 불안해하는　③ 기쁜　④ 화가 난　⑤ 지루해하는

여: 넌 사랑니를 뽑았니?
남: 응. 난 몇 년 전에 사랑니를 뽑았어.
여: 어땠어?
남: 솔직하게 말하자면, 너무 아팠어.
여: 정말? 난 내일 사랑니를 뽑으러 치과에 가. 난 정말 겁이 나.
남: 아, 괜찮을 거야.
여: 난 가기 싫어. 난 치과가 무서워.

wisdom tooth 사랑니
pull out ~ ~을 뽑다

06　그림상황에적절한대화찾기　　▶ 정답 ④

듣·기·대·본

① M: Do you like my new wallpaper?
　W: Yes. You <u>made a good choice</u>.
② M: I really need to go to the restroom.
　W: Oh, no. The nearest one is 15 minutes away.
③ M: I always forget the password for my cellphone.
　W: How about <u>writing it down</u> somewhere?
④ M: Could you give me the password for the restroom?
　W: Sure. It's <u>written on the wall</u> right here.
⑤ M: Where can I find the toilet paper?
　W: It's over there, in <u>aisle</u> 12.

우·리·말·해·석

① 남: 당신은 제 새 벽지가 마음에 드시나요?
　여: 네. 당신은 잘 선택했군요.
② 남: 저 정말로 화장실을 가고 싶어요.
　여: 오, 이런. 가장 가까운 곳이 15분 떨어져 있어요.
③ 남: 저는 항상 제 휴대폰 비밀번호를 잊어버려요.
　여: 그것을 어딘가에 적어 놓는 게 어때요?
④ 남: 화장실 비밀번호를 제게 알려주실 수 있으신가요?
　여: 물론이죠. 바로 여기 벽에 쓰여 있습니다.
⑤ 남: 제가 화장지를 어디서 찾을 수 있을까요?
　여: 저기 12번 통로에 있습니다.

make a choice 선택하다
write ~ down (기억하거나 기록하기 위해) ~을 적다
somewhere [sʌ́mhwὲər] 凰 어딘가에
aisle [ail] 몡 통로

07　부탁(요청)한일파악　　▶ 정답 ①

듣·기·대·본

W: Jason, do you have any plans this Friday?
M: Not yet.
W: <u>Would you mind</u> <u>filling in for</u> me at my part-time job at the café on Friday night?
M: Oh, sure. Is everything alright?
W: Yes. My brother is <u>starring in</u> a play that is <u>opening</u> this Friday, and I have to go.
M: You are a wonderful sister to support your brother's

career.
W: Thanks. I owe you big time.

우•리•말•해•석

여: Jason, 이번 금요일에 무슨 계획이라도 있니?
남: 아직 없어.
여: 금요일 밤에 카페에서 하는 내 아르바이트 일을 나 대신 해줄 수 있겠니?
남: 오, 물론이지. 무슨 일 없는 거지?
여: 응. 내 남동생이 이번 금요일에 개막하는 연극에서 주연을 맡아서 내가 가야 하거든.
남: 넌 남동생의 경력을 지지해주는 훌륭한 누나구나.
여: 고마워. 너한테 정말 크게 빚졌어.

단•어•및•표•현

fill in for ~ ~을 대신하여 일하다
owe [ou] [동] 빚지다

LISTENING ADVICE

'd'와 'y'가 만나면 'd' 소리는 'y' 소리에 동화되어, [ㄷ]가 아닌 [ㅈ] 소리로 발음됩니다. 따라서 'Would you mind ~'에서 'Would you'는 [우드 유]가 아닌 [우쥬]에 가깝게 들립니다. 'd'뿐만 아니라 't', 's', 'z' 등과 'y'가 만날 때에도 동화현상이 일어납니다.

08 담화미언급 ▶ 정답 ⑤

듣•기•대•본

M: Welcome to Pet Nation! We are here for your beloved companions. Our services include pet grooming, dog training, and vet services. We also have a pet hotel and a grooming salon inside the center. There are 4 branches around the city, so you can find us easily. We also sell a variety of pet snacks and accessories. We are open 24 hours, so call us or visit us anytime.

우•리•말•해•석

남: Pet Nation에 오신 것을 환영합니다! 저희는 여러분의 사랑하는 반려동물을 위해 여러분 곁에 있습니다. 저희 서비스는 반려동물 털 관리, 반려견 훈련, 동물 의료 서비스를 포함합니다. 저희는 또한 센터 안에 반려동물 호텔과 털 관리 살롱이 있습니다. 시 전역에 4개의 지점이 있으므로 저희를 쉽게 찾아오실 수 있습니다. 저희는 또한 다양한 종류의 반려동물 간식과 액세서리들을 판매합니다. 24시간 열려있으니 언제라도 전화하시거나 방문해 주세요.

단•어•및•표•현

beloved [bilʌ́vd] [형] 사랑하는
companion [kəmpǽnjən] [명] 반려자, 동반자

09 담화화제추론 ▶ 정답 ③

듣•기•대•본

W: This place sells many kinds of things. You can buy snacks, drinks, and even simple meals here. You can also buy daily necessities such as toothbrushes and toilet paper, just to name a few. In Korea, some medicines that don't require a prescription are sold here. This place usually takes the form of a small store and some are open 24 hours.

우•리•말•해•석

여: 이 장소는 많은 종류의 물건들을 팝니다. 당신은 이곳에서 과자나 음료수, 심지어 간단한 식사거리를 살 수 있습니다. 또한 몇 가지 말씀드리면 칫솔이나 화장지와 같은 생활필수품들을 살 수도 있어요. 한국에서는 처방전을 필요로 하지 않는 일부 약품들이 여기에서 팔립니다. 이 장소는 대개 작은 가게의 형태를 띠고 있고 일부는 24시간 영업을 합니다.

단•어•및•표•현

daily necessity 생활필수품
prescription [priskrípʃən] [명] 처방전

10 어색한대화찾기 ▶ 정답 ③

듣•기•대•본

① W: Have you heard of Chris Brown?
M: No. Who's that?
② W: What's the matter?
M: I broke my sister's mirror.
③ W: Can you give me a hand?
M: I'd love to hold your hand.
④ W: What are you going to do after school?
M: I'm going to play soccer.
⑤ W: How long will it take?
M: About 30 minutes.

우•리•말•해•석

① 여: 너 Chris Brown에 대해 들어본 적 있니?
남: 아니. 그게 누군데?
② 여: 무슨 일 있니?
남: 내가 누나의 거울을 깼어.
③ 여: 좀 도와줄래?
남: 나 네 손을 잡고 싶어.
④ 여: 방과 후에 뭐 할 거니?
남: 난 축구를 할 거야.
⑤ 여: 얼마나 걸리니?
남: 약 30분 정도.

단•어•및•표•현

give A a hand A를 도와주다

11 할일파악(대화직후) ▶ 정답 ①

듣•기•대•본

(*Telephone rings.*)
W: Hello, this is Quick Express Customer Service. How may I help you?
M: Hi, I want to check my package status.
W: Sure. Could you give me your tracking number?
M: Oh, I'm not sure if I have it.
W: Are you the sender?
M: Yes, I am.
W: Then, the tracking number should be on the receipt, or you would have received it as a text message.
M: Right. Let me check my phone. Just a second, I'll find it now.
W: Take your time.

우•리•말•해•석

(전화벨이 울린다.)
여: 안녕하세요, Quick Express 고객센터입니다. 어떻게 도와드릴까요?
남: 안녕하세요, 저는 제 택배의 (배송) 상황을 확인하고 싶어요.

여: 네, 저에게 당신의 운송장 번호를 알려주실 수 있나요?

남: 아, 제가 그걸 가지고 있는지 확실하지 않네요.

여: 발송인이신가요?

남: 네, 맞아요.

여: 그러면, 운송장 번호는 영수증에 있을 거예요, 혹은 당신은 그것을 문자 메시지로 받으셨을 거예요.

남: 맞아요. 제 휴대폰을 확인해볼게요. 잠시만요, 제가 그것을 지금 찾아볼게요.

여: 천천히 하세요.

단·어·및·표·현

status [stéitəs] 명 (진행 과정상의) 상황
tracking number 운송장 번호
sender [séndər] 명 발송인, 보내는 사람
receipt [risíːt] 명 영수증
receive [risíːv] 동 받다
take one's time 천천히 하다

12 도표정보파악 ▶ 정답 ④

듣·기·대·본

M: Christine, what are you <u>searching for</u> online?

W: I'm looking for a Bluetooth speaker. Can you help me choose one?

M: Sure. Are you searching for something <u>affordable</u>?

W: Yeah, I can't spend more than 150 dollars.

M: Okay. You'll be <u>carrying it around</u> in your backpack, right?

W: Yeah, I don't want it to be heavier than my laptop which is 800 grams.

M: Okay. You have two options left, then.

W: This one looks good. It has a longer battery life.

M: Yes, that seems like the better choice.

W: Thanks. I'll order this one then.

우·리·말·해·석

	모델	가격	무게	배터리 수명
①	A	100달러	950그램	20시간
②	B	120달러	900그램	20시간
③	C	130달러	750그램	30시간
④	D	140달러	700그램	40시간
⑤	E	160달러	600그램	40시간

남: Christine, 너는 온라인에서 무엇을 찾고 있니?

여: 나는 블루투스 스피커를 찾고 있어. 내가 하나 고르는 것을 도와줄 수 있니?

남: 물론이지. 너는 적당한 가격의 제품을 찾고 있니?

여: 응, 나는 150달러보다 많이 쓸 수 없어.

남: 알겠어. 너는 그것을 네 배낭에 넣고 다닐 거지, 맞지?

여: 맞아, 나는 그것이 800그램인 내 노트북 컴퓨터보다 더 무겁지 않으면 좋겠어.

남: 알겠어. 그럼 너는 두 개의 선택지가 남았어.

여: 이거 좋아 보인다. 이게 더 긴 배터리 수명을 가지고 있어.

남: 응, 그게 더 좋은 선택 같아 보여.

여: 고마워. 그럼 나는 이걸 주문하겠어.

단·어·및·표·현

search for ~을 찾다
affordable [əfɔ́ːrdəbl] 형 적당한 가격의, 감당할 수 있는

option [ápʃən] 명 선택(지)
battery life 배터리 수명

13 수치파악(날짜) ▶ 정답 ④

듣·기·대·본

M: Ellie, look at this picture! The leaves on the trees on Seorak Mountain have <u>started to turn</u> red and yellow.

W: Wow! It's really beautiful!

M: Why don't we go to Seorak Mountain to see the <u>beautiful scenery</u>?

W: Sounds good. How about this Saturday, October 4th?

M: Oh, not this Saturday. I'm playing soccer on the 4th. How about the 11th?

W: Sorry, I have a family gathering that day. Perhaps we can go on Sunday. How about the 12th?

M: You know what? That's a great idea. Let's go on the 12th.

W: Great. See you then.

우·리·말·해·석

남: Ellie, 이 사진을 봐! 설악산에 있는 나무들의 잎들이 붉고 노랗게 변하기 시작했어.

여: 와! 정말 아름답다!

남: 우리 아름다운 경치를 보기 위해서 설악산에 가는 게 어때?

여: 좋은 생각이야. 이번 주 토요일인 10월 4일은 어때?

남: 아, 이번 주 토요일은 안돼. 나는 4일에 축구를 해. 11일은 어때?

여: 미안하지만, 나는 그날 가족 모임이 있어. 아마 우리는 일요일에 갈 수 있을 거야. 12일은 어때?

남: 있잖아. 그건 정말 좋은 생각이야. 12일에 가자.

여: 좋아. 그때 보자.

단·어·및·표·현

turn [təːrn] 동 (~한 상태로) 변하다, 되다
scenery [síːnəri] 명 경치, 풍경
gathering [gǽðəriŋ] 명 (특정 목적을 위한) 모임
perhaps [pərhǽps] 부 아마, 어쩌면

14 한일파악 ▶ 정답 ③

듣·기·대·본

W: Sean, Kelvin and I are going to ride our bikes at the park. Do you want to join us?

M: I'd like to, but I need to do some research at the library.

W: <u>Weren't you supposed</u> to do it yesterday?

M: I was. But I got a call from my sister on my way to the library.

W: What was it about?

M: She asked me to babysit her son, Jason, because her babysitter called in sick.

W: I see. What did you do with your nephew yesterday?

M: We watched an animated film and I made him pancakes.

W: Sounds like you and Jason had a wonderful time together.

우·리·말·해·석

여: Sean, Kelvin하고 내가 공원에서 자전거를 탈 거야. 우리와 함께 할래?

남: 그러고 싶지만, 나는 도서관에서 조사를 해야 해.

여: 너는 그것을 어제 하기로 하지 않았니?

남: 그랬어. 하지만 도서관에 가는 길에 내 누나로부터 전화를 받았어.
여: 무엇에 관한 것이었어?
남: 그녀의 아이 봐주는 사람이 아파서 못 간다고 전화를 해서, 누나가 내
　게 누나의 아들 Jason을 봐달라고 부탁했어.
여: 알겠어. 너는 어제 네 남자 조카와 무엇을 했어?
남: 우리는 만화영화를 봤고 내가 그에게 팬케이크를 만들어 줬어.
여: 너와 Jason이 함께 멋진 시간을 보낸 것 같다.

단·어·및·표·현

join[dʒɔin] ⑧ 함께 하다
be supposed to + 동사원형 ~하기로 되어 있다
babysit[béibisit] ⑧ 아이를 봐주다
call in sick 전화로 아파서 못 간다고 하다

15 담화목적파악　　　　　　▶ 정답 ④

듣·기·대·본

M: Hello, students. This is your P.E. teacher, Garry Wills. I want to let you know that you're not allowed to use the outdoor basketball court until tomorrow. I'm aware that many of you love to play basketball during lunchtime, but the court was repainted today, and it won't be dry until the next day. You can use the court the day after tomorrow as usual. It's almost lunchtime now. I hope you have a wonderful time. Thank you.

우·리·말·해·석

남: 안녕하세요, 학생 여러분. 저는 여러분의 체육 선생님인 Garry Wills입니다. 저는 여러분에게 여러분이 내일까지 실외 농구 코트를 이용할 수 없음을 알려드리고 싶습니다. 저는 여러분 중 많은 사람들이 점심 시간에 농구를 하기를 좋아한다는 것을 알지만, 코트가 오늘 다시 페인트칠 되어 다음 날까지 마르지 않을 것입니다. 여러분은 모레 평상시처럼 코트를 이용할 수 있습니다. 이제 거의 점심 시간입니다. 저는 여러분이 좋은 시간을 갖기를 바랍니다. 감사합니다.

단·어·및·표·현

outdoor[áutdɔ̀ːr] ⑧ 실외의
the day after tomorrow 모레
as usual 평상시처럼

16 수치계산(금액)　　　　　　▶ 정답 ④

듣·기·대·본

M: Welcome to Beauty Boutique. How can I assist you?
W: Hi, I'm in need of some moisturizer.
M: Certainly. We have two options, regular and premium. The premium products have more powerful ingredients, so they work better.
W: That sounds great. How much are they?
M: A bottle of regular moisturizer is $20, while the premium one is $35.
W: I'll go for the premium option.
M: Great choice. If you buy two premium products, you'll get one additional product for free.
W: Oh, that's fantastic! I'll take two bottles of the premium moisturizer then.
M: Excellent decision. Here you go.
W: Thanks. Let me pay with my card.

우·리·말·해·석

남: Beauty Boutique에 오신 것을 환영합니다. 어떻게 도와드릴까요?

여: 안녕하세요, 저는 수분 로션이 좀 필요합니다.
남: 알겠습니다. 저희에겐 일반 그리고 고급 두 가지 선택지가 있습니다. 고급 제품들은 더 강력한 성분들로 되어 있어서 그것들은 더 효과가 있습니다.
여: 좋은데요. 그것들은 얼마인가요?
남: 일반 수분 로션 한 병은 20달러인 반면, 고급은 35달러입니다.
여: 저는 고급을 선택할게요.
남: 좋은 선택입니다. 만약 고급 제품을 2개 구매하시면, 한 개의 추가 제품을 무료로 받으실 수 있습니다.
여: 아, 멋지네요! 그러면 저는 고급 수분 로션을 두 병 살게요.
남: 훌륭하신 결정입니다. 여기 있습니다.
여: 감사해요. 제 카드로 결제할게요.

단·어·및·표·현

moisturizer[mɔ́istʃəràizər] ⑨ 수분 로션
premium[príːmiəm] ⑧ 고급의
ingredient[ingríːdiənt] ⑨ 성분, 재료
work[wəːrk] ⑧ 효과가 있다[나다]

17 알맞은응답찾기　　　　　　▶ 정답 ③

듣·기·대·본

W: I loved spending time with those children. How about you?
M: Me, too. I thought an orphanage would be a lot more of a depressing place, but the children were so nice and cute.
W: I'm a little tired, but I think it was nice to visit and do volunteer work there.
M: I agree. I want to go there next weekend, too. What do you think?
W: I don't think I can. But I can go there the week after that.
M: OK. Let's visit them in two weeks.

우·리·말·해·석

① 넌 그럴 필요가 없어.
② 난 너무 피곤해서 다시 거기에 갈 수 없어.
③ 알았어. 2주 후에 그들을 방문하자.
④ 난 네가 아이들을 좋아하지 않는지 몰랐어.
⑤ 아니. 난 네가 위험에 빠지는 걸 원하지 않아.

여: 나는 그 아이들과 함께 시간을 보내는 것이 아주 좋았어. 넌 어때?
남: 나도. 나는 고아원은 훨씬 더 우울한 곳일 거라고 생각했는데, 아이들이 아주 착하고 귀엽더라.
여: 나는 조금 피곤하지만, 거기에 방문해서 봉사 활동을 하는 것은 좋았다고 생각해.
남: 동의해. 나는 다음 주말에도 거기에 가고 싶어. 넌 어떻게 생각해?
여: 난 그럴 수 있을 것 같지 않아. 하지만 그 다음 주에는 거기에 갈 수 있어.
남: 알았어. 2주 후에 그들을 방문하자.

단·어·및·표·현

orphanage[ɔ́ːrfənidʒ] ⑨ 고아원
more of ~에 더 가까운

🎧 **LISTENING ADVICE**

'I don't think I can.'에서 'don't'는 [돈트]가 아닌 [도운]으로 발음됩니다. 이는 단어가 'nt'로 끝날 때 끝소리 [t]가 탈락되거나 약하게 발음되기 때문입니다.

듣·기·대·본

M: What's the matter, Kelly? You look upset.

W: Dad, I had a fight with Jessica today.

M: I thought you were best friends with her. What went wrong?

W: We were supposed to see a movie together, but she went to see it with other people.

M: That's not nice, but maybe she had a reason.

W: She said she went to a birthday party and everyone went to see the movie together.

M: Oh, I see. She couldn't help it, then.

W: I know, but I was so disappointed.

우·리·말·해·석

① 알아요, 하지만 저는 정말 실망했어요.
② 그럼요, 저는 파티에서 그녀를 도울 수 있어요.
③ 그래서 제가 그녀와 싸우지 않았던 거예요.
④ 맞아요, 그래서 그녀는 영화를 보지 않았어요.
⑤ 그건 사실이 아니에요. 그녀는 선택권이 없었어요.

남: 무슨 일 있니, Kelly? 기분이 안 좋아 보이는구나.
여: 아빠, 저 오늘 Jessica와 다퉜어요.
남: 내 생각엔 네가 그녀와 가장 친한 친구인 줄 알았는데. 뭐가 잘못된 거니?
여: 우리는 같이 영화를 보기로 했어요. 하지만 그녀가 다른 사람들과 그것을 보러 갔어요.
남: 그건 좋지 않구나, 하지만 아마도 그녀에게 이유가 있었을 거야.
여: 그녀가 생일 파티에 갔는데 모든 사람들이 같이 그 영화를 보러 갔대요.
남: 오, 그렇구나. 그러면, 그녀는 어쩔 수 없었겠네.
여: 알아요, 하지만 저는 정말 실망했어요.

단·어·및·표·현

wrong [rɔ(:)ŋ] ⑱ 잘못된

🗣 LISTENING ADVICE

'What went wrong?'에서 'wrong'은 'w'가 'r' 앞에서 묵음이 되어 [r] 발음만 소리가 나고 [롱]이라고 발음됩니다. 'w'가 묵음이 되는 다른 예로는 'wrap', 'wrist'가 있습니다.

● **wrong: How to pronounce [r]**

'r' 발음은 우리나라의 'ㄹ' 발음과 비슷하지만 발음하는 방법은 전혀 다릅니다. 혀끝을 잇몸의 바로 뒤 입천장의 앞쪽으로 말아 올리며 발음합니다.

듣·기·대·본

W: What are you doing, Sam?

M: I'm searching the web for a good-bye present for Muriel.

W: Right. I have to buy one, too.

M: Do you have anything in mind?

W: Not yet. What about you?

M: I want to get her a hat, but it's too expensive.

W: She's going to like it, hat or not.

M: Yeah, but this hat is something that she really wants.

W: Why don't we split the cost? I'll pay for half.

우·리·말·해·석

① 그녀가 떠난다니 정말 슬프다.
② 그러면, 작별 파티를 준비하자.
③ 나도 그 모자가 좋지만 그녀에게 먼저 물어봐야 해.
④ 걱정 마. 나는 비싼 선물들은 원하지 않아.
⑤ 비용을 나눠 내는 게 어때? 내가 반 낼게.

여: 뭐하고 있니, Sam?
남: Muriel을 위한 작별 선물을 인터넷에서 검색하고 있어.
여: 맞다. 나도 하나 사야 해.
남: 생각해 둔 것이 있니?
여: 아직 없어. 너는?
남: 나는 그녀에게 모자를 사주고 싶지만 그게 너무 비싸.
여: 모자든 아니든 그녀가 좋아할 거야.
남: 그래, 하지만 이 모자는 그녀가 정말로 원하는 거야.
여: 비용을 나눠 내는 게 어때? 내가 반 낼게.

단·어·및·표·현

search the web 인터넷 검색을 하다

듣·기·대·본

W: Julian has a close friend, Leah. They often hang out and take a lot of pictures together. One day, Julian notices that Leah's photos are looking much better than before. Leah explains that it's because of the new picture app on her phone. Julian thinks it's brilliant. So, he would like to ask her to tell him more about the app. In this situation, what would Julian most likely say to Leah?

Julian: Leah, could you let me know which photo app it is?

우·리·말·해·석

① 너의 새 핸드폰 정말 멋진 것 같아.
② 너의 친구에게 나를 소개해 줄 수 있어?
③ 난 너랑 방과 후에 노는 게 즐거워.
④ 그게 어떤 사진 앱인지 알려줄 수 있어?
⑤ 사진 포즈 더 잘 잡는 법 좀 가르쳐줄 수 있어?

여: Julian에게는 Leah라는 친한 친구가 있다. 그들은 자주 함께 어울려 놀고 많은 사진도 찍는다. 어느 날, Julian은 Leah의 사진이 예전보다 훨씬 나아 보인다는 걸 알아차린다. Leah는 그녀의 휴대폰에 있는 새로운 사진 앱 때문이라고 설명한다. Julian은 그것(앱)이 정말 멋지다고 생각한다. 그래서 그는 그녀에게 그 앱에 대해 더 알려달라고 부탁하고 싶어 한다. 이 상황에서, Julian은 Leah에게 뭐라고 말하겠는가?

Julian: Leah, 그게 어떤 사진 앱인지 알려줄 수 있어?

단·어·및·표·현

hang out 놀다, 시간을 보내다
brilliant [bríljənt] ⑱ 훌륭한, 멋진

Words & Expressions Review

1. 추가적인, 추가의	2. 훌륭한, 멋진	3. 효과가 있다[나다]
4. 고급의	5. 전화로 아파서 못 간다고 하다	6. ~을 찾다
7. 처방전	8. (진행 과정상의) 상황	9. 수분 로션
10. 아이를 봐주다	11. ~을 갖고 다니다	12. ~에서 주연을 맡다

13. 잘못된	14. (~한 상태로) 변하다, 되다	15. (특정 목적을 위한) 모임
16. 수납, 보관, 저장	17. 나누다	18. ~을 뽑다
19. 받다	20. 경치, 풍경	21. 우울한
22. 시간이 있는	23. 평상시처럼	24. 적당한 가격의, 감당할 수 있는
25. (명단/프로그램 등에 들어가는) 자리	26. A를 대신하여 일하다	27. 주제, 테마
28. 고아원	29. 필요로 하다, 필요하다	30. 시간을 보내다
31. 실외의	32. 선택(지)	33. 출판사
34. 자세한, 상세한	35. A를 도와주다	36. 안타깝게도, 불행하게도
37. 조직하다, 개최하다	38. 사랑니	39. 필요한
40. 봉사 활동	41. 영수증	42. 생활필수품
43. 통로	44. 선택하다	

Listening Test
영어듣기 모의고사 03회

|정|답|

01 ①	02 ④	03 ①	04 ④	05 ②
06 ④	07 ③	08 ④	09 ③	10 ④
11 ④	12 ③	13 ②	14 ④	15 ③
16 ③	17 ②	18 ②	19 ③	20 ⑤

01 그림정보파악(대화) ▶ 정답 ①

듣·기·대·본

M: Hello. May I help you?

W: Hi. I'd like a cotton candy, please. It's for my daughter.

M: Sure. We have bear-shaped ones and rabbit-shaped ones. You can take a look at the samples here.

W: I'll go for a rabbit-shaped cotton candy. I think she'd like a rabbit better than a bear.

M: Okay. And if you look carefully, you'll notice that some have small eyes, and some have big eyes. Which do you prefer?

W: Oh, the ones with big eyes look really pretty! Also, is it possible to put a ribbon on one ear?

M: Of course! I'll make one for you right away.

우·리·말·해·석

남: 안녕하세요. 도와드릴까요?

여: 안녕하세요. 저는 솜사탕을 원해요. 제 딸을 위한 거예요.

남: 그렇군요. 저희는 곰 모양인 것들과 토끼 모양인 것들이 있습니다. 여기서 샘플들을 보실 수 있습니다.

여: 저는 토끼 모양의 솜사탕으로 할게요. 제 생각에 그녀가 곰보다 토끼를 더 좋아할 것 같아요.

남: 알겠습니다. 그리고 잘 보시면, 어떤 것은 작은 눈을 가지고 있고, 어떤 것은 큰 눈을 가지고 있는 것을 알아차릴 것입니다. 어느 것을 더 선호하세요?

여: 오, 큰 눈을 가진 것들은 정말 예뻐 보이네요! 또한, 한쪽 귀에 리본을 다는 게 가능한가요?

남: 당연하죠! 지금 당장 하나 만들어 드릴게요.

단·어·및·표·현

cotton candy 솜사탕

sample [sǽmpl] 몡 샘플, 보기, 견본

go for ~으로 하다, ~을 고르다

notice [nóutis] 통 알아차리다, 인지하다

02 대화미언급 ▶ 정답 ④

듣·기·대·본

M: Charlotte, are you entering the Annual Jump Rope Contest?

W: I'm not sure yet. The contest is next Saturday, right?

M: Yes. It'll be held at Star Stadium. I'm entering the contest.

W: Oh, really? What kind of jumps will you do?

M: The alternate foot jump and the double unders jump.

W: Right. Are there any other categories?

M: Sure. There are many other categories you can compete in. You should try it.

W: Okay. Maybe I'll have a go.

M: Great. It'll be fun. Everyone will get a reusable bag as a participation prize, too.

W: That's nice. Do you want to practice together?

M: Yeah. Let's do that.

우·리·말·해·석

남: Charlotte, 너 매년 열리는 줄넘기 대회에 참가할 거니?

여: 아직 모르겠어. 그 대회는 다음 주 토요일이지, 맞지?

남: 응. 그것은 스타 경기장에서 개최될 거야. 나는 그 대회에 참가할 거야.

여: 오, 정말? 너는 어떤 종류의 줄넘기를 할 거니?

남: 번갈아 뛰기랑 2단 뛰기.

여: 그렇구나. 거기 다른 부문도 있니?

남: 그럼. 네가 참가할 수 있는 다른 많은 부문들이 있어. 너도 한번 시도해봐.

여: 그래. 나도 한번 해볼래.

남: 좋아. 재미있을 거야. 모두가 참가상으로 재사용이 가능한 가방도 받을 거야.

여: 그거 좋다. 같이 연습할래?

남: 그래. 그렇게 하자.

단·어·및·표·현

alternate foot jump 번갈아 뛰기

double unders jump 2단 뛰기

category [kǽtəgòːri] 몡 부문, 범주

compete in ~에 참가하다, 출전하다

have a go 한번 해보다, 시도하다

reusable [riúːzəbəl] 혱 재사용할 수 있는

03 전화목적파악 ▶ 정답 ①

듣·기·대·본

(Telephone rings.)

M: Hi, Annie. This is Tom.

W: Hi, Tom. What's up?

M: Annie, would you do me a favor?

W: Sure. What is it?

M: I need to print out my assignment for the English literature class. But I'm afraid my printer isn't working right now. Can I use your printer?

W: Sure. But I'm going to my friend's birthday party tonight, so come by here before seven, okay?

M: OK. Thank you very much.

우·리·말·해·석

(전화벨이 울린다.)

남: 안녕, Annie. 나 Tom이야.

여: 안녕, Tom. 무슨 일이니?

남: Annie, 내 부탁 좀 들어줄래?

여: 물론이지. 뭔데?

남: 나는 내 영문학 수업 숙제를 프린트해야 해. 그런데 내 프린터가 지금 작동하지 않는 것 같아. 네 프린터를 사용해도 돼?

여: 그럼. 하지만 나는 오늘 밤에는 친구의 생일 파티에 가니까 여기에 7시 전에는 와, 알았지?

남: 알았어. 정말 고마워.

단·어·및·표·현

literature [lítərətʃùər] 몡 문학

04 수치파악(시각) ▶ 정답 ④

듣·기·대·본

(Cellphone rings.)

M: Hello.

W: Cameron, it's me. Are you on the train now?

M: Yes, the train left on time, at 4 p.m.

W: That's nice. I'll be at the station at 6 p.m. to pick you up.

M: Come at 7. The train is delayed, and I need to take care of something at the station.

W: Oh, did the train stop in the middle of the route again?

M: Yes, there was a signal mix-up.

W: Okay. I'll be there at 7 then.

M: Thanks. See you soon.

우·리·말·해·석

(휴대폰이 울린다.)

남: 여보세요.

여: Cameron, 나야. 너 지금 기차에 타고 있니?

남: 응, 오후 4시, 제때에 기차가 떠났어.

여: 잘됐다. 나는 너를 데리러 오후 6시에 기차역에 있을게.

남: 7시에 와. 기차가 지연되었고 나는 역에서 뭔가를 처리해야 해.

여: 오, 기차가 또 중간에 멈췄어?

남: 응, 신호 혼동이 있었어.

여: 알았어. 그러면 7시에 갈게.

남: 고마워. 조금 이따 보자.

단·어·및·표·현

take care of ~ ~을 처리하다

mix-up 혼동

05 심정추론 ▶ 정답 ②

듣·기·대·본

M: Mom, I'm home.

W: Andy, how was your speech contest?

M: Good. I tried to do my best and I quite enjoyed the contest.

W: I'm glad to hear that.

M: And guess what? I won first prize!

W: Wow, good for you! I knew you could do it.

M: Thank you, Mom. I still can't believe that I won.

W: Oh, you deserve it. You practiced really hard. I'm so happy for you.

우·리·말·해·석

① 지루해하는　　　② 자랑스러운　　　③ 염려하는
④ 부러워하는　　　⑤ 실망스러운

남: 엄마, 다녀왔어요.

여: Andy, 말하기 대회는 어땠니?

남: 좋았어요. 저는 최선을 다하려 노력했고 대회를 꽤 즐겼어요.

여: 그걸 들으니 기쁘구나.

남: 그리고 무슨 일이 있었는지 맞춰보세요. 저 일등 했어요!

여: 와, 잘 됐구나! 나는 네가 할 수 있을 줄 알았어.

남: 감사해요. 엄마. 저는 아직도 제가 1등한 게 안 믿겨요.

여: 오, 너는 그것을 받을 자격이 있어. 너는 정말 열심히 연습했잖아. 정말 잘됐어.

단·어·및·표·현

try to + 동사원형 ~하려고 노력하다

do one's best 최선을 다하다

quite [kwait] 톤 꽤, 상당히

deserve [dizə́ːrv] 통 ~을 받을 자격이 있다, ~을 받을 만하다

06 그림상황에적절한대화찾기 ▶ 정답 ④

듣·기·대·본

① W: What time do you finish work here?
　M: I finish at 6 p.m.
② W: Can I have a cheese cake, please?
　M: Sorry. They are all sold out today.
③ W: Where is the elevator?
　M: It's down the hall.
④ W: Could you put my coffee in this tumbler, please?
　M: Sure, no problem.
⑤ W: I have a high fever and runny nose.
　M: You need to see a doctor.

우·리·말·해·석

① 여: 당신은 몇 시에 여기서 일이 끝나시나요?
　남: 저는 오후 6시에 끝나요.
② 여: 치즈 케이크 하나 주시겠어요?
　남: 죄송합니다. 그것들은 오늘 다 팔렸어요.
③ 여: 엘리베이터는 어디에 있나요?
　남: 그것은 복도 끝에 있어요.
④ 여: 제 커피를 이 텀블러에 넣어주시겠어요?
　남: 물론이죠. 문제없습니다.
⑤ 여: 저는 열이 높고 콧물이 나요.
　남: 당신은 병원에 가야 해요.

단·어·및·표·현

sold out 다 팔린, 매진된

put [put] 통 넣다, 놓다, 두다

tumbler [tʌ́mblər] 몡 텀블러

07 부탁(요청)한일파악 ▶ 정답 ③

듣·기·대·본

W: Dad, the washing machine isn't working properly.

M: What's wrong with it?

W: It's making a strange noise.

M: Have you tried turning it off and on again?

W: Yes, I have, but it didn't help. I think there might be a problem with the motor.

M: Have you checked out the customer service center's website? They provide specific instructions in case we have a problem.

W: No, I haven't. I have to go now because I have a violin lesson. Could you check it out for me?

M: Sure. No problem.

우·리·말·해·석

여: 아빠, 세탁기가 제대로 작동하지 않아요.

남: 무슨 문제라도 있니?

여: 이상한 소리가 나요.

남: 껐다가 다시 켜 봤니?

여: 네, 해 봤는데 도움이 안 됐어요. 모터에 문제가 있는 것 같아요.

남: 고객 서비스 센터의 웹사이트 확인해 봤니? 그들은 우리가 문제 있을 때를 대비해 구체적인 지침을 제공해.

여: 아니요, 안 해 봤어요. 바이올린 수업이 있어서 전 지금 가야 해요. 대신 확인해 주실 수 있어요?

남: 물론이지. 문제없어.

단·어·및·표·현

properly [prɑ́pərli] ㊊ 제대로, 적절히

check out 확인하다

specific [spisífik] ㊒ 구체적인

instruction [instrʌ́kʃən] ㊔ 지침, 설명

in case ~할 경우를 대비해서

08 담화미언급 ▶ 정답 ④

듣·기·대·본

W: Hello, everyone. Welcome to the International Woodcraft Fair at Riverside Complex. This event will run for two weeks until next Sunday. This year, over 200 woodcraft artists from 30 different countries are participating. It's a great chance to see world-class art. You can also buy beautiful wooden works at this fair. We give our thanks to our sponsor, Bailey Company. Enjoy!

우·리·말·해·석

여: 안녕하세요, 여러분. Riverside Complex에서 열리는 International Woodcraft Fair에 오신 것을 환영합니다. 이 행사는 다음 주 일요일까지 2주 동안 진행될 예정입니다. 올해는 30개국에서 온 200명 이상의 목각 예술가들이 참여합니다. 이것은 세계 수준의 예술을 볼 수 있는 아주 좋은 기회입니다. 여러분은 또한 이 박람회에서 아름다운 목재 작품들을 구입할 수도 있습니다. 우리는 우리의 후원 업체 Bailey Company에 감사를 전합니다. 즐기세요!

단·어·및·표·현

run [rʌn] ㊄ (공연, 전시, 박람회 등이) 진행되다, 계속되다

09 담화화제추론 ▶ 정답 ③

듣·기·대·본

M: This is a delicious Korean street food that many people enjoy worldwide. It's known for its spicy and flavorful taste, and you can have it as a snack or a meal. In Korea, it's a favorite for street food lovers. The great thing is, it's very easy to make. Just put some chewy rice cakes, fish cakes, and spicy sauce in a pan. Cook it until everything is soft and covered in sauce, and you're done.

우·리·말·해·석

남: 이것은 전세계적으로 많은 사람들이 즐기는 맛있는 한국의 길거리 음식입니다. 그것은 그것의 맵고 풍미 있는 맛으로 알려져 있고, 여러분은 그것을 간식이나 식사로 먹을 수 있습니다. 한국에서 그것은 길거리 음식 애호가들이 가장 좋아하는 것입니다. 좋은 점은, 그것이 매우 만들기 쉽다는 것입니다. 그저 쫄깃한 떡들과 어묵들, 그리고 매운 소스를 팬에 넣으세요. 모든 것이 부드러워지고 소스에 버무려질 때까지 그것을 요리하세요, 그러면 당신은 (요리를) 끝냈습니다.

단·어·및·표·현

delicious [dilíʃəs] ㊒ 맛있는

be known for ~로 알려져 있다

flavorful [fléivərfəl] ㊒ 풍미 있는, 맛 좋은

chewy [tʃúːi] ㊒ 쫄깃한

covered [kʌ́vərd] ㊒ 버무려진, 뒤덮인

10 어색한대화찾기 ▶ 정답 ④

듣·기·대·본

① M: How have you been?
W: I've been pretty good.

② M: What is your favorite subject?
W: I like science the most.

③ M: You know what? Jacob failed the exam.
W: You are kidding! I can't believe it.

④ M: What do you think about your English teacher?
W: I think so, too.

⑤ M: How often do you go to the library?
W: I'd say about three times a month.

우·리·말·해·석

① 남: 어떻게 지냈어?
여: 잘 지냈어.

② 남: 네가 제일 좋아하는 과목은 뭐야?
여: 나는 과학이 제일 좋아.

③ 남: 너 그거 알아? Jacob이 시험에 낙제했대.
여: 농담이지! 난 믿을 수가 없다.

④ 남: 너희 영어 선생님에 대해 너는 어떻게 생각하니?
여: 나도 그렇게 생각해.

⑤ 남: 도서관에 얼마나 자주 가니?
여: 내 생각에 한 달에 세 번 정도.

단·어·및·표·현

subject [sʌ́bdʒekt] ㊔ 과목

11 할일파악(대화직후) ▶ 정답 ④

듣·기·대·본

W: Eric, are you still on the school soccer team this semester?

M: Yes, but we lost two members who graduated last year.

W: Oh, then you must need more players for the next

tournament.

M: Exactly. We need at least one more member to join the team soon.

W: How about asking Brian? I mean the new boy in our class. I heard that he used to be a player at his previous school.

M: Really? I had no idea!

W: I think he'd be interested. You should ask him.

M: That's a good suggestion, Trisha. I'll talk to him right now.

우·리·말·해·석

여: Eric, 넌 이번 학기에도 여전히 학교 축구팀에 있어?

남: 응, 그런데 작년에 졸업한 두 명의 팀원이 떠났어.

여: 아, 그럼 다음 대회를 위해 더 많은 선수들이 필요하겠네.

남: 맞아. 우리는 곧 팀에 합류할 최소한 한 명의 팀원이 더 필요해.

여: Brian에게 물어보는 건 어때? 우리 반에 새로 온 남자애 말이야. 나는 그가 전 학교에서 선수였다고 들었어.

남: 정말? 난 전혀 몰랐어!

여: 난 그가 관심있을 것 같아. 네가 그에게 물어봐.

남: 좋은 제안이야, Trisha. 내가 지금 바로 그와 얘기해볼게.

단·어·및·표·현

semester[siméstər] 명 학기
graduate[grǽdʒueit] 동 졸업하다
tournament[túərnəmənt] 명 대회, 경기
at least 최소한
used to ~였다
previous[príːviəs] 형 이전의, 전의

12 도표정보파악 ▶ 정답 ③

듣·기·대·본

M: Chloe, I know you're an expert camper. Can you help me buy a tent?

W: Sure, that sounds fun. How many people will be sleeping in the tent?

M: There will be three of us.

W: Then, you should choose a tent that fits four or more people.

M: Okay, how much should I spend?

W: I wouldn't recommend spending more than $300.

M: Understood. Do you have any other suggestions?

W: You should also buy a tent which has at least two doors.

M: Thanks for your help. I'll buy this one then.

우·리·말·해·석

	모델	수용 인원	가격	문의 개수
①	A	2인용	200달러	1
②	B	4인용	250달러	1
③	C	4인용	280달러	2
④	D	6인용	330달러	3
⑤	E	6인용	360달러	4

남: Chloe, 나는 네가 캠핑 전문가라는 것을 알아. 내가 텐트를 사는 걸 도와줄 수 있니?

여: 그래, 재미있을 것 같네. 텐트에서 몇 명이나 잘 거니?

남: 세 명이 있을 거야.

여: 그럼, 너는 네 명 혹은 그 이상의 사람들이 들어갈 수 있는 텐트를 골

라야 해.

남: 알겠어, 내가 얼마나 써야 할까?

여: 나는 300달러보다 많이 쓰는 건 추천하지 않아.

남: 이해했어. 또 다른 제안이 있니?

여: 또한 너는 최소한 두 개의 문을 가진 텐트를 사야 해.

남: 도와줘서 고마워. 그럼 나는 이걸 살 거야.

단·어·및·표·현

expert[ékspəːrt] 명 전문가
fit[fit] 동 (공간적으로) 들어가다, 크기가 맞다
suggestion[sədʒéstʃən] 명 제안, 의견
at least 최소한, 적어도

13 수치파악(날짜) ▶ 정답 ②

듣·기·대·본

W: You look great in that coat.

M: I like it, too. I'll take it. However, the sleeves are a bit long.

W: We can shorten them for ten dollars.

M: That sounds good. How long will it take?

W: Today is February 2, so you can pick the coat up next Monday, February 6.

M: Hmm… I have an event on Sunday. Can I get it earlier?

W: Let's see. (pause) Okay. We can have it ready by Saturday, February 4 after 5 p.m.

M: That sounds OK. What about tomorrow, February 3?

W: Sorry, that's too soon. Saturday is the earliest possible date.

M: Okay, Saturday it is. Thank you.

우·리·말·해·석

여: 그 코트 당신에게 잘 어울리네요.

남: 저도 이것이 마음에 들어요. 이걸로 할게요. 그런데 소매들이 좀 길어요.

여: 저희는 10달러에 그것들을 줄여드릴 수 있어요.

남: 그거 좋네요. 얼마나 걸릴까요?

여: 오늘은 2월 2일이니까, 다음 주 월요일인 2월 6일에 코트를 찾아가실 수 있어요.

남: 음… 저는 일요일에 행사가 있어서요. 더 일찍 받을 수 있을까요?

여: 어디 봅시다. [잠시 후] 좋아요. 2월 4일 토요일 오후 5시 이후에 준비해드릴 수 있어요.

남: 괜찮네요. 내일, 2월 3일은 어떤가요?

여: 죄송하지만, 그건 너무 이릅니다. 토요일이 가장 빠른 가능한 날짜예요.

남: 알겠어요, 토요일로 할게요. 감사합니다.

단·어·및·표·현

sleeve[sliːv] 명 소매
shorten[ʃɔ́ːrtən] 동 줄이다
pick up 되찾다
possible[pásəbl] 형 가능한

14 한일파악 ▶ 정답 ④

듣·기·대·본

M: Alicia, are you all right?

W: What do you mean?

M: Ron told me he saw you at the hospital yesterday. Were you sick?

W: No, I'm perfectly fine. I was visiting my grandfather in

the hospital yesterday. He had surgery two days ago.
M: Oh, is he okay? Why did he need surgery?
W: He fell down and broke his arm. He's in recovery now.
M: That's a relief. When will he get out of the hospital?
W: Tomorrow. My sister and I are going to throw him a welcome home party.
M: Great!

우·리·말·해·석

남: Alicia, 너 괜찮니?

여: 무슨 말이야?

남: Ron이 어제 너를 병원에서 봤다고 내게 말했어. 너 아팠니?

여: 아니, 나는 완벽하게 괜찮아. 나는 어제 병원에서 내 할아버지께 병문안을 드리고 있는 중이었어. 그는 이틀 전에 수술을 받으셨어.

남: 오, 그분은 괜찮으셔? 그분이 왜 수술이 필요하셨어?

여: 그는 넘어져서 팔이 부러지셨어. 그는 지금 회복 중이셔.

남: 그렇다니 안심이네. 그분이 언제 병원에서 퇴원하셔?

여: 내일. 내 언니랑 내가 그에게 집으로 돌아오시는 것을 환영하는 파티를 열어드릴 거야.

남: 훌륭해!

단·어·및·표·현

have surgery 수술받다
in recovery 회복 중인
relief[rilíːf] 몡 안심
throw a party 파티를 열다

15 담화목적파악 ▶ 정답 ③

듣·기·대·본

M: Hello, students. I'm the school football coach. If you've always wanted to join the football team, now is your chance. We're holding tryouts this Saturday. In order to participate in the tryouts, you must register first. You can find the registration forms outside my office. After filling in the form, please hand it in to me by this Thursday. When your registration is complete, I'll inform you about the time and place for the tryouts.

우·리·말·해·석

남: 안녕하세요, 학생 여러분. 저는 학교 축구 코치입니다. 여러분이 축구 팀에 항상 가입하고 싶어했다면, 지금이 기회입니다. 우리는 이번 토요일에 테스트를 엽니다. 테스트에 참가하기 위해서는 여러분은 먼저 등록해야 합니다. 제 사무실 밖에서 등록 양식을 찾을 수 있습니다. 양식을 작성한 후, 이번 목요일까지 저에게 제출해주세요. 여러분의 등록이 완료되었을 때, 저는 테스트를 위한 시간과 장소를 여러분에게 알려 드리겠습니다.

단·어·및·표·현

tryout[tráiàut] 몡 테스트, 적성 시험
fill in (서식을) 작성하다

16 수치계산(금액) ▶ 정답 ③

듣·기·대·본

M: Welcome to Super Smoothies.
W: Hi! I'd like a green smoothie and a protein shake, please.
M: Of course! The green smoothie is 5 dollars, and the protein shake is 7 dollars.

W: Great! I'll take one of each. Oh, and do you have any energy bars?
M: Yes, they are 4 dollars each. But when you add one to a protein shake order, you can get it for 2 dollars.
W: That's a good deal! I'll take one energy bar as well.
M: Excellent! How would you like to pay?
W: Here's my credit card.

우·리·말·해·석

남: Super Smoothies에 오신 것을 환영합니다.

여: 안녕하세요! 그린 스무디 한 잔과 단백질 쉐이크 한 잔을 주문하고 싶어요.

남: 알겠습니다! 그린 스무디는 5달러이고 단백질 쉐이크는 7달러입니다.

여: 좋아요! 저는 한 잔씩 주문할게요. 아, 에너지 바도 있나요?

남: 네, 그것들은 개당 4달러입니다. 하지만 단백질 쉐이크 주문에 하나를 추가하시면 2달러에 구매하실 수 있습니다.

여: 괜찮은 가격이네요! 저는 에너지바도 한 개 구매할게요.

남: 좋습니다! 결제는 어떻게 하시겠어요?

여: 여기 제 신용카드입니다.

단·어·및·표·현

protein[próutiːn] 몡 단백질
add A to B A를 B에 더하다
a good deal 가성비가 좋은 거래

17 알맞은응답찾기 ▶ 정답 ②

듣·기·대·본

W: Thomas, I need help with my history presentation.
M: How can I help you?
W: I'm almost finished, but I need something in the introduction that will grab my audience's attention.
M: Okay. Can you include videos in your presentation?
W: Yeah, I think so. Do you think that would be helpful?
M: Yes. It's good to start with a short video to catch the interest of the audience.
W: That's a good idea. Can you help me find one?
M: Sure, let's look on the Internet.

우·리·말·해·석

① 오늘은 국경일이야.　　　　② 그럼, 인터넷에서 찾아보자.
③ 그의 발표는 무척 지루했어.　④ 우리의 역사를 아는 것은 중요해.
⑤ 우리는 우리 프로젝트를 거의 끝냈어.

여: Thomas, 나는 내 역사 발표에 대해 도움이 필요해.

남: 내가 어떻게 도와줄 수 있니?

여: 나는 거의 끝냈지만, 도입부에 내 청중들의 주의를 끌 수 있는 무언가가 필요해.

남: 좋아. 너는 네 발표에 비디오를 포함시킬 수 있니?

여: 응, 나는 그렇다고 생각해. 너는 그것이 도움이 된다고 생각해?

남: 응. 청중들의 관심을 끌기 위해 짧은 비디오로 시작하는 것이 좋아.

여: 그것은 좋은 생각이야. 내가 하나 찾는 것을 도와줄 수 있어?

남: 그럼, 인터넷에서 찾아보자.

단·어·및·표·현

grab attention 관심을 끌다
include[inklúːd] 통 포함시키다

18 알맞은응답찾기 ▶ 정답 ②

듣·기·대·본

(*Cellphone rings.*)

M: Hello?

W: Hi, this is Nadine's Flower Shop. Did you place an order for a dozen red roses?

M: Yes, that's correct. Is there an issue?

W: I'm afraid so. We've unexpectedly run out of red roses.

M: Oh, that's disappointing. My wife was really looking forward to them.

W: We sincerely apologize. You have the option to choose another flower arrangement or cancel your order.

M: Hmm... What other flower options do you have available?

W: We have lilies, daisies, and tulips. Would any of those interest you?

M: My wife loves tulips. I'll get them instead.

우·리·말·해·석

① 아니요, 저는 오늘 꽃을 가져갈 수 없어요.
② 제 아내는 튤립을 아주 좋아해요. 그것들로 대신 할게요.
③ 네. 메시지가 담긴 카드를 추가하고 싶습니다.
④ 꼭 시간 맞춰 배달해 주세요.
⑤ 화분에 꽃꽂이를 준비해 주시겠어요?

(휴대폰이 울린다.)

남: 여보세요?

여: 안녕하세요, Nadine's Flower Shop입니다. 빨간 장미 12송이를 주문하셨나요?

남: 네, 맞아요. 문제가 있나요?

여: 유감스럽게도 그렇습니다. 저희는 예상치 못하게 빨간 장미가 다 떨어졌어요.

남: 오, 실망스럽군요. 제 아내는 그것을 정말 기대하고 있었어요.

여: 진심으로 사과드립니다. 다른 꽃꽂이를 선택하시거나 주문을 취소한다는 선택지가 있습니다.

남: 흠... 구할 수 있는 다른 꽃에는 무엇이 있나요?

여: 백합, 데이지, 튤립이 있습니다. 그것들 중 어느 것이든 관심을 끄는 게 있을까요?

남: 제 아내는 튤립을 아주 좋아해요. 그것들로 대신 할게요.

단·어·및·표·현

issue [íʃuː] 몡 (걱정거리가 되는) 문제
look forward to ~을 기대하다
flower arrangement 꽃꽂이
available [əvéiləbl] 혱 구할 수 있는, 이용할 수 있는
make sure to + 동사원형 반드시 ~하도록 하다

19 알맞은응답찾기 ▶ 정답 ③

듣·기·대·본

W: Hi, Jack!

M: Hey, Emily! I saw you at the coffee shop yesterday.

W: Really? Why didn't you come over and say hi?

M: I wanted to, but you were with Sarah, so I changed my mind.

W: Why? What's wrong?

M: She found out that I like her and now I don't know how to act around her.

W: If you really like her, why don't you ask her out on a date?

M: I'm afraid she might say no.

우·리·말·해·석

① 나는 연기 수업을 받을 필요가 없어.
② 그냥 안심하고 너답게 행동해.
③ 나는 그녀가 싫다고 말할까 봐 두려워.
④ 네가 해보지 않는 이상 너는 절대 모를 거야.
⑤ 나는 어떤 질문도 없어.

여: 안녕, Jack!

남: 안녕, Emily! 나 어제 커피숍에서 너를 봤어.

여: 정말? 왜 와서 인사하지 않았니?

남: 그러고 싶었지만 네가 Sarah와 함께 있길래 마음을 바꿨어.

여: 왜? 뭐 잘못된 일이라도 있니?

남: 내가 그녀를 좋아한다는 것을 그녀가 알게 되어서 지금 나는 그녀 주위에서 어떻게 행동해야 할지 모르겠어.

여: 네가 만약 그녀를 정말 좋아한다면, 그녀에게 데이트 신청하는 것이 어때?

남: 나는 그녀가 싫다고 말할까 봐 두려워.

단·어·및·표·현

find out 알게 되다, 알아내다

20 상황에적절한말찾기 ▶ 정답 ⑤

듣·기·대·본

W: Chad is reading an article about eye health. It says staring at a digital screen for too long isn't good for your eyes. It also mentions that when your eyes feel dry, applying warm water to them can help. While reading the article, he remembers that his friend Bonnie uses her cellphone a lot and often complains about dry eyes. Chad would like to tell Bonnie to bathe her eyes with warm water whenever she has symptoms. In this situation, what would Chad most likely say to Bonnie?

Chad: Bonnie, washing your eyes with warm water may help you.

우·리·말·해·석

① 너는 네 눈을 검진 받아보는 게 좋을 거야.
② 너는 네 스마트폰을 너무 많이 사용하고 있어.
③ 찬물로 샤워를 하는 게 어때?
④ 너는 네 핸드폰으로 기사들을 쉽게 읽을 수 있어.
⑤ 따뜻한 물로 네 눈을 씻는 것이 너에게 도움이 될 거야.

여: Chad는 눈 건강에 관한 기사를 읽고 있다. 그것은 디지털 화면을 너무 오래 응시하는 것은 눈에 좋지 않다고 말한다. 그것은 또한 눈이 건조하다고 느낄 때, 그것들에 따뜻한 물을 대는 것이 도움이 될 수 있다고 언급한다. 기사를 읽으면서, 그는 그의 친구 Bonnie가 그녀의 핸드폰을 많이 사용하고 자주 건조한 눈에 대해 불평한 것을 떠올린다. Chad는 Bonnie에게 그녀에게 증상이 있을 때마다 그녀의 눈을 따뜻한 물로 씻으라고 말하고 싶다. 이 상황에서, Chad는 Bonnie에게 뭐라고 말할 것 같은가?

Chad: Bonnie, 따뜻한 물로 네 눈을 씻는 것이 너에게 도움이 될 거야.

단·어·및·표·현

stare [stɛər] 통 응시하다
apply [əplái] 통 (물건을) 대다, (약 등을) 바르다
complain [kəmpléin] 통 불평하다, 항의하다
bathe [beið] 통 씻다, 세척하다
whenever [hwenévər] 접 ~할 때마다
symptom [símptəm] 몡 증상

Words & Expressions Review

1. 재사용할 수 있는	2. 줄이다	3. 넣다, 놓다, 두다
4. 박람회	5. 졸업하다	6. 구체적인
7. 테스트, 적성 시험	8. 버무려진, 뒤덮인	9. 증상
10. 제대로, 적절히	11. 후원 업체, 후원자	12. 안심
13. 포함시키다	14. 다 팔린, 매진된	15. 세계 수준의
16. 최선을 다하다	17. 혼동, 혼란	18. 참여하다
19. 제안, 의견	20. 수술받다	21. A를 B에 더하다
22. 관심을 끌다	23. A를 (차에) 태우러 가다	24. 완료된, 완성된
25. ~하려고 노력하다	26. 이전의, 전의	27. (물건을) 대다, (약 등을) 바르다
28. 문학	29. 목각	30. 부문, 범주
31. ~을 받을 자격이 있다, ~을 받을 만하다	32. A에게 데이트를 신청하다	33. 숙제
34. (걱정거리가 되는) 문제	35. 알리다, 통지하다	36. (공연 등이) 진행되다
37. 맛있는	38. 풍미 있는, 맛 좋은	39. 쫄깃한
40. 꽤, 상당히	41. 최소한, 적어도	42. 전문가
43. 단백질	44. (공간적으로) 들어가다, 크기가 맞다	

Listening Test
영어듣기 모의고사 04회

|정|답|

01 ①	02 ④	03 ③	04 ④	05 ⑤
06 ④	07 ③	08 ⑤	09 ③	10 ③
11 ①	12 ②	13 ④	14 ④	15 ④
16 ④	17 ②	18 ④	19 ④	20 ④

01 그림정보파악(대화) ▶ 정답 ①

듣·기·대·본

M: Welcome to Happy Kids. How can I help you?

W: I'm looking for a T-shirt for my nephew. He's 4 years old.

M: Okay. Would you like a long-sleeved one or a short-sleeved one?

W: I think a short-sleeved one would be better because the weather is getting warmer.

M: True. How about this one with a dinosaur? It's very popular.

W: Um… No, I'm sure he would prefer a car.

M: Okay. You can choose between two types. One has a round neck and the other has a V-neck.

W: I'll take the one with the round neck. It looks nicer.

M: Sure. That's a good choice.

우·리·말·해·석

남: Happy Kids에 오신 것을 환영합니다. 어떻게 도와드릴까요?

여: 저는 제 조카를 위한 티셔츠를 찾고 있어요. 그는 4살이에요.

남: 그렇군요. 긴팔을 원하시나요 아니면 반팔을 원하시나요?

여: 제 생각엔 날씨가 더 따뜻해지고 있으니 반팔이 더 나을 것 같아요.

남: 맞습니다. 공룡이 있는 이 제품은 어떠세요? 그건 아주 인기가 많아요.

여: 음… 아뇨. 저는 그가 자동차를 더 좋아할 거라고 확신해요.

남: 알겠습니다. 당신은 두 가지 종류 중에 선택하실 수 있어요. 하나는 라운드넥이고 다른 건 브이넥이에요.

여: 저는 라운드넥인 것으로 할게요. 그게 더 좋아 보이네요.

남: 물론이죠. 아주 좋은 선택입니다.

단·어·및·표·현

long-sleeved 긴팔의, 긴 소매의
short-sleeved 반팔의, 짧은 소매의

02 대화미언급 ▶ 정답 ④

듣·기·대·본

W: Ryan, I saw an online advertisement about the Korea Apple Festival.

M: I saw that, too. It's an annual festival held in late September, right?

W: You're right. It's going to be held at Central Park this year.

M: Good. Will there be any interesting festival programs?

W: Yes, I'm hoping to participate in their apple pie baking program.

M: Great. I also heard that there will be free souvenirs.

W: Yes, they will be giving out free tumblers, but only for the first 100 visitors.

M: Okay. Let's go early on the first day then.

우·리·말·해·석

여: Ryan, 나는 한국 사과 축제에 대한 온라인 광고를 봤어.

남: 나도 그걸 봤어. 그건 9월 말에 열리는 연례 행사야, 맞지?

여: 맞아. 올해는 센트럴 파크에서 열릴 예정이야.

남: 좋네. 재미있는 축제 프로그램이 있을까?

여: 응, 나는 애플 파이 제빵 프로그램에 참여하고 싶어.

남: 좋다. 나는 또한 무료 기념품이 있을 거라고 들었어.

여: 응, 그들은 무료 텀블러를 나눠줄 예정이지만, 선착순 100명의 방문객들에게만 나눠줄 거야.

남: 그래. 그럼 첫째 날에 일찍 가자.

단·어·및·표·현

annual [ǽnjuəl] 휑 연례의
participate in ~ ~에 참여하다
souvenir [sùːvəníər] 뗑 기념품
give out (많은 사람들에게) ~을 나눠주다

03 전화목적파악 ▶ 정답 ③

듣·기·대·본

(*Telephone rings.*)

M: Hello? Is this "Fast Connect?"

W: Yes, how may I help you?

M: I would like to discontinue my Internet service.

W: OK. Is there a problem with your service?

M: No, not at all. I'm moving to another city.

W: I understand. Is there anything else I can help you with?

M: Oh, is there a penalty for terminating the contract?

W: No, you've used the service for more than 3 years. So, there won't be any penalties.

우·리·말·해·석

(전화벨이 울린다.)

남: 여보세요? 'Fast Connect'인가요?

여: 네, 어떻게 도와드릴까요?

남: 저는 제 인터넷 서비스를 중단하고 싶습니다.

여: 알겠습니다. 서비스에 문제가 있나요?

남: 아니요, 전혀 없습니다. 제가 다른 도시로 이사를 갈 거거든요.

여: 알겠습니다. 그 밖에 제가 도와드릴 수 있는 다른 것이 있나요?

남: 아, 계약을 해지하는 데에 대한 위약금이 있나요?

여: 아니요, 당신은 3년 이상 동안 서비스를 이용하셨어요. 그래서 위약금은 전혀 없을 것입니다.

단·어·및·표·현

discontinue [dìskəntínjuː] [동] (정기적으로 계속 하던 것을) 중단하다

penalty [pénəlti] [명] 위약금, 벌금

terminate [tə́ːrmənèit] [동] 해지하다, 끝내다

04 수치파악(시각) ▶ 정답 ④

듣·기·대·본

M: Mom, you're late for the dinner with your friends.

W: The dinner is at 7 p.m., honey. It's only 6. Aren't you going out, too?

M: Yes. I'm going to play basketball with Karl. I'm leaving now.

W: Okay. Oh, can you give the dog a bath when you get back?

M: Sure. But, she's going to have to wait. I won't be back until 8 p.m.

W: That's all right. Just don't forget to bathe her.

M: I'll bathe her at 9 p.m. after I take a shower.

W: All right. Have a good evening.

우·리·말·해·석

남: 엄마, 엄마는 친구분들과의 저녁 식사에 늦었어요.

여: 저녁은 오후 7시란다, 얘야. 겨우 6시야. 너도 외출하지 않니?

남: 네. 저는 Karl과 농구를 할 거예요. 저는 지금 나가요.

여: 알았다. 오, 돌아왔을 때 개를 목욕시킬 수 있니?

남: 그럼요. 하지만 개는 기다려야 할 거예요. 저는 오후 8시까지는 돌아오지 않을 거예요.

여: 그건 괜찮다. 개를 목욕시키는 것을 잊지만 마라.

남: 제가 샤워를 한 후 개를 오후 9시에 목욕시킬게요.

여: 좋아. 재미있는 저녁 시간 보내거라.

단·어·및·표·현

give a bath 목욕시키다

bathe [beið] [동] 목욕시키다, 씻기다

05 심정추론 ▶ 정답 ⑤

듣·기·대·본

W: Hey, Adam. Why the long face?

M: Candice, listen. You know I have a crush on this girl.

W: The new girl in our school? Sure.

M: I kind of asked her out the other day, and she said no.

W: I remember. Something happened?

M: Yeah, she is going out with Brian now!

W: Oh, dear. Brian from our class?

M: Yes! She said yes to him. I can't believe this. Don't I look better than Brian?

W: Um, I'm not going to answer that question.

M: I hate him. I envy him, and I hate him.

우·리·말·해·석

① 겁먹은 ② 편안한 ③ 신이 난
④ 자랑스러운 ⑤ 질투하는

여: 이봐, Adam, 왜 우울한 얼굴이니?

남: Candice, 들어봐. 너는 내가 이 소녀에게 반한 거 알잖아.

여: 우리 학교에 새로 온 여자애? 알지.

남: 내가 며칠 전에 그녀에게 일종의 데이트를 신청했는데, 그녀가 거절했잖아.

여: 기억 나. 무슨 일 있었어?

남: 응, 그녀가 지금 Brian이랑 사귀고 있어!

여: 오, 이런. 우리 반의 Brain?

남: 응! 그녀가 그의 고백을 받아줬대. 난 이걸 믿을 수가 없어. 내가 Brain보다 더 잘 생기지 않았어?

여: 음, 나는 그 질문에 대답하지 않을 거야.

남: 나는 그가 싫어. 나는 그가 부럽고, 나는 그가 싫어.

단·어·및·표·현

Why the long face? 왜 우울한 얼굴이니?

have a crush on A A에게 반하다

ask ~ out ~에게 데이트를 신청하다

go out with ~ ~와 사귀다, 교제하다

06 그림상황에적절한대화찾기 ▶ 정답 ④

듣·기·대·본

① M: You should be quiet when you're on public transportation.
W: Okay. I'll keep that in mind.

② M: Would you close your legs a little bit?
W: Oh, sorry. I was careless.

③ M: How many stops are left until Daehan Hospital?
W: There's only one more stop to go.

④ M: You can sit here, ma'am. I'm getting off at the next stop.
W: Thanks for giving me your seat.

⑤ M: Are you tired? You keep falling asleep.
W: Yes, I didn't sleep very well last night.

우·리·말·해·석

① 남: 넌 대중교통을 이용할 때 조용히 해야 해.
여: 알겠어요. 명심할게요.

② 남: 다리 좀 오므려 주실래요?
여: 오, 죄송합니다. 제가 부주의했네요.

③ 남: 대한병원까지 몇 정거장 남았나요?
여: 한 정거장만 더 가면 됩니다.

④ 남: 여기 앉으세요, 아주머니. 저는 다음 정거장에서 내려요.
여: 자리를 양보해 줘서 고맙구나.

⑤ 남: 너 피곤하니? 너는 계속 졸고 있어.
여: 응, 나는 어젯밤에 잠을 잘 못 잤어.

단·어·및·표·현

keep in mind 명심하다

careless[kέərlis] 혱 부주의한
give one's seat 자리를 양보하다

07 부탁(요청)한일파악 ▶ 정답 ③

듣·기·대·본

(Cellphone rings.)
W: Hello, Mark.
M: Hi, Karen. I'm afraid I have to <u>take the day off</u> today.
W: Is everything okay?
M: Well, I need to take my son to the hospital. He has a <u>high fever</u>.
W: I'm sorry to hear that. Then, I guess you won't be able to attend the meeting this afternoon.
M: No, so I <u>postponed</u> the meeting until tomorrow. I've just sent an e-mail to let people know.
W: I see. Is there anything else you need?
M: Yes. Could you <u>reserve</u> the meeting room for 2 p.m. tomorrow?
W: Sure, no problem.

우·리·말·해·석

(휴대폰이 울린다.)
여: 여보세요, Mark.
남: 안녕하세요, Karen. 미안하지만 제가 오늘 하루 휴가를 내야 할 것 같아요.
여: 다 괜찮은 거죠?
남: 음, 저는 아들을 병원에 데려가야 해요. 아들에게 고열이 있어요.
여: 그 말을 들으니 안타깝네요. 그럼 당신은 오늘 오후에 회의에 참석할 수 없겠군요.
남: 못 해요. 그래서 그 회의를 내일로 연기했어요. 사람들에게 알리기 위해서 방금 제가 이메일을 보냈어요.
여: 알겠어요. 다른 필요한 것이 있나요?
남: 네. 내일 2시로 회의실을 예약해 주시겠어요?
여: 물론이에요, 문제없어요.

단·어·및·표·현

take the day off 하루 휴가를 내다, 하루 쉬다
have a high fever 고열이 있다
postpone [poustpóun] 혱 연기하다, 미루다
reserve [rizə́:rv] 혱 예약하다

08 담화미언급 ▶ 정답 ⑤

듣·기·대·본

W: Hello, everyone. I'm proud to announce that the MT Short Film Competition is just <u>around the corner</u>. We accept short films no longer than 10 minutes of any genre. To enter the competition, you must <u>submit your film</u> as an MP4 file along with your application form. The submission period is from October 1st to November 30th. The winners will be announced on our website on December 15th. For more details, <u>feel free to</u> email us at shortfilm@mothertongue.com. Thanks!

우·리·말·해·석

여: 안녕하세요, 여러분. 저는 MT 단편영화 경연 대회가 코앞이라는 것을 자랑스럽게 알려드립니다. 우리는 10분을 넘지 않는 어떤 장르의 단편 영화라도 받습니다. 경연 대회에 참가하시려면, 지원서와 함께 여러분의 영화를 MP4 파일로 제출하셔야 합니다. 제출 기간은 10월 1일부터 11월 30일까지입니다. 우승작들은 12월 15일에 저희 웹사이트에 발표됩니다. 더 자세한 내용을 위해서는, shortfilm@mothertongue.com으로 마음 편히 이메일을 보내주세요. 감사합니다!

단·어·및·표·현

announce [ənáuns] 혱 알리다, 발표하다
submit [səbmít] 혱 제출하다

09 담화화제추론 ▶ 정답 ③

듣·기·대·본

W: People who have this job <u>lead a group of instrumentalists or singers to make music in a unified way</u>. They use their gestures to set the tempo, volume, rhythm and so on in a performance. They also <u>interpret the music and give directions</u> to the musicians. To have this job, you need to have broad knowledge about music and be skilled at many aspects of giving music performances.

우·리·말·해·석

여: 이 직업을 가진 사람들은 음악을 통합된 방식으로 만들기 위해 한 무리의 악기 연주자들이나 가수들을 이끕니다. 그들은 연주에서 박자, 음량, 리듬 등을 결정하기 위해 그들의 몸짓을 사용합니다. 그들은 또한 음악을 해석하고 음악가들에게 지시를 내립니다. 이 직업을 갖기 위해서는, 여러분은 음악에 대한 폭넓은 지식을 가지고 있어야 하고, 음악 연주의 많은 측면에 숙련돼야 합니다.

단·어·및·표·현

instrumentalist [ìnstrəméntəlist] 혱 악기 연주자
unified [júːnəfàid] 혱 통합된, 통일된
interpret [intə́ːrprit] 혱 해석하다, 설명하다
give directions to ~에게 지시를 내리다
be skilled at ~에 숙련되다, ~에 노련하다
aspect [ǽspekt] 혱 측면, 양상

10 어색한대화찾기 ▶ 정답 ③

듣·기·대·본

① M: I saw that movie last night with some friends.
　W: Do you <u>recommend</u> it?
② M: Do you think it will rain today?
　W: I honestly can't tell if it will.
③ M: Can you remember where you left your bag?
　W: My taste in bags and shoes is horrible.
④ M: I'm going to see Jeremy this afternoon.
　W: Really? Tell him I said "Hi."
⑤ M: When is Mr. Godfrey <u>coming back from</u> Bangkok?
　W: He said he won't return until Monday evening.

우·리·말·해·석

① 남: 나 저 영화를 어젯밤에 몇몇 친구들과 봤어.
　여: 너는 그것을 추천하니?
② 남: 오늘 비가 올 거라고 생각하니?
　여: 솔직히 나는 비가 올지 모르겠어.
③ 남: 너의 가방을 어디에 두었는지 기억하니?
　여: 가방과 신발에 관한 내 취향은 끔찍해.
④ 남: 나는 오늘 오후에 Jeremy를 만날 거야.
　여: 정말? 그에게 내 인사를 전해 줘.
⑤ 남: Godfrey 씨가 언제 방콕에서 돌아오니?
　여: 그는 다음 주 월요일 저녁까지는 돌아오지 않을 것이라고 말했어.

단·어·및·표·현

taste [teist] 몡 취향

11 할일파악 ▶ 정답 ①

듣·기·대·본

(Cellphone rings.)

M: Hello, Mom.

W: Hi, Nathan. Are you on your way?

M: Not yet. I'm still practicing for the dance contest.

W: I see. Can you buy some peaches on your way home?

M: Sure. Are you cooking dinner tonight?

W: No, your dad is cooking. It's going to be delicious!

M: Wow! I'm looking forward to it. By the way, is my favorite shirt washed? I want to wear it to tomorrow's practice.

W: It's not, but I'll wash it right away. It'll be dry by tomorrow.

M: Thanks, Mom. See you at home!

우·리·말·해·석

(휴대전화가 울린다.)

남: 여보세요, 엄마.

여: 여보세요, Nathan. 오는 중이니?

남: 아직이요. 춤 경연대회를 위해 아직 연습 중이에요.

여: 그렇구나. 집에 오는 길에 복숭아 몇 개 사다 줄 수 있겠니?

남: 물론이죠. 오늘 밤에 요리하실 거예요?

여: 아니, 아빠께서 하실 거야. 정말 맛있을 거야!

남: 우와! 기대돼요. 그런데, 제가 제일 좋아하는 셔츠 세탁하셨어요? 저 그거 내일 연습할 때 입고 싶어요.

여: 안 했는데, 바로 세탁해줄게. 내일이면 마를 거야.

남: 고맙습니다, 엄마. 집에서 봐요!

단·어·및·표·현

practice [prǽktis] 통 연습하다 몡 연습

🦻 LISTENING ADVICE

'shirt'와 'wash'의 'sh' 발음을 주의 깊게 들어보세요.

● **shirt, wash: How to pronounce [ʃ]**

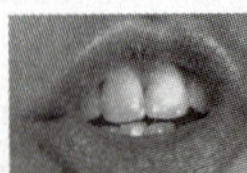

'sh' 소리는 발음기호로는 [ʃ]로 표기하며, '쉿!'이라고 말할 때와 같이 소리 냅니다.

---

12 도표정보파악 ▶ 정답 ②

듣·기·대·본

M: Hey, I'm thinking about buying a mini table. Can you give me some advice?

W: Sure! What do you want to use it for?

M: I need it for my small apartment, mainly as a compact workspace for my laptop.

W: OK. What's your budget for it?

M: I'm hoping to keep it under $100.

W: All right. How about the material? Wood or metal?

M: I prefer wood to metal because it looks nicer.

W: That's a good choice. Lastly, do you want a foldable table?

M: Of course. I have limited space, so a foldable one won't take up much room.

W: Great. Then you should order this one.

우·리·말·해·석

	모델	가격	소재	접이식 테이블
①	A	80달러	목재	X
②	B	85달러	목재	O
③	C	90달러	금속	X
④	D	110달러	목재	O
⑤	E	120달러	금속	X

남: 이봐, 나는 미니 테이블을 사는 것에 대해 생각 중이야. 내게 조언 좀 해줄 수 있어?

여: 물론이지! 너는 무엇을 위해 그것을 사용하고 싶어?

남: 난 그것이 나의 작은 아파트에 주로 내 노트북을 위한 작은 작업 공간으로 필요해.

여: 알겠어. 그것을 위한 너의 예산은 얼마야?

남: 나는 100달러 미만으로 유지하고 싶어.

여: 알겠어. 소재는 어때? 목재 또는 금속 어떤 게 좋아?

남: 나는 목재가 더 좋아 보여서 금속보다 목재를 선호해.

여: 좋은 선택이야. 마지막으로, 접이식 테이블을 원해?

남: 물론이야. 나는 제한된 공간을 갖고 있어서 접이식이 공간을 많이 차지하지 않을 거야.

여: 좋아. 그럼 너는 이걸 주문하는 게 좋겠어.

단·어·및·표·현

compact [kəmpǽkt] 혱 (공간이) 작은

workspace [wə́ːrkspèis] 몡 (특히 사무실 내의) 작업 공간

budget [bʌ́dʒit] 몡 예산, (지출 예상) 비용

material [mətí(ː)əriəl] 몡 (물건의) 소재, 재료

foldable [fóuldəbl] 혱 접을 수 있는, 접혀지는

13 수치파악(날짜) ▶ 정답 ②

듣·기·대·본

(Telephone rings.)

W: Thank you for calling Panda Chinese Restaurant. How may I help you?

M: I'd like to reserve a table for this Sunday evening, June 5.

W: I'm sorry, sir. We are fully booked on Sunday. However, we have just a few tables left on Friday evening.

M: You mean June 3?

W: Yes. I can give you a table by the window.

M: Sounds great. Please book a table under the name of Jason for 4 people at 6 p.m.

W: Thank you. Your reservation is confirmed for Friday at 6.

우·리·말·해·석

(전화벨이 울린다.)

여: Panda 중국음식점입니다. 어떻게 도와드릴까요?

남: 전 6월 5일 이번 일요일 저녁에 자리를 예약하고 싶습니다.

여: 죄송합니다, 손님. 저희는 일요일에 모두 예약이 꽉 찼습니다. 하지만 금요일 저녁에는 자리가 조금 남아 있습니다.

남: 6월 3일 말씀이신가요?

여: 네. 제가 창가 쪽에 자리를 드릴 수 있습니다.

남: 좋네요. Jason이라는 이름으로 오후 6시에 4자리 예약해 주세요.

여: 감사합니다. 금요일 6시에 예약이 확정되었습니다.

단·어·및·표·현
reserve a table 자리를 예약하다

14 한일파악　　　　　　　　▶ 정답 ④

듣·기·대·본

W: Mmm, smells good. What are you making, Tom?
M: I'm baking a cake. Today is my parents' <u>wedding anniversary</u>, so I am throwing them a party.
W: Aww, that's so sweet. Do you need any help? I'm free right now.
M: Thank you so much! Can you <u>decorate the table</u> with those flowers?
W: No problem. Wow, the flowers are beautiful!
M: My mom loves flowers, so I bought them this morning.
W: Your mom will be <u>so proud of you</u>.

우·리·말·해·석

여: 음, 냄새 좋다. 너는 무엇을 만들고 있니, Tom?
남: 나는 케이크를 굽고 있어. 오늘이 우리 부모님의 결혼기념일이어서, 나는 그들에게 파티를 열어줄 거야.
여: 아, 그것 참 다정하다. 너는 도움이 필요하니? 나는 지금 한가해.
남: 정말 고마워! 너는 저 꽃들로 테이블을 장식해 줄 수 있어?
여: 문제없어. 와, 꽃들이 예뻐!
남: 우리 엄마가 꽃들을 좋아하셔서 내가 오늘 아침에 그것들을 샀어.
여: 너의 엄마가 너를 무척 자랑스러워하시겠다.

단·어·및·표·현

anniversary [ǽnəvə́ːrsəri] 몡 기념일
decorate [dékərèit] 됭 장식하다

15 담화목적파악　　　　　　　▶ 정답 ④

듣·기·대·본

W: Good afternoon, visitors! Thank you for visiting Wonderland amusement park. Here are a few shows that will make your experience more special. First, a live music show by the award-winning musical group Mariachi begins at noon. Second, a Christmas Fantasy Parade will <u>take place</u> along Main Street at 4 p.m. Lastly, a <u>spectacular fireworks</u> show starts at 7 p.m. at the central castle. We hope you enjoy your time at Wonderland. Thank you.

우·리·말·해·석

여: 안녕하세요, 방문객 여러분! Wonderland 놀이공원을 방문해주셔서 감사합니다. 여기 여러분의 경험을 더욱 특별하게 해줄 몇 개의 쇼가 있습니다. 첫째, 상을 받은 뮤지컬 그룹 Mariachi에 의한 라이브 음악 쇼가 정오에 시작합니다. 둘째, Christmas Fantasy Parade가 오후 4시에 Main Street를 따라 벌어질 것입니다. 마지막으로, 장관인 불꽃놀이 쇼가 오후 7시에 중앙 성에서 시작합니다. 저희는 여러분이 Wonderland에서 즐거운 시간을 보내길 바랍니다. 감사합니다.

단·어·및·표·현

amusement park 놀이공원
take place 벌어지다, 일어나다
spectacular [spektǽkjələr] 혱 장관인, 장관을 이루는

16 수치계산(금액)　　　　　　▶ 정답 ④

듣·기·대·본

W: Welcome to the National History Museum.
M: How much is <u>a ticket for</u> an adult?
W: It's 12 dollars.
M: <u>How about</u> a kid? My son is five years old. Is he free?
W: I'm sorry. Only <u>kids under</u> three years old are free. It's six dollars for your son.
M: I see. Then I need two adult tickets and one child ticket for my son.
W: Okay. <u>Wait a minute</u>, please.

우·리·말·해·석

여: 국립 역사 박물관에 오신 것을 환영합니다.
남: 성인 표는 얼마인가요?
여: 12달러입니다.
남: 아이는 어떤가요? 제 아들은 5살입니다. 그 아이는 무료인가요?
여: 죄송합니다. 오직 3세 이하의 어린이만 무료입니다. 당신의 아들은 6달러입니다.
남: 그렇군요. 그럼 전 성인 표 2장이랑 제 아들을 위한 어린이 표 한 장이 필요해요.
여: 알겠습니다. 잠시만 기다려주세요.

단·어·및·표·현

Wait a minute, please. 잠시만 기다려주세요.

17 알맞은응답찾기　　　　　　▶ 정답 ②

듣·기·대·본

M: Hi, Lisa. How are you <u>getting on</u> with the yoga <u>postures</u> I taught you last week?
W: Hi, Matthew. I'm doing them every day! Thanks to you, I found the perfect exercises for me.
M: I'm glad you're <u>keeping up with it</u>.
W: You know what? It would be great if you'd make a video of the yoga postures and upload it online.
M: Why do you think so?
W: Because you teach so well! A lot of people are looking for simple exercises they can do at home.
M: That sounds interesting, but I don't know how to <u>edit videos</u>.
W: I can teach you how to do that.

우·리·말·해·석

① 너는 규칙적으로 운동해야 해.
② 내가 너에게 그것을 하는 방법을 가르쳐줄 수 있어.
③ 나는 정말 동영상 시청을 즐겼어.
④ 간단한 요가 자세를 하는 것은 쉬워.
⑤ 그럼 네가 야외에서 할 수 있는 운동을 해.

남: 안녕, Lisa. 내가 너에게 지난주에 가르쳐준 요가 자세는 어떻게 되어 가니?
여: 안녕, Matthew. 난 매일 그걸 하고 있어! 네 덕분에 나에게 완벽한 운동을 찾았어.
남: 네가 그것을 꾸준히 한다니 기뻐.
여: 너 그거 알아? 네가 요가 자세 동영상을 만들어서 온라인에 업로드하면 좋을 거야.
남: 왜 그렇게 생각해?
여: 왜냐하면 네가 아주 잘 가르치니까! 많은 사람들이 집에서 할 수 있는 간단한 운동을 찾고 있어.
남: 그것은 흥미롭게 들리지만 난 동영상을 편집하는 방법을 몰라.
여: <u>내가 너에게 그것을 하는 방법(동영상을 편집하는 방법)을 가르쳐줄</u>

수 있어.

단·어·및·표·현

get on with ~을 해나가다
posture [pάstʃər] (명) 자세, 태도
keep up with ~을 꾸준히 하다, ~을 따라잡다
edit [édit] (동) 편집하다

18 알맞은응답찾기 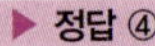 ▶ 정답 ④

듣·기·대·본

M: (Sneezing sound)
W: Ethan, please cover your mouth properly when you sneeze.
M: I did, Mom. I covered my mouth with my hands.
W: I know, but you might be spreading germs to others that way.
M: Oh, I didn't know that.
W: The proper etiquette for sneezing is to sneeze into the inside of your elbow.
M: Wait, Mom. I feel another sneeze coming up.
W: Remember what I just told you!
M: Okay. I'll sneeze into my elbow this time.

우·리·말·해·석

① 좋아요. 감기 걸리지 않도록 조심하세요.
② 코를 닦기 위해 티슈를 사용하세요.
③ 미안해요. 저는 엄마께 그것을 얘기한 것을 기억하지 못해요.
④ 알았어요. 저는 이번에는 제 팔꿈치 쪽으로 재채기할게요.
⑤ 저는 엄마가 말한 것처럼 꼭 마스크를 쓸게요.

남: (재채기 소리)
여: Ethan, 재채기할 때는 네 입을 제대로 가려줘.
남: 그랬어요, 엄마. 저는 제 입을 제 손으로 가렸어요.
여: 알아, 하지만 너는 그런 방식으로 다른 사람들에게 세균을 퍼뜨리고 있을 수도 있어.
남: 오, 저는 그것을 몰랐어요.
여: 재채기에 있어서 적절한 예의는 네 팔꿈치 안쪽에 재채기하는 거야.
남: 잠깐만요, 엄마. 또 재채기가 나오려는 것 같아요.
여: 내가 방금 네게 얘기한 것을 기억하렴!
남: 알았어요. 저는 이번에는 제 팔꿈치 쪽으로 재채기할게요.

단·어·및·표·현

sneeze [sniːz] (동) 재채기하다
spread [spred] (동) 퍼뜨리다
germ [dʒəːrm] (명) 세균

19 알맞은응답찾기 ▶ 정답 ④

듣·기·대·본

M: Welcome to City Museum. How may I help you?
W: I just saw the sign outside. Is it true that the Monet Room is closed?
M: Yes, ma'am. I'm afraid so.
W: No! Why? I came all the way from Chicago to see Monet's paintings!
M: We are really sorry. There was a small fire in that room yesterday.
W: Well, when will it reopen? I'm only staying in the city for a few days.

M: We do not know yet. It depends on the level of damage.

우·리·말·해·석

① 네, Monet의 그림은 진짜 놀라워요.
② 화재가 빠르게 진압되었고 아무도 다치지 않았습니다.
③ 당신은 운이 좋군요. 우리 박물관은 많은 훌륭한 그림들을 소장하고 있습니다.
④ 저희도 아직은 모릅니다. 그것의 손상 정도에 달려있습니다.
⑤ 어떤 그림들도 손상되지 않았지만, 저희는 안전상의 이유로 그 전시실을 닫았습니다.

남: City Museum에 오신 걸 환영합니다. 무엇을 도와드릴까요?
여: 저는 방금 밖에 있는 표지판을 봤어요. Monet Room이 닫혀있다는 게 사실인가요?
남: 네, 부인. 안타깝게도 그렇습니다.
여: 안 돼요! 왜요? 저는 Monet의 그림을 보기 위해 시카고에서 먼 길을 왔단 말이에요!
남: 정말 죄송합니다. 어제 그 전시실에서 작은 화재가 있었습니다.
여: 음, 언제 그것이 다시 열까요? 저는 이 도시에서 며칠 동안만 지낼 예정이거든요.
남: 저희도 아직은 모릅니다. 그것의 손상 정도에 달려있습니다.

단·어·및·표·현

reopen [riːóupən] (동) 다시 열다

20 상황에적절한말찾기 ▶ 정답 ④

듣·기·대·본

M: George is on the express bus on his way to see his grandparents. He falls asleep, and when he wakes up, the bus is arriving at his destination. As he prepares to get off, he finds a cellphone next to his seat. He thinks that someone must have dropped it. So, he decides to take it to the driver and tell him what has happened. In this situation, what would George most likely say to the driver?
George: I think someone left this cellphone on the bus.

우·리·말·해·석

① 운전기사는 버스를 무척 부드럽게 운전합니다.
② 버스가 언제 도착하는지 알려주시겠어요?
③ 혹시 제 휴대전화를 갖고 있으신가요?
④ 누군가가 이 휴대전화를 버스에 두고 간 것 같아요.
⑤ 저 뒤에 잠이 든 승객이 있습니다.

남: George는 그의 조부모님을 만나러 가는 중으로 고속버스를 타고 있다. 그는 잠이 들었고, 그가 깼을 때, 버스는 그의 목적지에 도착하고 있었다. 그가 내리려고 준비를 할 때, 옆자리에서 휴대전화를 발견한다. 그는 누군가가 그것을 떨어뜨렸음이 틀림없다고 생각한다. 그래서, 그는 그것을 운전기사에게 가져가 어떻게 된 건지 말하기로 결정한다. 이런 상황에서, George는 운전기사에게 뭐라고 말할 것 같은가?
George: 누군가가 이 휴대전화를 버스에 두고 간 것 같아요.

단·어·및·표·현

fall asleep 잠들다
destination [dèstənéiʃən] (명) 목적지
get off 내리다

Words & Expressions Review

1. 장관인, 장관을 이루는	2. 제출하다	3. 연기하다, 미루다
4. 긴팔의, 긴 소매의	5. ~에 달려 있다	6. 재채기하다
7. A를 목욕시키다	8. 벌어지다, 일어나다	9. A에게 반하다
10. 통합된, 통일된	11. 중단하다	12. 예약하다
13. 코앞에 와 있는, 아주 가까운	14. 무료의	15. 부주의한
16. 하루 쉬다, 하루 휴가를 내다	17. 기념일	18. ~과 함께
19. ~을 기대하다	20. 자세, 태도	21. ~을 해나가다
22. 자리를 양보하다	23. ~보다 길지 않은	24. 연례의
25. 예약	26. 잠들다	27. 세균, 병균
28. 명심하다	29. 취향, 맛	30. 마음 편히 ~하다
31. 목욕시키다, 씻기다	32. 다시 문을 열다	33. 놀이공원
34. 확정하다, 확인하다	35. 반팔의, 짧은 소매의	36. 해석하다, 설명하다
37. 내리다	38. 모두 예약된	39. (공간이) 작은
40. ~와 사귀다, 교제하다	41. 참석하다	42. (경연) 대회, 시합, 경쟁(자)
43. 제출	44. 끔찍한	

Listening Test
영어듣기 모의고사 05회

|정답|

01 ⑤	02 ②	03 ⑤	04 ②	05 ④
06 ④	07 ①	08 ④	09 ③	10 ④
11 ①	12 ②	13 ⑤	14 ③	15 ⑤
16 ④	17 ⑤	18 ②	19 ②	20 ④

01 그림정보파악(대화) ▶ 정답 ⑤

듣·기·대·본
W: May I help you?
M: Hi, I'm looking for a vegetable peeler.
W: Sure. What type of blade do you want—vertical or Y-shaped?
M: I'll take the Y-shaped one.
W: Would you like a striped handle or a plain one?
M: I'll take the striped one.
W: Do you want a hole at the end of the handle so you can hang it?
M: No, I don't need that feature.
W: Okay.

우·리·말·해·석
여: 무엇을 도와드릴까요?

남: 안녕하세요, 저는 채소 필러(껍질을 벗기는 칼)를 찾고 있어요.
여: 알겠습니다. 세로형 또는 Y자형 중 어떤 종류의 칼날을 원하시나요?
남: Y자형으로 할게요.
여: 손잡이에 줄무늬가 있는 걸로 하시겠어요, 아니면 민무늬 손잡이로 하시겠어요?
남: 줄무늬 있는 걸로 할게요.
여: 걸어둘 수 있게 손잡이 끝에 구멍이 있는 것을 원하세요?
남: 아니요, 그 기능은 필요하지 않아요.
여: 알겠습니다.

단·어·및·표·현
peeler [píːlər] 명 껍질 벗기는 칼
blade [bleid] 명 칼날
vertical [vɔ́ːrtikəl] 형 세로의, 수직의
hang [hæŋ] 동 걸다, 매달다
feature [fíːtʃər] 명 기능, 특징

02 대화미언급 ▶ 정답 ②

듣·기·대·본
(*Telephone rings.*)
M: Hello. Everyday Pilates Center. How may I help you?
W: Hi. I'd like to sign up for a one-on-one Pilates lesson.
M: Okay. Do you have a teacher in mind?
W: Yes. I read about Sarah Kim on your website.
M: Oh, Sarah is a popular teacher. She has a free slot at 4 p.m. on Saturdays.
W: That's perfect. I'd like a one-hour lesson every week. How much is it?
M: It's 40 dollars an hour.
W: Right. Is there anything I need to bring?
M: You just need to bring your own Pilates clothes. We have everything else you need here.
W: Okay. Thanks.

우·리·말·해·석
(전화벨이 울린다.)
남: 여보세요. Everyday Pilates Center입니다. 어떻게 도와드릴까요?
여: 안녕하세요. 저는 일대일 필라테스 수업을 등록하고 싶어요.
남: 네. 마음에 두고 있는 강사가 있으신가요?
여: 네. 저는 웹사이트에서 Sarah Kim 강사님에 대해 읽었어요.
남: 아, Sarah는 인기 있는 선생님이에요. 그녀는 토요일 오후 4시에 빈자리가 있네요.
여: 완벽하네요. 저는 매주 한 시간 수업을 받고 싶어요. 얼마예요?
남: 한 시간당 40달러입니다.
여: 알겠습니다. 제가 가져가야 할 것이 있나요?
남: 당신은 당신의 필라테스복만 가져오면 돼요. 그 밖의 당신이 필요로 하는 모든 것은 여기에 있어요.
여: 네. 감사해요.

단·어·및·표·현
sign up for ~ ~에 등록하다, 신청하다
one-on-one 1대 1의
have A in mind A를 마음에 두다, 염두에 두다
free slot 빈자리, 공석

03 전화목적파악 ▶ 정답 ⑤

듣·기·대·본
(*Cellphone rings.*)

M: Hi, Rachel. It's Joseph.
W: Hi. What's going on?
M: I have a bit of a dilemma. I'm supposed to pick up my parents from the airport tomorrow, but my car broke down.
W: Oh, no. What do you need?
M: I was wondering if you could give me a ride to the airport tomorrow morning.
W: Of course, I'd be happy to help. What time do you need to be there?
M: Their flight lands at 10 a.m., so if we leave by 9:00, that should give us plenty of time.
W: Sounds good. I'll be there at 9:00 sharp.
M: I owe you one, Rachel. Thanks a lot.

우·리·말·해·석
(휴대전화가 울린다.)
남: 안녕, Rachel. Joseph이야.
여: 안녕. 무슨 일이야?
남: 나는 약간 딜레마가 있어. 나는 내일 공항으로 나의 부모님을 데리러 가기로 되어 있지만, 내 차가 고장났어.
여: 오, 이런. 넌 무엇이 필요하니?
남: 나는 네가 내일 아침에 공항으로 나를 태워 줄 수 있는지 궁금했어.
여: 물론이지, 나는 도울 수 있어서 기뻐. 너는 그곳에 몇 시에 도착해야 해?
남: 그들의 항공편은 오전 10시에 착륙해. 그러니 우리가 9시까지 출발한다면 우리에겐 충분한 시간이 주어질 거야.
여: 좋은걸. 내가 그곳에 9시 정각에 갈게.
남: 내가 너에게 하나 빚졌어, Rachel. 정말 고마워.

단·어·및·표·현
be supposed to ~하기로 되어 있다
give A a ride A를 태워 주다
land [lænd] ⑧ 착륙하다
plenty of 충분한, 많은
sharp [ʃɑːrp] ⑨ 정각

04 수치파악(시각) ▶ 정답 ②
듣·기·대·본
W: Bradley, when does the football game start?
M: At 7 p.m., Mom. But, I have to get to the stadium by 6 p.m.
W: Why? Are you going to stop by the souvenir store?
M: Yes, we can get a discount with our tickets.
W: Good. It takes about an hour to get to the stadium. So, make sure to leave early.
M: I'll leave home at 5 p.m. Paul and I will take the subway.
W: Good idea. You can avoid the rush-hour traffic, then.
M: Yes! I'm so excited!

우·리·말·해·석
여: Bradley, 축구 경기는 언제 시작해?
남: 오후 7시요, 엄마. 하지만 저는 오후 6시까지 경기장에 도착해야 해요.
여: 왜? 기념품 가게에 들를 거니?
남: 네, 저희는 표로 할인을 받을 수 있어요.
여: 좋다. 경기장에 도착하는 데 약 한 시간이 걸려. 그러니까 꼭 일찍 떠나거라.
남: 저는 오후 5시에 집을 나갈 거예요. Paul과 저는 지하철을 탈 거예요.
여: 좋은 생각이야. 그러면 러시아워의 교통혼잡을 피할 수 있어.
남: 네! 저는 무척 흥분돼요!

단·어·및·표·현
souvenir [sùːvəníər] ⑨ 기념품
get a discount 할인을 받다

05 심정추론 ▶ 정답 ④
듣·기·대·본
W: Hey, Jim! Did you hear about the new movie, *Jinx*?
M: Of course! I've wanted to see that movie since I saw the trailer!
W: Really? Then, are you going to the premiere?
M: No... Unfortunately, I couldn't get a ticket.
W: Oh, really? Guess what I have?
M: You're pulling my leg! Do you have a ticket?
W: Yes! In fact, I have two tickets, so you can come with me!
M: Oh my gosh! This is too good to be true!

우·리·말·해·석
① 평화로운　　　② 화난　　　③ 침착한
④ 신이 난　　　⑤ 겁먹은

여: 이봐, Jim! 너는 새로운 영화 "징크스"에 대해 들어봤니?
남: 물론이지! 나는 예고편을 본 이후로 그 영화를 보고 싶었어!
여: 정말? 그러면, 너는 시사회에 가니?
남: 아니… 안타깝게도, 나는 표를 구할 수 없었어.
여: 아, 정말? 내가 뭘 가지고 있는지 맞춰볼래?
남: 너 나를 놀리는 거지! 너 표를 가지고 있니?
여: 응! 사실, 나는 표가 두 장 있어서 넌 나와 같이 가도 돼!
남: 세상에! 너무 좋아서 믿어지지 않는걸!

단·어·및·표·현
trailer [tréilər] ⑨ (영화·텔레비전 프로의) 예고편
premiere [primjɛ́ər] ⑨ (영화, 연극의) 시사회
pull one's leg 놀리다, 농담을 던지다
too good to be true 너무 좋아서 믿어지지 않는

06 그림상황에적절한대화찾기 ▶ 정답 ④
듣·기·대·본
① M: How much is this washing machine?
　W: It's 800 dollars.
② M: I'd like to buy some jeans.
　W: The jeans are right over there in aisle 6.
③ M: Can you pick up my jacket from the dry cleaner's?
　W: Sure. I'll pick it up after work.
④ M: Do you want me to help you with anything?
　W: Yes. Get the clean laundry out of the dryer and fold it.
⑤ M: I've spilled some soda on my shirt.
　W: We should get the stain out immediately.

우·리·말·해·석
① 남: 이 세탁기는 얼마인가요?
　여: 800달러입니다.
② 남: 청바지를 좀 사고 싶은데요.
　여: 청바지는 바로 저쪽 6번 통로에 있어요.
③ 남: 제 재킷을 세탁소에서 찾아 주실 수 있어요?
　여: 물론이지. 퇴근 후에 찾아 올게.
④ 남: 제가 뭘 좀 도와드릴까요?
　여: 응. 건조기에서 깨끗한 세탁물을 꺼내서 개줘.
⑤ 남: 제 셔츠에 탄산음료를 좀 흘렸어요.

여: 얼룩을 바로 제거해야 해.

단·어·및·표·현
aisle [ail] 뗑 (상점이나 극장 같은 곳의) 통로
dry cleaner's 세탁소
laundry [lɔ́:ndri] 뗑 세탁물
fold [fould] 똉 (옷 등을) 개다
spill [spil] 똉 (액체를) 흘리다, 쏟다
stain [stein] 뗑 얼룩, 오염
immediately [imí:diətli] 뛩 바로, 즉시

07 부탁(요청)한일파악 ▶ 정답 ①

듣·기·대·본
M: Hey, Katie. Are you ready to go?
W: Hi, Mike. Before we go, can I sit here for a few more minutes?
M: What's the matter?
W: Actually, my feet are really sore. I can barely move.
M: Oh, how did that happen?
W: It's because of these new shoes that I bought. They don't fit well.
M: Is there anything that I can do to help?
W: Could you buy me some bandages? I want to put some bandages on my heels.
M: Sure. Wait here for a minute.

우·리·말·해·석
남: 안녕, Katie. 갈 준비가 됐어?
여: 안녕, Mike. 우리가 가기 전에, 내가 여기에 조금 더 앉아 있을 수 있을까?
남: 뭐가 문제야?
여: 사실, 내 발이 정말 아파. 나는 거의 움직일 수가 없어.
남: 오, 어떻게 된 거야?
여: 그것은 내가 산 이 새 신발 때문이야. 그것들은 잘 맞지 않아.
남: 널 돕기 위해서 내가 할 수 있는 것이 있을까?
여: 나에게 반창고를 좀 사다 줄래? 나는 반창고를 발뒤꿈치에 좀 붙이고 싶어.
남: 그럼. 여기서 잠깐 기다려.

단·어·및·표·현
barely [béərli] 뛩 거의 ~ 아니게(없이), 간신히
bandage [bǽndidʒ] 뗑 반창고, 붕대

08 담화미언급 ▶ 정답 ④

듣·기·대·본
M: Hello, I'm Eric Kim, leader of the school band, Rock Stars. We're looking for new members now. If you're good at music, sign up for the audition by next Friday. The audition will be held on October 10 in the main hall. You'll be judged by two music teachers and us. The new members will be announced on October 11. For more information, check the notice on the school website.

우·리·말·해·석
남: 안녕하세요, 저는 학교 밴드 Rock Stars의 리더인 Eric Kim입니다. 저희는 지금 새로운 멤버를 찾고 있습니다. 만약 당신이 음악을 잘한다면, 다음 주 금요일까지 오디션에 등록하세요. 오디션은 10월 10일 메인홀에서 열릴 것입니다. 두 분의 음악 선생님들과 저희가 심사합니다. 새 멤버는 10월 11일에 발표됩니다. 더 많은 정보를 원하시면, 학교 홈페이지의 공지를 확인하세요.

단·어·및·표·현
judge [dʒʌdʒ] 똉 심사하다, 판단하다
announce [ənáuns] 똉 발표하다, 알리다

09 담화주제추론 ▶ 정답 ③

듣·기·대·본
W: This is an important place that is related to people's health. Many adults regularly receive physical examinations here. This place provides people with physical therapy and also mental therapy. Some people might stay at this place for multiple days to receive treatment. Mostly, people go to this place when they feel sick or when they get injured.

우·리·말·해·석
여: 이것은 사람들의 건강과 관련된 중요한 장소입니다. 많은 성인들은 정기적으로 여기서 신체검사를 받습니다. 이 장소는 사람들에게 물리 치료와 심리 치료도 또한 제공합니다. 어떤 사람들은 치료를 받기 위해 며칠 동안 이 장소에서 머물 수도 있습니다. 일반적으로, 사람들은 아프거나 다칠 때 이 장소에 갑니다.

단·어·및·표·현
be related to ~와 관련되다, 관계가 있다
physical examination 신체검사
provide A with B A에게 B를 제공하다
physical therapy 물리 치료
mental therapy 심리 치료

10 어색한대화찾기 ▶ 정답 ④

듣·기·대·본
① W: Excuse me. Where is the post office?
　M: Go straight and turn right at the corner.
② W: Hello. May I speak to John?
　M: Speaking. Who's this, please?
③ W: Who's that in the picture?
　M: That's Mahatma Gandhi. Don't you recognize him?
④ W: Have you ever heard about Mother Teresa?
　M: My mother doesn't listen to me.
⑤ W: Fall is a very beautiful season.
　M: Yes, it is. That's why it's my favorite season.

우·리·말·해·석
① 여: 실례합니다. 우체국이 어디죠?
　남: 직진하시다가 모퉁이에서 오른쪽으로 꺾으세요.
② 여: 여보세요. John이랑 통화할 수 있을까요?
　남: 전데요. 누구시죠?
③ 여: 사진 속의 저 사람은 누구야?
　남: Mahatma Gandhi(마하트마 간디)야. 그를 못 알아보겠니?
④ 여: Mother Teresa(테레사 수녀)에 대해 들어본 적 있니?
　남: 우리 엄마는 내 말을 듣지 않으셔.
⑤ 여: 가을은 매우 아름다운 계절이야.
　남: 응, 그래. 그게 바로 가을이 내가 가장 좋아하는 계절인 이유야.

단·어·및·표·현
season [síːzən] 뗑 계절

11 할일파악 ▶ 정답 ①

듣·기·대·본
W: Richard, are you invited to Valerie's birthday party?

M: Yes! You're coming, too, right?
W: Yes. Can you do me a favor? Can you pick up a cake at Molly's Bakery?
M: Sure. Is that your present for her?
W: Yes. I already paid for it. It's just that I don't have time to go pick it up.
M: Don't worry. I'll do it now. The bakery is not far from my house.
W: Thanks. What's your present?
M: I bought her a diary. I got her a book last year, but it seems that she likes writing better than reading!

우·리·말·해·석

여: Richard, 너는 Valerie의 생일 파티에 초대받았니?
남: 응! 너도 오지, 맞지?
여: 맞아. 너 내 부탁 하나만 들어줄 수 있니? 넌 Molly's Bakery에서 케이크를 찾아와줄 수 있니?
남: 그래. 그것은 그녀를 위한 네 선물이니?
여: 맞아. 나는 이미 그것에 대해 비용을 냈어. 단지 내가 그것을 찾으러 갈 시간이 없을 뿐이야.
남: 걱정 마. 내가 그것을 지금 할게. 그 빵집은 우리 집에서 멀지 않아.
여: 고마워. 너의 선물은 무엇이니?
남: 나는 그녀에게 일기장을 사줬어. 나는 작년에 그녀에게 책 한 권을 사줬는데, 그녀는 독서보다 글쓰기를 더 좋아하는 것 같아!

단·어·및·표·현

invite [inváit] [동] 초대하다, 초청하다
do somebody a favor ~의 부탁을 들어주다, ~에게 호의를 베풀다
pick up (어디에서) ~을 찾아오다
pay for ~에 대해 비용을 내다, 대금을 지불하다
far from ~와 거리가 먼

12 도표정보파악 ▶ 정답 ②

듣·기·대·본

W: Phil, what are you looking at online?
M: We need a new saucepan. Can you help me choose one?
W: Sure. I think an 8-inch to 10-inch saucepan would work for us.
M: You're right. 7-inch saucepans are too small, and 11-inch ones are too big. Now, let's choose the material.
W: I prefer aluminum saucepans. They are much lighter than stainless steel saucepans.
M: I agree. Look! There is a saucepan with a detachable handle.
W: Do you think we should buy that one?
M: Definitely! It will save storage space when we keep it in the cupboard.
W: That's an excellent point! Let's order it.

우·리·말·해·석

	모델	크기(인치)	재질	분리형 손잡이
①	A	7	알루미늄	X
②	B	8	알루미늄	O
③	C	9	알루미늄	X
④	D	10	스테인리스 스틸	O
⑤	E	11	스테인리스 스틸	X

여: Phil, 온라인에서 뭘 보고 있어?
남: 우리 새 냄비가 필요해. 하나 고르는 거 도와줄래?
여: 물론이지. 8인치에서 10인치 정도 되는 냄비면 우리한테 딱 좋을 것 같아.
남: 맞아. 7인치 냄비는 너무 작고, 11인치짜리는 너무 커. 이제 재질을 골라보자.
여: 나는 알루미늄 냄비가 더 좋아. 스테인리스 스틸 냄비보다 훨씬 가볍거든.
남: 동의해. 봐봐! 분리형 손잡이가 있는 냄비가 있어.
여: 우리 그걸로 사야 할 것 같아?
남: 당연하지! 찬장에 보관할 때 저장 공간을 절약할 수 있어.
여: 좋은 생각이야! 그걸로 주문하자.

단·어·및·표·현

saucepan [sɔ́:spæ̀n] [명] 냄비, 소스팬
work [wə:rk] [동] 효과가 있다, 잘 맞다
material [mətí(:)əriəl] [명] 재질
detachable [ditǽtʃəbl] [형] 분리할 수 있는
storage [stɔ́:ridʒ] [명] 저장, 보관

13 수치파악(날짜) ▶ 정답 ⑤

듣·기·대·본

(*Telephone rings.*)
M: Hello, Glamour Nail Studio. How can I assist you?
W: Hi, I'd like to schedule a manicure appointment. Do you have any availability on October 10th?
M: I'm sorry, but we're fully booked on that day. How about October 11th?
W: Unfortunately, I have a busy schedule on weekdays.
M: I understand. So, October 12th to the 15th won't work for you. How about October 16th?
W: Hmm. Can I book for Sunday, October 17th instead?
M: Certainly. Would 3 p.m. work for you?
W: Yes, that's perfect. Can you please book it under my name, Jasmine?
M: Absolutely. We'll see you then.

우·리·말·해·석

(전화벨이 울린다.)
남: 안녕하세요, Glamour Nail Studio입니다. 어떻게 도와드릴까요?
여: 안녕하세요, 매니큐어 예약을 하고 싶습니다. 10월 10일에 이용 가능한 시간이 있나요?
남: 죄송하지만 그날은 예약이 꽉 찼어요. 10월 11일은 어떠세요?
여: 안타깝게도 평일에는 바쁜 일정이 있어요.
남: 이해해요. 그러면 10월 12일부터 15일까지는 손님께 적합하지 않겠군요. 10월 16일은 어떠세요?
여: 흠. 대신 10월 17일 일요일에 예약할 수 있나요?
남: 물론입니다. 오후 3시 괜찮으실까요?
여: 네, 완벽하네요. 제 이름 Jasmine으로 예약해주실 수 있나요?
남: 물론이죠. 그때 뵙겠습니다.

단·어·및·표·현

assist [əsíst] [동] 돕다
schedule [skédʒu:l] [동] 일정을 잡다
appointment [əpɔ́intmənt] [명] (특히 업무 관련) 약속, 예약

availability [əvèiləbíləti] 명 이용 가능성
work for ~에게 문제없다, 괜찮다

14 한일파악 ▶ 정답 ③

듣•기•대•본

W: Hello! Did you have a <u>good weekend</u>?
M: Yes. I went to my grandmother's farm and helped her pick apples. How was your weekend?
W: Well, it <u>was terrible</u>.
M: Why? What happened?
W: My boyfriend and I <u>were supposed to</u> go to a concert, but we didn't go.
M: Why?
W: I had a huge fight with him. So I just stayed home and <u>did my assignment</u>.
M: Oh, has he called you yet?
W: No, not yet.

우•리•말•해•석

여: 안녕! 좋은 주말 보냈니?
남: 응. 난 할머니 농장에 가서 사과 따는 것을 도와드렸어. 넌 주말을 어떻게 보냈어?
여: 그게, 끔찍했어.
남: 왜? 무슨 일이 있었어?
여: 나랑 내 남자친구는 콘서트에 가기로 되어 있었는데, 우리는 가지 않았어.
남: 왜?
여: 그와 크게 싸웠어. 그래서 그냥 집에 있으면서 과제를 했어.
남: 아, 그가 너에게 전화를 했니?
여: 아니, 아직 안 했어.

단•어•및•표•현

be supposed to + 동사원형 ~하기로 되어 있다

🦻 **LISTENING ADVICE**

'wh'로 시작하는 의문사(where, when, which 등)와 단어(whale, wheat 등)를 발음할 때에 [h] 소리는 탈락되고 [w] 소리만 남습니다. 따라서 'why'는 [화이]가 아닌 [와이]로, 'what'은 [홧]이 아닌 [왓]으로 들립니다. 단, 'who'의 경우에는 [h] 소리를 꼭 발음합니다.

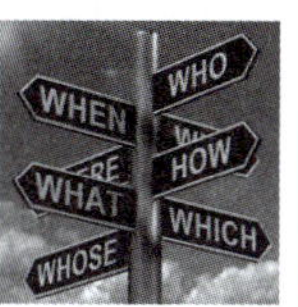

---

15 담화목적파악 ▶ 정답 ⑤

듣•기•대•본

M: Hello. This is *Save Our Blue Planet*. Thousands of sea animals are harmed by plastic waste. <u>Here are some ways to reduce plastic pollution</u>. First, take your own bags and containers to the grocery store. Second, say "no" to straws and get a <u>reusable coffee cup</u> instead of a paper cup. Third, buy as few packaged products as possible. Your small actions can <u>make a huge difference</u> and save animals in the ocean. Thank you.

우•리•말•해•석

남: 안녕하세요. Save Our Blue Planet(우리의 푸른 지구를 지켜라)입니다. 수천 마리의 바다 동물들이 플라스틱 쓰레기로 피해를 입습니다. 여기 플라스틱 오염을 줄이는 몇 가지 방법이 있습니다. 첫째, 여러분 자신의 가방과 용기를 식료품점에 가져가세요. 둘째, 빨대를 '거부'하고 종이컵 대신에 재사용할 수 있는 커피 컵을 받으세요. 셋째, 가능한 한 포장된 상품을 적게 사세요. 여러분의 작은 행동이 큰 차이를 만들고 바다의 동물들을 구할 수 있습니다. 감사합니다.

단•어•및•표•현

pollution [pəlú:ʃən] 명 오염
container [kəntéinər] 명 용기, 그릇
reusable [rì:jú:zəbl] 형 재사용할 수 있는

---

16 수치계산(금액) ▶ 정답 ④

듣•기•대•본

M: Welcome to Fresh Mart. How can I help you?
W: Hi. I'm looking to buy some coffee beans.
M: Sure. We have two options <u>available</u>, regular and premium. The premium beans are <u>freshly roasted</u>.
W: Sounds good. How much are they?
M: A bag of regular beans is $8, and <u>the premium beans are $12 per bag</u>.
W: I'll get the premium ones.
M: Great choice. We also have a <u>special promotion</u>. If you buy two bags of coffee beans, you get a third bag for <u>half</u> price.
W: That's fantastic! <u>I'll take three bags of premium beans in total</u>.
M: Wonderful. Here you go.
W: Thanks. Here's my credit card.

우•리•말•해•석

남: Fresh Mart에 오신 것을 환영합니다. 어떻게 도와드릴까요?
여: 안녕하세요. 저는 커피 원두를 좀 사려고 해요.
남: 물론이죠. 일반과 고급의 두 가지 이용 가능한 선택지가 있습니다. 고급 원두는 갓 볶은 원두입니다.
여: 좋은데요. 그것들은 얼마죠?
남: 일반 원두 한 봉지는 8달러이고, 고급 원두는 한 봉지당 12달러입니다.
여: 고급 제품으로 사겠습니다.
남: 훌륭한 선택이네요. 저희는 또한 특별 판촉 행사를 하고 있습니다. 만약 원두 두 봉지를 사시면 세 번째 봉지를 반값에 얻으실 수 있습니다.
여: 그거 굉장하네요! 저는 총 3봉지의 고급 원두를 가져갈게요.
남: 훌륭해요. 여기 있습니다.
여: 고마워요. 여기 제 신용카드요.

단•어•및•표•현

coffee beans 커피 원두
premium [prí:miəm] 형 고급의
freshly [fréʃli] 부 갓(막) …한
roast [roust] 동 (콩 등을) 볶다
promotion [prəmóuʃən] 명 판촉 (행사)
in total 총합으로

---

17 알맞은응답찾기 ▶ 정답 ⑤

듣•기•대•본

W: Hey, Nick. Why the <u>long face</u>?
M: I didn't get my driver's license yet. I've been trying <u>since last month</u>, but I just keep failing.
W: What's the problem?
M: The written test is easy, but I always <u>mess up</u> on the driving course.
W: Oh, you mean the one that looks like the letter, "S"?
M: Yes. <u>I will never pass</u> that course.

W: Take it easy. You'll get it next time.

우·리·말·해·석

① 그 말을 들어서 정말 기뻐.　② 넌 시험을 언제 봤니?
③ 그건 무시할 수 없는 것 같네.　④ 당연하지, 난 네가 가지 않길 바라지.
⑤ 마음 편히 가져. 다음번엔 딸 수 있을 거야.

여: 이봐, Nick. 왜 우울한 얼굴이니?
남: 나 아직도 운전면허를 못 땄어. 난 지난달부터 시도했지만, 계속 실패
　　하기만 해.
여: 문제가 뭔데?
남: 필기시험은 쉬운데, 난 주행 코스에서 항상 망쳐.
여: 아, 'S'자처럼 생긴 것 말이니?
남: 응. 난 그 코스를 절대 통과하지 못할 거야.
여: 마음 편히 가져. 다음번엔 딸 수 있을 거야.

단·어·및·표·현

mess up 망치다

18　알맞은응답찾기　▶ 정답 ②

듣·기·대·본

W: Mike, look at this news article! It says most students
　don't exercise at all and it's causing a lot of health
　problems.
M: I totally agree. I should work out as well, but I can't
　seem to find anything interesting to do.
W: Why don't you take a swimming class after school?
M: Swimming? That's a great idea!
W: I've been in a class since last year, and it helps me stay
　fit.
M: I didn't know you were in a swimming class. I'd love to
　join you.
W: You're going to love it! The class is on Wednesday and
　Friday.
M: All right! I can't wait to start.

우·리·말·해·석

① 너는 얼마나 자주 운동을 하니?
② 좋아! 나는 시작하는 것을 기다릴 수 없어. (너무 기대된다.)
③ 나는 매주 거기서 수영을 하곤 했어.
④ 건강은 가장 중요한 것이야.
⑤ 우리 학교는 많은 방과 후 학교 프로그램을 하고 있어.

여: Mike, 이 기사를 봐! 대부분의 학생들이 전혀 운동을 하지 않고 그것은
　　많은 건강 문제들을 야기한다고 되어 있어.
남: 나는 전적으로 동의해. 나도 운동해야 되는데, 나는 할 만한 흥미로운
　　것을 찾을 수가 없는 것 같아.
여: 방과 후에 수영 수업을 듣는 것은 어때?
남: 수영? 그거 좋은 생각이다!
여: 나는 작년부터 수업을 듣고 있는데, 그것은 내가 건강을 유지하는 데
　　도움이 돼.
남: 나는 네가 수영 수업을 듣고 있는지 몰랐어. 나도 너와 함께 하고 싶어.
여: 너는 그것을 분명 좋아할 거야! 수업은 수요일과 금요일에 있어.
남: 좋아! 나는 시작하는 것을 기다릴 수 없어. (너무 기대된다.)

단·어·및·표·현

news article 뉴스 기사
It says ~ (신문, 표지판, 문서의 내용을 말할 때 쓰는 표현) ~라고 되어
　　　　　　있어, ~라고 하네
not ~ at all 전혀 ~하지 않다

---

work out (건강·몸매 관리 등을 위해) 운동하다
be in a class 수업(과목)을 수강하다
stay fit 건강을 유지하다
join [ʤɔin] ⑧ 함께 하다
can't wait to + 동사원형 기다릴 수 없다, 너무 ~하고 싶다

19　알맞은응답찾기　▶ 정답 ②

듣·기·대·본

M: There are so many people over there. What's going on
　in the park?
W: I don't know. Is there a movie shooting?
M: There is! Look! I can see the actor. I forget his name.
W: Let me see. Oh! That's Ian Holland! I like him so much.
M: He is handsome in person.
W: He is handsome all the time.
M: Why don't you go and ask for his autograph?
W: I can't! How can I speak to him? I can't even look at
　him.
M: Shall I ask him for you?

우·리·말·해·석

① 그의 영화는 좋아.
② 내가 너 대신 물어볼까?
③ 너는 그를 언제라도 만날 수 있어.
④ 그는 그의 팬에게 별로 친절하지 않아.
⑤ 나는 그의 이름을 알 필요가 없어.

남: 저기에 사람이 많네. 공원에 무슨 일이 있는 거야?
여: 몰라. 영화를 찍고 있나?
남: 그러네! 봐! 배우가 보여. 그 사람 이름을 잊어버렸네.
여: 어디 봐. 오! Ian Holland잖아! 나는 그가 정말 좋아.
남: 직접 보니 잘생겼네.
여: 그는 늘 잘생겼어.
남: 가서 사인 해달라는 게 어때?
여: 못 해! 내가 어떻게 그에게 말을 걸어? 그를 쳐다볼 수도 없어.
남: 내가 너 대신 물어볼까?

단·어·및·표·현

What's going on? 무슨 일이야?

20　상황에적절한말찾기　▶ 정답 ④

듣·기·대·본

W: Jude and her friend Monica go shopping together. Jude
　wants to buy a nice jacket. After an hour shopping, she
　finds a jacket she likes. However, she can't decide
　on the color. She likes both the black and the blue, but
　she has to choose one. So she wants to hear Monica's
　opinion on the jacket. In this situation, what would Jude
　say to Monica?
Jude: Which color looks best on me?

우·리·말·해·석

① 오늘 쇼핑 어땠어?　② 넌 쇼핑 가는 것을 좋아하니?
③ 이 재킷을 사는 것이 어때?　④ 어떤 색이 내게 가장 잘 어울려?
⑤ 넌 파란색이 잘 어울린다.

여: Jude와 그녀의 친구 Monica는 함께 쇼핑을 간다. Jude는 좋은 재킷을
　　사고 싶어 한다. 한 시간 쇼핑 후, 그녀는 마음에 드는 재킷을 발견한
　　다. 하지만, 그녀는 색상을 결정하지 못한다. 검정색과 파란색 둘 다 마

음에 들지만 그녀는 하나만 선택해야 한다. 그래서 그녀는 재킷에 대한 Monica의 의견을 듣고 싶어 한다. 이러한 상황에서, Jude는 Monica에게 무엇이라고 말하겠는가?

Jude: 어떤 색이 내게 가장 잘 어울려?

단·어·및·표·현

decide on ~ ~을 결정하다

Words & Expressions Review

1. ~에 들르다	2. 판촉 (행사)	3. 놀리다, 농담을 던지다
4. 반창고, 붕대	5. 치료, 처치	6. 분리할 수 있는
7. 운동하다	8. 알아보다	9. (출퇴근) 혼잡 시간대
10. 운전면허	11. ~하기로 되어 있다	12. (상점이나 극장 같은 곳의) 통로
13. 심사하다, 판단하다	14. 총합으로	15. 반드시 (~하도록) 하다
16. ~과 거리가 먼	17. 신체검사	18. (콩 등을) 볶다
19. 발표하다, 알리다	20. 저장, 보관	21. 걸다, 매달다
22. 칼날	23. 우울한 얼굴	24. A와 싸우다
25. 결정하다	26. 촬영, 발사	27. 아픈, 따가운
28. (영화, 연극의) 시사회	29. 빈자리, 공석	30. 다치다, 부상을 입다
31. 재사용할 수 있는	32. 직접, 몸소	33. ~에 도착하다
34. 거의 ~ 아니게	35. 일정을 잡다	36. 얼룩, 오염
37. ~에게 문제없다, 괜찮다	38. (옷 등을) 개다	39. 건강을 유지하다
40. 갓[막] …한	41. 오염	42. 받다, 받아들이다
43. 효과가 있다, 잘 맞다	44. 치료, 요법	

영어듣기 모의고사 06회

|정|답|

01 ⑤	02 ④	03 ③	04 ⑤	05 ③
06 ④	07 ②	08 ④	09 ①	10 ④
11 ①	12 ③	13 ③	14 ②	15 ④
16 ③	17 ③	18 ③	19 ④	20 ③

01 　그림정보파악(대화)　　▶ 정답 ⑤

듣·기·대·본

W: Welcome to Fun Flowers. How can I help you?
M: Hi, I'd like to buy a flower pot.
W: Sure. We have round pots and square pots.
M: I think the round pots look prettier.
W: Okay. What do you think of the striped one? It's a popular model.
M: Hmm… I like the plain model more.

W: Sure. The pot comes in two styles. One has a hanger and the other does not.
M: I like the one with the hanger. I was thinking of hanging the flower pot on the wall.
W: Good choice! I'm sure you'll make good use of it.

우·리·말·해·석

여: Fun Flowers에 오신 것을 환영합니다. 어떻게 도와드릴까요?
남: 안녕하세요, 저는 화분을 사고 싶은데요.
여: 네. 둥근 화분과 정사각형의 화분이 있어요.
남: 저는 둥근 화분이 더 예뻐 보인다고 생각해요.
여: 네. 줄무늬가 있는 것은 어떻게 생각하세요? 그것은 인기 있는 모델입니다.
남: 음… 저는 무늬가 없는 것이 더 좋아요.
여: 네. 화분은 두 가지 스타일로 나옵니다. 하나는 고리가 있고, 다른 하나는 없어요.
남: 저는 고리가 있는 것이 좋아요. 저는 화분을 벽에 걸까 생각 중이었어요.
여: 좋은 선택입니다! 저는 당신이 그것을 잘 활용할 거라고 확신해요.

단·어·및·표·현

striped[straipt] [형] 줄무늬가 있는
hanger[hǽŋər] [명] (옷 따위를 거는) 고리, 걸이
make good use of ~을 잘 활용하다

02 　대화미언급　　▶ 정답 ④

듣·기·대·본

W: Jonathan, are you interested in going to a concert with me this Friday?
M: This Friday? Who's the singer?
W: It's Brian Jackson. Actually, I got two tickets from my aunt.
M: Really? He's my favorite!
W: Great! The concert starts at 7 p.m. and will be finished around 10 p.m.
M: That sounds great. Where should we meet?
W: The concert is at Robin's Hall on 16th Street. Why don't we meet at 6:30 in front of the hall?
M: Okay. Thank you, Susan.

우·리·말·해·석

여: Jonathan, 너 이번 주 금요일에 나랑 콘서트에 가는 데 관심 있니?
남: 이번 주 금요일? 가수가 누군데?
여: Brian Jackson이야. 사실, 내가 이모한테 티켓 두 장을 받았거든.
남: 정말? 그는 내가 가장 좋아하는 가수야!
여: 잘됐다! 콘서트는 오후 7시에 시작해서 저녁 10시쯤 끝날 거야.
남: 그거 좋네. 우리 어디서 만날까?
여: 콘서트는 16번가에 있는 Robin's Hall에서 열려. 우리 그 홀 앞에서 6시 30분에 보는 게 어때?
남: 알았어. 고마워, Susan.

단·어·및·표·현

be interested in ~ ~에 관심이 있다, 흥미가 있다
actually[ǽktʃuəli] [부] 사실은, 실제로는

03 　전화목적파악　　▶ 정답 ③

듣·기·대·본

(*Telephone rings.*)
M: Hello, this is Natural Beauty Salon.

W: Hello, my name is Tiffany Lee. I have an appointment at 6 p.m. today.
M: Yes, Tiffany. How can I help you?
W: I'm getting a perm today, and I was wondering about the price.
M: Well, it depends on the length of your hair.
W: Oh, I see.
M: If you come 10 minutes early, we can discuss it.
W: Thanks. Then, I'll be there at 5:50.

우·리·말·해·석

(전화벨이 울린다.)
남: 여보세요, Natural Beauty Salon입니다.
여: 여보세요, 제 이름은 Tiffany Lee입니다. 저는 오늘 오후 6시에 예약되어 있습니다.
남: 네, Tiffany 씨. 어떻게 도와드릴까요?
여: 오늘 파마를 하려고 하는데 가격이 궁금합니다.
남: 음, 그것은 머리 길이에 따라 다릅니다.
여: 아, 그렇군요.
남: 10분 일찍 오셔서, 상의하시면 됩니다.
여: 고마워요. 그러면 5시 50분에 갈게요.

단·어·및·표·현

beauty salon 미용실
length [leŋkθ] ⑱ 길이
discuss [diskʌ́s] ⑧ 상의하다

04 수치파악(시각) ▶ 정답 ⑤

들·기·대·본

M: Mary, did you register for tennis lessons yet?
W: Not yet, Dad. I haven't decided whether to take the 4 p.m. class or the 7 p.m. class.
M: Don't you think it'll be a little tight to take the 4 p.m. class?
W: Yeah, I might not make it to the class in time after school.
M: So, you shouldn't take the 4 p.m. class.
W: You're right. The 7 p.m. class is a better choice because I can eat dinner at 5 p.m. and then go to the class.
M: That's a good plan.
W: I'll go register now.

우·리·말·해·석

남: Mary, 너는 벌써 테니스 강습에 등록했니?
여: 아직 안 했어요, 아빠. 저는 오후 4시 강습을 받을지 오후 7시 강습을 받을지 결정하지 못했어요.
남: 오후 4시 강습을 받는 것은 약간 빠듯할 것 같지 않니?
여: 네, 저는 학교가 끝나고 제시간에 강습에 도착하지 못할 수도 있어요.
남: 그럼 너는 오후 4시 강습을 받아서는 안 돼.
여: 아빠 말이 맞아요. 오후 5시에 저녁을 먹고 나서 강습에 갈 수 있기 때문에 오후 7시가 더 나은 선택인 것 같아요.
남: 좋은 계획이구나.
여: 저는 지금 등록하러 갈게요.

단·어·및·표·현

register [rédʒistər] ⑧ 등록하다
tight [tait] ⑱ (여유가 없이) 빠듯한, 빡빡한
make it to 늦지 않게 ~에 도착하다, 간신히 ~에 도착하다
in time 제시간에, 시간 맞춰

05 심정추론 ▶ 정답 ③

들·기·대·본

M: Kimberly, can I talk to you for a second?
W: Sure. What's up?
M: Remember the book I borrowed from you last week?
W: *War and Peace*? Do you like it? It's a bit long, isn't it?
M: Um, yes, it's fine. I'm really sorry, but I can't return it to you.
W: Why?
M: My little cousin came over and drew pictures all over it when I was in another room.
W: Oh... it's my favorite novel.
M: I know. I'm so sorry. I'll buy you a new copy. I've already ordered one.
W: That's kind. Thank you, Dale.

우·리·말·해·석

① 마음이 편안한　　　② 부러워하는　　　③ 미안해하는
④ 만족하는　　　　　⑤ 행복한

남: Kimberly, 잠시 나랑 이야기할 수 있니?
여: 그래. 무슨 일이니?
남: 내가 지난주에 너에게 빌린 책 기억해?
여: "전쟁과 평화?" 그 책이 마음에 들어? 그거 좀 길지, 그렇지 않니?
남: 음, 맞아, 괜찮더라. 진짜 미안하지만 너에게 그걸 돌려줄 수 없어.
여: 왜?
남: 내 어린 사촌 동생이 와서 내가 다른 방에 있을 때 그것 곳곳에 그림을 그렸어.
여: 오… 그건 내가 가장 좋아하는 소설이야.
남: 나도 알아. 진짜 미안해. 내가 새 책으로 사줄게. 난 이미 하나를 주문했어.
여: 친절하구나. 고마워, Dale.

단·어·및·표·현

for a second 잠시
all over 곳곳에
copy [kápi] ⑱ (책·신문 등의) 한 부

06 그림상황에적절한대화찾기 ▶ 정답 ④

들·기·대·본

① M: Are you paying in cash or by credit card?
　 W: In cash. Here you are.
② M: Is this your first time visiting Korea?
　 W: Actually, this is my fifth visit to Korea.
③ M: Excuse me. Do you have this shirt in a smaller size?
　 W: Sure, let me get it for you.
④ M: How much money would you like to exchange?
　 W: I'd like to change 100 dollars into Korean won.
⑤ M: What is the purpose of your visit?
　 W: I'm here for business.

우·리·말·해·석

① 남: 현금으로 지불하시나요, 아니면 신용카드인가요?
　 여: 현금으로요. 여기 있습니다.
② 남: 이것이 당신의 한국 첫 방문입니까?
　 여: 사실, 이것은 저의 5번째 한국 방문입니다.
③ 남: 실례합니다. 이 셔츠 더 작은 사이즈로 있나요?
　 여: 그럼요, 제가 당신을 위해 그것을 가져다드릴게요.

④ 남: 얼마나 많은 돈을 환전하고 싶으세요?
여: 저는 100달러를 한국 원으로 바꾸고 싶어요.
⑤ 남: 당신의 방문 목적은 무엇입니까?
여: 저는 업무차 왔습니다.

단•어•및•표•현

exchange [ikstʃéindʒ] [동] 환전하다, 교환하다

07 부탁(요청)한일파악 ▶ 정답 ②

듣•기•대•본

M: Hey, Katelynn! What are you doing?
W: Well, I'm trying to fix the posters on the bulletin board.
M: Do you need my help?
W: Hmm… I can handle it.
M: I think the board is too high to reach.
W: I'll step onto the chair.
M: Okay, that will do!
W: Oh, wait… Could you cut the tape while I'm holding the poster?
M: Sure, why not?
W: Thank you!

우•리•말•해•석

남: 안녕, Katelynn! 뭐하고 있어?
여: 음, 나는 게시판에 포스터를 붙이려고 하는 중이야.
남: 내 도움이 필요하니?
여: 음… 내가 처리할 수 있어.
남: 내 생각엔 게시판이 손에 닿기엔 너무 높은 것 같아.
여: 나는 의자를 밟고 올라설 거야.
남: 그래, 그러면 되겠네!
여: 오, 잠깐만… 내가 포스터를 잡고 있을 동안 테이프를 좀 잘라줄래?
남: 물론이지, 왜 안 되겠어?
여: 고마워!

단•어•및•표•현

fix A on B A를 B에 붙이다, 고정하다
bulletin board 게시판

08 담화미언급 ▶ 정답 ④

듣•기•대•본

W: Hello, students. I'd like to remind you all about the Bake Sale we will be having on June 9. We are holding this event to raise funds for our local animal rescue. It will be held in our cafeteria. There will be a variety of baked goods such as brownies, cookies, cakes, and more. So, come to the bake sale and enjoy some delicious desserts. Please bring your family and friends as well. Thank you.

우•리•말•해•석

여: 안녕하세요, 학생 여러분. 저는 여러분 모두에게 우리가 6월 9일에 열 예정인 빵 판매 자선바자회에 대해서 다시 한번 알려드리려고 합니다. 우리는 우리 지역의 동물 구조를 위한 기금을 모으기 위해 이 행사를 열 것입니다. 그것은 우리 구내식당에서 열릴 것입니다. 브라우니, 쿠키, 케이크 등 오븐에 구운 다양한 상품이 있을 것입니다. 그러니 빵 바자회에 오셔서 맛있는 디저트들을 즐기세요. 여러분의 가족과 친구들도 데려오시기 바랍니다. 감사합니다.

단•어•및•표•현

remind [rimáind] [동] 다시 한번 알려주다, 상기시키다
bake sale (기금 모금을 위한) 빵 판매 자선바자회
raise funds 기금을 모으다, 자금을 조달하다
rescue [réskjuː] [명] 구조, 구출
a variety of 여러 가지의

09 담화화제추론 ▶ 정답 ①

듣•기•대•본

W: This is the world's most popular team sport. The game is played on a rectangular grass field and there is a goal at each end of the field. Two teams move the ball in order to kick it into the goal. The only player on each team who can touch the ball with his hands stands in front of the goal. The other players must use their feet, knees, head and chest to control the ball. If a player touches the ball with his hands, it is considered a foul and a free kick is given to the opposing team.

우•리•말•해•석

여: 이것은 세계적으로 가장 인기 있는 팀 스포츠입니다. 경기는 직사각형의 잔디 구장에서 열리며, 경기장 각 끝에는 골대가 있습니다. 두 팀은 골대 안으로 공을 차기 위해서 공을 움직입니다. 각각의 팀에서 손으로 공을 만질 수 있는 유일한 선수는 골대 앞에 섭니다. 다른 선수들은 공을 제어하기 위해서 발, 무릎, 머리, 그리고 가슴을 사용해야 합니다. 만약 선수가 손으로 공을 만진다면, 그것은 파울로 간주되며, 상대팀에게 프리킥이 주어집니다.

단•어•및•표•현

in order to + 동사원형 ~하기 위해
It is considered ~ ~로 간주되다

10 어색한대화찾기 ▶ 정답 ④

듣•기•대•본

① M: Would you like to order, ma'am?
W: I will have a chicken salad.
② M: What's wrong? You look upset.
W: I think I lost my wallet.
③ M: Who's calling, please?
W: This is Emily speaking.
④ M: When shall we meet?
W: In front of the concert hall.
⑤ M: May I help you?
W: Yes, please. I am looking for men's shirts.

우•리•말•해•석

① 남: 주문하시겠습니까, 부인?
여: 저는 치킨 샐러드로 할게요.
② 남: 무슨 일이야? 너 속상해 보여.
여: 나 지갑을 잃어버린 것 같아.
③ 남: 전화 주신 분이 누구신가요?
여: Emily입니다.
④ 남: 우리 언제 만날까?
여: 콘서트 홀 앞에서.
⑤ 남: 도와드릴까요?
여: 네, 저는 남성용 셔츠를 찾고 있어요.

단•어•및•표•현

upset [ʌpsét] [형] 속상한, 화난

듣·기·대·본

M: Hello, welcome to Nature Coffee.
W: Hi. Can I have a cup of white coffee, please?
M: Sure. Do you need anything else?
W: Um, actually, I have a bag of coffee beans. Can you grind them for me?
M: Of course.
W: How much is it to grind the beans?
M: Oh, there's no charge if you buy a cup of coffee.
W: That's great! Let me get the bag of beans right away. It's in my car.
M: Take your time.

우·리·말·해·석

남: 안녕하세요, Nature Coffee에 오신 것을 환영합니다.
여: 안녕하세요. 화이트 커피 한 잔 주시겠어요?
남: 그럼요. 다른 필요하신 것이 있으신가요?
여: 음, 사실, 저에게는 커피 원두 한 봉지가 있어요. 저를 위해 그것들을 갈아주실 수 있나요?
남: 물론이죠.
여: 원두를 가는 것은 얼마인가요?
남: 오, 커피 한 잔을 구매하시면, 무료입니다.
여: 좋네요! 제가 지금 바로 원두 봉지를 가져올게요. 그것은 제 차에 있어요.
남: 천천히 하세요.

단·어·및·표·현

coffee bean 커피 원두
grind [graind] ⑧ (곡식 등을 잘게) 갈다, 빻다
no charge 무료의, 무료인
take one's time 천천히 하다

듣·기·대·본

M: Hey, look at this schedule on the website. There are farm experience programs.
W: Oh, I like farms. Why don't we sign up for one over the weekend?
M: Sounds good. Which do you prefer, a morning or afternoon program?
W: An afternoon program. I want to sleep in this weekend.
M: Right. How about experiencing a milk cow feeding?
W: Sounds good. Do you want to do the tasting, too?
M: Sure. Then, let's sign up for this program.
W: Okay. It'll be fun.

우·리·말·해·석

	프로그램	시간	활동	우유/치즈 맛보기
①	A	9:00 ~ 11:00 a.m.	젖소 먹이 주기	X
②	B	9:00 ~ 11:30 a.m.	치즈 만들기	O
③	C	2:00 ~ 4:30 p.m.	젖소 먹이 주기	O
④	D	2:00 ~ 4:00 p.m.	젖소 먹이 주기	X
⑤	E	2:00 ~ 4:00 p.m.	치즈 만들기	X

남: 이봐, 웹사이트에서 이 스케줄을 봐. 농장 체험 프로그램들이 있어.
여: 오, 나는 농장을 좋아해. 우리 주말에 하나 신청하는 것 어때?
남: 좋아. 아침 프로그램, 아니면 오후 프로그램 중 어느 것이 더 좋아?
여: 오후 프로그램. 나는 이번 주말에는 늦잠을 자고 싶어.
남: 좋아. 젖소 먹이 주기 체험하는 것은 어때?
여: 좋아. 맛보기도 하고 싶어?
남: 그럼. 그러면 이 프로그램을 신청하자.
여: 좋아. 그것은 재미있을 거야.

단·어·및·표·현

sleep in 늦잠 자다

듣·기·대·본

W: Hi, Tom. What are you looking at on your laptop?
M: I'm checking out the Awesome Amusement Park website. They're opening a new rollercoaster soon.
W: Oh, really? I love rollercoasters! When is it opening?
M: It's opening on June 5th.
W: Great! We should definitely go ride it together.
M: Yeah, we should. How about going on June 15th? I think it'll be less crowded then.
W: Hmm... I have a student council meeting on the 15th. How about June 19th?
M: No problem! I'm free that day.

우·리·말·해·석

여: 안녕, Tom. 너는 네 노트북으로 무엇을 보고 있니?
남: 난 Awesome 놀이공원 웹사이트를 살펴보는 중이야. 그들은 곧 새로운 롤러코스터를 개장할 거야.
여: 오, 정말이야? 나 롤러코스터를 매우 좋아해! 그것은 언제 개장한대?
남: 그건 6월 5일에 개장할 거야.
여: 좋다! 우리는 반드시 함께 그것을 타러 가야 해.
남: 맞아, 우리는 그래야 해. 6월 15일에 가는 게 어때? 내 생각에 그때는 덜 붐빌 것 같아.
여: 음… 나는 15일에 학생회 회의가 있어. 6월 19일은 어때?
남: 문제없어! 난 그날 한가해.

단·어·및·표·현

check out (흥미로운 것을) 살펴보다, 확인하다
definitely [défənitli] ⑨ 반드시, 틀림없이
crowded [kráudid] ⑩ 붐비는, 복잡한

듣·기·대·본

M: Ella, how was your weekend? Didn't you say that you were going to a jazz concert?
W: Yeah, but the show got cancel(l)ed at the last minute.
M: Really? What happened?
W: The musician got food poisoning, so he couldn't perform.
M: I'm sorry to hear that. Did you do anything else?
W: Yes, I bought these new headphones. Here, give them a try.
M: Wow, the sound is amazing! I really like them.
W: Thanks. I really like them as well.

우·리·말·해·석

남: Ella, 네 주말은 어땠어? 너 재즈 콘서트에 갈 거라고 말하지 않았니?
여: 그래, 하지만 그 공연은 마지막 순간에 취소되었어.
남: 정말이야? 무슨 일이 있었는데?
여: 연주자가 식중독에 걸려서 공연할 수 없었어.

남: 그 말을 들으니 안됐다. 넌 그것 말고 다른 것을 했니?
여: 응, 난 이 새 헤드폰을 샀어. 여기, 그것들(헤드폰)을 한번 써봐.
남: 와, 소리가 굉장하다! 정말 마음에 들어.
여: 고마워. 나도 그것들(헤드폰)이 정말 좋아.

단•어•및•표•현

get cancel(l)ed 취소되다
at the last minute 마지막 순간에
food poisoning 식중독
perform [pərfɔ́ːrm] [동] 공연[연주]하다
give ~ a try ~을 한번 해보다

15 담화목적파악 ▶ 정답 ④

듣•기•대•본

W: Hello. This is *Today's Safety Tip*. When localized heavy rain is expected, don't go near streams, rivers or beaches. Try to stay indoors if you can, and close all the windows. Then, keep track of weather updates on TV, radio, or the Internet. On the road, avoid going near construction sites as things may fall from above. Heavy rain can be very dangerous. Stay safe, everyone.

우•리•말•해•석

여: 안녕하세요. 〈오늘의 안전 팁〉입니다. 국지성 호우가 예상될 때는 개천, 강, 또는 해변 근처에 가지 마세요. 할 수 있다면 실내에 머물도록 하시고 모든 창문을 닫으세요. 그러고 나서 TV, 라디오 또는 인터넷으로 최신 날씨 관련 정보를 놓치지 않도록 하세요. 도로에서는, 물건이 위에서 떨어질 수도 있으므로 공사장 근처로 가는 것을 피하세요. 호우는 매우 위험할 수 있습니다. 모두들, 안전하게 있으세요.

단•어•및•표•현

localized [lóukəlàizd] [형] 국지적인
keep track of ~ ~을 놓치지 않도록 하다
avoid [əvɔ́id] [동] 피하다

16 수치계산(금액) ▶ 정답 ③

듣•기•대•본

M: Hello, may I help you?
W: Hi, I'm looking for a Mother's Day present.
M: Do you have anything in mind?
W: Well... My mom likes tea. How much are these tea pots?
M: The big one is 20 dollars, and the small one is 15 dollars.
W: Then, I'd like to buy one of each.
M: Okay, your total will be 35 dollars.
W: Can I use this coupon?
M: Sure. You can get a five-dollar discount from the total price.
W: Okay. I'll pay by credit card.

우•리•말•해•석

남: 안녕하세요, 도와드릴까요?
여: 안녕하세요, 저는 어머니 날 선물을 찾고 있어요.
남: 당신이 염두에 두신 것이 있나요?
여: 음… 저희 어머니는 차를 좋아하세요. 이 찻주전자는 얼마인가요?
남: 큰 것은 20달러이고, 작은 것은 15달러입니다.
여: 그러면, 저는 각각 하나씩 사겠습니다.
남: 알겠습니다, 총액은 35달러 되겠습니다.
여: 제가 이 쿠폰을 사용할 수 있을까요?
남: 물론입니다. 전체 가격에서 5달러 할인을 받으실 수 있습니다.
여: 좋습니다. 신용카드로 지불하겠습니다.

단•어•및•표•현

have ~ in mind ~을 염두에 두다, ~에 관해 생각하고 있다
total [tóutl] [명] 총액, 합계 [형] 총, 전체의
get a discount 할인을 받다

17 알맞은응답찾기 ▶ 정답 ③

듣•기•대•본

W: Hi, Tom. How was your summer vacation?
M: Hi, Angela. I spent some time working at an animal shelter.
W: Wow! How did you decide to do that during your vacation?
M: I'm thinking of becoming a dog trainer so I wanted to have some real experience with dogs.
W: That's a very good idea. So, how was it?
M: It was very tough but extremely rewarding. I still miss some of the dogs I cared for there.
W: So, I guess you became more certain about what you want to do in the future?
M: Yes. I think I want to be a dog trainer.

우•리•말•해•석

① 아니. 나는 그 일을 하고는 돈을 받지 않았어.
② 맞아. 그들의 미래는 우리에게 달려 있어.
③ 그래. 나는 내가 개 훈련사가 되기를 원한다고 생각해.
④ 굉장해! 너는 너의 꿈을 따라야 해.
⑤ 물론이야. 너는 다음번에 나와 함께 갈 수 있어.

여: 안녕, Tom. 네 여름방학은 어땠어?
남: 안녕, Angela. 난 동물 보호소에서 일하면서 시간을 좀 보냈어.
여: 와! 어떻게 네 방학 동안 그렇게 하기로 결정한 거야?
남: 나는 개 훈련사가 될까 생각 중이어서 개와 함께하는 진짜 경험을 좀 하고 싶었어.
여: 그거 아주 좋은 생각이야. 그래서, 그것은 어땠어?
남: 그것은 아주 힘들었지만 정말 보람이 있었어. 나는 내가 거기서 돌보았던 개들 몇몇이 아직도 보고 싶어.
여: 그래서, 네가 미래에 하고 싶은 일에 대해서 더욱 확신하게 되었을 것 같은데?
남: 그래. 나는 내가 개 훈련사가 되기를 원한다고 생각해.

단•어•및•표•현

animal shelter 동물 보호소
rewarding [riwɔ́ːrdiŋ] [형] 보람 있는
care for ~를 보살피다, 돌보다
be certain about ~에 대해 확신하다

18 알맞은응답찾기 ▶ 정답 ③

듣•기•대•본

M: Sharon, did you know that the badminton club is looking for new members?
W: Yes, I saw the poster on the board.
M: Me, too. Would you like to join the club with me?
W: Sure. Sounds fun.
M: The poster says we need to bring our own racket. Do

you have one?

W: No, I have never played badminton before.

M: I don't have one, either.

W: Oh, I just remembered that the sporting goods store on Sierra Street is having a huge sale.

M: The one that has just opened? That's great. Let's go and check it out.

W: Okay. I hope we can get a good deal.

우·리·말·해·석

① 나는 일주일에 세 번 테니스를 쳐.
② 물론이지, 너는 내 것을 빌릴 수 있어.
③ 그래. 우리가 싸게 살 수 있으면 좋겠다.
④ 내가 그것을 도와줄 수 없어서 미안해.
⑤ 나는 네가 경기에서 이겼다고 들었어. 축하해!

남: Sharon, 너는 배드민턴 동아리가 새로운 회원을 찾고 있다는 것을 알고 있니?
여: 응, 나는 게시판에 붙은 포스터를 봤어.
남: 나도 봤어. 나와 함께 동아리에 가입할래?
여: 그래. 재밌겠다.
남: 포스터에는 우리가 우리의 라켓을 가져와야 한다고 쓰여 있어. 너는 하나 가지고 있니?
여: 아니, 나는 전에 배드민턴을 쳐본 적이 전혀 없어.
남: 나도 라켓이 없어.
여: 아, 나는 방금 Sierra 거리에 있는 스포츠 용품 가게에서 엄청난 세일을 하고 있다는 게 기억났어.
남: 이제 막 개업한 거기? 잘됐다. 가서 확인해보자.
여: 그래. 우리가 싸게 살 수 있으면 좋겠다.

단·어·및·표·현

look for ~을 찾다
join [dʒɔin] [동] 가입하다
racket [rǽkit] [명] (테니스 등의) 라켓
either [íːðər] [부] (부정문에서) …도 또한 그렇다
goods [gudz] [명] 용품, 상품, 제품
have a sale 세일하다
check ~ out ~을 확인하다, 살펴보다

19 알맞은응답찾기 ▶ 정답 ④

듣·기·대·본

M: Welcome to Sandy's Sandwiches. How may I help you?

W: Can you recommend a vegetarian sandwich for me?

M: How about the mushroom sandwich? It is one of our most popular menu items.

W: Do you have any other vegetarian options?

M: Yes, we have an avocado sandwich that is also quite popular.

W: Sounds good. I'll have that one.

M: Okay. What kind of sauce would you like?

W: Just a little bit of mustard, please.

우·리·말·해·석

① 내 친구들은 항상 배가 고파요.
② 저는 채식주의자를 위한 샌드위치를 먹을 거예요.
③ 그녀는 식재료들을 준비할 수 있어요.
④ 단지 약간의 머스타드만요.
⑤ 저는 약간의 감자 칩을 먹고 싶어요.

남: Sandy's Sandwiches에 오신 것을 환영합니다. 어떻게 도와드릴까요?
여: 저에게 채식주의자를 위한 샌드위치를 추천해주시겠어요?
남: 버섯 샌드위치는 어떠세요? 그것은 저희의 최고 인기 메뉴 품목 중 하나입니다.
여: 다른 채식주의자를 위한 선택이 있나요?
남: 네, 저희는 또한 꽤 인기 있는 아보카도 샌드위치가 있습니다.
여: 좋을 것 같네요. 저는 그것을 먹겠어요.
남: 알겠습니다. 어떤 종류의 소스를 원하세요?
여: 단지 약간의 머스타드만요.

단·어·및·표·현

recommend [rèkəménd] [동] 추천하다
vegetarian [vèdʒitɛ́(:)əriən] [형] 채식주의자의, 채식의

20 상황에적절한말찾기 ▶ 정답 ③

듣·기·대·본

M: David is having a birthday party at home. Allison, one of his friends, gets him a book as a present. There is even a beautiful handwritten message inside. However, when Allison finds the same book already on his shelf, her face falls. David hasn't read the book yet, and he bought it just a few days ago. So, he wants to tell her that he can just return the book he bought. In this situation, what would David most likely say to Allison?

David: Don't worry. I'm going to return the book.

우·리·말·해·석

① 말해줘. 너는 어떻게 그렇게 글을 잘 쓸 수 있어?
② 괜찮아. 나는 이미 그 책을 읽었어.
③ 걱정 마. 나는 그 책을 반품할 거야.
④ 고마워. 나는 모든 곳에서 그것을 찾고 있었어.
⑤ 너는 벌써 하나 갖고 있구나. 그것을 파는 게 어때?

남: David는 집에서 생일 파티를 열고 있다. 그의 친구 중 하나인 Allison이 그에게 선물로 책을 준다. 안에는 아름다운 손글씨 메시지도 있다. 하지만, Allison이 똑같은 책이 이미 그의 책꽂이에 있는 것을 발견했을 때, 그녀의 얼굴이 어두워진다. David는 그 책을 아직 읽지 않았고 그는 그것을 단지 며칠 전에 샀다. 그래서, 그는 그녀에게 그가 산 그 책을 그냥 반품하면 된다고 말하길 원한다. 이런 상황에서 David는 Allison에게 뭐라고 말할 것 같은가?
David: 걱정 마. 나는 그 책을 반품할 거야.

단·어·및·표·현

handwritten [hǽndrìtən] [형] 손으로 쓴
shelf [ʃelf] [명] 책꽂이
fall [fɔːl] [동] (안색이) 어두워지다

Words & Expressions Review

1. 줄무늬가 있는	2. 상대팀	3. 피하다
4. 손으로 쓴	5. (곡식 등을 잘게) 갈다, 빻다	6. 다시 한번 알려주다, 상기시키다
7. 미용실	8. ~을 놓치지 않도록 하다	9. ~쯤, 약
10. 잠시	11. 무료의, 무료인	12. 공연하다, 연주하다
13. (책 · 신문 등의) 한 부	14. 동물 보호소	15. 간주하다, 고려하다
16. 책꽂이	17. 일, 업무	18. (옷 따위를 거는) 고리, 걸이

19. 여러 가지의	20. 채식주의자의, 채식의	21. 사실은, 실제로는
22. 목적	23. 곳곳에	24. 붐비는, 복잡한
25. 취소되다	26. 공사장, 건설 현장	27. 기금을 모으다, 자금을 조달하다
28. 경기장, 들판	29. 보람 있는	30. (여유가 없이) 빠듯한, 빡빡한
31. 상의하다	32. 국지적인	33. 환전하다, 교환하다
34. 용품, 상품, 제품	35. ~을 잘 활용하다	36. 할인을 받다
37. 신용카드	38. 제시간에, 시간 맞춰	39. ~하기 위해
40. 길이	41. ~을 한번 해보다	42. 무늬가 없는, 밋밋한
43. 처리하다, 다루다	44. ~을 찾다	

Listening Test
영어듣기 모의고사 07회

|정|답|

01 ⑤	02 ④	03 ①	04 ④	05 ③
06 ③	07 ⑤	08 ③	09 ②	10 ①
11 ②	12 ②	13 ③	14 ③	15 ⑤
16 ④	17 ③	18 ②	19 ②	20 ④

01 그림정보파악(대화) ▶ 정답 ⑤

듣·기·대·본
M: Hello. What can I do for you?
W: Hi, I'm throwing a Christmas party and I'd like to buy some paper plates.
M: Okay. Here are the samples of what we have in stock. There are square ones and round ones.
W: Oh, I like the round plates. I'll choose from among those ones.
M: Sure. They come in two styles, plain and striped.
W: I like the striped ones more.
M: These ones have the words 'Merry Christmas' printed on them. Would you like to buy them?
W: Yes. That's just what I was looking for. I'll take them.
M: Okay.

우·리·말·해·석
남: 안녕하세요. 무엇을 도와드릴까요?
여: 안녕하세요, 저는 크리스마스 파티를 열 예정이라서 종이 접시를 좀 사고 싶어요.
남: 알겠습니다. 여기 재고가 있는 제품의 샘플들이 있습니다. 네모난 모양과 둥근 모양이 있습니다.
여: 오, 저는 둥근 접시가 좋아요. 저는 그것들 중에서 고를게요.

남: 좋습니다. 그것들은 무늬가 없는 것과 줄무늬가 있는 것, 두 가지 스타일로 나옵니다.
여: 저는 줄무늬가 있는 게 더 좋아요.
남: 이것들은 위에 'Merry Christmas'라는 말이 쓰여 있습니다. 이것들로 구매하시겠습니까?
여: 네. 딱 제가 찾던 거예요. 그것들을 살게요.
남: 알겠습니다.

단·어·및·표·현
throw a party 파티를 열다
have in stock 재고가 있다
plain [plein] 혱 무늬가 없는, 무지의

02 대화미언급 ▶ 정답 ④

듣·기·대·본
M: Do you watch the Heavenly Voice Contest program?
W: Yes. I'm really excited about the finals.
M: Who do you think will win between Daniel and Ella?
W: I'm cheering for Ella, so I hope she wins.
M: Me, too. She'll get a million dollars in prize money if she wins.
W: Right. I hope the judges will be generous with her this time.
M: Yes. They've been a little hard on her.
W: Let's see what happens this week. The program is on Saturday, right?
M: Yes. It's going to be so fun!

우·리·말·해·석
남: 너 '천상의 목소리 경연' 프로그램 보니?
여: 응. 난 결승전에 대해 정말 들떠 있어.
남: 넌 Daniel과 Ella 중에서 누가 우승할 거라고 생각하니?
여: 나는 Ella를 응원하고 있어서 그녀가 이기길 바라.
남: 나도 그래. 그녀는 우승하면 상금으로 백만 달러를 받게 될 거야.
여: 맞아. 이번에는 심사위원들이 그녀에게 너그럽길 바라.
남: 그래. 그들이 그녀에게 조금 심하게 대했어.
여: 이번 주에 어떻게 되나 보자. 그 프로그램은 토요일에 방영하지, 맞지?
남: 응. 그건 아주 재미있을 거야!

단·어·및·표·현
be excited about ~에 대해 들뜨다, 흥분하다
final [fáinəl] 혱 결승전
cheer for ~를 응원하다
be hard on ~에게 심하게 대하다

03 전화목적파악 ▶ 정답 ①

듣·기·대·본
(Telephone rings.)
M: Hello. This is City Outfitter.
W: Hello. I was at your shop this morning and I think I left my purse there.
M: Your purse? We do not have any purses in our lost and found.
W: Oh, no! Could you check the fitting room? I think I left it there.
M: One moment, please. (Pause) Is it a purple purse with a dog keychain on it?
W: Yes! That's mine!

M: We will <u>hold on to it</u> for you.
W: Thank you so much! I will be there soon!

우·리·말·해·석

(전화벨이 울린다.)
남: 여보세요. City Outfitter입니다.
여: 안녕하세요. 저는 오늘 아침에 당신의 가게에 갔는데, 제 지갑을 거기에 두고 온 것 같아요.
남: 지갑이요? 저희 분실물 보관소에는 어떤 지갑도 없어요.
여: 아, 안돼요! 탈의실을 확인해주실 수 있나요? 저는 거기에 두고 온 것 같아요.
남: 잠시만 기다려주세요. (잠시 후) 강아지 열쇠고리가 달린 보라색 지갑인가요?
여: 네! 제 거예요!
남: 저희가 당신을 위해 그것을 보관하고 있을게요.
여: 정말 감사해요! 곧 갈게요!

단·어·및·표·현

lost and found 분실물 보관소
hold on to ~ (남을 위해) ~을 보관하다, 맡아주다

04 수치파악(시각) ▶ 정답 ④

듣·기·대·본

[Cellphone rings.]
W: Good morning, Dad.
M: Hi, Jane. I <u>can't wait to</u> see you. When is your arrival time?
W: It was supposed to be 1 p.m., but the flight <u>has been delayed</u> due to a mechanical problem.
M: I'm sorry to hear that. Let me know what time to <u>pick you up</u>.
W: The flight attendant says the arrival time may be 3 p.m.
M: Okay. I'll wait for you in front of the <u>international arrivals</u> gate.
W: I need to find my luggage, so it will take me <u>about an hour</u>.
M: OK. Then, let's meet at 4 p.m.
W: Sure, Dad. I'll text you the flight number so you can find the gate number.

우·리·말·해·석

[휴대전화가 울린다.]
여: 좋은 아침이에요, 아빠.
남: 안녕, Jane. 나는 네가 빨리 보고 싶구나. 너의 도착 시간은 언제니?
여: 오후 1시로 되어 있었는데 비행기가 기계적인 문제 때문에 지연됐어요.
남: 그거 참 안됐구나. 몇 시에 차로 널 데리러 갈지 나에게 알려주렴.
여: 승무원은 도착 시간이 오후 3시일 거라고 해요.
남: 알았다. 나는 국제선 도착 게이트 앞에서 너를 기다리마.
여: 저는 제 수하물을 찾아야 해서, 약 한 시간 정도 걸릴 거예요.
남: 알았어. 그러면, 오후 4시에 만나자.
여: 네, 아빠. 아빠가 게이트 번호를 찾을 수 있도록 제가 항공편 번호를 문자로 보내드릴게요.

단·어·및·표·현

can't wait to + 동사원형 얼른 ~하고 싶다, ~가 기대되어 기다릴 수 없다
be supposed to + 동사원형 ~하기로 되어 있다
delay [diléi] ⑧ 지연시키다, 지체하게 하다
mechanical [məkǽnikəl] ⑧ 기계적인

flight attendant 승무원
international arrivals gate 국제선 도착 게이트

05 심정추론 ▶ 정답 ③

듣·기·대·본

W: David, why do you look so down?
M: I <u>yelled at</u> my little brother this morning. He cried a lot.
W: What happened?
M: He broke my old toy and I <u>got angry at</u> him.
W: Hmm, that can happen.
M: He's only five years old, and I was <u>too hard on him</u>.
W: Did you try to talk to him after that?
M: I tried, but he's still so down. <u>I shouldn't have yelled at him like that.</u>

우·리·말·해·석

① 신나는 ② 기쁜 ③ 후회하는 ④ 지루해 하는 ⑤ 질투하는

여: David, 너 왜 그렇게 우울해 보여?
남: 나는 오늘 아침에 내 남동생에게 소리를 질렀거든. 그가 많이 울었어.
여: 무슨 일 있었어?
남: 그가 내 오래된 장난감을 망가트려서 나는 그에게 화가 났어.
여: 흠, 그럴 수도 있지.
남: 그는 겨우 다섯 살인데, 내가 그에게 너무 심했어.
여: 너는 그 이후에 그와 대화하려 해 봤니?
남: 시도는 했지만, 그는 아직 우울해. 나는 그에게 그렇게 소리를 질러선 안 됐어.

단·어·및·표·현

pleased [pliːzd] ⑧ 기쁜, 만족해하는
regretful [rigrétfəl] ⑧ 후회하는
jealous [dʒéləs] ⑧ 질투하는, 시기하는

06 그림상황에적절한대화찾기 ▶ 정답 ③

듣·기·대·본

① W: May I <u>take your order</u>?
　 M: Yes, I'd like a vanilla latte, please.
② W: Hi, I'm here to interview for the part-time job.
　 M: Oh, I'll be with you in a moment.
③ W: <u>Excuse me, where can I find a straw?</u>
　 M: <u>Disposable</u> plastics <u>are banned</u> from cafés.
④ W: I think you got my order wrong.
　 M: I'm very sorry. I'll make your drinks again right away.
⑤ W: I'm sorry, but can I have these <u>drinks to go</u>?
　 M: Sure! No problem.

우·리·말·해·석

① 여: 주문하시겠습니까?
　 남: 네, 바닐라 라떼 한 잔 주세요.
② 여: 안녕하세요, 저는 아르바이트 면접을 보기 위해 여기 왔어요.
　 남: 오, 금방 가겠습니다.
③ 여: 실례합니다, 빨대는 어디서 찾을 수 있나요?
　 남: 카페에서 일회용 플라스틱은 사용이 금지되어 있습니다.
④ 여: 당신은 제 주문을 잘못 받은 것 같아요.
　 남: 정말 죄송합니다. 제가 바로 손님의 음료를 다시 만들어 드리겠습니다.
⑤ 여: 죄송하지만, 이 음료들을 포장해 주실 수 있나요?
　 남: 물론이죠! 문제없습니다.

take an order 주문을 받다
straw [strɔː] 똉 빨대
disposable [dispóuzəbl] 똉 일회용의
ban [bɑːn] 똉 금지하다
to go (음식을 식당에서 먹지 않고) 포장해 갈, 가지고 갈

07 부탁(요청)한일파악　▶ 정답 ⑤

듣·기·대·본

W: Pete, are you ready to <u>leave for our vacation</u> tomorrow?
M: I'm all set, but I have one problem.
W: The bus? Don't worry. I already bought the tickets.
M: No. It's the meeting I have tomorrow. It ends at five.
W: The bus leaves at six, so we <u>won't miss it</u>.
M: OK, then. But can you buy me a sandwich? I won't have time to buy anything before we <u>get on the bus</u>.
W: No problem.

우·리·말·해·석

여: Pete, 내일 휴가 갈 준비 됐니?
남: 준비 다 됐는데, 한 가지 문제가 있어.
여: 버스 말이야? 걱정하지 마. 내가 이미 표를 샀어.
남: 아니. 내일 있는 회의 말이야. 5시에 끝나.
여: 버스가 6시에 떠나니까, 놓치지 않을 거야.
남: 좋아, 그럼. 하지만 샌드위치 좀 사줄래? 나는 버스 타기 전에 뭘 살 시간이 없을 거야.
여: 문제없어.

단·어·및·표·현

get on ~ ~에 타다

🦻 **LISTENING ADVICE**

단어 가운데에 있는 [d]나 [t] 소리는 약화되어 발음되거나 탈락될 때가 많습니다. 따라서 'sandwich'는 [샌드위치]라고 발음되기보다는 [샌위치]에 가깝게 발음됩니다. [d] 소리의 탈락에 유의하며 다시 한 번 들어보고 발음해보세요.

---

08 담화미언급　▶ 정답 ③

듣·기·대·본

W: Hello, class. Today we'll learn about Ben Hicks, the famous space scientist. He was <u>born in Seattle in 1969</u>. He <u>grew up</u> in a poor family. But he found hope and joy in math and science. He <u>worked his way through</u> school and up to scholarships. He studied space science in college and started working at NASA. When he was 27, he became the youngest winner of the National Science Award. Since then, he has made many discoveries that <u>have helped advance</u> space travel.

우·리·말·해·석

여: 안녕하세요, 여러분. 오늘 우리는 유명한 우주 과학자인 Ben Hicks에 대해 배울 겁니다. 그는 1969년에 시애틀에서 태어났습니다. 그는 가난한 가정에서 자랐습니다. 하지만 그는 수학과 과학에서 희망과 기쁨을 찾았습니다. 그는 학교생활을 열심히 하며 장학금까지 탔습니다. 그는 대학에서 우주과학을 공부했고 NASA에서 일하기 시작했습니다. 그가 27살이었을 때, 그는 국가과학상 최연소 수상자가 되었습니다. 그때부터, 그는 우주여행 발전에 도움을 준 많은 발견을 해 왔습니다.

---

work one's way through 열심히 ~을 해 나가다, 고생하며 ~을 하다
scholarship [skάlərʃip] 똉 장학금
NASA 미합중국 항공우주국(National Aeronautics and Space Administration)
discovery [diskʌ́vəri] 똉 발견
advance [ədvǽns] 똉 발전, 진전

09 담화화제추론　▶ 정답 ②

듣·기·대·본

M: It is one of the most popular types of <u>electronic equipment</u>. The screen is located on the inside of the upper lid and the keyboard is on the inside of the lower lid. Sometimes the screens are <u>touchable</u>. It folds shut for transportation and it is <u>suitable for</u> mobile use. It can be used for many different purposes from gaming to writing a report. Its name originated from the fact that it can be placed on a person's lap when being used.

우·리·말·해·석

남: 그것은 가장 인기 있는 종류의 전자기기 중 하나입니다. 화면은 위쪽 덮개의 안쪽에 위치해 있고 키보드는 아래쪽 덮개의 안쪽에 있습니다. 때때로 화면은 터치가 가능합니다. 그것은 이동을 위해 접어서 닫게 되어 있고, 이동식 사용에 적합합니다. 그것은 게임에서 보고서 작성까지 많은 다양한 목적으로 사용될 수 있습니다. 그것의 이름은 그것이 사용될 때 사람의 무릎 위에 놓일 수 있다는 사실에서 유래됐습니다.

단·어·및·표·현

electronic equipment 전자기기
locate [lóukeit] 똉 위치해 있다
transportation [trænspərtéiʃən] 똉 이동, 운반
be suitable for ~에 적합하다
mobile [móubəl] 똉 이동식의, 이동하는
originate from ~에서 유래되다
lap [læp] 똉 무릎

10 어색한대화찾기　▶ 정답 ①

듣·기·대·본

① M: Do you know what this means?
　 W: Yes, I've <u>been there</u> once.
② M: Do you know who he is?
　 W: I have no idea.
③ M: Can you <u>teach me</u> how to drive a car?
　 W: I'm sorry, but I have no time.
④ M: Why do you think he's rude?
　 W: He talks <u>too loud</u> in the classroom.
⑤ M: Are you okay?
　 W: Sure. Don't worry.

우·리·말·해·석

① 남: 이게 무슨 뜻인지 아니?
　 여: 응, 나 거기 한 번 가본 적 있어.
② 남: 그가 누군지 알아?
　 여: 전혀 모르겠는데.
③ 남: 운전하는 법을 나에게 가르쳐 줄 수 있니?
　 여: 미안하지만, 난 시간이 없어.
④ 남: 왜 그가 무례하다고 생각하니?

여: 그는 교실에서 너무 큰 소리로 말해.
⑤ 남: 너 괜찮니?
　　여: 그럼. 걱정 마.

단·어·및·표·현
rude [ruːd] ⑧ 무례한

11 할일파악(대화직후)　　▶ 정답 ②

듣·기·대·본

M: Mom, I'm going to the park, now.
W: You mean now? We're supposed to pick up your dad at the airport at 4 o'clock, remember?
M: Is it today? I thought it was tomorrow.
W: Your dad is coming today. Sweetie, I told you yesterday at dinner.
M: At dinner? Oh, you're right. But, I'm supposed to play soccer with Brian at 3 o'clock today.
W: I think you'd better cancel that. Why don't you play soccer on the weekend?
M: Okay. I'll call him right away and tell him I can't play today.

우·리·말·해·석

남: 엄마, 저 지금 공원에 가요.
여: 지금 말이니? 우리 4시에 공항에 아빠 모시러 가기로 했잖아, 기억나니?
남: 그게 오늘이에요? 전 내일인 줄 알았어요.
여: 네 아빠는 오늘 오셔. 얘야, 내가 어제 저녁 먹을 때 이야기했잖니.
남: 저녁 먹을 때요? 아, 엄마 말이 맞아요. 그런데 전 오늘 3시에 Brian이랑 축구 하기로 했어요.
여: 내 생각에 네가 그것을 취소하는 것이 좋겠구나. 주말에 축구를 하지 그러니?
남: 알았어요. 지금 즉시 전화해서 오늘 (축구를) 못한다고 그 아이에게 이야기할게요.

단·어·및·표·현
be supposed to + 동사원형 ~하기로 되어 있다

12 도표정보파악　　▶ 정답 ②

듣·기·대·본

M: Honey, are you going to buy something online?
W: Yes, I'm looking for some hand soap. We're almost out of it.
M: OK, let's check together. I don't think we should spend more than $15.
W: I agree. I don't want to spend too much on hand soap.
M: Right. How about the fragrance?
W: Anything but vanilla. We've used vanilla for a long time.
M: Okay. Then, we have two options left.
W: How about getting foam soap? I prefer foam to liquid.
M: Me, too. Let's order it.

우·리·말·해·석

	제품	가격	향	유형
①	A	8달러	바닐라	액체
②	B	10달러	라벤더	거품
③	C	12달러	라벤더	액체
④	D	14달러	바닐라	거품
⑤	E	16달러	라벤더	액체

남: 여보, 당신은 온라인으로 무언가를 사려고 하나요?
여: 네, 저는 손 세정제를 좀 찾고 있어요. 우리는 그것을 거의 다 썼어요.
남: 알겠어요. 같이 확인해 보죠. 제 생각에 우리는 15달러보다 많이 쓰면 안 돼요.
여: 동의해요. 저도 손 세정제에 돈을 너무 많이 쓰고 싶지 않아요.
남: 맞아요. 향은 어떻게 할까요?
여: 바닐라만 아니면 돼요. 우리는 너무 오랫동안 바닐라 향을 사용해왔어요.
남: 알겠어요. 그러면, 우리는 두 개의 선택지가 남았군요.
여: 거품 비누를 사는 것은 어때요? 저는 액상보다 거품을 더 선호해요.
남: 저도요. 그걸로 주문하죠.

단·어·및·표·현
be out of ~ ~을 다 써서 없다, ~이 떨어지다
fragrance [fréigrəns] ⑧ 향, 향기
anything but ~이 결코 아닌
foam [foum] ⑧ 거품
prefer A to B B보다 A를 선호하다

13 수치파악(날짜)　　▶ 정답 ③

듣·기·대·본

W: Hi, Max! What are you up to?
M: Hey, Christine! I'm just checking out some event listings online. There's a music festival in the park next weekend.
W: Oh, that sounds like fun! When is it?
M: It's taking place from July 20th to July 24th.
W: Nice! We should definitely go together. How about July 21st?
M: July 21st sounds good, but I have a family gathering that day. How about July 22nd?
W: July 22nd works for me. Let's mark it on our calendars!
M: Okay. See you then.

우·리·말·해·석

여: 안녕, Max! 뭘 하고 있니?
남: 안녕, Christine! 지금 온라인에서 몇몇 이벤트 목록을 확인하고 있는 중이야. 다음 주말에 공원에서 음악 축제가 있어.
여: 오, 그거 재미있겠다! 그게 언제야?
남: 7월 20일부터 7월 24일까지 열려.
여: 좋은데! 우린 꼭 같이 가야 해. 7월 21일은 어때?
남: 7월 21일이 좋을 것 같은데, 하지만 난 그날 가족 모임이 있어. 7월 22일은 어때?
여: 7월 22일 좋아. 우리 달력에 표시해 두자!
남: 알았어. 그때 보자.

단·어·및·표·현
take place (준비되거나 계획된 일이) 개최되다, 열리다
definitely [défənitli] ⑨ 꼭, 분명히, 절대로
family gathering 가족 모임

14 한일파악　　▶ 정답 ③

듣·기·대·본

M: Where were you last week?
W: My whole family celebrated Chuseok in Daegu, which is my father's hometown. There were a lot of special events for Chuseok.
M: Sounds like you had fun. Did you join any events?

W: No, we didn't. We <u>were also supposed to</u> watch a dance, but it was cancelled because of the bad weather.

M: Oh, that's too bad.

W: It was okay. <u>I played games with</u> my cousins instead.

우·리·말·해·석

남: 지난주에 어디에 있었어?

여: 우리 가족 모두가 아빠 고향인 대구에서 추석을 보냈어. 많은 특별한 추석 행사가 있었어.

남: 네가 즐거운 시간을 보낸 거 같네. 참여한 행사가 있었니?

여: 아니, 그러지 못했어. 우리는 무용도 관람하기로 되어 있었는데, 날씨가 안 좋아서 취소됐어.

남: 오, 그거 참 안됐다.

여: 괜찮아. 대신 난 사촌들과 게임을 했어.

단·어·및·표·현

hometown [hóumtàun] 명 고향

because of ~ ~때문에

15 담화목적파악　▶ 정답 ⑤

듣·기·대·본

W: Good afternoon, students. The weather is getting warmer every day, and a lot of you are <u>spending time outdoors</u>. Getting fresh air is good for you and for your studies. However, it seems that many of you are enjoying your time outside while wearing your indoor shoes. This isn't <u>hygienic</u>, since your shoes bring all the dust and dirt from outside into your classrooms. Next time when you head outdoors, please <u>change your shoes</u>. You can protect everybody's health by doing so. Thank you.

우·리·말·해·석

여: 좋은 오후입니다, 학생 여러분. 날씨가 매일 점점 따뜻해지고 있고, 여러분 중 많은 사람은 밖에서 시간을 보내고 있습니다. 신선한 공기를 쐬는 것은 여러분과 여러분의 학업을 위해 좋습니다. 하지만, 여러분 중 많은 사람이 실내화를 신은 채 밖에서 즐겁게 시간을 보내고 있는 것 같습니다. 이것은 위생적이지 않은데요, 여러분의 신발이 외부의 모든 먼지를 여러분의 교실 안으로 가져오기 때문입니다. 다음번에 여러분이 밖에 나갈 때는 신발을 갈아 신기 바랍니다. 여러분은 그렇게 함으로써 모든 사람의 건강을 지킬 수 있습니다. 감사합니다.

단·어·및·표·현

outdoors [àutdɔ́ːrz] 부 야외에서

indoor [índɔ̀ːr] 형 실내의, 실내용의

hygienic [hàidʒiénik] 형 위생적인, 청결한

dust and dirt 먼지

protect [prətékt] 동 보호하다, 지키다

16 수치계산(금액)　▶ 정답 ④

듣·기·대·본

M: Welcome to Happy Mart.

W: Hi, I'm looking to buy some strawberries.

M: We have <u>two varieties available</u>: organic strawberries and locally grown strawberries. The organic ones are slightly larger <u>in size</u>.

W: How much are they?

M: A pound of organic strawberries is $5, while the locally grown ones are $4 per pound.

W: I'll take the organic strawberries.

M: Great choice! We also have a <u>special promotion</u>. If you buy three pounds of strawberries, you get one more pound <u>for free</u>.

W: Wonderful! I'll take three pounds of organic strawberries, then.

M: Here they are.

W: Thank you! I'll pay with cash.

우·리·말·해·석

남: Happy Mart에 오신 것을 환영합니다.

여: 안녕하세요, 저는 딸기를 좀 사려고 합니다.

남: 유기농 딸기와 현지에서 재배된 딸기, 두 가지 종류가 있습니다. 유기농 제품은 크기가 약간 더 큽니다.

여: 그것들은 얼마인가요?

남: 유기농 딸기 1파운드는 5달러인 반면, 현지에서 재배된 딸기는 파운드당 4달러입니다.

여: 유기농 딸기로 하겠습니다.

남: 훌륭한 선택이군요! 저희는 특별 프로모션도 있습니다. 만약 딸기 3파운드를 사시면 1파운드를 무료로 더 받으실 수 있습니다.

여: 정말 멋지네요! 그럼 유기농 딸기 3파운드를 사겠습니다.

남: 여기 있습니다.

여: 감사합니다! 현금으로 지불하겠습니다.

단·어·및·표·현

variety [vəráiəti] 명 종류

organic [ɔːrgǽnik] 형 유기농의

locally grown 현지에서 기른

17 알맞은응답찾기　▶ 정답 ③

듣·기·대·본

W: Hey, how was your trip over the weekend?

M: It was terrible. We <u>had a flat tire</u> on the way.

W: Oh, dear. So, what happened?

M: It was the <u>middle of the night</u> when we arrived.

W: You got to the hotel, anyway.

M: Yeah, but they <u>mixed up</u> our booking, and we had no room.

W: What?

M: So, we <u>borrowed a tent</u>, and the next morning it rained.

W: I'm so sorry to hear that.

M: Yeah, when it rains, it pours.

우·리·말·해·석

① 글쎄, 서두르면 일을 망쳐.　② 고생을 해야 얻는 게 있지.

③ 응, 안 좋은 일은 한꺼번에 닥치지.　④ 뭉치면 산다고 배웠어.

⑤ 아, 음, 돌다리도 두드려 보고 건너야지.

여: 안녕, 주말 동안 여행 어땠어?

남: 끔찍했어. 가는 도중에 타이어가 터지고 말았어.

여: 오, 저런. 그래서 어떻게 됐어?

남: 우리가 도착했을 때는 한밤중이었어.

여: 어쨌든 호텔에 도착했구나.

남: 응, 하지만 호텔에서 예약을 혼동해서, 우리는 방이 없었어.

여: 뭐라고?

남: 그래서, 우리는 텐트를 빌렸는데, 다음날 아침에 비가 왔어.

여: 정말 안됐다.

남: 응, 안 좋은 일은 한꺼번에 닥치지.

단·어·및·표·현

mix up ~ ~을 혼동하다, ~을 뒤섞다

borrow [bárou] 동 빌리다

18 알맞은응답찾기 ▶ 정답 ②

듣·기·대·본

W: Zack, what's that sound? I think it's coming from your phone.

M: Oh, it's my new app. It reminds me to drink water every two hours.

W: I heard that drinking plenty of water has a lot of health benefits.

M: That's right. It increases your energy and regulates body temperature.

W: I tried to do that before, but it wasn't easy.

M: It wasn't easy for me, either. That's why I've installed this app.

W: It sounds really useful.

M: It also sends you messages like "You must be thirsty by now."

W: That's really interesting.

M: You should try it out.

W: Good idea. I will download it right away.

우·리·말·해·석

① 알겠어. 물에 얼음을 많이 넣어줘.

② 좋은 생각이야. 바로 다운로드 받을게.

③ 나는 그것이 내 기운을 북돋우는 데 도움이 될 거라고 생각하지 않아.

④ 아닐 수도 있어. 나는 내 휴대폰을 너무 자주 사용해서는 안 돼.

⑤ 조언해 줘서 고마워. 내가 전화해서 예약할게.

여: Zack, 그거 무슨 소리야? 네 휴대폰에서 나는 것 같아.

남: 아, 그건 내 새로운 앱이야. 그것은 2시간마다 나에게 물을 마시라고 상기시켜 줘.

여: 나는 물을 많이 마시는 것이 건강에 많은 이점이 있다고 들었어.

남: 맞아. 그것은 에너지를 증가시키고 체온을 조절해줘.

여: 나는 전에 그렇게 해보려고 했지만 쉽지 않았어.

남: 나도 쉽지 않았어. 그게 내가 이 앱을 설치한 이유야.

여: 정말 유용할 것 같아.

남: 그것은 또한 "당신은 지금쯤 목이 마를 거예요."와 같은 메시지도 보내.

여: 정말 흥미롭네.

남: 너도 한번 해봐.

여: **좋은 생각이야. 바로 다운로드 받을게.**

단·어·및·표·현

remind [rimáind] 동 상기시키다, 생각나게 하다

plenty of 많은

benefit [bénəfit] 명 이점, 이득

regulate [régjəlèit] 동 조절하다, 조정하다

install [instɔ́:l] 동 설치하다

try ~ out (성능·효력을 알아보기 위해) ~을 한번 해보다

19 알맞은응답찾기 ▶ 정답 ②

듣·기·대·본

(*Cellphone rings.*)

W: Charlie? What's up?

M: Hey, Abigail. I'm at the shop. You wanted a chicken salad for lunch, right?

W: Yes. Is there a problem?

M: They ran out of chicken. Can I get you any other salad?

W: Sure. What do they have?

M: They have tuna, salmon, and egg.

W: Hmm, I'm allergic to salmon. Other than that, I'm fine with anything.

M: All right. I've picked up mine along with a tuna salad for you. I'll be there as soon as I can.

W: Thanks. I appreciate you taking care of it.

우·리·말·해·석

① 물론이지. 연어에는 건강한 지방이 들어있어.

② 고마워. 네가 그걸 처리해줘서 고맙게 생각해.

③ 맞아. 그 음식은 저녁 식사용이니까 서두르지 마.

④ 잠깐만. 그들이 잘못된 배송 주소를 갖고 있는 것 같아.

⑤ 아니. 닭고기를 먼저 요리하고 샐러드는 잊어버려.

(휴대폰이 울린다.)

여: Charlie? 무슨 일이야?

남: 안녕, Abigail. 나는 가게에 있어. 너는 점심으로 치킨 샐러드를 원했지, 그렇지?

여: 응. 무슨 문제가 있어?

남: 그들은 닭고기가 떨어졌어. 내가 뭔가 다른 샐러드를 사다 줘도 될까?

여: 물론이지. 그들은 무엇을 가지고 있어?

남: 그들은 참치, 연어, 달걀이 있어.

여: 음, 난 연어에 알레르기가 있어. 그 외에는 뭐든 괜찮아.

남: 알겠어. 나는 너를 위한 참치 샐러드와 함께 내 것을 골랐어. 최대한 빨리 거기에 갈게.

여: **고마워. 네가 그걸 처리해줘서 고맙게 생각해.**

단·어·및·표·현

run out of ~이 떨어지다(바닥나다), 소진되다

allergic [əlɔ́:rdʒik] 형 알레르기가 있는

contain [kəntéin] 동 ~이 들어[함유되어] 있다

20 상황에적절한말찾기 ▶ 정답 ④

듣·기·대·본

W: Peter and Jenna are studying at the study café. After a few hours, Peter starts to feel sleepy. He tries drinking cold water and doing some stretches to shake off his sleepiness, but he keeps falling asleep. Peter can't concentrate on his studies. He thinks it would be better if he took a nap for a few minutes. So, he wants to ask Jenna to wake him up after five minutes. In this situation, what would Peter most likely say to Jenna?

Peter: Can you wake me up after five minutes?

우·리·말·해·석

① 나는 가서 물을 좀 사야 해.

② 너는 너무 오랫동안 가만히 앉아있지 않는 게 좋아.

③ 너는 나랑 산책 가기를 원해?

④ 5분 뒤에 나를 깨워줄 수 있어?

⑤ 너는 여기서 먹고 마시는 것이 허용되지 않아.

여: Peter와 Jenna는 스터디 카페에서 공부를 하고 있다. 몇 시간 후에, Peter는 졸리다고 느끼기 시작한다. 그는 졸음을 떨쳐내기 위해 찬물

을 마시고 스트레칭을 좀 해보지만 계속 잠이 든다. Peter는 그의 공부에 집중할 수가 없다. 그는 몇 분 동안 낮잠을 잔다면 더 좋을 것이라고 생각한다. 그래서, 그는 Jenna에게 5분 뒤에 그를 깨워달라고 부탁하고 싶다. 이런 상황에서 Peter는 Jenna에게 뭐라고 말할 것 같은가?

Peter: 5분 뒤에 나를 깨워줄 수 있어?

단·어·및·표·현

sleepy [slíːpi] ⑱ 졸린
shake off 떨쳐내다
take a nap 낮잠 자다

Words & Expressions Review

1. 야외에서	2. 꼭, 분명히, 절대로	3. 바람 빠진 타이어
4. 무례한	5. 고향	6. ~이 들어[함유되어] 있다
7. 주문을 받다	8. 후회하는	9. 현지에서 기른
10. (준비되거나 계획된 일이) 개최되다, 열리다	11. 발견	12. 낮잠 자다
13. ~에 타다	14. 무늬가 없는, 무지의	15. 위생적인, 청결한
16. 표시하다, 기록하다	17. ~을 다 써서 없다, ~이 떨어지다	18. 승무원
19. 알레르기가 있는	20. ~를 응원하다	21. 기쁜
22. 종류	23. 장학금	24. 상기시키다, 생각나게 하다
25. 가족 모임	26. ~에 적합하다	27. 설치하다
28. 실내의, 실내용의	29. 준비가 다 되다	30. 유기농의
31. 일회용의	32. 조절하다, 조정하다	33. ~을 혼동하다
34. 예약	35. 향, 향기	36. 이동식의, 이동하는
37. ~이 결코 아닌	38. 심사위원, 심판	39. ~하기로 되어 있다
40. 이동, 운반	41. 무릎	42. 기계적인
43. 많은	44. 집중하다	

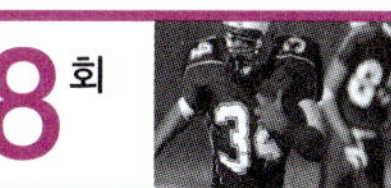

Listening Test
영어듣기 모의고사 08회

|정|답|

01	④	02	④	03	⑤	04	③	05	⑤
06	③	07	⑤	08	④	09	①	10	④
11	③	12	①	13	④	14	⑤	15	④
16	④	17	①	18	②	19	②	20	③

01   그림정보파악(대화)　　　▶ 정답 ④

듣·기·대·본

M: What can I do for you?
W: I can't decide on which one to buy. Every frame is so pretty and unique.

M: This oval shaped frame <u>with heart decorations</u> is very popular in our store.
W: It's pretty, but I have an oval frame <u>at home</u>. I want to try a rectangular frame this time.
M: Then how about this one with the stars?
W: <u>Its design</u> is too retro. I like this rectangular frame <u>with flowers.</u>
M: That's a good one, too. It <u>goes well</u> with classic furniture.
W: I think so, too. I'll take it.

우·리·말·해·석

남: 무엇을 도와드릴까요?
여: 전 어떤 것을 살지 결정하지 못하겠어요. 모든 액자가 너무 예쁘고 독특하네요.
남: 여기 하트 장식이 있는 타원형 액자가 저희 가게에서 아주 인기가 있어요.
여: 그것은 예쁘기는 한데 전 집에 타원형 액자가 있어요. 전 이번에는 직사각형 액자를 시도해보고 싶네요.
남: 그럼 별 장식이 있는 이것은 어떻습니까?
여: 그 디자인은 너무 복고풍이에요. 전 꽃 장식이 있는 이 직사각형 액자가 마음에 드네요.
남: 그것도 좋은 상품이에요. 그것은 고전적인 가구와 잘 어울려요.
여: 저도 그렇게 생각해요. 전 이것으로 할게요.

단·어·및·표·현

rectangular [rektǽŋgjulər] ⑱ 직사각형의

02   대화미언급　　　▶ 정답 ④

듣·기·대·본

W: Hi, I'd like to sign up for a personal training program.
M: Welcome. Let me help you with that. What's the purpose of your exercise?
W: <u>I want to lose some weight and get in shape.</u>
M: Okay. Do you have a specific weight goal in mind?
W: Well, <u>I want to weigh less than</u> 55 kg.
M: And how quickly do you want to achieve your goal?
W: <u>I hope I can get there within three to four months.</u>
M: Alright. Now let's talk about diet. Are you <u>controlling your nutrition</u>?
W: No, I'd like some help with that.
M: Okay, then. Let's check your <u>fitness level</u> and go over some more details.

우·리·말·해·석

여: 안녕하세요, 저는 개인 훈련(PT) 프로그램에 등록하고 싶습니다.
남: 어서 오세요. 제가 도와드리겠습니다. 당신의 운동 목적은 무엇인가요?
여: 저는 체중을 감량하고 몸매를 가꾸고 싶어요.
남: 알겠습니다. 생각해 둔 구체적인 목표 체중이 있으신가요?
여: 음, 저는 55kg보다 체중이 덜 나가길 원해요.
남: 그러면 목표를 얼마나 빨리 달성하길 원하시나요?
여: 저는 3~4개월 내에 거기에 도달할 수 있으면 좋겠어요.
남: 알겠습니다. 이제 식단에 대해 이야기해 봅시다. 당신은 영양 섭취를 조절하고 있나요?
여: 아니요, 그것에 대해 도움을 좀 원해요.
남: 알겠습니다. 당신의 체력 수준을 확인하고 좀 더 자세한 내용들을 살펴봅시다.

단·어·및·표·현

get in shape 몸매를 가꾸다, 몸을 단련하다
specific [spisífik] ⓗ 구체적인
weigh [wei] ⓥ 체중[무게]이 ~이다
diet [dáiət] ⓝ 식단, 식습관
nutrition [njuːtríʃən] ⓝ 영양 섭취
fitness [fítnis] ⓝ 체력, 건강
go over ~을 살펴보다, 점검하다

03 전화목적파악 ▶ 정답 ⑤

듣·기·대·본

[*Telephone rings.*]
M: Hello, this is Comfy Wear Company.
W: Hello, I ordered some pajamas online. Your website says they were delivered, but I never got them.
M: Really? Do you have your order number?
W: Yes, I have it here. It's PJ469.
M: [*Typing sound*] Oh, the package seems to be missing. We're very sorry. Would you like a refund or reshipping?
W: Please send them again.
M: Okay. We'll send your pajamas as soon as possible. We'll also send you a 30 percent discount coupon for a future order. We apologize again for the inconvenience.
W: That's okay. Thanks for the coupon.

우·리·말·해·석

[전화벨이 울린다.]
남: 안녕하세요, Comfy Wear 회사입니다.
여: 안녕하세요, 저는 온라인으로 잠옷을 좀 주문했어요. 당신의 웹사이트는 그것들이 배송되었다고 하는데, 저는 그것들을 받지 못했어요.
남: 정말요? 고객님의 주문번호를 갖고 계시나요?
여: 네, 여기 그것을 갖고 있어요. 그것은 PJ469예요.
남: [키보드 치는 소리] 오, 그 택배물은 분실된 것으로 보여요. 정말 죄송합니다. 환불해드릴까요, 아니면 재배송해드릴까요?
여: 그것들을 다시 보내주세요.
남: 알겠습니다. 저희는 고객님의 잠옷을 가능한 한 빨리 보내드리겠습니다. 저희는 또한 향후의 주문을 위한 30퍼센트 할인 쿠폰도 보내드리겠습니다. 불편을 끼친 점 다시 한번 사과드립니다.
여: 괜찮아요. 쿠폰 감사합니다.

단·어·및·표·현

pajamas [pədʒɑ́ːməz] ⓝ (바지와 상의로 된) 잠옷
seem to be + -ing ~한 것처럼 보이다
reship [riːʃíp] ⓥ 재배송하다, 재선적하다
inconvenience [ìnkənvíːnjəns] ⓝ 불편, 애로

04 수치파악(시각) ▶ 정답 ③

듣·기·대·본

M: Mina, did you hear that professor Kim's retirement ceremony will be held on Saturday afternoon?
W: Yes, I did. I'll definitely be there. I think that he is the best professor on campus.
M: I think so, too. How about we go together?
W: Sounds great! Do you know when the ceremony starts?
M: It starts at 5 p.m. When shall we meet?
W: It'll be held in the campus auditorium. So, how about at the main gate at 3 p.m.?
M: I think that's too early. What about 4 p.m.?
W: That's better. See you then.

우·리·말·해·석

남: Mina, 너는 토요일 오후에 김 교수님의 퇴임식이 열린다는 걸 들었어?
여: 응, 들었어. 나는 꼭 거기에 갈 거야. 나는 그가 교내에서 최고의 교수님이라고 생각해.
남: 나도 그렇게 생각해. 우리 같이 가는 게 어때?
여: 좋아! 너는 언제 그 퇴임식이 시작하는지 알아?
남: 오후 5시에 시작해. 우리 언제 만날까?
여: 그건 캠퍼스 강당에서 열릴 거야. 그러니까 오후 3시에 정문에서 보는 건 어때?
남: 그건 너무 이른 것 같아. 오후 4시 어때?
여: 그게 더 낫네. 그때 보자.

단·어·및·표·현

professor [prəfésər] ⓝ 교수
retirement ceremony 퇴임식
be held 열리다, 개최되다
on campus 교내에서, 대학에서
auditorium [ɔ̀ːditɔ́ːriəm] ⓝ 강당

05 심정추론 ▶ 정답 ⑤

듣·기·대·본

W: Josh, are you okay? You look pale.
M: What should I do? I can't enter the contest now.
W: The video contest? Why? What's wrong?
M: When I finished editing the video, my computer crashed.
W: Oh, no. Did you save the file?
M: I'm sure I did.
W: Then you'll be fine. The deadline for the contest is tomorrow.
M: Yeah, but the service center can't fix my computer until tomorrow.
W: Are you sure? Is there any way you can retrieve the file?
M: No. I don't know what to do. All my weeks of work are useless now.

우·리·말·해·석

① 지루해하는　　　　② 안도하는　　　　③ 질투하는
④ 만족하는　　　　⑤ 좌절감을 느끼는

여: Josh, 괜찮아? 너 창백해 보여.
남: 나 어떻게 해야 하지? 이제 나는 대회에 참가할 수 없어.
여: 영상 대회 말하는 거야? 왜? 뭐가 문제야?
남: 내가 영상 편집을 끝냈을 때, 내 컴퓨터가 고장났어.
여: 오, 이런. 파일은 저장했니?
남: 그랬다고 확신해.
여: 그럼 괜찮을 거야. 그 대회의 마감일은 내일이야.
남: 응, 하지만 서비스 센터에서 내 컴퓨터를 내일까지 고치지는 못해.
여: 확실해? 네가 파일을 복구할 수 있는 어떤 방법이 있니?
남: 아니. 나는 무엇을 해야 할지 모르겠어. 몇 주 간의 내 모든 노력이 이제 쓸모 없어졌어.

단·어·및·표·현

pale [peil] ⓗ (안색이) 창백한, 핼쑥한
crash [kræʃ] ⓥ (컴퓨터가) 고장나다
deadline [dédlàin] ⓝ 마감일, 기한

retrieve[ritríːv] ⑧ 복구하다, 되찾다
work[wəːrk] ⑱ 노력, 작업
useless[júːslis] ⑱ 쓸모 없는

06 그림상황에적절한대화찾기 ▶ 정답 ③

듣•기•대•본

① W: How much is this bottle of soda?
M: It's 3 dollars.
② W: Can you help me find my phone?
M: Sure. I think I see it under your seat.
③ W: May I see your ticket, please?
M: Sure, here it is.
④ W: I'm sorry I'm late.
M: It's okay. I arrived a little late, too.
⑤ W: It looks like it's going to rain.
M: Really? I didn't bring my umbrella.

우•리•말•해•석

① 여: 이 탄산음료 병은 얼마인가요?
남: 그것은 3달러입니다.
② 여: 당신은 제가 핸드폰 찾는 걸 도와줄 수 있나요?
남: 물론이죠. 제 생각엔 제가 그걸 당신 자리 밑에서 본 것 같아요.
③ 여: 표를 보여주시겠습니까?
남: 물론이죠, 여기 있습니다.
④ 여: 늦어서 미안해요.
남: 괜찮아요. 저도 조금 늦게 도착했어요.
⑤ 여: 비가 올 것 같아 보여요.
남: 정말요? 저는 제 우산을 가져오지 않았어요.

단•어•및•표•현

arrive[əráiv] ⑧ 도착하다
be going to ~할 것이다

07 부탁(요청)한일파악 ▶ 정답 ⑤

듣•기•대•본

(Cellphone rings.)
W: Hi, Hojin. Are we ready for Juri's birthday party?
M: Nearly. I've bought the cake, and you're bringing the present, right?
W: Yes. How about the balloons?
M: They're all set. We've decorated the room nicely.
W: Great. Is there anything else I can do?
M: Actually, that's why I called you. Can you buy a birthday card on your way here?
W: Sure. I'll get a really cute one!

우•리•말•해•석

(휴대전화가 울린다.)
여: 호진아, 안녕. 주리 생일 파티 준비는 다 됐니?
남: 거의 다 됐어. 내가 케이크를 샀고, 네가 선물을 가져올 거야, 맞지?
여: 응. 풍선들은?
남: 그것들은 모두 준비가 됐어. 우리가 방을 멋지게 꾸며놨어.
여: 잘했어. 내가 할 수 있는 다른 일은 없니?
남: 사실, 그게 내가 너에게 전화를 한 이유야. 네가 여기 오는 길에 생일카드 좀 사다 줄 수 있니?
여: 물론이지. 내가 정말 귀여운 걸로 사 갈게!

단•어•및•표•현

decorate[dékərèit] ⑧ 꾸미다, 장식하다

08 담화미언급 ▶ 정답 ④

듣•기•대•본

W: The Golden Science Fair is for middle school students across the country. It was initiated to help develop our future scientists. It's hosted by the Golden Science Center, and is held every May. This year, the fair was held at the Capital Convention Center. Around 600 students from 423 schools participated. They competed for awards totaling $5,000. Special thanks go to Triangle Corporation for their sponsorship and volunteer efforts.

우•리•말•해•석

여: Golden 과학 박람회는 전국의 중학생들을 위한 것입니다. 그것은 우리의 미래 과학자들을 양성하는 것을 돕기 위해 시작되었습니다. 그것은 Golden 과학 센터에 의해 주최되며 매년 5월에 열립니다. 올해에는 박람회가 Capital 컨벤션 센터에서 열렸습니다. 423개 학교에서 약 600명의 학생들이 참가했습니다. 그들은 총 5,000달러의 상금을 위해 경쟁했습니다. Triangle 기업의 후원과 자원봉사 노력에 특별히 감사 드립니다.

단•어•및•표•현

host[houst] ⑧ (행사 등을) 주최하다
sponsorship[spánsərʃip] ⑱ 후원

09 담화화제추론 ▶ 정답 ①

듣•기•대•본

W: This animal is a reptile that can be found in warm countries such as Australia and Africa. It has thick skin and a powerful jaw filled with sharp teeth. It has a long tail that helps it swim and move on land. It is a great swimmer and can hold its breath for a long time underwater. It is a good hunter and eats fish, birds, and mammals. Some people wear shoes and bags made from its skin.

우•리•말•해•석

여: 이 동물은 호주나 아프리카와 같은 따뜻한 나라에서 발견되는 파충류입니다. 그것은 두꺼운 가죽과 날카로운 이빨로 가득 찬 힘 있는 턱을 가지고 있습니다. 그것은 수영하고 육지에서 움직일 수 있도록 도와주는 긴 꼬리를 가지고 있습니다. 그것은 훌륭한 수영 선수이며, 물속에서 오랫동안 숨을 참을 수 있습니다. 그것은 훌륭한 사냥꾼이며, 물고기, 새, 그리고 포유동물들을 먹습니다. 몇몇 사람들은 그것의 가죽으로 만든 신발을 신거나 가방을 듭니다.

단•어•및•표•현

reptile[réptail] ⑱ 파충류
jaw[dʒɔː] ⑱ 턱
filled with ~ ~로 가득 찬
hold one's breath 숨을 참다, 숨을 멈추다
made from ~ ~으로 만든

10 어색한대화찾기 ▶ 정답 ④

듣•기•대•본

① M: I really want to take a picture of this scenery.
W: Oh, do you want me to be in it?
② M: How about going to the beach?
W: I'm not in the mood for that.

③ M: Do you know where James is?
W: He went to the restroom.
④ M: Do you have a bandage?
W: No, I don't like rock and roll music very much.
⑤ M: I didn't know that he had a daughter.
W: Me, neither.

우·리·말·해·석

① 남: 난 정말 이 풍경의 사진을 찍고 싶어.
여: 오, 나도 사진에 찍히길 원해?
② 남: 해변에 가는 게 어때?
여: 난 그럴 기분이 아니야.
③ 남: 너 James가 어디에 있는지 아니?
여: 그는 화장실에 갔어.
④ 남: 붕대 있니?
여: 아니, 나는 로큰롤 음악을 별로 좋아하지 않아.
⑤ 남: 나는 그에게 딸이 있는지 몰랐어.
여: 나도 몰랐어.

단·어·및·표·현

scenery [síːnəri] [명] 풍경, 경치
bandage [bǽndidʒ] [명] 붕대

11 할일파악(대화직후) ▶ 정답 ③

듣·기·대·본

W: Jake, I hear that a new AR experience park just opened in the area.
M: What's AR?
W: Augmented Reality. You can experience a whole new artificial world as if it were real.
M: Does it include gaming experience, too?
W: Of course. Do you want to check it out?
M: Sure. I'm free today. Let's go now.
W: Okay. By the way, we can get a student discount. Do you have your student ID?
M: I think I left it in my room. I'll go get it right now.
W: Okay. I'll meet you downstairs.

우·리·말·해·석

여: Jake, 이 지역에 새로운 AR 체험 공원이 막 문을 열었다고 들었어.
남: AR이 뭐야?
여: 증강 현실. 마치 현실인 것처럼 완전히 새로운 인공의 세계를 경험할 수 있어.
남: 그건 게임 경험도 포함하니?
여: 물론이지. 너 확인해 보고 싶어?
남: 응. 난 오늘 한가해. 지금 가자.
여: 알았어. 그런데 우린 학생 할인을 받을 수 있어. 너 학생증 갖고 있어?
남: 난 내 방에 그걸 두고 온 것 같아. 지금 당장 가서 가지고 올게.
여: 알았어. 아래층에서 만나.

단·어·및·표·현

augmented reality 증강 현실
artificial [ɑ̀ːrtəfíʃəl] [형] 인공[인조]의
as if 마치 …인 것처럼

12 도표정보파악 ▶ 정답 ①

듣·기·대·본

W: Patrick, I want to get a new bag for school. What do you think about this one?
M: You mean the red one? I think black would go with more of your outfits.
W: You're right. Black is easy to match. What about the size? Small or large?
M: I'd go with the large one. You carry a lot of books.
W: That makes sense. Do you think I should get one with a chest strap?
M: Yes, absolutely. My bag has a chest strap and it's really comfortable. It keeps the straps from slipping.
W: That sounds perfect. I'll choose that one.

우·리·말·해·석

	가방	색상	크기	가슴끈
①	A	검정	대형	O
②	B	검정	소형	X
③	C	검정	대형	X
④	D	빨강	대형	O
⑤	E	빨강	소형	X

여: Patrick, 학교에 가지고 다닐 새 가방을 사고 싶어. 이건 어떤 것 같아?
남: 빨간 것 말하는 거야? 나는 검정이 네 옷이랑 더 잘 어울릴 것 같아.
여: 맞아. 검정은 (색상을) 맞추기 쉬워. 크기는 어때? 작은 것 아니면 큰 것?
남: 나라면 큰 걸로 하겠어. 너 책 많이 들고 다니잖아.
여: 말이 되네. 너는 내가 가슴끈이 있는 것을 사야 한다고 생각해?
남: 응, 당연하지. 내 가방에 가슴끈이 있는데 그건 정말 편해. 끈이 흘러내리지 않게 해 줘.
여: 완벽하네. 그걸로 고를게.

단·어·및·표·현

go with ~와 어울리다
outfit [áutfit] [명] 옷차림, 복장
make sense 말이 되다, 타당하다
keep A from -ing A가 ~하지 못하게 하다

13 수치파악(날짜) ▶ 정답 ④

듣·기·대·본

M: I'm going to have a housewarming party soon. When would be good for you?
W: I'm off this Friday, November 27.
M: I have a dinner meeting with a client on that day. How about next Friday? I mean December 4.
W: Sorry, but I have other plans with my friends next Friday. I'm free on the next weekend, though.
M: Then, is Saturday evening okay for you? December 5?
W: Yes. I'm available anytime after 6 on that day.
M: Good. Then I'll see you next Saturday.

우·리·말·해·석

남: 난 곧 집들이를 할 거야. 넌 언제가 편하니?
여: 난 11월 27일, 이번 금요일에 쉬어.
남: 나는 그날 고객과 저녁 미팅이 있어. 다음 금요일은 어때? 12월 4일 말이야.
여: 미안해, 난 다음 금요일에 친구들과 다른 계획이 있어. 하지만 난 다음 주 주말에는 괜찮아.
남: 그럼, 토요일 저녁은 괜찮니? 12월 5일?
여: 그래. 난 그날 6시 이후에 언제든지 시간이 있어.
남: 좋아. 그럼 다음 토요일에 보자.

housewarming party 집들이
available [əvéiləbl] 형 시간이 있는, 이용 가능한

🔊 LISTENING ADVICE

'Then is Saturday evening okay for you? December 5?'에서 문장 끝을 올려 말하는 것을 들을 수 있습니다. 이렇게 문장을 말할 때 음을 높이거나 낮추는 것을 '억양'이라고 하는데 영어는 의미에 따라 억양도 다릅니다. 보통 평서문은 문장 끝을 내려서 말하고 의문문은 문장 끝을 올려서 말합니다.

14 한일파악 ▶ 정답 ⑤

듣·기·대·본

W: Bill, what are you going to do next Saturday?
M: I'm going to go to my grandmother's birthday party.
W: Oh, what present are you going to give to her?
M: I made her a photo album of our family members.
W: What a meaningful gift! How did you make it?
M: I ordered it by using an application yesterday. It was easy to make.
W: That sounds interesting. I can use it to make one for my mom's birthday.
M: Sure. I'll show you the application.

우·리·말·해·석

여: Bill, 너 다음 주 토요일에 뭐할 거니?
남: 나는 내 할머니 생신 파티에 갈 거야.
여: 오, 너는 그녀에게 무슨 선물을 드릴 거니?
남: 나는 그녀를 위한 우리 가족 사진 앨범을 만들었어.
여: 정말 의미 있는 선물이다! 너는 어떻게 그것을 만들었니?
남: 나는 어제 애플리케이션을 사용하여 그것을 주문했어. 그것은 만들기 쉬웠어.
여: 흥미로운데. 나도 그것을 사용하여 우리 엄마 생신에 하나 만들 수 있겠어.
남: 물론이지. 내가 너에게 애플리케이션을 보여줄게.

단·어·및·표·현

meaningful [míːniŋfəl] 형 의미 있는
application [æpləkéiʃən] 명 애플리케이션, 앱 (응용 프로그램, 실무처리용 소프트웨어)

15 담화목적파악 ▶ 정답 ④

듣·기·대·본

M: Good evening, guests. Thank you for visiting our shopping center today. The current time is 9:45 p.m. We wanted to let you know that the shopping center will be closing in 15 minutes. At this time, we ask that you bring your selected items to the cash registers. If you need any assistance, our staff members will be happy to serve you. Thank you for shopping with us. We hope you visit us again soon.

우·리·말·해·석

남: 안녕하세요, 손님 여러분. 오늘 저희 쇼핑 센터를 방문해 주셔서 감사합니다. 현재 시각은 오후 9시 45분입니다. 저희는 쇼핑 센터가 15분 후에 폐점함을 여러분에게 알려드리고 싶습니다. 이 시각에는 저희는 여러분이 선택하신 물품들을 계산대로 가져가시기를 부탁드립니다. 만약 어떤 도움이 필요하시다면, 저희 직원이 기꺼이 도와드릴 것입니다. 저희와 함께 쇼핑해 주셔서 감사합니다. 저희는 여러분이 곧 다시 방문해 주시길 바랍니다.

단·어·및·표·현

select [silékt] 동 선택하다
cash register 계산대
assistance [əsístəns] 명 도움
serve [səːrv] 동 (점원이 손님을) 돕다

16 수치계산(금액) ▶ 정답 ④

듣·기·대·본

W: Welcome! What would you like to order?
M: Hi, I would like to order a double cheeseburger combo.
W: That will be $7. Would you like to add any sides to your combo?
M: Let's see... How much is the salad?
W: It's $3 for the small salad and $5 for the large salad.
M: Okay. I'll have the small salad then.
W: Sure! Will that be all?
M: Yeah, that's it. Thank you.

우·리·말·해·석

여: 어서오세요! 무엇을 주문하시겠어요?
남: 안녕하세요. 저는 더블 치즈버거 콤보를 주문하고 싶어요.
여: 7달러 되겠습니다. 콤보에 다른 사이드 메뉴를 추가하시겠어요?
남: 어디 보자… 샐러드는 얼마예요?
여: 작은 샐러드가 3달러, 큰 샐러드가 5달러입니다.
남: 좋아요. 그러면 저는 작은 샐러드를 먹을게요.
여: 그럼요! 그것이 다인가요?
남: 네, 다예요. 고마워요.

단·어·및·표·현

order [ɔ́ːrdər] 동 주문하다
double [dʌ́bl] 형 두 배의
add [æd] 동 추가하다, 더하다

17 알맞은응답찾기 ▶ 정답 ①

듣·기·대·본

M: Lily, you are coming to our bowling club next week, aren't you?
W: Of course. I'm so excited. But I haven't bought shoes yet.
M: You can always borrow them from the bowling alley.
W: I want my own shoes, though. Do you know any stores that sell them?
M: Oh, I know a place where you can buy them at a discounted price.
W: Really? Where is it?
M: Wait! I have the store name and number in my phone. [Pause] Found it!
W: **Great! Please text it to me now.**

우·리·말·해·석

① 좋아! 그걸 지금 나에게 문자로 보내줘.
② 응. 나는 어제 한 켤레를 온라인으로 주문했어.
③ 너는 나에게 그 볼링장이 어디 있는지 알려줄 수 있어?
④ 그 동아리 모임이 화요일이니, 목요일이니?

08 회 모의고사

⑤ 그 신발들은 내가 생각했던 것보다 더 비싸.

남: Lily야, 너는 다음 주에 우리 볼링 동아리에 오는 거지, 그렇지 않아?
여: 물론이지. 난 너무 신나. 그런데 나는 아직 신발을 사지 않았어.
남: 너는 그것들을 그 볼링장에서 언제든지 빌릴 수 있어.
여: 그렇지만 나는 내 신발을 갖고 싶어. 너는 그것들을 파는 가게를 알아?
남: 아, 나는 네가 그것들을 할인된 가격으로 살 수 있는 곳을 알아.
여: 정말? 거기가 어딘데?
남: 잠깐만! 내 전화기에 그 가게 이름과 번호가 있어. [잠시 후] 그것을 찾았어!
여: 좋아! 그걸 지금 나에게 문자로 보내줘.

단·어·및·표·현

borrow [bárou] [동] 빌리다, 대여하다
bowling alley 볼링장
discounted price 할인된 가격

18 알맞은응답찾기 ▶ 정답 ②

듣·기·대·본

M: Hello, how can I help you?
W: Hi, I'd like to buy a plant for my home. Could you recommend something easy to grow?
M: How about this sansevieria? It's a popular plant for people who are new to gardening.
W: Why is it popular?
M: It cleans the air and relieves allergies, not to mention how easy it is to take care of.
W: Perfect! I'll take it. Can I have it delivered?
M: Certainly. Please write your address on this form.
W: Here you are. Are there any tips for caring for this plant?
M: **Place it in indirect sunlight and water it monthly.**

우·리·말·해·석

① 당신은 당신의 알레르기를 치료함으로써 재채기를 완화시킬 수 있어요.
② 그것을 햇빛이 간접적으로 드는 곳에 두고 한 달에 한 번 물을 주세요.
③ 그것은 집들이 선물로 완벽한 선택입니다.
④ 정원 가꾸기는 스트레스를 줄이는 데 도움이 됩니다.
⑤ 그것은 내일 배달될 것입니다.

남: 안녕하세요, 어떻게 도와드릴까요?
여: 안녕하세요, 저는 제 집에 둘 식물을 사고 싶어요. 기르기 쉬운 것을 추천해주시겠어요?
남: 이 산세베리아는 어떠세요? 그것은 정원 가꾸기에 처음인 사람들에게 인기 있는 식물이에요.
여: 그것이 왜 인기가 있어요?
남: 그것은 돌보기가 얼마나 쉬운지는 말할 것도 없고 공기를 깨끗이 하고 알레르기를 완화시켜요.
여: 완벽해요! 그것으로 할게요. 제가 그것을 배달받을 수 있나요?
남: 물론이죠. 이 양식에 당신의 주소를 적어주세요.
여: 여기 있습니다. 이 식물을 돌보는 데 필요한 조언이 있나요?
남: 그것을 햇빛이 간접적으로 드는 곳에 두고 한 달에 한 번 물을 주세요.

단·어·및·표·현

relieve [rilíːv] [동] 완화시키다
allergy [ǽlərdʒi] [명] 알레르기
not to mention ~ ~은 말할 것도 없이

19 알맞은응답찾기 ▶ 정답 ②

듣·기·대·본

M: Are you okay, Ashley? You are coughing a lot and look sick.
W: I feel terrible, Dad. I think I'm coming down with the flu.
M: You shouldn't have run home in the rain yesterday.
W: It wasn't raining hard, so I didn't think it would be a problem. Sorry.
M: You had better go and see the doctor now.
W: Now, Dad? What about school?
M: Your health is more important, Ashley.
W: I know, but my teachers and friends will worry about me.
M: **I'll call the school and explain the situation.**

우·리·말·해·석

① 이 약을 하루 세 번씩 먹으렴.
② 내가 학교에 전화해서 상황을 설명하마.
③ 나는 집에 오는 길에 비를 맞았어.
④ 학교에 늦는 것은 좋은 습관이 아니야.
⑤ 너는 네 친구들을 모두 초대해도 돼.

남: 너 괜찮니, Ashley? 너는 기침을 많이 하고 아파 보여.
여: 저는 몸이 안 좋아요, 아빠. 제 생각엔 독감에 걸린 것 같아요.
남: 너는 어제 빗속에 집에 뛰어오지 말았어야 했어.
여: 비가 심하게 오지 않아서, 저는 그것이 문제가 될 거라고 생각하지 않았어요. 죄송해요.
남: 너는 지금 의사에게 가보는 게 좋겠구나.
여: 지금요, 아빠? 학교는 어떡해요?
남: 네 건강이 더 중요하단다, Ashley.
여: 저도 알지만, 제 선생님과 친구들이 저를 걱정할 거예요.
남: 내가 학교에 전화해서 상황을 설명하마.

단·어·및·표·현

cough [kɔ(ː)f] [동] 기침하다
come down with (병에) 걸리다
habit [hǽbit] [명] 습관, 버릇
get caught in the rain 비를 맞다, 비를 만나다

20 상황에적절한말찾기 ▶ 정답 ③

듣·기·대·본

W: Emily and Liam are having lunch together at a restaurant. While they are eating, Liam talks to Emily while there is food in his mouth. She is annoyed with his behavior because some of the food comes out of his mouth. So, she wants to ask him to stop talking while he is eating. In this situation, what would Emily most likely say to Liam?
Emily: **Please stop talking with your mouth full.**

우·리·말·해·석

① 나에게 티슈 좀 건네줄래?
② 음식 하나를 더 주문하는 게 어때?
③ 입안이 가득 찬 채 말하는 것을 멈춰줘.
④ 나는 잠깐 화장실에 가야겠어.
⑤ 영화를 보는 동안 조용히 해줄래?

여: Emily와 Liam은 식당에서 함께 점심을 먹고 있다. 그들이 식사를 하는 동안, Liam은 그의 입안에 음식이 있는 채로 Emily에게 말을 건다. 그녀는 음식의 일부가 그의 입에서 나왔기 때문에 그의 행동에 짜증이 난다. 그래서, 그녀는 그에게 그가 먹는 동안 말하기를 멈추라고 요청하

고 싶다. 이런 상황에서, Emily는 Liam에게 뭐라고 말할 것 같은가?
Emily: 입안이 가득 찬 채 말하는 것을 멈춰줘.

단·어·및·표·현

annoyed [ənɔ́id] [형] 짜증이 난

Words & Expressions Review

1. 의미 있는	2. 불편, 애로	3. ~은 말할 것도 없이
4. 주문 번호	5. 빌리다, 대여하다	6. 마치 …인 것처럼
7. 몸매를 가꾸다, 몸을 단련하다	8. 교수	9. 재배송하다
10. 증강 현실	11. 애플리케이션	12. 인공[인조]의
13. 열리다	14. 성장시키다, 개발하다	15. 집들이
16. 두 배의	17. 복구하다, 되찾다	18. 행동
19. 계산대	20. ~으로 만든	21. 알레르기
22. 후원	23. 붕대	24. 시작하다, 개시하다
25. 완화시키다	26. 짜증이 난	27. 기분, 분위기
28. 도착하다	29. 꾸미다, 장식하다	30. 풍경, 경치
31. (안색이) 창백한, 핼쑥한	32. ~할 것이다	33. 교내에서, 대학에서
34. 볼링장	35. (병에) 걸리다	36. 추가하다, 더하다
37. 도움	38. 할인된 가격	39. 습관, 버릇
40. 주문하다, 명령하다	41. 선물	42. 파충류
43. 액자, 틀	44. 턱	

Listening Test

영어듣기 모의고사 09회

| 정 | 답 |

01 ①	02 ④	03 ③	04 ③	05 ②
06 ④	07 ②	08 ⑤	09 ③	10 ⑤
11 ②	12 ③	13 ④	14 ①	15 ⑤
16 ②	17 ①	18 ⑤	19 ①	20 ②

01 그림정보파악(대화) ▶ 정답 ①

듣·기·대·본

M: Hello, how can I help you?
W: I'm looking for a hand mirror for my friend.
M: We have square-shaped and round-shaped mirrors. Which one would your friend like?
W: I think she would like a round-shaped one. Oh, there are designs on the back.
M: Yes. These flower designs are popular.
W: I want a mirror with the flower design.
M: Good choice. We can also put your friend's name on it. It will only take a few minutes.
W: Wonderful! Put 'Alice' under the flower, please.
M: Okay. I'll be right back.

우·리·말·해·석

남: 안녕하세요, 어떻게 도와드릴까요?
여: 저는 제 친구를 위한 손 거울을 찾고 있어요.
남: 저희는 사각형과 원형 거울을 갖고 있어요. 당신의 친구는 어떤 걸 좋아할까요?
여: 그녀가 원형 거울을 좋아할 거라고 생각해요. 오, 뒷면에 디자인들이 있네요.
남: 네. 이 꽃 디자인들이 인기가 많아요.
여: 저는 꽃 디자인의 거울을 원해요.
남: 좋은 선택이에요. 우리는 또한 당신의 친구의 이름을 그것(손거울) 위에 넣을 수 있어요. 그건 단지 몇 분 밖에 안 걸릴 거예요.
여: 멋지네요! 꽃 밑에 'Alice'를 넣어 주세요.
남: 알겠어요. 저는 금방 돌아올게요.

단·어·및·표·현

look for ~을 찾다, 구하다
a few 조금의

02 대화미언급 ▶ 정답 ④

듣·기·대·본

W: Steve, did you know that the Technology Fair is going on right now?
M: Yes. The theme of the fair this year is 'AI and domestic robots.'
W: I'm really interested in domestic robots these days.
M: I'm sure you can get a lot of information there.
W: Do you know where the fair is taking place?
M: It's being held at Lincoln Center downtown.
W: Tickets are only 7 dollars each for students. Do you want to go with me?
M: Definitely.
W: How about going next weekend?
M: We have to go this weekend. The fair ends on August 25th.
W: I see. Let's go this weekend then.

우·리·말·해·석

여: Steve, 너 과학기술 박람회가 지금 진행 중인 거 알고 있었니?
남: 응. 올해 박람회의 주제는 '인공지능과 가정용 로봇'이야.
여: 나는 요즘 가정용 로봇에 관심이 많아.
남: 나는 네가 거기서 많은 정보를 얻을 수 있을 거라 확신해.
여: 너는 그 박람회가 어디서 열리고 있는지 아니?
남: 그것은 시내에 있는 링컨 센터에서 하고 있어.
여: 학생들에게 표는 1장당 7달러밖에 안 해. 나랑 같이 갈래?
남: 물론이지.
여: 다음 주말에 가는 게 어때?
남: 우리는 이번 주말에 가야 해. 그 박람회는 8월 25일에 끝나.
여: 그렇구나. 그럼 이번 주말에 가자.

단·어·및·표·현

technology [teknɑ́lədʒi] [명] (과학 · 공학과 관련된) 기술
fair [fɛər] [명] 박람회
go on (어떤 상황이) 계속되다
AI(Artificial Intelligence) 인공지능
domestic [dəméstik] [형] 가정용의, 집안의
take place 열리다, 주최되다
definitely [défənitli] [부] (강한 긍정 · 동의) 물론, 확실히 그래

듣·기·대·본

(*Telephone rings.*)

W: Good afternoon. City Library. How may I help you?

M: Hi. I'm planning to visit the library today, but I think I've lost my library card.

W: I'm sorry to hear that. May I have your full name, please?

M: Brian Johnson.

W: (*Typing sound*) Let me check that for you... Yes, I found your record in our system.

M: Can I get a new card?

W: Of course! But you'll need to visit the library with your ID. There's also a small fee of $2.

M: I understand. Thank you for your help.

우·리·말·해·석

(전화벨이 울린다.)

여: 안녕하세요. 시립 도서관입니다. 어떻게 도와드릴까요?

남: 안녕하세요. 오늘 도서관에 방문할 계획인데, 도서관 카드를 잃어버린 것 같아요.

여: 그렇다니 안타깝네요. 성함 전부를 알려 주시겠어요?

남: Brian Johnson입니다.

여: (키보드 치는 소리) 확인해 드릴게요... 네, 저희 시스템에서 당신의 정보를 찾았어요.

남: 새 카드를 받을 수 있을까요?

여: 물론이죠! 하지만 신분증을 가지고 도서관에 방문하셔야 해요. 그리고 약간의 수수료로 2달러가 있습니다.

남: 알겠습니다. 도와주셔서 감사합니다.

단·어·및·표·현

record [rékərd] 몡 정보, 기록

ID [àidí:] 몡 신분증(= identification)

fee [fi:] 몡 수수료, 요금

04 수치파악(시각)   ▶ 정답 ③

듣·기·대·본

W: Hello, how may I help you?

M: I'd like to buy four tickets for the express train to Busan this afternoon.

W: Okay. Would you like first class or economy class?

M: Economy class, please.

W: Sure. You can buy tickets for trains leaving at 12 p.m., 2 p.m. or 4 p.m.

M: What about the 1 p.m. train?

W: I'm afraid tickets are sold out for that one.

M: I see. The 12 p.m. train won't give us any time for lunch. So, I'll take the one leaving at 2 p.m.

W: Okay. Would you like four adult tickets?

M: That's right.

우·리·말·해·석

여: 안녕하세요, 어떻게 도와드릴까요?

남: 저는 오늘 오후 부산행 급행 열차표를 4장 사고 싶어요.

여: 네. 일등석으로 하시겠어요, 아니면 일반석으로 하시겠어요?

남: 일반석으로 주세요.

여: 네. 오후 12시, 2시, 아니면 4시에 출발하는 기차표를 구매하실 수 있어요.

남: 오후 1시 기차는요?

여: 유감이지만 그 시간 표는 다 팔렸어요.

남: 그렇군요. 오후 12시 기차는 저희에게 점심 먹을 시간을 주지(허락하지) 않을 거예요. 그래서, 저는 오후 2시에 출발하는 걸로 할게요.

여: 네. 성인표 4장으로 하시겠어요?

남: 맞아요.

단·어·및·표·현

express train 급행 열차

economy class 일반석, 이코노미 클래스

05 심정추론   ▶ 정답 ②

듣·기·대·본

W: Hi, Jiho. You don't look so well. Is there something wrong?

M: Hello, Mrs. Hills. I'm feeling uneasy about the school play tomorrow.

W: What's the matter?

M: During rehearsal last week, I forgot my lines several times. It was awful.

W: Don't be silly. You've practiced so much more since then. You'll be great tomorrow.

M: But what if I make the same mistakes again?

W: I don't think you will. But even if you forget some lines, just make something up and the audience won't notice.

M: I'm not sure if I'll be able to do that.

우·리·말·해·석

① 차분한　② 불안한　③ 안심한　④ 후회하는　⑤ 만족하는

여: 안녕, 지호야. 너 너무 안 좋아 보인다. 무슨 잘못된 것이 있니?

남: 안녕하세요, Hills 선생님. 저는 내일 학교 연극에 대해 불안함을 느껴요.

여: 뭐가 문제니?

남: 지난주 리허설 (하는) 동안, 저는 제 대사를 여러 번 잊었어요. 끔찍했어요.

여: 바보같이 굴지 마렴. 너는 그때 이후로 훨씬 더 많이 연습해왔잖니. 너는 내일 잘할 거야.

남: 하지만 만약 제가 또 같은 실수들을 하면요?

여: 네가 그럴 것 같지는 않구나. 하지만 네가 대사들을 좀 잊는다고 하더라도, 그냥 무언가를 지어내면 관객들은 알아채지 못할 거야.

남: 제가 그것을 할 수 있을지 모르겠어요.

단·어·및·표·현

uneasy [ʌníːzi] 몡 불안한, 우려되는

line [lain] 몡 (연극, 영화의) 대사

awful [ɔ́:fəl] 몡 끔찍한

silly [síli] 몡 바보같은, 어리석은

what if 만약 ~라면?

even if ~이라고 할지라도

make up 지어내다, 만들어내다

notice [nóutis] 통 알아채다

06 그림상황에적절한대화찾기   ▶ 정답 ④

듣·기·대·본

① W: That's a really ugly painting.

  M: Yeah, it does not suit this restaurant.

② W: You stepped on my foot.

M: Oh, I didn't know. I'm so sorry.
③ W: Why is it so noisy in here?
　　M: The TV is on. I'll turn the volume down.
④ W: My throat really hurts. I can't even drink water.
　　M: Okay, let me take a look. Say "Ah."
⑤ W: What seems to be the problem?
　　M: The oven is broken. It's okay, I'll fix it.

우·리·말·해·석
① 여: 저것은 정말 보기 흉한 그림이야.
　　남: 그래, 그것은 이 식당과 어울리지 않아.
② 여: 네가 내 발을 밟았어.
　　남: 오, 몰랐어. 정말 미안해.
③ 여: 여기 왜 이렇게 시끄러워?
　　남: TV가 켜져 있어. 내가 소리를 줄일게.
④ 여: 제 목이 정말 아파요. 저는 물도 마실 수 없어요.
　　남: 알겠습니다, 제가 한번 볼게요. "아" 하세요.
⑤ 여: 뭐가 문제인 것 같아?
　　남: 오븐이 고장났어. 괜찮아, 내가 그것을 고칠게.

단·어·및·표·현
suit [suːt] ⑧ 어울리다

07 부탁(요청)한일파악　　　▶ 정답 ②

듣·기·대·본
W: Hey, did you hear about the cooking class happening next Saturday?
M: No, I missed that. What cuisines will they be covering?
W: They're offering a variety, from Italian pasta dishes to Indian curries.
M: That sounds exciting! Should we sign up for it?
W: Definitely. The announcement mentioned that registration is now open online. Plus, there's a discount for early birds.
M: Oh, I'm usually good at online registration.
W: Perfect! In that case, could you register both of us?
M: Of course, I'll take care of it right now.

우·리·말·해·석
여: 이봐, 너는 다음 주 토요일에 있을 요리 교실에 대해 들었어?
남: 아니, 난 그것을 놓쳤어. 그들은 어떤 요리를 다룰 거래?
여: 그들은 이탈리아 파스타 요리부터 인도 카레까지 여러 가지를 제공할 거야.
남: 재밌겠는데! 우리 그것을 신청할까?
여: 물론이지. 공고에서 등록은 지금 온라인에서 가능하다고 언급했어. 게다가, 얼리버드(조기 등록자)에겐 할인이 있어.
남: 오, 나는 평소에 온라인 등록에 능숙해.
여: 완벽하네! 그렇다면, 네가 우리 둘 다 등록해 줄 수 있어?
남: 물론이지, 내가 지금 바로 그것을 처리할게.

단·어·및·표·현
cuisine [kwizíːn] ⑨ 요리
cover [kʌ́vər] ⑧ 다루다
variety [vəráiəti] ⑨ 여러 가지
sign up for ~을 신청하다
announcement [ənáunsmənt] ⑨ 공고, 고지
mention [ménʃən] ⑧ 언급하다, 말하다
registration [rèdʒistréiʃən] ⑨ 등록
early bird 얼리버드(재빨리 무언가를 시작하거나 특히 그렇게 함으로써 일종의 유리한 점을 얻는 사람)

take care of 처리하다, 수습하다

08 담화미언급　　　▶ 정답 ⑤

듣·기·대·본
W: Ladies and gentlemen, I am thrilled to announce this year's Food Festival. Thanks to the incredible support of our sponsors, it will be held at City Park. On September 15th, get ready to enjoy a feast like never before! The theme of the festival will be "Flavors of the World." Some lucky attendees will receive gourmet food baskets as special treats. Don't miss out on this opportunity to sample delicious dishes from various cultures!

우·리·말·해·석
여: 신사 숙녀 여러분, 올해의 음식 축제를 발표하게 되어 기쁩니다. 우리 후원자들의 엄청난 지원 덕분에 그것은 City Park에서 개최될 것입니다. 9월 15일에, 전에 없던 축제를 즐길 준비를 하세요! 축제의 주제는 '세계의 맛'이 될 겁니다. 일부 행운의 참석자들은 특별 선물로 고급 음식 바구니를 받을 것입니다. 다양한 문화의 맛있는 요리를 맛볼 수 있는 이 기회를 놓치지 마세요!

단·어·및·표·현
incredible [inkrédəbl] ⑱ 엄청난, 놀라운, 믿을 수 없는
sponsor [spánsər] ⑨ (방송 프로그램·스포츠 행사 등의) 후원사, 광고주
feast [fiːst] ⑨ 축제
like never before 전에 없이, 전과 다르게
attendee [ətendíː] ⑨ 참석자
gourmet food (미식가용) 고급 음식
treat [triːt] ⑨ 특별한 선물
miss out (좋은 기회를) 놓치다
sample [sǽmpl] ⑧ 맛보다, 시식하다

09 담화화제추론　　　▶ 정답 ③

듣·기·대·본
W: This is a natural underground space. It is created when slowly-moving water dissolves rocks. It is large enough to hold a person. Its size can be small like a single room, but it also can be a long tunnel-like passage. Animals like bats, fish, snakes and spiders are found in the dark parts of this. Also, ancient people often drew pictures on the walls of this.

우·리·말·해·석
여: 이것은 자연적으로 만들어진 지하 공간이다. 이것은 천천히 움직이는 물이 암석을 녹이면서 형성된다. 이것은 사람을 수용할 만큼 크다. 이것의 크기는 방 하나처럼 작을 수도 있으나 긴 터널과 같은 통로일 수도 있다. 박쥐, 물고기, 뱀 그리고 거미와 같은 동물들이 이것의 어두운 공간에서 발견되기도 한다. 또한 고대 사람들은 종종 이것의 벽에 그림을 그렸다.

단·어·및·표·현
dissolve [dizálv] ⑧ 녹이다, 용해하다

10 어색한대화찾기　　　▶ 정답 ⑤

듣·기·대·본
① M: I bought a box of chocolates for you on my trip.

W: Thank you. They're really delicious.
② M: How often do you work out?
　　W: I work out every day.
③ M: Which do you prefer, meat or fish?
　　W: I prefer meat to fish.
④ M: Who should I talk to about changing a reservation?
　　W: I can help you with that.
⑤ M: Can I call you back later?
　　W: Okay. Let's meet at 7.

우·리·말·해·석

① 남: 내가 여행에서 너를 위해 초콜릿 한 상자를 샀어.
　　여: 고마워. 그것은 정말 맛있어.
② 남: 너는 얼마나 자주 운동을 하니?
　　여: 나는 매일 운동해.
③ 남: 너는 어느 것을 더 좋아하니, 고기 아니면 생선?
　　여: 나는 생선보다 고기를 더 좋아해.
④ 남: 예약을 변경하는 것에 대해 누구에게 얘기해야 하나요?
　　여: 그것에 대해서는 제가 당신을 도와드릴 수 있습니다.
⑤ 남: 내가 나중에 다시 너에게 전화해도 될까?
　　여: 그래. 7시에 만나자.

단·어·및·표·현

reservation [rèzərvéiʃən] 몡 예약
call back (전화 걸어온 사람에게) 다시 전화하다

11 　할일파악　　　　　　▶ 정답 ②

듣·기·대·본

W: Honey, what are you doing?
M: I'm mowing the lawn. Our back yard is like a jungle.
W: Last night, you said our lawn mower was broken. Have you fixed it already?
M: No, I borrowed a lawn mower from Jerry next door.
W: That's very sweet of him. Do you need a hand?
M: It's okay. I'm done here. I'm about to return the machine to Jerry.
W: Wait. I'll bake some muffins. Take them with you. He loves them.
M: Okay. I'll go and take a shower, then.

우·리·말·해·석

여: 여보, 뭐해요?
남: 전 잔디를 깎고 있어요. 우리 뒷마당이 정글 같아요.
여: 어젯밤에, 당신은 우리 잔디 깎는 기계가 고장 났다고 했잖아요. 벌써 그것을 고쳤어요?
남: 아뇨, 옆집의 Jerry에게 잔디 깎는 기계를 빌렸어요.
여: 그는 매우 친절하네요. 도움이 필요해요?
남: 괜찮아요. 여기 다 했어요. 저는 Jerry에게 기계를 막 돌려주려던 참이에요.
여: 기다려요. 제가 머핀을 좀 구울게요. 그것들을 가져가요. 그는 그것들을 아주 좋아해요.
남: 알겠어요. 그럼 저는 가서 샤워해야겠어요.

단·어·및·표·현

mow the lawn 잔디를 깎다
lawn mower 잔디 깎는 기계
fix [fiks] 동 고치다
need a hand 도움이 필요하다
be about to + 동사원형 막 ~하려던 참이다

12 　도표정보파악　　　　　　▶ 정답 ③

듣·기·대·본

M: Honey, which television should we buy?
W: We should definitely get a large one. There's that saying, "The bigger, the better!"
M: I agree. Let's buy a 65-inch model.
W: Okay. Should we buy one with a curved screen?
M: No. I don't like curved screens. I believe that TV screens should be flat.
W: Then, we have two options left.
M: Let's choose the one that has the wireless connection.
W: Okay. Then we can connect the smartphone to the TV without cables. Let's buy that one.

우·리·말·해·석

	모델	사이즈(인치)	화면 형태	연결성
①	A	55	곡면형	무선
②	B	55	평면형	HDMI 케이블
③	C	65	평면형	무선
④	D	65	평면형	HDMI 케이블
⑤	E	65	곡면형	무선

남: 여보, 우리는 어떤 텔레비전을 사야 할까요?
여: 우리는 확실히 큰 것을 사야 해요. 그런 말이 있잖아요, "더 클수록 더 좋다!"
남: 나도 동의해요. 65인치 모델을 삽시다.
여: 알겠어요. 우린 곡면형 화면인 것을 사야 할까요?
남: 아뇨. 나는 곡면형 화면을 좋아하지 않아요. 나는 TV 화면은 평평해야 한다고 생각해요.
여: 그럼, 우리에게 두 개의 선택지가 남아 있어요.
남: 무선 연결을 하는 것을 선택합시다.
여: 좋아요. 그러면 우리는 케이블 없이 TV에 스마트폰을 연결할 수 있어요. 저것을 삽시다.

단·어·및·표·현

definitely [défənitli] 뷔 확실히, 분명히
saying [séiiŋ] 몡 옛말, 속담
curved screen 곡면형 화면
option [ɑ́pʃən] 몡 선택지, 선택(권)
wireless [wáiərlis] 혱 무선(의)
cable [kéibl] 몡 케이블, 전선

13 　수치파악(날짜)　　　　　　▶ 정답 ④

듣·기·대·본

(Telephone rings.)
M: Hello, this is Denny's Pizzeria.
W: Hello, this is Sarah Simpson and I'm a journalist at K magazine.
M: Oh, hello. How can I help you?
W: I've heard your restaurant serves great food and I'd like to write an article about it.
M: Thank you. That would be wonderful.
W: So, can I visit the restaurant on August 11 around 3?
M: Um... We'll be closed from August 10 to 12 for vacation. Can you make it on August 13 instead?
W: I'm only available after 5 p.m. on that day. Will that be okay?

M: No problem. I'll see you on August 13 at 5 p.m.
W: Okay, see you then.

우·리·말·해·석

(전화벨이 울린다.)

남: 여보세요. Denny's Pizzeria입니다.

여: 여보세요. 저는 Sarah Simpson이고 K 잡지의 기자입니다.

남: 오, 안녕하세요. 제가 어떻게 도와드릴까요?

여: 저는 당신의 식당이 훌륭한 음식을 제공한다고 들었고 그것에 대해 기사를 쓰고 싶습니다.

남: 감사합니다. 그러면 정말 좋을 것 같습니다.

여: 그래서, 제가 8월 11일 3시쯤에 식당을 방문할 수 있을까요?

남: 음… 저희는 8월 10일부터 12일까지 휴가로 문을 닫습니다. 대신에 8월 13일에 오실 수 있나요?

여: 저는 그날은 오후 5시 이후로만 시간이 있습니다. 그래도 괜찮을까요?

남: 문제없습니다. 8월 13일 오후 5시에 뵙겠습니다.

여: 좋아요, 그때 뵙겠습니다.

단·어·및·표·현

journalist [ʤɔ́ːrnəlist] 몡 기자
available [əvéiləbl] 쀉 (만날) 시간이 있는

14 한일파악 ▶ 정답 ①

듣·기·대·본

M: Olivia, how was your weekend? You said that you were going to visit your grandmother.
W: Yes, but she told me not to come.
M: Why would she say that? What happened?
W: She caught the flu, so she didn't want to infect me.
M: I see… I hope she gets well soon. How did you spend your weekend then?
W: I just stayed at home and read some comic books.
M: Oh, what did you read?
W: I read *The Fabulous Five*. You should read it, too!

우·리·말·해·석

남: Olivia, 주말 어땠어? 너는 너희 할머니를 방문할 거라고 했잖아.

여: 응, 그런데 할머니가 나에게 오지 말라고 하셨어.

남: 할머니가 왜 그렇게 말씀하셨을까? 무슨 일이야?

여: 할머니는 독감에 걸리셨고, 그래서 나에게 병을 옮기고 싶지 않으셨던 거야.

남: 그렇구나… 할머니께서 곧 나으시길 바라. 그러면 너는 주말을 어떻게 보냈어?

여: 나는 그냥 집에 있었고 만화책 몇 권을 읽었어.

남: 오, 너는 무엇을 읽었어?

여: "The Fabulous Five"를 읽었어. 너도 그거 읽어봐!

단·어·및·표·현

catch the flu 독감에 걸리다
infect [infékt] 몡 병을 옮기다, 감염시키다
get well 병이 낫다, (몸을) 회복하다

15 담화목적파악 ▶ 정답 ⑤

듣·기·대·본

W: Good afternoon, students. We're happy to announce that we have finished renovating our school library. Our library now has more space to accommodate more books. If there are books that you want the library to purchase, please let us know. You can make a request on our school website. Please fill out and submit the book purchase request form that can be found on the online library menu. Your requests will be reviewed by our librarian and then considered for purchase. Thank you.

우·리·말·해·석

여: 좋은 오후입니다, 학생 여러분. 우리는 학교 도서관 수리가 끝났음을 알리게 되어 기쁩니다. 우리 도서관은 현재 더 많은 책을 수용할 수 있는 더 넓은 공간을 갖게 되었습니다. 만약 도서관이 구입하기를 원하는 책이 있다면, 우리에게 알려주세요. 여러분은 우리 학교의 웹사이트에서 요청할 수 있습니다. 온라인 도서관 메뉴에서 찾을 수 있는 도서 구매 요청서를 작성해서 제출해주세요. 여러분의 요청은 사서에게 검토되고, 그러고 나서 구입이 고려될 것입니다. 감사합니다.

단·어·및·표·현

renovate [rénəvèit] 몡 수리하다, 개조하다
accommodate [əkámədèit] 몡 수용하다, 공간을 제공하다
purchase [pɔ́ːrtʃəs] 몡 구매하다
make a request 요청하다

16 수치계산(금액) ▶ 정답 ②

듣·기·대·본

W: May I help you?
M: I'm looking for a T-shirt.
W: Then, please come this way. This is the men's section.
M: Hmm, I like this grey one. How much is this?
W: It's 60 dollars, sir.
M: That's a little expensive. I thought this store was having a sale.
W: I'm really sorry, but the sale is only on women's clothing.
M: I see. I guess I'll take it anyway. Here's a 100 dollars.
W: Thank you. Here's your change.

우·리·말·해·석

여: 도와드릴까요?

남: 전 티셔츠를 찾고 있어요.

여: 그럼 이쪽으로 오세요. 여기가 남성 코너입니다.

남: 흠, 이 회색 옷이 좋네요. 이건 얼마죠?

여: 60달러입니다, 손님.

남: 약간 비싸네요. 이 가게가 세일하는 중인 줄 알았는데요.

여: 정말 죄송합니다만, 세일은 여성 옷에만 해당됩니다.

남: 그렇군요. 어쨌든 그냥 사겠어요. 여기 100달러요.

여: 감사합니다. 여기 거스름돈이요.

단·어·및·표·현

change [tʃeinʤ] 몡 거스름돈, 잔돈, 변화

17 알맞은응답찾기 ▶ 정답 ①

듣·기·대·본

W: Hey, Michael. What are you going to do tomorrow?
M: I'm not sure yet. Why?
W: I just thought that maybe we could go to the amusement park tomorrow.
M: Oh, sorry, but I can't. I just remembered that I'm visiting my aunt tomorrow as usual.
W: As usual? You mean, you visit her every weekend? Why?

M: She lives alone since all her children have moved abroad. I don't want her to be lonely.
W: Oh. That's so sweet of you.
M: Thanks. I just do what I can.

우·리·말·해·석
① 고마워. 내가 할 수 있는 걸 하는 것뿐인걸.
② 너 굉장히 귀여운 남자아이구나.
③ 아니, 난 그녀를 매일 보지 않아.
④ 아니, 난 사탕을 다 먹지 않았어.
⑤ 게다가, 내 사촌들은 정말 다정하거든.

여: 얘, Michael. 내일 뭐 할거니?
남: 아직 잘 모르겠어. 왜?
여: 우리가 어쩌면 내일 놀이공원에 갈 수도 있지 않을까 하고 방금 생각했어.
남: 아, 미안하지만 난 못 가. 내일 내가 평소처럼 우리 고모를 방문한다는 게 방금 생각났어.
여: 평소처럼? 주말마다 고모를 방문한단 말이니? 왜?
남: 고모의 자녀들이 모두 해외로 이주했기 때문에 고모는 혼자 사시거든. 난 고모가 외로워하는 걸 바라지 않아.
여: 아. 너 굉장히 다정하구나.
남: 고마워. 내가 할 수 있는 걸 하는 것뿐인걸.

단·어·및·표·현
amusement park 놀이공원
as usual 평소처럼
abroad [əbrɔ́ːd] ⓐ 해외로, 해외에(서)

🎧 LISTENING ADVICE
한 단어 내에 동일한 자음이 연속될 때, 앞의 자음은 탈락하고 뒤에 오는 자음만 발음합니다. 따라서 'tomorrow'는 [투머르러우]가 아니라 [투머러우]로 들립니다. 이와 같은 발음규칙이 적용되는 단어들로는 'impossible'[임파서블], 'messenger'[메신저러] 등이 있습니다.

---

18 알맞은응답찾기   ▶ 정답 ⑤

듣·기·대·본
W: This bus is slow.
M: It's the traffic. Don't worry. We won't be late.
W: How many more stops before we get to the theater?
M: Hmm… three. Oh, look at that man in the car!
W: In the second lane? What's he doing?
M: He's driving and talking on his cellphone at the same time.
W: Isn't that dangerous, even if the traffic is slow?
M: Of course it is. I hope he stops doing that.
W: He should pull over if he wants to use his cellphone.

우·리·말·해·석
① 글쎄, 우리는 어쨌든 급하지 않아.
② 걱정 마. 극장은 늦게까지 열어.
③ 그래도, 운전자들이 항상 친절할 필요는 없어.
④ 내 말이 그 말이야. 그는 그렇게 빠르게 운전해서는 안 돼.
⑤ 휴대폰을 사용하고 싶다면 그는 차를 세워야 해.

여: 이 버스 느리네.
남: 교통량 때문이야. 걱정 마. 우리 늦지 않을 거야.
여: 극장에 도착할 때까지 몇 정거장 더 있지?
남: 음… 셋. 아, 차 안에 있는 저 남자를 봐!
여: 두 번째 차선? 그 사람 뭐하고 있어?
남: 그 사람은 운전하면서 동시에 휴대폰으로 통화도 하고 있어.
여: 교통이 느리더라도 그건 위험하지 않아?
남: 물론 그렇지. 그가 그 행동을 멈췄으면 좋겠다.
여: 휴대폰을 사용하고 싶다면 그는 차를 세워야 해.

단·어·및·표·현
at the same time 동시에

---

19 알맞은응답찾기   ▶ 정답 ①

듣·기·대·본
M: Welcome to Sunnyside Hotel. Did you make a reservation?
W: Yes, a twin-bed room under the name of Lee.
M: Let me see… I'm sorry, but we're out of twin-bed rooms. Is a double-bed room okay?
W: No. There are two of us, and I booked twin beds.
M: Right. It's our fault. So, if you stay in a double-bed room just for tonight, we'll make it up to you.
W: How?
M: We'll move you to a twin-bed room tomorrow, and give you free breakfast for your entire stay.
W: That sounds good. I'll take the deal.

우·리·말·해·석
① 좋은 것 같네요. 제안을 받아들이겠습니다.
② 알겠습니다. 저는 그냥 새 침대를 사고 싶었어요.
③ 고맙습니다만, 더블 침대도 괜찮습니다.
④ 괜찮습니다. 머무시는 동안 즐거운 시간 보내시기 바랍니다.
⑤ 죄송하지만 호텔을 잘못 예약하셨습니다.

남: Sunnyside Hotel에 오신 것을 환영합니다. 예약하셨나요?
여: 네, Lee라는 이름으로 트윈룸을 예약했습니다.
남: 어디 볼게요… 죄송하지만 트윈룸이 다 찼네요. 더블룸은 괜찮으신가요?
여: 아니요. 저희는 두 명이고, 저는 트윈 베드를 예약했습니다.
남: 맞습니다. 저희 잘못입니다. 그러니 오늘 밤만 더블룸에 묵으시면 저희가 보상해 드리겠습니다.
여: 어떻게요?
남: 내일 트윈룸으로 옮겨 드리고 전체 숙박 기간 동안 무료로 아침 식사를 제공해 드리겠습니다.
여: 좋은 것 같네요. 제안을 받아들이겠습니다.

단·어·및·표·현
make a reservation 예약하다
be out of 품절되다, ~이 바닥나다
make it up to ~에게 보상하다
entire [intáiər] ⓐ 전체의

---

20 상황에적절한말찾기   ▶ 정답 ②

듣·기·대·본
W: Mary is studying for a midterm exam with her friend, Peter. They are in a coffee shop. She's using her laptop to look up class materials for the exam, but the battery is low. Peter uses the same model as Mary's, and his laptop seems fully charged. So, Mary decides to ask Peter if she can use his charger. In this situation, what would Mary most likely say to Peter?
Mary: Would it be okay if I borrowed your charger?

우·리·말·해·석

① 내 노트북 컴퓨터를 사용하면서 문제가 발생하고 있어.

② 내가 네 충전기를 빌려도 괜찮을까?

③ 내가 커피 한 잔을 더 마셔도 괜찮을까?

④ 노트북 사용이 편한 커피숍을 어디에서 찾을 수 있을까?

⑤ 너는 언제 정리하고 집에 가려고 생각하고 있니?

여: Mary는 그녀의 친구 Peter와 함께 중간 고사 공부를 하고 있다. 그들은 커피숍에 있다. 그녀는 시험을 위한 수업 자료를 찾아보기 위해 그녀의 노트북 컴퓨터를 사용하고 있지만, 배터리가 거의 없다. Peter는 Mary의 것과 같은 모델을 사용하고 있고, 그의 노트북 컴퓨터는 충전이 완전히 되어 있는 것 같다. 그래서 Mary는 Peter에게 그녀가 그의 충전기를 쓸 수 있는지 물어보기로 결정한다. 이 상황에서, Mary는 Peter에게 뭐라고 말하겠는가?

Mary: 내가 네 충전기를 빌려도 괜찮을까?

단·어·및·표·현

look up (정보를) 찾아보다

material [mətí(ː)əriəl] 명 자료

Words & Expressions Review

1. 찾아보다	2. 수용하다, 공간을 제공하다	3. ~에게 보상하다
4. 조금의	5. 구매하다	6. 옛말, 속담
7. 잔디를 깎다	8. 맛보다, 시식하다	9. (좋은 기회를) 놓치다
10. 등록	11. 일반석, 이코노미 클래스	12. 참석자
13. 가정용의, 집안의	14. 급행 열차	15. 자료
16. 알리다	17. 축제	18. 불안한, 우려되는
19. 통로, 복도	20. 차선, 도로	21. 병을 옮기다, 감염시키다
22. 가다, 참석하다	23. 독감에 걸리다	24. 고대의
25. 어울리다	26. 요청하다	27. 시간이 있는
28. 기자	29. 요리	30. 교통(량)
31. 거스름돈, 변화	32. 충전하다	33. 녹이다, 용해하다
34. 끔찍한	35. 해외로, 해외에(서)	36. 박쥐, 방망이
37. 지하의	38. 지어내다, 만들어내다	39. 도움이 필요하다
40. 동시에	41. 수리하다, 개조하다	42. 차를 세우다
43. 예약	44. 정보, 기록	

|정|답|

01 ③	02 ③	03 ⑤	04 ⑤	05 ②
06 ②	07 ②	08 ③	09 ①	10 ④
11 ②	12 ⑤	13 ④	14 ③	15 ⑤
16 ②	17 ⑤	18 ④	19 ④	20 ④

01 그림정보파악(대화)   ▶ 정답 ③

듣·기·대·본

W: Welcome to The Flag Company.

M: Hello. Can I order 25 spirit flags for my students?

W: Certainly! We have ready-made options, or you can design your own.

M: I'd prefer to design the flags myself.

W: Excellent! What shape would you like, square or triangular?

M: Triangular, please.

W: Should they have decorations like stars or hearts on them?

M: Stars would be nice.

W: Do you want to add any text or a slogan?

M: Yes, please print the class number, 2, in the middle of each flag.

W: Perfect. We'll have your order completed by next Friday.

우·리·말·해·석

여: The Flag Company에 오신 것을 환영합니다.

남: 안녕하세요. 제 학생들을 위해 응원 깃발 25개를 주문할 수 있을까요?

여: 물론이죠! 저희는 기성 제품들이 있고, 아니면 직접 디자인할 수도 있어요.

남: 제가 직접 그 깃발들을 디자인하고 싶어요.

여: 훌륭합니다! 네모나 세모 중, 어떤 모양으로 하시겠어요?

남: 세모 모양으로 해 주세요.

여: 그것들은 별이나 하트 같은 장식이 있어야 할까요?

남: 별이 있으면 좋겠어요.

여: 글자나 구호를 추가하시겠어요?

남: 네, 각 깃발의 중앙에 반 번호인 2를 인쇄해 주세요.

여: 좋습니다. 다음 주 금요일까지 당신의 주문을 완료해 드릴게요.

단·어·및·표·현

flag [flæg] 명 깃발

spirit [spírit] 명 기운, 열성

decoration [dèkəréiʃən] 명 장식(품)

slogan [slóugən] 명 구호

complete [kəmplíːt] 통 완료하다, 끝마치다

02 대화미언급   ▶ 정답 ③

듣·기·대·본

M: Hey, Sue. What do you think of Oracle Bath Salt? I think I'll get some for Grace.

W: That's a good idea. Its relaxing effects are really helping me.

M: Really? Grace said she wanted something just like that.

W: It's packed with minerals and natural oils, so she'll like it.

M: Do you recommend any scents?

W: Lavender and rosemary are popular, although I prefer peppermint.

M: I see. Do you know how much it is?

W: Yeah. It's 12 dollars a bottle, but it's totally worth it.

M: Okay. Thanks.

우·리·말·해·석

남: 이봐, Sue. 너는 오라클 목욕 소금에 대해 어떻게 생각해? 나는 Grace

를 위해 좀 살까 생각해.
여: 좋은 생각이야. 그것의 긴장을 풀어주는 효과는 내게 정말 도움이 되고
있어.
남: 정말? Grace는 그녀도 딱 그런 것을 원한다고 말했어.
여: 그것은 미네랄과 천연기름으로 가득해서 그녀는 그것을 좋아할 거야.
남: 너는 어떤 향을 추천하니?
여: 라벤더와 로즈마리가 인기 있지만, 나는 페퍼민트를 선호해.
남: 그렇구나. 너는 그것이 얼마인지 아니?
여: 응. 그것은 한 병에 12달러지만, 그것은 완전히 그만한 가치가 있어.
남: 알겠어. 고마워.

relaxing [riléksiŋ] 형 긴장을 풀어주는, 마음을 느긋하게 해 주는
packed with ~로 가득한
recommend [rèkəménd] 동 추천하다
scent [sent] 명 향, 향기
worth [wəːrθ] 형 ~의 가치가 있는

03 전화목적파악 ▶ 정답 ⑤

듣·기·대·본
(*Telephone rings.*)
W: Yellow Shopping Mall. How may I help you?
M: Hello. My name is Chris Walker. I'm calling about the
order I made for a shirt.
W: (*Typing sound*) Yes, Mr. Walker. I see that you ordered a
shirt on June 2nd.
M: That's right. I got a text message saying the delivery
was complete, but I never received the package.
W: Really? It's possible there was a mistake with the
delivery. We'll send you another shirt.
M: How long will it take?
W: Two days. Or, would you like a refund?
M: No, I can wait. Could you send it right away?
W: Of course. We're very sorry. And thank you for your
patience.

우·리·말·해·석
(전화벨이 울린다.)
여: Yellow 쇼핑몰입니다. 어떻게 도와드릴까요?
남: 안녕하세요. 제 이름은 Chris Walker예요. 제가 주문한 셔츠 건으로 전
화드렸어요.
여: (키보드 치는 소리) 네, Walker 씨. 6월 2일에 셔츠를 주문하신 걸로 확
인됩니다.
남: 맞아요. 저는 배송이 완료되었다는 문자를 받았는데, 택배를 받은 적이
없어요.
여: 정말요? 배송에 실수가 있었을 수 있어요. 저희가 당신께 또 하나의 셔
츠를 보내드릴게요.
남: 그건 얼마나 걸릴까요?
여: 이틀이요. 아니면, 환불을 원하시나요?
남: 아뇨, 전 기다릴 수 있어요. 당신은 그것을 바로 보내주실 수 있나요?
여: 물론이죠. 정말 죄송합니다. 그리고 당신의 인내에 감사드립니다. (기다
려주셔서 감사합니다.)

package [pækidʒ] 명 택배, 소포
refund [ríːfʌnd] 명 환불
patience [péiʃəns] 명 인내, 참을성

04 수치파악(시각) ▶ 정답 ⑤

듣·기·대·본
W: Hey, David. Are you going to go work out at the gym
today?
M: Yeah, I think I will go work out around 3 p.m. Why?
W: I was going to ask if you wanted to go work out
together.
M: Sure! I'll go with you. What time were you planning to
go?
W: I was thinking around 5 p.m. Would that work for you?
M: I'm afraid not. I am going to have dinner with my friends
at that time.
W: How about after dinner? Maybe at 8 p.m.?
M: I think I can make it then.
W: Okay! I'll see you at the gym.

우·리·말·해·석
여: 이봐, David. 너 오늘 체육관에 운동하러 갈 거니?
남: 응. 난 오후 3시쯤에 운동하러 갈 생각이야. 왜?
여: 나는 네가 같이 운동하러 가고 싶은지 물어보려고 했어.
남: 물론이지! 너와 같이 갈게. 너는 몇 시에 갈 계획이었니?
여: 나는 오후 5시쯤을 생각 중이었어. 그게 너에게 괜찮겠니?
남: 나는 안 될 것 같아. 나는 내 친구들과 그 시간에 저녁을 먹을 거야.
여: 저녁 먹은 후에는 어때? 아마 오후 8시쯤?
남: 나는 그때 갈 수 있을 것 같아.
여: 좋아! 체육관에서 보자.

go work out 운동하러 가다
around [əráund] 부 ~쯤, 약
make it 제시간에 도착하다, (어떤 곳에 간신히) 시간 맞춰 가다

05 심정추론 ▶ 정답 ②

듣·기·대·본
W: Look! The girl in the yellow swimsuit swims very fast.
M: Yeah, she is an excellent swimmer.
W: Yes, I can see that.
M: She also won the swimming contest last month.
W: Oh, you know her well!
M: Of course I do. She is my youngest daughter.
W: That's why you keep smiling!

우·리·말·해·석
① 슬픈   ② 자랑스러운   ③ 짜증이 난   ④ 충격을 받은   ⑤ 미안한

여: 봐요! 노란 수영복 입은 저 여자아이 정말 빠르게 수영하네요.
남: 네, 그녀는 뛰어난 수영 선수예요.
여: 네, 정말 그렇군요.
남: 그녀는 또한 지난달 수영 대회에서 우승했어요.
여: 오, 그녀에 대해 잘 알고 있군요!
남: 물론이죠. 그녀는 제 막내딸인걸요.
여: 그래서 당신이 계속 미소 짓고 있는 거군요.

keep -ing 계속 ~하다

LISTENING ADVICE

'swimmer'와 'swimming'은 한 단어 내에 동일한 자음이 연속되어 앞 자음 소리가 탈락하고 뒤에 오는 자음만 발음하여 각각 [스위머ㄹ], [스위밍]으로 발음됩니다.

06 그림상황에적절한대화찾기 ▶ 정답 ②

듣·기·대·본

① W: What are you doing now?
M: I'm playing with my daughter.
② W: Honey, did we buy soy sauce?
M: Hold on. Let me check the cart.
③ W: That'll be 87 dollars in total.
M: What? I think there must be a mistake.
④ W: Do you have a coin? We need one for the cart.
M: Yeah. I have one right here.
⑤ W: I can't find my phone. Can you call it?
M: Okay. I'm calling now.

우·리·말·해·석

① 여: 당신은 지금 뭐하고 있나요?
남: 저는 제 딸과 놀고 있어요.
② 여: 여보, 우리 간장을 샀나요?
남: 잠깐만요. 제가 카트를 확인해볼게요.
③ 여: 모두 합해서 87달러입니다.
남: 뭐라고요? 제 생각에 뭔가 실수가 있는 것 같아요.
④ 여: 당신은 동전이 있나요? 우리는 카트를 위해 하나 필요해요.
남: 네. 바로 여기 하나 있어요.
⑤ 여: 제 휴대폰을 찾을 수 없어요. 그것에 전화를 걸어줄 수 있어요?
남: 알겠어요. 지금 전화할게요.

단·어·및·표·현

soy sauce 간장
check [tʃek] [동] 확인하다, 알아보다
in total 모두 합해서, 총

07 부탁(요청)한일파악 ▶ 정답 ②

듣·기·대·본

(Cellphone rings.)
M: Hello?
W: Hello, Mr. Bowman, this is Mike's mother.
M: Oh, hi, Mrs. Myers.
W: I'm sorry, but can I pick my son up from school an hour early today?
M: May I ask what this is about?
W: It's my fault. I had forgotten that classes end late today when I made Mike's dentist appointment.
M: It's OK. His last class is biology. I'll let the teacher know. By the way, I'm very happy with Mike's grades. He's doing well.
W: Thank you very much.

우·리·말·해·석

(휴대전화가 울린다.)
남: 여보세요?
여: 여보세요, Bowman 선생님, Mike의 엄마입니다.
남: 아, 안녕하세요, Myers 부인.
여: 죄송하지만, 오늘 제 아이를 한 시간 일찍 데려갈 수 있나요?
남: 무슨 일인지 여쭤봐도 될까요?
여: 제 잘못입니다. Mike의 치과 예약을 할 때 오늘 수업이 늦게 끝난다는 것을 깜빡했습니다.
남: 괜찮습니다. 그의 마지막 수업은 생물입니다. 선생님에게 알리겠습니다. 그건 그렇고, 저는 Mike의 성적에 매우 기분이 좋습니다. 잘하고 있어요.
여: 정말 감사합니다.

단·어·및·표·현

make an appointment 예약하다, 만날 약속을 하다

08 담화미언급 ▶ 정답 ③

듣·기·대·본

W: Hello, listeners! Cornville Community Center's Autumn Program begins next week. This long-awaited program has been delayed because of the recent typhoons. Still, it will run for 10 weeks as usual, and end in late November. The program will offer many classes such as farming, gardening, and even creative writing. The program is for those who are 12 years of age and older. Please visit the website to learn more.

우·리·말·해·석

여: 안녕하세요, 청취자 여러분! Cornville 지역사회 센터의 가을 프로그램이 다음 주에 시작합니다. 오래 기다려온 이 프로그램이 최근 태풍으로 인해 지연되어 왔습니다. 그래도, 그것은 예전처럼 10주간 운영되고 11월 말에 끝날 것입니다. 프로그램은 농사, 정원 관리와 창의적 글쓰기 같은 많은 강좌들을 제공할 것입니다. 프로그램은 12세 이상을 위한 것입니다. 더 많은 것을 알아보시려면 홈페이지를 방문해주세요.

단·어·및·표·현

offer [ɔ́(:)fər] [동] 제공하다

09 담화화제추론 ▶ 정답 ①

듣·기·대·본

M: This is a sport that uses a ball. This sport is usually played on a wooden court. You can score points by putting the ball through the opponent's hoop. The hoop is round and it is 10 feet above the ground. You need to use your hands to control the ball, however, you are not allowed to touch the ball with your feet.

우·리·말·해·석

남: 이것은 공을 사용하는 운동입니다. 이 운동은 나무로 된 코트에서 보통 경기가 이루어집니다. 당신은 공을 상대방의 링에 통과시켜 넣음으로써 점수를 얻을 수 있습니다. 링은 둥근 모양이고 땅 위 10피트에 있습니다. 공을 제어하기 위해 당신의 손을 사용해야 합니다. 그러나 당신의 발로 공을 건드리는 것은 허용되지 않습니다.

단·어·및·표·현

hoop [hu:p] [명] (농구의) 링, 테, 고리

10 어색한대화찾기 ▶ 정답 ④

듣·기·대·본

① M: The weather is getting cold.
W: Yeah. It is almost winter.
② M: You must not eat this food.
W: What's wrong with it?
③ M: What should I do to lose weight?
W: How about changing your eating habits?

④ M: What are you going to do this summer vacation?
　W: It was fantastic. I went to Jejudo with my family.
⑤ M: Will you watch the new James Bond movie with me today?
　W: I am sorry. I have plans today.

우·리·말·해·석

① 남: 날씨가 점점 추워진다.
　여: 응, 거의 겨울이야.
② 남: 너 이 음식을 먹어서는 안 돼.
　여: 이 음식에 무슨 문제가 있는데?
③ 남: 체중을 줄이기 위해 내가 무엇을 해야 하지?
　여: 너의 식습관을 바꿔보는 건 어때?
④ 남: 이번 여름 방학에 뭐 할 거니?
　여: 대단했어. 나는 가족과 함께 제주도에 갔었어.
⑤ 남: 오늘 나랑 같이 새로 나온 James Bond 영화 볼래?
　여: 미안해. 나는 오늘 계획이 있어.

단·어·및·표·현

lose weight 체중을 줄이다

11 할일파악(대화직후)　▶ 정답 ②

듣·기·대·본

M: Torrie, we've been in the library for two hours now. I can't focus anymore.
W: Yeah, me, either. Let's go outside and get some coffee.
M: Okay. Oh, wait. I need to bring this cup with me.
W: Why?
M: Well, if we bring our own cup to the cafe, they give us a discount on coffee.
W: Really? That's brilliant. It's to help protect the environment, right?
M: Yes. If you have a spare cup with you…
W: I have one in my locker. I'll go get it right away.
M: Sure. Take your time.

우·리·말·해·석

남: Torrie, 우리는 지금 도서관에 두 시간 동안 있었어. 난 더 이상 집중할 수가 없어.
여: 응, 나도 마찬가지야. 밖에 나가서 커피 좀 마시자.
남: 좋아. 오, 잠깐만. 난 이 컵을 가지고 가야 해.
여: 왜?
남: 음, 우리가 카페에 우리 컵을 가져가면 그들은 우리에게 커피를 할인해 줘.
여: 정말? 그거 멋지다. 그건 환경을 보호하기 위해서지, 그렇지?
남: 응. 네가 여분의 컵이 있으면…
여: 내 사물함에 하나 있어. 바로 가서 가져올게.
남: 그래. 천천히 해.

단·어·및·표·현

focus [fóukəs] ⑧ 집중하다
spare [spɛər] ⑧ 여분의
take one's time 천천히 하다

12 도표정보파악　▶ 정답 ⑤

듣·기·대·본

M: Honey, which mattress should we buy?
W: Let's buy a large mattress. Our old mattress felt a bit small.

M: I agree. Let's get a king size mattress then.
W: Okay. Should we choose a hard mattress?
M: Yes. I definitely get a better sleep when using a hard mattress.
W: Then, we have two options to choose from.
M: Let's choose the one that offers the longer trial period.
W: Yes. Then, we'll have more time to test out the mattress before deciding if we want to keep it.

우·리·말·해·석

	모델	크기	단단함	체험 기간
①	A	퀸	단단한	100일
②	B	퀸	푹신한	60일
③	C	킹	단단한	60일
④	D	킹	푹신한	100일
⑤	E	킹	단단한	100일

남: 여보, 우리는 어떤 매트리스를 사야 할까요?
여: 큰 매트리스를 삽시다. 우리의 낡은 매트리스는 다소 작게 느껴졌어요.
남: 동의해요. 그러면 킹 사이즈 매트리스를 사요.
여: 알겠어요. 우리는 단단한 매트리스를 선택해야 할까요?
남: 네. 저는 단단한 매트리스를 사용할 때 확실히 더 잠을 잘 자요.
여: 그러면, 우리에게는 고를 수 있는 두 가지 선택이 있네요.
남: 더 긴 체험 기간을 제공하는 걸로 골라요.
여: 네. 그러면, 그것을 가지고 있고 싶은지를 결정하기 전에 우리는 그 매트리스를 체험할 수 있는 시간이 더 많겠어요.

단·어·및·표·현

hard [ha:rd] ⑧ 단단한, 딱딱한
definitely [défənitli] ⑨ 확실히, 분명히
trial period 체험 기간

13 수치파악(날짜)　▶ 정답 ③

듣·기·대·본

M: Would you like to go see a movie tomorrow?
W: I'd love to, but I'm busy all day tomorrow. How about this Saturday?
M: You mean October 11? It's my grandmother's birthday.
W: Then how about Wednesday, October 8?
M: We can't see a movie on Wednesday. We have a math test on Thursday.
W: You're right. Then let's see a movie on Thursday after the test. So it's going to be October 9.
M: That's a good idea. I'll buy tickets on Thursday around 7.

우·리·말·해·석

남: 내일 영화를 보러 갈래?
여: 나도 그러고 싶지만, 난 내일 하루 종일 바빠. 이번 토요일은 어때?
남: 10월 11일 말이야? 그날은 우리 할머니 생신이야.
여: 그럼 10월 8일 수요일은 어때?
남: 우리는 수요일에 영화를 볼 수 없어. 목요일에 수학 시험이 있잖아.
여: 네 말이 맞다. 그럼 시험 끝나고 목요일에 영화를 보자. 그러니까 10월 9일에 말이야.
남: 그거 좋은 생각이다. 내가 목요일 7시쯤 표를 구매할게.

단·어·및·표·현

all day 하루 종일

14 한일파악 ▶ 정답 ③

듣·기·대·본

M: Caroline, did you hear the news about Mia?
W: Yes. She won an award at the city art contest.
M: There's a special exhibition going on for the winners.
W: That's right. It's at the city art center.
M: I want to go and see her painting. Do you want to come with me?
W: Thanks for asking, but I already saw the exhibition with my sister last Saturday.
M: Really? How did you like it?
W: It was very interesting. I'm sure you'll enjoy it.
M: OK. I'll make sure I go.

우·리·말·해·석

남: Caroline, 너 Mia에 대한 소식 들었어?
여: 응. 그녀는 시립 미술 대회에서 상을 탔잖아.
남: 우승자들을 위해 진행되고 있는 특별전이 있어.
여: 맞아. 그것은 시립 예술 회관에서 열리고 있어.
남: 나는 가서 그녀의 그림을 보고 싶어. 나랑 같이 갈래?
여: 물어봐 줘서 고맙지만, 나는 이미 지난 토요일에 내 여동생과 전시회를 봤어.
남: 정말? 어땠어?
여: 매우 흥미로웠어. 네가 그것(전시회)을 즐길 거라고 확신해.
남: 응. 꼭 갈게.

단·어·및·표·현

win an award 상을 타다
exhibition [èksəbíʃən] [명] 전시회
make sure 꼭 ~하다, 확실하게 하다

15 담화목적파악 ▶ 정답 ⑤

듣·기·대·본

W: Attention, visitors to Elm National Park. During your visit, please follow these rules. First, keep to the trail so you don't get lost. Second, fires are prohibited. Third, take any trash back home with you so we can keep the park clean. I hope you have fun. Safe trekking!

우·리·말·해·석

여: Elm 국립 공원 방문객 여러분께 알려드립니다. 방문 중에는 다음 규칙들을 따라 주시기 바랍니다. 첫째, 길을 잃지 않도록 코스를 따라 가세요. 둘째, 불은 금지되어 있습니다. 셋째, 공원을 깨끗하게 유지할 수 있도록 모든 쓰레기는 집으로 가져가주세요. 즐거운 시간 되시기 바랍니다. 안전한 트레킹하세요!

단·어·및·표·현

trail [treil] [명] (특정 목적을 위해 따라 가는) 코스, 루트
prohibit [prouhíbit] [동] 금지하다
trekking [trékiŋ] [명] 트레킹, 등산

16 수치계산(금액) ▶ 정답 ②

듣·기·대·본

W: Welcome to Meow Pet Store.
M: Hi there. I need to purchase some cat food.
W: We have two options available: regular brand and premium brand. The premium brand contains more nutrients.
M: How much does each brand cost?
W: The regular brand is $15 per bag, and the premium brand is $25 per bag.
M: I'll go with the regular brand. Any discounts available?
W: Yes, if you buy two bags, you can get $5 off the total price.
M: In that case, I'll take two bags of the regular brand.
W: Great! Anything else you need?
M: No, that will be all.

우·리·말·해·석

여: Meow Pet Store에 오신 것을 환영합니다.
남: 안녕하세요. 저는 고양이 사료를 좀 사야 해요.
여: 일반 브랜드와 고급 브랜드 두 가지 선택지가 있습니다. 고급 브랜드는 더 많은 영양소를 포함하고 있습니다.
남: 각 브랜드의 가격은 얼마인가요?
여: 일반 브랜드는 봉지당 15달러이고, 고급 브랜드는 봉지당 25달러입니다.
남: 일반 브랜드로 할게요. 가능한 할인이 있나요?
여: 네, 두 봉지를 사시면 총 가격에서 5달러를 할인받으실 수 있습니다.
남: 그렇다면 일반 브랜드 두 봉지를 사겠습니다.
여: 좋습니다! 그 밖에 필요한 것이 있으세요?
남: 아니요, 그게 전부예요.

단·어·및·표·현

purchase [pə́ːrtʃəs] [동] 구입하다
contain [kəntéin] [동] ~이 들어[함유되어]있다, 포함하다
nutrient [njúːtriənt] [명] 영양소, 영양분
available [əvéiləbl] [형] 이용할 수 있는

17 알맞은응답찾기 ▶ 정답 ⑤

듣·기·대·본

M: Are you doing anything special this weekend, Katie?
W: I'm going to do volunteer work at a nursing home.
M: That's nice. What do you do there?
W: Nothing special. I help to serve meals and clean the rooms.
M: Isn't it hard?
W: Caring for others is not always easy, but it's worth it. It feels great to see the happy faces of those I have helped.
M: Oh, I see now. Can I come with you next time?
W: Of course. We always welcome a helping hand.

우·리·말·해·석

① 고마워. 너는 많은 도움이 되었어.
② 문제없어. 내가 널 도와줄 수 있어.
③ 미안해. 난 봉사활동을 좋아하지 않아.
④ 알겠어. 식사를 제공하기 전에 네 손을 씻어.
⑤ 물론이지. 우리는 언제나 도움의 손길을 환영해.

남: 이번 주말에 뭐 특별한 일 있니, Katie?
여: 나는 양로원에서 자원봉사를 할 거야.
남: 그거 좋네. 너는 거기서 무엇을 하니?
여: 특별한 건 없어. 나는 식사를 제공하고 방을 청소하는 것을 도와.
남: 그건 힘들지 않니?
여: 다른 사람들을 돌보는 것이 항상 쉬운 것은 아니지만, 그만한 가치가 있어. 내가 도와준 사람들의 행복한 얼굴을 보는 것은 기분이 좋아.

남: 아, 이제 알겠어. 다음에 나도 같이 가도 될까?
여: **물론이지. 우리는 언제나 도움의 손길을 환영해.**

단·어·및·표·현
serve [səːrv] ⑧ (음식을) 제공하다, 차려주다
care for ~를 돌보다, 보살피다
worth [wəːrθ] ⑱ ~할 가치가 있는
helping hand 도움의 손길, 도움

18 알맞은응답찾기　▶ 정답 ④

듣·기·대·본
W: Excuse me. Can you help me please?
M: What can I do for you, ma'am?
W: I saw a toy here yesterday that was just right for my son,
　but I can't find it now.
M: What does it look like?
W: It's a train with animals that sit on top.
M: It seems that all of the trains we had on display are sold
　out.
W: Oh, no. I really want that toy for my son's birthday.
M: I'll go and see if we have any stock left in storage.

우·리·말·해·석
① 고객님을 돕는 것이 저희의 기쁨입니다.
② 네, 장난감 기차는 요즘 매우 인기가 있습니다.
③ 걱정 마세요. 아드님이 선물을 좋아할 것입니다.
④ 창고에 재고가 남아있는지 가서 알아보겠습니다.
⑤ 저와 같이 가시겠어요? 제가 파티를 주선할 수 있습니다.

여: 실례합니다. 좀 도와주시겠어요?
남: 무엇을 도와드릴까요, 손님?
여: 어제 여기서 제 아들에게 꼭 맞는 장난감을 봤는데, 지금은 찾을 수가
　없어요.
남: 그것은 어떻게 생겼나요?
여: 동물들이 위에 앉아 있는 기차였어요.
남: 진열되었던 모든 기차들이 품절된 것 같습니다.
여: 아, 안 되는데. 저는 제 아들의 생일 선물로 그 장난감을 정말로 원해요.
남: **창고에 재고가 남아있는지 가서 알아보겠습니다.**

단·어·및·표·현
sold out 품절된

19 알맞은응답찾기　▶ 정답 ④

듣·기·대·본
W: Hello. Welcome to Sweet Home Furniture Store. What
　can I do for you?
M: Hi, I'm looking for a dining table.
W: Okay. We have many sizes of dining tables. For
　example, the smallest one seats 2 people, and the
　biggest one will seat 10 to 12 people.
M: I need one that comes with 4 chairs.
W: Alright. What shape would you prefer, a rectangular one
　or an oval one?
M: I would prefer a rectangular one.
W: Okay. Do you have a price range in mind?
M: I'd like to spend as little as possible.

우·리·말·해·석
① 저는 네 명 자리를 예약했습니다.
② 나무 테이블이 딱 좋을 것입니다.
③ 죄송하지만 그것은 지금 세일 중이 아닙니다.
④ 저는 가능한 한 적게 쓰고 싶습니다.
⑤ 그것은 잘못된 주소로 배송되었습니다.

여: 안녕하세요. Sweet Home 가구점에 오신 것을 환영합니다. 무엇을 도
　와 드릴까요?
남: 안녕하세요, 저는 식탁을 찾고 있어요.
여: 네. 저희는 다양한 크기의 식탁이 있습니다. 예를 들어, 가장 작은 것
　은 2인이 앉을 수 있고, 가장 큰 것은 10명에서 12명까지 앉을 수 있
　습니다.
남: 저는 의자 4개가 함께 제공되는 것이 필요해요.
여: 알겠습니다. 직사각형과 타원형 중 어떤 모양을 선호하시나요?
남: 저는 직사각형 모양을 더 선호합니다.
여: 네. 생각하고 있는 가격대가 있으신가요?
남: **저는 가능한 한 적게 쓰고 싶습니다.**

단·어·및·표·현
look for ~을 찾다
dining table 식탁
seat [siːt] ⑧ 좌석이 있다
rectangular [rektǽŋgjələr] ⑱ 직사각형의
oval [óuvəl] ⑱ 타원형의
price range 가격대

20 상황에적절한말찾기　▶ 정답 ④

듣·기·대·본
W: Sally is at the park. She is having a good time with her
　friends. It is getting late and they are about to leave.
　One of her friends, Joe, is about to leave his empty
　water bottle on the bench. After noticing what he is
　about to do, she thinks it's wrong. So, she decides to
　tell Joe that he should pick up his trash. In this situation,
　what would Sally most likely say to Joe?
Sally: Joe, **you shouldn't leave the bottle behind.**

우·리·말·해·석
① 너는 이 근처에서 쓰레기통을 본 적이 있어?
② 우리는 다음 주에 여기에 다시 와야 해.
③ 내가 내 책을 네 빈 가방에 넣어도 될까?
④ 너는 그 병을 두고 가면 안 돼.
⑤ 너는 물 좀 마실래?

여: Sally는 공원에 있다. 그녀는 그녀의 친구들과 좋은 시간을 보내는 중
　이다. (시간이) 늦어지고 있고 그들은 막 떠나려는 참이다. 그녀의 친구
　들 중 한 명인 Joe는 벤치에 그의 빈 물병을 두고 가려고 한다. 그가 무
　엇을 하려고 하는지 알아차린 후, 그녀는 그것이 잘못됐다고 생각한다.
　그래서, 그녀는 Joe에게 그가 그의 쓰레기를 치워야 한다고 말하기로
　결정한다. 이러한 상황에서, Sally가 Joe에게 뭐라고 말하겠는가?
Sally: Joe, **너는 그 병을 두고 가면 안 돼.**

단·어·및·표·현
get [get] ⑧ ~해지다
be about to + 동사원형 (막) ~하려는 참이다, ~하려고 하다
pick up ~ ~을 치우다
trash can (옥외용) 쓰레기통
leave ~ behind ~을 두고 가다

Words & Expressions Review

1. ~해지다	2. 향, 향기	3. 운영하다, 달리다
4. ~할 가치가 있는	5. 기운, 열성	6. 좌석이 있다
7. 가격대	8. 잘못, 단점	9. 간장
10. 예약하다, 만날 약속을 하다	11. ~을 치우다	12. ~를 돌보다, 보살피다
13. ~을 찾다	14. 타원형의	15. 트레킹, 등산
16. 제공하다	17. 생물학	18. 환불
19. 운동하러 가다	20. 직사각형의	21. (음식을) 제공하다, 차려주다
22. 체험 기간	23. 금지하다	24. 피트(길이의 단위로 약 30cm)
25. 하루 종일	26. ~을 두고 가다	27. 깃발
28. 확인하다, 알아보다	29. 나무로 된, 목재의	30. 뛰어난, 훌륭한
31. 재고(품)	32. ~으로 가득한	33. 집중하다
34. 구호	35. 태풍	36. 택배, 소포
37. ~쯤, 약	38. 영양소, 영양분	39. 확실히, 분명히
40. 오래 기다려온	41. 쓰레기통	42. 체중을 줄이다
43. 인내, 참을성	44. 제시간에 도착하다	

Listening Test

영어듣기 모의고사 11회

|정|답|

01 ②	02 ④	03 ④	04 ⑤	05 ④
06 ③	07 ②	08 ④	09 ③	10 ③
11 ①	12 ⑤	13 ③	14 ①	15 ②
16 ④	17 ④	18 ④	19 ⑤	20 ②

01 그림정보파악(대화) ▶ 정답 ②

듣·기·대·본

M: Stacy, what are you making with that clay?

W: I'm making a pot mat for my kitchen.

M: You made a really good heart.

W: Thanks. I first tried to make a star, but it didn't work out so well. So, I changed the shape.

M: I see. Is that a cat on it?

W: Yes! I wanted to put my cat, Luna's face on it.

M: That's lovely. Why don't you add her name to it?

W: Good idea. I'll write her name right away.

우·리·말·해·석

남: Stacy, 그 점토로 무엇을 만들고 있어?

여: 나는 내 부엌용 냄비 받침을 만들고 있어.

남: 하트를 정말 잘 만들었네.

여: 고마워. 나는 처음에 별을 만들려고 시도했지만, 그것은 썩 잘되지 않았어. 그래서, 모양을 바꿨어.

남: 알겠어. 그 위에 있는 건 고양이니?

여: 응! 나는 내 고양이 Luna의 얼굴을 거기에 넣고 싶었어.

남: 그것은 사랑스럽다. 고양이의 이름을 추가하지 그래?

여: 좋은 생각이야. 나는 당장 그녀의 이름을 쓸게.

단·어·및·표·현

pot mat 냄비 받침

work out (일이) 잘 풀리다

02 대화미언급 ▶ 정답 ④

듣·기·대·본

W: Randy, you should come to the Sunshine Bazaar with me.

M: What's the Sunshine Bazaar?

W: It's a sales event designed to raise money for a local charity.

M: Sounds interesting. Tell me more.

W: The profits will go to a foundation for children.

M: Great. When is it?

W: It'll be held this weekend from 10 a.m. to 6 p.m.

M: Do you know what kinds of items we can buy?

W: Yes. From pencils to clothes, all kinds of items will be sold. I even heard there will be secondhand gadgets such as headsets and tablets.

M: Cool. I've been thinking of buying a headset. I'll definitely be there.

우·리·말·해·석

여: Randy, 넌 나와 Sunshine 바자회에 가야 해.

남: Sunshine 바자회가 뭐야?

여: 지역 자선 단체를 위해 모금하려고 마련된 판매 행사야.

남: 흥미로운걸. 내게 더 얘기해줘.

여: 수익은 어린이들을 위한 재단으로 갈 거야.

남: 좋네. 그게 언제야?

여: 이번 주말에 오전 10시부터 오후 6시까지 열릴 거야.

남: 너는 우리가 어떤 종류의 물품들을 살 수 있는지 아니?

여: 응. 연필들부터 옷까지, 모든 종류의 물품들이 팔릴 거야. 나는 심지어 헤드셋이나 태블릿 같은 중고 기기들도 있을 거라 들었어.

남: 멋진데. 나는 헤드셋을 하나 사는 것을 생각해왔어. 나는 무조건 그곳에 갈 거야.

단·어·및·표·현

bazaar [bəzɑ́ːr] [명] 바자회

designed [dizáind] [형] 설계된, 계획된

raise money 모금하다

charity [tʃǽrəti] [명] 자선[구호] 단체

profit [prɑ́fit] [명] 수익, 이익

foundation [faundéiʃən] [명] 재단

hold [hould] [동] 열다, 개최하다

secondhand [sékəndhǽnd] [형] 중고의

gadget [gǽdʒit] [명] 기기, 기계 장치

03 전화목적파악 ▶ 정답 ④

듣·기·대·본

(*Telephone rings.*)

W: Hello, this is Midtown Boxing Academy.

M: Hi, I'm in the boxing class that's starting this Friday. I'd like to check if I need to bring anything to the class.

W: Which level are you in?

11회 모의고사

M: Basic level.

W: Then, there's nothing you need to bring to the class. We provide everything that you will need.

M: Really? Not even gloves? I was going to bring my brother's old ones.

W: We have gloves for beginners here, but you can bring your own if you prefer. Just remember to wear something comfortable.

M: I will. Thank you.

우·리·말·해·석

(전화벨이 울린다.)

여: 여보세요, Midtown Boxing 학원입니다.

남: 안녕하세요, 저는 이번 주 금요일에 시작하는 복싱 수업을 들어요. 저는 수업에 가져가야 할 것이 있는지 확인하고 싶어서요.

여: 어느 단계이신가요?

남: 기초 단계입니다.

여: 그러면, 수업에 가져오실 것은 아무것도 없습니다. 당신에게 필요한 것은 모두 저희가 제공해드려요.

남: 정말요? 장갑도 필요 없나요? 저는 저희 형의 오래된 장갑을 가져가려고 했어요.

여: 초보자들을 위한 장갑은 여기 있지만, 당신이 선호하신다면 당신의 것을 가지고 오셔도 돼요. 편안한 옷을 입으시는 것만 기억해 주세요.

남: 그럴게요. 감사합니다.

단·어·및·표·현

bring [briŋ] [동] 가져오다

provide [prəváid] [동] 제공하다

comfortable [kʌ́mfərtəbl] [형] 편안한, 편한

04 수치파악(시각) ▶ 정답 ⑤

듣·기·대·본

M: Hey, Bridget. What time do you want to work on our history project together?

W: Umm… Do you have time after school today? Because I am free after 4 p.m.

M: I have to go to the volunteer center after school, so I can't meet today. Are you free on the weekend?

W: Yeah! I have tennis practice from 11 a.m. to 1 p.m. on Saturday, but other than that I am free.

M: Okay! Then, do you want to meet at 2 p.m. on Saturday?

W: Let's meet at 3 p.m., just to be safe. Sometimes tennis practice ends later than usual.

M: Sounds good! I will see you then.

우·리·말·해·석

남: 이봐, Bridget. 너는 몇 시에 우리 역사 과제를 같이 하고 싶니?

여: 음… 너는 오늘 방과 후에 시간 있니? 왜냐하면 나는 오후 4시 이후에 한가하거든.

남: 나는 방과 후에 자원봉사 센터에 가야 해서 오늘은 만날 수 없어. 너는 이번 주말에 시간 있니?

여: 응! 나는 토요일 오전 11시부터 오후 1시에 테니스 연습이 있지만 그것을 제외하면 한가해.

남: 알겠어! 그럼, 토요일 오후 2시에 만날래?

여: 오후 3시에 만나자, 혹시 모르니까. 때때로 테니스 연습은 평소보다 늦게 끝나.

남: 좋아! 그때 보자.

단·어·및·표·현

work on (과제 · 프로젝트 등) ~을 하다

free [friː] [형] 한가한, 다른 계획[약속]이 없는

other than that 그것을 제외하고는, 그거 말고는

just to be safe 혹시 모르니까, 만약을 위해서

05 심정추론 ▶ 정답 ④

듣·기·대·본

W: Hello. Welcome to Lily's Cake House.

M: Hi. I'm here to pick up a cake I ordered a few days ago.

W: Okay. May I have your name?

M: Tom Bradley. It's a wedding anniversary cake.

W: Oh, I remember. Please wait a minute. [*Pause*] Here's your cake.

M: Wow! It's beautiful. It's amazing how you put our photo on the cake.

W: That's our specialty. I'm glad you like it.

M: It's perfect. I'm sure my wife will be very impressed with this.

W: Great! Have a nice day.

우·리·말·해·석

① 속상한 ② 지루해하는 ③ 후회하는
④ 만족한 ⑤ 당황스러운

여: 안녕하세요. Lily's Cake House에 오신 것을 환영합니다.

남: 안녕하세요. 저는 며칠 전에 제가 주문한 케이크를 찾으러 여기 왔어요.

여: 네. 성함이 어떻게 되세요?

남: Tom Bradley예요. 결혼기념일 케이크예요.

여: 아, 기억해요. 잠시만 기다려주세요. [잠시 후] 여기 당신의 케이크입니다.

남: 우와! 아름다워요. 당신이 어떻게 우리 사진을 케이크에 올려놓으셨는지 놀랍네요.

여: 그건 저희 전문입니다. 좋아해 주셔서 기쁘네요.

남: 완벽해요. 저는 제 아내가 이것에 매우 감동받을 거라고 확신해요.

여: 좋네요! 좋은 하루 보내세요.

단·어·및·표·현

pick up (어디에서) ~을 찾다[찾아오다]

anniversary [æ̀nəvə́ːrsəri] [명] 기념일

specialty [spéʃəlti] [명] 전문, 특기

be impressed with ~에 감동받다

06 그림상황에적절한대화찾기 ▶ 정답 ③

듣·기·대·본

① W: It's so hot outside.
M: Yes, it is. Maybe we shouldn't ride a bike today.

② W: I just got back from the department store.
M: Did you buy me a bike?

③ W: Please don't let go of me.
M: I won't. You don't have to worry.

④ W: Did you see that car?
M: I did. The driver is very careless.

⑤ W: Does this come with an adjustable back?
M: Yes. It also comes with a front basket of your choice.

우·리·말·해·석

① 여: 밖은 너무 더워.

남: 응, 그러네. 아마 우리는 오늘 자전거를 타면 안 될 것 같아.
② 여: 나는 백화점에서 방금 돌아왔어.
남: 내게 줄 자전거를 샀니?
③ 여: 제발 저를 놓지 마세요.
남: 그렇게 안 할게. 걱정할 필요 없어.
④ 여: 너는 그 차를 보았니?
남: 봤어. 운전사가 매우 부주의해.
⑤ 여: 이것은 조절 가능한 등받이가 딸려 있나요?
남: 네. 고객님이 직접 선택하실 수 있는 앞바구니도 드린답니다.

단·어·및·표·현

careless [kέərlis] [형] 부주의한

LISTENING ADVICE

단어가 'nd' 혹은 'nt'로 끝날 때 끝소리 [d]와 [t] 소리는 탈락되거나 약하게 발음됩니다. 예를 들어 'don't'는 [돈트]보다는 [돈ㅌ] 또는 [돈]으로 들리고, 'shouldn't'는 [슈든트]가 아닌 [슈든ㅌ] 혹은 [슈든]으로 들리지요. 또, 'won't'는 [원트]가 아닌 [원ㅌ]나 [원]으로 들립니다. 'nt'로 끝나는 단어들의 소리에 집중하여 다시 들어보세요.

07 부탁(요청)한일파악 ▶ 정답 ②

듣·기·대·본

W: Thank you for coming, Shawn. So, what do you think?
M: It's very nice! You must have worked hard to open this bakery.
W: It wasn't easy at the beginning. But then I started to get a few regular customers.
M: I'm so proud of you. I'm sure you'll get more regulars sooner or later.
W: Thank you. Speaking of which, could you help me to get more customers?
M: Sure! What can I do for you?
W: Can you write a review of my bakery on your blog?
M: Sure thing. No problem.

우·리·말·해·석

여: 와 줘서 고마워, Shawn. 그래서, 어떻게 생각해?
남: 매우 멋져! 너는 이 빵집을 열기 위해 열심히 일했겠구나.
여: 그것은 처음에는 쉽지 않았어. 하지만 그 후 나는 몇 명의 단골손님을 갖기 시작했어.
남: 나는 네가 무척 자랑스럽다. 나는 너에게 언젠가는 단골들이 더 많이 생길 거라고 확신해.
여: 고마워. 그 말이 나와서 말인데, 너는 내가 더 많은 손님들을 얻게 나를 도와줄 수 있어?
남: 그럼! 내가 너를 위해 무엇을 할까?
여: 네가 네 블로그에 내 빵집에 대한 리뷰를 써줄 수 있을까?
남: 물론이지. 문제없어.

단·어·및·표·현

regular customer 단골손님
speaking of which 말이 나와서 말인데

08 담화미언급 ▶ 정답 ④

듣·기·대·본

W: Good afternoon! Are you looking for quality books for your kids? Then, come to Sunnyside Children's Bookstore, located in downtown Chicago. We are open Monday through Saturday from 10 a.m. to 9 p.m. We are closed on Sunday. We have thousands of picture books, non-fiction books, middle-grade novels, and even selected novels for adults. If you apply for a membership on our website, you can get a 10% discount. For more information, visit our website, www.thescbookstore.com. Thank you.

우·리·말·해·석

여: 안녕하세요! 여러분은 여러분의 아이들을 위한 양질의 책들을 찾고 있습니까? 그렇다면, 시카고 시내에 위치한 Sunnyside Children's Bookstore로 오세요. 저희는 월요일부터 토요일까지 오전 10시부터 오후 9시까지 엽니다. 저희는 일요일에는 닫습니다. 저희는 수천 권의 그림책들, 비소설 도서들, 중등 소설, 그리고 어른들을 위한 선별된 소설들도 있습니다. 저희 웹사이트에서 회원 신청을 하시면, 10% 할인을 받을 수 있습니다. 더 많은 정보를 위해 저의 웹사이트 www.thescbookstore.com을 방문하세요. 감사합니다.

단·어·및·표·현

downtown [dàuntáun] [형] 시내의, 도심의
apply for ~ ~을 신청하다

09 담화화제추론 ▶ 정답 ③

듣·기·대·본

W: This is an electronic home device. You can use this to clean floors. It usually looks like a rectangle or a tube. You can change the suction power based on what you're cleaning. People use it to suck up dust, dirt, and messes from carpets and floors. It's easy to use and helps you clean up quickly. That's why almost everyone has one at home or uses one for cleaning jobs.

우·리·말·해·석

여: 이것은 가정용 전자 기기입니다. 여러분은 이것을 바닥을 청소하는 데 사용하실 수 있습니다. 이것은 보통 직사각형 또는 튜브처럼 보입니다. 여러분은 여러분이 무엇을 청소하는지에 따라 흡입력을 변경할 수 있습니다. 사람들은 카펫과 바닥에서 먼지, 때, 그리고 지저분한 것들을 빨아들이려고 이것을 사용합니다. 이것은 사용하기 쉽고 당신이 빠르게 청소하도록 도와줍니다. 그래서 거의 모든 사람들이 집에 하나씩 가지고 있거나 청소 작업에 (하나씩) 사용합니다.

단·어·및·표·현

device [diváis] [명] 기기, 장치, 기구
suction [sʌ́kʃən] [명] 흡입, 빨아들이기
based on ~에 따라
suck up 빨아들이다
dust [dʌst] [명] 먼지
dirt [dəːrt] [명] 때, 먼지
mess [mes] [명] 더러운 것, 흘린 것

10 어색한대화찾기 ▶ 정답 ③

듣·기·대·본

① M: You know John, don't you?
W: Of course, I do. He is one of my best friends.
② M: Do you have any plans this afternoon?
W: Not really. Why?
③ M: Shall we stop here?
W: No, I don't.

④ M: Will you join the science club?
W: No, I'd rather join the drama club.
⑤ M: Where do you usually have lunch?
W: At school.

우·리·말·해·석

① 남: 너는 John을 알지, 그렇지 않니?
여: 물론 알지. 그는 나의 제일 친한 친구들 중 하나야.
② 남: 오늘 오후에 계획이라도 있니?
여: 딱히 없는데. 왜?
③ 남: 여기서 멈출까?
여: 아니, 난 아냐.
④ 남: 과학 동아리에 가입할 거니?
여: 아니, 난 차라리 연극 동아리에 들어가겠어.
⑤ 남: 넌 보통 점심을 어디서 먹니?
여: 학교에서.

단·어·및·표·현

join [dʒɔin] [동] 가입하다, 합류하다

11 할일파악 ▶ 정답 ①

듣·기·대·본

W: Ted, did you finish your history report?
M: Yes, I just need to print it.
W: You do know that the printer at the computer lab is broken, right?
M: What? This is the first time I've heard about this.
W: It's been broken for about a week.
M: I'd better run to Ms. Smith's office to see if I can submit the report by e-mail.
W: Hurry, class starts in 15 minutes.

우·리·말·해·석

여: Ted, 역사 리포트 끝냈니?
남: 응, 프린트만 하면 돼.
여: 너 컴퓨터실에 있는 프린터가 망가진 거는 알고 있지, 그렇지?
남: 뭐라고? 난 그거 처음 듣는 말인데.
여: 거의 일주일 동안 망가진 상태야.
남: Smith 선생님 교무실에 빨리 가서 이메일로 리포트를 제출해도 되는지 알아봐야겠다.
여: 서둘러. 수업이 15분 후에 시작해.

단·어·및·표·현

submit [səbmít] [동] 제출하다

12 도표정보파악 ▶ 정답 ⑤

듣·기·대·본

W: Jonathan, I'm picking out a hat for the summer. How do you like this blue one?
M: I think beige would match your outfits better.
W: You're right. Beige is more neutral. Should I get a wide brim or a short brim?
M: Go for a wide brim. It'll protect you from the sun.
W: That's a good idea. Do you think I need one with a chin strap?
M: Definitely. It'll stay on even when it's windy.
W: Great. I'll get that one.

우·리·말·해·석

	모델	색상	챙	턱끈
①	A	베이지	넓은 것	X
②	B	베이지	짧은(좁은) 것	O
③	C	파랑	넓은 것	O
④	D	파랑	짧은(좁은) 것	X
⑤	E	베이지	넓은 것	O

여: Jonathan, 난 여름용 모자를 고르고 있어. 이 파란 것은 어때?
남: 베이지색이 네 옷이랑 더 잘 어울릴 것 같아.
여: 맞아. 베이지가 더 중립적인(튀지 않는) 색이지. 챙이 넓은 걸 사야 할까, 짧은(좁은) 걸 사야 할까?
남: 챙 넓은 걸로 해. 햇빛으로부터 보호해 줄 거야.
여: 좋은 생각이야. 내가 턱끈이 있는 게 필요하다고 생각하니?
남: 당연하지. 바람이 불 때조차도 모자가 그대로 있게(벗겨지지 않게) 해 줄 거야.
여: 좋아. 그걸로 살게.

단·어·및·표·현

match [mætʃ] [동] (색깔 · 무늬 등이 서로) 어울리다, 맞다
outfit [áutfit] [명] 옷차림, 복장
neutral [njú:trəl] [형] 중립적인, 중간색의
brim [brim] [명] (모자의) 챙
chin strap (모자의) 턱끈

13 수치파악(날짜) ▶ 정답 ③

듣·기·대·본

(Telephone rings.)
W: Wellington's Chocolate Factory. How may I help you?
M: Hello. This is Harry Winters from Leigh Middle School. I'd like to book a tour for my students.
W: Hello, Mr. Winters. There's a tour every Tuesday in May, beginning on May 4th.
M: Can I book a tour for May 11th?
W: Of course. But if you can make it on May 18th, that would be better.
M: Why? What's special about that day?
W: On that day, you'll have a chance to taste our new line of chocolate products.
M: Wonderful. We'll visit on May 18th, then.
W: Good choice.

우·리·말·해·석

(전화벨이 울린다.)
여: Wellington의 초콜릿 공장입니다. 어떻게 도와드릴까요?
남: 안녕하세요. 저는 Leigh 중학교의 Harry Winters입니다. 저는 저희 학생들을 위해 견학을 예약하고 싶습니다.
여: 안녕하세요, Winters 씨. 5월은 5월 4일에 시작해서 매주 화요일에 견학 코스가 있습니다.
남: 5월 11일로 견학을 예약할 수 있나요?
여: 물론이죠. 그런데 만약 5월 18일에 참석하실 수 있다면, 그것이 더 나을 겁니다.
남: 왜요? 그날은 무엇이 특별한가요?
여: 그날, 저희의 새로운 종류의 초콜릿 제품들을 맛볼 수 있는 기회가 있을 겁니다.
남: 좋네요. 그럼 5월 18일에 방문할게요.
여: 좋은 선택입니다.

단·어·및·표·현

book[buk] 통 예약하다
make it 참석하다, 가다
have a chance to + 동사원형 ~할 기회가 있다
line[lain] 명 (상품의) 종류

14 한일파악 ▶ 정답 ①

듣·기·대·본

W: Daniel, how was your summer vacation? You said you were going to learn how to cook, right?
M: Oh, my uncle was going to teach me but he couldn't do it.
W: Why not?
M: He's a cook and his restaurant got very busy.
W: I see. Then did you do something else?
M: Yes. I wanted to try something new, so I went fishing with my dad.
W: Sounds fun! How was it?
M: It was great. I had so much fun.

우·리·말·해·석

여: Daniel, 네 여름 방학은 어땠어? 너는 요리하는 법을 배울 거라고 말했었잖아, 맞지?
남: 오, 내 삼촌이 나를 가르쳐주기로 했었는데 그러지 못했어.
여: 왜 못 했어?
남: 삼촌은 요리사인데 삼촌네 식당이 매우 바빠졌어.
여: 그렇구나. 그러면 너는 또 다른 일을 했니?
남: 응. 새로운 것을 시도해보고 싶어서 아빠랑 낚시하러 갔었어.
여: 재밌었겠다! 어땠어?
남: 좋았어. 너무 재미있었어.

단·어·및·표·현

cook[kuk] 통 요리하다 명 요리사
go fishing 낚시하러 가다

15 담화목적파악 ▶ 정답 ②

듣·기·대·본

W: Good morning, students. To make school life easier for our students, we're opening a borrowing service called 'School Market.' You can borrow pens, slippers, umbrellas, soccer balls and many more items from the market. There's no charge, but you need to return the items on time and take good care of them. To borrow items, please go to the student meeting room. The market will be open daily during lunchtime. I hope many of you will benefit from it. Thank you.

우·리·말·해·석

여: 좋은 아침입니다, 학생 여러분. 우리 학생들의 학교 생활을 편하게 만들기 위해, 저희는 '학교 시장'이라 불리는 대여 서비스를 시작할 예정입니다. 여러분은 시장에서 펜, 슬리퍼, 우산, 축구공과 더 많은 물건들을 빌릴 수 있습니다. 요금은 없지만, 물건을 제때에 반납해야 하고 잘 관리하셔야 합니다. 물건을 빌리려면 학생 회의실로 가세요. 시장은 매일 점심시간 동안 열릴 것입니다. 많은 분들이 그것으로부터 혜택을 받길 바랍니다. 감사합니다.

단·어·및·표·현

charge[tʃɑːrdʒ] 명 요금

on time 제때에, 시간을 어기지 않고
daily[déili] 부 매일

16 수치계산(금액) ▶ 정답 ④

듣·기·대·본

W: Welcome to Blossom Flower Shop. How can I assist you?
M: Hi, I'm looking for some flowers for a special occasion.
W: Absolutely! We have two choices: a bouquet of mixed flowers or a bouquet of just one type of flower like roses or lilies.
M: How much are they?
W: The mixed bouquet is $30, while the single flower arrangements range from $20 to $25.
M: I'll go for the mixed bouquet. Can I get a discount if I buy two bouquets?
W: Certainly! If you purchase two bouquets, we offer a 10% discount.
M: Perfect! I'll take two of the mixed bouquets.
W: Excellent choice! Let me help you pay at the counter.

우·리·말·해·석

여: Blossom 꽃집에 온 것을 환영합니다. 어떻게 도와드릴까요?
남: 안녕하세요, 저는 특별한 날을 위한 꽃을 좀 찾고 있어요.
여: 물론이죠! 저희에겐 혼합 꽃다발이나 장미나 백합 같은 단 한 종류의 꽃으로 된 꽃다발, 두 가지 선택지가 있어요.
남: 그것들은 얼마인가요?
여: 혼합 꽃다발은 30달러인 반면, 단일 꽃다발은 20달러에서 25달러 사이예요.
남: 전 혼합 꽃다발을 선택할게요. 만약 제가 두 개의 꽃다발을 사면 할인 받을 수 있나요?
여: 물론이죠! 만약 두 개의 꽃다발을 구매하시면, 저희는 10% 할인을 제공해드립니다.
남: 완벽하네요! 저는 혼합 꽃다발을 두 개 살게요.
여: 훌륭한 선택입니다! 카운터에서 결제하시도록 도와드리겠습니다.

단·어·및·표·현

special occasion 특별한 날(때, 행사)
bouquet[boukéi] 명 꽃다발, 부케
flower arrangement 꽃꽂이
range from A to B (범위가) A에서 B 사이이다
go for ~을 선택하다

17 알맞은응답찾기 ▶ 정답 ④

듣·기·대·본

W: That's a nice canvas bag you have there, Stewart.
M: Thanks, Tiffany. I really like it. Amazingly, it is one-hundred percent hand-made.
W: Really? Where did you get it?
M: I bought it at the night market in Riverside Park.
W: I thought they only sold food.
M: No, they sell all kinds of stuff. Their hand-made items are especially good.
W: Why didn't I know that? I should go there. They're open every weekend, right?
M: Yes. But be aware that they close if it rains.

우·리·말·해·석

① 아뇨. 이 가방은 수제가 아니에요.
② 음, 저는 중고품을 사는 걸 좋아하지 않아요.
③ 맞아요. 당신의 물건은 인기 있을 거예요.
④ 네. 하지만 비가 오면 그들은 문을 닫는다는 걸 알아 두세요.
⑤ 미안해요. 저는 이번 주말에 공원에 갈 수 없어요.

여: 당신은 멋진 천 가방을 가지고 있군요, Stewart.
남: 고마워요, Tiffany. 저는 그것을 정말 좋아해요. 놀랍게도, 그것은 100% 수제예요.
여: 정말요? 당신은 그것을 어디서 샀나요?
남: 저는 그것을 Riverside 공원에서 열린 야시장에서 샀어요.
여: 저는 그들이 음식만 파는 줄 알았어요.
남: 아뇨, 그들은 온갖 종류의 물건을 팔아요. 그들의 수제품들이 특히 좋아요.
여: 전 왜 그걸 몰랐을까요? 저는 거기에 가야겠어요. 그들은 주말마다 열죠, 맞죠?
남: 네. 하지만 비가 오면 그들은 문을 닫는다는 걸 알아 두세요.

단·어·및·표·현

amazingly [əméizŋli] [부] 놀랍게도
night market 야시장
all kinds of 온갖 종류의
aware [əwέər] [형] 알고 있는, 의식하고 있는

18 알맞은응답찾기 ▶ 정답 ④

듣·기·대·본

(Door keypad lock opening sound)
W: Honey, I'm home.
M: Hey, why are you panting?
W: The elevator is out of order, so I had to walk up the stairs.
M: Oh, honey, it's only six flights of stairs. You really need to exercise more.
W: Thanks for pointing that out. But, we have a bigger issue at hand.
M: What's that?
W: Our groceries will be delivered soon. So, someone has to go down and come back up again.
M: Okay. That someone must be me, I guess?
W: Could you? I'll make you a nice, big dinner.

우·리·말·해·석

① 말도 안 돼요. 계단들이 너무 미끄러워요.
② 전혀요. 당신은 장 보러 갈 수 있어요.
③ 좋은 생각이에요. 내일 운동을 시작하죠.
④ 그래 줄 수 있어요? 제가 당신에게 맛있고, 푸짐한 저녁식사를 차려 줄게요.
⑤ 맞아요. 엘리베이터는 지금 잘 작동하고 있어요.

(도어 키패드 잠금 장치 열리는 소리)
여: 여보, 저 왔어요.
남: 여보, 당신은 왜 숨을 헐떡이고 있어요?
여: 엘리베이터가 고장이 나서 저는 계단들을 걸어 올라와야 했어요.
남: 오, 여보, 계단은 6층밖에 안 돼요. 당신은 정말 운동을 더 해야 해요.
여: 그것을 지적해줘서 고마워요. 하지만, 우리는 바로 앞에 더 큰 문제가 있어요.
남: 그게 뭔가요?
여: 우리 식료품들이 곧 배달될 거예요. 그래서, 누군가 내려갔다가 다시 올라와야 해요.
남: 네. 추측건대 그 누군가는 제가 틀림없겠죠?
여: 그래 줄 수 있어요? 제가 당신에게 맛있고, 푸짐한 저녁식사를 차려 줄게요.

단·어·및·표·현

pant [pænt] [동] (숨을) 헐떡이다
out of order 고장 난
flight [flait] [명] (층과 층 사이의) 계단, 층계
point out 지적하다, 가리키다
at hand 바로 앞에, 머지 않아
slippery [slípəri] [형] 미끄러운

19 알맞은응답찾기 ▶ 정답 ⑤

듣·기·대·본

M: Hi, Gemma! What club are you in at school?
W: I'm in the robotics club. We make and control robots.
M: Cool! I'm thinking about joining, too.
W: That'd be great! We can work on robot projects as a team and enter competitions together.
M: Yeah, it sounds fun. But I don't know much about robots.
W: Don't worry! Our club is open to everyone. We'll teach you all about robotics.
M: Thanks, that's reassuring. I'll think about joining.
W: If you need help, I can introduce you to our club leader. He knows a lot about robots.
M: Thanks! That'd be helpful.
W: Sure! I'll give you his phone number so you can call him.

우·리·말·해·석

① 코딩으로, 너는 로봇을 움직이게 할 수 있어.
② 우리는 현재 신규 회원을 받지 않고 있어.
③ 아마 다음 번에. 나는 지금은 좀 바빠.
④ 나는 대회에서 우승한 것에 대해 널 축하하고 싶어.
⑤ 물론! 네가 그에게 전화할 수 있도록 내가 너에게 그의 전화번호를 줄게.

남: 안녕, Gemma! 너는 학교에서 무슨 동아리에 있어?
여: 나는 로봇 공학 동아리에 있어. 우리는 로봇을 만들고 조종해.
남: 멋진걸! 나도 가입할까 생각 중이야.
여: 그거 좋겠다! 우리는 한 팀으로 로봇 프로젝트를 진행하고 함께 대회에 참가할 수 있어.
남: 응, 재밌을 것 같아. 하지만 난 로봇들에 대해 잘 몰라.
여: 걱정 마! 우리 동아리는 모두에게 열려 있어. 우리가 너에게 로봇 공학에 대한 모든 것을 가르쳐 줄 거야.
남: 고마워, 그거 안심된다. 나는 가입하는 것에 대해 생각해 볼게.
여: 만약 네가 도움이 필요하다면, 내가 너를 우리 동아리 장에게 소개해 줄 수 있어. 그는 로봇에 대해 많이 알고 있어.
남: 고마워! 그것은 도움이 되겠다.
여: 물론! 네가 그에게 전화할 수 있도록 내가 너에게 그의 전화번호를 줄게.

단·어·및·표·현

robotics [roubátiks] [명] 로봇 공학
competition [kàmpitíʃən] [명] 대회
reassuring [rìːəʃúəriŋ] [형] 안심시키는
currently [kə́ːrəntli] [부] 현재, 지금
at the moment 지금

20 상황에적절한말찾기 ▶ 정답 ②

듣·기·대·본

M: Dean <u>plans to go</u> to the water park tomorrow with his friend Ted. Before he goes, he checks the weather report for tomorrow. Unfortunately, it says it's going to rain <u>all day tomorrow</u>. He's very disappointed, but <u>he calls his friend to cancel the appointment.</u> In this situation, what would Dean most likely say to his friend?

Dean: <u>Why don't we go some other time?</u>

우·리·말·해·석

① 나랑 함께 할래?
② 우리 다음번에 가는 것이 어때?
③ 넌 거기에 제시간에 올 수 있어?
④ 우산을 꼭 가지고 오도록 해.
⑤ 난 내일 다른 약속이 있어.

남: Dean은 친구 Ted와 내일 워터파크에 갈 계획이다. 그는 가기 전에 내일 일기예보를 확인한다. 안타깝게도, 내일 하루 종일 비가 올 것이라고 한다. 그는 매우 실망했지만 약속을 취소하기 위해 친구에게 전화를 한다. 이러한 상황에서, Dean은 그의 친구에게 무엇이라고 말하겠는가?

Dean: 우리 다음번에 가는 것이 어때?

단·어·및·표·현

appointment[əpɔ́intmənt] 몡 약속

Words & Expressions Review

1. 기기, 장치, 기구	2. 기념일	3. 제때에, 시간을 어기지 않고
4. ~로부터 혜택을 입다	5. 시내의, 도심의	6. (색깔·무늬 등이 서로) 어울리다, 맞다
7. 편안한, 편한	8. 흡입, 빨아들이기	9. ~을 놓다
10. 꽃다발, 부케	11. 선별된, 엄선된	12. 조절 가능한
13. 요금	14. 참석하다, 가다	15. 중립적인, 중간색의
16. 모양	17. 중고의	18. 온갖 종류의
19. 가져오다	20. 알고 있는, 의식하고 있는	21. (일이) 잘 풀리다
22. 안타깝게도	23. 냄비 받침	24. 자선[구호] 단체
25. 제공하다	26. 현재, 지금	27. 고장 난
28. 단골손님	29. 제출하다	30. 예약하다
31. 안심시키는	32. 가입하다, 합류하다	33. (모자의) 챙
34. ~을 신청하다	35. 놀랍게도	36. 옷차림, 복장
37. 돌아오다	38. (숨을) 헐떡이다	39. 회의실
40. 재단	41. 점토	42. 바자회
43. 말이 나와서 말인데	44. 부주의한	

영어듣기 모의고사 12^회

|정|답|

01 ⑤	02 ③	03 ②	04 ⑤	05 ①
06 ③	07 ⑤	08 ①	09 ③	10 ③
11 ④	12 ①	13 ②	14 ③	15 ①
16 ④	17 ②	18 ⑤	19 ①	20 ②

01 그림정보파악(대화) ▶ 정답 ⑤

듣·기·대·본

W: Hi, Jake. What are you <u>looking at</u>?
M: Hi, Letty. I'm looking at swimming caps. I need a new one. Can you <u>help me choose one</u>?
W: Sure. Let's see. How would you like a dolphin on the cap?
M: Sure, I like dolphins. They are <u>great swimmers</u>.
W: Okay. There are caps with one dolphin and caps with two dolphins.
M: The caps with two dolphins look nice.
W: Good. How about this one that says 'SPLASH'?
M: It's nice. I'll get that one. Thanks for your help.

우·리·말·해·석

여: 안녕, Jake. 넌 뭘 보고 있어?
남: 안녕, Letty. 나는 수영모를 보고 있는 중이야. 나는 새 것이 필요해. 너는 내가 하나를 고를 수 있게 도와줄 수 있어?
여: 물론이지. 어디 보자. 모자에 돌고래가 있는 건 어때?
남: 응, 나는 돌고래들을 좋아해. 그들은 수영을 아주 잘해.
여: 자. 한 마리의 돌고래가 있는 모자와 두 마리의 돌고래가 있는 모자가 있어.
남: 두 마리 돌고래가 있는 모자가 멋져 보이네.
여: 좋아. 'SPLASH'라고 써 있는 이건 어때?
남: 멋지다. 나는 그걸로 살래. 도와줘서 고마워.

단·어·및·표·현

look at ~ ~을 보다
choose[tʃuːz] 동 고르다, 선택하다
dolphin[dάlfin] 몡 돌고래
say[sei] 동 ~라고 쓰여 있다, 나타내다

02 대화미언급 ▶ 정답 ③

듣·기·대·본

W: Jamie, have you heard about Super Soccer Class?
M: Yeah, I love soccer so I'm interested in the class. How about you?
W: Me, too. I think it's a good chance to learn how to play soccer.
M: The class runs from August 3 to 14, right?
W: Yes, it is from 8 to 9:30 every weekday morning.
M: What's more, the class is free!
W: Sounds great. How can we sign up for the class?
M: We need to fill out the form on the website.
W: Let's <u>sign up</u> right away.

여: Jamie, 너는 Super Soccer 수업에 대해 들어본 적 있어?
남: 응, 나는 축구를 아주 좋아해서 그 수업에 흥미가 있어. 너는 어때?
여: 나도, 축구하는 법을 배울 수 있는 좋은 기회라고 생각해.
남: 그 수업은 8월 3일부터 14일까지 운영해, 맞지?
여: 응, 매일 평일 아침 8시부터 9시 30분까지야.
남: 게다가, 그 수업은 무료야!
여: 좋은데. 어떻게 그 수업에 등록해?
남: 우리는 웹사이트에 있는 양식을 작성해야 해.
여: 지금 바로 등록하자.

단·어·및·표·현

run [rʌn] 동 운영하다, 제공하다
what's more 게다가
sign up 등록하다, 가입하다

03 전화목적파악 ▶ 정답 ②

들·기·대·본

(Telephone rings.)
W: Hello. This is Forest Restaurant. How can I help you?
M: Hi. I have some questions about your menu.
W: Okay. What would you like to know?
M: My daughter is vegan. Do you have any vegan options?
W: Yes, we have some dishes with tofu.
M: Oh, okay. Also, I am allergic to peanuts, so is there anything on the menu without peanuts in it?
W: Yes, we do have a peanut-free menu as well.
M: That's a relief. Okay, thank you so much.
W: No problem. Just ask your waiter about the items on the menu and he can explain them in more detail.

우·리·말·해·석

(전화벨이 울린다.)
여: 안녕하세요. 여기는 Forest 식당입니다. 어떻게 도와드릴까요?
남: 안녕하세요. 저는 당신의 메뉴에 대해 질문이 좀 있어요.
여: 네. 당신은 무엇이 알고 싶으신가요?
남: 제 딸은 완전 채식주의자예요. 완전 채식주의자가 선택할 수 있는 것이 있나요?
여: 네, 저희는 두부로 된 음식이 좀 있어요.
남: 아, 알겠어요. 또한, 제가 땅콩에 알레르기가 있어서 그러는데 땅콩이 들어가지 않은 것이 메뉴에 있나요?
여: 네, 저희는 땅콩이 없는 메뉴도 있습니다.
남: 그것 참 다행이네요. 네, 정말 감사합니다.
여: 천만에요. 그저 웨이터에게 메뉴에 있는 항목에 대해 물어보시면 그가 더 자세하게 그것들을 설명할 수 있어요.

단·어·및·표·현

vegan [víːgən] 명 완전 채식주의자(고기는 물론 우유, 달걀도 먹지 않음) 형 동물성 식품을 포함하지 않은
option [ápʃən] 명 선택(할 수 있는 것)
be allergic to ~ ~에 알레르기가 있다
peanut-free 땅콩이 없는
as well ~도, 또한, 역시
that's a relief 그것 참 다행이다
in detail 자세하게

04 수치파악(시각) ▶ 정답 ⑤

들·기·대·본

M: I'm thinking about learning how to play the guitar.
W: That's great. I can give you some tips if you'd like.
M: Really? I didn't know you played the guitar. It would be really helpful if you could.
W: Why don't we talk in more detail after school?
M: That sounds good. How about we meet at 5:00 p.m.?
W: I can't. I have to go to the dentist at 4:30 p.m. I'll be done by 5:30 p.m.
M: Oh, okay. Does 6:00 p.m. work for you?
W: Sure, see you then. We can have dinner while we talk.
M: All right. Dinner is on me.

우·리·말·해·석

남: 나는 기타 치는 법을 배울까 생각 중이야.
여: 멋지네. 네가 원하면 내가 몇 가지 조언을 줄 수 있어.
남: 정말? 나는 네가 기타를 치는 줄 몰랐어. 네가 그래 준다면 정말 도움이 될 거야.
여: 우리 방과 후에 좀 더 자세히 얘기하는 게 어때?
남: 좋은 생각이야. 우리 오후 5시에 만나는 게 어때?
여: 안 돼. 나는 오후 4시 30분에 치과에 가야 해. 오후 5시 30분까지는 끝날 거야.
남: 오, 알겠어. 오후 6시는 괜찮니?
여: 그래, 그때 보자. 우리 얘기하면서 저녁 먹으면 되겠다.
남: 좋아. 저녁은 내가 살게.

단·어·및·표·현

tip [tip] 명 (실용적인, 작은) 조언

05 심정추론 ▶ 정답 ①

들·기·대·본

M: Sally, you look so upset. What's up?
W: I went to piano class today.
M: And?
W: There was a little boy, and he kept bothering me.
M: Oh, no. What did you do?
W: I told the teacher to stop him, but she scolded me for not being patient with him.
M: That's so unfair. You must have been very mad.

우·리·말·해·석

① 화난 ② 슬픈 ③ 행복한 ④ 고마워하는 ⑤ 신난

남: Sally, 너 매우 화나 보인다. 무슨 일이야?
여: 오늘 피아노 수업에 갔었어.
남: 그런데?
여: 작은 남자아이가 있었는데, 그 애가 나를 계속 괴롭혔어.
남: 오, 이런. 넌 뭘 했어?
여: 나는 선생님께 그 애가 그만하도록 해 달라고 말했는데, 그녀는 그를 참을성 있게 대하지 못했다며 나를 혼내셨어.
남: 그건 정말 불공평해. 넌 굉장히 화가 났었겠구나.

단·어·및·표·현

scold [skould] 동 혼내다
patient [péiʃənt] 형 참을성 있는
unfair [ʌnféər] 형 불공평한

06 그림상황에적절한대화찾기 ▶ 정답 ③

들·기·대·본

① W: Do we have milk? I want to have some cereal.

M: Why don't you check the fridge?
② W: Would you like plastic or paper bags?
   M: Plastic bags, please. Thank you.
③ W: This product is buy one, get one free.
   M: Oh, really? I'll go grab another one.
④ W: The pears are on sale online.
   M: Let's order some right now.
⑤ W: There's more space on the top shelf.
   M: Let's put these books there then.

우·리·말·해·석

① 여: 우리 우유 있나요? 저는 시리얼을 좀 먹고 싶어요.
   남: 당신이 냉장고를 확인해 보는 게 어때요?
② 여: 비닐봉지를 드릴까요, 아니면 종이봉투를 드릴까요?
   남: 비닐봉지로 주세요. 고마워요.
③ 여: 이 상품은 하나를 사면 하나를 무료로 드려요.
   남: 아, 정말요? 제가 가서 다른 하나를 가져올게요.
④ 여: 온라인에서 배를 할인 중이에요.
   남: 지금 당장 좀 주문하죠.
⑤ 여: 선반 맨 위에 공간이 더 있어요.
   남: 그러면 이 책들을 거기에 놓죠.

단·어·및·표·현

fridge [friʤ] 몡 냉장고
plastic bag 비닐봉지
buy one, get one free 한 개 사면 한 개는 공짜
grab [græb] 용 가져오다
on sale 할인 중인

07   부탁(요청)한일파악   ▶ 정답 ⑤

듣·기·대·본

W: Honey, when did you say we're going to get our car back from the repair shop?
M: It won't be ready until next week. Why are you asking about it?
W: Didn't I tell you that my parents are coming to visit this weekend?
M: Oh, right! Are they taking the train?
W: Yes, they are. So, we definitely need a car to pick them up at the station and drive them around.
M: We should rent a car for the weekend then.
W: Could you take care of it, please?
M: Okay, I will.

우·리·말·해·석

여: 여보, 우리가 자동차를 정비소에서 언제 찾아온다고 했지?
남: 다음 주까지는 준비가 안 될 거야. 왜 그것에 대해 물어보는 거야?
여: 이번 주말에 우리 부모님이 방문하러 오신다고 내가 말 안 했어?
남: 아, 맞다! 기차 타고 오시는 거야?
여: 응, 그래. 그래서 우리가 그분들을 역에서 모셔오고, 여기저기 태워 드리려면 차가 꼭 필요해.
남: 그럼 이번 주말 동안 차를 빌려야겠다.
여: 그거 좀 처리해 줄래?
남: 알겠어, 내가 할게.

단·어·및·표·현

repair shop 정비소, 수리점
rent [rent] 용 빌리다

08   담화미언급   ▶ 정답 ①

듣·기·대·본

W: Are you looking for a new experience, or a way to relax? Whatever you want, you can find it at Warm Glow. We produce a wide range of 100% handmade candles. Our candles are different because they are long-lasting and highly scented. Visit our website now. You can place an order online, or over the phone. Also, our members always receive discounts.

우·리·말·해·석

여: 여러분은 새로운 경험이나 휴식을 취할 방법을 찾고 계십니까? 무엇을 원하시든, Warm Glow에서 찾으실 수 있습니다. 저희는 다양한 종류의 100% 수제 양초를 생산합니다. 저희 양초는 오래 지속되고 향이 풍부하기 때문에 다릅니다. 지금 저희 홈페이지를 방문해주세요. 인터넷이나 전화로 주문하실 수 있습니다. 또한 회원분들은 항상 할인을 받습니다.

단·어·및·표·현

long-lasting 오래 지속되는
highly scented 향이 풍부한

> 🔊 **LISTENING ADVICE**
>
> 'visit'의 [v] 발음은 [b] 발음과 헷갈릴 수 있습니다. 그러나 둘은 같은 발음이 아니기 때문에 주의하여야 합니다.
>
> ● **How to pronounce [b], [v]**
> [b]는 우리말 [브] 발음과 같고, [v] 발음은 [f] 발음과 같이 윗니로 아랫입술을 살짝 물었다가 [브]라고 발음하면 됩니다.

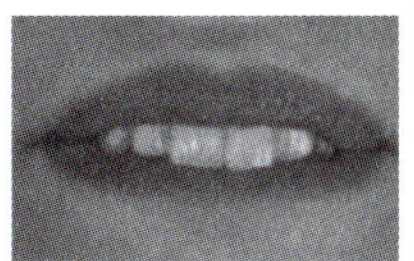

09   담화화제추론   ▶ 정답 ③

듣·기·대·본

W: This is a bird. It has excellent eyesight and hearing. It has very powerful claws to help it catch and kill prey. It can rotate its neck 270 degrees. It is very active at night and its night vision allows it to catch prey at night. Its feathers allow it to fly silently. It is known for its hooting sound.

우·리·말·해·석

여: 이것은 새입니다. 그것은 뛰어난 시력과 청력을 가지고 있습니다. 그것은 먹이를 잡고 죽이는 것을 돕는 매우 강력한 발톱을 가지고 있습니다. 그것은 그것의 목을 270도 회전할 수 있습니다. 그것은 밤에 매우 활동적이고 그것의 야간 시력은 밤에 먹이를 잡는 것을 가능하게 해줍니다. 그것의 깃털은 그것이 조용히 나는 것을 가능하게 해줍니다. 그것은 그것의 부엉부엉 소리로 알려져 있습니다.

단·어·및·표·현

claw [klɔː] 몡 (동물·새의) 발톱
prey [prei] 몡 (사냥 동물의) 먹이, 사냥감
rotate [róuteit] 용 회전하다
degree [digríː] 몡 (각도의 단위인) 도
silently [sáiləntli] 뷔 조용히
be known for ~ ~로 알려져 있다
hoot [huːt] 용 (부엉이가) 부엉부엉 하다

듣·기·대·본

① W: Would you please help me <u>do the dishes</u>?
　 M: Sure. I'd be glad to.
② W: Can you tell me the way to the post office?
　 M: Sorry, I'm new here, too.
③ W: <u>Have you been to New York?</u>
　 M: <u>You're really good.</u>
④ W: I decided to learn Japanese.
　 M: That's a <u>great</u> idea.
⑤ W: What are you reading?
　 M: A story about a <u>famous</u> painter.

우·리·말·해·석

① 여: 내가 설거지 하는 것 좀 도와줄래?
　 남: 물론. 기꺼이 도와줄게.
② 여: 우체국 가는 길 좀 가르쳐 주시겠어요?
　 남: 죄송하지만, 저도 여기가 처음인데요.
③ 여: 뉴욕에 가본 적이 있니?
　 남: 넌 정말 멋져.
④ 여: 나 일본어를 배우기로 결정했어.
　 남: 그거 참 좋은 생각이다.
⑤ 여: 무엇을 읽고 있어?
　 남: 유명한 화가에 대한 이야기야.

단·어·및·표·현

decide[disáid] ⑧ 결정하다, 결심하다

11 할일파악(대화직후) ▶ 정답 ④

듣·기·대·본

W: Hi, how are you today? What can I do for you?
M: I'd like to change my hairstyle.
W: Do you have <u>anything special in mind</u>?
M: I was thinking of getting a perm, but I'm not sure if that's the right choice.
W: Here, <u>take a look at our stylebook.</u> It has photos of different hairstyles.
M: Wow, thanks. There are lots of photos here!
W: <u>Take your time.</u> You can choose what style you prefer and show it to me.
M: Okay, I will. Give me a minute, please.

우·리·말·해·석

여: 안녕하세요, 오늘 어떠세요? 무엇을 해드릴까요?
남: 제 머리 스타일을 바꾸고 싶어요.
여: 어떤 특별한 것을 마음에 두고 있나요?
남: 파마를 하려고 생각하고 있었지만 그게 맞는 선택인지 확신이 없어요.
여: 여기, 저희 스타일북을 보세요. 다른 머리 스타일의 사진들이 있어요.
남: 와, 고마워요. 여기 사진이 많네요!
여: 서두르지 마세요. 어떤 스타일이 더 좋은지 고르시고 저에게 보여주세요.
남: 좋아요, 그럴게요. 잠시만 시간을 주세요.

단·어·및·표·현

Take your time. 서두르지 마세요. 천천히 하세요.
give ~ a minute ~에게 잠시 시간을 주다

12 도표정보파악 ▶ 정답 ①

듣·기·대·본

M: Hello, I'm looking for some vitamins for my son.
W: Do you have anything <u>particular</u> in mind?
M: He says his eyes <u>get tired</u> easily these days. Do you have anything for that?
W: Vitamin A is really good for your eyes. Vitamin A comes in two types: jellies and pills.
M: My son would love the jellies. Then, he won't have <u>any trouble taking them.</u>
W: Great! Do you want the smaller quantity, just in case he doesn't like them?
M: Okay. I will take that one.

우·리·말·해·석

	제품	비타민	유형	수량
①	A	비타민A	젤리형	30
②	B	비타민A	젤리형	60
③	C	비타민A	알약형	30
④	D	비타민C	알약형	60
⑤	E	비타민C	알약형	30

남: 안녕하세요, 저는 제 아들에게 줄 비타민을 찾고 있습니다.
여: 당신이 생각해 놓은 특정한 것이 있나요?
남: 그는 요즘 그의 눈이 쉽게 피로해진다고 말합니다. 그것을 위한 것이 있을까요?
여: 비타민A가 눈에 정말로 좋습니다. 비타민A는 2가지 종류인 젤리와 알약으로 나옵니다.
남: 제 아들은 젤리를 엄청 좋아할 거예요. 그렇다면, 그가 그것들을 복용하는 데 아무런 어려움을 겪지 않을 것입니다.
여: 아주 좋네요! 당신은 그가 그것들을 좋아하지 않을 경우를 대비하여, 더 작은 양을 원하시나요?
남: 좋습니다. 저는 그것으로 할게요.

단·어·및·표·현

have ~ in mind ~를 생각하다, ~를 염두에 두다
pill[pil] ⑨ 알약
have trouble -ing ~하는 데 어려움을 겪다
take[teik] ⑧ 복용하다, 섭취하다
quantity[kwántəti] ⑨ 양, 수량
just in case ~한 경우에 대비해서, 만약을 위해서

13 수치파악(날짜) ▶ 정답 ②

듣·기·대·본

M: Have you thought about when we should take <u>our pottery class</u>?
W: Not yet. What about you, Fred?
M: I'm still deciding. Why don't we plan it together for next month?
W: Sounds like a good idea. How about Saturday, July 27th?
M: Well... Saturdays are usually busy for me. What about July 28th?
W: Hmm... I have a friend's birthday party on the 28th. Does July 26th work for you?
M: July 26th <u>works perfectly.</u> I don't have any other plans then.
W: Okay, <u>let's make it</u> July 26th for our pottery class.

우·리·말·해·석

남: 우리 도자기 수업 언제 들을지 생각해 봤어?

여: 아직. 너는, Fred?
남: 나도 아직 결정하는(고민하는) 중이야. 우리 다음 달로 같이 계획해 보는 건 어때?
여: 좋은 생각이네. 7월 27일 토요일은 어때?
남: 글쎄... 난 토요일에 보통 바빠. 7월 28일은 어때?
여: 음... 28일엔 친구 생일 파티가 있어. 7월 26일은 괜찮아?
남: 7월 26일 완전 괜찮아. 그때는 다른 약속 없어.
여: 좋아, 그럼 도자기 수업은 7월 26일로 하자.

단·어·및·표·현
pottery [pɑ́təri] 몡 도자기
work for + 사람 (일정이나 계획이) ~에게 맞다, 괜찮다
make it (약속 시간이나 장소를) ~로 정하다

14 한일파악 ▶ 정답 ③

듣·기·대·본
W: Hey, Dave. How was your weekend?
M: Oh, hey, Cindy! It was very meaningful.
W: Why? What did you do?
M: I took part in this event called the Hand-in-Hand Mini Olympics.
W: What's that?
M: It's an event for kids with disabilities. I volunteered to help them complete the games as a team.
W: That's so nice of you. It must have been worth it.
M: It really was. I'm going to participate next year as well.

우·리·말·해·석
여: 안녕, Dave. 네 주말은 어땠어?
남: 오, 안녕, Cindy! 아주 의미가 있었어.
여: 왜? 넌 뭘 했는데?
남: '손에 손을 잡은 미니 올림픽'이라고 불리는 이 행사에 참가했어.
여: 그게 뭐야?
남: 장애가 있는 아이들을 위한 행사야. 난 그들이 한 팀으로서 경기들을 끝내는 것을 도우려고 자원했어.
여: 그렇다니 너 정말 다정하구나. 그것은 그만한 가치가 있었을 게 틀림없어.
남: 정말 그랬어. 난 내년에도 참가할 예정이야.

단·어·및·표·현
meaningful [míːniŋfəl] 혱 의미 있는, 중요한
take part in ~에 참가하다, 참여하다
disability [dìsəbíləti] 몡 (신체적, 정신적) 장애
volunteer to + 동사원형 ~하겠다고 자원하다
complete [kəmplíːt] 통 끝마치다, 완료하다
worth [wəːrθ] 혱 ~할 가치가 있는

15 담화목적파악 ▶ 정답 ①

듣·기·대·본
W: Hello and welcome to ABC Cinema. Before you enjoy your movie, let me go over a few rules to keep in mind. First, don't kick the seat in front of you. Second, please avoid using your cellphone. The light from your phone can be very distracting for other people. Lastly, put all trash in the trash can when you exit the theater. Please keep these rules in mind to ensure for everyone's comfort. Have a good time.

우·리·말·해·석
여: 안녕하세요, 그리고 ABC 시네마에 오신 것을 환영합니다. 영화를 즐기기 전에, 명심해야 할 몇 가지 규칙을 살펴보도록 하겠습니다. 우선, 당신 앞의 좌석을 발로 차지 마세요. 둘째, 핸드폰 사용은 피해주세요. 핸드폰에서 나오는 빛이 다른 사람들에게 매우 방해가 될 수 있습니다. 마지막으로, 극장에서 나갈 때 모든 쓰레기는 쓰레기통에 넣으세요. 모두의 편안함을 보장하기 위해 이 규칙들을 명심하세요. 좋은 시간 보내세요.

단·어·및·표·현
go over 살펴보다, 검토하다
distracting [distrǽktiŋ] 혱 방해가 되는
ensure [inʃúər] 통 보장하다, 확보하다
comfort [kʌ́mfərt] 몡 편안함, 안락

16 수치계산(금액) ▶ 정답 ④

듣·기·대·본
M: Excuse me, I'd like to buy two adult bus tickets to New York.
W: They are 10 dollars each.
M: Can I buy return tickets here, too?
W: Yes, it'll cost 8 dollars more for each person.
M: Okay, I'll buy two return tickets. How much is it in total?
W: It's 36 dollars.
M: I have a two-dollar discount coupon here. Can I use it?
W: Let me see. (pause) Yes, you can.
M: All right. Here's my credit card.

우·리·말·해·석
남: 실례합니다, 저는 뉴욕으로 가는 성인 버스표 두 장을 사고 싶어요.
여: 그것들은 각 10달러입니다.
남: 여기서 왕복표도 살 수 있나요?
여: 네, 한 사람당 8달러씩 더 듭니다.
남: 알겠어요, 왕복표 두 장을 살게요. 총 얼마죠?
여: 36달러입니다.
남: 저는 여기 2달러 할인 쿠폰을 가지고 있어요. 제가 그걸 사용할 수 있나요?
여: 어디 볼게요. (잠시 후) 네, 가능합니다.
남: 좋아요. 여기 제 신용카드요.

단·어·및·표·현
return ticket 왕복표
cost [kɔ(ː)st] 통 비용이 들다

17 알맞은응답찾기 ▶ 정답 ②

듣·기·대·본
(Telephone rings.)
M: Hello, Happy Mall lost-and-found.
W: Hello. I'm calling about my purse. I think I left it in the washroom on the first floor.
M: Okay. What does your purse look like?
W: It's purple with a gold button.
M: I have one purse that looks like that. What's in it?
W: Some cash, a student ID, and a family photo.
M: Please tell me your name.
W: Tina Evans.
M: Okay, I have what you're looking for.

W: **You saved my life! I'll be there soon.**

우·리·말·해·석
① 네, 보라색은 제가 제일 좋아하는 색입니다.
② 저를 살려주셨습니다! 제가 곧 거기로 가겠습니다.
③ 정말 감사합니다. 그 지갑을 사겠습니다.
④ 쇼핑몰에 사람들이 너무 많았습니다.
⑤ 좋아요, 내가 좋아하는 것을 찾기 어려우니까요.

(전화벨이 울린다.)
남: 여보세요, Happy Mall 분실물 센터입니다.
여: 여보세요. 제 지갑 때문에 전화했습니다. 제가 그것을 1층 화장실에 두고 온 것 같아요.
남: 알겠습니다. 지갑이 어떻게 생겼나요?
여: 금색 단추가 있는 보라색입니다.
남: 그것처럼 보이는 지갑을 하나 갖고 있습니다. 안에 뭐가 들어있죠?
여: 현금 약간, 학생증, 그리고 가족 사진이요.
남: 이름을 말씀해 주세요.
여: Tina Evans입니다.
남: 네, 당신이 찾고 있는 것이 제게 있네요.
여: **저를 살려주셨습니다! 제가 곧 거기로 가겠습니다.**

단·어·및·표·현
purse [pəːrs] 몡 지갑

18 알맞은응답찾기 ▶ 정답 ⑤

듣·기·대·본
M: Hey, Alice. Are you doing anything after school?
W: No, I don't have any plans. What about you?
M: I'm thinking of going shopping at the mall.
W: What are you shopping for?
M: I want to look at some hiking shoes.
W: I didn't know you liked to go hiking.
M: Yeah, I went for the first time last week, and it was really fun.
W: Well, I could use some new shoes as well. Can I come with you?
M: Sure, we can go together.

우·리·말·해·석
① 나는 방과 후에 바빠.
② 미안, 나는 기억이 안 나.
③ 내일 등산하러 가자.
④ 나는 저번 주에 신발을 샀어.
⑤ 물론이지, 우리는 같이 갈 수 있어.

남: 이봐, Alice. 방과 후에 뭐 할 거 있니?
여: 아니, 아무 계획도 없어. 너는?
남: 쇼핑몰로 쇼핑하러 갈까 생각 중이야.
여: 무엇을 사려고?
남: 등산화를 좀 보고 싶어서.
여: 나는 네가 등산을 좋아하는지 몰랐어.
남: 응, 저번 주에 처음 갔는데, 그건 정말 재미있었어.
여: 나도 새 신발이 있으면 좋겠어. 너랑 같이 가도 될까?
남: **물론이지, 우리는 같이 갈 수 있어.**

단·어·및·표·현
go hiking 등산하다
could use A A가 있었으면 좋겠다, A가 필요하다
as well ~도, 또한

19 알맞은응답찾기 ▶ 정답 ①

듣·기·대·본
W: Hi, Patrick. What's wrong? You look worried.
M: Hi, Amy. I was just thinking about how to improve my Chinese pronunciation.
W: Oh, I see.
M: How come your pronunciation is so good?
W: Didn't I tell you that my sister is majoring in Chinese in college?
M: Wow! Cool!
W: She is helping me on weekends. Why don't you join us this weekend?
M: That would be awesome! I hope she'll be okay with it.
W: I'm sure she won't mind me bringing a friend. I will call you this Saturday.
M: **Great! I can't wait to meet her.**

우·리·말·해·석
① 좋아! 나는 그녀를 빨리 만나고 싶어.
② 알겠어. 그것을 사전에서 찾아보자.
③ 내 가족은 중국에서 5년 동안 살았어.
④ 나는 보통 주말에 영화를 봐.
⑤ 이것을 중국어로 어떻게 발음하니?

여: 안녕, Patrick. 무슨 일이야? 너 걱정이 있는 표정이야.
남: 안녕, Amy. 나는 그저 어떻게 하면 내 중국어 발음을 향상시킬 수 있는지 생각 중이었어.
여: 오, 그렇구나.
남: 어째서 네 발음은 그렇게 좋니?
여: 내 언니가 대학에서 중국어를 전공하고 있다고 내가 말하지 않았니?
남: 우와! 멋지다!
여: 그녀는 주말마다 나를 도와주고 있어. 이번 주말에 함께 하지 않을래?
남: 너무 멋진데! 난 그녀가 그것에 대해 괜찮길 바라.
여: 그녀는 내가 친구를 데려오는 것에 대해 개의치 않을 거라고 확신해. 내가 이번 주 토요일에 너에게 전화할게.
남: **좋아! 나는 그녀를 빨리 만나고 싶어.**

단·어·및·표·현
improve [imprúːv] 통 향상시키다, 개선하다
pronunciation [prənÀnsiéiʃən] 몡 발음
How come ~? 어째서, 왜 ~?
major in ~을 전공하다
mind [maind] 통 개의하다, 언짢아하다
look up (사전 · 컴퓨터 등에서 정보를) 찾아보다
pronounce [prənáuns] 통 발음하다

20 상황에적절한말찾기 ▶ 정답 ②

듣·기·대·본
W: Naomi is a middle school student. Today is class photo day. When the photographer sets up the shot, Phil, one of her classmates, is standing in the row in front of her. Phil happens to be a tall boy, and Naomi fears that he will block her in the photo. So, she would like to ask Phil to change places with her. In this situation, what would Naomi most likely say to Phil?
Naomi: Phil, **I think we need to change rows.**

우·리·말·해·석

① 네가 우리 사진을 찍어줄 수 있니?
② 내 생각엔 우리가 줄을 바꿔야 할 것 같아.
③ 너는 그 카메라를 통해서 나를 볼 수 있니?
④ 너는 언제 교실을 청소했니?
⑤ 너는 단체 사진을 위해 차려입어야 해.

여: Naomi는 중학교 학생이다. 오늘은 반 사진 촬영일이다. 사진사가 촬영을 준비할 때, 그녀의 반 친구 중 하나인 Phil이 그녀의 앞 줄에 서 있다. Phil은 공교롭게도 키가 큰 남자아이였고, Naomi는 그가 사진에서 그녀를 가릴 것을 우려한다. 그래서, 그녀는 Phil에게 그녀와 자리를 바꾸자고 부탁하고 싶다. 이 상황에서, Naomi가 Phil에게 뭐라고 말하겠는가?

Naomi: Phil, 내 생각엔 우리가 줄을 바꿔야 할 것 같아.

단·어·및·표·현

set up 준비하다
shot [ʃat] 명 사진
row [rou] 명 (사람·사물들이 옆으로 늘어서 있는) 줄, 열
happen to be 공교롭게도[우연히·때마침] ~이다
fear [fiər] 통 (~일까 봐) 우려[염려]하다

Words & Expressions Review

1. (일정이나 계획이) ~에게 맞다, 괜찮다	2. (동물·새의) 발톱	3. 주문하다
4. 살펴보다, 검토하다	5. 혼내다	6. 보장하다, 확보하다
7. 회전하다	8. ~에 알레르기가 있다	9. 다양한, 광범위한
10. 몹시 화가 난, 미친	11. 어째서, 왜 ~?	12. ~을 전공하다
13. ~에게 잠시 시간을 주다	14. 향이 풍부한	15. 비용이 들다
16. 의미 있는, 중요한	17. 발음하다	18. 편안함, 안락
19. (실용적인, 작은) 조언	20. 분실물 센터	21. 불공평한
22. 괴롭히다, 귀찮게 하다	23. 참을성 있는, 환자	24. 피하다, 회피하다
25. ~을 생각하다	26. 수제의	27. (사냥 동물의) 먹이, 사냥감
28. 도자기	29. 조용히	30. 운영하다, 제공하다
31. 생산하다	32. 빌리다	33. (신체적, 정신적) 장애
34. 냉장고	35. ~할 가치가 있다	36. 정비소, 수리점
37. 오래 지속되는	38. 양, 수량	39. ~하려고 생각하다
40. 자세하게	41. 준비하다	42. 가져오다
43. 줄, 열	44. 방해가 되는	

영어듣기 모의고사 13회

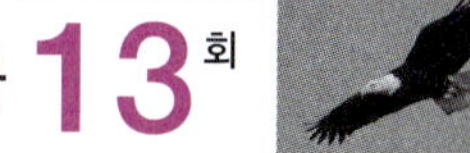

|정|답|

01 ⑤	02 ③	03 ①	04 ④	05 ③
06 ③	07 ⑤	08 ⑤	09 ④	10 ①
11 ②	12 ④	13 ⑤	14 ⑤	15 ②
16 ④	17 ③	18 ①	19 ②	20 ⑤

01 그림정보파악(대화) ▶ 정답 ⑤

듣·기·대·본

W: Hi, Roger. What are you doing here?
M: Hey, Brittany. I need to buy a rubber powered model airplane kit for Science Day at school. Can you help me choose one?
W: Sure. How many sets of wings do you want for your model airplane?
M: I'd like 2 sets of wings.
W: Then let's look at the design. Would you like star decorations on the wings?
M: Yes. I think stars will make it look awesome.
W: Okay. Then how about this one with four stars?
M: Cool! I'll get that one. Thanks for helping me.

우·리·말·해·석

여: 안녕, Roger. 너는 여기서 뭐 하고 있니?
남: 안녕, Brittany. 나는 학교 과학의 날을 위해 고무 동력 모형 비행기 키트를 사야 해. 너는 내가 고르는 걸 도와줄 수 있니?
여: 당연하지. 너는 네 모형 비행기에 몇 쌍의 날개를 원하니?
남: 나는 2쌍의 날개를 원해.
여: 그럼, 디자인을 좀 보자. 너는 날개 위에 별 장식을 원하니?
남: 응. 별들은 그것을 더 멋있게 보이게 할 것 같아.
여: 알겠어. 그럼 별 네 개가 있는 이건 어떠니?
남: 멋있다! 나는 그걸로 할게. 도와줘서 고마워.

단·어·및·표·현

rubber powered 고무 동력의
decoration [dèkəréiʃən] 명 장식, 무늬
awesome [ɔ́ːsəm] 형 아주 멋진, 굉장한

02 대화미언급 ▶ 정답 ③

듣·기·대·본

M: Are you excited about Eco Adventure Day?
W: Absolutely! It'll take place at Blue Forest Park on June 3.
M: What time does the program begin?
W: It starts at 8:30 a.m.
M: What are we going to do there?
W: We'll plant trees and clean up the hiking trail.
M: Sounds meaningful!
W: By the way, they said we should wear waterproof boots because the paths might be muddy.
M: Good to know.

우·리·말·해·석

남: 넌 Eco Adventure Day(환경 체험의 날)가 기대되니?

여: 물론이지! 6월 3일 Blue Forest 공원에서 열릴 거야.
남: 프로그램은 몇 시에 시작해?
여: 오전 8시 30분에 시작해.
남: 우리는 거기서 뭘 하게 돼?
여: 우리는 나무들을 심고 등산로를 청소할 거야.
남: 의미 있겠다!
여: 그런데, 그들은 길이 진흙투성이일 수 있어서 방수 부츠를 신어야 한다고 했어.
남: 알게 되어서 좋네.

단·어·및·표·현

clean up ~을 청소하다, 정리하다
hiking trail 등산로
by the way 그런데
waterproof [wɔ́:tərprù:f] [형] 방수의
muddy [mʌ́di] [형] 진흙투성이의, 진흙의

03 전화목적파악 ▶ 정답 ①

듣·기·대·본

(*Cellphone rings.*)
W: Hello?
M: Hi, this is Chris calling from Sunshine Library. Am I speaking with Emily Parker?
W: Yes, speaking.
M: The book you requested, *The Secret Plan*, has arrived and is ready for pickup.
W: Oh, that's great news! Can I pick it up tomorrow?
M: Sure! We're open from 9 a.m. to 6 p.m., so you can drop by anytime during those hours.
W: Perfect! Is there anything I need to bring with me?
M: No. You only need to bring your library card.
W: Thank you, Chris. I appreciate the call.

우·리·말·해·석

(휴대전화가 울린다.)
여: 여보세요?
남: 안녕하세요, 저는 Sunshine 도서관에서 전화를 건 Chris입니다. Emily Parker이신가요?
여: 네, 말씀하세요.
남: 당신이 요청하신 책 "The Secret Plan"이 도착하여 찾아가실 준비가 되었습니다.
여: 아, 좋은 소식이네요! 제가 그것을 내일 찾아가도 될까요?
남: 물론이죠! 저희는 오전 9시부터 오후 6시까지 문을 여니, 당신은 그 시간 동안 언제든 잠깐 들르실 수 있습니다.
여: 완벽하네요! 제가 가져가야 할 것이 있나요?
남: 아뇨, 당신은 당신의 도서관 카드만 가져오시면 됩니다.
여: 감사해요, Chris. 전화주셔서 감사해요.

단·어·및·표·현

be ready for ~ ~할 준비가 되다
pickup [píkʌ̀p] [명] (물건을) 찾으러 감
pick up (어디에서) ~을 찾다[찾아오다]
drop by 잠깐 들르다, 불시에 찾아가다
anytime [énitàim] [부] 언제든지
appreciate [əprí:ʃièit] [동] 고마워하다

04 수치파악(시각) ▶ 정답 ④

듣·기·대·본

(*Telephone rings.*)
W: VR Electronics Service Center. How may I help you?
M: Hi. My air conditioner isn't working. Could you send a repairperson?
W: Sure. The earliest we can send someone is Thursday. Is that okay?
M: Yes. But I won't be home in the morning.
W: I see. Then, is 2 p.m. okay for you?
M: I'm afraid not. Could you make it 6 p.m. instead?
W: I'm sorry, but they get off at 6.
M: I see. Then how about 5 p.m.?
W: Okay. I'll set you up at 5.
M: Thank you.

우·리·말·해·석

(전화벨이 울린다.)
여: VR전자 서비스 센터입니다. 어떻게 도와드릴까요?
남: 안녕하세요. 제 에어컨이 작동이 안 돼요. 수리기사님을 보내주실 수 있나요?
여: 물론이죠. 저희가 누군가를 보낼 수 있는 가장 빠른 날은 목요일입니다. 괜찮으신가요?
남: 네. 하지만 저는 아침에 집에 없을 거예요.
여: 그렇군요. 그럼 오후 2시는 괜찮으신가요?
남: 유감스럽게도 안 돼요. 대신 오후 6시로 해주실 수 있나요?
여: 죄송하지만 그들은 6시에 퇴근합니다.
남: 그렇군요. 그럼 오후 5시는요?
여: 가능합니다. 5시로 잡아 놓겠습니다.
남: 감사합니다.

단·어·및·표·현

work [wəːrk] [동] (기계장치 등이) 작동되다, 기능하다
repairperson [ripέərpə̀:rsn] [명] 수리기사, 수리공
instead [instéd] [부] 대신에
get off 퇴근하다
set ~ up (약속 · 회의 등을) 잡다, 마련하다

05 심정추론 ▶ 정답 ③

듣·기·대·본

W: So, how did it go with the doctor?
M: What do you mean?
W: You said you were taking your cat to the vet.
M: Oh, right! He's fine. Thank goodness.
W: Nothing is wrong with him, then? You were so worried.
M: Well, he is over-weight, and he is being lazy. That's why he isn't moving very much.
W: He just needs to go on a diet.
M: Exactly. It's a huge weight off my chest. I really thought he was sick.
W: Well, I'm glad he's fine.

우·리·말·해·석

① 걱정하는 ② 지루해하는 ③ 안도하는
④ 궁금해하는 ⑤ 자랑스러워하는

여: 그래서, 병원에 간 건 어떻게 됐어요?
남: 무슨 말이에요?
여: 당신은 당신의 고양이를 수의사에게 데려간다고 했잖아요.
남: 아, 맞아요! 그는 괜찮아요. 정말 다행이에요.
여: 그럼, 그에게 아무 이상이 없는 거예요? 당신은 엄청 걱정했잖아요.

남: 음, 그는 과체중이고, 게을러요. 그것이 그가 별로 움직이지 않는 이
  유죠.

여: 그는 단지 다이어트가 필요한 거네요.

남: 정확해요. 제 마음에서 큰 짐을 덜었어요. 저는 정말 그가 아프다고 생
  각했어요.

여: 아이고, 그가 괜찮아서 다행이에요.

단·어·및·표·현

vet[vet] 뗑 수의사

over-weight 과체중의, 비만의

go on a diet 다이어트를 하다

weight[weit] 뗑 (무거운 책임감 같은) 짐, 부담

06 그림상황에적절한대화찾기　▶ 정답 ③

듣·기·대·본

① W: Look at that tiger in the cage. It looks so scary.
   M: Yes, it is. Let's take a picture of it.
② W: Hello, sir. Can I help you?
   M: Yes. I'm looking for a teddy bear for my daughter.
③ W: Do you want me to take your picture?
   M: Yes, first as a bear, then as a tiger.
④ W: Did you watch the documentary on bears last night?
   M: Yes, I did. It was so touching.
⑤ W: Can I feed this baby tiger?
   M: No, you are not allowed to do it.

우·리·말·해·석

① 여: 우리 안에 있는 저 호랑이를 좀 봐. 그것은 무척 무섭게 보인다.
   남: 응, 그러네. 그것의 사진을 찍자.
② 여: 안녕하세요, 손님. 도와드릴까요?
   남: 네. 저는 제 딸을 위한 곰 인형을 찾고 있습니다.
③ 여: 내가 너의 사진을 찍어줄까?
   남: 네, 처음에는 곰, 그 다음에는 호랑이로요.
④ 여: 지난밤에 곰에 관한 다큐멘터리를 봤니?
   남: 응, 그랬어. 그것은 정말 감동적이었어.
⑤ 여: 제가 이 아기 호랑이에게 먹이를 줄 수 있나요?
   남: 아니요, 그렇게 하는 것은 허락되지 않습니다.

단·어·및·표·현

take a picture 사진을 찍다

allow[əláu] 통 허락하다, 허용하다

🔊 LISTENING ADVICE

'd' 혹은 't'가 연속되는 두 단어의 자음 사이에 올 때 [d]와 [t] 소리
는 탈락되어 발음됩니다. 따라서 'Do you want me to take ~'에서
'want me'는 [원트 미]라고 발음되지 않고 [원미]에 가깝게 소리 납니
다. 미국식 영어에서는 이러한 [d], [t] 소리의 탈락현상이 자주 발생
합니다.

---

07 부탁(요청)한일파악　▶ 정답 ⑤

듣·기·대·본

(Cellphone rings.)

M: Hi, Karen.

W: Hi, Joel. Are you still at the library?

M: Yeah, I just finished up with my study group. I'm about
   to leave. Why?

W: I got a message that the book I reserved is now
   available, but I can't go pick it up today.

M: Oh, really? Do you want me to get it for you?

W: Could you, please? I'll send my library card to your
   phone.

M: Sure. Just one book?

W: Yes. I owe you big time.

M: Hey, no problem. I'll bring it to you later.

우·리·말·해·석

(휴대전화가 울린다.)

남: 안녕, Karen.

여: 안녕, Joel. 너 아직 도서관에 있어?

남: 응. 방금 스터디 그룹이 끝났어. 이제 막 나가려던 참이야. 왜?

여: 내가 예약한 책이 이제 이용 가능하다는 메시지를 받았는데, 나는 오늘
  찾으러 갈 수가 없어.

남: 아, 정말? 내가 너를 위해 대신 받아주길 원해?

여: 그래 줄 수 있어? 내 도서관 카드를 네 휴대폰으로 보낼게.

남: 좋아. 책 한 권뿐이야?

여: 응. 너한테 정말 큰 신세 진다.

남: 에이, 괜찮아. 나중에 너한테 가져다줄게.

단·어·및·표·현

be about to + 동사원형 막 ~하려던 참이다

reserve[rizə́ːrv] 통 예약하다

available[əvéiləbl] 형 이용 가능한

owe + 사람 + big time ~에게 큰 신세를 지다

08 담화미언급　▶ 정답 ⑤

듣·기·대·본

W: Hello, students. Let me tell you about tomorrow's class
   field trip to Daehan Youth Sports Center. You need to
   be there by 9 a.m. You can take bus number 23 or 38 to
   get there. You're going to have a chance to experience
   exciting sports such as indoor rock climbing. Please
   wear casual clothes or athletic wear for the programs.
   And, don't forget to bring your lunch. Thank you.

우·리·말·해·석

여: 안녕하세요, 학생 여러분. 제가 내일 있을 Daehan Youth Sports Center
  현장학습에 대해 말씀드리겠습니다. 여러분은 오전 9시까지 와야 합니
  다. 그곳에 가려면 23번이나 38번 버스를 타면 됩니다. 여러분은 실내
  암벽 등반 같은 신나는 스포츠를 체험할 기회를 가질 것입니다. 그 프
  로그램들을 위해 간편한 옷이나 운동복을 입으세요. 그리고 점심 가져
  오는 것 잊지 마세요. 감사합니다.

단·어·및·표·현

indoor[índɔ̀ːr] 형 실내의

rock climbing 암벽 등반

09 담화화제추론　▶ 정답 ②

듣·기·대·본

M: This is a food. Many people eat this as a meal. It's very
   convenient and easy to eat. So, many people reach for
   it when they are busy. There are various recipes for this,
   depending on the ingredients. To make this, spread rice
   on a dried sheet of seaweed. Then, put eggs, carrots,
   ham and all the other ingredients on top, and roll it up.
   Finally, slice it into bite-sized pieces so you can eat it.

우·리·말·해·석

남: 이것은 음식이다. 많은 사람들은 이것을 식사로 먹는다. 이것은 매우

간편하고 먹기 쉽다. 그래서 많은 사람들이 바쁠 때 이것을 찾는다. 이것은 재료에 따라 다양한 조리법이 있다. 이것을 만들기 위해서는 마른 김 위에 밥을 펴 바른다. 그 다음에, 계란, 당근, 햄과 다른 모든 재료들을 위에 올리고 말아준다. 마지막으로, 그것을 먹을 수 있도록 한입 크기의 조각으로 자른다.

단·어·및·표·현

convenient [kənvíːnjənt] [형] 간편한, 편리한
reach for ~을 찾다, 손을 뻗다
seaweed [síːwìːd] [명] (김 · 미역 등의) 해조, 해초
ingredient [ingríːdiənt] [명] 재료, 구성 요소
bite-sized 한입 크기의

10 어색한대화찾기 ▶ 정답 ①

듣·기·대·본

① M: Do they allow dogs in this apartment building?
W: There's a nearby pet shop where I get all my supplies.
② M: My elbows are swollen and they really hurt.
W: Soak them in warm water. That'll ease the pain.
③ M: Do you need money for your school trip?
W: No, it's okay. Everything will be provided for us.
④ M: How did you get to be that good at singing?
W: I've been practicing every day since I was nine years old.
⑤ M: What's the specialty of this restaurant?
W: I think they serve a fusion of Asian and European foods.

우·리·말·해·석

① 남: 이 아파트 건물에서 개를 허용해 주나요?
여: 제가 모든 용품들을 사는 가까운 반려동물 가게가 있어요.
② 남: 제 양 팔꿈치가 부어서 정말 아파요.
여: 팔꿈치를 따뜻한 물에 담그세요. 그게 고통을 덜어 줄 거예요.
③ 남: 너 수학여행을 위해 돈이 필요하니?
여: 아니요, 괜찮아요. 모든 것이 우리를 위해 제공될 거예요.
④ 남: 너 어떻게 그렇게 노래를 잘하게 되었니?
여: 나는 9살 이후로 매일 연습해왔어.
⑤ 남: 이 식당의 전문 요리가 뭐니?
여: 그들은 아시아와 유럽의 퓨전 음식을 제공하는 것 같아.

단·어·및·표·현

nearby [níərbài] [형] 가까운, 인근의

11 할일파악(대화직후) ▶ 정답 ②

듣·기·대·본

W: Hey, Chris. Did you hear about the cheerleading team tryout at our school?
M: No, I didn't.
W: Well, there is going to be one, and I'm going to try out.
M: Good for you! How are you going to prepare for it?
W: I need to practice my tumbling skills, and make up some dance routines.
M: Wow, that's a lot of work. Are you going to the practice room right now?
W: Actually, I'm going to the principal's office. I have to submit my application first.

우·리·말·해·석

여: 이봐, Chris. 너 우리 학교의 응원단 선발 시험에 대해 들었어?
남: 아니, 못 들었어.
여: 그러니까, 테스트가 있을 거야. 그래서 나는 시도해볼 거야.
남: 잘됐다! 어떻게 준비할 거야?
여: 공중제비 기술을 연습하고, 몇 가지 춤 동작들을 만들어야 해.
남: 와, 할 게 많구나. 너는 지금 바로 연습실에 갈 거야?
여: 실은, 교장실에 갈 거야. 먼저 신청서를 제출해야 해.

단·어·및·표·현

submit [səbmít] [동] 제출하다

12 도표정보파악 ▶ 정답 ④

듣·기·대·본

M: Hey, why don't we learn a foreign language this winter?
W: Good idea. Actually, I want to learn French. I'd like to go to France someday.
M: Me, too. Will three classes a week be too much?
W: Not at all. It's better to learn fast, and winter break is not that long.
M: Right. How about taking classes in the morning?
W: That works for me.
M: Okay. Let's go and sign up now.

우·리·말·해·석

	수업	언어	수업 수(주당)	시간
①	A	이탈리아어	3번	9:00 ~ 11:00 a.m.
②	B	이탈리아어	2번	2:00 ~ 4:00 p.m.
③	C	프랑스어	3번	2:00 ~ 4:00 p.m.
④	D	프랑스어	3번	9:00 ~ 11:00 a.m.
⑤	E	프랑스어	2번	2:00 ~ 4:00 p.m.

남: 이봐, 우리 이번 겨울에 외국어를 배우는 게 어때?
여: 좋은 생각이야. 사실, 나는 프랑스어를 배우고 싶어. 나는 언젠가 프랑스에 가고 싶어.
남: 나도. 일주일에 세 번 수업이 너무 많을까?
여: 아니, 전혀. 빨리 배우는 것이 더 좋고, 겨울 방학이 그렇게 길지 않아.
남: 맞아. 아침에 수업을 듣는 것이 어때?
여: 나는 괜찮아.
남: 좋아. 지금 가서 신청하자.

단·어·및·표·현

work [wəːrk] [동] 괜찮다, 효과가 있다

13 수치파악(날짜) ▶ 정답 ⑤

듣·기·대·본

W: Mr. Park, when are you available for your next dental appointment?
M: Do you have anything available on April 12?
W: I'm afraid we don't. Dr. Lee is fully booked all day.
M: Then how about April 13?
W: I'm sorry, he's off that day. Are you available on April 14?
M: Yes, I am. How about 11 o'clock?
W: Let me check the schedule. (*pause*) Oh, we have 11 o'clock open. I'll schedule you at 11 next week.

우·리·말·해·석

여: 박 선생님, 다음 치과 진료 예약은 언제 가능하세요?
남: 4월 12일날 가능한 시간이 있나요?
여: 죄송하게도, 없습니다. 이 박사님께서 하루 종일 예약이 되어 있으세요.

남: 그럼 4월 13일은요?

여: 죄송합니다만, 그날은 박사님께서 쉬세요. 4월 14일은 가능하신가요?

남: 네, 가능해요. 11시는 어떤가요?

여: 제가 스케줄을 확인해볼게요. (잠시 후) 아, 11시가 비어있네요. 제가 다음 주 11시로 예약해놓을게요.

단·어·및·표·현
all day 하루 종일

14 한일파악 ▶ 정답 ⑤
듣·기·대·본
W: Hey, Brandon. What's up?

M: Hey, Cathy. Have you heard about the school promotional video contest?

W: Yeah, I saw the notice a few days ago.

M: I thought you would be interested. So, are you applying?

W: Of course! In fact, I turned in the application yesterday.

M: Really? Who is on your team?

W: Nick and Becky.

M: Wow! You guys are the dream team. I hope your team wins first place.

우·리·말·해·석
여: 안녕, Brandon. 잘 지내?

남: 안녕, Cathy. 너 학교 홍보 영상 공모전에 대해 들어봤니?

여: 응, 며칠 전에 공지를 봤어.

남: 네가 관심 있을 거라 생각했어. 그래서, 너 지원하니?

여: 당연하지! 사실은 나 어제 그 신청서를 냈어.

남: 정말? 너의 팀에는 누가 있는데?

여: Nick과 Becky.

남: 우와! 너희들은 드림팀이다. 나는 너희 팀이 1등을 하길 바라.

단·어·및·표·현
promotional [prəmóuʃənl] 형 홍보의
contest [kántest] 명 공모전, 대회, 시합
notice [nóutis] 명 공지, 공지사항
turn in ~을 제출하다
application [æ̀pləkéiʃən] 명 신청서, 지원서

15 담화목적파악 ▶ 정답 ②
듣·기·대·본
W: Welcome to Sunset Beach. Before you start swimming in the ocean, let me remind you of a few things. First, please don't go into the water except during the hours when swimming is allowed. At other times, the ocean may be dangerous to swim in or the lifeguards may not be there to help you. Second, make sure you always wear your life jacket when participating in water activities. Have a good time and stay safe, everyone!

우·리·말·해·석
여: Sunset Beach에 오신 것을 환영합니다. 바다에서 수영을 시작하기 전에, 제가 여러분께 몇 가지를 상기시켜드리겠습니다. 우선, 수영이 허용되는 시간 이외에는 물에 들어가지 마십시오. 다른 때에는, 바다는 수영하기에 위험할 수 있고 안전 요원들이 여러분들을 돕기 위해 그곳에 있지 않을 수도 있습니다. 둘째, 수상활동에 참여할 때에는 반드시 항상 구명조끼를 입으십시오. 좋은 시간 보내시고 안전하게 계십시오, 모두들!

단·어·및·표·현
remind A of B A에게 B를 상기시키다
lifeguard [láifgɑ̀ːrd] 명 안전 요원, 구조원
participate in ~에 참여하다, 참가하다

16 수치계산(금액) ▶ 정답 ④
듣·기·대·본
M: Good morning. How can I help you?

W: I'd like to buy tickets for the music concert tomorrow.

M: Great. Tickets are 70 dollars for VIP seats and 40 dollars for standard seats.

W: Two standard seats, please.

M: Thank you. The total comes to 80 dollars.

W: Oh, is this a catalog for the concert program?

M: Yes, it is. The price of the catalog is 5 dollars.

W: I'll take one catalog. Here's a 100-dollar bill.

우·리·말·해·석
남: 좋은 아침입니다. 어떻게 도와드릴까요?

여: 내일 있는 음악 콘서트 티켓을 사고 싶어요.

남: 좋습니다. VIP 좌석은 70달러이고, 일반석은 40달러입니다.

여: 일반석 두 장 주세요.

남: 감사합니다. 총 80달러입니다.

여: 오, 이것은 콘서트 프로그램의 카탈로그인가요?

남: 네, 맞아요. 카탈로그의 가격은 5달러입니다.

여: 카탈로그 하나 주세요. 여기 100달러짜리 지폐입니다.

단·어·및·표·현
standard [stǽndərd] 형 일반적인, 보통의
bill [bil] 명 지폐

17 알맞은응답찾기 ▶ 정답 ③
듣·기·대·본
W: Hi, Alex! Have you finished your essay for writing class?

M: No, not yet. We still have time. Isn't it due next Friday?

W: I don't think so. It's due this Friday.

M: Let me check. [Pause] Oh, you're right! I often get confused about deadlines.

W: Why don't you use a time management app?

M: A time management app? Please tell me more about it.

W: It reminds you of the deadlines for all your important tasks.

M: That sounds really helpful!

W: I've been using it for quite a while now and I find it very useful.

M: Thanks for the tip. I should definitely try it out.

우·리·말·해·석
① 축하해! 네가 합격해서 기뻐.

② 걱정 마. 나는 네가 잘 해낼 거라고 확신해!

③ 조언 고마워. 난 꼭 한번 그걸 사용해 봐야겠어.

④ 멋지다! 그건 틀림없이 내 작문 실력을 향상시킬 거야.

⑤ 동의해. 우리 선생님께 마감일에 대해 얘기해보자.

여: 안녕, Alex! 너는 작문 수업 과제를 다 끝냈니?

남: 아니, 아직 다 못했어. 우린 아직 시간이 있잖아. 다음 주 금요일까지 아냐?

여: 난 그렇게 생각하지 않아. 이번 주 금요일까지야.

남: 확인해볼게. [잠시 후] 아, 네가 맞아! 나는 종종 마감일을 헷갈려.
여: 시간 관리 앱을 사용해보는 건 어때?
남: 시관 관리 앱? 내게 그것에 대해 좀 더 말해줘.
여: 그건 너의 모든 중요한 과제의 마감일을 너에게 상기시켜줘.
남: 정말 도움이 될 것 같다!
여: 나는 지금까지 그걸 꽤 오랫동안 사용해왔고 매우 유용하다고 생각해.
남: **조언 고마워. 난 꼭 한번 그걸 사용해 봐야겠어.**

단·어·및·표·현
confused[kənfjúːzd] 휑 헷갈려 하는, 혼란스러워하는
deadline[dédlàin] 휑 마감일
management[mǽnidʒmənt] 휑 관리
remind A of B A에게 B를 상기시키다, 생각나게 하다

18 　알맞은응답찾기　▶ 정답 ①

들·기·대·본
W: Good morning, how may I help you?
M: Hi. I bought this shirt yesterday, and I'd like to exchange
   it for another.
W: Sure. May I ask why you would like to exchange it?
M: It's a little tight for me. I think I've gained weight
   recently.
W: I see. Then I'll get you a bigger one right away.
M: Actually, I want to take a look around and find a different
   shirt. Is that OK?
W: Sure. Feel free to look around.

우·리·말·해·석
① 물론이죠. 편하게 둘러보세요.
② 문제없어요. 더 작은 것들도 있어요.
③ 유감이지만 더 큰 사이즈는 없습니다.
④ 죄송합니다만, 환불은 해드릴 수 없어요.
⑤ 네, 이건 크기만 다른 같은 셔츠예요.

여: 안녕하세요, 무엇을 도와드릴까요?
남: 안녕하세요. 제가 어제 이 셔츠를 샀는데, 다른 것으로 교환하고 싶어요.
여: 그래요. 왜 교환을 원하시는지 여쭤봐도 될까요?
남: 그건 제게 좀 작아요. 제 생각엔 제가 최근에 살이 찐 것 같아요.
여: 알겠습니다. 그러면 지금 바로 좀 더 큰 걸로 가져다 드릴게요.
남: 사실, 제가 한번 둘러보고 다른 셔츠를 찾아보고 싶어요. 괜찮을까요?
여: **물론이죠. 편하게 둘러보세요.**

단·어·및·표·현
exchange[ikstʃéindʒ] 图 교환하다
actually[ǽktʃuəli] 图 사실은

19 　알맞은응답찾기　▶ 정답 ②

들·기·대·본
M: Honey, are you all packed for our trip?
W: No, I still have to pack a few more things. Have you
   finished packing your stuff?
M: Yeah, I'm finished. Do you need any help?
W: Well… Can you find my passport for me? I can't seem
   to find it.
M: Did you lose your passport? That's bad news.
W: I don't think I actually lost it. It should be around here
   somewhere.
M: Did you check the drawers in the living room? I think I
   saw it there.

W: Thanks, I'll go check the drawers.

우·리·말·해·석
① 나는 우리 여행에 대해 무척 신나요.
② 고마워요, 내가 가서 서랍들을 확인할게요.
③ 당신은 당신의 핸드폰 충전기를 챙겼어요?
④ 우리는 두 시간 후에 집을 나서야 해요.
⑤ 당신은 당신의 여권 없이 비행기에 탑승할 수 없어요.

남: 여보, 당신은 우리 여행을 위한 짐을 다 챙겼어요?
여: 아니요, 나는 아직 몇 가지 것들을 더 챙겨야 해요. 당신은 당신의 물건
   을 다 챙겼어요?
남: 네, 나는 끝났어요. 당신은 도움이 필요한가요?
여: 글쎄요… 나를 위해 내 여권을 찾아 줄 수 있어요? 나는 그것을 찾을
   수 없을 것 같아요.
남: 당신은 당신의 여권을 잃어버렸어요? 그것은 안 좋은 소식이네요.
여: 나는 내가 그것을 실제로 잃어버렸다고 생각하지 않아요. 그것은 여기
   어딘가에 있을 거예요.
남: 당신은 거실에 있는 서랍들을 확인했어요? 나는 그것을 거기서 봤다고
   생각해요.
여: **고마워요, 내가 가서 서랍들을 확인할게요.**

단·어·및·표·현
packed[pækt] 휑 짐을 챙긴
somewhere[sʌ́mhwɛ̀ər] 图 어딘가에

20 　상황에적절한말찾기　▶ 정답 ⑤

들·기·대·본
M: Steve is a middle school student. He is worried about
   the math test next week. He didn't do very well last
   time, and he wants to make up for it this time. He knows
   that one of his classmates, Katie, is really good at math.
   She always gets an A. So, he would like to ask Katie if
   she can help him prepare for the test. In this situation,
   what would Steve most likely say to Katie?
Steve: Katie, can you give me a hand with the test next
   week?

우·리·말·해·석
① 나는 내 무례한 행동을 만회할 거야.
② 시험은 내가 예상했던 것보다 더 어려웠어.
③ 시험 결과에 실망하지 마.
④ 나는 수학이 너의 가장 좋아하는 과목이라는 것을 몰랐어.
⑤ 너는 다음 주 시험(준비)을 도와줄 수 있니?

남: Steve는 중학생이다. 그는 다음 주에 있을 수학 시험에 대해 걱정한다.
   그는 지난번에 별로 잘하지 못했고, 이번에는 만회하기를 원한다. 그는
   그의 반 친구 중 한 명인 Katie가 수학을 정말 잘하는 것을 알고 있다.
   그녀는 항상 A를 받는다. 그래서, 그는 Katie에게 그가 시험을 준비하
   는 것을 도와줄 수 있는지 물어보고 싶다. 이 상황에서 Steve는 Katie
   에게 뭐라고 말하겠는가?
Steve: Katie, 너는 다음 주 시험(준비)을 도와줄 수 있니?

단·어·및·표·현
make up for ~을 만회하다
give A a hand A를 도와주다

Words & Expressions Review

1. 실내의	2. 진흙투성이의, 진흙의	3. 자르다
4. 감동적인	5. 허용된, 허가받은	6. 홍보의
7. 해조, 해초	8. 공모전, 대회	9. 이용 가능한
10. ~을 만회하다	11. 예약하다	12. (짐승의) 우리, 새장
13. 아주 멋진, 굉장한	14. 퇴근하다	15. 휴가, 휴식
16. 서랍	17. 방수의	18. (근무·일을) 쉬는
19. (배·기차·버스·비행기 등에) 타다	20. 준비하다	21. 전문, 특제품
22. (고통 등을) 덜어주다	23. 한입 크기의	24. (약속·회의 등을) 잡다, 마련하다
25. 재료, 구성요소	26. 신청서, 지원서	27. 일반적인, 보통의
28. 암벽 등반	29. 그런데	30. 간편한, 편리한
31. ~을 찾다, 손을 뻗다	32. 다이어트를 하다	33. 예약, 약속
34. 살찌다, 체중이 늘다	35. 교환하다	36. 부푼, 부어오른
37. 물품	38. ~을 제출하다	39. 헷갈려 하는, 혼란스러워하는
40. 수의사	41. 장식, 무늬	42. 잠깐 들르다, 불시에 찾아가다
43. ~에 참가하다	44. 테스트, 적성시험	

Listening Test

영어듣기 모의고사 14회

|정|답|

01 ①	02 ④	03 ②	04 ④	05 ③
06 ③	07 ③	08 ⑤	09 ④	10 ⑤
11 ④	12 ④	13 ④	14 ⑤	15 ⑤
16 ④	17 ③	18 ③	19 ③	20 ④

01 그림정보파악(대화) ▶ 정답 ①

듣·기·대·본

M: How may I help you?

W: I'm looking for some winter boots for myself.

M: Okay. These tall boots are popular this year. They look very trendy.

W: Well, I prefer shorter ones. Do you have any?

M: Sure. How about these ones with zippers on the side?

W: Oh, they look very nice! I think the zippers will be convenient, too.

M: We also have the same design with heels.

W: Um... I like the flat ones better, without the heels. I'll take those ones.

M: Sure. That's a good choice.

우·리·말·해·석

남: 어떻게 도와드릴까요?

여: 저는 제가 신을 겨울 부츠를 찾고 있어요.

남: 그러시군요. 올해는 이 긴 부츠가 인기가 많습니다. 아주 최신 유행으로 보이기도 하고요.

여: 글쎄요, 저는 짧은 것을 더 선호해요. 그런 게 있나요?

남: 그럼요. 옆에 지퍼가 달린 이 제품은 어떠신가요?

여: 오, 아주 좋아 보이네요! 지퍼도 편리할 것 같아요.

남: 저희는 같은 디자인으로 굽이 있는 것도 가지고 있습니다.

여: 음… 저는 굽이 없는 평평한 것이 더 좋아요. 저는 저걸로 할게요.

남: 알겠습니다. 좋은 선택이네요.

단·어·및·표·현

trendy [tréndi] 휑 최신 유행의

convenient [kənvíːnjənt] 휑 편리한

flat [flæt] 휑 평평한, 납작한

02 대화미언급 ▶ 정답 ④

듣·기·대·본

W: Hey, Nathan. You use the wireless earphones, 'Cosypod', don't you?

M: Yes, I use them all the time. Why?

W: I'm tired of dealing with earphone cords. So, I'm thinking of getting new wireless ones.

M: Good idea. They're really comfortable, and mine only cost $50.

W: That's cheaper than I thought. How long do they stay charged?

M: They last for 5 hours once charged.

W: That will be long enough. Do they have any additional functions?

M: Well, they provide noise cancellation and they are waterproof.

W: I see. What colors do they come in?

M: They're available in white, black and gold.

W: Okay, thanks.

우·리·말·해·석

여: 안녕, Nathan. 너는 무선 이어폰, Cosypod를 사용하지, 그렇지 않니?

남: 응, 난 그것들을 항상 써. 왜?

여: 나는 이어폰 줄을 다루는 것에 지쳤어. 그래서 나는 새 무선 이어폰을 살까 생각 중이야.

남: 좋은 생각이야. 그것들은 정말 편하고, 내 것은 50달러밖에 안 들었어.

여: 그것은 내가 생각했던 것보다 더 싸네. 그것들은 충전된 상태로 얼마나 오래 가?

남: 그것들은 한 번 충전되면 5시간 동안 지속돼.

여: 그것은 충분히 길겠네. 그것들은 어떤 부가적인 기능들이 있니?

남: 음, 그것들은 외부 소음 제거를 제공하고 방수야.

여: 그렇구나. 그것들은 어떤 색깔로 나오니?

남: 그것들은 흰색, 검은색 그리고 금색으로 구할 수 있어.

여: 알겠어, 고마워.

단·어·및·표·현

wireless [wáiərlis] 휑 무선의

deal with ~을 다루다, 처리하다

earphone cords 이어폰 줄

stay charged 충전된 상태로 유지되다

noise cancellation 외부 소음 제거

waterproof [wɔ́:tərprù:f] [형] 방수의, 물이 새어들지 않는
available [əvéiləbl] [형] ~을 구할[이용할] 수 있는

03 전화목적파악 ▶ 정답 ②

듣·기·대·본

(*Telephone rings.*)
M: Hi, Karen. It's me, Alex.
W: Oh, hi. Are you okay? Ms. Gage told us that you couldn't come to school because you were sick.
M: I feel much better now. Thank you for asking.
W: You're welcome. Why did you call me?
M: I wanted to ask you what today's homework is.
W: It is reading our history textbook from page 11 to 15.
M: Thanks. See you tomorrow!

우·리·말·해·석

(전화벨이 울린다.)
남: 안녕, Karen. 나 Alex야.
여: 오, 안녕. 너 괜찮은 거니? Gage 선생님께서 네가 아파서 학교에 나오지 못했다고 그러셨는데.
남: 이제는 훨씬 나아졌어. 물어봐 줘서 고마워.
여: 천만에. 왜 전화했니?
남: 오늘 숙제가 뭔지 물어보고 싶어서.
여: 역사 교과서를 11쪽부터 15쪽까지 읽는 거야.
남: 고마워. 내일 보자!

단·어·및·표·현

feel better (병세 등이) 나아지다

04 수치파악(시각) ▶ 정답 ④

듣·기·대·본

(*Telephone rings.*)
W: Hello, Daymoon Community Center.
M: Hi, I'd like to register for the basic swimming lesson program on Monday and Wednesday.
W: Okay. What time do you want to register for?
M: I want the morning class. Either 6 a.m. or 7 a.m. is fine.
W: Sorry, but the morning classes are both full.
M: Oh, I see. Then which class is available?
W: There are still a few spots available for evening lessons.
M: Then, I'd like to sign up for the 7 p.m. class.
W: Sure. Can I have your name, please?
M: It's Kevin Lee.
W: All right. Please bring your ID card on the first day.

우·리·말·해·석

(전화벨이 울린다.)
여: 여보세요, Daymoon 커뮤니티 센터입니다.
남: 안녕하세요, 저는 월요일과 수요일에 하는 기초 수영 강습 프로그램에 등록하고 싶은데요.
여: 알겠습니다. 몇 시로 등록하고 싶으세요?
남: 저는 아침 수업을 원해요. 오전 6시나 7시 둘 중 어떤 것도 괜찮아요.
여: 죄송합니다만 아침 수업은 둘 다 만원입니다.
남: 아, 그렇군요. 그럼 어떤 수업이 자리가 있죠?
여: 저녁 수업들은 아직 몇 자리 여유가 있습니다.
남: 그러면 저는 오후 7시 수업에 등록하고 싶어요.
여: 좋습니다. 성함을 알려주시겠어요?
남: Kevin Lee입니다.
여: 알겠습니다. 첫날에는 신분증을 지참해 주세요.

단·어·및·표·현

register for ~에 등록하다
available [əvéiləbl] [형] 이용할 수 있는, 구할 수 있는
sign up for (강좌에) 등록하다

05 심정추론 ▶ 정답 ③

듣·기·대·본

W: Ron, what's wrong?
M: You know my parents adopted a dog last week, right?
W: Yes, I remember. You were so excited.
M: He is very sick. I don't think his previous owner took care of him properly.
W: Oh, no! But, will he be okay?
M: I'm not sure. I just wish there were more I could do for him.
W: I'm so sorry, Ron.
M: I don't know what I'd do without him.

우·리·말·해·석

① 지루해하는 ② 행복한 ③ 속상한
④ 질투하는 ⑤ 놀란

여: Ron, 무슨 일이야?
남: 너는 내 부모님이 지난주에 강아지를 한 마리 입양한 거 알지, 그렇지?
여: 응, 나는 기억해. 너 정말 신났었잖아.
남: 그가 매우 아파. 내가 생각하기에 그의 전 주인이 그를 제대로 돌보지 않았던 것 같아.
여: 오, 저런! 그런데, 그가 괜찮아질까?
남: 잘 모르겠어. 나는 단지 내가 그를 위해 할 수 있는 게 더 있었으면 좋겠어.
여: 유감이야, Ron.
남: 나는 그가 없이 뭘 어떻게 해야 할지 모르겠어.

단·어·및·표·현

adopt [ədάpt] [동] 입양하다
previous [prí:viəs] [형] 이전의
owner [óunər] [명] 주인, 소유자
properly [prάpərli] [부] 제대로, 적절히

06 그림상황에적절한대화찾기 ▶ 정답 ③

듣·기·대·본

① W: Hello, how may I help you?
M: I'm here to get fitted for new contact lenses.
② W: Excuse me. You dropped your wallet.
M: Oh, my. Thank you for letting me know.
③ W: Can you cover your right eye and read this letter?
M: Um... I can't read that letter.
④ W: Oh, no. I forgot to bring my glasses.
M: Don't worry. I'll show you my notes later.
⑤ W: Can you show me to the cafeteria?
M: Sure. It's this way.

우·리·말·해·석

① 여: 안녕하세요, 어떻게 도와드릴까요?
남: 저는 새 콘택트렌즈를 맞추러 왔습니다.
② 여: 실례합니다. 당신은 당신의 지갑을 떨어뜨렸습니다.
남: 아, 이런. 알려주셔서 감사합니다.

③ 여: 당신의 오른쪽 눈을 가리고 이 글자를 읽을 수 있나요?
　　남: 음… 전 그 글자를 읽을 수가 없어요.
④ 여: 아, 이런. 제 안경을 가져오는 것을 잊었네요.
　　남: 걱정하지 마세요. 나중에 제 메모를 보여 드리겠습니다.
⑤ 여: 저를 식당까지 안내해 주실 수 있나요?
　　남: 물론이죠. 이쪽입니다.

get fitted for ~을 맞추다
drop [drɑp] 동 떨어뜨리다
letter [létər] 명 글자, 문자
note [nout] 명 (기억을 돕기 위한) 메모
show [ʃou] 동 (장소로) 안내[인도]하다

07 부탁(요청)한일파악 ▶ 정답 ③

듣·기·대·본

W: John, are you going to the gym?
M: Yes, I am. Why?
W: I'm thinking of joining.
M: That's great. Let's go together.
W: Not today. I have to take my brother to the hospital.
M: Right. Can I give you a ride on my way?
W: It's OK. We're taking a taxi. But can you bring me a brochure from the gym?
M: Sure, no problem.

우·리·말·해·석

여: John, 너 체육관에 가는 거니?
남: 응, 그래. 왜?
여: 나도 다닐까 생각 중이야.
남: 그것 잘됐네. 함께 가자.
여: 오늘은 안 돼. 내 남동생을 병원에 데려다줘야 해.
남: 알겠어. 내가 가는 길에 너희를 태워줄까?
여: 괜찮아. 우리는 택시를 탈 거야. 하지만 나한테 체육관 안내 책자를 가져다줄 수 있니?
남: 물론이지, 문제없어.

단·어·및·표·현

on one's way 가는 길에

08 담화미언급 ▶ 정답 ⑤

듣·기·대·본

W: Do you want to have some excitement this summer? Then, come to the Venice Water Park. Our new park will open for the summer on May 30. It's conveniently located in Venice, and is easily accessible from the city. You can enjoy a variety of facilities at the park including swimming pools, water slides, water playgrounds, and more. As an opening special, we will offer 40% off tickets until June 30. Please visit our website to find out more!

우·리·말·해·석

여: 이번 여름을 즐겁게 보내고 싶으신가요? 그렇다면, Venice 워터 파크에 오세요. 우리 워터 파크는 올여름 5월 30일에 새롭게 개장합니다. 그것은 도시로부터 쉽게 접근할 수 있는 Venice에 편리하게 위치해 있습니다. 당신은 수영장과 물 미끄럼틀, 물 놀이터 등을 포함하여 다양한 시설들을 워터파크에서 즐길 수 있습니다. 개장 특가로서 우리는 6월 30일까지 40%할인권을 제공합니다. 저희 웹사이트에 방문하셔서

더 많은 것을 알아보세요!

단·어·및·표·현

a variety of 다양한, 각종
special [spéʃəl] 명 (상점·식당의) 특별가, 특별할인가

09 담화화제추론 ▶ 정답 ④

듣·기·대·본

W: This is a method of transportation. You use it to go up and down between floors. It is usually square in shape. You can press the number button on the wall inside to set the floor you want to go to. People use this instead of taking the stairs in a building. It's very convenient and saves time. That's why most tall buildings these days have one of these inside.

우·리·말·해·석

여: 이것은 이동수단이다. 당신은 층 사이를 오르내리기 위해서 이것을 이용한다. 이것은 보통 네모난 모양이다. 당신은 가고 싶은 층을 설정하기 위해서 안쪽 벽에 있는 숫자 버튼을 누를 수 있다. 사람들은 건물 내 계단을 이용하는 대신에 이것을 이용한다. 이것은 매우 편리하고 시간을 절약해준다. 그래서 대부분의 고층빌딩들이 요즘 건물 내에 이것들 중 하나를 가지고 있다.

단·어·및·표·현

method of transportation 이동수단, 교통수단
instead of ~ 대신에
convenient [kənvíːnjənt] 형 편리한

10 어색한대화찾기 ▶ 정답 ⑤

듣·기·대·본

① W: How long do I have to wait to get my order?
　 M: It will arrive in two days.
② W: Why don't we take a break for 30 minutes?
　 M: That sounds great.
③ W: I can't start my computer.
　 M: Have you checked that it's plugged in?
④ W: Isn't it cold in here?
　 M: I'll get you something to put on.
⑤ W: Where is the fitting room?
　 M: I'll clean my room later this evening.

우·리·말·해·석

① 여: 제가 주문한 것을 받기 위해 얼마나 기다려야 하나요?
　 남: 그것은 2일 후에 도착할 것입니다.
② 여: 우리 30분 동안 쉬는 게 어때?
　 남: 그거 좋은 생각이야.
③ 여: 나는 내 컴퓨터를 시작할 수가 없어.
　 남: 너는 그것의 플러그가 꽂혀 있는지 확인했어?
④ 여: 여기 춥지 않니?
　 남: 내가 입을 것을 너에게 가져다 줄게.
⑤ 여: 탈의실이 어디예요?
　 남: 저는 이따 오늘 저녁에 제 방을 청소할 거예요.

단·어·및·표·현

put on 입다

11 할일파악 ▶ 정답 ④

듣·기·대·본

14
회
모
의
고
사

W: Honey, aren't we supposed to clear out the attic today?

M: You're right. I've already brought some boxes up to put things in.

W: Then let's do it now. Oh, what do you want to do with the books?

M: The books in the attic? We don't read them anymore, so let's sell them.

W: Good idea. Are the boxes upstairs?

M: Yes, I'll move them to the attic.

W: Then, I'll bring the vacuum cleaner. There must be lots of dust.

우·리·말·해·석

여: 여보, 우리 오늘 다락을 청소하기로 하지 않았나요?

남: 당신 말이 맞아요. 나는 이미 물건들을 넣을 상자들을 가져왔어요.

여: 그러면 지금 그것을 해요. 오, 당신은 그 책들로 무엇을 하고 싶어요?

남: 다락에 있는 책들이요? 우리는 그것들을 더 이상 읽지 않으니까, 그것들을 팔아요.

여: 좋은 생각이에요. 상자들은 위층에 있나요?

남: 네, 내가 그것들을 다락으로 옮길게요.

여: 그러면, 나는 진공청소기를 가져올게요. 틀림없이 많은 먼지가 있을 거예요.

단·어·및·표·현

clear out 청소하다

attic[ǽtik] 명 다락

12 그림정보파악(배치도) ▶ 정답 ④

듣·기·대·본

W: The school food festival is next week. Where shall we set up our sandwich booth?

M: I think we should avoid setting up next to the barbecue booth.

W: I agree. There could be too much smoke.

M: How about the place on the other side of the pancake booth?

W: Well, let's try to avoid the sections at the far end. We'll sell more if we're closer to the entrance.

M: Right. Then we have two choices left.

W: Why don't we go directly next to the coffee and tea booth? Those drinks go well with our sandwiches.

M: Sounds perfect!

우·리·말·해·석

여: 학교 음식 축제가 다음 주야. 우리 샌드위치 부스를 어디에 설치할까?

남: 바비큐 부스 옆에 설치하는 건 피해야 할 것 같아.

여: 동감이야. 연기가 너무 많이 날 수 있어.

남: 팬케이크 부스의 반대편 장소는 어때?

여: 글쎄, 맨 끝쪽 구역은 피하도록 하자. 입구에 더 가까우면 더 많이 팔 거야.

남: 맞아. 그러면 우리에겐 두 가지 선택이 남았어.

여: 우리 커피와 차 부스 바로 옆으로 가는 게 어때? 그 음료들은 우리의 샌드위치와 잘 어울려.

남: 완벽해!

단·어·및·표·현

set up 설치하다

entrance[éntrəns] 명 입구

13 수치파악(날짜) ▶ 정답 ④

듣·기·대·본

W: Hey, Liam. How about going to the National Museum on our trip?

M: But we are traveling to a rural area. The National Museum is in Seoul.

W: They opened another branch. It's right in the city we are visiting.

M: Oh, good. Then, let's go there on May 17th.

W: That's the first day of our trip. We won't have time.

M: How about the day after? On the 18th.

W: We booked a visit to a petting zoo on the 18th. How about May 24th?

M: That's the last day of the trip. Sounds great.

우·리·말·해·석

여: 이봐, Liam. 우리 여행 중에 국립 박물관에 가는 거 어때?

남: 하지만 우린 지방으로 여행 갈 거야. 국립 박물관은 서울에 있어.

여: 그들은 또 다른 지점을 개관했어. 그건 바로 우리가 방문할 도시에 위치해 있어.

남: 오, 좋네. 그럼, 5월 17일에 거기에 가자.

여: 그날은 우리 여행의 첫 날이야. 우리에겐 시간이 없을 거야.

남: 그 다음날은 어때? 18일 말이야.

여: 우리는 18일에 동물을 만질 수 있는 동물원 방문을 예약했어. 5월 24일 어때?

남: 그날은 여행의 마지막 날이잖아. 좋은 것 같아.

단·어·및·표·현

rural area 지방, 시골 지역

the day after 그 다음날, 익일

petting zoo 동물을 만질 수 있는 동물원

14 한일파악 ▶ 정답 ⑤

듣·기·대·본

W: Thomas, I can't remember the title of the book you recommended.

M: Which one do you mean? The book about travel to Peru?

W: No. It was science fiction. Something about space travel.

M: Oh, it's *Mike 8*. That's the title.

W: Right. Can I borrow it from you?

M: You can. But you'll have to wait for a couple of days.

W: Why? Did someone else borrow it?

M: No, I lost it. So I ordered another copy online yesterday.

W: I see. You really like the book!

우·리·말·해·석

여: Thomas, 나는 네가 추천해준 책의 제목이 기억이 안 나.

남: 어떤 걸 말하는 거야? 페루 여행에 관한 책?

여: 아니. 공상 과학 소설이었어. 우주 여행에 관한 것.

남: 아, "Mike 8"이야. 그게 제목이야.

여: 맞아. 내가 너에게 그것을 빌릴 수 있을까?

남: 빌릴 수 있지. 하지만 너는 이틀 정도 기다려야 할 거야.

여: 왜? 다른 누군가가 그것을 빌렸어?

남: 아니, 난 그걸 잃어버렸어. 그래서 나는 어제 온라인으로 다른 한 부를 주문했어.

여: 그렇구나. 너는 그 책을 정말 좋아하는구나!

recommend[rèkəménd] 통 추천하다
a couple of days 이틀 정도
copy[kápi] 명 (책, 신문 등의) 한 부

15 담화목적파악 ▶ 정답 ⑤

듣·기·대·본

W: Attention, students! This is Mrs. Clarkson, your school principal. We have a field trip planned next Wednesday to Seoul Botanic Park and I'd like to provide you with some important guidelines. First, we'll meet in the school courtyard at 8:30 a.m. Second, wear comfortable clothing and footwear since we'll be walking around a lot. Finally, bring a packed lunch and a water bottle as we will be spending the whole day outdoors. Let's all stay safe and have fun!

우·리·말·해·석

여: 주목해주세요, 학생 여러분! 저는 여러분 학교 교장인 Clarkson 선생님입니다. 우리는 다음 주 수요일 서울 식물원으로의 현장학습이 예정되어 있고, 저는 여러분께 몇 가지 중요한 지침을 안내하고자 합니다. 첫째, 우리는 오전 8시 30분에 학교 안뜰에서 만날 것입니다. 둘째, 많이 걸어 다녀야 하기 때문에 편안한 옷과 신발을 착용하세요. 마지막으로, 우리는 하루 종일 야외에서 시간을 보낼 것이기 때문에 도시락과 물병을 가져오세요. 모두 안전하고 즐거운 시간 보냅시다!

botanic park 식물원
guideline[gáidlàin] 명 지침, 가이드라인
courtyard[kɔ́ːrtjàːrd] 명 안뜰, 안마당
packed lunch 도시락

16 수치계산(금액) ▶ 정답 ③

듣·기·대·본

W: Hello, sir. How can I help you?

M: How much is it for the chocolate cake and the muffins?

W: The chocolate cake is $6 a piece and muffins are $5 each.

M: I'd like three pieces of chocolate cake and two peanut butter muffins, please.

W: Okay. If you install our application and get a membership, you can get $5 off the total.

M: Oh, I'll do it then. [Pause] I've done it.

W: Can I see your phone, please? Okay, now you can get the discount.

M: Thanks. I'll pay by credit card.

우·리·말·해·석

여: 안녕하세요, 손님. 어떻게 도와드릴까요?

남: 초콜릿 케이크와 머핀은 얼마입니까?

여: 초콜릿 케이크는 한 조각에 6달러이고 머핀은 각각 5달러입니다.

남: 초콜릿 케이크 3조각과 땅콩버터 머핀 2개 주세요.

여: 알겠습니다. 만약 손님이 우리의 앱을 설치하고 회원 가입을 하신다면, 전체에서 5달러를 할인받으실 수 있습니다.

남: 오, 그렇다면 저는 그렇게 하겠습니다. [잠시 후] 다 했습니다.

여: 제가 손님의 휴대폰을 볼 수 있을까요? 네, 이제 할인을 받으실 수 있

습니다.

남: 감사합니다. 저는 신용 카드로 결제할게요.

install[instɔ́ːl] 통 설치하다
application[æpləkéiʃən] 명 앱, 애플리케이션
get a membership 회원 가입을 하다, 회원권을 얻다
credit card 신용 카드

17 알맞은응답찾기 ▶ 정답 ③

듣·기·대·본

M: Hi, Laura. Why didn't you come to school yesterday?

W: My grandmother was in a car accident, so my family went to see her.

M: I'm sorry to hear that. I hope she didn't get hurt too badly.

W: Luckily, she didn't get hurt at all. She was just a little shocked by the accident.

M: I understand. So, you went to comfort her.

W: That's right. I think she felt much better after seeing us.

M: Yes. Being with family is the best thing.

우·리·말·해·석

① 알아. 나는 네가 곧 회복하길 바라.

② 그래서 네가 그녀를 방문할 수 없었구나.

③ 응. 가족과 함께 있는 것이 가장 좋지.

④ 그녀가 자동차 사고를 당하지 않은 것은 다행이야.

⑤ 너의 할머니께서 심하게 다치셨다니 유감이야.

남: 안녕, Laura. 너 어제 왜 학교에 안 왔니?

여: 우리 할머니가 자동차 사고를 당하셔서, 우리 가족이 그녀를 만나러 갔어.

남: 정말 안됐다. 나는 그녀가 심하게 다치지 않았기를 바라.

여: 운이 좋게도, 그녀는 전혀 다치지 않았어. 단지 그녀는 사고로 인해 약간 충격을 받으셨어.

남: 이해해. 그래서, 네가 그녀를 위로해 드리러 갔구나.

여: 맞아. 내 생각에 그녀가 우리를 만난 후 훨씬 나아지신 것 같아.

남: 응. 가족과 함께 있는 것이 가장 좋지.

comfort[kʌ́mfərt] 통 위로하다

18 알맞은응답찾기 ▶ 정답 ③

듣·기·대·본

W: Josh, are you going on the camping trip next month?

M: No, I'm afraid not. How about you?

W: I'm going. It'll be really exciting, and I'm looking forward to it. Why aren't you going?

M: I really want to, but I forgot to hand in the application form. I'm very disappointed.

W: Well, I heard that Kevin handed in the form but can't go because he has a family trip.

M: Really? Then I should go and talk to Mrs. Park about it.

W: Yes. You might be able to take Kevin's place.

우·리·말·해·석

① 나는 그렇게 생각하지 않아. 나는 가족여행이 있어.

② 응. 내가 너와 함께 여행을 갈 수 있다면 좋을 텐데. (실제로는 못 간다는 의미)

③ 그래. 네가 Kevin의 자리를 대신할 수 있을지도 몰라.

④ 그럼. 하지만 너는 이미 신청서를 제출했잖아.

⑤ 네 말이 맞아. 그녀는 그 여행에 대해 아무것도 알지 못해.

여: Josh, 너 다음 달에 캠핑 여행 가니?
남: 아니, 아쉽지만 안 가. 너는?
여: 나는 갈 예정이야. 그건 정말 재미있을 거고, 나는 그것을 아주 기대하
　　고 있어. 넌 왜 안 가니?
남: 난 정말 가고 싶어. 하지만 신청서 제출하는 것을 깜빡했어. 나는 무척
　　실망했어.
여: 음, 나는 Kevin이 신청서를 제출했지만 가족 여행이 있어서 캠핑에 가
　　지 못한다고 들었어.
남: 정말? 그러면 내가 가서 Park 선생님께 그것에 대해 말해봐야겠다.
여: 그래. 네가 Kevin의 자리를 대신할 수 있을지도 몰라.

단·어·및·표·현
look forward to ~ ~을 기대하다
hand in ~ ~을 제출하다

19 알맞은응답찾기　　　　　▶ 정답 ③

듣·기·대·본
M: Hi, Sally! Have you signed up for the computer coding
　　class?
W: Unfortunately, it was already fully booked when I tried.
M: I couldn't register, either. I guess a lot of students
　　wanted to take that class.
W: What are you going to do now?
M: I'm thinking of taking it online.
W: There's an online coding class?
M: Yes, but if we want to take it online, we are required to
　　consult with Mr. Smith first.
W: I see. Then let's go together to talk to him now. Do you
　　know where his office is?
M: It's on the fifth floor in this building.
W: That's great! I hope he will allow us to take it.

우·리·말·해·석
① 안됐다. 다음엔 더 나을 거야.
② 문제없어. 나는 너를 위해 그걸 할 수 있어.
③ 잘됐다! 나는 그가 우리가 그것을 수강하는 걸 허락하길 바라.
④ 네가 맞아! 계단을 이용하는 것이 훨씬 더 빠를 거야.
⑤ 신경 쓰지 마. 나는 이미 다른 수업에 등록했어.

남: 안녕, Sally! 너는 컴퓨터 코딩 수업에 등록했어?
여: 안타깝게도, 내가 시도했을 때 그건 이미 예약이 꽉 차 있었어.
남: 나도 등록할 수 없었어. 많은 학생들이 그 수업을 수강하고 싶어했던
　　것 같아.
여: 너는 이제 뭘 할 거야?
남: 나는 그걸 온라인으로 수강할까 생각 중이야.
여: 온라인 코딩 수업이 있어?
남: 응, 하지만 만약 우리가 그걸 온라인으로 수강하고 싶다면, 우리는 먼
　　저 Smith 선생님과 상의하도록 되어 있어.
여: 그렇구나. 그럼 지금 그에게 이야기하러 같이 가자. 그의 교무실이 어
　　디인지 알아?
남: 이 건물의 5층에 있어.
여: 잘됐다! 나는 그가 우리가 그것을 수강하는 걸 허락하길 바라.

단·어·및·표·현
sign up for ~에 등록하다, 신청하다
register [rédʒistər] 통 등록하다
be required to + 동사원형 ~하도록 되어있다, 요구되다

---

consult [kənsʌ́lt] 통 상의하다, 상담하다

20 상황에적절한말찾기　　　　　▶ 정답 ④

듣·기·대·본
M: Nick is a middle school student. Today, he is on his way
　　home from school by bus as usual. Claire, his classmate
　　is sitting in the seat in front of him. The window by her
　　seat is wide open. The wind is blowing pretty hard and
　　after a few minutes, Nick starts to feel cold. So, he
　　would like to ask Claire if she could close the window
　　beside her. In this situation, what would Nick most likely
　　say to Claire?
Nick: Claire, would you mind closing the window, please?

우·리·말·해·석
① 나랑 자리 좀 바꿔줄래?
② 버스가 학교에 언제 도착하니?
③ 잠깐 창문 좀 열어도 될까?
④ 창문 좀 닫아줄 수 있니?
⑤ 나는 우리가 학교에 지각할까 봐 걱정돼.

남: Nick은 중학생이다. 오늘 그는 평소대로 버스를 타고 학교에서 집으로
　　돌아가는 길이다. 그의 반 친구 Claire가 그의 앞 자리에 앉아 있다. 그
　　녀의 자리 옆에 있는 창문은 활짝 열려 있다. 바람이 꽤 세게 불어오고
　　몇 분 후, Nick은 춥다고 느끼기 시작한다. 그래서 그는 Claire에게 그
　　녀의 옆에 있는 창문을 닫아 줄 수 있는지 물어보려고 한다. 이 상황에
　　서, Nick이 Claire에게 뭐라고 말하겠는가?
Nick: Claire, 창문 좀 닫아줄 수 있니?

단·어·및·표·현
on one's way home 집으로 돌아가는 길에
as usual 평소대로, 늘 그렇듯이
wide open 활짝 열린, 크게 벌어진
pretty [príti] 틧 꽤, 어느 정도

Words & Expressions Review

1. ~을 다루다, 처리하다	2. 입양하다	3. 추천하다
4. 플러그를 꽂다, 전원을 연결하다	5. 이틀 정도	6. 다락
7. 설치하다	8. 다양한, 각종	9. 체육관
10. 이용할 수 있는, 구할 수 있는	11. (안내용) 책자	12. ~을 제출하다
13. (기억을 돕기 위한) 메모	14. 신청서	15. 청소하다
16. 지방, 시골 지역	17. ~에 위치하다	18. 안뜰, 안마당
19. 최신 유행의	20. ~에 등록하다, 신청하다	21. 집으로 돌아가는 길에
22. 활짝 열린, 크게 벌어진	23. 편리한	24. (책, 신문 등의) 한 부
25. 글자, 문자	26. 방수의	27. 설치하다
28. 이전의	29. 식물원	30. 평소대로, 늘 그렇듯이
31. ~에 등록하다	32. 위로하다, 위로 편안	33. 제대로, 적절히
34. 도시락	35. 위층에, 2층에	36. 진공청소기

37. 그 다음날, 익일	38. 지침, 가이드라인	39. 상의하다, 상담하다
40. 꽤, 어느 정도	41. A를 태워주다	42. 충격을 받은
43. 교과서	44. 주인, 소유자	

Listening Test

영어듣기 모의고사 15회

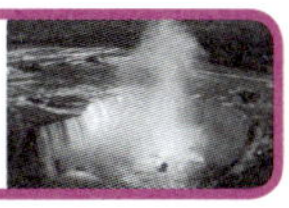

| 정 | 답 |

01 ①	02 ④	03 ③	04 ⑤	05 ④
06 ②	07 ③	08 ④	09 ④	10 ④
11 ③	12 ①	13 ④	14 ④	15 ⑤
16 ③	17 ②	18 ③	19 ④	20 ④

01 그림정보파악(대화) ▶ 정답 ①

듣•기•대•본

M: What are you looking for, Daisy?

W: Hey, Jim. I want to buy a snow globe as a souvenir of Paris. I collect snow globes.

M: I didn't know that. Then, how about this snow globe with a French girl holding the flag? It looks cute.

W: Well, I would prefer a globe with the Eiffel Tower.

M: What about this one? It has a flag beside the tower.

W: Cool. And I like the word 'PARIS' written on the snow globe. I'll buy this one.

우•리•말•해•석

남: 너는 무엇을 찾고 있니, Daisy?

여: 이봐, Jim. 나는 파리 기념품으로 스노글로브를 사고 싶어. 나는 스노글로브를 모아.

남: 나는 그것을 몰랐어. 그러면, 프랑스 소녀가 국기를 들고 있는 이 스노글로브는 어때? 그것은 귀여워 보여.

여: 글쎄, 나는 에펠탑이 있는 스노글로브가 더 좋겠어.

남: 이것은 어때? 그것은 에펠탑 옆에 국기가 있어.

여: 괜찮은데. 그리고 나는 스노글로브에 쓰여 있는 'PARIS'라는 말이 좋아. 나는 이것을 살 거야.

단•어•및•표•현

snow globe 스노글로브(흔들면 눈이 내리는 것처럼 보이는 유리 공)
souvenir [sùːvəníər] [명] 기념품
flag [flæg] [명] 국기, 깃발

02 대화미언급 ▶ 정답 ④

듣•기•대•본

M: Felicity, I'm going to take skating lessons. Are you interested?

W: Yeah, I am. When are the lessons?

M: They're every Saturday, from 10 a.m. to 12 p.m.

W: Cool. They're at the Central Ice Rink, right?

M: That's right. Have you been there?

W: No, I've never skated. How much do we have to pay?

M: It's 10 dollars per session. We can learn all the basic skills during 4 sessions.

W: Okay. Is there anything we need to bring?

M: No. We can borrow all the gear there.

W: Great. Let's sign up!

우•리•말•해•석

남: Felicity, 나는 스케이트 강습을 받을 거야. 너 관심 있니?

여: 응, 관심 있어. 강습은 언제야?

남: 매주 토요일 오전 10시부터 오후 12시까지야.

여: 좋아. 그것은 Central 아이스 링크장에서 하지, 맞지?

남: 맞아. 너는 거기에 가 본 적이 있니?

여: 아니, 나는 스케이트를 타 본 적이 없어. 우리는 얼마를 내야 하니?

남: 수업 한 회당 10달러야. 우리는 4회의 수업 동안 기초 기술들을 모두 배울 수 있어.

여: 알겠어. 우리가 가져가야 하는 것이 있니?

남: 아니. 우리는 모든 장비를 거기서 빌릴 수 있어.

여: 좋다. 등록하자!

단•어•및•표•현

session [séʃən] [명] 수업[강의] 시간
gear [giər] [명] (특정 활동에 필요한) 장비
sign up 등록하다

03 전화목적파악 ▶ 정답 ③

듣•기•대•본

(*Telephone rings.*)

W: Hello, is this Andrew Bint's phone?

M: Yes, who's this, please?

W: Hi, this is Michelle from your voice recording agency. Is it a good time to talk?

M: Sure, what can I do for you?

W: I'd like to change your recording schedule. Can we record on Friday from 1:30 to 3:30 instead of Wednesday? The scripts are not ready yet. Sorry.

M: That's all right. Let me check my schedule first. (*pause*) I think I can. So the recording is on Friday.

W: Right. Thanks a lot. Have a nice day!

우•리•말•해•석

(전화벨이 울린다.)

여: 안녕하세요. Andrew Bint 씨의 전화인가요?

남: 네. 누구시죠?

여: 안녕하세요. 성우 회사의 Michelle이에요. 지금 통화하기 좋은 시간인가요?

남: 그럼요. 무엇을 도와드릴까요?

여: 당신의 녹음 일정을 변경하고 싶어서요. 수요일 대신 금요일 1:30부터 3:30까지 녹음할 수 있을까요? 대본이 아직 준비되지 않아서요. 죄송합니다.

남: 괜찮아요. 제 일정을 먼저 확인해 보죠. (잠시 후) 할 수 있을 것 같아요. 그러면 녹음은 금요일이네요.

여: 맞아요. 감사합니다. 좋은 하루 되세요!

단•어•및•표•현

script [skript] [명] 대본

04 수치파악(시각) ▶ 정답 ⑤

듣•기•대•본

[*Telephone rings.*]

W: This is Selena's pet salon. How can I help you?
M: Hi, I'd like to get my dog groomed. Can I make a reservation at 9 a.m. tomorrow?
W: Sorry, but we open at 10 a.m. And we are fully booked tomorrow morning.
M: Then, is there a time available in the afternoon?
W: We have openings at 3 p.m. and 5 p.m.
M: I can come in at 5. I'll visit then.
W: All right. Can I have your dog's name, please?
M: Her name is Coco.
W: I've got Coco on the list. We'll see you tomorrow.

우·리·말·해·석

[전화벨이 울린다.]
여: Selena의 애견 미용실입니다. 어떻게 도와드릴까요?
남: 안녕하세요, 저는 개에게 미용을 해주고 싶어요. 내일 오전 9시에 예약할 수 있을까요?
여: 죄송합니다만, 저희는 오전 10시에 문을 엽니다. 그리고 저희는 내일 오전 예약이 꽉 찼습니다.
남: 그러면, 오후에는 가능한 시간이 있을까요?
여: 저희는 오후 3시와 오후 5시에 빈자리가 있습니다.
남: 저는 5시에 갈 수 있어요. 그때 방문할게요.
여: 알겠습니다. 손님의 개의 이름을 알려주시겠습니까?
남: 그녀의 이름은 Coco예요.
여: Coco를 명단에 넣었습니다. 내일 뵙겠습니다.

단·어·및·표·현

groom [gru(:)m] 동 (동물의 외관을) 손질하다, 다듬다
fully booked 예약이 꽉 찬, 모두 예약된
available [əvéiləbl] 형 시간이 있는, 이용할 수 있는
opening [óupəniŋ] 명 빈자리[공석]

05 심정추론 ▶ 정답 ④

듣·기·대·본

W: Bill, you look different today.
M: I'm a whole new person, Martha. I got onto the school basketball team finally!
W: Really? That's great! You really wanted to join the team.
M: I practiced hard last summer. And the coach selected me this time.
W: I'm so happy for you. So, can I see you on court at the next match?
M: I hope so. I can't wait for the first practice!
W: Good luck to you!

우·리·말·해·석

① 무서운　　　　② 수줍은　　　　③ 후회하는
④ 신나는　　　　⑤ 실망스러운

여: Bill, 너 오늘 달라 보여.
남: 나는 완전히 새로운 사람이야, Martha. 나 마침내 학교 농구팀에 들어갔어!
여: 정말? 잘됐다! 너는 정말로 그 팀에 들어가고 싶어했잖아.
남: 나는 지난 여름에 열심히 연습했어. 그리고 코치님이 이번에 나를 선택해줬어.
여: 정말 기쁜 일이야. 그럼, 다음 경기 때 경기장에서 너를 볼 수 있는 거야?
남: 그러길 바라. 빨리 첫 연습을 하고 싶어.
여: 너에게 행운을 빌게!

단·어·및·표·현

whole [houl] 부 완전히
select [silékt] 동 선택하다, 고르다
regretful [rigrétfəl] 형 후회하는

06 그림상황에적절한대화찾기 ▶ 정답 ②

듣·기·대·본

① W: Shall we go to an art gallery today?
　M: Maybe next time. I'm too tired today.
② W: I'm afraid you're not allowed to take photos here.
　M: Oh, I didn't see the sign. Sorry.
③ W: What are you going to draw for the art contest?
　M: I'm going to draw some flowers in a vase.
④ W: Excuse me. Could you take a picture for us?
　M: Sure. Let me have your camera.
⑤ W: You shouldn't use your cell phone during the concert.
　M: Don't worry. I've already turned it off.

우·리·말·해·석

① 여: 우리 오늘 미술관에 갈래?
　남: 다음에 가자. 오늘 너무 피곤해.
② 여: 죄송합니다만, 여기는 사진을 찍는 것이 허용되지 않습니다.
　남: 오, 저는 그 표시를 못 봤어요. 죄송합니다.
③ 여: 미술대회를 위해 무엇을 그릴 거니?
　남: 꽃병에 있는 약간의 꽃들을 그릴 거야.
④ 여: 실례합니다. 저희 사진 좀 찍어주실 수 있나요?
　남: 물론이죠. 카메라 주세요.
⑤ 여: 콘서트 동안에 핸드폰을 사용하면 안 돼.
　남: 걱정 마. 나는 이미 그것을 껐어.

단·어·및·표·현

art gallery 미술관, 화랑
vase [veis] 명 꽃병

07 부탁(요청)한일파악 ▶ 정답 ③

듣·기·대·본

M: Hey, where are you off to?
W: I'm going to the market for some fruit.
M: Can you get me some, too?
W: No problem.
M: Thanks. I had my checkup at the hospital last week, and the doctor said that I need to eat healthy.
W: That's what I've been telling you every day.
M: I know. I'm really going to try to change my lifestyle this time.

우·리·말·해·석

남: 이봐, 어디에 가는 길이야?
여: 과일을 사러 시장에 가고 있어.
남: 나한테도 좀 사다 줄 수 있니?
여: 문제없어.
남: 고마워. 지난주에 병원에서 건강 검진을 받았는데, 의사가 난 좀 더 건강하게 먹어야 한다고 했어.
여: 그게 바로 내가 매일 네게 해온 말이잖아.
남: 알아. 이번에는 정말 내 생활 방식을 바꾸려고 노력할 거야.

단·어·및·표·현

be off to ~ ~로 가다
checkup [tʃékʌp] 명 건강 검진

'd' 혹은 't'가 연속되는 두 단어의 자음 사이에 올 때 [d]와 [t] 소리
는 탈락되어 발음됩니다. 따라서 'Can you get me some, too?'에
서 'get me'는 [겟트 미]가 아닌 [게미]로 소리 납니다. 'I need to
eat healthy'에서도 마찬가지로 'eat healthy'는 [잇트 헬씨]가 아닌
[잇 헬씨]로 들립니다.

08 담화미언급 ▶ 정답 ④

듣·기·대·본

M: May I have your attention, please? We've found
a cellphone. It was found on a chair in the school
cafeteria right after lunch time. It is a black smartphone
with cute puppy stickers on the back. If you are looking
for a phone like this, you will be able to find your phone
at the principal's office on the second floor.

우·리·말·해·석

남: 주목해 주세요. 우리는 휴대폰을 하나 발견했습니다. 점심 시간 직후에
학교 식당의 의자 위에서 발견되었습니다. 뒷면에 귀여운 강아지 스티
커가 있는 검은색 스마트폰입니다. 만약 이런 전화기를 찾고 있다면, 2
층 교장실에서 전화기를 찾을 수 있습니다.

단·어·및·표·현

school cafeteria 학교[교내] 식당
principal[prínsəpəl] 영 교장 형 주요한

09 담화화제추론 ▶ 정답 ④

듣·기·대·본

M: This is an electric home device. You usually use this
during the summer. It comes in many different shapes.
It sometimes can be hung on the wall or ceiling. People
commonly use this when they need to cool the room.
Sometimes, it is used to bring the humidity down.
However, if you use this device too much, you could get
sick. Moreover, your electricity bill could end up being
very high if you use it too much.

우·리·말·해·석

남: 이것은 가전제품이다. 당신은 보통 이것을 여름 동안 사용한다. 이것은
많은 다양한 모양으로 출시된다. 때때로 이것은 벽이나 천장에 걸릴 수
있다. 사람들은 흔히 방을 시원하게 할 필요가 있을 때 이것을 사용한
다. 때때로 이것은 습도를 낮추기 위해 사용된다. 하지만, 당신이 이 장
치를 너무 많이 사용하면, 아프게 될 수도 있다. 더욱이 당신이 이것을
너무 많이 사용하면 당신의 전기요금은 매우 많이 나올 수 있다.

단·어·및·표·현

hang[hæŋ] 동 걸리다, 걸다, 매달리다
commonly[kámənli] 부 흔히, 보통
bring ~ down ~을 낮추다, 줄이다
humidity[hju:mídəti] 명 습도
end up (결국) ~이 되다

10 어색한대화찾기 ▶ 정답 ④

듣·기·대·본

① M: What did you do on Sunday?
　 W: I played video games all day.
② M: How long does it take to get to school?
　 W: It takes about 15 minutes on foot.
③ M: Do you make your bed in the morning?
　 W: No, I usually don't have time to do that.
④ M: Why didn't you come to basketball practice today?
　 W: One of my hobbies is playing basketball.
⑤ M: Where did you buy that scarf?
　 W: I didn't buy it. I made it by myself.

우·리·말·해·석

① 남: 너는 일요일에 무엇을 했니?
　 여: 나는 하루 종일 비디오 게임을 했어.
② 남: 학교에 가는 데 얼마나 걸려?
　 여: 걸어서 15분 정도 걸려.
③ 남: 너는 아침에 침대를 정리하니?
　 여: 아니, 나는 보통 그걸 할 시간이 없어.
④ 남: 너는 왜 오늘 농구 연습에 안 왔니?
　 여: 내 취미 중 하나는 농구를 하는 거야.
⑤ 남: 너 그 목도리 어디서 샀어?
　 여: 나는 이것을 사지 않았어. 내가 직접 만들었어.

단·어·및·표·현

on foot 걸어서
make (the) bed 침대[잠자리]를 정리하다
by oneself 직접, 도움을 받지 않고

11 할일파악(대화직후) ▶ 정답 ③

듣·기·대·본

M: Maria, are you planning to participate in the school
badminton tournament?
W: I wanted to, but all the singles matches are already full.
M: Oh, that's too bad. What about the mixed doubles?
W: I'd love to try that, but I don't have a partner.
M: How about asking Allen? He's really good at badminton.
W: That's a great idea! Do you think he would want to be
my partner?
M: I'm sure he would. You should ask him before someone
else does.
W: You're right. I'll go ask him right now.

우·리·말·해·석

남: Maria, 너는 학교 배드민턴 대회에 참가할 계획이야?
여: 그러고 싶었는데, 모든 단식 경기는 이미 다 찼어.
남: 아, 안타깝네. 혼합 복식은 어때?
여: 시도해보고 싶긴 한데, 나는 파트너가 없어.
남: Allen에게 물어보는 건 어때? 그는 배드민턴을 정말 잘하잖아.
여: 좋은 생각이야! 너는 그가 내 파트너가 되고 싶어할 것 같아?
남: 나는 그가 그럴 거라 확신해. 다른 사람이 하기 전에 네가 그에게 물어
봐야 해.
여: 맞아. 난 지금 바로 그에게 가서 물어볼게.

단·어·및·표·현

participate in ~ ~에 참가하다
single match 단식 경기, 단일 경기
mixed doubles 혼합 복식

12 도표정보파악 ▶ 정답 ①

듣·기·대·본

W: Hi, how may I help you?
M: Hello, I'm looking for a table fan for my desk.
W: All right. We have two sizes, 17 cm and 13 cm.

M: I think the bigger one would be better.
W: Okay. The fans are <u>portable</u>, and they can <u>run for</u> 9 hours or 7 hours.
M: I'm in the office for at least 8 hours, so, I'd prefer the one that runs <u>the longest</u>.
W: Sure. There are two colors, blue and white.
M: I'll take the blue one.
W: Okay. Please wait a second.

우·리·말·해·석

	탁상용 선풍기	선풍기 크기	작동 시간	색상
①	A	17 cm	9시간	파란색
②	B	17 cm	9시간	흰색
③	C	17 cm	7시간	파란색
④	D	13 cm	9시간	흰색
⑤	E	13 cm	7시간	파란색

여: 안녕하세요. 어떻게 도와드릴까요?
남: 안녕하세요, 저는 제 책상에 놓을 탁상용 선풍기를 찾고 있어요.
여: 알겠습니다. 저희는 17센티미터와 13센티미터, 두 가지 크기가 있습니다.
남: 제 생각엔 더 큰 게 좋을 것 같아요.
여: 네. 그 선풍기들은 휴대용이고, 그것들은 9시간 혹은 7시간 동안 작동할 수 있습니다.
남: 저는 사무실에 최소한 8시간은 있어서 가장 오래 작동하는 것이 좋을 것 같아요.
여: 그러시군요. 파란색과 흰색 두 가지 색상이 있습니다.
남: 저는 파란색으로 할게요.
여: 알겠습니다. 잠시만 기다려주세요.

단·어·및·표·현

table fan 탁상용 선풍기
portable [pɔ́ːrtəbl] ⑱ 휴대용의
run [rʌn] ⑧ 작동하다, 기능하게 하다
at least 최소한, 적어도

13 수치파악(날짜) ▶ 정답 ④

듣·기·대·본

M: Brenda, have you decided where <u>to volunteer</u>?
W: I'm thinking of helping out at a local farm. What about you, Nick?
M: I'm thinking of doing the same. You know, August 7th is blueberry <u>picking day</u>.
W: Oh, I can't volunteer that day. Why don't you join me the week after that? We can still pick other fruit.
M: I have a cooking class on August 14th. What about August 21st?
W: <u>August 21st works for me</u>!
M: Then, let's go on that day.

우·리·말·해·석

남: Brenda, 너 어디서 자원봉사 할지 정했니?
여: 나는 지역 농장에서 일을 도울 생각이야. 너는 어때, Nick?
남: 나도 같은 것을 할 생각이야. 너도 알겠지만, 8월 7일은 블루베리를 따는 날이야.
여: 아, 나 그날은 자원봉사 못해. 그다음 주에 나랑 같이 하는 게 어때? 우리는 여전히 다른 과일을 딸 수 있어.
남: 나는 8월 14일에 요리 수업이 있어. 8월 21일은 어때?
여: 난 8월 21일 괜찮아!

남: 그러면, 그날에 가자.

단·어·및·표·현

help out 도와주다
local [lóukəl] ⑱ 지역의, 현지의
pick [pik] ⑧ (과일 등을) 따다, 수확하다
work for ~에게 문제없다, 좋다

14 한일파악 ▶ 정답 ④

듣·기·대·본

W: Hey, Glen. I didn't see you at the <u>academy</u> yesterday.
M: Hi, Diane. Yeah, I couldn't go.
W: Why not?
M: Two days ago, I played basketball after school with some friends, and I <u>sprained my ankle</u>.
W: Oh, no! Are you okay?
M: I'm okay, but I went to the hospital yesterday <u>just in case</u>.
W: What did the doctor say?
M: The doctor said that it's not a serious injury.
W: That's a relief.

우·리·말·해·석

여: 이봐, Glen. 나는 어제 너를 학원에서 보지 못했어.
남: 안녕, Diane. 맞아, 나는 갈 수 없었어.
여: 왜?
남: 이틀 전에, 나는 방과 후에 몇몇의 친구들과 농구를 하다가 발목을 삐었어.
여: 오, 저런! 너 괜찮니?
남: 나는 괜찮아, 하지만 혹시나 해서 나는 어제 병원에 갔어.
여: 의사가 뭐라고 했어?
남: 의사는 그것이 심각한 부상은 아니라고 했어.
여: 다행이다.

단·어·및·표·현

academy [əkǽdəmi] ⑱ 학원
sprain [sprein] ⑧ (특히 팔목·발목을) 삐다, 접지르다
just in case 만약을 위해서, 혹시나 해서
injury [índʒəri] ⑱ 부상, 상처
that's a relief 다행이다, 안심이다

15 담화목적파악 ▶ 정답 ⑤

듣·기·대·본

W: Hello, students. Attention, please. As you already know, we will be renovating our main gate. Starting Monday, you won't be able to use the main gate for two weeks. We're sorry for the inconvenience, but it's <u>necessary</u> for your safety. You can use the back gate from July 6th to 20th. Detailed information is <u>available</u> on our school website. If you have any questions, please contact your teacher or come to the teachers' office.

우·리·말·해·석

여: 안녕하세요, 학생 여러분. 주목해 주십시오. 여러분이 이미 알고 있다시피, 우리는 정문을 수리할 것입니다. 월요일부터, 여러분은 2주 동안 정문을 사용할 수 없을 것입니다. 불편을 드려 죄송하지만, 그것은 여러분의 안전을 위해서 필요합니다. 여러분은 7월 6일부터 20일까지 후문을 사용할 수 있습니다. 자세한 정보는 우리 학교 웹사이트에서 이용하실 수 있습니다. 문의사항이 있으시면, 여러분의 선생님께 연락하시거

나 교무실로 오세요.

renovate [rénəvèit] 동 수리하다, 개조하다
inconvenience [ìnkənví:njəns] 명 불편, 애로
necessary [nésəsèri] 형 필요한, 피할 수 없는
detailed [ditéild / díteild] 형 자세한, 상세한

16 수치계산(금액) ▶ 정답 ③

듣·기·대·본

W: Welcome to Speedy Car Rental!
M: Hi, how much does it cost to rent a car for one day?
W: It's 80 dollars.
M: I also need insurance.
W: Insurance is 30 dollars, but we offer a 10% discount on the car rental if you are renting the car for just one day.
M: Oh, that's nice. You mean I can get a discount on the total price?
W: The 10% discount applies to the car rental only. The insurance isn't included in the discount.
M: All right, that's clear. I'll use my card to pay.

우·리·말·해·석

여: Speedy 렌터카에 오신 것을 환영합니다!
남: 안녕하세요, 하루 동안 차를 빌리는 데 비용이 얼마나 드나요?
여: 80달러입니다.
남: 전 보험도 필요해요.
여: 보험은 30달러이고, 만약 당신이 차를 딱 하루만 빌리신다면 저희는 차 렌트비에서 10% 할인을 제공해드려요.
남: 오, 좋네요. 당신은 제가 전체 금액에서 할인받을 수 있다는 말씀이신 거죠?
여: 10% 할인은 차 렌트비에만 적용돼요. 보험료는 할인에 포함되지 않아요.
남: 알겠어요, 명확하네요. 저는 제 카드로 결제할게요.

단·어·및·표·현

cost [kɔ(:)st] 동 (값, 비용이) ~이다[들다]
insurance [inʃú(:)ərəns] 명 보험, 보험료
apply to ~ ~에 적용되다

17 알맞은응답찾기 ▶ 정답 ②

듣·기·대·본

M: Welcome to Bright Electronics. How can I help you?
W: Hi, I'm interested in purchasing a new laptop.
M: Sure. Are you looking for a standard size or something more compact like a notebook?
W: I need a standard size laptop.
M: All right. Do you prefer a touchscreen or a regular display?
W: I think a regular display will suit my needs better.
M: Great. Would you also like to add any accessories like a mouse or a laptop bag?
W: Yes, a laptop bag would be convenient to have.

우·리·말·해·석

① 저는 신용카드로 결제하고 싶습니다.
② 네, 노트북 가방이 있으면 편리할 것 같아요.
③ 노트북을 구매하고 무선마우스를 무료로 받으세요!
④ 그럼, 저는 이 노트북으로 할게요. 도와주셔서 감사합니다.

⑤ 아니요, 터치스크린은 일반 디스플레이보다 더 많은 전력을 소비합니다.

남: Bright Electronics에 오신 것을 환영합니다. 어떻게 도와 드릴까요?
여: 안녕하세요, 저는 새 노트북 컴퓨터를 구입하는 것에 관심 있어요.
남: 알겠습니다. 표준 크기를 찾고 계신가요, 아니면 노트처럼 좀 더 작은 것을 찾고 계신가요?
여: 표준 크기의 노트북 컴퓨터가 필요해요.
남: 알겠습니다. 터치스크린을 선호하시나요 아니면 일반 디스플레이를 선호하시나요?
여: 일반 디스플레이가 저의 필요에 더 잘 맞을 것 같아요.
남: 좋습니다. 마우스나 노트북 가방과 같은 부속물들 또한 추가하시겠습니까?
여: 네, 노트북 가방이 있으면 편리할 것 같아요.

단·어·및·표·현

laptop [læptap] 명 노트북 컴퓨터
compact [kəmpækt] 형 소형의[간편한], 작은
accessory [əksésəri] 명 부속물, 부속품, 액세서리
consume [kənsjú:m] 동 소비하다

18 알맞은응답찾기 ▶ 정답 ③

듣·기·대·본

W: Honey, how was your checkup this morning?
M: The doctor said everything's fine, but he did mention that I needed to exercise more.
W: He's definitely right about that. You haven't exercised in ages.
M: Okay, I'll start exercising, but I don't know where to start.
W: You can always start with some jogging.
M: I think you're right. Why don't you start jogging with me as well?
W: Hmm… Okay. Then let's start tonight, shall we?
M: I feel tired today. Let's start tomorrow.

우·리·말·해·석

① 오늘 저녁 식사는 뭐예요? 저 배고파요.
② 나는 마라톤 선수였어요.
③ 오늘은 피곤해요. 내일 시작합시다.
④ 하루에 사과 한 알이면 의사가 필요 없어요.
⑤ 나는 한 번도 당신을 헬스장에서 본 적이 없어요.

여: 여보, 오늘 아침 건강 검진 어땠어요?
남: 의사 선생님이 다 괜찮은데, 내가 더 운동할 필요가 있다고 말하셨어요.
여: 그것에 대해서는 그의 말이 정말 맞아요. 당신은 오랫동안 운동을 하지 않았어요.
남: 좋아요, 나는 운동을 시작할 거예요. 하지만 어디서 시작해야 할지 모르겠어요.
여: 당신은 조깅으로 항상 시작할 수 있어요.
남: 당신이 옳다고 생각해요. 당신도 나와 함께 조깅을 시작하는 게 어때요?
여: 음… 좋아요. 그럼 오늘 밤에 시작해요, 그럴래요?
남: 오늘은 피곤해요. 내일 시작합시다.

단·어·및·표·현

mention [ménʃən] 동 말하다, 언급하다
as well ~도, 또한

19 알맞은응답찾기 ▶ 정답 ④

듣·기·대·본

W: I'm so nervous. I wonder if I should just back out of the play.

M: What's the matter? You've been waiting to be in this play for so long.

W: I know, but I'm afraid I might mess up.

M: We both know how much you wanted to get the part in the school play. Don't let this opportunity pass you by. You're a great performer!

W: You really think so?

M: Of course!

W: Hmm… You're right. I should grab this chance. Thanks a lot, Phil.

M: Just believe in yourself. Go for it!

우·리·말·해·석

① 그거 아주 좋은 생각이야. 그 연극을 보러 가자.
② 나는 네가 그 캐릭터에 공감하지 않는다고 생각해.
③ 나는 학교에 늦게 도착할 거야.
④ 그냥 너 자신을 믿어. 힘내!
⑤ 나는 내가 잘 못할까 봐 두려워.

여: 나 너무 불안해. 내가 그냥 이 연극에서 빠져야 할지 어떨지 모르겠어.
남: 무슨 일이야? 넌 아주 오랫동안 이 연극에 출연하기를 기다려왔잖아.
여: 알아. 하지만 난 내가 망칠까 봐 두려워.
남: 네가 학교 연극에서 배역을 맡기를 얼마나 많이 원했는지 우리 둘 다 알잖아. 이번 기회를 놓치지 마. 너는 훌륭한 연기자야!
여: 정말 그렇게 생각해?
남: 물론이지!
여: 흠… 네가 맞아! 나는 이번 기회를 잡아야 해. 정말 고마워, Phil.
남: 그냥 너 자신을 믿어. 힘내!

단·어·및·표·현

nervous [nə́ːrvəs] 형 불안해하는, 초조해하는
back out of (하기로 했던 일에서) 빠지다
mess up 망치다, 엉망으로 만들다

20 상황에적절한말찾기 ▶ 정답 ④

듣·기·대·본

M: Erin gets a hamster from her parents on her birthday. She always wanted a pet, so she is thrilled. But she doesn't know how to take care of a hamster. Erin asks her classmate, Kevin, who also has a pet hamster, where to start. When Kevin first got his pet, he got a lot of help from video clips on the Internet. So, Kevin would like to suggest to Erin that she watch video clips online. In this situation, what would Kevin most likely say to Erin?

Kevin: Erin, there are many useful video clips on the Internet.

우·리·말·해·석

① 네 생일에 햄스터를 받고 싶니?
② 너는 동물들을 정말 잘 돌본다.
③ 반려동물을 돌보는 것은 많은 시간과 노력이 들어.
④ 인터넷에 많은 유용한 영상 클립들이 있어.
⑤ 영상을 보는 것이 새로운 것을 배우는 가장 좋은 방법은 아니야.

남: Erin은 그녀의 생일에 그녀의 부모님으로부터 햄스터 한 마리를 받는다. 그녀는 항상 반려동물을 원했기 때문에 그녀는 매우 기쁘다. 하지만 그녀는 햄스터를 어떻게 돌보아야 하는지 모른다. Erin은 마찬가지로 반려 햄스터를 가지고 있는 그녀의 반 친구 Kevin에게 어디서부터 시작할지 물어본다. Kevin이 처음 반려동물을 가졌을 때, 그는 인터넷에 있는 영상 클립들로부터 많은 도움을 받았다. 그래서 Kevin은 Erin에게 온라인 영상 클립들을 볼 것을 제안하려고 한다. 이 상황에서 Kevin은 Erin에게 뭐라고 말하겠는가?

Kevin: Erin, 인터넷에 많은 유용한 영상 클립들이 있어.

단·어·및·표·현

thrilled [θrild] 형 매우 기뻐하는, 흥분된
effort [éfərt] 명 노력, 수고

Words & Expressions Review

1. (특정 활동에 필요한) 장비	2. 다행이다, 안심하다	3. 교장, 주요한
4. 휴대용의	5. 예전에는 ~이었다 [했다]	6. (결국) ~이 되다
7. 깃발	8. ~로 가다	9. 생활 방식
10. 보험, 보험료	11. 걸어서	12. 대본
13. 학교 식당	14. 후회하는	15. 이용할 수 있는
16. 말하다, 언급하다	17. 빼다, 접지르다	18. ~에 참가하다
19. 직접, 도움을 받지 않고	20. (전기·가스·수도 등을) 끄다	21. 소비하다
22. 빈자리, 공석	23. 회사, 기관	24. 습도
25. 침대[잠자리]를 정리하다	26. 지역의, 현지의	27. 노력, 수고
28. 사진을 찍다	29. 부상, 상처	30. 걸리다, 걸다, 매달리다
31. ~에게 문제없다, 좋다	32. 사무실	33. 녹음하다
34. 수업[강의] 시간	35. 오랫동안	36. 망치다, 엉망으로 만들다
37. 자세한	38. 손질하다, 다듬다	39. 건강 검진, 대조, 검사
40. 수리하다, 개조하다	41. 작동하다	42. 매우 기뻐하는, 흥분된
43. 기념품	44. ~을 낮추다, 줄이다	

Listening Test
영어듣기 모의고사 16회

|정|답|

01 ⑤	02 ③	03 ③	04 ③	05 ①
06 ③	07 ⑤	08 ④	09 ②	10 ③
11 ③	12 ①	13 ③	14 ③	15 ⑤
16 ④	17 ④	18 ②	19 ④	20 ⑤

01 그림정보파악(대화) ▶ 정답 ⑤

듣·기·대·본

W: Welcome to the Home Market. How can I help you?

M: I'm looking for a trash can for my house.

W: I see. Would you <u>prefer</u> a big one or a smaller one?

M: I'll be putting the trash can in my bedroom, so I think a smaller one would be nice.

W: All right. Would you prefer a rectangular one or a round one?

M: The round one looks more stylish. The design will match my room.

W: Okay. It <u>comes in</u> two styles. One has a pedal and the other doesn't.

M: I'll take the one with a pedal. It is more <u>convenient</u> to use.

W: Good choice.

우·리·말·해·석

여: Home Market에 오신 것을 환영합니다. 어떻게 도와드릴까요?

남: 저는 저희 집에 둘 쓰레기통을 찾고 있어요.

여: 그렇군요. 당신은 큰 것이 좋나요, 아니면 더 작은 것이 좋나요?

남: 저는 쓰레기통을 제 침실에 둘 것이라서 더 작은 것이 좋겠네요.

여: 좋아요. 당신은 직사각형의 것이 좋나요, 아니면 둥근 것이 좋나요?

남: 둥근 것이 더 세련되어 보이네요. 그 디자인은 제 방과 어울릴 거예요.

여: 네. 그것은 두 가지 스타일로 나와요. 하나는 페달이 있고, 다른 것은 없어요.

남: 저는 페달이 달린 것으로 살게요. 그게 쓰기 좀 더 편해요.

여: 좋은 선택이에요.

단·어·및·표·현

look for ~ ~을 찾다

stylish [stáiliʃ] 혱 세련된, 멋진

match [mætʃ] 동 어울리다, (색깔·무늬·스타일이 서로) 맞다

come in ~ (물품, 상품 등이) ~으로 나오다

convenient [kənví:njənt] 혱 편리한, 간편한

02 대화미언급 ▶ 정답 ③

듣·기·대·본

(Telephone rings.)

M: Hello. This is Green Art Workshop.

W: Hi. I'm <u>interested in</u> the art workshop. When does it begin?

M: It begins on August 5th.

W: How long does it last?

M: It <u>runs for</u> two days, from 10:00 a.m. to 3:00 p.m.

W: That's great. What kind of activities are included?

M: Participants can try pottery, watercolor painting, and collage making.

W: Sounds fun! How much is the fee for the two-day workshop?

M: It's 50 dollars per person.

W: Wonderful! I'll <u>sign up for</u> it.

우·리·말·해·석

(전화벨이 울린다.)

남: 안녕하세요. Green Art Workshop입니다.

여: 안녕하세요. 저는 그 미술 워크숍에 관심이 있어요. 그건 언제 시작하나요?

남: 8월 5일에 시작해요.

여: 기간은 얼마나 되나요?

남: 이틀 동안 진행되고, 오전 10시부터 오후 3시까지예요.

여: 좋네요. 어떤 종류의 활동들이 포함되어 있나요?

남: 참가자들은 도자기, 수채화, 그리고 콜라주 만들기를 해볼 수 있어요.

여: 재밌겠네요! 이틀간의 워크숍 비용은 얼마예요?

남: 인당 50달러예요.

여: 멋지네요! 저는 그것을 신청할게요.

단·어·및·표·현

be interested in ~ ~에 관심이 있다

run [rʌn] 동 (서비스, 강좌 등을) 운영하다, 제공하다

participant [pɑːrtísəpənt] 혱 참가자

pottery [pátəri] 혱 도자기, 도예

watercolor painting 수채화

collage [kəlá:ʒ] 혱 콜라주, 모음

sign up for ~을 신청하다

03 전화목적파악 ▶ 정답 ③

듣·기·대·본

(Cellphone rings.)

W: Hello?

M: Hi, is this Sarah? This is John from FlexFit Gym.

W: Hi, John. Yes, this is Sarah.

M: Due to a pipe <u>leakage</u> issue, our showers will be <u>closed for maintenance</u> starting tomorrow.

W: Oh, no! How long will the showers be closed?

M: Approximately one week.

W: I guess I'll have to go home to shower during the repairs. Thanks for the <u>heads up</u>, though.

M: I'm so sorry. As compensation for the inconvenience, we'll <u>extend</u> your membership by one week.

W: Thank you, John. I appreciate it.

우·리·말·해·석

(휴대폰이 울린다.)

여: 여보세요?

남: 안녕하세요, Sarah 씨 맞나요? 저는 FlexFit 체육관의 John이라고 합니다.

여: 안녕하세요, John 씨. 네, Sarah 맞아요.

남: 저희 샤워실은 배관 누수 문제로 인하여 내일부터 보수를 위해 폐쇄될 예정입니다.

여: 오, 저런! 샤워실은 얼마나 오랫동안 폐쇄되나요?

남: 대략 일주일입니다.

여: 보수 기간 동안은 샤워하려면 집에 가는 수밖에 없을 것 같네요. 그래도 미리 알려주셔서 감사합니다.

남: 정말 죄송합니다. 불편을 끼친 것에 대한 보상으로 저희는 당신의 회원권을 일주일 연장해 드릴 것입니다.

여: 감사합니다, John. 저는 그것에 대해 고맙게 생각합니다.

단·어·및·표·현

leakage [lí:kidʒ] 혱 누수

maintenance [méintənəns] 혱 보수, 정비

approximately [əpráksəmətli] 부 대략, 거의

repair [ripɛ́ər] 혱 보수, 수리

heads up 알림, 경고

compensation [kàmpənséiʃən] 혱 보상

inconvenience [ìnkənví:njəns] 혱 불편(함), 성가심

extend [iksténd] 동 연장하다

appreciate [əprí:ʃièit] 동 고맙게 생각하다

16 회 모의고사

04　수치파악(시각)　▶ 정답 ③

듣·기·대·본

(*Telephone rings.*)

W: Dr. Howard's office. May I help you?
M: Yes. This is Brad Lee. I'm not going to be able to make it to my appointment today.
W: No problem, Mr. Lee. Would you like to reschedule?
M: Yes. Can I come in next Tuesday at 5 p.m.?
W: I'm sorry, but 5 p.m. is already booked. Does 3 p.m. work for you?
M: No, I could get there by 4 p.m., though.
W: 4 p.m. works for us, too. I'll reschedule your appointment to 4 p.m. next Tuesday, then.
M: Great. Thanks a lot.

우·리·말·해·석

(전화벨이 울린다.)

여: Howard 선생님 병원입니다. 어떻게 도와드릴까요?
남: 네. 저는 Brad Lee입니다. 저는 오늘 제 예약시간에 못 갈 것 같아요.
여: 괜찮습니다, Lee 씨. 일정을 변경하시겠어요?
남: 네. 다음 주 화요일 오후 5시에 가도 될까요?
여: 죄송하지만 오후 5시는 이미 예약되었습니다. 오후 3시는 괜찮으신가요?
남: 아니요, 그렇지만 저는 오후 4시까지는 거기에 갈 수 있어요.
여: 저희도 오후 4시는 괜찮습니다. 그럼 당신의 예약을 다음 주 화요일 오후 4시로 변경하겠습니다.
남: 좋아요. 감사합니다.

단·어·및·표·현

make it 시간 맞춰 가다
appointment [əpɔ́intmənt] 몡 (병원·미용실 따위의) 예약
reschedule [rìːskédʒuːl] 통 일정을 변경하다
book [buk] 통 예약하다
work for ~에게 문제없다, 좋다

05　심정추론　▶ 정답 ①

듣·기·대·본

M: What's wrong, Nina? Why are you just standing in front of your locker?
W: Jay, the lock on my locker is broken.
M: What? What happened?
W: I don't know. I just came from class and found it like this.
M: Somebody picked the lock?!
W: I think so. Now I'm afraid to open it.
M: But you need to check if anything is missing.
W: I'm more afraid that somebody put something in there.
M: Like what?
W: How should I know? It could be anything.

우·리·말·해·석

① 겁먹은　　② 안도하는　　③ 행복한
④ 슬픈　　　⑤ 질투하는

남: 무슨 일이야, Nina? 너는 왜 네 사물함 앞에 그냥 서 있니?
여: Jay, 내 사물함의 자물쇠가 부서졌어.
남: 뭐? 무슨 일이 있던 거야?
여: 나도 모르겠어. 막 수업에서 돌아왔는데 이렇게 돼 있는 걸 발견했어.

여: 그런 것 같아. 지금 나는 이것을 열어보는 것이 두려워.
남: 하지만 너는 무언가 없어진 것이 있는지 확인해야 해.
여: 나는 누군가 거기에 뭔가를 넣어 놓았을까 봐 더 두려워.
남: 예를 들면 어떤 거?
여: 내가 어떻게 알아? 그것은 뭐든지 될 수 있다고.

단·어·및·표·현

lock [lɑk] 몡 자물쇠
pick a lock (철사 같은 것을 이용하여) 자물쇠를 따다
missing [mísiŋ] 혱 없어진, 실종된

06　그림상황에적절한대화찾기　▶ 정답 ③

듣·기·대·본

① W: You should go to bed.
　M: I know, but let me just finish this drawing first.
② W: Do you want to go for a walk?
　M: Not now. I prefer taking a walk at night.
③ W: Your music is too loud. Can you turn it down?
　M: Sure. I'll do it right away.
④ W: Where can I buy headphones?
　M: You should go to the music section over there.
⑤ W: You shouldn't play your musical instrument at night.
　M: I'm sorry. I won't do it again.

우·리·말·해·석

① 여: 너는 자러 가야 해.
　남: 알아. 하지만 먼저 이 그림만 다 그리게 해줘.
② 여: 너는 산책하러 가길 원하니?
　남: 지금은 아니야. 나는 밤에 산책하는 것을 더 좋아해.
③ 여: 너의 음악은 너무 시끄러워. 줄여줄 수 있니?
　남: 물론. 지금 당장 줄일게.
④ 여: 헤드폰을 어디서 살 수 있나요?
　남: 저쪽에 있는 음악 코너로 가야 합니다.
⑤ 여: 밤에 악기를 연주하면 안 돼.
　남: 미안해. 다시는 안 할게.

단·어·및·표·현

turn ~ down ~를 줄이다[낮추다]
musical instrument 악기

07　부탁(요청)한일파악　▶ 정답 ⑤

듣·기·대·본

W: Nathan, what's up? You look a bit anxious.
M: Hi, Amy. I have a presentation this afternoon and I can't stop thinking about it.
W: Don't worry. You'll do fine.
M: I'm really nervous. I don't think I practiced enough.
W: If your presentation is in the afternoon, why don't you practice now?
M: Maybe I should. Can you help me practice?
W: Sure! What do you want me to do?
M: Could you listen to my practice presentation and give me some feedback?
W: Sure, no problem.

우·리·말·해·석

여: Nathan, 무슨 일 있어? 너 약간 불안해 보여.
남: 안녕, Amy. 오늘 오후에 발표가 있는데, 그것에 대해 생각하는 걸 멈출

수 없어.

여: 걱정 마. 너는 잘할거야.

남: 난 정말 긴장돼. 나는 충분히 연습했다고 생각하지 않아.

여: 너의 발표가 오후에 있다면, 지금 연습하는 게 어때?

남: 해야겠다. 내가 연습하는 거 도와줄 수 있어?

여: 물론이지! 내가 뭘 하기를 원하니?

남: 나의 연습 발표를 듣고 나에게 피드백을 해 줄 수 있어?

여: 물론, 문제없어.

단·어·및·표·현
feedback[fíːdbæk] 몡 피드백, 의견, 반응

08 담화미언급   ▶ 정답 ④

듣·기·대·본
W: Hello, students. This is Anna, the president of the student council. I'm happy to invite you to a concert to raise funds to help our friend Helen, who is bravely fighting cancer. The concert will take place on July 11th from 6 to 8 p.m. in the school auditorium. You can now get tickets for $20 from the student council. During the concert, our school orchestra and a school band will play beautiful music. Thank you.

우·리·말·해·석
여: 안녕하세요, 학생 여러분. 저는 학생회 회장인 Anna입니다. 저는 용감하게 암과 싸우고 있는, 우리의 친구 Helen을 돕기 위한 기금을 모으기 위한 콘서트에 여러분을 초대하게 되어 기쁩니다. 콘서트는 7월 11일 오후 6시부터 8시까지 학교 강당에서 열릴 것입니다. 여러분은 지금 학생회로부터 20달러에 표를 사실 수 있습니다. 콘서트 동안, 우리 학교 오케스트라와 학교 밴드가 아름다운 음악을 연주할 것입니다. 감사합니다.

단·어·및·표·현
student council 학생회
raise funds 기금을 모으다
auditorium[ɔ̀ːditɔ́ːriəm] 몡 강당

09 담화화제추론   ▶ 정답 ②

듣·기·대·본
M: This is a familiar object seen everywhere. It allows you to view your own reflection. It is made of glass, so it is breakable. When you look at yourself in this, the image you see is reversed. In other words, you see everything on the opposite side from how another person sees you. It is also placed in every car. You can see on the right, left and in the back with this while driving. What is it?

우·리·말·해·석
남: 이것은 어디서나 볼 수 있는 친숙한 물건입니다. 이것은 당신이 당신의 모습을 볼 수 있게 해줍니다. 이것은 유리로 만들어져서, 깨지기 쉽습니다. 당신이 이것으로 당신의 모습을 볼 때, 당신이 보는 이미지는 반대입니다. 다시 말해서 당신은 다른 사람이 당신을 보는 것과는 반대로 모든 것을 보게 됩니다. 이것은 또한 모든 차에도 달려 있습니다. 당신은 운전 중에 이것으로 오른쪽, 왼쪽, 뒤를 볼 수 있습니다. 이것은 무엇인가요?

단·어·및·표·현
be made of ~ ~으로 만들어지다, 구성되다
reversed[rivə́ːrst] 혱 반대의, 뒤집힌

10 어색한대화찾기   ▶ 정답 ③

듣·기·대·본
① M: What are you studying now?
　W: I'm studying science for an exam next week.
② M: Do you mind if I turn off the air conditioner?
　W: Not at all. I was feeling a bit cold myself.
③ M: Which bus goes to the airport?
　W: It will take an hour to get there.
④ M: It was the best musical I've ever seen.
　W: I totally agree with you.
⑤ M: May I borrow your book?
　W: Sure. I'll give it to you when I'm done.

우·리·말·해·석
① 남: 너는 지금 무엇을 공부하고 있어?
　여: 다음 주 시험을 위해 과학을 공부하고 있어.
② 남: 제가 에어컨을 끄면 싫으세요?
　여: 전혀 그렇지 않아요. 저도 약간 춥다고 느끼고 있었어요.
③ 남: 어느 버스가 공항에 가나요?
　여: 거기에 도착하는 데 1시간이 걸릴 것입니다.
④ 남: 그것은 내가 지금까지 본 뮤지컬 중에서 최고였어.
　여: 나도 네 말에 완전 동의해.
⑤ 남: 내가 너의 책을 빌려도 될까?
　여: 물론이지. 내가 다 읽으면 너에게 줄게.

단·어·및·표·현
air conditioner 에어컨

11 할일파악(대화직후)   ▶ 정답 ③

듣·기·대·본
W: Anton, what should we do for the science fair?
M: I'm not sure. I don't want to make an app like last time.
W: Yeah, me, neither. What about making something visually attractive, like fireworks?
M: That sounds interesting! It'll definitely draw attention.
W: And I'm sure we can borrow materials from the school, too.
M: Great. But, wait. Are we allowed to demonstrate fireworks? The fair is indoors.
W: Why not? As long as we follow safety protocols it should be okay.
M: I think we should ask our teacher first, to be certain.
W: Okay. I'll do it right now.

우·리·말·해·석
여: Anton, 과학 박람회를 위해 우리가 뭘 해야 할까?
남: 잘 모르겠어. 지난번처럼 앱을 만들고 싶진 않아.
여: 나도. 불꽃놀이처럼 시각적으로 눈길을 끄는 것을 만드는 게 어때?
남: 그거 흥미로운데! 확실히 주목을 끌 거야.
여: 그리고 학교에서 재료도 빌릴 수 있을 거라고 확신해.
남: 좋아. 근데, 잠깐. 우리가 불꽃놀이를 시연하는 게 허용돼? 박람회는 실내에서 열리잖아.
여: 왜 안 돼? 우리가 안전 수칙만 잘 지키면 괜찮을 거야.
남: 확실히 하려면 선생님께 먼저 여쭤봐야 할 것 같아.
여: 알겠어. 내가 지금 바로 할게.

단·어·및·표·현
visually[víʒuəli] 囝 시각적으로

16 회 모의고사

attractive [ətrǽktiv] 혱 매력적인, 멋진
draw [drɔː] 동 (주의·흥미 등을) 끌다
attention [əténʃən] 혱 주의, 주목
demonstrate [démənstrèit] 동 시연하다, 보여주다
safety protocol 안전 수칙

12 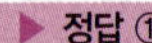 도표정보파악　　　　　▶ 정답 ①

들·기·대·본

M: Honey, have you decided which summer skirt to buy for our daughter, Sally?

W: It's harder than I thought. I could use your opinion.

M: No problem. It is for summer, so a linen skirt would be much better.

W: I agree. Linen absorbs moisture and dries quickly, which makes it perfect for the summer.

M: Okay. Should we get a skirt with an elastic waistband or one with a zipper?

W: Sally would feel more comfortable with an elastic waistband.

M: You're right. Now, we have two options left. Do you want one with pockets or no pockets?

W: In my opinion, the skirt with pockets doesn't look as nice.

M: You have a point. Let's order this one, then.

우·리·말·해·석

	모델	소재	특징	주머니
①	A	리넨	고무 허리밴드	X
②	B	리넨	고무 허리밴드	O
③	C	리넨	지퍼	X
④	D	면직물	고무 허리밴드	O
⑤	E	면직물	지퍼	X

남: 여보, 우리 딸 Sally에게 어떤 여름 치마를 사줄지 정했나요?

여: 제가 생각했던 것보다 더 어려워요. 저는 당신의 의견이 필요해요.

남: 문제없어요. 여름용이니 리넨 치마가 훨씬 더 낫겠어요.

여: 동의해요. 리넨은 습기를 흡수하고 빨리 마르는데, 그 점이 그것을 여름용으로 딱 맞게 만들어주는 거죠.

남: 네. 우리는 고무 허리밴드인 치마를 살까요, 아니면 지퍼로 된 것을 살까요?

여: Sally는 고무 허리밴드를 더 편하게 느낄 거예요.

남: 당신이 맞아요. 이제, 우리에겐 두 가지 선택지가 남았네요. 당신은 주머니가 있는 것을 원해요 아니면 주머니가 없는 것을 원해요?

여: 제 의견으로는 주머니들이 있는 치마는 멋있게 보이지 않아요.

남: 일리 있네요. 그럼, 이걸로 주문하죠.

단·어·및·표·현

absorb [əbsɔ́ːrb] 동 흡수하다
moisture [mɔ́istʃər] 혱 수분, 습기
elastic [ilǽstik] 혱 고무로 된
waistband [wéistbæ̀nd] 혱 허리 밴드
comfortable [kʌ́mfərtəbl] 혱 편한, 편안한
have a point 일리 있다

13 수치파악(날짜)　　　　　▶ 정답 ③

들·기·대·본

M: Look, Heather! The Han River night market is finally back.

W: Really? Why don't we go there together?

M: Yeah, sure! Let's see. It will be running every Sunday for one month only starting on May 7th.

W: How about going on the first day, May 7th? The night market will feel so alive with all the crowds.

M: True, but I can't go that night. I have plans with my family on the 7th. How about the 14th?

W: I can't go on the 14th. I'm going to a musical that night.

M: Then, is the 21st okay with you?

W: Yeah, the 21st sounds fine. Let's go then.

우·리·말·해·석

남: 봐, Heather! 한강 야시장이 드디어 돌아왔어.

여: 정말? 우리 같이 거기 가보지 않을래?

남: 응, 물론이지! 어디 보자. 그것은 5월 7일에 시작해서 딱 한 달 동안 매주 일요일에 운영될 거야.

여: 첫날인 5월 7일에 가는 건 어때? 야시장은 많은 사람으로 엄청 활기찰 거야.

남: 맞아, 하지만 난 그날 밤에는 갈 수 없어. 난 7일에 가족들과 약속이 있어. 14일은 어때?

여: 나는 14일에 못 가. 난 그날 밤에 뮤지컬 보러 갈 거야.

남: 그럼, 21일은 괜찮아?

여: 응, 21일은 괜찮을 것 같아. 그때 가자.

단·어·및·표·현

night market 야시장
alive [əláiv] 혱 활기찬, 생기 있는
crowd [kraud] 혱 사람들, 군중, 무리

14 한일파악　　　　　▶ 정답 ③

들·기·대·본

M: Katelyn, have you finished the literature homework?

W: Not yet. How about you?

M: I haven't even started. It's too hard. How can I pick the right book?

W: Well, the list our teacher gave us is very long. So, I went to the library yesterday.

M: And?

W: I asked the librarian to point out the least popular books. And I came home with one of them.

M: How did it help you?

W: At the very least, it saved me time choosing a book.

M: Okay. Not a bad idea. I think I'll do the same.

우·리·말·해·석

남: Katelyn, 너는 문학 숙제를 끝냈니?

여: 아직 못 끝냈어. 너는 어때?

남: 나는 시작조차 안 했어. 그것은 너무 어려워. 어떻게 내가 적절한 책을 고를 수 있을까?

여: 음. 우리 선생님께서 우리에게 주신 목록은 너무 길어. 그래서 나는 어제 도서관에 갔어.

남: 그리고?

여: 나는 사서에게 가장 인기 없는 책들을 알려달라고 요청했어. 그리고 나는 그것들 중 하나를 가지고 집에 왔어.

남: 그것이 너에게 어떻게 도움이 됐니?

여: 최소한 그것은 내가 책을 고르는 시간을 아껴줬어.

남: 그렇구나. 나쁘지 않은 생각이네. 나도 똑같이 해봐야겠어.

literature [lítərətʃùər] 명 문학
point out 알려주다, 가리키다
at the very least 최소한, 적어도

15 담화목적파악　　　▶ 정답 ⑤

듣·기·대·본

W: Good afternoon, students. This is your teacher Mrs. Hill speaking. A valuable item was just turned into our school's Lost and Found. It's a smartphone of the Milky Way brand. It's white with gold star stickers on the back. It was found in the women's restroom on the second floor. It's locked, so the owner will need to unlock it to prove that it belongs to her. If the phone belongs to you, come to my office as soon as you can. Thank you.

우·리·말·해·석

여: 좋은 오후입니다, 학생 여러분. 저는 여러분의 교사인 Hill 선생님입니다. 우리 학교의 분실물 센터에 귀중품 하나가 막 들어왔습니다. 그것은 Milky Way 브랜드의 스마트폰입니다. 그것은 하얀색이고 뒤에 금색 별 스티커가 붙어있습니다. 그것은 이층의 여자 화장실에서 발견되었습니다. 그것은 잠겨 있으므로 주인은 본인의 것임을 증명하기 위해 잠금을 해제해야 할 것입니다. 만약 그 전화기가 자신의 것이라면, 가능한 한 빨리 제 사무실로 오세요. 감사합니다.

단·어·및·표·현

valuable item 귀중품
Lost and Found 분실물 센터
restroom [réstrùm] 명 (공공장소의) 화장실
unlock [ʌ̀nlák] 동 잠금 해제하다, 열다
belong to ~ 것이다, 소유이다

16 수치계산(금액)　　　▶ 정답 ④

듣·기·대·본

W: What can I do for you, sir?
M: I'm looking for a present for my sister.
W: Okay. How about this blouse? It's the most popular item.
M: It looks nice. How much is it?
W: The original price is 50 dollars, but we're giving a 20% discount this week.
M: Oh, that's great. I'll take it.
W: Do you want it gift-wrapped? It will cost one more dollar.
M: Yes, please.

우·리·말·해·석

여: 뭘 도와드릴까요, 손님?
남: 여동생을 위한 선물을 찾고 있는데요.
여: 알겠습니다. 이 블라우스는 어떠세요? 가장 인기 있는 상품이에요.
남: 괜찮은데요. 얼마입니까?
여: 정가는 50달러인데요, 이번 주에는 20% 할인해 드린답니다.
남: 오, 잘됐군요. 그걸로 하겠습니다.
여: 선물용 포장을 원하십니까? 그건 1달러가 더 듭니다.
남: 네, 해주세요.

단·어·및·표·현

give a discount 할인해 주다

17 알맞은응답찾기　　　▶ 정답 ④

듣·기·대·본

W: Hi, Carl. Did you see the sports documentary on TV last night?
M: No. What was it about?
W: It was about the famous Brazilian soccer player, Pele.
M: I've never heard of him. Can you tell me something about him?
W: He was an amazing goal scorer.
M: Was he the best?
W: Well, he holds the world record for most goals.
M: Really? What is the record?
W: He scored over 1,200 goals.

우·리·말·해·석

① 그는 지금 브라질에 살아.
② 그는 가장 빠른 선수야.
③ 그는 공을 패스하는 것을 좋아했어.
④ 그는 1,200골 이상을 득점했어.
⑤ 그는 그의 팀에서 최고였어.

여: 안녕, Carl. 지난밤 TV에서 스포츠 다큐멘터리를 봤어?
남: 아니. 뭐에 대한 거였는데?
여: 그건 유명한 브라질 축구 선수인 Pele에 대한 거였어.
남: 나는 그에 대해 들어본 적이 없어. 그에 대해 좀 말해줄 수 있어?
여: 그는 놀라운 골 득점자였어.
남: 그가 최고였어?
여: 음, 그는 최다골로 세계 기록을 보유하고 있어.
남: 정말? 기록이 어떻게 되는데?
여: 그는 1,200골 이상을 득점했어.

단·어·및·표·현

hear of + 명사 ~에 대해 듣다
hold [hould] 동 (기록, 타이틀 등을) 보유하다

18 알맞은응답찾기　　　▶ 정답 ②

듣·기·대·본

W: Hi, Adrian! How is your history report going?
M: Hi, Joyce! I've just finished my first draft. I've put a lot of effort into it.
W: I'm sure you have.
M: But I think I need someone to give me some feedback.
W: Oh, why don't you ask your brother? Isn't he a college student?
M: He is, but he's doing part-time work these days. I hardly see him.
W: Then, I will ask my sister. She loves history.
M: Are you sure? I would be grateful for her help.
W: No problem. I'm sure she will be happy to help you.
M: That's great! I would really appreciate it.

우·리·말·해·석

① 알겠어. 같이 보고서를 작성하자.
② 좋다! 그렇게 해준다면 정말 고마울 거야.
③ 너무 안됐다. 너는 네 언니를 많이 그리워하는 것이 틀림없어.
④ 그런 경우에는, 너는 선생님께 말씀드리는 게 좋아.
⑤ 물론이지. 그는 내 보고서에 긍정적인 피드백을 주었어.

여: 안녕, Adrian! 네 역사 보고서는 어떻게 되어 가니?

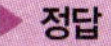

16
회
모
의
고
사

남: 안녕, Joyce! 나는 막 초고를 완성했어. 나는 그것에 많은 노력을 기울였어.

여: 나는 네가 그랬을 거라고 확신해.

남: 하지만 나는 나에게 피드백을 줄 누군가가 필요하다고 생각해.

여: 오, 네 형에게 물어보는 게 어때? 그는 대학생이지 않니?

남: 맞아, 하지만 그는 요즘 아르바이트를 하고 있어. 나는 그를 거의 못 봐.

여: 그럼, 내가 내 언니한테 물어볼게. 그녀는 역사를 정말 좋아해.

남: 그게 정말이야? 그녀가 도와준다면 나는 정말 고마울 거야.

여: 문제없어. 나는 그녀가 너를 기꺼이 도와줄 것이라고 확신해.

남: **좋다! 그렇게 해준다면 정말 고마울 거야.**

단·어·및·표·현

draft [dræft] 명 초고, 초안

put effort 노력을 기울이다, 공을 들이다

hardly [háːrdli] 부 거의 ~할 수 없다

grateful [gréitfəl] 형 고마워하는, 감사하는

19 알맞은응답찾기 ▶ 정답 ④

듣·기·대·본

M: You seem to be busy with your phone these days. What are you doing?

W: I've been learning Spanish with a new language app.

M: Oh, really? Is it better than the app you used before?

W: Definitely. It has fun games and short lessons that keep you motivated.

M: That sounds interesting. Is it free to use?

W: Yes, the basic version is free, and you can pay for extra features if you want. You should try it.

M: That's a great idea. Does it work for other languages, too?

W: Yes, they have over 20 languages to choose from.

M: All right, I'll give it a shot. Thanks for telling me about it.

우·리·말·해·석

① 그러면 좋겠어. 하지만 (내 휴대폰에는) 저장 공간이 충분하지 않아.

② 나는 온라인 게임에 중독되고 싶지 않아.

③ 나는 예전에 스페인에서 살았어서, 스페인어를 잘해.

④ 알겠어, 한번 시도해 볼게. 그것에 대해 알려줘서 고마워.

⑤ 외국어를 배우는 것은 네 기억력을 향상시키는 데에 도움이 돼.

남: 너 요즘 휴대폰 하느라 바쁜 것 같아. 뭐 하고 있어?

여: 나는 새 언어 앱으로 스페인어를 배우고 있었어.

남: 오, 정말? 네가 전에 쓰던 앱보다 더 좋아?

여: 확실히 좋아. 그건 계속 동기를 부여해주는 재미있는 게임들과 짧은 수업들이 있어.

남: 흥미롭다. 그걸 사용하는 것은 무료야?

여: 응, 기본 버전은 무료이고, 원한다면 추가 기능을 (이용하기) 위해 돈을 지불할 수도 있어. 너도 해봐.

남: 좋은 생각이다. 그거 다른 언어도 되니?

여: 응, 그들은 선택할 수 있는 20개 이상의 언어를 가지고 있어.

남: **알겠어, 한번 시도해 볼게. 그것에 대해 알려줘서 고마워.**

단·어·및·표·현

motivate [móutəvèit] 동 동기를 부여하다

extra [ékstrə] 형 추가의, 여분의

feature [fíːtʃər] 명 기능

---

give it a shot 한번 해 보다, 시도해 보다

storage [stɔ́ːridʒ] 명 저장, 보관

addict [ǽdikt] 동 중독되게 하다

improve [imprúːv] 동 향상시키다, 개선하다

20 상황에적절한말찾기 ▶ 정답 ⑤

듣·기·대·본

W: Helen is visiting an art gallery with her friend. Taking pictures is allowed in most parts of the gallery, so they take a lot of pictures. However, when they enter one room, there is a sign saying that they shouldn't take pictures in that particular room. Not noticing this sign, her friend starts to take pictures as in other rooms. So, Helen wants to ask her friend to read the sign. In this situation, what would Helen most likely say to her friend?

Helen: **Please look at that sign. We can't take pictures here.**

우·리·말·해·석

① 왜 이 방에서 사진(촬영)이 금지되지?

② 너는 미술관에서 얼마나 오래 머물고 싶어?

③ 너는 어느 그림을 사진 찍고 싶어?

④ 너는 또 다른 방에 있는 그림들을 보길 원해?

⑤ 저 표지판 좀 봐줘. 우리는 여기서 사진을 찍을 수 없어.

여: Helen은 그녀의 친구와 함께 미술관을 방문하고 있다. 미술관의 대부분에서 사진 찍는 것이 허용되어서, 그들은 많은 사진을 찍는다. 그렇지만, 그들이 한 방에 들어갈 때, 그들이 그 특정한 방에서는 사진을 찍어서는 안 된다고 하는 표지판이 있다. 이 표지판을 알아채지 못하고, 그녀의 친구는 다른 방들에서처럼 사진을 찍는다. 그래서, Helen은 그녀의 친구에게 표지판을 읽으라고 요청하고 싶다. 이런 상황에서, Helen은 그녀의 친구에게 뭐라고 말하겠는가?

Helen: **저 표지판 좀 봐줘. 우리는 여기서 사진을 찍을 수 없어.**

단·어·및·표·현

particular [pərtíkjələr] 형 특정한

notice [nóutis] 동 알아채다

Words & Expressions Review

1. 보수, 정비	2. 할인해 주다	3. 초고, 초안
4. 콜라주, 모음	5. 보상	6. 최소한, 적어도
7. 고마워하는, 감사하는	8. 특정한	9. 동기를 부여하다
10. (기록, 타이틀 등을) 보유하다	11. 활기찬, 생기 있는	12. (상품 등이) ~으로 나오다
13. ~을 줄이다	14. 알아채다	15. 피드백, 반응, 의견
16. 선물용으로 포장된	17. 수채화	18. 세련된, 멋진
19. 흡수하다	20. 어울리다	21. 산책하다
22. 누수	23. 일정을 변경하다	24. ~ 것이다, 소유이다
25. 매력적인, 멋진	26. 없어진, 실종된	27. 강당
28. 알림, 경고	29. 거의 ~할 수 없다	30. 시각적으로
31. 기금을 모으다	32. 고무로 된	33. (전기 · 가스 · 수도 등을) 끄다
34. 불안한, 걱정하는	35. 반대의, 뒤집힌	36. ~에 대해 듣다

37. 주의, 주목	38. 반대의, ~ 맞은편의	39. 에어컨
40. 분실물 센터	41. 자물쇠	42. 알려주다, 가리키다
43. 잠금 해제하다	44. (거울에 비친) 모습, 반사	

Listening Test

영어듣기 모의고사 17회

| 정 | 답 |

01 ⑤	02 ⑤	03 ⑤	04 ②	05 ③
06 ①	07 ①	08 ⑤	09 ③	10 ③
11 ②	12 ①	13 ③	14 ③	15 ①
16 ④	17 ⑤	18 ④	19 ②	20 ②

01 그림정보파악(대화) ▶ 정답 ⑤

듣·기·대·본

W: Hi, Carl. What are you doing on your laptop?

M: I'm creating a sticker using a photo of my dog. Can you help me out?

W: Sure. Let's choose the sticker shape first. Do you want a circle-shaped sticker?

M: Yes, that sounds good.

W: It seems that you can add other pictures like flowers and rainbows to the sticker as well.

M: Okay. I'll add a picture of a rainbow then.

W: Good. Your dog's name is 'Max,' isn't it? Why don't you put his name on the sticker as well?

M: That's a great idea. I think we're done! I'll print this out.

우·리·말·해·석

여: 안녕, Carl. 너는 네 노트북으로 뭐 하고 있어?

남: 나는 내 개의 사진을 이용해서 스티커를 만들고 있어. 너는 나를 도울 수 있니?

여: 물론. 먼저 스티커 모양부터 정하자. 너는 원형 스티커를 원하니?

남: 그래, 그거 좋다.

여: 너는 스티커에 꽃이나 무지개 같은 다른 그림들 또한 추가할 수 있는 것 같아 보여.

남: 응. 그러면 나는 무지개 그림을 추가할게.

여: 좋아. 너의 개의 이름은 'Max'야, 그렇지 않니? 너는 그의 이름 또한 스티커에 넣는 게 어때?

남: 그거 좋은 생각이야. 다 된 것 같아! 나는 이걸 출력할게.

단·어·및·표·현

create [kriéit] [동] 만들어 내다
as well 또한, 역시

02 대화미언급 ▶ 정답 ⑤

듣·기·대·본

M: Mia, are you participating in this year's Junior Cooking Challenge?

W: Yes! It'll be held at the Downtown Culinary School this Saturday.

M: Do you know when it starts?

W: The challenge begins at 2 p.m.

M: What are we going to make?

W: We'll bake cupcakes and decorate cookies.

M: Yum! That sounds delicious.

W: Oh, and remember to tie back your hair for safety and sanitation.

M: Good tip.

우·리·말·해·석

남: Mia, 너는 올해 청소년 요리 챌린지에 참가하니?

여: 응! 이번 주 토요일 Downtown 요리 학교에서 열릴 거야.

남: 넌 그게 언제 시작하는지 알아?

여: 챌린지는 오후 2시에 시작해.

남: 우리는 뭘 만들 거야?

여: 우리는 컵케이크를 굽고 쿠키들을 꾸밀 거야.

남: 냠냠! 맛있겠다.

여: 아, 그리고 안전과 위생을 위해 네 머리를 뒤로 묶는 것을 기억해.

남: 좋은 조언이네.

단·어·및·표·현

participate in ~ ~에 참여하다
culinary [kʌ́linəri, kjú:lənèri] [형] 요리의
decorate [dékərèit] [동] 꾸미다, 장식하다
tie [tai] [동] (끈 등으로) 묶다, 묶어 두다[놓다]
safety [séifti] [명] 안전
sanitation [sæ̀nitéiʃən] [명] 위생

03 전화목적파악 ▶ 정답 ⑤

듣·기·대·본

(*Cellphone rings.*)

M: Hi, Emily.

W: Hi, David. I have a question for you. Are you still interested in volunteer work?

M: Of course. I love giving back to the community. Why do you ask?

W: Our local animal shelter is organizing an adoption event, and we need volunteers to help with the preparations.

M: Oh, that's wonderful.

W: Would you like to join us? I know that you love animals.

M: Well, let me think about it. When do you need to know by?

W: We need to finalize the volunteer schedule by this Friday.

M: OK. I'll let you know by tomorrow.

우·리·말·해·석

(휴대폰이 울린다.)

남: 안녕, Emily.

여: 안녕, David. 나는 네게 질문이 하나 있어. 너는 아직도 자원봉사 활동에 관심이 있니?

남: 당연하지. 나는 지역 사회에 돌려주는 것을 정말 좋아해. 왜 물어봐?

여: 우리 지역 동물 보호소가 입양 행사를 준비하고 있는데 우리는 그 준비를 도와줄 자원봉사자들이 필요해.

남: 오, 그거 멋진걸.

여: 우리와 함께 할래? 나는 네가 동물들을 정말 좋아한다는 것을 알아.

남: 음, 그것에 대해 생각해 볼게. 언제까지 알려줘야 해?
여: 우리는 이번 주 금요일까지 자원봉사자 일정을 마무리 지어야 해.
남: 알겠어. 난 내일까지 네게 알려줄게.

단·어·및·표·현
organize [ɔ́ːrɡənàiz] 통 준비하다, 조직하다
adoption [ədápʃən] 명 입양
preparation [prèpəréiʃən] 명 준비
finalize [fáinəlàiz] 통 마무리 짓다

04 수치파악(시각) ▶ 정답 ②

듣·기·대·본
W: Harry, have you decided which swimming class to take?
M: Mom, I'm thinking about taking the afternoon class at 5 p.m.
W: Don't you think you will be too tired after school?
M: School finishes around 4 p.m., so I can rest for about an hour.
W: But you often meet up with your classmates after school to work on school projects.
M: Hm… You're right, Mom.
W: Why don't you take a morning lesson? They have classes at 6 a.m. and 7 a.m.
M: That's a better idea. 6 a.m. is too early for me. I will sign up for the 7 a.m. class.
W: Sounds good.

우·리·말·해·석
여: Harry, 너는 어떤 수영 수업을 들 건지 결정했니?
남: 엄마, 저는 오후 5시 수업을 들을까 생각중이에요.
여: 방과 후에 너는 너무 피곤할 것 같지 않니?
남: 학교는 오후 4시쯤에 끝나니까 저는 대략 한 시간 정도 쉴 수 있어요.
여: 하지만 너는 방과 후에 종종 학교 과제를 하기 위해 반 친구들과 만나잖니.
남: 흠… 엄마 말이 맞아요, 엄마.
여: 오전 수업을 듣는 게 어떠니? 그들은 오전 6시와 오전 7시에 수업이 있어.
남: 그게 더 좋은 생각이네요. 오전 6시는 제게 너무 일러요. 저는 오전 7시 수업에 등록할게요.
여: 좋은 생각이구나.

단·어·및·표·현
rest [rest] 통 쉬다
meet up with ~와 만나다
work on ~에 대한 작업을 하다

05 심정추론 ▶ 정답 ③

듣·기·대·본
M: Ms. Wallace, thank you for coming by our shop.
W: Thank you for calling me. So, where is it?
M: Here. It just came in from abroad. Is this the clock you were looking for?
W: Oh, my! Yes!
M: It wasn't easy to find a clock this old in working order.
W: I can imagine. This antique clock looks the same as the one in my grandparents' photo.
M: Will you take it?
W: Of course! I can't wait to present it to my granny.

M: I'm so glad you like it.
W: Thank you for finding this. It means so much to me.

우·리·말·해·석
① 속상한　　　　② 후회하는　　　　③ 아주 기뻐하는
④ 지루해하는　　　⑤ 당황스러운

남: Wallace 씨, 저희 가게에 들러 주셔서 감사합니다.
여: 제게 연락해 주셔서 감사해요. 그래서, 그것은 어디에 있나요?
남: 여기 있습니다. 이것은 막 해외에서 도착했습니다. 이것이 당신이 찾던 시계가 맞나요?
여: 어머나! 맞아요!
남: 정상적으로 작동하는 이렇게 오래된 시계를 찾는 것은 쉽지 않았어요.
여: 그럴 것 같아요. 이 골동품 시계는 제 조부모님의 사진에 있는 것과 똑같아 보여요.
남: 그것을 구매하시겠어요?
여: 그럼요! 저는 이것을 제 할머니께 빨리 드리고 싶어요.
남: 손님이 그것을 마음에 들어하시니 기쁘네요.
여: 이것을 찾아주셔서 감사해요. 그것은 제게 큰 의미가 있어요.

단·어·및·표·현
come by 잠깐 들르다
come in 도착하다, 들어오다
abroad [əbrɔ́ːd] 부 해외에서
in working order 정상적으로 작동하고 있는
antique [æntíːk] 형 골동품인
mean [miːn] 통 (~에게) …의 의미[가치]가 있다

06 그림상황에적절한대화찾기 ▶ 정답 ①

듣·기·대·본
① M: Can I help you with anything?
　W: Sure. Please stir the soup for me, will you?
② M: Can you do the dishes while I clean the living room?
　W: I can't. I'm taking care of the baby.
③ M: We need to buy some beef for dinner.
　W: Okay. Let's go to the meat section over there.
④ M: There's something in my soup.
　W: Oh, no. I'll call the waiter and complain.
⑤ M: What are you doing in the kitchen?
　W: I'm trying to fix the oven. It's not working.

우·리·말·해·석
① 남: 내가 뭐라도 도와줄까?
　여: 그래. 나를 위해 수프를 저어줄래?
② 남: 내가 거실을 청소하는 동안 네가 설거지를 해줄 수 있어?
　여: 나는 할 수 없어. 나는 아기를 돌보고 있어.
③ 남: 우리는 저녁 식사를 위해 약간의 소고기를 살 필요가 있어.
　여: 알았어. 저기에 있는 고기 섹션으로 가자.
④ 남: 내 수프에 뭔가 있어.
　여: 오, 이런. 내가 웨이터를 불러서 항의할게.
⑤ 남: 부엌에서 뭐하고 있어?
　여: 나는 오븐을 고치고 있어. 그것은 작동이 안 돼.

단·어·및·표·현
stir [stəːr] 통 젓다, (저어 가며) 섞다
complain [kəmpléin] 통 항의하다, 불평하다

07 부탁(요청)한일파악 ▶ 정답 ①

듣·기·대·본

(*Telephone rings.*)
M: Hello.
W: Honey, it's me. Are you on your way home?
M: Yeah, I'm on the subway. I think I'll be home in 30 minutes.
W: Good. I'm making spaghetti for dinner.
M: That sounds delicious. I can't wait to get home.
W: I was trying to make a salad as well, but I'm out of ingredients.
M: Oh, what are you missing? I can buy whatever you need.
W: Then, can you buy some tomatoes on your way home?
M: No problem. Leave it to me.

우•리•말•해•석
(전화벨이 울린다.)
남: 여보세요.
여: 여보, 나야. 당신 집에 오는 길이야?
남: 응, 지하철이야. 30분 후에 집에 도착할 거 같아.
여: 좋아. 저녁 식사로 스파게티를 만들고 있어.
남: 맛있겠다. 빨리 집에 가고 싶다.
여: 샐러드도 만들려고 하고 있었는데, 재료가 떨어졌어.
남: 오, 뭐가 없는데? 당신이 필요한 게 뭐든 내가 살 수 있어.
여: 그럼, 집에 오는 길에 토마토 좀 사 올 수 있어?
남: 문제없어. 내게 맡겨.

단•어•및•표•현
on one's way home 집에 오는 길에
can't wait to + 동사원형 ~하기를 기다릴 수 없다, 빨리 ~하고 싶다

08 담화미언급 ▶ 정답 ⑤

듣•기•대•본
W: Good morning, students! Our school now has a Student Computer Lab. There are personal computers, printers, and scanners available for all students. The lab is on the second floor, inside the library. It is open during library hours. When using the lab, please do not store files or user names. Also, you cannot bring food or drinks inside the lab. To access the wireless network, please ask our librarian, Mr. Banks.

우•리•말•해•석
여: 안녕하세요, 학생 여러분! 우리 학교에 이제 학생 컴퓨터실이 생겼습니다. 모든 학생들이 PC와 프린터, 스캐너를 사용할 수 있습니다. 컴퓨터실은 2층 도서관 내에 있습니다. 도서관 이용 시간에 개방됩니다. 컴퓨터실을 이용할 때, 파일이나 사용자 이름을 저장하지 마세요. 또한, 컴퓨터실 안으로 음식이나 음료를 가지고 들어갈 수 없습니다. 무선 네트워크에 접속하려면, 사서인 Banks 씨에게 요청하세요.

단•어•및•표•현
access [ǽksès] [동] 접속하다, 접근하다

09 담화화제추론 ▶ 정답 ③

듣•기•대•본
W: This sport first started out as a skill used in hunting and in battle. Now it is one of the most popular Olympic sports. A player aims to shoot an arrow at a target with the use of a bow. To win, a player needs to shoot arrows as close to the center of a target as possible. Determination and concentration are very important for the players of this sport.

우•리•말•해•석
여: 이 스포츠는 사냥이나 전투에서 사용되던 기술로 처음 시작되었습니다. 이제는 가장 인기 있는 올림픽 스포츠 중 하나입니다. 선수는 활을 사용하여 화살을 과녁에 맞추는 것을 목표로 합니다. 이기기 위해서는, 선수는 과녁 중앙에 가능한 한 가장 가깝게 화살을 쏴야 합니다. 결단력과 집중력은 이 스포츠의 선수들에게 매우 중요합니다.

단•어•및•표•현
aim to + 동사원형 ~하는 것을 목표로 하다
arrow [ǽrou] [명] 화살

LISTENING ADVICE
● 'shoot': How to pronounce [ʃ]
'sh'는 입을 모으고 입술은 붙이지 않은 채로 성대를 울리지 않은 채 바람소리를 내듯이 소리를 냅니다. '쉬' 혹은 '쉿'이라고 말할 때와 비슷하게 발음하는 것으로, [s]와는 다른 소리가 납니다.

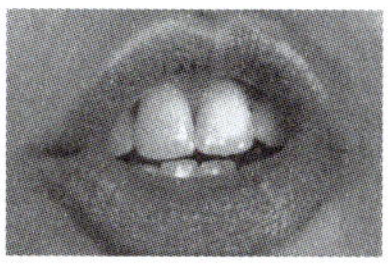

10 어색한대화찾기 ▶ 정답 ③

듣•기•대•본
① M: Hello. Can I speak to Minji?
W: Speaking. Who's calling, please?
② M: What did the weather forecast say?
W: It's going to be sunny and warm.
③ M: Where shall we meet?
W: Tomorrow at three o'clock.
④ M: May I see your ticket and passport, please?
W: Yes. Here you are.
⑤ M: What are you listening to?
W: Beethoven's 3rd symphony.

우•리•말•해•석
① 남: 여보세요. 민지와 통화할 수 있나요?
여: 전데요. 누구세요?
② 남: 일기 예보에서 뭐라고 말했니?
여: 맑고 따뜻할 거래.
③ 남: 어디에서 만날까?
여: 내일 3시에.
④ 남: 표와 여권 좀 볼 수 있을까요?
여: 네. 여기 있어요.
⑤ 남: 뭘 듣고 있니?
여: 베토벤의 제3번 교향곡.

단•어•및•표•현
passport [pǽspɔːrt] [명] 여권

11 할일파악 ▶ 정답 ②

듣•기•대•본
M: Hey, Becky. Is our booth all set for the school food festival?
W: Almost. The ice cream machine is fantastic!
M: That's cool. Do we have a box for the money?
W: Dan will bring us one.
M: Great. Oh, we don't have any chairs to sit on.

W: Can you bring some from our classroom? I'll make a sign for the ice cream prices.

M: Sure. But Jenny's already made the sign. Why don't you get some syrup for the ice cream?

W: OK. I'll go and buy some.

M: Thanks.

우·리·말·해·석

남: 이봐, Becky. 학교 음식 축제를 위한 우리 부스 준비는 다 됐어?

여: 거의 다 됐어. 아이스크림 기계는 정말 끝내줘!

남: 아주 좋아. 돈을 넣을 박스는 있어?

여: Dan이 하나를 가져올 거야.

남: 훌륭해. 오, 앉을 의자가 하나도 없네.

여: 네가 우리 교실에서 몇 개 가져다줄 수 있니? 나는 아이스크림 가격을 적은 표지판을 만들게.

남: 그래. 하지만 Jenny가 이미 표지판을 만들었어. 너는 아이스크림 만드는 데 필요한 시럽을 사오는 게 어때?

여: 알았어. 내가 가서 사올게.

남: 고마워.

단·어·및·표·현

price[prais] 명 가격

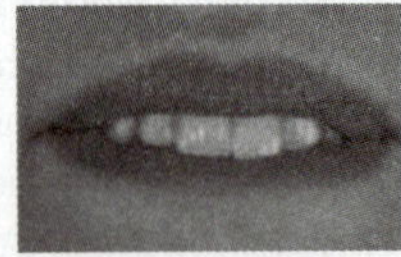

LISTENING ADVICE

'festival'과 'fantastic'의 [f] 발음을 주의 깊게 들어보세요.

● **festival, fantastic: How to pronounce [f]**

f는 윗니로 아랫입술을 살짝 물어서 바람을 내보내면서 [프] 하고 발음합니다.

12 도표정보파악 ▶ 정답 ①

듣·기·대·본

M: Honey, what are you doing?

W: I'm looking for a tablet PC for our daughter. Can we decide on one together?

M: Sure. Do you have anything in mind?

W: Not yet. Do you think we should buy one with a bigger screen?

M: I guess 11 inches will be big enough for her.

W: Okay. The 11-inch models come in two colors. She said she likes white better than grey.

M: Then we should choose the white one. How about the storage?

W: She will mainly use it for taking lectures online. She won't need a lot of storage space for that.

M: I agree. Let's get her the one with less storage.

W: Great. Let's order this one.

우·리·말·해·석

	모델	화면 크기(인치)	색상	용량(GB)
①	A	11	흰색	128
②	B	11	회색	128
③	C	11	흰색	256
④	D	13	회색	128
⑤	E	13	회색	256

남: 여보, 뭐하고 있어요?

여: 저는 우리 딸에게 줄 태블릿 PC를 찾고 있어요. 우리 같이 하나 정할까요?

남: 물론이죠. 당신은 염두에 둔 것이 있나요?

여: 아직요. 당신은 우리가 더 큰 화면의 것을 사야 한다고 생각하나요?

남: 저는 그녀에게 11인치면 충분히 클 거라고 생각해요.

여: 네. 11인치 모델들은 두 가지 색으로 나오네요. 그녀는 회색보다 흰색이 더 좋다고 했어요.

남: 그러면 우리는 흰색의 것을 골라야겠어요. 용량은 어때요?

여: 그녀는 그것을 주로 온라인 강의를 듣기 위해 사용할 거예요. 그녀는 그것을 위해 많은 저장 공간이 필요하지 않을 거예요.

남: 동의해요. 그녀에게 더 적은 용량의 것으로 사 주죠.

여: 좋아요. 이것으로 주문하죠.

단·어·및·표·현

decide on ~을 정하다, 결정하다

have A in mind A를 염두에 두다

come in (상품 등이) 나오다

mainly[méinli] 부 주로

take a lecture 강의를 듣다

storage space 저장 공간

13 수치파악(날짜) ▶ 정답 ③

듣·기·대·본

M: Hey, Nicole. What are you doing?

W: Oh, hey, Paul. I was looking at this pop-up store's Instagram account.

M: What kind of pop-up store is it?

W: It's a clothing brand known for street fashion.

M: I like street fashion. Can I go with you?

W: Sure. The pop-up store will be open from September 10th to 20th.

M: I would like to go on the weekend. Does either the 16th or 17th work for you?

W: I have something on the 17th. But I think the 16th would work for me.

M: Perfect!

우·리·말·해·석

남: 이봐, Nicole. 뭐 하고 있니?

여: 오, 안녕, Paul. 나는 이 팝업 스토어의 인스타그램 계정을 보고 있었어.

남: 그게 무슨 종류의 팝업 스토어인데?

여: 이것은 스트릿 패션으로 유명한 의류 브랜드야.

남: 나 스트릿 패션 좋아해. 내가 너와 함께 가도 되니?

여: 물론이지. 그 팝업 스토어는 9월 10일부터 20일까지 열릴 거야.

남: 나는 주말에 가고 싶어. 16일이나 17일 둘 중 너에게 괜찮은 날이 있니?

여: 나는 17일에 일이 있어. 하지만 16일은 괜찮을 것 같아.

남: 완벽해!

단·어·및·표·현

account[əkáunt] 명 (정보 서비스) 계정

known for ~으로 유명한

either A or B A나 B 둘 중 하나

work for ~에게 문제없다, 좋다

14 한일파악 ▶ 정답 ③

듣·기·대·본

M: Leona, how was your weekend? Did you go to the farm like you'd planned?

W: Yes. The farm is my aunt and uncle's. It was so nice!

M: Sounds like you had a good time.

W: I helped them out a lot. I'm just sorry that it rained. We couldn't have a campfire.

M: Oh, too bad. What did you do to help them?

W: I did some work in the fields. I planted new blueberry bushes, too.

M: That's nice. I've never been to a farm.

W: Come with me next time.

우·리·말·해·석

남: Leona, 네 주말은 어땠니? 네가 계획했던 대로 그 농장에 갔었니?

여: 응. 그 농장은 내 이모와 이모부네 농장이야. 정말 좋았어!

남: 너는 좋은 시간을 보낸 것 같구나.

여: 나는 그들을 많이 도와드렸어. 나는 그저 비가 와서 유감이었어. 우리는 캠프파이어를 하지 못했거든.

남: 오, 안됐네. 너는 그들을 돕기 위해 무엇을 했니?

여: 나는 밭에서 일을 좀 했어. 나는 새 블루베리 관목도 심었어.

남: 잘했네. 나는 농장에 한 번도 가본 적이 없어.

여: 다음에 나랑 같이 가자.

단·어·및·표·현

like[laik] 웹 ～대로[처럼]

field[fi:ld] 뎽 밭, 들판

plant[plænt] 뎽 (나무·씨앗 등을) 심다

bush[buʃ] 뎽 관목, 덤불

15 담화목적파악 ▶ 정답 ①

듣·기·대·본

W: Welcome to Sports Village, the best indoor sports center in town! Before you start your exciting adventure, let me tell you about our rules. First, you should be 120 cm or over to use our facilities. Second, if you wear inappropriate shoes like slippers or high heels, you will not be able to participate in some sports activities for safety reasons. Third, no outside food or drink is allowed. Have a great time.

우·리·말·해·석

여: 도시 내 최고의 실내 스포츠센터인 Sports Village에 오신 것을 환영합니다! 여러분이 신나는 모험을 시작하시기 전에 제가 이곳의 규칙에 대해 말씀드리겠습니다. 첫째, 저희 시설을 이용하기 위해서 여러분은 120cm 이상이어야 합니다. 둘째, 만약 여러분이 슬리퍼나 하이힐 같은 부적합한 신발을 신고 계신다면, 여러분은 안전상의 이유로 몇몇 스포츠 활동들에 참여하실 수 없을 것입니다. 셋째, 외부 음식이나 음료는 허용되지 않습니다. 즐거운 시간 되십시오.

단·어·및·표·현

indoor[índɔ̀ːr] 뎽 실내의, 실내용의

adventure[ədvéntʃər] 뎽 모험

facility[fəsíləti] 뎽 시설, 기관

inappropriate[ìnəpróupriit] 뎽 부적합한, 부적절한

participate in ～에 참여하다, 참가하다

16 수치계산(금액) ▶ 정답 ④

듣·기·대·본

M: Welcome to Happy Camping. How may I help you?

W: I'd like to book a campsite for this weekend.

M: It's 25 dollars for four people. The cost of electricity is included.

W: I'll take it. Can I rent a tent?

M: It's 15 dollars. You can also get a grill for 10 dollars.

W: I'll just take the tent. Can I use this discount coupon?

M: Sure. You can get 5 dollars off with the coupon.

W: Okay, here's my credit card.

우·리·말·해·석

남: Happy Camping에 오신 것을 환영합니다. 어떻게 도와드릴까요?

여: 저는 이번 주말 캠핑 자리를 예약하고 싶어요.

남: 4인에 대해 25달러입니다. 전기 요금이 포함되어 있습니다.

여: 그것으로 할게요. 제가 텐트를 빌릴 수 있나요?

남: 15달러입니다. 10달러에 그릴도 빌리실 수 있습니다.

여: 저는 텐트만 할게요. 제가 이 할인 쿠폰을 사용할 수 있나요?

남: 물론입니다. 쿠폰으로 5달러를 할인받으실 수 있습니다.

여: 좋아요, 여기 제 신용카드예요.

단·어·및·표·현

book[buk] 뎽 예약하다

campsite[kǽmpsàit] 뎽 캠핑 자리

electricity[ilektrísəti] 뎽 전기

rent[rent] 뎽 빌리다

17 알맞은응답찾기 ▶ 정답 ⑤

듣·기·대·본

W: Hello, how can I help you?

M: Hi, I'd like to order a birthday cake for my daughter.

W: Fantastic! How old is she?

M: She'll be 6 this Friday.

W: Excellent! We have vanilla, chocolate and strawberry cakes. Which one do you want?

M: I'll go with a vanilla cake. And can I have strawberry filling in it?

W: Of course. Would you like to put a message on the cake?

M: Yes, please write "Happy Birthday, Amy" on it.

우·리·말·해·석

① 이번 주 금요일에 찾으러 올게요.

② 초 여섯 개가 필요해요.

③ 아니요, 저는 어떤 메시지도 받지 않았어요.

④ 제 딸은 딸기를 아주 좋아해요.

⑤ 네, "생일 축하한다, Amy"라고 그 위에 써주세요.

여: 안녕하세요, 무엇을 도와드릴까요?

남: 안녕하세요, 제 딸을 위한 생일 케이크를 주문하고 싶습니다.

여: 멋지시군요! 그녀는 몇 살인가요?

남: 그녀는 이번 주 금요일에 6살이 됩니다.

여: 잘됐군요! 저희는 바닐라, 초콜릿, 그리고 딸기 케이크가 있어요. 어떤 것을 원하세요?

남: 바닐라 케이크로 하겠습니다. 그리고 그 안에 딸기 소를 넣어주실 수 있나요?

여: 물론이죠. 케이크 위에 메시지를 넣으시겠습니까?

남: 네, "생일 축하한다, Amy"라고 그 위에 써주세요.

단·어·및·표·현

filling[fíliŋ] 뎽 (파이 등 음식의) 소[속]

듣·기·대·본

M: Hi. What can I do for you?

W: Hi, I'm looking for the new Max series sneakers. I heard that you sell them.

M: Yes, we do. What size do you need? We're out of size 240 at the moment.

W: Oh, no. I wear size 240. When will you get more in?

M: Probably by tomorrow morning.

W: Alright. I'll come back then.

M: Before you come back, I'd recommend that you download our app. You can get discount coupons on it.

W: Oh, I didn't know that. Thanks for the tip.

우·리·말·해·석

① 다행이네요. 고객님의 사이즈는 재고가 있어요.

② 좋습니다. 제가 스니커즈가 꼭 들어오도록 할게요.

③ 멋져요. 저는 지금 바로 한 켤레 살게요.

④ 오, 저는 그것을 몰랐어요. 조언 주셔서 감사해요.

⑤ 물론이죠. 고객님은 오늘 그 쿠폰들을 사용하실 수 있습니다.

남: 안녕하세요. 무엇을 도와드릴까요?

여: 안녕하세요, 저는 새로운 Max 시리즈 스니커즈를 찾고 있어요. 저는 여기서 그것을 판다고 들었어요.

남: 네, 그렇습니다. 고객님은 어떤 사이즈를 원하시나요? 현재 240 사이즈는 품절입니다.

여: 오, 이런. 저는 240을 신어요. 언제 더 입고되나요?

남: 아마 내일 아침까지는 입고될 것입니다.

여: 알겠습니다. 저는 그때 다시 올게요.

남: 다시 오시기 전에, 저희 앱을 다운 받으시길 추천드립니다. 고객님은 거기서 할인 쿠폰을 받으실 수 있습니다.

여: 오, 저는 그것을 몰랐어요. 조언 주셔서 감사해요.

단·어·및·표·현

be out of ～이 품절되다, 떨어지다

at the moment 현재, 바로 지금

get ~ in (식품·물자 등을) 들여오다, 사오다

probably [prάbəbli] ⑨ 아마

듣·기·대·본

W: Mr. Austin, you know I'm in charge of the School Career Day, right?

M: Sure, Ms. Webster. What's the matter?

W: I want to invite a fashion designer as one of the lecturers, and I hear that you have one as a close friend.

M: Oh, yes. A shoe designer. Do you want me to call him?

W: Could you, please?

M: No problem. When is the event?

W: It's October 10th. Am I asking too early?

M: Not at all. He's a pretty busy man, so I think it's safe to ask early on. Just give me a day or so.

W: Of course. I owe you a big one.

우·리·말·해·석

① 좋아요. 그는 그가 올 수 있다고 말했어요.

② 그럼요. 제가 당신에게 큰 빚을 졌네요.

③ 정말요? 저는 그가 당신의 전화에 답을 해서 기뻐요.

④ 물론이죠. 저는 당신의 행사에서 강연을 할 수 있어요.

⑤ 죄송해요. 우리는 10월까지 기다려야 할 거예요.

여: Austin 선생님, 당신은 제가 학교 진로의 날을 담당하고 있는 거 아시죠, 그렇죠?

남: 물론이죠, Webster 선생님. 무엇이 문제인가요?

여: 저는 강연자 중 한 명으로 패션 디자이너를 초청하고 싶은데, 당신이 친한 친구로 (패션 디자이너) 한 명이 있다고 들었어요.

남: 오, 네. 신발 디자이너예요. 당신은 제가 그에게 전화 걸기를 바라나요?

여: 그래 주실 수 있나요?

남: 문제없어요. 행사가 언제죠?

여: 10월 10일이에요. 제가 너무 일찍 물어보는 건가요?

남: 전혀요. 그는 매우 바쁜 사람이니 일찍 물어보는 게 안전한 것 같아요. 제게 하루 정도만 (시간을) 주세요.

여: 그럼요. 제가 당신에게 큰 빚을 졌네요.

단·어·및·표·현

be in charge of ～을 담당하다

invite [inváit] ⑧ 초청하다, 초대하다

lecturer [léktʃərər] ⑨ 강연자, 강사

or so ～정도, 쯤

give a lecture 강연하다

듣·기·대·본

M: Elliot and Sarah are close friends. Elliot finds out that Sarah will spend her whole summer vacation in a faraway province with her family. He is a little disappointed that he cannot spend any time with her for the next few months. So, he wants to ask her to contact him over the phone as often as possible. In this situation, what would Elliot most likely say to Sarah?

Elliot: Let's call or text each other often.

우·리·말·해·석

① 너는 우리 집에 머물면 어때?　② 서로 자주 전화나 문자 하자.

③ 나는 먼 지방으로 이사 갈 거야.　④ 너와 같이 시간을 보내는 것이 신나.

⑤ 너는 여름 동안 뭔가 계획이 있어?

남: Elliot과 Sarah는 친한 친구이다. Elliot는 Sarah가 그녀의 여름 휴가 전체를 그녀의 가족들과 먼 지방에서 보낼 것이라는 것을 알게 된다. 그는 다음 몇 달 동안 그녀와 조금도 시간을 같이 보낼 수 없다는 것에 약간 실망한다. 그래서, 그는 그녀에게 가능한 한 자주 전화로 그에게 연락하라고 부탁하고 싶다. 이런 상황에서, Elliot은 Sarah에게 뭐라고 말하겠는가?

Elliot: 서로 자주 전화나 문자 하자.

단·어·및·표·현

faraway [fάːrəwèi] ⑨ 먼

province [prάvins] ⑨ 지방

disappointed [dìsəpɔ́intid] ⑨ 실망한

contact [kάntækt] ⑧ 연락하다

Words & Expressions Review

1. 마무리 짓다	2. ～에 대한 작업을 하다	3. 표지판
4. ～으로 유명한	5. 관목, 덤불	6. (상품 등이) 나오다
7. 해외에서	8. A의 재고가 있다	9. 위생

10. ~을 찾다 [찾아오다]	11. 교향곡	12. 캠핑 자리
13. 실내의, 실내용의	14. 구역, 구획	15. 접속하다, 접근하다
16. ~와 만나다	17. 사서	18. 밭, 들판
19. 쉬다	20. ~정도, 쯤	21. 골동품인
22. 먼	23. 연락하다	24. 활
25. 여권	26. (정보 서비스) 계정	27. 잠깐 들르다
28. 지방	29. 준비하다, 조직하다	30. 젓다, 섞다
31. (파이 등 음식의) 소[속]	32. 강연하다	33. 집중력, 집중
34. 만들어 내다	35. 화살	36. ~이 떨어지다, 품절되다
37. 요리의	38. 초청하다, 초대하다	39. 무선의
40. 실망한	41. 주로	42. 집에 오는 길에
43. 전기	44. 결단력, 결정	

Listening Test

영어듣기 모의고사 18회

| 정 | 답 |

01 ④	02 ④	03 ⑤	04 ②	05 ③
06 ①	07 ①	08 ⑤	09 ①	10 ③
11 ⑤	12 ③	13 ⑤	14 ②	15 ②
16 ④	17 ④	18 ⑤	19 ⑤	20 ④

01 그림정보파악(대화) ▶ 정답 ④

듣·기·대·본

W: I'm looking for a bicycle for my son. Can you recommend any?

M: Can he ride a two-wheel bicycle?

W: No, he needs a four-wheel bicycle.

M: Okay, ma'am. This four-wheel bicycle with a front basket is nice.

W: I see. Do you have any other models?

M: Yes. Please come this way. This four-wheel bicycle has an adjustable back, so a child can rest in the bike seat. It has a front basket, too.

W: Oh, I like it. I'll take it.

우·리·말·해·석

여: 전 제 아들을 위한 자전거를 찾고 있어요. 추천해 주실래요?

남: 그는 두발자전거를 탈 수 있나요?

여: 아니요, 그는 네발자전거가 필요해요.

남: 알겠습니다, 손님. 앞 바구니가 있는 이 네발자전거가 좋아요.

여: 그렇군요. 다른 모델도 있나요?

남: 네. 이쪽으로 오세요. 이 네발자전거는 조정 가능한 등받이가 있어서 아이가 자전거 안장에 앉아 기댈 수 있어요. 이것도 앞 바구니가 있고요.

여: 아, 이것이 마음에 드네요. 전 이것으로 할게요.

단·어·및·표·현

adjustable [ədʒʌ́stəbl] [형] 조정 가능한

02 대화미언급 ▶ 정답 ④

듣·기·대·본

W: Paul, are you interested in Summer Sports Camp?

M: Oh, I love summer sports. When is it?

W: It starts on July 20th.

M: How long is the camp?

W: It's a week, from Monday to Sunday.

M: I think I can join. So, you mean we'll be doing summer sports like scuba-diving and waterskiing?

W: Exactly. And the program also includes safety education.

M: Sounds good! I'll ask my mom if I can attend the camp.

W: Tell Mr. Anderson if you want to apply for the camp. He'll give you more details about it.

우·리·말·해·석

여: Paul, 너는 여름 스포츠 캠프에 관심 있니?

남: 오, 난 여름 스포츠를 정말 좋아해. 그게 언제야?

여: 그것은 7월 20일에 시작해.

남: 캠프 기간은 얼마나 돼?

여: 그것은 월요일부터 일요일까지, 일주일이야.

남: 나 참가할 수 있을 것 같아. 그럼, 네 말은 우리가 스쿠버다이빙과 수상스키 같은 여름 스포츠를 하게 될 거란 거지?

여: 정확해. 그리고 이 프로그램에는 안전교육도 포함돼 있어.

남: 좋은데! 나는 엄마에게 내가 캠프에 참석할 수 있는지 물어볼 거야.

여: 만약 네가 캠프에 신청하고 싶다면 Anderson 선생님에게 말해. 그가 네게 그것에 대한 세부 사항들을 알려줄 거야.

단·어·및·표·현

attend [əténd] [동] 참석하다

details [ditéilz] [명] 세부 사항, 정보

03 전화목적파악 ▶ 정답 ⑤

듣·기·대·본

(*Telephone rings.*)

W: Hello, can I speak to Michael?

M: This is he. Who's calling, please?

W: Hi, it's me, Anne. Do you have any plans today?

M: Not really. I just need to pick up some books from the library. Why?

W: Would you like to go to a hip hop concert tonight? I got free tickets.

M: I'm sorry, but I don't like hip hop music very much.

W: Oh, I didn't know that. Hmm, whom should I go with, then?

M: Ask Kenny. I heard that he's really into hip hop.

W: Really? Great! Thanks, Michael.

우·리·말·해·석

(전화벨이 울린다.)

여: 여보세요, Michael과 통화할 수 있을까요?

남: 전데요. 누구세요?

여: 안녕, 나야, Anne. 너 오늘 무슨 계획 있니?

남: 별로. 그냥 도서관에서 책 몇 권만 빌려오면 돼. 왜?

여: 오늘 밤에 힙합 콘서트에 갈래? 나 공짜 표가 생겼거든.

남: 미안하지만, 난 힙합 음악을 그다지 좋아하지 않아.
여: 아, 그런지 몰랐어. 흠, 그럼 누구랑 같이 가지?
남: Kenny한테 물어봐. 걔가 힙합 음악에 정말 빠져 있다고 들었어.
여: 정말? 잘됐다! 고마워, Michael.

단·어·및·표·현
be into ~ ~에 빠져 있다

04 수치파악(시각) ▶ 정답 ②

듣·기·대·본
M: Hey, Diane. You like the actor Kim Dong Hun, right?

W: Yes, I love him. Why?

M: I have two tickets for the premiere of his latest movie. Would you like to go with me?

W: I'd love to! When is it?

M: It's at 2 p.m. this Saturday. It takes about an hour to get there from my place, so we should meet up at 1 p.m.

W: Hmm… How about we meet a little earlier and have lunch together before we go?

M: That sounds great! Let's meet at 12 p.m. at my place.

W: Okay, I'll see you then.

우·리·말·해·석
남: 이봐, Diane. 너 김동훈 배우 좋아하지, 맞지?

여: 맞아, 난 그를 정말 좋아해. 왜?

남: 나 그의 최신 영화 시사회 표가 두 장 있어. 나랑 같이 가고 싶니?

여: 그러고 싶어! 그게 언제인데?

남: 이번 주 토요일 오후 2시야. 우리 집에서 거기에 도착하는 데 한 시간 정도 걸리니까 우리는 오후 1시에 만나야 해.

여: 흠… 우리 조금 더 일찍 만나서 가기 전에 같이 점심 먹는 건 어때?

남: 그거 좋다! 우리 집에서 오후 12시에 만나자.

여: 알겠어, 그때 보자.

단·어·및·표·현
premiere [primjέər] 몡 시사회, 초연
Would you like to + 동사원형? (제안) 너는 ~하고 싶니?

05 심정추론 ▶ 정답 ③

듣·기·대·본
M: Mom, can I hang out with Mike on Friday evening?

W: Sure. Just don't be out too late.

M: But this is special. Guess what, Mom? I'm going to the football match!

W: Really? You said the tickets were sold out.

M: Mike got the tickets as a birthday present, and he's taking me!

W: That's amazing. You really wanted to go to the match.

M: I know. I'm so excited that he asked me.

W: That's great news. Is any adult coming along?

M: Yeah, Mike's dad is taking us.

W: Good.

우·리·말·해·석
① 속상한   ② 미안한   ③ 행복한
④ 지루해하는   ⑤ 당황스러운

남: 엄마, 저 금요일 저녁에 Mike와 놀아도 돼요?

여: 그럼. 단지 너무 늦게까지 밖에 있지는 말렴.

남: 하지만 이번엔 특별해요. 그거 알아요, 엄마? 저 미식축구 경기에 갈 거예요!

여: 정말이니? 너는 표가 매진되었다고 했잖니.

남: Mike가 생일 선물로 표를 받았는데 그가 저를 데려간대요!

여: 놀랍구나. 너는 정말 그 경기에 가고 싶어 했잖니.

남: 맞아요. 저는 그가 제게 물어봐 줘서 정말 신나요.

여: 좋은 소식이구나. 누군가 어른이 함께 가니?

남: 네, Mike의 아버지가 저희를 데려가실 거예요.

여: 좋구나.

단·어·및·표·현
hang out with ~와 놀다, 시간을 보내다, 어울리다
sold out 표가 매진된
come along 함께 가다

06 그림상황에적절한대화찾기 ▶ 정답 ①

듣·기·대·본
① W: What seems to be the problem?
   M: I'll have to open it up and check what's wrong.
② W: Where can I get my laptop fixed?
   M: You'll need to take it to the computer repair shop.
③ W: Where did you buy that scarf?
   M: I didn't buy it. My girlfriend made it for me.
④ W: Don't forget to turn off the lights when you leave the room.
   M: Okay. I won't forget.
⑤ W: I'd like to order a cheeseburger and a Diet Coke.
   M: Okay, that will be 10 dollars.

우·리·말·해·석
① 여: 뭐가 문제인 거 같나요?
   남: 그것을 열어서 무엇이 잘못됐는지 확인해야 합니다.
② 여: 어디서 제 노트북을 고칠 수 있나요?
   남: 그것을 컴퓨터 수리점에 가져가야 합니다.
③ 여: 그 스카프 어디서 샀어요?
   남: 이거 제가 안 샀어요. 제 여자 친구가 저를 위해 만들었어요.
④ 여: 그 방을 나갈 때 불을 끄는 것을 잊지 마세요.
   남: 알았어요. 안 잊을게요.
⑤ 여: 치즈 버거와 다이어트 콜라를 주문하고 싶어요.
   남: 알겠습니다, 10달러입니다.

단·어·및·표·현
laptop [lǽptὰp] 몡 노트북 컴퓨터

07 부탁(요청)한일파악 ▶ 정답 ①

듣·기·대·본
W: Hey, Adam. Did you hear about the new play at the community theater?

M: No, what is it about?

W: It's a comedy about student life. I saw a short preview video online, and it looked really funny.

M: Sounds interesting. Are tickets on sale already?

W: Yes. And there's a 15 percent discount for members of the community learning center.

M: Really? I'm a member!

W: Great! Could you book tickets for both of us, then?

M: Sure thing. I'll do it right away.

우·리·말·해·석
여: 안녕, Adam. 지역 극장에서 하는 새 연극에 대해 들었어?

남: 아니, 무엇에 관한 것인데?

여: 학생 생활에 관한 코미디야. 온라인에서 짧은 예고편 영상을 봤는데, 정말 재미있어 보였어.

남: 재미있겠다. 벌써 표를 판매하고 있어?

여: 응. 그리고 지역 교육 센터 회원을 위한 15% 할인이 있어.

남: 정말? 나 회원이야!

여: 잘됐다! 그럼 우리 둘을 위한 표를 예약해 줄 수 있어?

남: 물론이지. 바로 할게.

단·어·및·표·현

preview[príːvjùː] 몡 예고편

on sale 판매 중인

discount[diskáunt] 몡 할인

book[buk] 동 예약하다

08 담화미언급 ▶ 정답 ⑤

듣·기·대·본

W: Good afternoon, Jefferson Middle School students. This is Colin from the school broadcasting club. Starting next week, we will air a series of Special Jefferson Interviews every Friday. It'll be from 12 p.m. to 12:30 p.m. The guests will be our own fellow students. They will talk about topics such as grades, activities, friends, and more. You can join us via school-wide broadcasting, or on the school app. Thank you.

우·리·말·해·석

여: 좋은 오후입니다, Jefferson 중학교 학생 여러분. 저는 학교 방송부의 Colin입니다. 다음 주부터, 저희는 매주 금요일에 특별한 Jefferson 인터뷰 시리즈를 방송할 것입니다. 그것은 오후 12시부터 오후 12시 반까지 진행될 것입니다. 초대 손님은 우리 학우 여러분들이 될 것입니다. 그들은 성적이나, 활동, 친구 등과 같은 주제에 대해 이야기할 것입니다. 여러분은 전교 방송 또는 학교 앱을 통해 참여하실 수 있습니다. 감사합니다.

단·어·및·표·현

broadcasting[brɔ́ːdkæstiŋ] 몡 방송

air[ɛər] 동 방송하다

fellow[félou] 혱 학우의, 동등한 위치의

via[váiə] 졘 (특정한 사람·시스템 등을) 통하여

09 담화화제추론 ▶ 정답 ①

듣·기·대·본

M: This is a type of stationery. You can use this to convey messages. It is usually square in shape. You can write or draw anything on this. People usually use this when they need to leave a message or make a note of something. Some of these are sticky on the back. It's usually packaged in bundles so you can tear off a page from the whole pack.

우·리·말·해·석

남: 이것은 문구류의 한 종류이다. 당신은 메시지를 전달하기 위해 이것을 사용할 수 있다. 이것은 주로 네모난 모양이다. 당신은 이것에 무엇이든 쓰거나 그릴 수 있다. 사람들은 주로 이것을 메시지를 남기거나 무언가를 필기할 때 사용한다. 이것들 중 일부는 뒷면이 끈적거린다. 이것은 주로 묶음으로 포장되어 있어서 당신은 전체 묶음에서 한 장을 떼어낼 수 있다.

단·어·및·표·현

stationery[stéiʃənèri] 몡 문구류

convey[kənvéi] 동 전달하다

make a note of ~을 필기하다, 노트에 적다

sticky[stíki] 혱 끈적거리는

package[pǽkidʒ] 동 포장하다

bundle[bʌ́ndl] 몡 묶음, 꾸러미

tear off 떼어내다, 찢어내다

10 어색한대화찾기 ▶ 정답 ③

듣·기·대·본

① M: Do you have tickets for the show at 2:30?
   W: I'm sorry, sir. We're all sold out.
② M: May I check your baggage?
   W: Sure, here you are.
③ M: How much is it to send a letter to China?
   W: It will arrive tomorrow.
④ M: Could you show me the way to Seoul City Hall?
   W: Sure. It's not far from here.
⑤ M: I'm looking for something for my father's birthday.
   W: How about this watch?

우·리·말·해·석

① 남: 2시 30분 공연 입장권이 있습니까?
   여: 죄송합니다, 손님. 모두 다 팔렸습니다.
② 남: 짐을 확인해 봐도 되겠습니까?
   여: 물론이죠, 여기 있습니다.
③ 남: 중국으로 편지를 보내는 데 얼마입니까?
   여: 내일 도착할 것입니다.
④ 남: 서울 시청으로 가는 길 좀 알려주시겠습니까?
   여: 물론이죠. 여기서 멀지 않습니다.
⑤ 남: 아버지 생신 선물로 뭔가 찾고 있는데요.
   여: 이 시계는 어떠세요?

단·어·및·표·현

arrive[əráiv] 동 도착하다

11 할일파악 ▶ 정답 ⑤

듣·기·대·본

M: Mom, do you need any help cleaning the house?

W: Are you sure? Aren't you going out with your friends?

M: Nah, I just want to stay home today.

W: Wow, that's a first. Did you make your bed?

M: Yes. I also put the dirty clothes in the laundry.

W: I'm impressed. Help me wash the dishes then. Oh wait, you might drop the plates.

M: Hahaha... You're right. How about I just mop the floor?

W: That's a great idea.

우·리·말·해·석

남: 엄마, 집을 청소하는 데 어떤 도움이라도 필요하세요?

여: 너 진심이니? 너 친구들과 밖에 나가는 거 아니었니?

남: 아니요, 전 오늘은 그냥 집에 머물고 싶어요.

여: 와, 그건 처음 있는 일이구나. 너 침대는 정리했니?

남: 네, 또한 세탁물에 더러워진 옷들을 넣어놨어요.

여: 감동이구나. 그럼 설거지하는 것을 도와주렴. 오, 기다려, 네가 접시를 떨어뜨릴지도 모르겠다.

남: 하하하… 엄마가 옳아요. 그냥 제가 바닥을 걸레로 닦는 게 어때요?

여: 그거 아주 좋은 생각이야.

단·어·및·표·현
make one's bed 침대를 정리하다

12 도표정보파악 ▶ 정답 ③

듣·기·대·본
W: Honey, I think we need a clothes dryer.
M: I agree. It will be <u>convenient</u> in any type of weather. Let's find one online.
W: How much can we <u>afford</u>?
M: I don't think we can afford to spend more than $900.
W: You're right. Look, some of the dryers have smart functions.
M: With the smart functions, we can check <u>the drying process</u> on our app.
W: Then we should get one with those functions.
M: Now, we have two options left.
W: A black one would go well with our <u>home decor</u>.
M: I agree! Let's order this one.

우·리·말·해·석

	모델	가격	스마트 기능	색상
①	A	720달러	X	흰색
②	B	760달러	O	흰색
③	C	810달러	O	검은색
④	D	860달러	X	검은색
⑤	E	950달러	O	흰색

여: 여보, 제가 생각하기에 우리는 의류 건조기가 필요한 것 같아요.
남: 나도 그렇게 생각해요. 그것은 어떤 날씨에도 편리할 거예요. 온라인으로 하나 찾아봐요.
여: 우리는 얼마까지 감당할 수 있을까요?
남: 우리는 900달러 이상은 지불할 여유가 안 될 것 같아요.
여: 당신 말이 맞아요. 보세요, 몇몇 건조기는 스마트 기능을 가지고 있어요.
남: 스마트 기능으로 우리는 앱에서 건조 과정을 확인할 수 있어요.
여: 그럼 우리는 그런 기능이 있는 걸로 사야겠네요.
남: 이제 두 가지 선택지가 남았어요.
여: 검은색이 우리 집 실내 장식과 잘 어울릴 거예요.
남: 맞아요! 이걸로 주문합시다.

단·어·및·표·현
convenient [kənví:njənt] 휑 편리한, 가까운
afford [əfɔ́:rd] 동 ~을 감당하다, ~을 지불할 여유가 되다
decor [deikɔ́:r] 명 실내 장식

13 수치파악(날짜) ▶ 정답 ⑤

듣·기·대·본
(*Telephone rings.*)
W: Hello?
M: Hello. This is Jason from J's Hair Salon. You <u>made a reservation</u> on March 15 at 9 o'clock, right?
W: Yes, I did.
M: I'm really sorry, but I'll be <u>out of town</u> on business that day. So I'm calling to reschedule you for another day and time.
W: I see. Do you have <u>any openings</u> on March 16 or March 18?

M: How about March 18 at 11?
W: That sounds good. I'll see you <u>next week</u> then.

우·리·말·해·석
(전화벨이 울린다.)
여: 여보세요?
남: 여보세요. 전 J 미용실의 Jason입니다. 3월 15일 9시에 예약을 하셨죠, 맞나요?
여: 네, 그랬어요.
남: 정말 죄송합니다만, 제가 그날 출장을 가게 되었어요. 그래서 다른 날 다른 시간으로 일정을 변경해 드리려고 전화했어요.
여: 그렇군요. 3월 16일이나 3월 18일에 비는 자리가 있나요?
남: 3월 18일 11시 어떠세요?
여: 좋아요. 그럼 다음 주에 뵐게요.

단·어·및·표·현
I'm calling to + 동사원형 ~하려고 전화했어요

14 한일파악 ▶ 정답 ②

듣·기·대·본
W: Hey, Nate. What's up?
M: Hi, Brenda. Have you heard about the classical music camp?
W: Yeah. I saw a poster on the school website. Are you going?
M: Yes. I need to <u>upgrade</u> my trumpet skills.
W: Me, too. I haven't practiced the violin <u>for a while</u>. How about practicing together?
M: Sure, but not today. My trumpet is at the <u>instrument repair shop</u>.
W: Why? What happened?
M: It's broken so I took it there yesterday.
W: I see. I hope it's <u>fixed</u> soon.

우·리·말·해·석
여: 이봐, Nate. 뭐해?
남: 안녕, Brenda. 너 클래식 음악 캠프에 대해 들어봤니?
여: 응. 나는 학교 웹사이트에서 포스터를 봤어. 너 갈 거니?
남: 응. 나는 내 트럼펫 실력을 향상시켜야 해.
여: 나도. 나는 한동안 바이올린 연습을 하지 않았어. 같이 연습하는 게 어때?
남: 좋아, 하지만 오늘은 안 돼. 내 트럼펫은 악기 수리점에 있거든.
여: 왜? 무슨 일 있었어?
남: 그것이 고장 나서 어제 내가 그것을 거기에 가져갔어.
여: 그렇구나. 그것이 금방 고쳐지길 바라.

단·어·및·표·현
classical [klǽsikəl] 휑 (음악이) 클래식의, 고전적인
upgrade [ʌ́pgréid] 동 개선하다, 향상시키다
for a while 한동안, 잠시 동안
instrument [ínstrəmənt] 명 악기
fix [fiks] 동 수리하다

15 담화목적파악 ▶ 정답 ②

듣·기·대·본
W: Hello, students. This is your vice principal. I have a special <u>announcement</u> today. As you know, we have a <u>student exchange program</u> with Franklin Middle School in Arizona. This September, we will have three

exchange students, so we are looking for families to host the students. They will be staying from September until the end of November. This will be a great opportunity for you to learn about a new culture. If you are interested, please contact Mr. Harbour.

우·리·말·해·석

여: 안녕하세요, 학생 여러분. 저는 여러분의 교감 선생님입니다. 저는 오늘 특별한 소식이 있습니다. 여러분들도 아시다시피, 우리에게는 애리조나 주에 있는 Franklin 중학교와 교환 학생 프로그램이 있습니다. 이번 9월에 3명의 교환 학생이 있을 것이고, 그래서 우리는 학생들을 묵게 할 가정들을 찾고 있습니다. 그들은 9월부터 11월 말까지 머무를 것입니다. 이것은 여러분이 새로운 문화에 대해 배울 수 있는 좋은 기회가 될 것입니다. 만약 여러분이 관심 있으시다면, Harbour 선생님께 연락해주십시오.

단·어·및·표·현

vice principal 교감 선생님
announcement[ənáunsmənt] 몡 소식, 발표
student exchange program 교환 학생 프로그램
host[houst] 몡 (손님을) 묵게 하다, 접대하다
opportunity[ὰpərtjúːnəti] 몡 기회

16 수치계산(금액) ▶ 정답 ④

듣·기·대·본

W: May I take your order?
M: One cheeseburger and one Coke, please.
W: Okay. Your total comes to 8 dollars.
M: Oh, wait. Do you have any combo meals?
W: Yes. For a dollar more, you can add French fries to your order.
M: Great. I'll have that combo meal.
W: Thank you. For here or to go?
M: To go, please. I can get a two-dollar discount on the to-go order, right?
W: Oh, I'm sorry, that discount event ended last month.
M: All right. Here's my credit card.

우·리·말·해·석

여: 주문하시겠습니까?
남: 치즈 버거 한 개랑 콜라 한 잔 주세요.
여: 네. 총 8달러입니다.
남: 오, 잠시만요. 세트 메뉴가 있나요?
여: 네. 1달러를 더 내시면, 당신의 주문에 감자튀김을 추가하실 수 있습니다.
남: 좋네요. 저는 그 세트 메뉴로 할게요.
여: 감사합니다. 여기서 드실 건가요, 아니면 가져가실 건가요?
남: 가져갈게요. 포장 주문하면 2달러 할인을 받을 수 있는 거죠, 맞죠?
여: 오, 죄송합니다만 그 할인 이벤트는 지난달에 끝났어요.
남: 그렇군요. 여기 제 신용카드요.

단·어·및·표·현

come to (총계가) ~가 되다
For here or to go? 여기서 드실 건가요, 아니면 가져가실 건가요?
end[end] 몡 끝나다, 끝내다

17 알맞은응답찾기 ▶ 정답 ④

듣·기·대·본

(Cellphone rings.)

M: Hello?
W: Hi, this is Sushi King. Did you place an order for two sushi combos for delivery?
M: Yes, I did. Is there a problem?
W: We're swamped with orders, and our delivery drivers are overwhelmed at the moment.
M: Oh, no! Does that mean my order won't be delivered?
W: We're doing our best to manage the situation, but it might take an extra 45 minutes for your order to arrive.
M: I see. We're really craving sushi, so we'll wait for it.
W: Thanks for waiting. Your order will arrive soon.

우·리·말·해·석

① 유감스럽게도 저는 그렇게 오래 기다릴 수는 없습니다.
② 죄송하지만 저희는 초밥이 다 떨어졌습니다.
③ 저는 다른 곳에서 초밥을 사야겠습니다.
④ 기다려주셔서 감사합니다. 당신의 주문이 곧 도착할 겁니다.
⑤ (주문을) 혼동해서 죄송합니다. 저희가 맞는 것으로 가져다 드리겠습니다.

(휴대폰이 울린다.)
남: 여보세요?
여: 안녕하세요, Sushi King입니다. 당신은 배달로 초밥 콤보 2개를 주문하셨나요?
남: 네, 주문했어요. 문제가 있습니까?
여: 주문이 빗발쳐서 저희 배달 기사들이 지금 어쩔 줄 모르고 있어요.
남: 오, 이런! 그건 제 주문이 배달되지 않을 거란 뜻인가요?
여: 저희는 상황에 대처하기 위해 최선을 다하고 있지만, 당신의 주문이 도착하는 데 추가로 45분 정도 더 걸릴 수 있습니다.
남: 그렇군요. 우리는 초밥을 정말 먹고 싶으니까, 그것을 기다리겠습니다.
여: 기다려주셔서 감사합니다. 당신의 주문이 곧 도착할 겁니다.

단·어·및·표·현

be swamped with orders 주문이 빗발치다
overwhelm[òuvərhwélm] 몡 (너무 많은 일로) 어쩔 줄 모르게 만들다
at the moment 지금
do one's best 최선을 다하다
crave[kreiv] 몡 갈망하다

18 알맞은응답찾기 ▶ 정답 ⑤

듣·기·대·본

M: Jessica, how is your school presentation going?
W: I've finished writing it, but I need some practice presenting it.
M: What's your topic?
W: I'm going to talk about how to make scented candles and how they affect our emotions.
M: That sounds interesting! My topic is the benefits of having indoor plants.
W: Philip! Why don't we get together and review each other's work?
M: That's a very good idea. Then we can make improvements to our presentations.
W: Since the presentations are tomorrow, let's meet after school today.
M: Sounds great! I'll wait for you at the main gate.

우·리·말·해·석

① 나는 발표를 하는 것이 어려워.

② 내가 얼마나 자주 식물에 물을 줘야 하니?
③ 내가 너에게 내가 만든 양초를 좀 줄게.
④ 걱정하지 마. 너는 다음번에 더 잘할 거야.
⑤ 좋아! 정문에서 너를 기다릴게.

남: Jessica, 네 학교 발표는 어떻게 돼가니?
여: 나는 그것을 다 썼지만, 그것을 발표하는 연습이 좀 필요해.
남: 너의 주제가 무엇인데?
여: 나는 향초를 만드는 방법과 그것들이 우리의 감정에 어떻게 영향을 미치는지에 대해 말할 거야.
남: 흥미로운데! 내 주제는 실내 식물을 기르는 것의 이점이야.
여: Philip! 우리 모여서 서로의 작업물을 검토해주는 게 어때?
남: 매우 좋은 생각이야. 그럼 우리는 우리의 발표를 개선할 수 있어.
여: 발표가 내일이니까, 오늘 수업 끝나고 만나자.
남: **좋아! 정문에서 너를 기다릴게.**

단·어·및·표·현
scented[séntid] 혱 강한 향기가 나는, 향기로운
benefit[bénəfit] 몡 이점, 이익
improvement[imprúːvmənt] 몡 개선, 호전, 향상

19 알맞은응답찾기 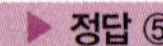 ▶ 정답 ⑤

듣·기·대·본
W: Mr. Yoon, <u>you've been on</u> that computer for hours now.
M: I'm looking for a file, but I can't find it.
W: Is the file for a class?
M: Yes, it's for the third grade. <u>I'm worried that</u> I lost it.
W: What is it about?
M: It's about Korean history.
W: Isn't that the one you e-mailed to all of the history teachers last week? I got it.
M: Did I? Oh, yes! Did you save it?
W: **Of course I did.**
M: **Thank goodness! Can you send it to me, please?**

우·리·말·해·석
① 저는 역사 수업에서 낙제할 것입니다.
② 당신은 매우 친절하시군요. 하지만 사양합니다.
③ 전에 저에게 또 다른 이메일을 보내셨어요?
④ 잘됐네요. 당장 파일을 이메일로 보내드리겠습니다.
⑤ 정말 다행이에요! 그걸 저에게 보내주시겠어요?

여: Yoon 선생님, 지금 몇 시간째 그 컴퓨터 앞에 앉아 계시네요.
남: 파일을 찾고 있는데, 찾을 수가 없어요.
여: 수업 시간에 쓰실 파일인가요?
남: 네, 3학년 거예요. 제가 잃어버린 것일까 봐 걱정입니다.
여: 무엇에 관한 거예요?
남: 한국사에 대한 것입니다.
여: 지난주에 모든 역사 선생님들에게 이메일로 보내셨던 거 아닌가요? 제가 갖고 있어요.
남: 제가 보냈나요? 아, 그래요! 저장하셨어요?
여: 물론 했습니다.
남: **정말 다행이에요! 그걸 저에게 보내주시겠어요?**

단·어·및·표·현
history[hístəri] 몡 역사

20 상황에적절한말찾기 ▶ 정답 ④

듣·기·대·본

M: Tiffany is on the field hockey team. During a practice a month ago, she injured her ankle. She has missed practice since then and has <u>patiently undergone treatment</u>. Now, a tournament is coming up and she feels she cannot just rest any longer. **So, she decides to tell her coach, Mr. Wilson that she would like to get back to practicing.** In this situation, what would Tiffany most likely say to Mr. Wilson?
Tiffany: Mr. Wilson, <u>I think it's time for me to start practicing again.</u>

우·리·말·해·석
① 죄송합니다만, 저는 다리를 다쳤어요.
② 시합에서 우리는 더 잘할 수 있다고 믿어요.
③ 유감이지만 저는 그 대회에 참여하지 못할 것 같아요.
④ 이제 제가 다시 연습을 시작할 때인 것 같아요.
⑤ 저는 우리 마을에서 대회가 열린다고 들었어요.

남: Tiffany는 필드하키 팀에 있다. 한 달 전 연습 도중에, 그녀는 발목을 다쳤다. 그 후로 그녀는 연습에 빠지게 되었고 끈기 있게 치료를 받아왔다. 이제, 대회는 다가오고 있고 그녀는 더 이상 쉴 수 없다고 느낀다. 그래서, 그녀는 그녀의 코치인 Wilson 선생님에게 다시 연습하고 싶다고 말하기로 결심한다. 이 상황에서, Tiffany는 Wilson 선생님에게 뭐라고 말하겠는가?
Tiffany: Wilson 선생님, **이제 제가 다시 연습을 시작할 때인 것 같아요.**

단·어·및·표·현
injure[índʒər] 통 다치게 하다, 부상을 입히다
ankle[ǽŋkl] 몡 발목
patiently[péiʃəntli] 분 끈기 있게, 참을성 있게
treatment[tríːtmənt] 몡 치료

Words & Expressions Review

1. 침대를 정리하다	2. 저장하다, 구하다	3. (너무 많은 일로) 어쩔 줄 모르게 만들다
4. 세부 사항, 정보	5. 조정 가능한	6. 공짜 표
7. 판매 중인	8. 감동을 받은	9. 방송하다
10. (특정한 사람·시스템 등을) 통하여	11. 일정을 변경하다	12. 할인
13. 노트북, 휴대용 컴퓨터	14. 한동안	15. 악기
16. 포장하다	17. ~을 신청하다	18. (전기·가스·수도 등을) 끄다
19. 실내 장식	20. 학우의, 동등한 위치의	21. 떼어내다, 찢어내다
22. ~을 열다, 따다, 펴다	23. (손님을) 묵게 하다	24. 추천하다
25. 끈기 있게, 참을성 있게	26. 도시를 떠나 있다	27. 개선하다
28. 예고편	29. 전달하다	30. 클래식의, 고전의
31. 고장 난	32. 시사회	33. 수리하다
34. 너는 ~하고 싶니?	35. 함께 가다	36. ~에 빠져 있다
37. 세탁물	38. 문구류	39. 교감 선생님
40. (대걸레로) 바닥을 닦다	41. (시간이) 걸리다	42. 짐, 수하물
43. 방송	44. 수리점	

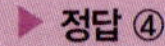

영어듣기 모의고사 19회

|정답|

01 ④	02 ④	03 ①	04 ④	05 ②
06 ①	07 ⑤	08 ⑤	09 ②	10 ②
11 ④	12 ③	13 ③	14 ①	15 ④
16 ④	17 ②	18 ④	19 ①	20 ⑤

01 그림정보파악(대화) ▶ 정답 ④

듣·기·대·본

M: Joan, what is that <u>dangling from your bag</u>?
W: It's a key chain. I make key chains as a hobby. They're really easy to make.
M: Wow! It looks great. <u>I like the cherries on it.</u>
W: Well, I thought <u>adding cherries</u> would give it a refreshing energy. Besides, it is my favorite fruit.
M: I see. And there's <u>even a flower on it.</u>
W: Yes. I wanted to add a strap, but I was <u>running out of</u> them. So, I put a flower on it instead.
M: That's awesome.

우·리·말·해·석

남: Joan, 네 가방에 매달려 있는 저게 뭐야?
여: 그것은 열쇠 고리야. 나는 취미로 열쇠 고리를 만들어. 그것들은 정말 만들기 쉬워.
남: 와! 그것은 좋아 보여. 나는 그것에 있는 체리가 좋아.
여: 음, 나는 체리를 추가하는 것이 그것에 산뜻한 기운을 줄 거라고 생각했어. 게다가, 그것은 내가 가장 좋아하는 과일이야.
남: 알겠어. 그리고 심지어 그것에 꽃도 있네.
여: 응. 나는 끈을 추가하기를 원했지만, 나는 그것들이 다 떨어졌어. 그래서, 나는 대신에 그것에 꽃을 두었어.
남: 그것은 멋져.

단·어·및·표·현

dangle[dǽŋgl] 통 매달리다, 달랑거리다
refreshing[rifréʃiŋ] 형 산뜻한, 신선한
besides[bisáidz] 부 게다가
strap[stræp] 명 끈
run out of ~이 다 떨어지다

02 대화미언급 ▶ 정답 ④

듣·기·대·본

M: Sarah, have you heard about the <u>upcoming</u> English speech contest at our school?
W: Yeah, the contest is next Wednesday, isn't it?
M: Yes, it's going to be held in the school auditorium.
W: Can the students <u>deliver speeches</u> about anything they want?
M: No, they must speak about a topic <u>related to education.</u>
W: Interesting. Are you participating in the contest?
M: Yes, I'm planning to talk about the importance of reading books.
W: That's a great topic. Will there be any prizes for the winners?

M: Yes, the top three contestants <u>will be awarded certificates and scholarships.</u>
W: Oh, I might consider participating, too.
M: Good luck if you decide to join!

우·리·말·해·석

남: Sarah, 너는 우리 학교에서 곧 있을 영어 연설 대회에 대해 들었니?
여: 응, 그 대회는 다음 주 수요일이야, 그렇지 않니?
남: 그래. 그것은 학교 강당에서 열릴 거야.
여: 학생들은 그들이 원하는 어떤 것에 대해서든 연설할 수 있니?
남: 아니, 그들은 교육에 관련된 주제에 대해 말해야 해.
여: 흥미로운데. 너는 대회에 참가할 거니?
남: 응, 나는 독서의 중요성에 대해서 얘기할 계획이야.
여: 그거 멋진 주제다. 우승자들을 위한 상이 있니?
남: 응, 상위 3명의 대회 참가자들에게는 증명서와 장학금이 수여될 거야.
여: 오, 나도 참가하는 것을 고려해 볼까 봐.
남: 만약 참가하기로 결정한다면 행운을 빌게!

단·어·및·표·현

upcoming[ʌ́pkʌ̀miŋ] 형 곧 있을, 다가오는
deliver a speech 연설을 하다
award[əwɔ́ːrd] 통 수여하다
certificate[sərtífəkit] 형 증명서, 증서
scholarship[skɑ́lərʃìp] 명 장학금

03 전화목적파악 ▶ 정답 ①

듣·기·대·본

(*Telephone rings.*)
M: Hello. Denny and George's. How may I help you?
W: Hi. I bought <u>a pair of</u> pants at your store, and I found that a part of it was torn.
M: I'm sorry, ma'am. Would you like to get an <u>exchange</u> or a refund?
W: <u>I want to get a refund.</u>
M: Okay, ma'am. Do you have the receipt?
W: Yes, I have it.
M: Well, come by the store <u>anytime</u> and we'll give you a refund.
W: OK. Thanks.

우·리·말·해·석

(전화벨이 울린다.)
남: 안녕하십니까. Denny and George's입니다. 어떻게 도와 드릴까요?
여: 안녕하세요. 제가 당신의 가게에서 바지를 한 벌 샀는데요, 일부분이 찢겨져 있는 걸 발견했어요.
남: 죄송합니다. 고객님. 교환을 원하십니까, 환불을 원하십니까?
여: 환불을 받고 싶은데요.
남: 알겠습니다. 고객님. 영수증이 있으신가요?
여: 네, 있어요.
남: 그럼, 아무 때나 가게에 들르시면 환불해 드리겠습니다.
여: 네. 감사합니다.

단·어·및·표·현

tear[tɛər] 통 찢다
receipt[risíːt] 명 영수증

04 수치파악(시각) ▶ 정답 ④

듣·기·대·본

[*Cellphone rings.*]

19회 모의고사

M: Hey, Phoebe.
W: Hi, Carl. You promised to teach me how to skateboard. Can we start tomorrow?
M: Tomorrow sounds good. When do you want to meet?
W: I was thinking 10 a.m. Are you free then?
M: I'm afraid not. I have to finish my homework by noon. What about 1 p.m.?
W: I'm having lunch with Sylvia at that time. Is 3 p.m. okay?
M: Yeah. See you then at Gate Park. Don't forget to bring your skateboard!
W: Sure thing. Bye.

우•리•말•해•석

[휴대전화가 울린다.]
남: 이봐, Phoebe.
여: 안녕, Carl. 너 내게 스케이트보드 타는 법을 가르쳐 주기로 약속했잖아. 우리 내일 시작할 수 있을까?
남: 내일 좋은데. 너는 언제 만나고 싶니?
여: 나는 오전 10시를 생각하고 있었어. 너는 그때 한가하니?
남: 안 될 것 같아. 나는 정오까지 내 숙제를 끝내야 해. 오후 1시는 어때?
여: 나는 그 시간에 Sylvia와 점심을 먹기로 했어. 오후 3시는 괜찮아?
남: 응. 그때 Gate 공원에서 만나. 네 스케이트보드를 가져오는 것을 잊지 마!
여: 물론이지. 안녕.

단•어•및•표•현

skateboard [skéitbɔ̀ːrd] [동] 스케이트보드를 타다
free [friː] [형] 한가한, 다른 계획이 없는

05 심정추론 ▶ 정답 ②

듣•기•대•본

M: I got an "A" on my English test.
W: Really? That's great. Please don't ask me what I got.
M: Is it that bad?
W: Well, I got a "C" on my test. I think my mom will be really disappointed.
M: Cheer up! You'll do better next time.
W: Well, to be honest with you, I didn't study hard enough for the test. I played mobile games every night.
M: You know what? There is a saying, "As you sow, so you reap."
W: I know that, too. Whew… I should have studied harder. What should I do now?

우•리•말•해•석

① 만족하는 ② 후회하는 ③ 외로운 ④ 행복한 ⑤ 지루한

남: 난 영어 시험에서 A를 받았어.
여: 정말? 그거 잘됐다. 난 무엇을 받았는지 제발 묻지 말아줘.
남: 그렇게 나빠?
여: 그게, 난 시험에서 C를 받았어. 내 생각에 엄마가 많이 실망하실 거 같아.
남: 기운 내! 넌 다음번에 더 잘할 거야.
여: 그게, 솔직히 말하자면, 난 시험공부를 충분히 열심히 하지 않았어. 난 매일 밤 휴대폰 게임을 했어.
남: 너 그거 아니? '뿌린 만큼 거둔다.'라는 속담이 있어.
여: 나도 알아. 휴… 난 공부를 더 열심히 했어야 했어. 이제 난 어떻게 해야 되지?

단•어•및•표•현

Cheer up! 기운 내!
to be honest (with you) 솔직히 말하자면

06 그림상황에적절한대화찾기 ▶ 정답 ①

듣•기•대•본

① W: Our car is parked on what floor?
M: It's on the 2nd basement floor. I'll press the button.
② W: Do you mind opening the window?
M: Of course not.
③ W: What time and where should we meet?
M: How about six?
④ W: Do you need anything from the market?
M: Oh, can you get some ice cream?
⑤ W: This escalator is slow.
M: Yes. I wish it went faster.

우•리•말•해•석

① 여: 우리 차가 몇 층에 주차되어 있지?
남: 지하 2층이에요. 제가 버튼을 누를게요.
② 여: 창문을 열어도 괜찮겠니?
남: 물론이죠.
③ 여: 우리 몇 시에 어디서 만나야 할까?
남: 6시는 어때요?
④ 여: 시장에서 뭐 필요한 것이 있니?
남: 아, 아이스크림 좀 사다 주시겠어요?
⑤ 여: 이 에스컬레이터는 느려.
남: 그러네요. 저는 그것이 더 빨리 가면 좋겠어요.

단•어•및•표•현

park [pɑːrk] [동] 주차하다

07 부탁(요청)한일파악 ▶ 정답 ⑤

듣•기•대•본

M: Honey, will you be coming straight home after work tonight?
W: No. I have to pick up some groceries.
M: Do you have anything else to do after that?
W: Not really, why?
M: Can you make a trip to the auto repair shop as well?
W: Why's that?
M: It's time to change the oil.
W: Okay. I'll take care of it.

우•리•말•해•석

남: 여보, 오늘 밤에 일 끝나고 바로 집으로 와요?
여: 아니요. 식료품을 좀 사와야 하는데요.
남: 그거 다음에 다른 거 할 거 있어요?
여: 그렇진 않은데요, 왜요?
남: 자동차 정비소도 들를 수 있나요?
여: 왜 그러는데요?
남: 오일을 바꿀 때가 돼서요.
여: 좋아요. 내가 처리할게요.

단•어•및•표•현

take care of ~ ~를 처리하다, ~에 신경 쓰다

08 담화미언급 ▶ 정답 ⑤

듣•기•대•본

M: Hello, listeners. The Hands Foundation is looking for enthusiastic teenagers. The Foundation's summer volunteer program is now recruiting students to help out at farms during the busiest time of the year. The activities will take place in mid-southern areas. The program starts on June 1st, and ends on the 14th. It's open to all students between the ages of 13 and 17. Please register by May 20th.

우·리·말·해·석

남: 안녕하세요, 청취자 여러분. Hands 재단에서는 열정적인 십대들을 찾고 있습니다. 재단의 여름 자원봉사 프로그램에서 한 해 중 가장 바쁜 시기에 농장 일을 도울 학생들을 지금 모집하고 있습니다. 활동은 중남부 지역에서 이뤄질 것입니다. 프로그램은 6월 1일에 시작해서 14일에 끝납니다. 그것은 13세에서 17세 사이의 모든 학생들에게 열려 있습니다. 5월 20일까지 등록하세요.

단·어·및·표·현

enthusiastic [inθjùːziǽstik] 형 열정적인, 열렬한
recruit [rikrúːt] 동 모집하다, (사람을) 모으다

09 담화화제추론 ▶ 정답 ②

듣·기·대·본

M: This animal lives in the ocean but is not a fish. It uses lungs to breathe and must come to the surface for air. It is very intelligent and often travels in groups. It is known for its friendly image. It swims gracefully in the water. People enjoy watching it jump and spin out of the water. It is widely loved, researched, and protected.

우·리·말·해·석

남: 이 동물은 바다에 살지만 물고기는 아닙니다. 폐를 사용해 숨을 쉬며, 공기를 (마시기) 위해 수면 위로 올라와야 합니다. 이것은 아주 똑똑하며, 자주 무리를 지어 이동합니다. 이것은 친근한 이미지로 잘 알려져 있습니다. 이것은 물속에서 우아하게 헤엄칩니다. 사람들은 이것이 물 밖으로 뛰어오르고 회전하는 것을 보는 걸 즐깁니다. 이것은 널리 사랑받고, 연구되며, 보호받습니다.

단·어·및·표·현

lung [lʌŋ] 명 폐
breathe [briːð] 동 숨 쉬다
surface [sə́ːrfis] 명 표면, 수면
intelligent [intélidʒənt] 형 똑똑한, 지능이 높은
be known for ~로 알려져 있다
gracefully [ɡréisfəli] 부 우아하게
research [risə́ːrtʃ] 동 연구하다
protect [prətékt] 동 보호하다

10 어색한대화찾기 ▶ 정답 ②

듣·기·대·본

① W: Can I borrow this book for a few days?
　 M: Of course.
② W: I'm looking forward to seeing her again.
　 M: You don't have to look for it.
③ W: Do you sell blue jeans?
　 M: Sure. What's your size?
④ W: I have a job interview tomorrow.
　 M: I hope everything goes well.
⑤ W: How would you like your steak?
　 M: Well-done, please.

우·리·말·해·석

① 여: 내가 며칠간 이 책 좀 빌려도 될까?
　 남: 물론이지.
② 여: 그녀를 다시 보기를 고대하고 있어.
　 남: 넌 그거 찾을 필요가 없어.
③ 여: 청바지 파나요?
　 남: 물론이지요. 사이즈가 어떻게 됩니까?
④ 여: 내일 취업 면접이 있어.
　 남: 모든 게 잘 되길 바라.
⑤ 여: 스테이크는 어떻게 해 드릴까요?
　 남: 바싹 익혀 주세요.

단·어·및·표·현

look forward to -ing ~하기를 고대하다

11 할일파악(대화직후) ▶ 정답 ④

듣·기·대·본

W: Dad, Mom's birthday is coming up. We should get something special for her.
M: Okay. What do you have in mind?
W: Let's throw her a surprise birthday party at home. We should also surprise Mom by inviting Grandma.
M: I like that idea! We'll need to decorate the house and prepare some food then.
W: I'll take care of the decorations. Can you help me with the menu? What should we make?
M: Hmm… I'll think about the menu.
W: Okay. While you're thinking, I'm going to call Grandma.
M: Good idea.

우·리·말·해·석

여: 아빠, 엄마의 생일이 다가오고 있어요. 우리는 엄마를 위해 특별한 무언가를 준비해야 해요.
남: 알았다. 너는 무엇을 염두에 두고 있니?
여: 집에서 엄마에게 깜짝 생일파티를 열어드리죠. 우리는 할머니도 초대해서 엄마를 놀라게 해야 해요.
남: 그 아이디어 좋구나! 그러면 우리는 집을 꾸미고 음식을 좀 준비할 필요가 있어.
여: 제가 장식을 책임질게요. 메뉴에 관해 도와주실 수 있나요? 우리가 무엇을 만들어야 할까요?
남: 흠… 내가 메뉴를 생각해보마.
여: 알았어요. 아빠가 생각하시는 동안, 저는 할머니에게 전화를 할게요.
남: 좋은 생각이야.

단·어·및·표·현

come up 다가오다
have ~ in mind ~을 염두에 두다
throw a party 파티를 열다
invite [inváit] 동 초대하다
decorate [dékərèit] 동 장식하다
take care of ~을 책임지다, 처리하다
decoration [dèkəréiʃən] 명 장식

12 도표정보파악 ▶ 정답 ③

듣·기·대·본

M: Honey, are you still browsing for desk lamps online?
W: Yes. I'm trying to choose the right one for our son's desk. Can you help me?

M: Sure. Let's see. I think spending more than $30 is too much.

W: I agree. Let's look for ones that are cheaper than $30. Should we choose one with an adjustable arm or a fixed arm?

M: An adjustable arm would be better because then the light can be directed.

W: Okay. Then, two options are left, a lamp with brightness adjustment or one without.

W: Let's get one with brightness adjustment. That way, he can adjust it according to his needs.

W: Good idea. Let's order this one.

우·리·말·해·석

	모델	가격	거치대	밝기 조정
①	A	39달러	고정	O
②	B	35달러	조절 가능	X
③	C	25달러	조절 가능	O
④	D	20달러	조절 가능	X
⑤	E	15달러	고정	X

남: 여보, 당신은 아직도 온라인에서 책상용 스탠드를 검색하고 있나요?

여: 네. 저는 우리 아들의 책상에 알맞은 것을 고르기 위해 노력 중이에요. 당신이 저를 도와줄 수 있어요?

남: 물론이죠. 어디 봐요. 전 30달러보다 더 소비하는 건 너무 과한 것 같아요.

여: 동의해요. 30달러보다 저렴한 것들로 찾아보죠. 우리는 조절 가능한 거치대가 있는 것을 골라야 할까요, 아니면 고정된 거치대가 있는 것을 골라야 할까요?

남: 빛(의 방향)을 돌릴 수 있기 때문에 조절 가능한 거치대가 더 나을 것 같아요.

여: 네. 그러면, 밝기 조정이 가능한 램프와 아닌 램프, 두 가지 선택지가 남았네요.

남: 밝기 조정이 가능한 것으로 사죠. 그렇게 하면, 그는 그의 필요에 따라 그것을 조정할 수 있어요.

여: 좋은 생각이에요. 이걸로 주문하죠.

단·어·및·표·현

browse [brauz] [동] 검색하다
adjustable [ədʒʌ́stəbl] [형] 조절 가능한
arm [ɑːrm] [명] 거치대
direct [dirékt] [동] (어떤 방향으로) 돌리다
brightness adjustment 밝기 조정
according to ~에 따라

13 수치파악(날짜) ▶ 정답 ③

듣·기·대·본

W: Dad, the International Air Show is finally starting next month.

M: You've been looking forward to it for so long! Let's buy tickets right away.

W: Great! It starts on October 9th and ends on the 18th.

M: Should we go on opening day?

W: Sorry, Dad. I have to go to Eric's birthday party that day.

M: Then what about the 17th?

W: Look, Dad. We should go on the 16th instead of the 17th. On that day, visitors can get in the planes that are on display.

M: Awesome! Let's book the tickets for that day.

우·리·말·해·석

여: 아빠, 국제 에어쇼가 드디어 다음 달에 시작해요.

남: 너는 정말 오랫동안 그것을 기대해 왔잖니! 지금 바로 표를 사자.

여: 좋아요! 그것은 10월 9일에 시작해서 18일에 끝나요.

남: 우리 개최하는 날 갈까?

여: 죄송해요, 아빠. 저는 그날 Eric의 생일 파티에 가야 해요.

남: 그럼 17일은 어떠니?

여: 보세요, 아빠. 우리는 17일 대신 16일에 가야 해요. 그날에는 방문자들이 전시되어 있는 비행기들에 들어가 볼 수 있어요.

남: 멋지구나! 그날로 표를 예약하자.

단·어·및·표·현

international [ìntərnǽʃənəl] [형] 국제적인
display [displéi] [명] 전시, 진열

14 한일파악 ▶ 정답 ①

듣·기·대·본

M: Hi, Abby. How was your cooking class today?

W: Hi, Peter. I learned how to make chicken soup. I'll make it for our next family dinner.

M: Sounds yummy. It makes me feel hungry.

W: Have you had lunch yet?

M: No. I was too busy doing my part-time job.

W: I wish I had some soup left. I do have some pie left, though instead. I baked it yesterday. Would you like it?

M: Of course! Thanks. You're a life saver.

W: You're welcome.

우·리·말·해·석

남: 안녕, Abby. 오늘 네 요리 수업은 어땠어?

여: 안녕, Peter. 나는 오늘 닭고기 수프를 만드는 방법을 배웠어. 다음 우리 가족 저녁 식사에 내가 그것을 만들 거야.

남: 맛있겠다. 그러니까 배가 고파지네.

여: 너는 점심을 이미 먹었니?

남: 아니. 나는 아르바이트 하느라 너무 바빴어.

여: 수프가 조금 남았으면 좋았을 텐데. 대신에 내가 남은 파이를 좀 가지고 있어. 나는 그것을 어제 구웠어. 그거 먹을래?

남: 물론이지! 고마워. 너는 생명의 은인이야.

여: 천만에.

단·어·및·표·현

part-time job 아르바이트
instead [instéd] [부] 대신에
life saver 생명의 은인, (곤경에서) 건져내 주는 사람[것]

15 담화목적파악 ▶ 정답 ④

듣·기·대·본

W: Good afternoon, students. This is an announcement from your student council. First of all, congratulations on your graduation! We also wanted to take this opportunity to remind you once again to return all books to the library. The librarian delivered the list of students with outstanding library items a week ago, but some graduates still have not returned their books. All books borrowed from the library should be processed before your graduation ceremony. We would appreciate the return of these items as soon as possible. Thank you.

우•리•말•해•석

여: 좋은 오후입니다, 학생 여러분. 이것은 여러분의 학생회의 공지입니다. 우선, 여러분의 졸업을 축하합니다! 저희는 또한 이 기회를 빌려 여러분에게 다시 한번 도서관에 모든 책들을 반납하라고 상기시키고 싶었습니다. 사서가 일주일 전에 반납 처리되지 않은 도서관 물품들이 있는 학생들 명단을 전달했지만 몇몇 졸업생들은 아직 그들의 책들을 반납하지 않았습니다. 도서관에서 빌려 간 모든 책들은 졸업식 전에 처리되어야 합니다. 저희는 가능한 한 빠르게 이 물품들이 반납되면 감사하겠습니다. 감사합니다.

단•어•및•표•현

remind [rimáind] [동] 상기시키다, 다시 한번 알려주다
outstanding [àutstǽndiŋ] [형] 아직 처리되지 않은, 미해결된
process [práses] [동] 처리하다
appreciate [əpríːʃièit] [동] 고마워하다, 환영하다

16 수치계산(금액) ▶ 정답 ④

듣•기•대•본

M: Hi, can I help you?
W: I'm looking for toys for my twin daughters. They are 4.
M: How about these stuffed animals?
W: How much are they?
M: The small ones are $30 each, and the big ones are $40 each.
W: That's quite expensive.
M: We have a special promotion this week. You can get a $10 discount if you spend more than $50.
W: Oh, great. I'll take two large ones, please. Here is my credit card.

우•리•말•해•석

남: 안녕하세요, 도와드릴까요?
여: 저는 제 쌍둥이 딸들에게 줄 장난감들을 찾고 있습니다. 그들은 4살입니다.
남: 이 봉제 동물 인형들은 어떻습니까?
여: 그것들은 얼마인가요?
남: 작은 것들은 각각 30달러이고, 큰 것들은 각각 40달러입니다.
여: 꽤 비싸네요.
남: 저희는 이번 주에 특별한 판촉 활동을 하고 있어요. 당신이 50달러 이상 쓴다면 10달러 할인을 받으실 수 있습니다.
여: 오, 좋네요. 저는 큰 것들 2개를 살게요. 여기 제 신용카드입니다.

단•어•및•표•현

stuffed animal 봉제 동물 인형
promotion [prəmóuʃən] [명] 홍보 활동, 판촉, 광고
credit card 신용카드

17 알맞은응답찾기 ▶ 정답 ②

듣•기•대•본

M: Kelly, did you hear about John's K-pop audition?
W: I heard that he passed the first round.
M: Wow! I'm so proud of him.
W: Yes, but he still needs to pass the second round of the audition.
M: Well, he is marvelous at singing, so I'm sure he'll pass the next round.
W: I heard that he is allotted more time for this round, so he has to dance as well.
M: I see. I hope he doesn't make any mistakes.
W: Let's keep our fingers crossed for him.

우•리•말•해•석

① 난 케이팝 콘서트에 가고 싶어.
② 그에게 행운을 빌어주자.
③ 오디션이 취소되어서 실망했어.
④ 나는 세계적으로 유명한 가수가 되고 싶어.
⑤ 절대 크게 떠들지 말아주세요.

남: Kelly, 너 John의 케이팝 오디션에 대해 들었니?
여: 나는 그가 1라운드를 통과했다고 들었어.
남: 와! 나는 그가 정말 자랑스러워.
여: 그래, 하지만 아직 오디션의 2라운드를 통과해야 해.
남: 음, 그는 노래를 놀라울 정도로 잘하니까 다음 라운드에서도 통과할 거라고 확신해.
여: 이번 라운드에서는 그에게 더 많은 시간이 할당되어서 춤도 춰야 한다고 들었어.
남: 그렇구나. 나는 그가 어떤 실수도 하질 않길 바라.
여: 그에게 행운을 빌어주자.

단•어•및•표•현

proud of ~ ~을 자랑스러워하는
marvelous [máːrvələs] [형] 훌륭한, 놀라운
allot [əlát] [동] 할당하다

18 알맞은응답찾기 ▶ 정답 ④

듣•기•대•본

(*Telephone rings.*)
M: Hello, Charley's Electronics Store.
W: Hi, I ordered a laptop computer through the Internet but it hasn't been delivered yet.
M: OK. May I have your name, please?
W: It's Elena Park. I placed the order three days ago, on Sunday evening.
M: I see. Well, I think the delivery has been delayed because the order came through on the weekend. I'm very sorry.
W: That's OK. Can you check when it will be delivered?
M: It will certainly arrive by tomorrow.

우•리•말•해•석

① 제 생각에는 어제 배달된 것 같은데요.
② 당신의 컴퓨터는 수리되었어요.
③ 저희는 일요일에 주문을 받았어요.
④ 내일까지는 틀림없이 도착할 겁니다.
⑤ 왜 배달이 안 된 건지 잘 모르겠습니다.

(전화벨이 울린다.)
남: 안녕하세요, Charley's Electronics Store입니다.
여: 안녕하세요, 제가 인터넷으로 노트북 컴퓨터를 주문했는데 아직 배달이 안 됐어요.
남: 알겠습니다. 성함이 어떻게 되시나요?
여: Elena Park입니다. 저는 3일 전, 일요일 저녁에 주문을 했어요.
남: 알겠습니다. 음, 제 생각엔 주말에 주문이 들어와서 배달이 지연된 것 같아요. 정말 죄송합니다.

여: 괜찮습니다. 그것이 언제 배달될지 확인해주실 수 있나요?
남: <u>내일까지는 틀림없이 도착할 겁니다.</u>

단·어·및·표·현
delay[diléi] ⑧ 지연시키다, 미루다

19 알맞은응답찾기 ▶ 정답 ①

듣·기·대·본

W: Owen, what happened to your hand? It looks like it's <u>bandaged up</u>!
M: Oh, it's nothing serious. I accidentally cut it while cooking yesterday.
W: That sounds painful. How did it happen?
M: I was <u>chopping vegetables</u> and I accidentally <u>nicked</u> my finger with the knife.
W: Ouch, that must have hurt. Did you get it checked by a doctor?
M: Yeah, the doctor said it's <u>just a minor cut</u> and would heal quickly.
W: That's good to hear. Is it <u>bothering you</u> a lot?
M: It's a bit sore, but I'll manage.

우·리·말·해·석

① 조금 아프지만, 난 견뎌낼 거야.
② 너도 요리하는 법을 배워야 해.
③ 아니, 난 병원에 갈 필요는 없어.
④ 물론이야! 내가 너에게 야채 다지는 법을 가르쳐 줄게.
⑤ 주방에서는 안전이 최우선이라는 것을 잊지 마.

여: Owen, 네 손이 왜 그래? 붕대를 감은 것 같네!
남: 오, 심각한 건 아니야. 나는 어제 요리하다가 실수로 그것을 베었어.
여: 아플 것 같은데. 어떻게 그 일이 일어난 거야?
남: 난 야채를 다지고 있었는데 실수로 칼로 손가락을 베었어.
여: 아야, 그거 틀림없이 아팠겠구나. 너는 의사에게 그것을 진료받았니?
남: 응, 의사가 그저 가벼운 상처라 빨리 나을 거라고 말했어.
여: 그거 다행이다. 그게 널 많이 신경 쓰이게 하니?
남: <u>조금 아프지만, 난 견뎌낼 거야.</u>

단·어·및·표·현

bandage up 붕대를 감다
accidentally[æksidéntəli] ⑨ 실수로, 우연히
chop[tʃap] ⑧ 다지다, 썰다
nick[nik] ⑧ (칼로) 베다
bother[báðər] ⑧ 신경 쓰이게 하다
sore[sɔːr] ⑩ 아픈[따가운]
come first 최우선 고려 사항이다, 가장 먼저다

20 상황에적절한말찾기 ▶ 정답 ⑤

듣·기·대·본

W: Cynthia is <u>in class</u> now. However, she doesn't feel well. She has a <u>high fever</u> and a headache. Her teacher tells her to go home and <u>take a rest</u>. So Cynthia decides to call her mom to say that she's sick. <u>She wants her mom to come to school</u> and take her home. In this situation, what would Cynthia say to her mom?
Cynthia: <u>Can you pick me up at school now?</u>

우·리·말·해·석

① 제가 병원에 가야 하나요?

② 전 집에 곧 갈 거예요.
③ 절 학교에 내려 주시겠어요?
④ 갈 준비가 되셨나요?
⑤ 지금 학교에 절 데리러 와주시겠어요?

여: Cynthia는 지금 수업 중이다. 하지만 그녀는 몸이 좋지 않다. 고열과 두통이 있다. 그녀의 선생님은 그녀에게 집에 가서 쉬라고 말한다. 그래서 Cynthia는 엄마에게 전화해서 아프다고 말하기로 결정한다. 그녀는 엄마가 학교에 와서 그녀를 집으로 데리고 가기를 원한다. 이러한 상황에서, Cynthia는 엄마에게 무엇이라고 말하겠는가?
Cynthia: <u>지금 학교에 절 데리러 와주시겠어요?</u>

단·어·및·표·현

fever[fíːvər] ⑩ 열, 발열
take a rest 쉬다, 휴식하다

Words & Expressions Review

1. 홍보 활동	2. 등록하다	3. 열정적인, 열렬한
4. 한 벌의, 한 쌍의	5. 증명서, 증서	6. 훌륭한, 놀라운
7. ~이 다 떨어지다	8. 고마워하다	9. ~도, ~뿐만 아니라
10. 거치대	11. 아직 처리되지 않은	12. ~을 자랑스러워하는
13. 열, 발열	14. 게다가, ~ 외에	15. 속담, 격언
16. 전시, 진열	17. 똑똑한, 지능이 높은	18. 솔직히 말하자면
19. 거두다, 수확하다	20. 뿌리다, 심다	21. 다지다, 썰다
22. 장학금	23. 에스컬레이터	24. 식료품류
25. 주문을 하다	26. 모집하다	27. 파티를 열다
28. (고기가) 잘 익혀진	29. 잠깐 들르다	30. ~을 처리하다
31. (어떤 방향으로) 돌리다	32. 봉제 동물 인형	33. 지하층
34. 지연시키다, 미루다	35. 교환하다	36. 생명의 은인
37. (칼로) 베다	38. 할당하다	39. 숨 쉬다
40. 수여하다	41. 찢다	42. 기운 내!
43. 다가오다	44. 매달리다, 달랑거리다	

Listening Test

영어듣기 모의고사 20회

|정|답|

01 ③	02 ②	03 ①	04 ③	05 ④
06 ③	07 ③	08 ④	09 ③	10 ③
11	12 ⑤	13 ④	14 ③	15 ③
16 ③	17 ②	18 ①	19 ③	20 ②

01 그림정보파악(대화) ▶ 정답 ③

듣·기·대·본

M: Hello. Welcome to Everything Backpack! How can I help you?
W: Hi. I am <u>looking for</u> a backpack for my daughter.

M: Okay. Here are the backpack selections. Would you like a backpack with wheels or without wheels?

W: I think the ones with wheels will be better, because her backpack can be very heavy sometimes.

M: I see… So, would your daughter like a backpack with a cat or a rabbit?

W: Oh, definitely a rabbit! She loves rabbits!

M: Okay, sounds good! Would you like a backpack with or without side pockets?

W: I will take the one with side pockets. Thank you.

우·리·말·해·석

남: 안녕하세요. Everything Backpack에 오신 것을 환영합니다! 어떻게 도와드릴까요?

여: 안녕하세요. 저는 제 딸을 위한 책가방을 찾고 있습니다.

남: 네. 여기 책가방 전시품들이 있습니다. 바퀴가 있는 책가방을 원하시나요, 아니면 바퀴가 없는 책가방을 원하시나요?

여: 저는 바퀴가 있는 것이 더 나을 것 같아요, 왜냐하면 그녀의 책가방은 가끔 아주 무거울 수 있기 때문이에요.

남: 그렇군요… 그러면, 따님이 고양이가 그려진 책가방을 좋아할까요, 아니면 토끼가 그려진 것을 좋아할까요?

여: 아, 확실히 토끼예요! 그녀는 토끼를 아주 좋아해요!

남: 네, 좋네요! 옆 주머니가 있는 책가방을 원하시나요, 아니면 옆 주머니가 없는 걸 원하시나요?

여: 저는 옆 주머니가 있는 걸로 살게요. 고마워요.

단·어·및·표·현

selection [silékʃən] 뎽 (선택 · 구매 따위를 위한) 전시품
definitely [défənitli] 遇 확실히, 분명히
side pocket 옆 주머니, 옆쪽에 달린 호주머니

02 대화미언급   ▶ 정답 ②

듣·기·대·본

(*Telephone rings.*)

M: Hello, ABC Scooter Rental. How can I assist you today?

W: Hi, I'm interested in renting a scooter for the weekend. How much is the rental fee?

M: Our rental fees start at $30 per day.

W: That sounds reasonable. What are your operating hours?

M: We are open from 9 a.m. to 6 p.m.

W: Great, and where is your shop located?

M: We are located on Main Street, right next to the park.

W: Excellent. Do I need to bring anything when renting a scooter?

M: Yes, you need to bring your driver's license.

W: I see. Thank you, I'll come by this weekend.

M: You're welcome. We look forward to seeing you.

우·리·말·해·석

(전화벨이 울린다.)

남: 안녕하세요, ABC 스쿠터 대여점입니다. 오늘 제가 당신을 어떻게 도와드릴까요?

여: 안녕하세요, 저는 주말 동안 스쿠터를 대여하는 것에 관심 있어요. 대여료가 얼마인가요?

남: 저희 대여료는 하루당 30달러부터 시작합니다.

여: 합리적인 것 같네요. 영업시간이 어떻게 되나요?

남: 저희는 오전 9시부터 오후 6시까지 엽니다.

여: 좋아요, 그러면 가게가 어디에 위치해 있나요?

남: 저희는 공원 바로 옆, Main Street에 위치해 있습니다.

여: 완벽해요. 제가 스쿠터를 대여할 때 무언가 가져가야 하는 게 있나요?

남: 네, 손님은 손님의 운전면허증을 가져오셔야 합니다.

여: 그렇군요. 감사합니다. 이번 주말에 들를게요.

남: 천만에요. 뵙기를 기대하고 있겠습니다.

단·어·및·표·현

rental fee 대여료, 사용료
reasonable [ríːzənəbl] 뎽 (가격이) 합리적인, 적정한
operating hours 영업시간
located [lóukeitid] 뎽 ~에 위치한
come by (잠깐) 들르다

03 전화목적파악   ▶ 정답 ①

듣·기·대·본

(*Telephone rings.*)

M: Hello, this is Every Kind of Clothes You Can Think of.

W: Hi, I'm calling about the shipping address for my online order.

M: Okay. How can I help you?

W: I just made a purchase from your online store, but I accidentally used my old address as my shipping address.

M: So, you need to switch your shipping address?

W: Yes. Would that be possible?

M: Of course. Can I get your order number and the new shipping address?

W: My order number is 158347 and the new shipping address is 303 Madison St., New York City.

M: Okay. I've changed the address for your order.

우·리·말·해·석

(전화벨이 울린다.)

남: 여보세요, 'Every Kind of Clothes You Can Think of' 옷가게입니다.

여: 안녕하세요, 저는 제 온라인 주문 건의 배송지 때문에 전화를 드렸어요.

남: 그렇군요. 어떻게 도와드릴까요?

여: 저는 방금 당신의 온라인 상점에서 구매했는데, 실수로 제 예전 주소를 배송지로 사용했어요.

남: 그러니까, 고객님은 고객님의 배송지를 변경하셔야 하는 거죠?

여: 네. 그것이 가능할까요?

남: 물론이죠. 고객님의 주문번호와 새 배송지를 알려주시겠어요?

여: 제 주문번호는 158347이고 새 배송지는 New York City의 303 Madison가예요.

남: 알겠습니다. 고객님 주문 건의 주소를 변경했습니다.

단·어·및·표·현

make a purchase 구매하다, 구입하다
accidentally [æksidéntəli] 遇 실수로, 잘못하여
switch [switʃ] 동 변경하다, 바꾸다

04 수치파악(시각)   ▶ 정답 ③

듣·기·대·본

W: Hey, Mike! The movie, *Adventure Galaxy* will be released this Saturday.

M: I know! Let's watch it together in 3D.

W: Of course. Let me check the times on my phone.

M: Are there any shows in the morning?

W: Hmm… There's one at 9 a.m. and another at 11 a.m., but they're not in 3D.

M: Is there anything before 6 p.m.?

W: There's one at 2 p.m., and it's in 3D. The tickets for 4 p.m. are sold out.

M: All right. 2 p.m. works for me.

W: Me, too. Let's buy the tickets now.

우•리•말•해•석

여: 이봐, Mike! 영화 "은하 모험"이 이번 주 토요일에 개봉할 거야.

남: 나도 알아! 3D로 그것을 같이 보자.

여: 물론이지. 내가 휴대폰으로 시간을 확인해 볼게.

남: 아침에 하는 상영이 있니?

여: 흠… 오전 9시에 하나 그리고 오전 11시에 하나가 있지만, 그것들은 3D가 아니야.

남: 오후 6시 전에는 있니?

여: 오후 2시에 하나 있고 그것은 3D야. 오후 4시 표는 매진됐어.

남: 좋아. 난 오후 2시 괜찮아.

여: 나도. 지금 표를 사자.

단•어•및•표•현

release [rilíːs] [동] 개봉하다, 공개[발표]하다

sold out 표가 매진된, 다 팔린

work for (특정 일시 · 상황 등이) ~에게 문제없다, 좋다

05 심정추론 ▶ 정답 ④

듣•기•대•본

M: Hello, Angela. Is there something wrong?

W: Hi, Matthew. It's my sister again.

M: What happened?

W: Did I tell you before that she keeps wearing my clothes and shoes?

M: Yes, you did. What did she take this time?

W: My new trainers. I was really looking forward to wearing them today.

M: Oh, no. I guess she didn't even ask you if she could wear them.

W: She never does. I think it is so rude.

M: I agree. You should talk to her about this.

W: I will. I've had enough.

우•리•말•해•석

① 미안한 ② 신나는 ③ 질투하는 ④ 화난 ⑤ 고마운

남: 안녕, Angella. 무슨 문제 있니?

여: 안녕, Matthew. 또 내 여동생이야.

남: 무슨 일인데?

여: 전에 내가 너에게 그녀가 계속 내 옷들을 입고 신발을 신는다고 말했었나?

남: 응, 말했었어. 그녀가 이번엔 무엇을 가져간 거야?

여: 내 새 운동화. 나는 오늘 그것들을 신는 것을 정말 기대하고 있었어.

남: 아, 저런. 그녀는 심지어 너에게 그것들을 신어도 되냐고 묻지도 않았나 보구나.

여: 그녀는 절대 그러지 않아. 너무 무례한 것 같아.

남: 동의해. 너는 그녀에게 이것에 대해 얘기해야 해.

여: 그럴 거야. 난 더 이상 못 참아.

단•어•및•표•현

trainer [tréinər] [명] 운동화

look forward to ~을 기대하다

have had enough 더 이상 못 참다, 지긋지긋하다

06 그림상황에적절한대화찾기 ▶ 정답 ③

듣•기•대•본

① M: Can I help you?
W: Yes, I'm looking for a laptop.

② M: What are you doing now?
W: I'm studying for the test.

③ M: Why the long face?
W: I got a poor grade in English.

④ M: I've lost some weight.
W: Good for you. You look much healthier.

⑤ M: You look so happy. Why is that?
W: Guess what? I got a perfect score on the English test.

우•리•말•해•석

① 남: 도와드릴까요?
여: 네, 저는 노트북을 찾고 있어요.

② 남: 너는 지금 무엇을 하고 있니?
여: 저는 시험을 위해 공부하고 있어요.

③ 남: 왜 우울한 얼굴이니?
여: 저는 영어에서 나쁜 성적을 받았어요.

④ 남: 나는 살이 좀 빠졌어.
여: 잘됐네요. 더 건강해 보이세요.

⑤ 남: 너 무척 행복해 보이는구나. 왜 그러니?
여: 그거 아세요? 저는 영어시험에서 만점을 받았어요.

단•어•및•표•현

long face 우울한 얼굴

LISTENING ADVICE

● 'I got a poor grade': How to pronounce [r]

[r]은 혀끝을 구부려 입천장 가까이 가져가서, 천장에 닿지 않은 상태로 소리를 냅니다. 따라서 'poor'는 [푸어]나 [푸얼]이 아닌 [푸어ㄹ]로 들리며, 'grade'는 [그뤠이ㄷ]로 들립니다.

07 부탁(요청)한일파악 ▶ 정답 ③

듣•기•대•본

W: Hey, Patrick. How was your trip to Europe?

M: Hey, Gina. It was fantastic. I want to go again soon.

W: What was the best thing about your trip?

M: I would say it was the beautiful scenery.

W: I guess that's what trips are for. I'm planning a trip to Europe myself.

M: Oh, you are?

W: Yeah. So, can you share your itinerary and budget with me? I want to have some information for when I plan my own trip.

M: Sure. I have organized everything in one file. I'll send it to you when I get home.

W: Thanks.

우•리•말•해•석

여: 얘, Patrick. 네 유럽 여행은 어땠니?

남: 이봐, Gina. 그것은 환상적이었어. 나는 머지않아 또 가고 싶어.

여: 네 여행에서 가장 좋은 것은 무엇이었니?

남: 그것은 아름다운 풍경이었다고 말하고 싶어.

여: 난 그게 여행의 목적이라고 생각해. 나도 혼자 유럽 여행을 계획 중이야.

남: 오, 그래?

여: 응. 그래서 말인데, 너는 네 여행 일정이랑 예산을 나에게 공유해 줄 수 있니? 나는 내 여행을 계획할 때 정보가 좀 있으면 해.

남: 물론이지. 나는 모든 것을 하나의 파일에 정리해 놓았어. 내가 집에 가면 너에게 그것을 보내줄게.

여: 고마워.

단·어·및·표·현

scenery[sí:nəri] 명 풍경, 경치
itinerary[aitínərèri] 명 여행 일정(표)
budget[bʌ́dʒit] 명 예산

08 담화미언급 ▶ 정답 ④

듣·기·대·본

M: Welcome to River Opera House. We opened in 1999 as a hub for local artists. Besides two concert halls, we house three exhibition rooms, as well as training facilities. You can enjoy all of these amenities at a discounted price when you become a member of the River Opera House. The annual membership fee is $200. We also run various educational programs for the general public. For more information, please visit our website.

우·리·말·해·석

남: River 오페라 하우스에 오신 것을 환영합니다. 저희는 1999년에 지역 예술가들을 위한 중심지로서 문을 열었습니다. 두 개의 콘서트 홀 외에도 우리는 교육훈련시설뿐만 아니라 세 개의 전시실을 갖추고 있습니다. River 오페라 하우스의 회원이 되시면 이 모든 편의시설을 할인된 가격에 즐기실 수 있습니다. 연간 회원비는 200달러입니다. 저희는 또한 일반 대중을 위해 다양한 교육 프로그램을 운영합니다. 더 많은 정보를 위해서는 저희 웹사이트를 방문하세요.

단·어·및·표·현

amenity[əménəti] 명 (주로 복수로) 편의 시설

09 담화화제추론 ▶ 정답 ③

듣·기·대·본

M: This is a method of transportation. It allows you to travel long distances. It can accommodate hundreds of people. It can go across not only continents but also oceans. Its design is inspired by birds. People usually take this to go to foreign countries. There are staff who attend to people's needs on it while cruising.

우·리·말·해·석

남: 이것은 교통수단이다. 이것은 당신이 먼 거리를 여행하는 것을 가능하게 해준다. 이것은 수백 명의 사람들을 수용할 수 있다. 이것은 대륙뿐만 아니라 바다도 횡단할 수 있다. 이것의 디자인은 새들에게 영감을 받았다. 사람들은 주로 외국에 갈 때 이것을 탄다. 순항 중에는 사람들의 요구에 응대하는 직원들이 있다.

단·어·및·표·현

accommodate[əkɑ́mədèit] 동 수용하다, 충분한 공간을 제공하다

not only A but also B A뿐만 아니라 B도
inspire[inspáiər] 동 영감을 주다
attend to ~을 응대하다, 돌보다
cruise[kru:z] 동 순항하다

10 어색한대화찾기 ▶ 정답 ③

듣·기·대·본

① M: What course do you want to take in college?
　W: Maybe music or fine arts.
② M: Are you ready? We're leaving in five minutes.
　W: Wait, I'll just get my jacket.
③ M: Where did you spend spring break?
　W: We are going to visit our grandfather in Italy.
④ M: Are you going to the cafeteria for lunch?
　W: No, I brought my own food.
⑤ M: Oh no, I left my homework at home!
　W: Let's go back and get it.

우·리·말·해·석

① 남: 대학에서 어떤 과정을 듣고 싶어?
　여: 아마도 음악이나 순수 미술.
② 남: 준비되었니? 우리는 5분 뒤에 떠날 거야.
　여: 잠깐, 내 재킷을 가져올게.
③ 남: 어디에서 봄 방학을 보냈어?
　여: 우리는 이탈리아에 계신 할아버지를 방문하러 갈 거야.
④ 남: 점심 먹으러 매점에 갈 거야?
　여: 아니, 난 내 음식을 가져왔어.
⑤ 남: 아, 이런, 숙제를 집에 놓고 왔어!
　여: 돌아가서 가져오자.

단·어·및·표·현

spend[spend] 동 (시간을) 보내다, 쓰다

11 할일파악 ▶ 정답 ⑤

듣·기·대·본

M: Hey, Pippa! What are you doing here?
W: I'm going to meet up with my friend. What about you?
M: I just bought some books.
W: I see. Do you want to join us? We're going to have lunch at Steakland.
M: Mmm. I don't think I can.
W: Come on. We might watch a movie after, too.
M: Nah, maybe next time. I have to be home early. It's my sister's birthday today.
W: Oh, okay. Tell her Happy Birthday for me then. See you around.

우·리·말·해·석

남: 이봐, Pippa! 너 여기서 무엇을 하고 있니?
여: 난 친구를 만나기로 했어. 너는?
남: 그냥 책을 좀 샀어.
여: 그렇구나. 너도 우리와 함께할래? 우리는 Steakland에서 점심을 먹을 거야.
남: 음. 난 그럴 수 있을 거 같지 않아.
여: 그러지 말고. 우리는 그 후에 영화도 볼지 몰라.
남: 아니야, 다음에. 나는 집에 일찍 가야 해. 오늘이 내 여동생 생일이야.
여: 오, 알겠어. 그럼 그녀에게 나 대신 생일 축하한다고 말해줘. 또 보자.

단·어·및·표·현

meet up with A A를 만나다

12 도표정보파악 ▶ 정답 ⑤

듣·기·대·본

W: Honey, don't you need some T-shirts? They are on sale.

M: Great! I need some for this summer. What kind of T-shirts do they have?

W: They have T-shirts with two types of neck lines, U-neck and V-neck.

M: I prefer V-necks. I look thinner in V-necks.

W: What color do you want, white or black?

M: I want white T-shirts.

W: Then, you have two options left. Do you need T-shirts made of cooling cotton?

M: Sure. They are helpful in the summer.

W: I agree. Then, pick that one.

우·리·말·해·석

	모델	목둘레선	색상	쿨링 코튼
①	A	U자 모양	흰색	O
②	B	U자 모양	검은색	X
③	C	V자 모양	검은색	O
④	D	V자 모양	흰색	X
⑤	E	V자 모양	흰색	O

여: 여보, 당신은 티셔츠가 좀 필요하지 않나요? 그것들이 세일 중이에요.

남: 좋아요! 저는 이번 여름을 위해 몇 벌 필요해요. 어떤 종류의 티셔츠가 있나요?

여: 목둘레선이 U자 모양인 것과 V자 모양인 것으로 두 종류의 티셔츠가 있어요

남: 저는 V자 모양을 선호해요. 저는 V자 모양인 것을 입었을 때 더 말라 보여요.

여: 당신은 흰색과 검은색 중 어떤 색을 원해요?

남: 저는 흰색 티셔츠를 원해요.

여: 그럼, 당신은 두 가지 선택지가 남았어요. 당신은 쿨링 코튼으로 만든 티셔츠가 필요한가요?

남: 네. 그것들은 여름에 도움이 돼요.

여: 맞아요. 그럼, 그것으로 선택해요.

단·어·및·표·현

on sale 세일 중인

thin [θin] [형] (사람 · 몸 등이) 마른, 가는

made of ~으로 만든

13 수치파악(날짜) ▶ 정답 ④

듣·기·대·본

M: Honey, did you hear that there's going to be a baby fair in town this summer?

W: Oh, really? We should go check it out. When is it taking place?

M: It's being held from August 9th to 13th.

W: How about going on August 10th? Do you have any plans for that day?

M: Yes, I have a dinner appointment with a client on the 10th. What about the 11th?

W: We have a family gathering scheduled for the 11th. Are you free on August 12th?

M: Yes, it's a Saturday. We can spend the whole day exploring the fair together.

우·리·말·해·석

남: 여보, 이번 여름에 시내에서 베이비 페어가 있을 거라는 거 들었어요?

여: 오, 정말요? 우리는 살펴보러 가야 해요. 그것은 언제 열리나요?

남: 그것은 8월 9일부터 13일까지 열릴 거예요.

여: 8월 10일에 가는 것은 어때요? 그날 어떤 계획이 있나요?

남: 네, 저는 10일에 고객과 저녁 약속이 있어요. 11일은 어때요?

여: 우리는 11일에 가족 모임이 예정되어 있잖아요. 8월 12일에는 시간 돼요?

남: 네, 그날은 토요일이죠. 우리는 온종일 함께 페어를 답사하면서 보낼 수 있어요.

단·어·및·표·현

check ~ out (흥미로운 것을) 살펴보다

take place (회의 · 행사 등이) 열리다, 개최되다

appointment [əpɔ́intmənt] [명] (특히 업무 관련) 약속

scheduled [skédʒu:ld] [형] 예정된, 계획된

explore [iksplɔ́:r] [동] 답사하다, 탐험하다

14 한일파악 ▶ 정답 ③

듣·기·대·본

W: Jake, I have something for you.

M: Wow, chocolate cookies? What a surprise! Thank you.

W: I remember you saying that you love chocolate cookies.

M: That's really nice of you. Where did you buy these?

W: Actually, I made them myself yesterday.

M: What? You must be talented at baking.

W: Well, it's not that difficult if you have a good recipe.

M: Oh, really? How long did it take to make these?

W: About an hour.

우·리·말·해·석

여: Jake, 나에게 너를 위한 무언가가 있어.

남: 와, 초콜릿 쿠키야? 놀라워라! 고마워.

여: 네가 초콜릿 쿠키를 아주 좋아한다고 말한 것을 기억해.

남: 너 정말 다정하구나. 너 이것들을 어디서 샀어?

여: 실은 내가 어제 직접 그것들을 만들었어.

남: 뭐라고? 너는 제빵에 재능이 있는 게 틀림없어.

여: 음, 네가 좋은 조리법을 갖고 있다면 그렇게 어렵지 않아.

남: 아, 정말? 이것들을 만드는 데 얼마나 오래 걸렸어?

여: 한 시간 정도.

단·어·및·표·현

What a surprise! (감탄문) 놀라워라!, 깜짝이야!

talented [tǽləntid] [형] (타고난) 재능이 있는

recipe [résəpi:] [명] 조리법

15 담화목적파악 ▶ 정답 ③

듣·기·대·본

M: Hello, students. This is Mr. Anderson, your principal. The fine dust problem is getting worse these days. Today, I'd like to tell you what to do when the fine dust level is high. First of all, close all the windows and turn on the air purifier in the classroom. Second, drink plenty of water as often as possible. Finally, make sure to wear

a mask when you go out. Keep these tips in mind to
<u>protect your health</u>. Thank you.

우·리·말·해·석
남: 안녕하세요, 학생 여러분. 저는 여러분의 교장선생님 Anderson입니다.
요즘 미세 먼지 문제가 점점 악화되고 있습니다. 오늘 저는 여러분께
미세 먼지 수치가 높을 때 무엇을 해야 하는지 말해주고자 합니다. 가
장 먼저, 모든 창문을 닫고 교실 안의 공기 청정기를 켜세요. 둘째, 가
능한 한 자주 많은 양의 물을 마시세요. 마지막으로, 밖에 나갈 때 꼭
마스크를 착용하세요. 이 조언들을 명심하여 여러분의 건강을 보호하
세요. 감사합니다.

단·어·및·표·현
fine dust 미세 먼지
air purifier 공기 청정기
plenty of 많은, 다량의
keep ~ in mind 명심하다, 유념하다

16 수치계산(금액) ▶ 정답 ③

듣·기·대·본
M: Hello. How can I help you?
W: Hi. I'd like to pay for my PC bang <u>session</u>.
M: Sure. Can you tell me your seat number?
W: I used PC number 11.
M: [*Typing sounds*] Okay, you <u>were logged in to</u> the PC for
  five hours, so it's five dollars. Did you order food?
W: Yes, I ordered two cup noodles.
M: Okay, that's three dollars for the cup noodles and five
  dollars for your PC session.
W: All right. Here you go.

우·리·말·해·석
남: 안녕하세요. 어떻게 도와드릴까요?
여: 안녕하세요. 저는 제 PC방 (이용)시간 결제를 하고 싶습니다.
남: 알겠습니다. 저에게 손님의 좌석 번호를 말씀해 주실 수 있나요?
여: 저는 11번 PC를 사용했습니다.
남: [타자 치는 소리] 알겠습니다. 손님은 PC에 5시간 동안 접속되어 있었
  으니 5달러입니다. 음식을 주문하셨나요?
여: 네, 저는 컵라면 2개를 주문했습니다.
남: 네, 컵라면은 3달러이고 PC (이용)시간은 5달러입니다.
여: 알겠습니다. 여기 있습니다.

단·어·및·표·현
pay for 돈을 내다, 대금을 결제하다
session [séʃən] 몡 (특정 활동을 위한) 시간, 기간
log in 접속하다, 로그인하다
order [ɔ́ːrdər] 통 주문하다

17 알맞은응답찾기 ▶ 정답 ②

듣·기·대·본
W: Hi, Peter! Are you busy at the moment?
M: Not really. Do you need some help?
W: Yes. Can you help me look for <u>a place to rent</u>?
M: Oh, are you thinking of moving out?
W: Yes. I'm having some problems with my roommate.
M: That's too bad. Can I ask what the problem is?
W: She doesn't <u>clean up</u>. The living room and the kitchen
  are always <u>messy</u>.

M: Have you talked to her about it?
W: No, I haven't. Do you think I should?
M: Of course. I'm sure you can <u>resolve the issue</u> through
  communication.
W: OK. I will have a <u>heart-to-heart talk with her</u>.

우·리·말·해·석
① 나는 시도해 봤지만, 그녀는 내 말을 들으려 하지 않아.
② 알겠어. 난 그녀와 솔직한 대화를 나눠볼게.
③ 문제없어. 나는 네가 새집 찾는 것을 도와줄 거야.
④ 바로 그거야. 나는 지금 당장 새 장소를 찾는 것이 낫겠어.
⑤ 그것을 깨끗이 유지하는 방법에 대한 조언 고마워.

여: 안녕, Peter! 너는 지금 바쁘니?
남: 아니 별로 바쁘지 않아. 뭔가 도움이 필요하니?
여: 응. 내가 셋집을 찾는 것을 도와줄 수 있니?
남: 오, 너 이사 갈 생각이니?
여: 응. 나는 내 룸메이트와 문제를 좀 겪고 있어.
남: 안됐다. 무엇이 문제인지 내가 물어봐도 되니?
여: 그녀는 청소를 안 해. 거실과 주방이 항상 지저분해.
남: 그것에 대해 그녀에게 이야기해 봤니?
여: 아니, 안 해봤어. 내가 그래야 한다고 생각하니?
남: 당연하지. 나는 네가 소통을 통해 그 문제를 해결할 수 있다고 확신해.
여: **알겠어. 난 그녀와 솔직한 대화를 나눠볼게.**

단·어·및·표·현
at the moment 지금
rent [rent] 통 (집세·사용료 등을 내고) 세내다, 임차하다
move out 이사를 나가다
messy [mési] 혱 지저분한, 엉망인
resolve [rizálv] 통 (문제 등을) 해결하다
heart-to-heart 솔직한, 마음을 터놓고 하는

18 알맞은응답찾기 ▶ 정답 ①

듣·기·대·본
W: Hi, Andy. Who is <u>in your group</u> for the history project?
M: Actually, I was thinking about you. We worked together
  last year and we did an excellent job.
W: I was thinking the same! I have so many good ideas for
  this project.
M: I knew <u>you would</u>, but we still need one more person.
  Do you know anyone?
W: How about Paul? I heard him say he <u>is really interested</u>
  <u>in history</u>.
M: That's great! Do you know his phone number?
W: Yes. I'll call him right now.
M: Okay. I hope he says yes.

우·리·말·해·석
① 알겠어. 나는 그가 좋다고 하길 바라.
② 내 과제는 다음 주 금요일까지야.
③ 역사는 내가 가장 좋아하는 과목이야.
④ 나는 내가 그 시험에서 C를 받은 것을 믿을 수 없어.
⑤ 우리는 그 과제를 지금 바로 시작하는 게 좋겠어.

여: 안녕, Andy. 역사 과제를 위한 너희 조에는 누가 있니?
남: 사실, 나는 너를 생각하고 있었어. 우리는 작년에 같이 했고 우리 아주
  잘 해냈잖아.
여: 나도 같은 생각이었어! 나는 이 과제를 위한 좋은 아이디어들이 정말

많아.

남: 네가 그럴 줄 알았어, 하지만 우리는 아직 한 명이 더 필요해. 아는 사람 있니?

여: Paul은 어때? 나는 그가 역사에 정말 관심이 있다고 말하는 것을 들었어.

남: 좋아! 너는 그의 전화번호를 아니?

여: 응. 내가 그에게 지금 바로 전화할게.

남: 알겠어. 나는 그가 좋다고 하길 바라.

단·어·및·표·현

project [prádʒekt] [명] 과제, 연구 프로젝트

actually [ǽktʃuəli] [부] 사실은, 실제로

be interested in ~에 관심이 있다

be due (제출 기한이) ~까지이다

had better + 동사원형 ~하는 게 좋겠다

19 알맞은응답찾기 ▶ 정답 ③

들·기·대·본

W: Hey, Mike. Can you please do me a favor?

M: Yeah, sure. What is it?

W: Can you keep an eye on my bags? I'll just leave them here beside you.

M: Why? Where are you going?

W: I'm just going to the bathroom.

M: Okay. Hmmm. Can you get me a soda afterwards? There's a food stall near the bathroom.

W: Sure. Is there anything else you want?

M: No. I just want something to drink.

우·리·말·해·석

① 오. 이 음식은 아주 맛있어.
② 너는 내게 거스름돈 주는 것을 잊어버렸어.
③ 아니. 나는 그저 마실 것을 원해.
④ 물론이지. 내가 거기로 널 따라갈게.
⑤ 그냥 똑바로 가다가 왼쪽으로 돌아.

여: 이봐, Mike. 부탁 하나만 들어 줄래?

남: 응, 물론이지. 뭔데?

여: 내 가방들 좀 봐 줄래? 여기 네 옆에다가 그냥 내 가방들을 놔둘게.

남: 왜? 너 어디에 갈 건데?

여: 나는 그저 화장실에 가려는 것뿐이야.

남: 알았어. 흠. 나중에 내게 탄산음료 좀 사다 줄 수 있니? 화장실 근처에 음식 가판대가 있어.

여: 물론이지. 그 밖에 더 필요한 거 있어?

남: 아니. 나는 그저 마실 것을 원해.

단·어·및·표·현

favor [féivər] [명] 부탁, 호의

stall [stɔːl] [명] 매점, 노점

20 상황에적절한말찾기 ▶ 정답 ②

들·기·대·본

W: Ms. Lee is a Taekwondo coach. She is coaching one of her students, Bruce for the local Taekwondo tournament. 15-year-old Bruce has practiced hard for three months. On the day of the tournament, Ms. Lee sees that Bruce is very nervous and his kick isn't as good as usual. So, Ms. Lee would like to tell him that he has the power to win. In this situation, what would Ms. Lee most likely say to Bruce?

Ms. Lee: Bruce, you have all that is needed inside you.

우·리·말·해·석

① 너는 네 발차기를 더 연습해야 해.
② 너는 필요한 모든 것을 네 안에 가지고 있어.
③ 태권도는 멋진 스포츠야, 그렇지 않니?
④ 그 대회는 순식간에(네가 알기도 전에) 끝날 거야.
⑤ 나는 네가 대회에 출전했었는지 몰랐어.

여: 이 선생님은 태권도 사범이다. 그녀는 그녀의 제자 중 한 명인 Bruce를 지역 태권도 대회를 위해 지도하고 있다. 15살의 Bruce는 세 달 동안 열심히 연습했다. 대회 당일에, 이 선생님은 Bruce가 매우 긴장해서 그의 발차기가 평소만큼 좋지 않다는 걸 알아본다. 그래서, 이 선생님은 그에게 그는 이길 힘이 있다고 말하고 싶다. 이 상황에서, 이 선생님은 Bruce에게 뭐라고 말하겠는가?

이 선생님: Bruce, 너는 필요한 모든 것을 네 안에 가지고 있어.

단·어·및·표·현

tournament [túərnəmənt] [명] 토너먼트(승자 진출전), 경기, 대회

as + 원급 + as ~ ~만큼 …한

Words & Expressions Review

1. 편의 시설	2. ~을 계속 지켜보다	3. 옆 주머니
4. ~으로 만든	5. A를 만나다	6. 실수로, 잘못하여
7. ~를 응대하다, 돌보다	8. 예정된, 계획된	9. 운동화
10. 더 이상 못 참다, 지긋지긋하다	11. 봄 방학	12. 살이 빠지다, 체중이 줄다
13. 표가 매진된	14. 토너먼트	15. (제출기한이) ~까지이다
16. 평소의	17. 과제, 연구 프로젝트	18. (가격이) 합리적인, 적정한
19. 일어나다, 발생하다	20. 풍경, 경치	21. 명심하다, 유념하다
22. 시간, 기간	23. 중심지	24. 여행 일정(표)
25. 접속하다, 로그인하다	26. 순항하다	27. 재능이 있는
28. (흥미로운 것을) 살펴보다	29. 우울한 얼굴	30. 대여료, 사용료
31. 영감을 주다	32. 또 봐., 잘 있어.	33. 미세먼지
34. 변경하다, 바꾸다	35. (문제 등을) 해결하다	36. 전시품
37. 솔직한, 마음을 터놓고 하는	38. 이사를 나가다	39. 매점, 노점
40. 나중에, 그 뒤에	41. 공기청정기	42. (시간을) 보내다, 쓰다
43. (사람·몸 등이) 마른, 가는	44. 구매하다, 구입하다	

영어듣기 모의고사 21^회

|정|답|

01 ③	02 ③	03 ④	04 ①	05 ③
06 ③	07 ④	08 ⑤	09 ③	10 ②
11 ①	12 ③	13 ③	14 ③	15 ⑤
16 ③	17 ①	18 ②	19 ③	20 ④

01 그림정보파악(대화)　▶ 정답 ③

듣·기·대·본

M: Hello, do you need some help?

W: Hello, I'm looking for a grocery cart for my grandmother.

M: How about this one with bears on it?

W: It's cute, but I think it's too young for my grandma. I like that flower-patterned one.

M: Okay. It comes in two types, one with a zipper and one with a buckle.

W: Hmm… I prefer the one that closes with a zipper.

M: All right. What about the wheels? I recommend the three-wheel design. It can climb stairs.

W: Sure, I'll take your suggestion. Please give me the one with the three-wheel design.

M: Excellent choice.

우·리·말·해·석

남: 안녕하세요, 도움이 필요하세요?

여: 안녕하세요, 저는 제 할머니를 위한 쇼핑 카트를 찾고 있어요.

남: 곰 그림이 있는 이것은 어떠세요?

여: 그것은 귀엽지만, 저는 그것이 제 할머니에게는 너무 젊다고 생각해요. 저는 저 꽃무늬인 것이 좋아요.

남: 알겠습니다. 그것은 두 가지 형태로 나오는데, 지퍼가 있는 것과 버클이 있는 것입니다.

여: 음… 저는 지퍼로 닫는 것이 더 좋아요.

남: 좋습니다. 바퀴는 어떠세요? 저는 세 바퀴 디자인을 추천합니다. 그것은 계단을 올라갈 수 있습니다.

여: 그럼요, 저는 당신의 제안을 받아들일게요. 저에게 세 바퀴 디자인인 것을 주세요.

남: 훌륭한 선택이십니다.

단·어·및·표·현

grocery [ɡróusəri] 명 식료품점

buckle [bʌ́kl] 명 버클, 잠금장치

recommend [rèkəménd] 동 추천하다

02 대화미언급　▶ 정답 ③

듣·기·대·본

M: Chloe, does the new Max Energy Drink help wake you up?

W: Yes, I drank a can of it a few hours ago and I still don't feel sleepy.

M: What does it taste like?

W: Similar to orange juice, but it has a more bitter taste.

M: I should drink one as well. How much is it?

W: One can is five dollars, but don't drink more than one can per day.

M: Oh, are there side effects?

W: Yes, if you drink too much of it, it might make you dizzy.

M: OK. I'll take note of that.

우·리·말·해·석

남: Chloe, 그 새로운 Max 에너지 드링크가 너의 잠을 깨우는 데 도움이 되니?

여: 응, 나는 몇 시간 전에 그것을 한 캔 마셨는데 아직도 나는 졸리지 않아.

남: 그것은 맛이 어때?

여: 오렌지 주스와 비슷하지만, 그것은 더 쓴맛이 나.

남: 나도 하나 마셔야겠어. 그것은 얼마니?

여: 한 캔에 5달러인데, 하루에 한 캔 이상 마시지 마.

남: 오, 부작용이 있니?

여: 응, 만약 네가 그것을 너무 많이 마시면, 그것은 너를 어지럽게 할 수도 있어.

남: 알겠어. 주의할게.

단·어·및·표·현

bitter [bítər] 형 (음식 등이) 맛이 쓴

as well (…뿐만 아니라) ~도, 또한

side effect 부작용

dizzy [dízi] 형 어지러운

take note of ~에 주의하다, 참고하다

03 전화목적파악　▶ 정답 ④

듣·기·대·본

(*Cellphone rings.*)

M: Hi, Olivia.

W: Hi, Daniel. Can I ask you something?

M: Of course. What is it?

W: I think you said once that you used to sing in a choir as a tenor. Is that right?

M: Yes. It was about two years ago. Why do you ask?

W: Well, someone in my choir has moved to a different city and now we're short of a tenor.

M: Oh, I see.

W: How about joining the choir? We sing at concerts and have lots of fun.

M: Sounds interesting. Do I have to decide right now?

W: No, you can take a few days to think about it.

M: Okay. Then I'll let you know by Monday.

우·리·말·해·석

(휴대전화가 울린다.)

남: 안녕, Olivia.

여: 안녕, Daniel. 뭐 좀 물어봐도 될까?

남: 물론이지. 뭔데?

여: 네가 전에 합창단에서 테너로 노래를 불렀다고 말한 적이 있는 것 같은데. 맞니?

남: 맞아. 약 2년 전이었어. 왜 물어보는 거니?

여: 있잖아, 우리 합창단의 누군가가 다른 도시로 이사 가서 이제 우리는 테너가 부족해.

남: 아, 그렇구나.

여: 합창단에 들어오는 건 어때? 우리는 연주회에서 노래도 부르고 매우 즐거운 시간을 보내.

남: 재미있을 것 같아. 내가 지금 당장 결정해야 하니?

여: 아니, 넌 그것에 대해 며칠 동안 생각해봐도 돼.
남: 알겠어. 그럼 내가 월요일까지 알려줄게.

단·어·및·표·현
used to + 동사 (과거 한때는) ~했다, ~하곤 했다
choir[kwáiər] 몡 합창단, 성가대
be short of ~이 부족하다

04 수치파악(시각) ▶ 정답 ①

듣·기·대·본
(*Cellphone rings.*)
W: Hi, Ben! What's up?
M: Hey, Emily! I just found out about an outdoor concert happening tonight. Are you underlined interested in going?
W: Oh, that sounds fun! When does it start and end?
M: It starts at 6 p.m. and goes until 10 p.m.
W: Hmm, I have a dance class at 8 p.m. Can we go earlier?
M: Sure, we can catch the opening acts. How about meeting up at 6 p.m.?
W: Let's meet earlier than that. I want to grab a front row seat in advance.
M: Okay, sounds good. Let's meet near the main stage around 5 p.m.
W: All right, see you there!

우·리·말·해·석
(휴대전화가 울린다.)
여: 여보세요, Ben! 무슨 일이야?
남: 여보세요, Emily! 나는 오늘 밤 열리는 야외 콘서트에 대해 방금 알았어. 너는 가는 데 관심이 있니?
여: 오, 재밌게 들리는걸! 그것은 언제 시작하고 언제 끝나?
남: 오후 6시에 시작해서 오후 10시까지 계속해.
여: 음, 나는 오후 8시에 춤 수업이 있어. 우리가 조금 더 빨리 갈 수 있을까?
남: 물론이지, 우리는 개막 공연을 볼 수 있어. 오후 6시에 만나는 거 어때?
여: 그것보다 좀 더 일찍 만나자. 나는 미리 앞줄 좌석을 잡고 싶어.
남: 그래, 좋은데. 오후 5시쯤에 메인 무대 근처에서 만나자.
여: 좋아, 거기서 보자!

단·어·및·표·현
catch[kætʃ] 통 ~을 보다[듣다], ~에 참석하다
opening act 개막 공연
grab[græb] 통 잡다
in advance 미리, 사전에

05 심정추론 ▶ 정답 ③

듣·기·대·본
W: Hello, I booked a table under the name of Darla.
M: Miss Darla? I was about to call you. I'm afraid we cannot serve you this evening.
W: Really? What's wrong?
M: There was a small fire in the kitchen. We have to close the restaurant for safety reasons.
W: Oh, dear. Is anyone hurt?
M: Thankfully, no. But this will ruin your plans for the evening.
W: Don't worry about it. We can eat somewhere else.

M: All the same, I do apologize. Hopefully we'll see you again soon.

우·리·말·해·석
① 화난 ② 신난 ③ 미안한 ④ 수줍은 ⑤ 만족하는

여: 안녕하세요, 저는 Darla라는 이름으로 테이블을 예약했습니다.
남: Darla 씨? 저는 당신께 막 전화 드리려고 했습니다. 죄송합니다만 저희는 오늘 저녁 당신에게 식사를 제공할 수 없게 되었습니다.
여: 정말요? 무슨 일이 있나요?
남: 주방에 작은 불이 났습니다. 저희는 안전상의 이유로 식당을 닫아야 합니다.
여: 오, 저런. 다친 사람이 있나요?
남: 다행히도 없습니다. 하지만 이것이 당신의 저녁 계획을 망치게 되었네요.
여: 걱정하지 마세요. 저희는 어딘가 다른 곳에서 먹어도 돼요.
남: 그래도 사과 드립니다. 곧 다시 뵙기를 바랍니다.

단·어·및·표·현
be about to + 동사원형 막 ~하려고 하다
ruin[rú(:)in] 통 망치다, 파괴하다
all the same 그래도, 그럼에도 불구하고

06 그림상황에적절한대화찾기 ▶ 정답 ③

듣·기·대·본
① W: I feel like an egg sandwich for lunch.
   M: I'm afraid we don't have any eggs.
② W: What are you doing right now?
   M: I'm ordering some dishes online.
③ W: Shall I put these eggs back in the fridge?
   M: Yes, please. I won't need any more of them.
④ W: Where is the refrigerator section?
   M: It's over there. Please follow me.
⑤ W: Can you make some fried eggs for me?
   M: Sorry, but I'm busy washing the dishes.

우·리·말·해·석
① 여: 난 점심으로 계란 샌드위치를 먹고 싶어.
   남: 유감이지만, 우리는 계란이 하나도 없어.
② 여: 넌 지금 뭐 하고 있어?
   남: 난 온라인으로 그릇을 몇 개 주문하고 있어.
③ 여: 내가 이 계란들을 냉장고에 다시 넣을까?
   남: 응, 부탁해. 난 더 이상 그것들이 필요 없을 것 같아.
④ 여: 냉장고 코너는 어디에 있어요?
   남: 저쪽에 있어요. 저를 따라오세요.
⑤ 여: 너는 날 위해 계란프라이를 좀 해줄 수 있어?
   남: 미안하지만, 난 지금 설거지하느라 바빠.

단·어·및·표·현
put ~ back ~을 다시 제자리에 갖다 놓다
fridge[fridʒ] 몡 냉장고
section[sékʃən] 몡 부분, 부문, 구획
be busy ~ing ~하느라 바쁘다

07 부탁(요청)한일파악 ▶ 정답 ④

듣·기·대·본
M: Hello, are you moving into this apartment?
W: Yes. I'm Katelin. It's nice to meet you.
M: Hi, I'm Rick. I live in 203. That's a lot of boxes! Let me help you.

W: That's very kind, but my friends are helping, so it's OK.
M: Well, welcome anyway. If you need anything, just let me know.
W: Actually, I don't know how to work the built-in heater. Can you come inside and show me how?
M: No problem.

우·리·말·해·석

남: 안녕하세요. 이 아파트로 이사 들어오시나요?
여: 네. 저는 Katelin입니다. 만나서 반갑습니다.
남: 안녕하세요. 저는 Rick입니다. 203호에 살아요. 상자가 많네요! 도와드릴게요.
여: 정말 친절하시네요, 하지만 제 친구들이 돕고 있으니 괜찮습니다.
남: 그럼, 어쨌든 환영합니다. 필요한 것이 있으면 알려주세요.
여: 실은, 저는 붙박이로 된 난방기를 어떻게 조작해야 할지 모르겠습니다. 들어오셔서서 어떻게 하는 건지 보여주실 수 있으세요?
남: 문제없습니다.

단·어·및·표·현

actually [ǽktʃuəli] ⑨ 실은, 실제로

08 담화미언급 ▶ 정답 ⑤

듣·기·대·본

M: Cornell Fitness Club is looking for new members! We just opened on July 3. We have top-quality exercise equipment, lockers, shower rooms, and a lounge. The club is conveniently located in the city center. We have both group and personal exercise programs for all ages. You can enjoy all of these services with our annual membership. Visit us today, and find out more.

우·리·말·해·석

남: Cornell 헬스클럽이 새 회원을 찾고 있습니다. 저희는 7월 3일에 막 열었습니다. 저희는 최상급의 운동 장비와 사물함, 샤워실, 휴게실이 있습니다. 클럽은 도심부의 편리한 위치에 있습니다. 저희는 모든 연령을 위한 단체와 개인 운동 프로그램을 모두 갖추고 있습니다. 연간 회원권으로 이 서비스들을 모두 즐기실 수 있습니다. 오늘 저희를 방문하셔서 더 많은 것을 알아보세요.

단·어·및·표·현

be located in ~ ~에 위치하다, ~에 있다

09 담화화제추론 ▶ 정답 ③

듣·기·대·본

W: This is usually eaten during one of the Korean holidays. It is a rice cake and it is shaped like a half-moon. It is usually filled with sesame seeds, chestnut paste, or beans. When you cook this, you steam it over a layer of pine needles. There is a belief that if you make this pretty, you will have pretty children and a good-looking partner in the future.

우·리·말·해·석

여: 이것은 보통 한국의 명절 중 한 명절에 먹는다. 이것은 떡이며, 반달 모양이다. 이것은 보통 참깨, 밤 으깬 것, 혹은 콩으로 채워져 있다. 당신은 이것을 요리할 때, 솔잎을 깔아서 그 위에다 이것을 찐다. 만약 당신이 이것을 예쁘게 만들면, 미래에 예쁜 아이와 잘생긴 배우자를 가질 수 있다는 속설이 있다.

단·어·및·표·현

good-looking ⑧ 잘생긴, 보기 좋은

10 어색한대화찾기 ▶ 정답 ②

듣·기·대·본

① M: Why don't we go hiking tomorrow?
　 W: That sounds like a great idea.
② M: Who runs faster?
　 W: I'm running a business.
③ M: What's the matter? You look worried.
　 W: My mom is very sick.
④ M: What's your favorite subject?
　 W: I like English best.
⑤ M: How much does it cost?
　 W: It costs 20 dollars.

우·리·말·해·석

① 남: 내일 하이킹 가는 게 어때?
　 여: 그거 아주 좋은 생각인 것 같아.
② 남: 누가 더 빨리 달리니?
　 여: 난 사업체를 경영하고 있어.
③ 남: 왜 그러니? 걱정스러워 보인다.
　 여: 엄마가 매우 편찮으셔.
④ 남: 네가 제일 좋아하는 과목이 뭐야?
　 여: 난 영어를 제일 좋아해.
⑤ 남: 그것은 얼마예요?
　 여: 20달러예요.

단·어·및·표·현

run [rʌn] ⑧ 달리다, 운영하다

11 할일파악(대화직후) ▶ 정답 ①

듣·기·대·본

W: Hi, what can I get you?
M: Hi, one cappuccino, please.
W: All right. It's 3 dollars. Do you have a stamp card?
M: No. What is it?
W: We give you one stamp for each coffee that you buy. When you collect eight stamps, you get one coffee for free.
M: That's good. How can I get the stamp card?
W: First, you need to download our application on your cellphone.
M: Okay. I'll do it now.

우·리·말·해·석

여: 안녕하세요. 무엇을 드릴까요?
남: 안녕하세요. 카푸치노 하나 주세요.
여: 알겠습니다. 3달러입니다. 당신은 도장 카드를 가지고 있나요?
남: 아니요. 그게 무엇인가요?
여: 우리는 당신이 구매한 각각의 커피에 대해 도장을 하나씩 드립니다. 당신이 도장 여덟 개를 모으면, 당신은 커피 한 잔을 무료로 받습니다.
남: 그거 좋네요. 제가 도장 카드를 어떻게 받을 수 있을까요?
여: 먼저, 당신은 당신의 핸드폰에 우리 앱을 내려받아야 합니다.
남: 알겠어요. 지금 할게요.

단·어·및·표·현

stamp [stæmp] ⑨ 도장
for free 무료로
download [dáunlòud] ⑧ (파일, 앱 등을) 내려받다
application [æ̀pləkéiʃən] ⑨ 앱, 응용프로그램

12 도표정보파악 ▶ 정답 ③

듣·기·대·본

M: Bella, I'm planning to buy a drone for our son as a birthday gift.

W: Do you have one in mind?

M: I'm thinking of buying one on this list. Can you help me choose one?

W: Sure. What about range of control?

M: I think we need over 75 m of range of control.

W: Right. And our son doesn't need more than 30 minutes of flying time.

M: Okay. Then we have two options left.

W: Let's get the cheaper one.

M: Okay. I'll order this one.

우·리·말·해·석

	모델	조종 범위	비행 시간	가격
①	A	50 m	5분	30 달러
②	B	70 m	5분	50 달러
③	C	100 m	10분	90 달러
④	D	150 m	20분	100 달러
⑤	E	200 m	40분	150 달러

남: Bella, 저는 우리 아들에게 생일 선물로 드론을 사줄 계획이에요.
여: 생각해 둔 게 있나요?
남: 이 목록 중에서 하나를 살까 생각 중이에요. 제가 하나를 고르는 걸 도와줄 수 있나요?
여: 물론이죠. 조종 범위는 어떤 걸로 할까요?
남: 저는 75m 이상의 조종 범위가 필요하다고 생각해요.
여: 맞아요. 그리고 우리 아들은 30분 이상의 비행 시간은 필요하지 않아요.
남: 그렇죠. 그럼 우리에게 두 가지 선택지가 남아 있네요.
여: 더 저렴한 것으로 구매합시다.
남: 알겠어요. 이걸로 주문할게요.

단·어·및·표·현

have ~ in mind ~을 생각하다, 염두에 두다
range of control 조종 범위

13 수치파악(날짜) ▶ 정답 ③

듣·기·대·본

M: Hey, Julie! I'm going to visit Matt in the hospital. Do you want to join me?

W: Of course I do. Why don't we go the day after tomorrow? I mean on August 21.

M: Sorry, I can't go that day, but I can make time on Friday, August 23.

W: Friday is the busiest day for me. Well, can you go either on Thursday, August 22 or Saturday, August 24?

M: Thursday is fine with me.

W: That's good. I'm free on Thursday, too.

우·리·말·해·석

남: 이봐, Julie! 난 병원에 있는 Matt를 보러 갈 거야. 나랑 함께 갈래?
여: 물론 가야지. 내일모레 가는 것은 어때? 내 말은 8월 21일 말이야.
남: 미안해, 난 그날 갈 수 없어, 하지만 난 8월 23일 금요일에 시간을 낼 수 있어.
여: 금요일은 내게 가장 바쁜 날이야. 그럼, 8월 22일 목요일이나 8월 24일 토요일에 갈 수 있어?
남: 목요일은 괜찮아.
여: 그거 잘됐다. 나도 목요일에 시간이 돼.

단·어·및·표·현

the day after tomorrow 내일모레(= 모레)
make time (~하는 데) 시간을 내다

LISTENING ADVICE

문장 내에서 의미전달에 중요한 역할을 담당하는 내용어들은 정확하고 강하게 발음되는 한편, 그 자체만으로는 큰 의미가 없는 기능어들은 비교적 짧고 약하게 발음됩니다. 위 문제에서도 날짜나 요일에 해당하는 단어들은 강조되어 들리는 반면에 'on', 'or', 'is' 등의 단어들은 비교적 약하게 들리지요. 문장의 의미를 잘 파악하기 위해서는 강하게 발음되는 단어들에 집중해야 합니다.

14 한일파악 ▶ 정답 ③

듣·기·대·본

M: Amy, I heard you're applying to join our table tennis club.

W: Yeah. I submitted my application form last week. You've been in the club for a while, right?

M: Yes, for a year now. It's fun but you need to practice on a regular basis.

W: I know. I've been watching tutorial videos to learn the basic techniques.

M: That's a good start.

W: Also, yesterday, I bought new table tennis shoes at the sports store.

M: Good for you! If you need anything else, just let me know.

W: Thanks. I'm excited to start playing with everyone!

우·리·말·해·석

남: Amy, 너 우리 탁구 동아리에 가입 신청할 거라고 들었어.
여: 응. 지난주에 신청서를 제출했어. 너 꽤 오래 동아리에 있었지, 맞지?
남: 응, 이제 1년 됐어. 재미있긴 한데 정기적으로 연습해야 해.
여: 알아. 기본 기술을 배우려고 설명 영상을 보고 있어.
남: 좋은 시작이야.
여: 그리고 어제는 스포츠용품점에서 새 탁구화를 샀어.
남: 잘했네! 다른 필요한 거 있으면 그냥 알려줘.
여: 고마워. 모두와 함께 치기 시작하는 게 기대돼!

단·어·및·표·현

apply 신청하다, 지원하다
submit [səbmít] [동] 제출하다
application form 신청서
tutorial [tju(:)tɔ́:riəl] [명] 설명, 지도, 학습

15 담화목적파악 ▶ 정답 ⑤

듣·기·대·본

M: Hello, passengers. Our train is fully air-conditioned, but due to individual preferences regarding temperature, we have compartments with milder air-conditioning. Depending on the compartment you are in, you might feel cold. If you are sensitive to the cold, please move to a compartment with milder air-conditioning. We appreciate your cooperation and understanding in creating a comfortable environment for <u>everyone on board</u>.

남: 안녕하세요, 승객 여러분. 저희 열차는 완전히 냉방 중이지만, 온도에 관한 개인별 선호도 때문에 저희는 약냉방칸들이 있습니다. 여러분이 계신 칸에 따라, 여러분은 춥다고 느끼실 수도 있습니다. 만약 여러분이 추위에 민감하다면, 약냉방칸으로 이동하여 주시기 바랍니다. 저희는 탑승한 모든 고객을 위한 편안한 환경을 조성하는 데 있어서 여러분의 협조와 이해에 감사드립니다.

단·어·및·표·현

due to ~때문에

individual [ìndəvídʒuəl] ⑧ 개인의, 개별의

regarding [rigáːrdiŋ] ⑳ ~에 관하여

compartment [kəmpáːrtmənt] ⑧ 칸, 객실

mild [maild] ⑧ (심하거나 강하지 않고) 약한, 가벼운

sensitive [sénsətiv] ⑧ 민감한, 예민한

cooperation [kouàpəréiʃən] ⑧ 협조, 협력

16 수치계산(금액) ▶ 정답 ③

듣·기·대·본

M: Hello. Welcome to Healthy Bites Cafe.

W: Hi. I'd like an avocado salad and a grilled chicken wrap, please.

M: <u>Certainly</u>. The avocado salad is 9 dollars, and the grilled chicken wrap is 6 dollars. Do you need <u>anything else</u>?

W: How much is a banana smoothie?

M: It's 5 dollars. But if you order it with your salad and wrap, it's only 3 dollars.

W: That's <u>a good deal</u>. I'll <u>add</u> a banana smoothie to my order as well.

M: Great choice. How would you like to pay?

W: I'll <u>pay with</u> my credit card.

남: 안녕하세요. Healthy Bites 카페에 오신 것을 환영합니다.

여: 안녕하세요. 아보카도 샐러드와 구운 치킨랩 주세요.

남: 알겠습니다. 아보카도 샐러드는 9달러이고 구운 치킨랩은 6달러입니다. 그 밖에 또 필요한 것이 있으신가요?

여: 바나나 스무디는 얼마인가요?

남: 5달러입니다. 하지만 샐러드와 랩과 함께 주문하시면 3달러밖에 하지 않습니다.

여: 괜찮은 가격이네요. 제 주문에 바나나 스무디도 추가할게요.

남: 탁월한 선택입니다. 결제는 어떻게 하시겠어요?

여: 신용카드로 결제할게요.

단·어·및·표·현

grilled [grild] ⑧ 구운

as well ~도, 또한

17 알맞은응답찾기 ▶ 정답 ①

듣·기·대·본

M: What's that?

W: I'm just <u>looking at</u> some room design ideas.

M: Oh, are you going to redo your bedroom?

W: I'm planning on it. I need <u>more storage</u> for my clothes.

M: Sounds like a big project.

W: It is. By the way, do you have a <u>tape measure</u> that I can

borrow? I need to see how much space I have for new drawers.

M: **Sure thing. Let me just get it for you.**

① 물론. 너를 위해 지금 가져다줄게.

② 나에게 줄자를 빌려줘서 고마워.

③ 왜 너는 네 방을 다시 디자인할 거니?

④ 알았어. 우리는 내일 서랍장을 살 거야.

⑤ 응, 그것은 네 서랍장에 충분한 공간인 것 같아.

남: 그것은 뭐니?

여: 그냥 방 디자인 아이디어 몇 개를 보고 있는 중이야.

남: 오, 너 네 방을 리모델링할 거니?

여: 나는 그렇게 계획하고 있어. 내 옷들을 위한 수납공간이 더 필요해.

남: 큰 프로젝트인 것 같아.

여: 맞아. 그건 그렇고, 너한테 내가 빌릴 수 있는 줄자가 있니? 나는 새로운 서랍장을 위해 얼마나 공간이 있는지 봐야 하거든.

남: **물론. 너를 위해 지금 가져다줄게.**

단·어·및·표·현

storage [stɔ́ːridʒ] ⑧ 수납공간, 창고

by the way 그건 그렇고, 그런데

🎧 **LISTENING ADVICE**

한 단어 내에서 동일한 자음이 연속될 때, 앞의 자음은 탈락하고 뒤에 오는 자음만 발음합니다. 그러므로 'planning'은 [플래닝]이 아닌 [플래닝]으로 발음되며 'borrow'는 [바르러우]가 아닌 [바러우]로 발음됩니다.

---

18 알맞은응답찾기 ▶ 정답 ②

듣·기·대·본

M: Hello. May I help you?

W: Yes, I'd like to buy a bag.

M: Sure. We have <u>a beautiful collection</u> of bags this season. What size are you looking for?

W: I'd like a small one with a long strap.

M: Okay. Would you like a <u>metal</u> strap or a <u>leather</u> strap?

W: Oh, a leather strap would be better for me. Metal straps <u>tend to get caught</u> on my clothes.

M: Sure. Do you also need <u>pockets for cards</u> inside the bag?

W: **Yes. It would be useful to have them.**

① 문제없어요. 저는 현금으로 지불할 수 있어요.

② 네. 그것들이 있는 것이 유용할 거예요.

③ 아뇨, 제 옷에는 어떤 주머니도 없어요.

④ 저는 금속 끈이 있는 가방에 대한 환불을 원해요.

⑤ 죄송하지만 저희는 어울리는 옷이 전혀 없습니다.

남: 안녕하세요. 도와드릴까요?

여: 네, 저는 가방을 하나 사고 싶어요.

남: 알겠습니다. 저희는 이번 시즌의 아름다운 가방 컬렉션이 있습니다. 고객님은 어떤 사이즈를 찾고 계신가요?

여: 저는 끈이 긴 작은 것을 원해요.

남: 알겠습니다. 고객님은 금속 끈을 원하시나요, 가죽 끈을 원하시나요?

여: 오, 가죽 끈이 저에게 더 나을 것 같아요. 금속 끈은 제 옷에 걸리는 경향이 있어요.

남: 알겠습니다. 고객님은 가방 안에 카드를 위한 주머니도 필요하신가요?
여: 네. 그것들이 있는 것이 유용할 거예요.

단·어·및·표·현

collection [kəlékʃən] 몡 신상품들, 컬렉션
strap [stræp] 몡 끈, 줄
metal [métəl] 몡 금속
leather [léðər] 몡 가죽
tend to + 동사원형 ~하는 경향이 있다
get caught on (손가락·옷자락 등이) 걸리다, 끼다

19 알맞은응답찾기 ▶ 정답 ③

듣·기·대·본

W: This is awful.
M: What's the matter, Miranda?
W: It's this news article that I'm reading.
M: What is it about?
W: It's about a factory that's <u>dumping chemicals</u> into the river.
M: Dumping chemicals? That's terrible! There are people who <u>live along the river</u>.
W: Tell me about it. The article says the factory has been doing it for years.
M: How can they do it? <u>Don't they know it's against the law?</u>
W: <u>Well, they obviously chose to ignore the law.</u>

우·리·말·해·석

① 그래, 법은 중요한 주제라고 생각해.
② 그들은 좋은 사람들이니까 알고 있어.
③ 음, 그들은 분명히 법을 무시하기로 했어.
④ 너는 공장들에 대해 기사를 더 써야 해.
⑤ 그것은 단지 하나의 뉴스일 뿐이야. 너무 많은 의미를 두려고 하지 마.

여: 이거 끔찍하다.
남: 무슨 일이야, Miranda?
여: 내가 읽고 있는 이 뉴스 기사 말이야.
남: 뭐에 대한 거야?
여: 화학 약품들을 강에 버리는 공장에 관한 것이야.
남: 화학 약품들을 버린다고? 끔찍하다! 강가에 사는 사람들이 있잖아.
여: 그러게 말이야. 기사에 따르면 그 공장은 몇 년 동안 그렇게 해왔대.
남: 어떻게 그럴 수 있어? 그들은 그것이 불법이라는 것을 몰랐나?
여: 음, 그들은 분명히 법을 무시하기로 했어.

단·어·및·표·현

dump [dʌmp] 통 버리다

20 상황에적절한말찾기 ▶ 정답 ④

듣·기·대·본

W: Suji is in a clothing shop. She <u>decides to buy</u> the T-shirt she really likes. When she is about to pay for it, she finds a small stain on it. She asks the <u>clerk</u> to give her another one, but the clerk says it is <u>the last one</u> in stock. She really wants to buy that T-shirt, even if there's a stain on it. <u>So she wants to ask the clerk if she can get a discount.</u> In this situation, what would Suji say to the clerk?
Suji: <u>Can you lower the price a little bit?</u>

우·리·말·해·석

① 전 현금으로 계산할게요.
② 얼룩 제거제가 있나요?
③ 전 이것을 싸게 샀어요.
④ 가격을 좀 낮춰 주실 수 있나요?
⑤ 세일은 언제 시작하나요?

여: 수지는 옷 가게에 있다. 그녀는 정말 마음에 드는 티셔츠를 사기로 결정한다. 그녀가 막 계산을 하려는 찰나에 티셔츠에 있는 작은 얼룩을 발견한다. 그녀는 점원에게 다른 것으로 달라고 했지만, 점원은 이것이 마지막 재고 상품이라고 말한다. 그녀는 얼룩이 있어도 정말로 그 티셔츠를 사고 싶다. 그래서 그녀는 할인을 받을 수 있는지 점원에게 물어보고 싶다. 이러한 상황에서, 수지는 점원에게 무엇이라 말하겠는가?
수지: 가격을 좀 낮춰 주실 수 있나요?

단·어·및·표·현

be about to + 동사원형 막 ~하려고 하다
get a discount 할인 받다

Words & Expressions Review

1. 망치다, 파괴하다	2. 사실은, 실제로	3. 맛이 쓴
4. 미리, 사전에	5. 설명, 지도, 학습	6. 줄자
7. 무료로	8. ~을 다시 제자리에 갖다 놓다	9. ~을 보다[듣다], ~에 참석하다
10. 신청하다, 지원하다	11. 다시 하다	12. ~이 부족하다
13. 분명히	14. 운동 장비	15. 막 ~하려고 하다
16. 달리다, 운영하다	17. 버리다	18. 제출하다
19. 부작용	20. ~으로 가득 차다	21. 싼값으로
22. 개인의, 개별의	23. 수납공간, 창고	24. 구운
25. 냉장고	26. 식료품점	27. 이유, 까닭
28. 편리하게	29. 내일모레	30. 끈, 줄
31. 부분, 부문, 구획	32. 그래도, 그럼에도 불구하고	33. ~을 생각하다, 염두에 두다
34. 무시하다	35. ~에 위치하다	36. (~하는 데) 시간을 내다
37. 민감한, 예민한	38. 얼룩	39. 추천하다
40. 어울리다	41. 합창단, 성가대	42. ~로 이사[이동]하다
43. 도장	44. 찌다, 증기	

|정|답|

01 ①	02 ⑤	03 ⑤	04 ④	05 ②
06 ③	07 ⑤	08 ④	09 ④	10 ⑤
11 ②	12 ①	13 ⑤	14 ③	15 ③
16 ④	17 ④	18 ⑤	19 ①	20 ③

01 그림정보파악(대화) ▶ 정답 ①

듣·기·대·본

M: Hello, how can I assist you today?

W: Hi, I'm looking for a nice chair for my computer desk.
M: We have chairs with wheels and chairs without wheels. Which type do you prefer?
W: I need a chair that has wheels. It will help me move more freely within my room.
M: All right. Do you need a chair that has armrests to support your arms and hands?
W: Yes, I need armrests, but I don't want a headrest. I've found that a headrest lowers my productivity.
M: I understand. Then, I think this chair would be perfect for you.
W: Yes, that looks perfect. I'll take it.

우•리•말•해•석

남: 안녕하세요. 오늘 어떻게 도와드릴까요?
여: 안녕하세요. 저는 제 컴퓨터 책상을 위한 좋은 의자를 하나 찾고 있어요.
남: 저희는 바퀴가 있는 의자들과 바퀴가 없는 의자들이 있습니다. 어떤 종류를 선호하세요?
여: 저는 바퀴가 달린 의자가 필요해요. 그것은 제 방 안에서 제가 더 자유롭게 움직이는 데 도움이 될 거예요.
남: 알겠습니다. 손님은 팔과 손을 지탱해줄 팔걸이가 있는 의자가 필요하신가요?
여: 네, 저는 팔걸이가 필요하지만 머리 받침대는 원하지 않아요. 저는 머리 받침대가 제 생산성을 낮춘다는 것을 알았거든요.
남: 알겠습니다. 그렇다면 제 생각에 이 의자가 손님에게 꼭 맞을 것 같아요.
여: 네, 그것은 완벽해 보이네요. 그것으로 할게요.

단•어•및•표•현

assist [əsíst] [동] 돕다, 도와주다
armrest [ɑ́ːrmrèst] [명] 팔걸이
headrest [hédrèst] [명] 머리 받침대
productivity [pròudəktívəti] [명] 생산성
perfect [pə́ːrfikt] [형] 꼭 맞는, 완벽한

02 대화미언급 ▶ 정답 ⑤

듣•기•대•본

W: Honey, look at this poster about the World Camping Fair.
M: Oh, it's in the first week of next month. We should go.
W: Yes. It'll be held at the Grand Convention Center. That's only 10 minutes away by car.
M: Great. Will there be any programs for kids?
W: Yes, it says here that there's a tumbler printing program.
M: Cool. Our kids will love that.
W: Yeah. And we'd better book our tickets in advance. They are 9 dollars each.
M: Okay. Let's buy them today!

우•리•말•해•석

여: 여보, 세계 캠핑 박람회에 관한 이 포스터를 봐요.
남: 오, 그것은 다음 달 첫 주에 있네요. 우리는 가야 해요.
여: 그래요. 그것은 그랜드 컨벤션 센터에서 열릴 거예요. 그곳은 차로 10분밖에 걸리지 않아요.
남: 잘됐네요. 거기에는 아이들을 위한 프로그램이 있을까요?
여: 네, 여기에 텀블러 인쇄 프로그램이 있다고 쓰여 있어요.
남: 멋져요. 우리 아이들은 그것을 정말 좋아할 거예요.
여: 맞아요. 그리고 우리는 사전에 우리 표를 예매하는 게 좋겠어요. 그것들은 각각 9달러예요.
남: 알겠어요. 오늘 그것들을 사죠!

단•어•및•표•현

fair [fɛər] [명] 박람회
be held 열리다, 개최되다
had better + 동사원형 ~하는 게 좋겠다
book a ticket 표를 예매하다
in advance 사전에, 미리

03 전화목적파악 ▶ 정답 ⑤

듣•기•대•본

(*Cellphone rings.*)
W: Hello?
M: Hello, this is Fast Delivery Service. Is this Natalia Shin?
W: Yes, this is she.
M: I am calling to let you know that your delivery will be delayed.
W: Oh no… Could I ask why? And how long is it going to be delayed?
M: Because of the heavy rain, our storage area flooded. So, it will be at least a week before we ship out any products.
W: I see… I guess I have no choice but to wait. Thank you for calling me to let me know.
M: Thank you. I'm very sorry for the inconvenience.

우•리•말•해•석

(휴대전화가 울린다.)
여: 여보세요?
남: 안녕하세요, Fast Delivery 서비스입니다. Natalia Shin님 맞으세요?
여: 네, 맞습니다.
남: 저는 고객님의 배송이 지연될 것을 알려드리기 위해 전화드렸습니다.
여: 오 이런... 왜인지 물어봐도 되나요? 그리고 얼마나 오래 지연될까요?
남: 폭우 때문에, 저희 창고가 침수됐어요. 따라서, 저희는 어떤 제품이든 발송하기까지 최소한 일주일은 걸릴 것입니다.
여: 그렇군요... 저는 기다릴 수밖에 없을 것 같네요. 알려주기 위해 전화주셔서 감사해요.
남: 감사합니다. 불편을 드려 정말 죄송합니다.

단•어•및•표•현

delay [diléi] [동] 지연하다, 연기하다
storage area 창고
flood [flʌd] [동] 침수되다, 물에 잠기다
ship out ~을 발송하다, 보내다
have no choice but to + 동사원형 ~할 수밖에 없다
inconvenience [ìnkənvíːnjəns] [명] 불편, 애로

04 수치파악(시각) ▶ 정답 ④

듣•기•대•본

(*Telephone rings.*)
M: Hello, Herington Dance Studio. How may I help you?
W: Hi, this is Julia Dunkin, and I'd like to change my class time tomorrow.
M: Okay. What time is your class?
W: 7 a.m. but I'd like to change it to sometime in the evening.

M: Sure. What time?
W: Can I join the 5 p.m. class?
M: I'm afraid that class is already full.
W: Oh, that's too bad. How about the 6 p.m. class?
M: You are in luck. We have one spot left. I will sign you up for that class.
W: That's great! Thank you so much.

우•리•말•해•석

(전화벨이 울린다.)
남: 여보세요, Herington Dance Studio입니다. 어떻게 도와드릴까요?
여: 여보세요, 저는 Julia Dunkin이고, 저는 내일 제 수업 시간을 변경하고 싶어요.
남: 알겠습니다. 고객님의 수업은 몇 시인가요?
여: 오전 7시지만 저는 저녁 시간대로 변경하고 싶어요.
남: 네. 몇 시로요?
여: 제가 오후 5시 수업에 참여할 수 있나요?
남: 유감스럽게도 그 수업은 이미 찼어요.
여: 아, 안됐네요. 오후 6시 수업은 어때요?
남: 고객님은 운이 좋네요. 한 자리 남았어요. 저는 고객님을 그 수업에 등록할게요.
여: 잘됐네요! 정말 감사해요.

단•어•및•표•현

be in luck 운이 좋다, 재수가 좋다
spot [spɑt] [명] 자리, 장소
sign up for ~ ~에 등록하다, 신청하다

05 심정추론 ▶ 정답 ②

듣•기•대•본

W: Hey, why didn't you come to our club meeting yesterday?
M: My brother was sick. I had to take him to the hospital.
W: I'm sorry to hear that. What did the doctor say?
M: The doctor said it's a severe cold.
W: That's too bad. Is he okay now?
M: His fever's down, but he still has a bad cough. I feel sorry for him.
W: Oh, I hope he gets well soon.
M: Thanks.

우•리•말•해•석

① 부끄러운 ② 걱정하는 ③ 지루한
④ 긴장한 ⑤ 기쁜

여: 얘, 넌 어제 우리 동아리 모임에 왜 안 왔니?
남: 내 남동생이 아팠어. 나는 그를 병원에 데려가야 했어.
여: 유감이야. 의사가 뭐래?
남: 의사는 심한 감기라고 했어.
여: 너무 안됐다. 그는 지금은 괜찮니?
남: 그의 열은 내려갔지만 그는 여전히 기침이 심해. 그가 불쌍해.
여: 아, 그가 얼른 낫기를 바라.
남: 고마워.

단•어•및•표•현

severe [sivíər] [형] (태풍 · 병 등이) 심한, 중한
fever [fíːvər] [명] 열
cough [kɔ(ː)f] [명] 기침(이 나는 병)
feel sorry for ~를 불쌍하게 여기다
get well (병이) 낫다, 회복하다

06 그림상황에적절한대화찾기 ▶ 정답 ③

듣•기•대•본

① M: I am starving. I need food right now!
W: Okay, calm down! Let's go get some food.
② M: Excuse me, where can I find the restroom?
W: Oh, the restroom is right next to the entrance.
③ M: Would you like a paper or plastic bag for your items?
W: I will have a paper bag, please. Thank you.
④ M: Where can I find light bulbs?
W: You can find them in aisle number 7.
⑤ M: Can I have a cup of black coffee with sugar on the side?
W: Sure, no problem. Here you go.

우•리•말•해•석

① 남: 저는 몹시 배가 고파요. 전 지금 당장 음식이 필요해요!
여: 알겠어요, 진정해요! 음식을 좀 먹으러 가요.
② 남: 실례합니다만, 화장실은 어디에 있나요?
여: 아, 화장실은 입구 바로 옆에 있어요.
③ 남: 당신의 물건을 (담기) 위해 종이봉투 혹은 비닐봉투를 원하세요?
여: 종이봉투로 주세요. 감사해요.
④ 남: 전구는 어디에 있나요?
여: 당신은 그것들을 7번 통로에서 찾을 수 있어요.
⑤ 남: 블랙 커피 한 잔에 설탕을 따로 주시겠어요?
여: 네, 물론이죠. 여기 있습니다.

단•어•및•표•현

starve [stɑːrv] [동] 몹시 배고프다, 굶주리다
aisle [ail] [명] 통로
on the side (위에 얹지 않고) 따로 제공되는

07 부탁(요청)한일파악 ▶ 정답 ⑤

듣•기•대•본

W: Honey, what's wrong?
M: My laptop's not working.
W: What happened?
M: It froze while I was updating this software, and I don't have time to fix it myself.
W: You have to go to work, don't you?
M: Yes. Could you take my laptop to the computer repair shop while I'm at work?
W: Of course, I'm happy to help.

우•리•말•해•석

여: 여보, 무슨 일이에요?
남: 내 노트북 컴퓨터가 작동하지 않아요.
여: 무슨 일이 있었죠?
남: 이 소프트웨어를 업데이트 하는 동안 멈춰 버렸는데, 내가 직접 고칠 시간이 없어요.
여: 당신 일하러 가야 하잖아요, 그렇지 않아요?
남: 그래요. 내가 일하는 동안 당신이 컴퓨터 수리점에 내 노트북 컴퓨터를 가져다줄 수 있어요?
여: 물론이죠. 기꺼이 도와줄게요.

단•어•및•표•현

laptop [lǽptɑ̀p] [명] 노트북 컴퓨터
be at work 일하다

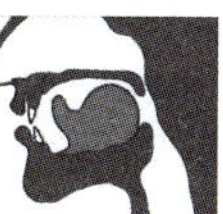

LISTENING ADVICE

- 'Could you take my laptop to the computer repair shop while I'm at work?' : How to pronounce [r]

[r]은 혀끝을 구부려 입천장 가까이 가져가서, 천장에 닿지 않은 상태로 소리를 냅니다. [r] 소리에 유의하며 위 문장을 다시 한 번 들어보고 읽어보세요.

08 담화미언급 ▶ 정답 ④

듣·기·대·본

W: Attention, class. I have a new assignment for you called Future of the Environment. You will write an essay about what our natural environment will be like in the future. The essay should be no more than 1,000 words. Pick out a book on the topic, write a review of it and submit your review before the end of the term. Grades will be based on clarity of presentation, flow of ideas, and correct sentence structure. I will post additional details on the school website.

우·리·말·해·석

여: 주목하세요, 학생 여러분. 여러분에게 환경의 미래라고 불리는 새로운 과제가 있습니다. 여러분은 미래에 우리의 자연 환경이 어떻게 될 것인지에 대한 에세이를 쓸 것입니다. 그 에세이는 1,000단어를 넘지 않아야 합니다. 이 주제에 대한 책을 고르고, 그것에 대한 보고서를 쓰고, 학기가 끝나기 전에 보고서를 제출하세요. 성적은 표현의 명확성, 아이디어의 흐름, 그리고 올바른 문장 구조에 기초할 것입니다. 저는 추가적인 세부 사항을 학교 홈페이지에 게시하겠습니다.

단·어·및·표·현

assignment [əsáinmənt] 몡 과제
essay [ései] 몡 에세이, 수필
submit [səbmít] 통 제출하다
term [təːrm] 몡 학기
be based on ~ ~에 기초하다
clarity [klǽrəti] 몡 명확성, 명료성
detail [ditéil] 몡 세부 사항

09 담화화제추론 ▶ 정답 ④

듣·기·대·본

M: This is a common electronic device that can be found in the house. Usually, this can be found in the kitchen. People use this to store food and drinks. It comes in many different designs and sizes, but usually, it is rectangular. People can use this to keep things cold and even freeze things. Its cold temperature lowers bacteria reproduction and reduces the rate of spoilage.

우·리·말·해·석

남: 이것은 집에서 찾을 수 있는 흔한 전자기기이다. 보통, 이것은 주방에서 찾을 수 있다. 사람들은 이것을 음식과 마실 것을 보관하기 위해 사용한다. 이것은 많은 다른 디자인과 크기로 나오지만, 보통 직사각형이다. 사람들은 음식을 차갑게 하고 심지어 얼리기 위해 이것을 사용한다. 이것의 차가운 온도는 박테리아 번식을 낮추고 부패 속도를 감소시킨다.

단·어·및·표·현

store [stɔːr] 통 보관하다, 저장하다

lower [lóuər] 통 낮추다[내리다]
reproduction [rìːprədʌ́kʃən] 몡 번식, 생식
reduce [ridjúːs] 통 감소시키다, 줄이다
rate [reit] 몡 속도
spoilage [spɔ́ilidʒ] 몡 (음식·식품의) 부패[손상]

10 어색한대화찾기 ▶ 정답 ⑤

듣·기·대·본

① M: It looks like it's going to rain.
　 W: Oh, no! I didn't bring my umbrella.
② M: What time do you normally go to bed?
　 W: Somewhere between 11 p.m. and midnight.
③ M: I think these shoes are too tight for me.
　 W: Let's try on some bigger shoes then.
④ M: What did you think of the movie?
　 W: It wasn't a good movie, but I've seen worse.
⑤ M: How long can you hold your breath underwater?
　 W: I can hold onto your things for you.

우·리·말·해·석

① 남: 비가 올 것처럼 보이네.
　 여: 오, 안 돼! 난 내 우산을 가져오지 않았어.
② 남: 너는 보통 몇 시에 자?
　 여: 오후 11시와 자정 그 사이 어딘가.
③ 남: 이 신발들은 나에게 너무 꽉 조이는 것 같아.
　 여: 그러면 좀 더 큰 신발들로 신어보자.
④ 남: 너는 그 영화에 대해 어떻게 생각했어?
　 여: 좋은 영화는 아니었지만, 나는 더 심한 것도 봤어.
⑤ 남: 너는 물 속에서 얼마나 오래 숨을 참을 수 있어?
　 여: 나는 너를 위해 너의 물건을 맡아줄 수 있어.

단·어·및·표·현

tight [tait] 톙 꽉 조이는, 딱 붙는
hold one's breath 숨을 참다
underwater [ʌ̀ndərwɔ́ːtər] 튄 물 속에서
hold onto ~을 맡아두다, 간수하다

11 할일파악(대화직후) ▶ 정답 ②

듣·기·대·본

M: Mom, what's all this?
W: Hi, honey. I'm preparing a special dinner. Your father got promoted!
M: That's great! Is there anything I can help you with?
W: Can you slice some carrots for me?
M: I'm on it. Are they for the salad?
W: Yes. The potatoes and steaks are ready, but I can't find any cheese for the salad.
M: Oh, I ate the last piece. I'll go and buy some at the store.
W: Thanks, honey. I'll have the soup ready when you get back.

우·리·말·해·석

남: 엄마, 이게 다 뭐예요?
여: 안녕, 얘야. 나는 특별한 저녁을 준비 중이란다. 네 아버지가 승진하셨어!
남: 잘됐네요! 제가 뭐 도와드릴 일이 있을까요?
여: 너는 나를 위해 당근을 좀 썰어줄 수 있겠니?
남: 알겠어요. 그것들은 샐러드용이에요?

22 회 모의고사

여: 응. 감자와 스테이크는 준비가 되었는데, 샐러드에 넣을 치즈를 못 찾겠네.

남: 아, 제가 마지막 한 조각을 먹었어요. 제가 가게에 가서 좀 사올게요.

여: 고맙구나, 얘야. 네가 돌아올 때 수프를 준비해 둘게.

prepare[pripɛ́ər] 통 준비하다, 마련하다
promote[prəmóut] 통 승진[진급]시키다
slice[slais] 통 (얇게) 썰다, 자르다
I'm on it. 알겠어요, 제가 할게요.

12 도표정보파악 ▶ 정답 ①

듣·기·대·본

M: Natalie, what are you looking at on your phone?

W: I'm trying to buy a smartwatch. You have one; can you help me choose one?

M: Sure. Let's choose the face of the watch first. Which do you prefer, round or square?

W: I'd like a round one better.

M: OK. Then, what about the battery life?

W: I don't want to have to charge it too often.

M: Then, why don't you choose one that lasts at least 48 hours?

W: Great. Leather straps go well with casual outfits, right?

M: Yes. Leather straps are a better fit for casual outfits than metal straps.

W: All right. I'll order this one.

우·리·말·해·석

	모델	(시계의) 앞면 모양	배터리 수명	(시계) 줄
①	A	원형	48시간	가죽
②	B	원형	36시간	가죽
③	C	원형	60시간	금속
④	D	정사각형	48시간	가죽
⑤	E	정사각형	36시간	금속

남: Natalie, 넌 네 전화로 뭘 보고 있니?

여: 나는 스마트워치를 사려고 하고 있어. 너는 하나 있으니까, 내가 하나 고르는 것을 도와줄 수 있니?

남: 물론이지. 먼저, 시계의 앞면(모양)을 고르자. 너는 어떤 것을 더 선호해, 원형 아니면 정사각형?

여: 나는 원형의 것이 더 좋아.

남: 응. 그러면, 배터리 수명은 어때?

여: 나는 그것을 너무 자주 충전해야 하는 걸 원하지 않아.

남: 그러면, 최소 48시간 지속되는 것을 고르는 건 어때?

여: 좋아. 가죽 줄들은 평상복에 잘 어울려, 그렇지?

남: 응. 가죽 줄들은 금속 줄들보다 평상복에 더 잘 어울려.

여: 좋아. 난 이걸로 주문해야겠다.

face[feis] 명 (시계의) 앞면 (모양)
prefer[prifə́ːr] 통 선호하다
charge[tʃɑːrdʒ] 통 충전하다
last[læst] 통 지속되다
at least 최소한
leather[léðər] 명 가죽
go well with ~와 잘 어울리다
metal[métəl] 명 금속

---

casual outfit 평상복
fit[fit] 명 어울림, 조화 형 어울리는

13 수치파악(날짜) ▶ 정답 ⑤

듣·기·대·본

M: Hi, Mandy. Have you heard that a Cup Noodles Museum is opening in Seoul?

W: Yes. It was really popular in Japan, and I'm so glad that it's coming to Seoul.

M: Do you know when it will open?

W: On October 14th. Would you like to go together?

M: Sounds great! Are you free on October 16th?

W: I'm afraid not. I have to do some volunteer work that day. How about October 22nd?

M: I'm going camping with my dad on the 22nd. Are you available on the 25th?

W: October 25th works for me. I will see you then.

우·리·말·해·석

남: 안녕, Mandy. 너는 서울에서 컵라면 박물관이 열린다는 것을 들었어?

여: 응. 그건 일본에서 매우 인기 있었고 나는 그것이 서울로 와서 너무 기뻐.

남: 너는 그것이 언제 열리는지 알아?

여: 10월 14일에. 너 같이 갈래?

남: 좋은걸! 너는 10월 16일에 한가해?

여: 안타깝게도 아니야. 나는 그날 자원봉사 일을 좀 해야 해. 10월 22일은 어때?

남: 나는 22일에 아빠랑 캠핑을 가. 넌 25일에 시간이 있니?

여: 10월 25일은 나에게 괜찮아. 그때 보자.

do volunteer work 자원 봉사 일을 하다
available[əvéiləbl] 형 시간이 있는
work for (특정 일시·상황 등이) ~에게 괜찮다, 문제없다

14 한일파악 ▶ 정답 ③

듣·기·대·본

W: Richard, do you have any plans for the summer?

M: I'm thinking of travel(l)ing a bit. How about you?

W: I'm taking piano lessons. My cousin says playing the piano is a good hobby.

M: I think your cousin is right.

W: Where are you planning to go, by the way?

M: To the southern part of the country.

W: Will you visit the islands, too?

M: Of course. I just booked my train ticket yesterday.

W: Cool. I'm sure you'll have a wonderful vacation.

우·리·말·해·석

여: Richard, 너는 여름에 무언가 계획이 있니?

남: 나는 여행을 좀 갈까 생각 중이야. 너는?

여: 나는 피아노 레슨을 받을 거야. 내 사촌이 말하길 피아노를 치는 것은 좋은 취미래.

남: 나는 네 사촌 말이 맞다고 생각해.

여: 그런데, 너는 어디로 갈 계획이니?

남: 남부 지방으로.

여: 너는 섬들도 방문할 거니?

남: 당연하지. 나는 바로 어제 내 기차표를 예매했어.

여: 멋지다. 나는 네가 아주 멋진 방학을 보낼 거라고 확신해.

a bit 조금, 약간
by the way 그런데

15 담화목적파악 ▶ 정답 ③

W: Good afternoon, residents! This is Alice Walker from the management office. We have been receiving many complaints from residents about disturbances caused by people who are moving out. So, I'd like to ask you to follow these guidelines when you move out. First, contact the management office to reserve an elevator two weeks before moving out. Second, do not park your moving truck in front of the building entrance. Finally, put all oversized garbage in the proper area for pickup. Thank you for your cooperation.

여: 안녕하세요, 주민 여러분! 관리사무소의 Alice Walker입니다. 저희는 이사를 가시는 분들로 인해 유발된 소란에 대해 거주민들로부터 많은 항의를 받고 있습니다. 그래서 여러분이 이사를 가실 때 이 지침들을 따라 주시기를 부탁드립니다. 먼저 이사를 가시기 2주 전에 엘리베이터를 예약하기 위해 관리사무소로 연락 주시기 바랍니다. 둘째, 이사 트럭을 건물 입구 앞에 주차하지 마세요. 마지막으로, 모든 대형 쓰레기는 수거를 위한 적절한 장소에 놓아주세요. 협조해 주셔서 감사합니다.

resident [rézidənt] 명 주민, 거주자
complaint [kəmpléint] 명 항의, 불편
disturbance [distə́:rbəns] 명 소란, 소동, 방해
move out 이사 가다
cooperation [kouὰpəréiʃən] 명 협조, 협력, 협동

16 수치계산(금액) ▶ 정답 ④

M: Hello! Welcome to Paws Pet Supplies.
W: Hi. I'm looking to buy a leash for my dog.
M: Sure. We have two types. One is a basic leash, and the other is a retractable leash.
W: How much does each cost?
M: The basic leash is 10 dollars, and the retractable leash is 15 dollars.
W: I'll buy the retractable leash.
M: Sure! When you purchase a leash, you can also get a chew toy for 2 dollars.
W: That's perfect. I'll buy one chew toy, too.
M: Okay. How would you like to pay?
W: I'll pay with cash.

남: 안녕하세요! Paws Pet Supplies에 오신 것을 환영합니다.
여: 안녕하세요. 저는 제 개의 목줄을 사려고 하고 있습니다.
남: 네. 저희는 두 가지 종류를 갖고 있습니다. 하나는 기본 목줄이고, 다른 하나는 (자유자재로 줄 길이를 조절할 수 있는) 자동 리드 목줄입니다.
여: 각각 얼마인가요?
남: 기본 목줄은 10달러이고, 자동 리드 목줄은 15달러입니다.

여: 저는 자동 리드 목줄로 살게요.
남: 네! 목줄을 구매하시면, 또한 씹을 수 있는 장난감을 2달러에 구매하실 수 있습니다.
여: 완벽하네요. 씹을 수 있는 장난감도 한 개 살게요.
남: 네. 지불은 어떻게 하시겠어요?
여: 현금으로 낼게요.

leash [li:ʃ] 명 (동물 등을 매는) 줄, 가죽끈
retractable leash (자유자재로 줄 길이를 조절할 수 있는) 자동 리드 목줄
chew toy 어린아이나 반려동물이 씹을 수 있는 장난감

17 알맞은응답찾기 ▶ 정답 ④

W: Napoli Restaurant. How may I help you?
M: Hi there! I'd like to reserve a table for dinner tonight, please.
W: Sure. For how many, sir?
M: Seven.
W: Okay. We have one available table for you. May I get your name?
M: I'm John Powell. Powell is spelled P-O-W-E-L-L.
W: Okay. Got it, sir. Oh, I forgot to ask, what time will you be arriving?
M: We'll be there at around 6:30.

① 죄송하지만 제 시계는 고장 났어요.
② 종업원이 저희에게 엉뚱한 음식을 줬어요.
③ 나는 이미 늦지 않았기를 바라요.
④ 저희는 그곳에 6시 30분쯤에 도착할 거예요.
⑤ 제가 몇 시에 점심을 먹었는지 확실히 모르겠어요.

여: Napoli 식당입니다. 무엇을 도와드릴까요?
남: 안녕하세요! 오늘 저녁을 위해 테이블을 예약하고 싶어요.
여: 물론이죠. 몇 분이시죠, 손님?
남: 일곱 명이요.
여: 알겠습니다. 손님이 쓰실 수 있는 테이블 하나가 있네요. 성함이 어떻게 되십니까?
남: 저는 John Powell입니다. Powell의 철자는 P-O-W-E-L-L이에요.
여: 네. 잘 알겠습니다, 손님. 오, 몇 시쯤에 도착하실지 여쭤보는 것을 잊었네요.
남: 저희는 그곳에 6시 30분쯤에 도착할 거예요.

ask [æsk] 동 물어보다

18 알맞은응답찾기 ▶ 정답 ⑤

W: Hi, Daniel, where are you going?
M: I'm on my way to the blood donation center. I donate blood on a regular basis.
W: Blood donation?
M: I think it's a great way to help other people. Plus there are several health benefits for the donor as well.
W: Really?
M: At the blood donation center they will check your pulse, blood pressure, body temperature, and more. They will

tell you if anything seems unusual.
W: I hadn't thought about that. Can I join you?
M: Sure. They always need more people.
W: Thank you so much for telling me about this.

우·리·말·해·석

① 너는 병원에 가 보는 게 좋겠어.
② 나는 책과 옷을 조금 기부할 거야.
③ 걱정하지 마. 우리는 시간 내에 거기에 도착할 거야.
④ 네 접시에 있는 야채들을 다 먹도록 해.
⑤ 내게 이것에 대해 말해줘서 정말 고마워.

여: 안녕, Daniel, 어디 가는 중이니?
남: 나는 헌혈 센터에 가는 중이야. 나는 정기적으로 헌혈을 해.
여: 헌혈?
남: 나는 그것이 남을 돕는 아주 좋은 방법이라고 생각해. 게다가 헌혈자에게도 몇 가지 건강상 이점이 있어.
여: 정말?
남: 헌혈 센터에서 그들이 네 맥박과 혈압, 체온 등을 확인할 거야. 만약 무언가 이상해 보이는 게 있으면 네게 말해줄 거야.
여: 그것에 대해서는 생각해 본 적이 없었어. 내가 너와 같이 가도 될까?
남: 물론이지. 그들은 항상 더 많은 사람이 필요해.
여: 내게 이것에 대해 말해줘서 정말 고마워.

단·어·및·표·현

donate [dóuneit] [동] 기부하다, 기증하다
on a regular basis 정기적으로
donor [dóunər] [명] 헌혈자, 기증자
pulse [pʌls] [명] 맥박
blood pressure 혈압
on time (시간을 어기지 않고) 정시에

19 알맞은응답찾기 ▶ 정답 ①

듣·기·대·본

M: Joyce, did you know that there's an AI robot show at the City Tech Center?
W: Yes. Actually, I was thinking of checking it out.
M: I've already seen it twice, but I'd love to go again.
W: Oh, I didn't know you were into robots and AI.
M: I'm fascinated by how much the technology has advanced. Do you enjoy things like that too?
W: Absolutely. I find it amazing how smart and lifelike robots are becoming.
M: Me, too. Would you like to see the show together?
W: That sounds great. Let's plan a visit.

우·리·말·해·석

① 그거 정말 좋겠다. 방문 계획을 세우자.
② 미안해, 난 그 쇼를 이미 봤어.
③ 괜찮아. 거기 어떻게 가는지 알려 줄게.
④ 나도 동의해. 로봇이 우리를 여러 가지로 도와줄 거야.
⑤ 물론이지. 너랑 같이 과학 동아리에 가입하고 싶어.

남: Joyce, 시립 기술 센터에서 AI 로봇 쇼가 있는 거 알고 있었어?
여: 응, 사실 나도 한번 가 볼까 생각 중이었어.
남: 난 벌써 두 번 봤는데, 또 가고 싶어.
여: 오, 네가 로봇이랑 AI에 관심 있는 줄 몰랐네.
남: 난 기술이 얼마나 진보했는지에 매료되었어. 너도 그런 거 좋아해?
여: 물론이지. 로봇들이 얼마나 똑똑해지고 실제처럼 되어 가고 있는지가 놀라워.
남: 나도 그래. 같이 그 쇼 보러 갈래?
여: 그거 정말 좋겠다. 방문 계획을 세우자.

단·어·및·표·현

check it out (직접 가서) 보다, 확인하다
fascinate [fǽsənèit] [동] 매료시키다
advance [ədvǽns] [동] (지식 · 기술 등이) 진보하다
lifelike [láiflaik] [형] 실제 같은, 진짜 같은

20 상황에적절한말찾기 ▶ 정답 ③

듣·기·대·본

M: Huisu is supposed to meet his girlfriend for lunch at 12 o'clock. However, he gets up late in the morning. He gets ready in a hurry and takes a taxi. Unfortunately, he soon gets stuck in a traffic jam. It's already 11:45. Now he wants to get off the taxi to transfer to the subway. In this situation, what would Huisu say to the taxi driver?
Huisu: Can you drop me off here?

우·리·말·해·석

① 천천히 운전해 주실래요?
② 거기까지 가는 데 얼마나 걸릴까요?
③ 절 여기서 내려주시겠어요?
④ 제일 가까운 버스 정류장이 어디에 있나요?
⑤ 다른 길로 가주시겠어요?

남: 희수는 여자친구와 12시에 점심을 위해 만나기로 되어있다. 하지만 그는 아침에 늦게 일어난다. 그는 서둘러 준비하고 택시를 탄다. 불행하게도 그는 곧 교통체증에 갇혀 꼼짝 못한다. 이미 11시 45분이다. 이제 그는 지하철로 갈아타기 위해 택시에서 내리고 싶다. 이러한 상황에서, 희수는 택시 기사에게 무엇이라고 말하겠는가?
희수: 절 여기서 내려주시겠어요?

단·어·및·표·현

get stuck in a traffic jam 교통체증에 갇혀 꼼짝 못하다

Words & Expressions Review

1. 교통체증	2. ~을 맡아두다, 간수하다	3. ~을 발송하다, 보내다
4. 몹시 배고프다, 굶주리다	5. 자원봉사 일을 하다	6. 서둘러
7. 금속	8. (병이) 낫다, 회복하다	9. 소란, 소동, 방해
10. 명확성, 명료성	11. 박람회	12. 자리, 장소
13. (음식의) 부패	14. 지속되다	15. 항의, 불편
16. 일하고 있다	17. 승진[진급]시키다	18. 물 속에서
19. 숨을 참다	20. 이용할 수 있는	21. (태풍 · 병 등이) 심한, 중한
22. 사전에, 미리	23. 통로	24. 주민, 거주자
25. 운이 좋다, 재수가 좋다	26. 생산성	27. 예약하다
28. 돕다, 도와주다	29. 협조, 협력, 협동	30. ~에 기초하다
31. 침수되다, 물에 잠기다	32. 알겠어요., 제가 할게요.	33. 가죽
34. 철자를 말하다	35. ~를 불쌍하게 여기다	36. 정기적으로

37. 보관하다, 저장하다	38. (지식·기술 등이) 진보하다	39. 속도
40. 멈추다, 얼다	41. 실제 같은, 진짜 같은	42. 매료시키다
43. 헌혈자, 기증자	44. 지연하다, 연기하다	

Listening Test
영어듣기 모의고사 23회

|정답|

01 ④	02 ③	03 ③	04 ④	05 ⑤
06 ④	07 ①	08 ⑤	09 ③	10 ④
11 ①	12 ②	13 ②	14 ④	15 ④
16 ③	17 ①	18 ②	19 ②	20 ③

01 그림정보파악(대화) ▶ 정답 ④

듣·기·대·본

W: Chris, we have to buy some balloons for Judy's welcome home party. Which kind do you like?
M: How about these heart-shaped ones?
W: Hmm… I think the round ones look better. How about these ones with the dots on them?
M: Well, I think they are too simple. Hey, look at these.
W: Which ones do you mean? The ones with stars, or the ones with flowers?
M: The ones with stars look nice to me.
W: Oh, I think so, too. Let's buy them right now.

우·리·말·해·석

여: Chris, 우리는 Judy의 귀가 환영 파티를 위해 풍선들을 좀 사야 해. 너는 어떤 종류가 좋아?
남: 이 하트 모양 풍선들은 어때?
여: 흠… 나는 둥근 것들이 더 좋아 보인다고 생각해. 점이 있는 이것들은 어때?
남: 글쎄, 나는 그것들이 너무 단순하다고 생각해. 이봐, 이것들을 봐.
여: 어느 것을 말하는 거야? 별이 있는 거, 아니면 꽃이 있는 거?
남: 별이 있는 것들이 내게는 멋져 보여.
여: 오, 나도 그렇게 생각해. 그것들을 당장 사자.

단·어·및·표·현

heart-shaped 하트 모양의
round [raund] 웹 둥근, 원형의

02 대화미언급 ▶ 정답 ③

듣·기·대·본

W: Justin! I heard that the Youth Festival is being held at Han River Park.
M: What is a Youth Festival?
W: It's a festival for youth between the ages of 15 and 24! There are many things to eat and events to participate in.

M: Okay. That's it?
W: No! There will be famous artists coming to perform and they are screening movies, too.
M: So, when is this festival?
W: It starts today and ends next Friday. Do you want to go with me?
M: Sure, why not?
W: But, there is an entrance fee of $10. Are you okay with that?
M: No problem!

우·리·말·해·석

여: Justin! 나는 한강공원에서 Youth Festival이 열린다고 들었어.
남: Youth Festival이 뭐야?
여: 15세에서 24세 사이의 청년들을 위한 축제야! 먹을 것과 참여할 수 있는 행사들이 많이 있어.
남: 응. 그게 다야?
여: 아니! 유명한 음악가들이 공연하러 올 것이고, 그들은 영화 상영도 할 거야.
남: 그래서, 이 축제는 언젠데?
여: 오늘 시작해서 다음 주 금요일에 끝나. 나랑 같이 갈래?
남: 물론이지, 왜 안되겠어.
여: 하지만, 입장료가 10달러 있어. 넌 그게 괜찮아?
남: 문제없어!

단·어·및·표·현

youth [ju:θ] 웹 청년, 젊은이
perform [pərfɔ́ːrm] 통 공연하다, 연주하다
screen [skriːn] 통 (영화를) 상영하다
entrance fee 입장료

03 전화목적파악 ▶ 정답 ③

듣·기·대·본

(*Telephone rings.*)
M: Hello, this is The Grill Restaurant. How can I help you?
W: Hi, I would like to make a reservation for four people at 8 p.m. tomorrow.
M: Sure, I'll check. (*pause*) I'm afraid all the tables are booked for 8 p.m.
W: Well… Is there another time that is available?
M: How about 7?
W: That sounds good! I'll make a reservation under the name Brown.
M: Okay, may I have your phone number, please?
W: 310-555-9024.

우·리·말·해·석

(전화벨이 울린다.)
남: 여보세요. Grill Restaurant입니다. 무엇을 도와드릴까요?
여: 안녕하세요. 내일 저녁 8시에 4명 예약을 하고 싶은데요.
남: 물론이죠. 확인해 보겠습니다. (잠시 후) 안타깝게도 저녁 8시에 모든 테이블이 예약되어 있네요.
여: 음… 예약 가능한 다른 시간이 있나요?
남: 7시는 어떠세요?
여: 좋아요! Brown이라는 이름으로 예약할게요.
남: 알겠습니다. 전화번호 좀 알려주실 수 있나요?
여: 310-555-9024입니다.

make a reservation 예약하다
available [əvéiləbl] 톙 이용할 수 있는, 구할 수 있는
under the name (of) ~라는 이름으로

04 수치파악(시각) ▶ 정답 ④

듣·기·대·본

(*Cellphone rings.*)

M: OZ Wireless, how can I help you?
W: Hi, I'm calling because I've lost my Internet connection.
M: We're very sorry for the inconvenience. Have you tried rebooting your computer?
W: Yes, even the router, but nothing has changed.
M: I see. We'll send someone to your house. Are you available on Saturday at 9 a.m.?
W: No, I have a yoga lesson in the morning. How about at 1 p.m.?
M: Sorry, that time's already booked. What about at 3 p.m.?
W: That's fine by me.
M: All right. Someone will visit you then.
W: Okay, thanks.

우·리·말·해·석

(휴대전화가 울린다.)

남: OZ Wirelss입니다, 무엇을 도와드릴까요?
여: 안녕하세요, 저는 인터넷 연결이 끊겨서 연락드렸어요.
남: 불편을 드려 정말 죄송합니다. 컴퓨터를 재부팅해보셨나요?
여: 네, 공유기까지요, 하지만 변한 건 없어요.
남: 그렇군요. 저희가 고객님 댁으로 사람을 보내겠습니다. 토요일 오전 9시에 시간이 되시나요?
여: 아뇨, 아침에 요가 수업이 있어요. 오후 1시는 어떨까요?
남: 죄송하지만 그 시간은 이미 예약되어 있습니다. 오후 3시는 어떠신가요?
여: 저는 좋아요.
남: 네. 누군가가 그때 고객님을 방문할 겁니다.
여: 네, 감사합니다.

단·어·및·표·현

lose Internet connection 인터넷 연결이 끊기다
reboot [ri:bú:t] 동 재부팅하다
router [ráutər] 명 공유기, 라우터(네트워크에서 데이터의 전달을 촉진하는 중계 장치)
available [əvéiləbl] 톙 시간[여유]이 있는

05 심정추론 ▶ 정답 ⑤

듣·기·대·본

M: Evelyn, is there something wrong?
W: Yes, Lucas. I was finishing off my résumé for a job application, but it's completely disappeared.
M: What do you mean?
W: Well, I edited it for the last time, but then deleted everything in the file by mistake.
M: Did you save the file with everything deleted?
W: That's right. And the deadline to submit it is in 10 minutes.
M: Oh, no. What can you do?

W: It's hopeless. I can't rewrite my résumé in 10 minutes.
M: Is there no solution to this?
W: No. I can't believe I ruined my application in this way.

우·리·말·해·석

① 자랑스러운　　② 지루한　　③ 질투하는
④ 안도하는　　⑤ 좌절한

남: Evelyn, 무슨 일 있어?
여: 응, Lucas. 나는 입사 지원을 위해 이력서를 마무리하고 있었는데, 그것이 완전히 사라졌어.
남: 무슨 말이야?
여: 음, 나는 마지막으로 그걸 수정했는데, 실수로 파일에 있는 모든 것을 삭제했어.
남: 모든 것을 삭제한 상태로 그 파일을 저장했어?
여: 맞아. 그리고 제출 기한은 10분 후야.
남: 아, 안 돼. 넌 뭘 할 수 있어?
여: 가망이 없어. 나는 10분 안에 이력서를 다시 쓸 수 없어.
남: 이것에 대한 해결책은 없어?
여: 없어. 내가 이런 식으로 내 지원을 망쳤다니 믿을 수 없어.

단·어·및·표·현

finish off ~ ~을 마무리하다
résumé [rézumèi] 명 이력서
disappear [dìsəpíər] 동 사라지다, 없어지다
hopeless [hóuplis] 톙 가망 없는, 절망적인
solution [səljú:ʃən] 명 해결책, 해법
ruin [rú(:)in] 동 망치다

06 그림상황에적절한대화찾기 ▶ 정답 ④

듣·기·대·본

① W: Stephen, where are you going?
　 M: I'm going to the library to return some books.
② W: How long have you been in sales?
　 M: I've worked in sales for 6 years.
③ W: Hello. How may I help you?
　 M: I'd like to return this shirt. It's too small for me.
④ W: You have to extend your arm further than that.
　 M: I'm trying my best, but it's difficult.
⑤ W: Do you know the way to the gym?
　 M: Yes, go straight down this road and turn left at the corner.

우·리·말·해·석

① 여: Stephen, 너는 어디에 가고 있니?
　 남: 나는 책을 좀 반납하기 위해 도서관에 가는 중이야.
② 여: 당신은 얼마나 오래 영업부에 있었나요?
　 남: 저는 6년 동안 영업부에서 일해왔습니다.
③ 여: 안녕하세요. 어떻게 도와드릴까요?
　 남: 저는 이 셔츠를 반품하려고 해요. 그것은 제게 너무 작아요.
④ 여: 당신은 그것보다 더 멀리 당신의 팔을 뻗어야 해요.
　 남: 저는 최선을 다하고 있지만, 그것은 어렵네요.
⑤ 여: 당신은 체육관으로 가는 길을 아시나요?
　 남: 네, 이 길을 따라 쭉 가서 모퉁이에서 왼쪽으로 도세요.

단·어·및·표·현

sales [seilz] 명 영업부, 매출(량)
extend [iksténd] 동 뻗다, 늘이다
further than ~보다 더 멀리
try one's best 최선을 다하다

07 부탁(요청)한일파악 ▶ 정답 ①

듣·기·대·본

M: What are you doing, Sojin?
W: I'm working on my English homework.
M: Is it going well?
W: Yes, but I have to read some more books.
M: I see. I'm on my way to the library. Do you need anything?
W: It's OK. I have all the books I need. Can you just turn on the heat as you go out?
M: Sure. It's really cold in here.

우·리·말·해·석

남: 뭘 하고 있니, 소진아?
여: 영어 숙제를 하는 중이야.
남: 잘 되어가니?
여: 응, 하지만 책을 좀 더 읽어야 해.
남: 그렇구나. 난 도서관에 가는 길이야. 뭐 필요한 거라도 있니?
여: 괜찮아. 필요한 책은 다 갖고 있어. 그냥 나가면서 난방을 켜 줄래?
남: 물론이지. 여긴 정말 춥구나.

단·어·및·표·현

go well (일이) 잘 되어가다

LISTENING ADVICE

문장을 말할 때 음을 높이거나 낮추는 것을 '억양'이라고 하는데, 영어에서는 문장의 의미에 따라 억양이 달라지기도 합니다. 주로 평서문은 문장 끝을 내려서 말하고 의문문은 문장 끝을 올려서 말하지요. 따라서 억양만으로도 대강의 의미를 유추할 수 있습니다. 억양 차이에 유의하며 대화를 다시 한번 들어보세요.

08 담화미언급 ▶ 정답 ⑤

듣·기·대·본

M: Thank you for using National Express. We own 200 well-maintained buses. Putting safety first, we run 11 repair centers for these vehicles. We recently added two extra lines, and now we operate 30 express bus lines all over the country. You can buy tickets through our website, or by calling our 24-hour customer service center. We value our customers' satisfaction above all.

우·리·말·해·석

남: National Express를 이용해 주셔서 감사합니다. 저희는 관리가 잘 된 200대의 버스를 소유하고 있습니다. 안전을 우선으로 하는 저희는 이 차량들을 위한 11개의 수리점을 운영합니다. 저희는 최근 두 개의 노선을 추가하였고 현재 전국에 걸쳐 30개의 고속버스 노선을 가동합니다. 여러분은 저희 웹사이트를 통하시거나, 24시간 고객 서비스 센터에 전화를 걸어 표를 구매하실 수 있습니다. 저희는 무엇보다 저희 고객들의 만족을 소중히 여깁니다.

단·어·및·표·현

own [oun] 통 소유하다
satisfaction [s`ætisf`ækʃən] 명 만족

09 담화화제추론 ▶ 정답 ③

듣·기·대·본

W: This is a traditional Korean dish. It is a bowl of rice topped with various vegetables, eggs, and beef. Before eating it, you need to mix all the ingredients together. It's basically served with red pepper paste, but other sauces like soy sauce may replace it. A spoon of sesame oil is also a common addition. The city of Jeonju is well known for the most popular version of this.

우·리·말·해·석

여: 이것은 한국의 전통적인 음식입니다. 그것은 다양한 채소, 달걀, 그리고 소고기를 함께 올린 한 그릇의 밥입니다. 그것을 먹기 전에, 당신은 모든 재료를 함께 섞어야 합니다. 그것은 기본적으로 고추장과 함께 나오지만, 간장 같은 다른 소스들이 그것을 대체해도 됩니다. 참기름 한 숟갈 역시 흔하게 추가됩니다. 전주시는 이것의 가장 인기 있는 버전으로 유명합니다.

단·어·및·표·현

traditional [trədíʃənəl] 형 전통적인
ingredient [ingrí:diənt] 명 재료

10 어색한대화찾기 ▶ 정답 ④

듣·기·대·본

① W: Is it OK if I sit here?
  M: I'm sorry but this seat is taken.
② W: Thank you so much for your kindness.
  M: Don't mention it.
③ W: Would you do me a favor?
  M: Sure. What is it?
④ W: What is your favorite subject?
  M: I love reading novels.
⑤ W: How was the exam?
  M: It wasn't difficult.

우·리·말·해·석

① 여: 제가 여기에 앉아도 될까요?
  남: 죄송합니다만 이 자리는 주인이 있습니다.
② 여: 친절에 정말 감사드려요.
  남: 천만에요.
③ 여: 부탁 좀 해도 될까?
  남: 물론이지. 뭔데?
④ 여: 네가 가장 좋아하는 과목이 뭐니?
  남: 난 소설책 읽는 것을 좋아해.
⑤ 여: 시험은 어땠니?
  남: 어렵지 않았어.

단·어·및·표·현

favor [féivər] 명 부탁, 호의

11 할일파악(대화직후) ▶ 정답 ①

듣·기·대·본

W: Welcome to Sunny Beach Resort. How can I assist you?
M: Hi, I'd like to rent a beach chair and umbrella.
W: Sure. Would you prefer a full-day rental or a half-day?
M: Just a half-day, please.
W: All right. We offer a discount for seniors.
M: Oh, that's wonderful to know.
W: Could you please show me your ID to verify your age?

M: Of course. Give me a second to find it in my purse.

W: Take your time.

우·리·말·해·석

여: Sunny Beach Resort에 오신 것을 환영합니다. 어떻게 도와드릴까요?

남: 안녕하세요, 저는 해변용 의자와 파라솔을 빌리고 싶어요.

여: 네. 종일 대여를 원하시나요, 아니면 한나절 대여를 원하시나요?

남: 그냥 한나절이요.

여: 알겠습니다. 저희는 고령자분들에게 할인을 제공합니다.

남: 오, 알게 되니 좋네요.

여: 연령을 확인하기 위해 저에게 손님의 신분증을 보여주실 수 있나요?

남: 물론이죠. 제 지갑에서 그것을 찾도록 저에게 잠시만 시간을 주세요.

여: 천천히 하세요.

단·어·및·표·현

umbrella [ʌmbrélə] 몡 파라솔

senior [síːnjər] 몡 고령자, 노인

verify [vérəfài] 통 확인하다, 입증하다

take one's time 천천히 하다

12 도표정보파악 ▶ 정답 ②

듣·기·대·본

M: Hey, Grace. It's 3 o'clock now and we need to reserve our movie tickets.

W: Oh, right. We were going to watch that new animated movie.

M: Yes. So, the next one starts at 4:00 p.m. and then there's another one at 4:45 p.m.

W: 4:00 p.m. would be better. I don't want to wait until 4:45 p.m.

M: Okay. Then, do you want 3D or just a regular movie?

W: They have 3D? 3D sounds really good to me!

M: Do you prefer a subtitled or dubbed movie?

W: Subtitles, of course! I want to hear the real actors' voices.

M: Me, too. I'll book the tickets now.

우·리·말·해·석

	영화	시간	3D / 일반	더빙 / 자막
①	A	오후 4시	3D	더빙
②	B	오후 4시	3D	자막
③	C	오후 4시	일반	자막
④	D	오후 4시 45분	3D	더빙
⑤	E	오후 4시 45분	일반	자막

남: 얘, Grace. 지금은 3시고 우리는 우리 영화표를 예약해야 해.

여: 오, 맞아. 우리 그 새로운 애니메이션 영화 보기로 했었지.

남: 맞아. 자, 다음 것은 오후 4시에 시작하고 그 다음에는 오후 4시 45분에 또 다른 것이 있어.

여: 오후 4시가 나을 것 같아. 나는 오후 4시 45분까지 기다리고 싶지 않아.

남: 알겠어. 그럼, 3D를 원하니, 아니면 그냥 일반 영화를 원하니?

여: 3D가 있어? 나는 3D가 정말 좋을 것 같아!

남: 너는 자막이 있는 영화를 선호하니, 아니면 더빙된 영화를 선호하니?

여: 당연히 자막이지! 나는 실제 배우들의 목소리를 듣고 싶어.

남: 나도야. 이제 내가 표를 예매할게.

단·어·및·표·현

reserve [rizə́ːrv] 통 예약하다

animated movie 애니메이션 영화

subtitled [sʌbtáitəld] 몡 자막 처리가 된

dubbed [dʌbd] 몡 (영화 등이 다른 언어로) 더빙된

13 수치파악(날짜) ▶ 정답 ②

듣·기·대·본

M: Lizzy! I heard Joanna Swift is going to have a concert in Seoul this summer. Do you want to go together?

W: Yes, I would love to! I love her songs. When are the dates?

M: Let's see. The concert dates are July 27th through 31st.

W: Are there any seats available on July 29th or 30th?

M: Unfortunately, tickets for the weekend are sold out. How about Friday, July 28th?

W: Well, that's not the best date for me, but I have something scheduled for July 27th. So, Friday it is!

M: Okay. Sounds good. I will book two seats for that day.

우·리·말·해·석

남: Lizzy! 나는 이번 여름에 Joanna Swift가 서울에서 콘서트를 한다고 들었어. 같이 가고 싶어?

여: 응, 그러고 싶어! 나는 그녀의 노래를 매우 좋아해. 날짜가 언제야?

남: 어디 보자. 콘서트 날짜는 7월 27일부터 31일까지야.

여: 7월 29일이나 30일에 이용할 수 있는 좌석이 있어?

남: 안타깝게도, 주말 표는 매진되었어. 7월 28일 금요일은 어때?

여: 음, 나에게 가장 좋은 날은 아니야, 하지만 난 7월 27일에 예정된 일이 있어. 그러니, 금요일로 하자!

남: 응, 좋아. 내가 그날로 두 좌석 예약할게.

단·어·및·표·현

available [əvéiləbl] 몡 이용할 수 있는

scheduled [skédʒuːld] 몡 예정된

14 한일파악 ▶ 정답 ④

듣·기·대·본

W: David, did you participate in the school volunteer day yesterday?

M: No, I didn't.

W: Really? I thought you had signed up for it!

M: I was in my garage all day yesterday.

W: Oh, were you cleaning it out?

M: No. I was fixing my old bicycle that had been broken for months.

W: Isn't it hard to do that yourself?

M: I watched a bicycle repair video online last weekend. It didn't look too difficult, so I tried it on my own.

W: That's awesome! Why don't we go for a bike ride sometime?

M: Great idea.

우·리·말·해·석

여: David, 어제 학교 자원봉사 날에 참여했어?

남: 아니, 안 했어.

여: 정말? 네가 신청했을 거라고 생각했는데!

남: 어제 하루 종일 차고에 있었거든.

여: 아, 차고 청소하고 있었어?

남: 아니, 몇 달 동안 고장 나 있던 내 오래된 자전거를 고치고 있었어.

여: 그거 직접 하기는 어렵지 않아?

남: 지난 주말에 온라인에서 자전거 수리 영상을 봤거든. 그렇게 어려워 보이지 않아서 혼자 해 봤어.
여: 멋지다! 조만간 자전거 타러 갈래?
남: 좋은 생각이야.

단·어·및·표·현

participate in ~에 참여하다
sign up for ~에 신청[등록]하다
clean out 깨끗이 치우다
fix [fiks] 통 고치다

15 담화목적파악 ▶ 정답 ④

듣·기·대·본

M: Good morning, students! Welcome to our weekly school broadcast, "Food for Thought." Today, we'd like to talk about food waste. Did you know that a large amount of food is wasted every day? This has become a serious problem for our environment. However, we students can make a difference. Let's start by taking only what we need and finishing our meals in the school cafeteria. Let's think twice before wasting food.

우·리·말·해·석

남: 좋은 아침입니다, 학생 여러분! 주간 학교 방송인 "Food for Thought"에 오신 것을 환영합니다. 오늘, 우리는 음식 쓰레기에 대해 얘기하고자 합니다. 여러분들은 매일 많은 양의 음식이 낭비된다는 것을 알고 계십니까? 이것은 우리 환경에 심각한 문제가 되었습니다. 하지만, 우리 학생 여러분은 변화를 가져올 수 있습니다. 학교 식당에서 필요한 것만 가져와서 식사를 끝내는 것부터 시작합시다. 음식을 낭비하기 전에 신중히 생각해봅시다.

단·어·및·표·현

waste [weist] 명 쓰레기, 낭비 통 낭비하다
a large amount of 많은 양의 ~
make a difference 변화를 가져오다, 차별을 두다
think twice 신중히 생각하다, 재고하다, 숙고하다

16 수치계산(금액) ▶ 정답 ③

듣·기·대·본

W: Hello, what can I get for you?
M: Hi, I'd like to order one medium popcorn and one large Coke.
W: Sure, that will be $8. Do you need anything else?
M: Hmm… I'm sorry, but I'd like to change my order. One large popcorn and one large Coke, please.
W: No problem. That will be $10. By the way, if you show us your movie ticket, you can get a one dollar discount.
M: Oh, really? That's great! Here's my movie ticket.
W: Thanks! So, one large popcorn and one large Coke, right?
M: That's right.

우·리·말·해·석

여: 안녕하세요, 무엇을 주문하시겠어요?
남: 안녕하세요. 미디엄 사이즈 팝콘 하나랑 라지 사이즈 콜라 하나를 주문하고 싶은데요.
여: 물론이죠, 8달러입니다. 다른 건 필요하신 거 없으세요?
남: 음… 죄송하지만 주문한 것을 바꾸고 싶은데요. 라지 사이즈 팝콘 하나랑 라지 사이즈 콜라 하나로 부탁드려요.

여: 그럼요. 10달러입니다. 그런데, 영화 티켓을 보여주시면 1달러를 할인받으실 수 있어요.
남: 아, 정말요? 그거 아주 좋네요! 여기 제 티켓이요.
여: 감사합니다! 그럼, 라지 사이즈 팝콘 하나랑 라지 사이즈 콜라 맞으시죠?
남: 맞아요.

단·어·및·표·현

What can I get for you? (상점에서) 무엇을 주문하시겠어요?
anything else 그 밖의 다른 것

17 알맞은응답찾기 ▶ 정답 ①

듣·기·대·본

M: Hey, Jenny. How was your mid-term exam?
W: Awful! I think I failed my math test.
M: Don't worry. I'm sure you did fine. (*pause*) By the way, if you need any help, I know this online tutoring website that I found really helpful.
W: Online tutoring?
M: Yeah, the tutoring teachers make difficult subjects easy to understand. I improved my score through this tutoring site.
W: Hmm… Maybe I should get some help.
M: If you are interested, I can send you the link.
W: Sure! My e-mail is jenny@gmail.com.

우·리·말·해·석

① 물론이지! 내 이메일은 jenny@gmail.com이야.
② 걱정하지 마. 나는 혼자서 집에 걸어갈 수 있어.
③ 알았어. 우리는 수요일에 그 영화를 볼 수 있어.
④ 나는 컴퓨터가 고장나서 마칠 수 없었어.
⑤ 고맙지만 괜찮아. 나는 이미 친구들과 점심을 먹었어.

남: 이봐, Jenny. 중간고사 어땠어?
여: 끔찍했어. 내 생각에는 수학 시험을 망친 것 같아.
남: 걱정하지 마. 네가 잘했을 거라고 확신해. (잠시 후) 그런데 혹시 네가 도움이 필요하다면, 내가 정말 도움이 되는 온라인 튜터링 웹사이트를 알고 있어.
여: 온라인 튜터링?
남: 응. 튜터링 선생님들이 어려운 과목들을 이해하기 쉽게 해주셔. 나는 이 튜터링 사이트를 통해 성적을 많이 향상시켰어.
여: 음… 아마도 나는 도움을 좀 받아야 할 것 같아.
남: 혹시 네가 관심이 있다면, 내가 링크를 보내줄 수 있어.
여: 물론이지! 내 이메일은 jenny@gmail.com이야.

단·어·및·표·현

fail a test 시험을 망치다, 시험에 낙제하다
improve [imprúːv] 통 향상시키다, 개선하다

18 알맞은응답찾기 ▶ 정답 ②

듣·기·대·본

W: Dan, did you pick which club you want to join?
M: No, I'm still working on it. There are too many clubs at our school.
W: What are your hobbies? I'm sure there must be a club for you.
M: I like singing and listening to music.
W: Oh, there's an opera club where they sing classical music.
M: Uh… I'm actually more interested in pop songs.
W: Then how about joining the band? I saw a poster that

says the band is recruiting a new singer.

M: **That sounds good. I'll check it out later.**

우·리·말·해·석

① 나는 한 번도 오페라를 좋아해본 적이 없어.

② 그거 좋네. 내가 나중에 확인해볼게.

③ 맞아. 내 생각엔 네가 정말로 그 동아리를 그만둬야 할 것 같아.

④ 문제없어! 혹시 도움이 더 필요하다면 나에게 알려줘.

⑤ 미안해. 나는 악기를 연주하는 데 관심이 없어.

여: Dan, 너 어떤 동아리에 들 건지 골랐니?

남: 아니, 나는 아직도 고민 중이야. 우리 학교에 동아리가 너무 많아.

여: 너의 취미가 뭔데? 나는 너에게 맞는 동아리가 있을 거라고 확신해.

남: 나는 노래 부르는 것과 음악 듣는 것을 좋아해.

여: 오, 거기에 클래식 음악을 노래하는 오페라 동아리가 있어.

남: 어… 사실 나는 대중음악에 좀 더 관심이 있어.

여: 그러면 밴드에 들어가는 건 어때? 나는 밴드에서 새로운 가수를 모집
하고 있다는 포스터를 봤어.

남: **그거 좋네. 내가 나중에 확인해볼게.**

단·어·및·표·현

recruit [rikrúːt] ⑧ 모집하다, 채용하다

19 알맞은응답찾기 ▶ 정답 ②

듣·기·대·본

W: Hi, Mark! You'll never guess who I ran into yesterday!

M: I have no idea. Who did you meet?

W: I met Mr. Watterson, our elementary school home room
teacher! You remember him, right?

M: Of course, how could I forget? I haven't seen him in
ages. How is he?

W: He's retired now, and he just moved into our
neighborhood a couple of days ago.

M: Really? I should get in touch with him. Did you get his
cell number?

W: **Yes, I'll text you his number right now.**

우·리·말·해·석

① 아니, 나는 어제 집에 있었어.

② 응, 내가 지금 당장 그분의 번호를 문자로 보내줄게.

③ 미안해. 나는 내일 너와 함께 갈 수 없어.

④ 알았어, 나는 다음 주에 다른 도시로 이사를 가.

⑤ 아주 좋아! 나는 너희가 서로 잘 알게 되기를 바라.

여: 안녕, Mark! 너는 내가 어제 누굴 마주쳤는지 짐작도 못할 거야!

남: 전혀 모르겠어. 누구를 만났는데?

여: 우리 초등학교 담임 선생님이셨던 Watterson 선생님을 만났어! 너 그분
기억하지, 그치?

남: 당연하지, 내가 어떻게 잊겠어? 나는 오랫동안 그분을 보지 못했어. 그
분은 어떻게 지내셔?

여: 이제 퇴직하셨고, 며칠 전에 우리 동네로 막 이사 오셨어.

남: 정말? 나는 그분과 연락해야겠어. 너 그분의 핸드폰 번호 받았니?

여: **응, 내가 지금 당장 그분의 번호를 문자로 보내줄게.**

단·어·및·표·현

run into ~ ~와 (우연히) 마주치다, 만나다

retired [ritáiərd] ⑧ 퇴직한, 은퇴한

20 상황에적절한말찾기 ▶ 정답 ③

듣·기·대·본

W: Peter went to the café to read some books. He ordered
a blueberry muffin and an iced latte. However, when his
order came out, he noticed that the drink wasn't an iced
latte, but a chocolate drink instead. He realized that
the waiter had mixed up the orders and given him the
wrong drink. So, Peter wants to ask if he could get his
original drink. In this situation, what would Peter most
likely say to the waiter?

Peter: **Excuse me, I think I received the wrong drink.**

우·리·말·해·석

① 이 카페는 몇 시에 문을 열고 닫나요?

② 제가 블루베리 머핀 하나를 더 얻을 수 있을까요?

③ 실례합니다만, 제가 잘못된 음료를 받은 것 같은데요.

④ 제가 시험 공부를 할 만한 조용한 장소가 있을까요?

⑤ 실례합니다만, 화장실이 어디인지 아시나요?

여: Peter는 책을 읽기 위해 카페에 갔다. 그는 블루베리 머핀과 아이스 라
테를 주문했다. 그러나 그가 주문한 것이 나왔을 때, 그는 음료가 아이
스 라테가 아니라 초콜릿 음료라는 것을 알아차렸다. 그는 웨이터가 주
문을 착각해서 그에게 잘못된 음료를 주었다는 것을 깨달았다. 그래서,
Peter는 자신이 원래 주문했던 음료를 받을 수 있는지 묻고 싶다. 이러
한 상황에서, Peter가 웨이터에게 무엇이라고 말하겠는가?

Peter: **실례합니다만, 제가 잘못된 음료를 받은 것 같은데요.**

단·어·및·표·현

realize [rí(ː)əlàiz] ⑧ 깨닫다, 알아차리다

mix up 착각하다, 혼동하다

Words & Expressions Review

1. (식당 · 호텔 등을) 예약하다	2. (상점에서) 무엇을 주문하시겠어요?	3. 부탁, 호의
4. (영화를) 상영하다	5. ~을 마무리하다	6. 이해하다
7. 소중히 여기다, 가치	8. 뻗다, 늘이다	9. 고르다, 선택하다
10. 재료	11. 가망 없는, 절망적인	12. 재부팅하다
13. 깨끗이 치우다	14. 퇴직한, 은퇴한	15. 심각한, 진지한
16. 확인하다, 입증하다	17. ~에 노력을 들이다	18. 알게 되다
19. 전통적인	20. 무엇보다도	21. 망치다
22. 둥근, 원형의	23. 향상시키다, 개선하다	24. 깨닫다, 알아차리다
25. 친절	26. 만족	27. 이사하다, 이주하다
28. 예정된	29. 그 밖의 다른 것	30. 공연하다, 연주하다
31. 자막 처리가 된	32. 입장료	33. 쓰레기, 낭비, 낭비하다
34. 모집하다, 채용하다	35. 이력서	36. (일이) 잘 되어 가다
37. 고치다	38. 신중히 생각하다, 재고하다, 숙고하다	39. 대신에
40. 변화를 가져오다, 차별을 두다	41. 더빙된	42. 할인을 받다
43. 청년, 젊은이	44. 최선을 다하다	

M: "The Razor Tower"? That's an interesting name. How tall is it?
W: It's 500 meters in height.
M: Wow! How many floors are there?
W: It says on their website that there are 100 floors.
M: Incredible! I wonder how long it took to build that thing.
W: Their website says that it took eight years to complete the building.
M: That's a lot of hard work.

우·리·말·해·석
여: 자기야, 난 우리가 이 시내관광에 참여해서 기뻐. 재미있지 않아?
남: 정말 재미있어. 저기 저 건물은 뭐야? 정말 높다!
여: 내가 내 스마트폰으로 찾아볼게. (잠시 후) 저건 'Razor 타워'임이 분명해.
남: 'Razor 타워'? 흥미로운 이름이네. 얼마나 높아?
여: 그것의 높이는 500미터야.
남: 우와! 몇 층이야?
여: 그들의 웹사이트에 100층이라고 나와 있어.
남: 믿을 수 없군! 저것을 짓는 데 얼마나 오래 걸렸는지 궁금해.
여: 그들의 웹사이트에 그 건물을 완성하는 데 8년이 걸렸다고 나와 있어.
남: 정말 힘든 일이네.

단·어·및·표·현
height[hait] 몧 높이
complete[kəmplíːt] 통 ~을 완료하다, 마무리짓다

03 전화목적파악 ▶ 정답 ⑤

듣·기·대·본
(*Telephone rings.*)
M: Hello. This is Happy Chicken. How can I help you?
W: Hi. I ordered a fried chicken and a chicken salad for delivery about 30 minutes ago.
M: Yes, your order is on the way.
W: Great. Could I ask you a favor?
M: Sure, what is it?
W: There's a baby sleeping at home. Please tell the delivery person not to ring the doorbell.
M: Of course. I'll tell him to text you when he arrives.
W: Thank you so much. That would really help.

우·리·말·해·석
(전화벨이 울린다.)
남: 여보세요. 행복 치킨입니다. 어떻게 도와드릴까요?
여: 안녕하세요. 약 30분 전에 프라이드 치킨 하나와 치킨 샐러드 하나를 배달 주문했어요.
남: 네, 고객님의 주문은 배달 중입니다.
여: 다행이네요. 부탁 하나 드려도 될까요?
남: 물론이죠, 무엇인가요?
여: 집에 자고 있는 아기가 있어요. 배달원에게 초인종을 누르지 말아 달라고 해 주세요.
남: 알겠습니다. 그가 도착하면 고객님께 문자 보내 드리라고 전하겠습니다.
여: 정말 감사합니다. 큰 도움이 될 거예요.

단·어·및·표·현
order[ɔ́ːrdər] 통 주문하다 몧 주문
delivery[dilívəri] 몧 배달
on the way 가는 중인

영어듣기 고난도 모의고사 High Level 24회

|정|답|

01 ⑤	02 ④	03 ⑤	04 ④	05 ③
06 ④	07 ④	08 ④	09 ①	10 ⑤
11 ②	12 ③	13 ①	14 ④	15 ⑤
16 ②	17 ④	18 ⑤	19 ④	20 ④

01 그림정보파악(대화) ▶ 정답 ⑤

듣·기·대·본
W: Welcome to the Desert Gift Shop. Did you enjoy your trip?
M: I did. Thank you. The desert was great. I want to buy a magnet to remember it by.
W: Sure. We have camel-shaped and triangle-shaped magnets. Both designs are popular.
M: I'll choose the triangle-shaped one. It reminds me of the pyramids.
W: Good choice. They come in two styles, plain and checkered.
M: Oh, the checkered style looks nice.
W: All right. Then, how about this one with the word "Pharaoh" on it? It represents the ancient rulers.
M: Great! I'll take it.

우·리·말·해·석
여: Desert 선물 가게에 오신 것을 환영합니다. 당신은 당신의 여행을 즐기셨나요?
남: 즐겼어요. 감사해요. 사막은 멋졌어요. 저는 그것을 기억하기 위해 자석을 사고 싶어요.
여: 네. 저희에겐 낙타 모양의 자석과 삼각형 모양의 자석이 있어요. 두 디자인 모두 인기 있어요.
남: 전 삼각형 모양의 것을 고를게요. 그것은 저에게 피라미드를 생각나게 해요.
여: 좋은 선택이에요. 그것들은 민무늬와 체크무늬 두 가지 스타일로 나와요.
남: 오, 체크 무늬 스타일이 좋아 보이네요.
여: 알겠습니다. 그러면, 그것 위에 "Pharaoh(파라오)"라는 단어가 있는 이것은 어떠신가요? 그것은 고대 통치자를 나타내요.
남: 좋네요! 전 그걸로 할게요.

단·어·및·표·현
remind A of B A에게 B를 생각나게 하다
plain[plein] 톙 민무늬의, 무늬가 없는
represent[rèprizént] 통 나타내다, 상징하다
ancient[éinʃənt] 톙 고대의
ruler[rúːlər] 몧 통치자, 지배자

02 대화미언급 ▶ 정답 ④

듣·기·대·본
W: Honey, I am glad that we joined this city tour. Isn't it fun?
M: It's really entertaining. What's that building over there? It's really tall!
W: I'll look it up on my smartphone. (*pause*) That must be

듣·기·대·본

(*Telephone rings.*)

W: Good evening, Happy Hair Salon. How may I help you?

M: Hello, I'd like to make a haircut appointment for this Sunday.

W: Let me check, please. (*pause*) The only time we have on Sunday is in the morning.

M: That's fine. What time do you open?

W: We open at 11 a.m. on weekdays and 9 a.m. on weekends. Would you like to come at 9 a.m.?

M: No, that's way too early. Can I make an appointment for 10 a.m.?

W: Okay. May I have your name, please?

M: It's Owen Wilson.

W: Thank you, Mr. Wilson. We'll see you on Sunday.

우·리·말·해·석

(전화벨이 울린다.)

여: 안녕하세요, Happy 미용실입니다. 어떻게 도와드릴까요?

남: 안녕하세요, 저는 이번 일요일에 커트 예약을 하고 싶어요.

여: 확인해보겠습니다. (잠시 후) 일요일에 있는 유일한 시간은 오전입니다.

남: 그것은 괜찮습니다. 몇 시에 여나요?

여: 저희는 주중에는 오전 11시, 주말에는 오전 9시에 열어요. 오전 9시에 오시겠어요?

남: 아니요, 그것은 너무 일러요. 오전 10시로 예약할 수 있어요?

여: 좋아요. 고객님의 이름을 알 수 있을까요?

남: Owen Wilson입니다.

여: 감사합니다, Wilson 씨. 일요일에 뵙겠습니다.

단·어·및·표·현

make an appointment 약속을 잡다, 예약하다

way [wei] ⑤ 너무, 훨씬

듣·기·대·본

W: Mr. Bates, you wanted to see me?

M: Yes, Hannah. What do you think of being a model for our school leaflet?

W: Me? But, there are better looking students than me.

M: It's not all about looks. I think you'd be a great representative of our school.

W: Wow, that's a nice surprise! I feel honored.

M: I'll take that as a yes.

W: Yes, sir. I can't believe you picked me.

M: I wasn't the only one.

우·리·말·해·석

① 불안해하는   ② 미안한   ③ 놀란

④ 지루해하는   ⑤ 부러워하는

여: Bates 선생님, 저를 보자고 하셨다고요?

남: 응, Hannah. 네가 우리 학교 홍보 책자의 모델이 되는 것에 대해 어떻게 생각하니?

여: 제가요? 하지만 저보다 외모가 더 나은 학생들이 있잖아요.

남: 외모가 전부는 아니란다. 내 생각에 너는 우리 학교의 훌륭한 대표가 될 것 같아.

여: 와, 정말 놀랍네요! 영광입니다.

남: 승낙한 것으로 받아들일게.

여: 네, 선생님. 선생님께서 저를 뽑아 주셨다니 믿을 수가 없어요.

남: 너뿐만이 아니었단다.

단·어·및·표·현

leaflet [líːflit] ⑱ 홍보 책자, 전단

representative [rèprizéntətiv] ⑱ 대표, 대리인

honored [ánərd] ⑱ 영광스러운, 명예로운

듣·기·대·본

① M: Your dog is so cute. What's his name?

　W: Thanks! His name is "Cookies."

② M: May I pet your dog?

　W: I'm sorry, but he doesn't like being petted by strangers.

③ M: Do you know where Central Park is?

　W: Sure! You just need to walk straight ahead for 5 minutes.

④ M: Excuse me, ma'am. No dogs are allowed in this park.

　W: I'm sorry. I'll leave right away.

⑤ M: Why don't we go for a jog tomorrow?

　W: Okay! Let's meet at the park.

우·리·말·해·석

① 남: 당신의 개가 무척 귀엽네요. 이름이 뭐예요?

　여: 고마워요! 그의 이름은 "Cookies"예요.

② 남: 당신의 개를 쓰다듬어도 될까요?

　여: 미안하지만 그는 낯선 사람이 쓰다듬는 것을 좋아하지 않아요.

③ 남: Central Park가 어디 있는지 아세요?

　여: 그럼요! 당신은 단지 5분 동안 앞으로 똑바로 걷기만 하면 돼요.

④ 남: 실례합니다. 이 공원에는 개가 허용되지 않습니다.

　여: 죄송합니다. 바로 떠날게요.

⑤ 남: 내일 조깅하러 가는 거 어때?

　여: 좋아! 공원에서 만나자.

단·어·및·표·현

pet [pet] ⑧ 쓰다듬다

ahead [əhéd] ⑨ 앞으로

듣·기·대·본

W: Hi, Ben. What happened to your arm?

M: Hi, Nancy. I broke it yesterday during a basketball game.

W: Oh, no! It must hurt a lot.

M: It's okay, but it's so inconvenient. I really need to finish my science assignment, but I can't do very much with this arm.

W: We have to submit the assignment by tomorrow, don't we? Well, I'm free this afternoon if you need any help.

M: Oh, then can you help me write up my report? I can't do any typing on my computer.

W: Sure! Let's go to your house and do it right now.

M: Great. Thanks!

우·리·말·해·석

여: 안녕, Ben. 네 팔에 무슨 일이 있었어?

남: 안녕, Nancy. 어제 농구 경기 동안 부러졌어.

여: 오, 안 돼! 그것은 많이 아프겠다.

남: 괜찮지만, 무척 불편해. 나는 정말로 내 과학 숙제를 끝내야 하지만 나

는 이 팔로는 많이 할 수가 없어.

여: 우리는 그 숙제를 내일까지 제출해야 해, 그렇지? 음, 네가 어떤 도움이라도 필요하다면 나는 오늘 오후에 시간이 있어.

남: 오, 그러면 내 보고서를 다 쓰는 것을 도와줄 수 있어? 나는 내 컴퓨터로 타이핑을 할 수가 없어.

여: 물론이지! 네 집에 가서 바로 그것을 하자.

남: 좋아. 고마워!

단·어·및·표·현

inconvenient[ìnkənví:njənt] 휑 불편한

submit[səbmít] 통 제출하다

08 담화미언급 ▶ 정답 ④

듣·기·대·본

W: Hello, students. Welcome to Han Sports Center. I'm Nicole Newman, the manager of the center. Let me tell you about our facilities. Right inside the hallway, you can find a gym where you can exercise. On the second floor, there's a hall where you can learn yoga. We also have an indoor swimming pool. Please make sure to wear the proper clothing for each facility. Showers and lockers are located on the ground floor. Thank you for listening.

우·리·말·해·석

여: 안녕하세요, 학생 여러분. Han Sports Center에 오신 것을 환영합니다. 저는 센터의 관리자인 Nicole Newman입니다. 저희 시설들에 대해 얘기해 드리겠습니다. 복도의 바로 안쪽에서 여러분이 운동할 수 있는 체육관을 볼 수 있습니다. 2층에는 여러분이 요가를 배울 수 있는 홀이 있습니다. 저희는 또한 실내 수영장도 있습니다. 꼭 각 시설에 맞는 적당한 옷을 입도록 해주세요. 샤워실과 사물함은 1층에 위치해 있습니다. 들어주셔서 감사합니다.

단·어·및·표·현

facility[fəsíləti] 휑 시설

hallway[hɔ́:lwèi] 휑 복도

09 담화화제추론 ▶ 정답 ①

듣·기·대·본

W: This is a wild animal, but you can also see it in a zoo. This animal is usually found in Africa. It's the tallest animal living on earth. It is famous for its beautiful long neck. It has big eyes and two little horns. It also has a unique pattern on its body. It likes to eat leaves and fruit. It's a peaceful animal on the savannah.

우·리·말·해·석

여: 이것은 야생동물이지만 당신은 동물원에서도 그것을 볼 수 있다. 이 동물은 주로 아프리카에서 발견된다. 그것은 지구에 사는 가장 키가 큰 동물이다. 그것은 아름다운 긴 목으로 유명하다. 그것은 큰 눈과 두 개의 작은 뿔을 가지고 있다. 그것은 자신의 몸에 독특한 무늬도 가지고 있다. 그것은 잎과 과일을 먹는 것을 좋아한다. 그것은 사바나에 사는 온순한 동물이다.

단·어·및·표·현

horn[hɔ:rn] 휑 뿔

unique[ju:ní:k] 휑 독특한

10 어색한대화찾기 ▶ 정답 ⑤

듣·기·대·본

① W: I have a presentation to make at the meeting tomorrow.

　　M: Good luck. I'm sure you'll do well.

② W: Why don't we play basketball after lunch?

　　M: Sounds good. I'll meet you at the gym.

③ W: Excuse me. This is not what I ordered.

　　M: I'm sorry. There must have been a mistake.

④ W: Could you show me how to use this machine?

　　M: Of course. Just press the red button on the top.

⑤ W: How long have you been living in Seoul?

　　M: It is a great place to live.

우·리·말·해·석

① 여: 나는 내일 회의에서 발표할 게 있어.

　　남: 행운을 빌어. 나는 네가 잘할 거라고 확신해.

② 여: 우리 점심 후에 농구를 하는 게 어때?

　　남: 좋은 생각이야. 체육관에서 만나자.

③ 여: 실례합니다. 이것은 제가 주문한 것이 아닙니다.

　　남: 죄송합니다. 착오가 있었던 것 같습니다.

④ 여: 이 기계를 사용하는 법을 저에게 보여주시겠어요?

　　남: 물론이죠. 꼭대기의 빨간 버튼을 누르기만 하세요.

⑤ 여: 너는 서울에서 얼마나 오래 살아왔니?

　　남: 그곳은 살기에 훌륭한 곳이야.

단·어·및·표·현

presentation[prì:zəntéiʃən] 휑 발표

11 할일파악(대화직후) ▶ 정답 ②

듣·기·대·본

W: Colin, don't you need to get a haircut?

M: I'm getting it tomorrow, Mom.

W: Isn't your graduation photo shoot tomorrow?

M: It's the day after tomorrow.

W: Oh, right. Then, I'll iron your school uniform tomorrow.

M: Thanks, Mom. I'm going to hang out with my friends now.

W: Put on your black sneakers. I'll wash your white ones right now.

M: Oh, are they for the photo shoot?

W: Yes. I think they'll look better with your uniform.

M: Okay. See you, Mom!

우·리·말·해·석

여: Colin, 너는 이발해야 하지 않니?

남: 전 내일 그것을 받을 거예요, 엄마.

여: 너의 졸업 사진 촬영이 내일 아니니?

남: 그건 모레예요.

여: 오, 그렇구나. 그러면, 내가 내일 너의 학교 교복을 다림질할게.

남: 감사해요, 엄마. 전 지금 제 친구들과 시간을 보내러 갈 거예요.

여: 네 검은 운동화를 신으렴. 나는 지금 당장 네 흰 운동화를 세탁할 거야.

남: 아, 그것들은 사진 촬영을 위해선가요?

여: 응. 네 교복에는 그것들이 더 보기 좋을 것 같아.

남: 네. 이따 봐요, 엄마!

단·어·및·표·현

graduation[grædʒuéiʃən] 휑 졸업

the day after tomorrow (내일) 모레

iron[áiərn] 통 다림질하다

hang out with ~와 시간을 보내다, 놀다

put on ~을 신다

12 도표정보파악　　　　▶ 정답 ③

듣·기·대·본

M: Maya, I'm trying to buy a robot vacuum cleaner. Can you help me out?

W: Sure. Have you narrowed down your options?

M: Yes. I'm considering buying one of these.

W: What's your budget?

M: I can spend up to 900 dollars.

W: Alright. The noise level should be low so it won't disturb your pets.

M: Great point. I think a noise level lower than 70dB will do. What controller type should I choose?

W: Get one that can be controlled by a mobile app. It'll be more useful than a remote controller.

M: Okay. I'll order this one.

우·리·말·해·석

	모델	가격	소음 수준	조종 장치 유형
①	A	600달러	75 데시벨	리모컨
②	B	700달러	68 데시벨	리모컨
③	C	800달러	68 데시벨	모바일 앱
④	D	1,000달러	65 데시벨	모바일 앱
⑤	E	1,100달러	65 데시벨	모바일 앱

남: Maya, 나는 로봇 진공청소기를 사려고 해. 나를 도와줄 수 있니?

여: 물론이지. 네 선택지는 좁혔니?

남: 응. 나는 이것들 중 하나를 살까 생각 중이야.

여: 네 예산은 얼마니?

남: 나는 900달러까지 쓸 수 있어.

여: 알았어. 소음 수준은 네 반려동물을 방해하지 않도록 낮아야 해.

남: 좋은 지적이야. 내 생각에 소음 수준이 70dB 이하이면 될 것 같아. 내가 어떤 유형의 조종 장치를 골라야 할까?

여: 모바일 앱으로 조종할 수 있는 것을 사. 리모컨보다 더 유용할 거야.

남: 알겠어. 나는 이걸로 주문할게.

단·어·및·표·현

narrow down 좁히다, 줄이다

budget [bʌ́dʒit] 뗑 예산, 비용

disturb [distə́ːrb] 통 방해하다, 어지럽히다

13 수치파악(날짜)　　　　▶ 정답 ①

듣·기·대·본

(Cellphone rings.)

W: Hello?

M: Hello, this is Ashley Furniture. Is this Ms. Bennett?

W: Yes, hi. This is about the sofa, right?

M: Yes, it is. I'm sorry, but I'm afraid we won't be able to deliver your sofa on January 20.

W: Is there a problem?

M: There was a system error. Can we deliver it on the 21st instead?

W: I'm out of town on that day. How about January 22?

M: Well, if you are available in the morning, we could make it on the 19th.

W: That sounds good! Can you come by 10 a.m.?

M: Sure! We'll see you on January 19, then.

W: Thank you.

우·리·말·해·석

(핸드폰이 울린다.)

여: 여보세요?

남: 여보세요. Ashely 가구입니다. Bennett 씨인가요?

여: 네, 안녕하세요. 소파에 대한 거죠, 맞죠?

남: 네, 맞습니다. 죄송합니다만, 저희가 1월 20일에 고객님의 소파를 배송할 수 없을 것 같아요.

여: 문제가 있나요?

남: 시스템 에러가 있었어요. 대신에 저희가 21일에 그것을 배송해도 될까요?

여: 저는 그날 도시에 없어요. 1월 22일은 어떤가요?

남: 음, 아침에 시간이 있으시다면, 저희는 19일에 갈 수 있어요.

여: 그것이 좋은 것 같아요! 오전 10시까지 오실 수 있어요?

남: 그럼요! 그러면 저희가 1월 19일에 뵙겠습니다.

여: 감사합니다.

단·어·및·표·현

out of town 도시를 떠난, 도시에 없는

14 한일파악　　　　▶ 정답 ④

듣·기·대·본

W: Hi, Jeff. How was your movie club gathering yesterday?

M: Oh, it didn't happen.

W: You didn't go to the movies?

M: No, the theater was being renovated, so we just put it off.

W: I'm sorry to hear that. You were really looking forward to this movie.

M: It's okay. We had a good time anyway.

W: Oh, did you and your club members do something fun?

M: Yeah, we went to Riverside Park, and enjoyed a little picnic.

W: That's nice!

우·리·말·해·석

여: 안녕, Jeff. 어제 네 영화 동아리 모임이 어땠어?

남: 오, 그거 안 했어.

여: 어제 영화 보러 안 갔어?

남: 응. 극장이 개조 중이어서, 우리는 그냥 그것을 연기했어.

여: 그렇다니 안됐다. 너는 이 영화를 정말로 기대했었지.

남: 괜찮아. 우리는 어쨌든 즐거운 시간을 가졌어.

여: 오, 너와 네 동아리 회원들이 무언가 재미있는 것을 했어?

남: 응. 우리는 Riverside 공원으로 가서 작은 소풍을 즐겼어.

여: 그거 멋지다!

단·어·및·표·현

renovate [rénəvèit] 통 수리하다, 개조하다

put ~ off ~을 연기하다, 미루다

15 담화목적파악　　　　▶ 정답 ⑤

듣·기·대·본

W: Hello, new students. Your health and wellbeing are very important to us, so we ask you to let us know if you have any allergies or medical conditions. Here is how to do it: go to your teacher, or any teacher, and tell them about your health concerns. Emails are also welcome. If you don't want to do it yourself, ask one of your parents to do it for you. Any information you share with us will be kept confidential. So, don't be shy. Let us help you! Thank you.

여: 안녕하십니까, 신입생 여러분. 여러분의 건강과 행복은 우리에게 매우 중요합니다. 그래서 우리는 여러분이 어떤 알레르기나 질병이 있다면 우리에게 알려줄 것을 요청드립니다. 여기 (알리는) 방법이 있는데 여러분의 선생님, 또는 아무 선생님에게 가서 그들에게 여러분의 건강에 관한 걱정거리들을 말하십시오. 이메일도 환영합니다. 만약 여러분이 직접 하기 싫다면 여러분의 부모님 중 한 분이 여러분을 대신하여 그것을 하도록 부탁하십시오. 여러분이 우리와 공유하는 어떤 정보라도 비밀로 유지될 것입니다. 그러니, 부끄러워 마세요. 우리가 여러분을 돕게 해주세요! 감사합니다.

단·어·및·표·현

medical condition 질병, 질환

16 수치계산(금액)　　　▶ 정답 ②

듣·기·대·본

(Telephone rings.)

M: Best Mobile, how may I help you?

W: Hi, I'm using the $30 <u>monthly plan</u>, but I'm always <u>short of data</u>.

M: Okay, then you could get the unlimited data plan priced at $100.

W: That's too expensive.

M: Then, how about the $50 plan that includes 12GB of data?

W: Great! I'll <u>switch</u> my plan to $50. So, how much <u>should I pay</u> for this month?

M: Today is September 15, so you'll have to pay half of the monthly bill for both the old and new plans.

W: Okay, then it would be $15 plus $25.

M: That's correct.

우·리·말·해·석

(전화벨이 울린다.)

남: Best Mobile입니다. 어떻게 도와드릴까요?

여: 안녕하세요, 저는 월 30달러의 요금제를 사용하고 있지만, 항상 데이터가 모자라요.

남: 알겠습니다, 그러면 100달러 가격의 무제한 데이터 요금제를 사용하실 수 있습니다.

여: 그것은 너무 비싸요.

남: 그렇다면, 12GB의 데이터를 포함하는 50달러 요금은 어떠세요?

여: 훌륭해요! 제 요금제를 50달러로 바꿀게요. 그러면, 제가 이번 달에 얼마를 지불해야 하죠?

남: 오늘이 9월 15일이니까, 구 요금제와 신 요금제 두 개의 월 청구액의 반을 내셔야 할 것입니다.

여: 좋아요, 그러면 그것은 15달러 더하기 25달러겠네요.

남: 맞습니다.

단·어·및·표·현

short of ~ ~이 부족한

17 알맞은응답찾기　　　▶ 정답 ④

듣·기·대·본

M: Hello, is this where I can <u>sign up</u> for the community choir?

W: Yes, you've come to the right place. Which one are you here to join?

M: You mean there is more than one?

W: Of course! We have a mixed choir as well as single-gender choirs.

M: They all sound inviting, but I don't have a specific preference. Are there any <u>empty spots left</u>?

W: We happen to have open spots in all three choirs, actually. But you'll have to audition for the mixed-gender choir. It is short on tenors.

M: <u>It so happens that</u> I am a tenor! I have a couple of years of experience in my church choir as well.

W: <u>Sounds great.</u> Would you like to sign up for an audition over the weekend?

M: <u>Unfortunately, I don't have time during the weekend.</u>

우·리·말·해·석

① 제가 그런 보컬 수업을 받는 것은 불가능해요.

② 주말에 하는 테너들을 위한 무료 강의를 선택할게요.

③ 네, 혼성 합창단에 제 친구를 추천하고 싶어요.

④ 유감스럽게도, 주말에는 시간이 나지 않아요.

⑤ 저와 합창단을 함께 하고 싶으신가 봐요.

남: 안녕하세요, 지역 합창단에 신청하는 곳이 여기 맞나요?

여: 네, 제대로 찾아오셨어요. 어떤 합창단에 참여 하시려고요?

남: 합창단이 더 있다는 말씀이세요?

여: 당연하지요! 단일 합창단뿐만 아니라 혼성 합창단도 있습니다.

남: 전부 다 좋아 보이지만, 특별히 선호하는 건 없어요. 빈자리가 있나요?

여: 사실, 세 합창단 전부 자리가 있어요. 그런데 혼성 합창단은 오디션을 봐야 해요. 테너들이 부족하거든요.

남: 마침 제가 테너인걸요! 교회 합창단에서 몇 년간의 경력도 있어요.

여: 좋아요. 그럼 주말에 있을 오디션에 등록하시겠어요?

남: <u>유감스럽게도, 주말에는 시간이 나지 않아요.</u>

단·어·및·표·현

be short on ~ ~가 부족하다

18 알맞은응답찾기　　　▶ 정답 ⑤

듣·기·대·본

M: Ruth, what's wrong? You look <u>concerned</u>.

W: Hi, Jim. I'm sure you know about Linda's birthday party this weekend.

M: Of course. All our classmates are invited.

W: Yes… The problem is that I haven't decided <u>what to</u> give her.

M: Don't worry. You know Linda. She will like whatever you give her.

W: We're best friends and we have known <u>each other</u> since we were babies. It's <u>getting harder</u> to choose presents for her.

M: I see. Actually, I haven't bought her anything yet, either. Let's go to the mall together this Friday.

W: <u>Wonderful! I could use a fresh pair of eyes.</u>

우·리·말·해·석

① 그녀를 도와주다니 너는 정말 친절하구나.

② 나는 파티에 가지 못할 것 같아.

③ 알겠어. 내가 전화해서 예약할게.

④ 그거 좋은 생각이다! 그녀는 케이크를 좋아할 거야.

⑤ 훌륭해! 나는 새로운 시각이 필요해.

남: Ruth, 무슨 일이야? 너 걱정스러워 보여.

여: 안녕, Jim. 나는 네가 이번 주말 Linda의 생일 파티에 대해 알고 있을 거라고 확신해.

남: 물론이지. 우리 반 모든 친구들이 초대받았잖아.

여: 응… 문제는 내가 그녀에게 무엇을 줄지 못 정했다는 거야.

남: 걱정하지 마. 너 Linda 알잖아. 그녀는 네가 그녀에게 무엇을 주든 좋아 할 거야.

여: 우리는 가장 친한 친구이고, 우리가 아기였을 때부터 서로 알고 지냈 어. 그녀에게 줄 선물을 고르는 것이 점점 더 어려워지고 있어.

남: 그렇구나. 사실, 나도 아직 그녀에게 줄 것을 사지 않았어. 이번 금요일 에 같이 쇼핑몰에 가자.

여: **훌륭해! 나는 새로운 시각이 필요해.**

단·어·및·표·현

concerned[kənsə́ːrnd] ⑬ 걱정하는, 염려하는

each other 서로

get + 비교급 점점 더 ~해지다

make it (모임 등에) 참석하다

make a reservation 예약하다

19 알맞은응답찾기　　　　　▶ 정답 ④

듣·기·대·본

W: About our friend Andy's move, you're coming <u>to help out</u>, right?

M: That's right. Are you coming, too?

W: Yes. But, I just heard bad news. Andy says there's no elevator in the building.

M: Uh-oh. What floor is he <u>moving to</u>?

W: Third.

M: That's not that bad. I think we'll need some extra help, though.

W: Yes, especially with the furniture and appliances. Any suggestions?

M: **Why don't we make some calls and gather a few more friends?**

우·리·말·해·석

① Andy는 새로운 곳으로 이사를 가는 데 어려움이 있을 거야.

② 나는 수리 기사에게 엘리베이터를 고쳐달라고 전화해야 할 것 같아.

③ 너는 정직해야 하고 네가 받을 수 있는 도움을 다 받아야 해.

④ 우리 전화를 좀 해서 친구들을 몇 명 더 모으는 건 어때?

⑤ 나는 그에게 집들이 선물로 실내용 식물을 사줄까 생각 중이야.

여: 우리의 친구 Andy의 이사에 대해서 말인데, 너는 도와주러 올 거지, 그렇지?

남: 맞아. 너도 올 거야?

여: 응. 하지만, 나는 막 나쁜 소식을 들었어. Andy가 말하길 그 건물에는 엘리베이터가 없대.

남: 이런. 그가 이사 가는 곳이 몇 층이지?

여: 3층.

남: 그렇게 나쁘진 않네. 하지만, 우리는 추가적인 도움이 좀 필요할 것 같아.

여: 맞아, 특히 가구와 가전제품들에 있어서 말이야. 제안이라도 있어?

남: **우리 전화를 좀 해서 친구들을 몇 명 더 모으는 건 어때?**

단·어·및·표·현

help out 도와주다

appliance[əpláiəns] ⑬ 가전제품

have difficulty ~ing ~하는 데 어려움이 있다[겪다]

repair person 수리 기사, 수리공

housewarming[háuswɔ̀ːrmiŋ] ⑬ 집들이

20 상황에적절한말찾기　　　　　▶ 정답 ④

듣·기·대·본

M: Hazel is going to register for the practical AI workshop that'll be held at the local youth education center. She wants to get as much information as possible about <u>cutting-edge</u> artificial intelligence. She is excited to learn about how best to use AI and how it'll change jobs in the future. She <u>finds out</u> that her friend, Patrick is also interested in this field. So, she would like to suggest that Patrick <u>register for</u> the workshop as well. In this situation, what would Hazel most likely say to Patrick?

Hazel: Patrick, <u>why don't you sign up for the AI workshop with me?</u>

우·리·말·해·석

① 혼자서 워크숍을 조직해보는 건 어때?

② 나는 네가 언젠가 훌륭한 AI 교육자가 될 거라고 생각해.

③ 너는 그 과정을 완료한 후 수료증을 받을 수 있어.

④ 나와 같이 AI 워크숍에 등록하는 건 어때?

⑤ 현장 경험은 구직할 때 이점이야.

남: Hazel은 지역 청소년 교육 센터에서 열릴 실용적인 AI 워크숍에 등록하 려고 한다. 그녀는 최첨단 인공지능에 대해 가능한 한 많은 정보를 얻 고 싶어 한다. 그녀는 AI를 가장 잘 활용하는 방법과 그것이 미래의 직 업들을 어떻게 바꿀지를 배우는 것에 신이 나 있다. 그녀는 그녀의 친 구인 Patrick도 이 분야에 관심이 있다는 것을 알게 된다. 그래서 그녀 는 Patrick도 워크숍에 등록하라고 제안하고 싶어 한다. 이 상황에서, Hazel은 Patrick에게 뭐라고 말하겠는가?

Hazel: Patrick, **나와 같이 AI 워크숍에 등록하는 건 어때?**

단·어·및·표·현

AI(artificial intelligence) 인공 지능

practical[præktikəl] ⑬ 실용적인

cutting-edge 최첨단의

by oneself 혼자서

Words & Expressions Review

1. 홍보 책자, 전단	2. (시간·날짜를) 연기하다, 미루다	3. 독특한, 특이한
4. 합창단	5. 졸업	6. 모임
7. 알레르기	8. ~이 부족한	9. 불편한, 곤란한
10. 질병	11. 타자를 치다	12. 특정한, 구체적인
13. 매월의	14. 오류, 실수	15. A를 신청하다
16. 높이	17. 예산, 비용	18. 재미있는, 즐거움을 주는
19. 적절한, 적당한	20. 좁히다, 줄이다	21. 배달하다
22. 시설	23. 뿔	24. 시간이 있는
25. 영광스러운, 명예로운	26. 포함시키다	27. 수리하다, 개조하다
28. 온화한, 평온한, 조용한	29. 예약하다, 만날 약속을 하다	30. 최첨단의
31. 가전제품	32. 실용적인	33. 다림질하다
34. 걱정하는, 염려하는	35. 주문하다, 주문	36. 통치자, 지배자
37. 누르다	38. 착오, 실수, 잘못	39. 과제, 임무
40. (내일) 모레	41. 선호	42. A에게 B를 생각나게 하다
43. 대표, 대리인	44. (정보를) 찾아보다, 검색하다	

중학영어듣기 필수 표현 📝

중요도 최상 ★★★ 상 ★★ 중 ★

길 안내하기

중요도	주요표현	해석
★★	(In fact) It's ~	(사실) 그것은 ~에 있습니다.
★★	(In that case,) Go(Cross, Turn, Follow)~.	(그럴 경우엔,) ~가십시오. (~건너십시오, ~도세요, ~따라가십시오.)
★	(Excuse me.) Can you tell me the way ~	(실례합니다.) ~가는 길 좀 알려주시겠어요?
★	Can you tell me where ~ is?	~가 어디인지 알려주시겠어요?
★	Excuse me. Where's the ~?	실례합니다. ~가 어디 있죠?
★	Where can I find ~?	~를 어디에서 찾을 수 있죠?
★	How can I get there?	어떻게 거기에 갈 수 있죠?
★	Is this the right way to ~?	이 길이 ~가는 길 맞죠?
★	It's (just) down the road.	그것은 (바로) 길 아래에 있습니다.
★	That road leads you to ~	저 길로 가면 ~에 도착합니다.
★	Let's go straight. We can walk across ~	직진합시다. 우리는 ~를 건너갈 수 있습니다.
★	You can see it on your ~	당신의 ~에서 그것을 볼 수 있습니다.
★	You have to go straight ~	직진하셔야 합니다.

기억/경험 묻고 말하기

중요도	주요표현	해석
★★	Do you remember ~?	~기억납니까?
★★	I'll never forget ~	나는 ~를 결코 잊지 않을 거야.
★★	I've (actually) never p.p. ~	(사실) 나는 ~한 적이 결코 없습니다.
★	Is that really true?	그게 정말 사실입니까?
★	Have you forgotten ~?	~잊으셨습니까?
★	Sure.	물론이야.
★	I forgot about that.	나 그거 잊어버렸어.
★	I didn't know that. That's amazing!	나는 그거 몰랐어. 놀라워라!
★	I find it hard to believe ~.	나는 ~을 믿기 어렵습니다.
★	Have you ever ~ p.p.?	~한 적이 있습니까?
★	I've (actually) p.p. ~	(사실) 나는 ~한 적이 있습니다.
★	(Actually,) I have had (done) the same experience (before).	(사실,) 나는 똑같은 경험이 있습니다.

마더텅 100%실전대비 MP3 중학영어듣기 24회 모의고사 3학년

정답표

1회

1	2	3	4	5	6	7	8	9	10
③	④	③	②	③	④	⑤	③	③	⑤

11	12	13	14	15	16	17	18	19	20
①	①	④	⑤	⑤	④	②	⑤	②	⑤

2회

1	2	3	4	5	6	7	8	9	10
④	④	②	⑤	②	④	①	⑤	③	③

11	12	13	14	15	16	17	18	19	20
①	④	④	③	④	④	③	①	⑤	④

3회

1	2	3	4	5	6	7	8	9	10
①	④	①	④	②	④	③	④	③	④

11	12	13	14	15	16	17	18	19	20
④	③	②	④	③	③	②	②	③	⑤

4회

1	2	3	4	5	6	7	8	9	10
①	④	③	④	⑤	④	③	⑤	③	③

11	12	13	14	15	16	17	18	19	20
①	②	②	④	④	④	②	④	④	④

5회

1	2	3	4	5	6	7	8	9	10
⑤	②	⑤	②	④	④	①	④	③	④

11	12	13	14	15	16	17	18	19	20
①	②	⑤	③	⑤	④	⑤	②	②	④

6회

1	2	3	4	5	6	7	8	9	10
⑤	④	③	⑤	③	④	②	④	①	④

11	12	13	14	15	16	17	18	19	20
①	③	③	②	④	③	③	③	④	③

7회

1	2	3	4	5	6	7	8	9	10
⑤	④	①	④	③	③	⑤	③	②	①

11	12	13	14	15	16	17	18	19	20
②	②	③	③	⑤	④	③	②	②	④

8회

1	2	3	4	5	6	7	8	9	10
④	④	⑤	③	⑤	③	⑤	④	①	④

11	12	13	14	15	16	17	18	19	20
③	①	④	⑤	④	④	①	②	②	③

9회

1	2	3	4	5	6	7	8	9	10
①	④	③	③	②	④	②	⑤	③	⑤

11	12	13	14	15	16	17	18	19	20
②	③	④	①	⑤	②	①	⑤	①	②

10회

1	2	3	4	5	6	7	8	9	10
③	③	⑤	⑤	②	②	②	③	①	④

11	12	13	14	15	16	17	18	19	20
②	⑤	③	②	⑤	②	⑤	④	④	④

11회

1	2	3	4	5	6	7	8	9	10
②	④	④	⑤	④	③	②	④	③	③

11	12	13	14	15	16	17	18	19	20
①	⑤	③	①	②	④	④	④	⑤	②

12회

1	2	3	4	5	6	7	8	9	10
⑤	③	②	⑤	①	③	⑤	①	③	⑤

11	12	13	14	15	16	17	18	19	20
④	①	②	③	①	④	②	⑤	①	②

13회

1	2	3	4	5	6	7	8	9	10
⑤	③	④	⑤	④	⑤	②	③	①	②

11	12	13	14	15	16	17	18	19	20
②	④	⑤	⑤	②	③	②	①	③	⑤

14회

1	2	3	4	5	6	7	8	9	10
④	①	③	③	②	③	④	⑤	③	⑤

11	12	13	14	15	16	17	18	19	20
④	②	①	②	③	⑤	③	③	③	④

15회

1	2	3	4	5	6	7	8	9	10
①	④	③	②	⑤	②	④	③	⑤	④

11	12	13	14	15	16	17	18	19	20
③	①	④	④	③	②	③	③	②	②

16회

1	2	3	4	5	6	7	8	9	10
⑤	③	③	④	①	③	⑤	④	②	③

11	12	13	14	15	16	17	18	19	20
③	①	③	④	⑤	④	④	②	④	⑤

17회

1	2	3	4	5	6	7	8	9	10
⑤	⑤	⑤	②	②	①	①	⑤	③	③

11	12	13	14	15	16	17	18	19	20
②	①	③	③	①	④	⑤	④	②	②

18회

1	2	3	4	5	6	7	8	9	10
④	④	⑤	②	③	②	⑤	①	⑤	①

11	12	13	14	15	16	17	18	19	20
③	②	②	④	②	④	⑤	⑤	④	④

19회

1	2	3	4	5	6	7	8	9	10
④	④	①	②	②	④	⑤	⑤	③	④

11	12	13	14	15	16	17	18	19	20
④	③	④	⑤	④	④	②	③	⑤	⑤

20회

1	2	3	4	5	6	7	8	9	10
④	②	③	④	⑤	②	③	④	②	②

11	12	13	14	15	16	17	18	19	20
⑤	②	③	④	④	③	①	②	②	③

21회

1	2	3	4	5	6	7	8	9	10
③	③	④	①	③	②	④	④	⑤	②

11	12	13	14	15	16	17	18	19	20
③	②	⑤	③	⑤	②	③	④	①	②

22회

1	2	3	4	5	6	7	8	9	10
①	②	③	⑤	③	④	②	④	①	⑤

11	12	13	14	15	16	17	18	19	20
②	①	⑤	③	③	④	④	⑤	①	③

23회

1	2	3	4	5	6	7	8	9	10
③	②	③	⑤	④	④	②	⑤	①	②

11	12	13	14	15	16	17	18	19	20
①	②	②	④	④	③	①	②	②	③

24회

1	2	3	4	5	6	7	8	9	10
⑤	④	⑤	④	③	④	④	①	⑤	⑤

11	12	13	14	15	16	17	18	19	20
②	③	①	④	⑤	②	④	⑤	④	④

중학영어듣기 필수 표현 📋

중요도 최상 ★★★ 상 ★★ 중 ★

질문/대답하기

중요도	주요표현	해석
★★★	I'm(We're) planning to + 동사원형	나는(우리는) ~할 계획이야.
★★★	I'm going to + 동사원형	나는 ~할 계획이야.
★★★	Have you heard of/about ~?	~에 대해 들어본 적 있어?
★★★	What are you planning to do?	무엇을 할 생각이야? (계획이 뭐야?)
★★★	Could/Can you (please) tell me ~?	~에 대해 말해 줄 수 있어?
★★	What would you like to + 동사원형?	너 무엇을 ~하고 싶어?
★★	Have you (ever) p.p. ~?	너 ~해본 적 있어?
★	What are you going to do?	너 뭐 할거야?
★	Do you know ~?	너 ~에 대해 알아?
★	Do you want to + 동사원형?	너 ~하고 싶어?
★	Are you planning to + 동사원형?	너 ~할 계획이야?
★	Do you have any plans?	어떤 계획이라도 있어?
★	I've never p.p. ~	나는 ~해본 적이 없어.
★	I have to ~	나는 ~해야만 해.
★	How did you + 동사원형?	어떻게 ~했어?
★	What is ~?	~는 무엇이야?
★	Who + 과거동사 ~?	누가 ~했어?
★	What did he + 동사원형 ~?	그가 무엇을 ~했어?
★	When + 동사 ~?	언제 ~야?
★	Why ~?	왜 ~야?
★	Did you + 동사원형 ~?	너 ~했어?
★	What do you do to + 동사원형 ~?	~하기 위해 너는 무엇을 해?
★	What do you call + 명사 ~?	너는 ~를 뭐라고 불러?
★	What A do you want to + 동사원형?	어떤 A를 ~하기 원해?
★	Which A do you like most?	어떤 A를 너는 가장 좋아해?
★	Which A would you like to + 동사원형?	어떤 A를 ~하고 싶어?
★	What do you want to be in the future?	너는 커서 무엇이 되고 싶어?
★	Would you like to + 동사원형 ~?	너 ~하고 싶어?
★	What kind of A do you prefer?	어떤 종류의 A를 너는 선호해?

감사/칭찬

중요도	주요표현	해석
★	I couldn't have p.p. without you.	네가 없었다면 나는 ~할 수 없었을 거야. (정말 고마워.)
★	Thanks (so much).	(매우) 감사합니다.
★	Thank you for + 명사	~에 대해 감사드립니다.
★	I appreciate it.	그것에 대해 감사드립니다.
★	It's (very) nice of you to + 동사원형	~를 해주셔서 (매우) 감사드립니다.
★	Terrific!	정말 멋졌어! (정말 잘했어!)
★	Excellent!	정말 멋졌어! (정말 잘했어!)
★	You did a good(great) job!	너 정말 훌륭했어!
★	I like(liked) your + 명사	나는 너의 ~가 좋아(좋았어).
★	You are such a friendly person.	너는 매우 친절하구나.
★	I'm glad you like it.	네가 그것을 좋아하니 기쁘다.
★	Don't mention it.	별말씀을요. (그렇게 말해 주니 고마워요.)

불가능 표현하기

중요도	주요표현	해석
★★★	I have no idea how ~	나는 어떻게 ~ 하는지 잘 모르겠어. (못하겠어.)
★	It's/That's/A is (almost) impossible!	그것은(A는) 불가능해!
★	I can't.	나는 할 수 없어.
★	That won't be possible.	그것은 불가능해.
★	I don't think I can.	내가 할 수 있다고 생각하지 않아. (못해.)
★	I /We won't be able to + 동사원형	나는(우리는) ~ 할 수 없어요.
★	I'm not good at ~	나는 ~를 잘하지 못해요.
★	There is no/a chance ~	~ 인 가능성은 없어. (있어.)
★	I have no time to + 동사원형	나는 ~ 할 시간이 없어.